A Nation Conceived in Liberty

U.S. History for the Georgia Milestones EOC Assessment

Mark Jarrett, Ph.D.

First Choice Educational Publishing

Copyright © 2022 by First Choice Educational Publishing

All rights reserved. Copying or projecting this book or posting on the Internet in any form without permission of the publisher is a violation of federal copyright law. An exception is granted to teachers who wish to project pages of this program if their district has purchased the program or an entire class set of ancillary books is present and in use by students at the time of such projection. All other unauthorized copying, projecting, or posting of this material will be prosecuted by the publisher to the fullest extent permitted by law. For permission requests, write to the publisher, addressed "Attention: Permissions Coordinator," at the address below.

First Choice Educational Publishing
10 Folin Lane
Lafayette, CA 94549
Tel: (925) 906-9742   Fax: (925) 939-6557   www.georgiasocialstudies.net

First Choice Educational Publishing and its logo are registered trademarks.

ISBN 978-0-9988117-3-4

24 23 22   10 9 8 7 6 5 4

2019 Edition

> *"Four score and seven years ago our fathers brought forth, on this continent, a new nation, conceived in Liberty, and dedicated to the proposition that all men are created equal."*
> —President Abraham Lincoln at Gettysburg, November 19, 1863

About the Author

Mark Jarrett lives in Lafayette, California, and is a current member of the State Bar of California. He studied at Columbia University (B.A.), the London School of Economics (M.A. in international history), Stanford University (Ph.D. in history), and the University of California at Berkeley, where he received a law degree with honors (Order of the Coif). He was an editor of the school's law review and received the American Jurisprudence Award for Comparative Legal History. He studied constitutional law with Robert Post, former dean of the Yale Law School. Mark has taught at Hofstra University, at the Mander Portman School in London, and in the New York City Public Schools. He has served as a test writer for the New York State Board of Regents, and practiced law in the San Francisco office of Baker & McKenzie, the world's largest law firm. He is the co-author of more than thirty test preparation books and textbooks including state-adopted textbooks in Florida and California. James Sheehan, past president of the American Historical Association, describes Mark's recent book, *The Congress of Vienna and its Legacy* (London: I. B. Tauris, 2013), as "beautifully written" and providing "a fine sense of political structures without losing the human element," while Robert Jervis, past president of the American Political Science Association, calls his book a "model treatment." Charles Maier of Harvard University writes that "Jarrett's massive and impressively researched volume promises to become our generation's authoritative study of the peace settlements of 1814–1815." John Bew of King's College, London, concurs, finding it to be the "most detailed and thoroughly researched study of the making of the Treaty of Vienna of 1815 and the European Congress system ever written."

The Cover

Declaration of Independence, a painting by John Trumbull

A NATION CONCEIVED IN LIBERTY:
U.S. HISTORY FOR THE GEORGIA EOC ASSESSMENT

Table of Contents

Acknowledgments		iv
Introduction		v
Chapter 1	Colonial Foundations	1
Chapter 2	The American Revolution	33
Chapter 3	The Story of Our Constitution	73
Chapter 4	The First Presidents of the New Republic	113
Chapter 5	The Age of Jackson	143
Chapter 6	The Civil War	173
Chapter 7	The Reconstruction Era	207
Chapter 8	The Rise of Industrial America	227
Chapter 9	The Last Frontier	263
Chapter 10	The Progressive Era	285
Chapter 11	American Imperialism	313
Chapter 12	The United States in World War I	337
Chapter 13	The Roaring Twenties	359
Chapter 14	The Great Depression and the New Deal	383
Chapter 15	America in World War II	417
Chapter 16	The Truman and Eisenhower Years: Cold War, Prosperity, and Civil Rights	453
Chapter 17	The Kennedy and Johnson Years: Cuba, Civil Rights, the Great Society, and Vietnam	489
Chapter 18	The Presidency in Crisis: Presidents Nixon, Ford, and Carter	525
Chapter 19	America in Recent Times: Presidents Reagan, George H.W. Bush, Clinton, George W. Bush, and Obama	551
	Index	585

Dedication

To my wife, Gośka, and our children Alex and Julia.
—Mark Jarrett

"I have a dream that one day on the Red Hills of Georgia, the sons of former slaves and the sons of former slave owners will be able to sit down together at the table of brotherhood."
—Dr. Martin Luther King, Jr., August 28, 1963.

Dr. King was born in Atlanta, Georgia. He attended both high school and college in Atlanta, and was buried there.

Acknowledgments

The author wishes to thank Mr. Robert Yahng for earlier drafts of sections of this book on the Bill of Rights, economics, and nineteenth-century Asian immigration to the United States, and Dr. Herman J. Viola for his insights on American Indian tribes. The author also wishes to thank the following individuals for their generous help and advice, either directly on this book or in the course of many discussions on the nature and goals of social studies education over several years: Jeff Burns of Henry County Schools; Ben Smalley of DeKalb County School District; Dr. Eddie Bennett of the Georgia Council for the Social Studies; Ms. Angela Miller, former Social Studies Supervisor for the Houston Independent School District; Ms. Jackie Viana, District Social Studies Supervisor of Miami-Dade County Public Schools; Dr. Montra Rogers, Social Studies Director for Houston Independent School District; Mr. Adam Motter, Social Studies Supervisor for Akron Public Schools; Mr. Corbin Moore, Social Studies Supervisor of Hamilton School District; Ms. Polly Schlosser, former Social Studies Supervisor of Plano Independent School District; Ms. Amy Thibaut, former Social Studies Director of Spring Branch Independent School District; and Dr. Rosemary Morrow, former Director of Social Studies for the Texas Education Agency. In addition, the author would like to thank Dr. Peter Stansky of Stanford University, Dr. Robert Post of the Yale Law School, the late Gordon Craig and Alexander George of Stanford University, the late Ken Bourne of the London School of Economics, and the late J. M. W. Bean of Columbia University, for attempting to teach him something about history, law, and international relations. Finally, the author would like to thank Ms. Małgorzata Jarrett, Mr. Alex Jarrett, Ms. Julia Jarrett, and Ms. KrisAnne Nuguid for a multitude of services in completing this book from finding images and typing to researching topics; Ms. Nina Tyksinski for her excellent work as proofreader; Ms. Helen Stirling of Inverness, Scotland, for her superb maps; Ms. Jerianne Van Dijk for her original drawings; and Mr. Jonathan Peck and Ms. Joan Keyes of Dovetail Publishing Services for their creativity in the design and layout of this book. This is not to be taken as an endorsement of this product by any of these individuals. In fact, in some cases I was not able to follow all of their recommendations. Any remaining errors are therefore my own.

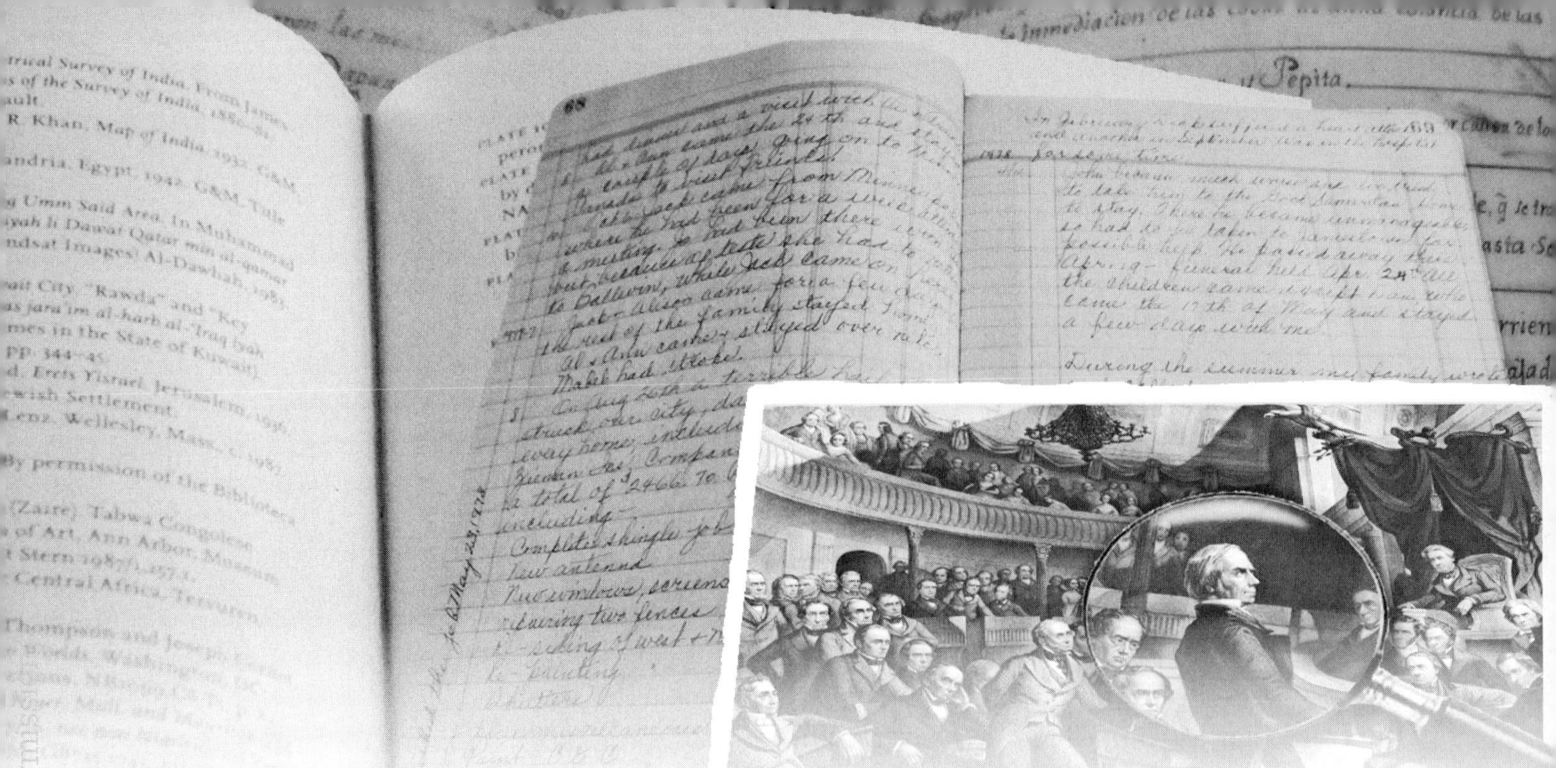

Introduction

This year you will be studying United States History. You will also be taking the Georgia Milestones United States History End-of-Course ("EOC") Assessment at the end of your course. This assessment will test your knowledge of 23 Georgia Standards of Excellence for United States History. Each learning standard has from two to six parts.

The test will be given in two sections. You will have up to 70 minutes to complete each section.

The questions on the Georgia Milestones EOC Assessment for United States History will be distributed as follows:

Time Period (Reporting Category)	Georgia Standards of Excellence	Percentage of Test	Number of Points on the Test	Chapters in *A Nation Conceived in Liberty*
Colonization through the Constitution	SSUSH 1–5	16%	10	1–3
New Republic through Reconstruction	SSUSH 6–10	20%	12	4–7
Industrialization, Reform, and Imperialism	SSUSH 11–14	15%	10	8–11
Establishment as a World Power	SSUSH 15–19	24%	14	12–15
Post-World War II to the Present	SSUSH 20–23	24%	14	16–19

This book, *A Nation Conceived in Liberty*, can help you learn about American history and perform your very best on the EOC Assessment.

Special Features of *A Nation Conceived in Liberty*

A Nation Conceived in Liberty includes many special learning features to make United States history easier to learn.

Every content chapter in this book begins by telling you what the chapter is about. The title of the chapter identifies its topic or theme. This is followed by a series of questions, identified by number, that are closely tied to the Georgia Standards of Excellence. These questions identify the particular learning standards covered in the chapter. They also establish the issues you should think about as you read through it.

This is followed by a list of *Names and Terms You Should Know*. If some of the words on this list are unknown to you, you may want to learn their meanings before you read the chapter. Many of the terms are found in the standards themselves.

The next section is the *Georgia "Peaches" of Wisdom*. No, these aren't real Georgia peaches, as delicious as they are! They are simply the "peaches" of wisdom found in the chapter. This section provides a one-page overview of the most important ideas and facts you will encounter. It serves as a one-page summary of the chapter. You should study this overview carefully before you read the chapter text. See how many of these "peaches" you already know. The rest of the chapter expands on these key ideas and facts. Once you have finished the chapter, you can read these "peaches" a second time. If you find that you don't understand or remember any of these "peaches," you may want to look back at the more detailed discussion in the chapter. Finally, you can review all of the *Georgia "Peaches" of Wisdom* just before you take the Georgia Milestones EOC Assessment.

The *Georgia "Peaches"* are followed by the main text of the chapter. Each chapter is divided into sections, accompanied by illustrations, charts, graphs, and maps. Information in the chapter is organized around core concepts and events to make American history more exciting and fun to learn.

In some cases, this book includes background information that will ***not*** be tested on the Georgia Milestones EOC Assessment. We have often included a short note telling you when a section includes information that is not tested, but that is nevertheless important for understanding the topic of the chapter. For example, we have included information about the outbreak of World War II in Europe that is useful to know but that will not be tested on the EOC Assessment. You may find it helpful to read these sections when you first read the chapter, but you may not want to look at these sections again when you are reviewing for the EOC Assessment.

At the end of each major section of the text, you will find *The Historian's Apprentice*. This feature recommends activities for you and your classmates to complete under the supervision of your teacher. In these activities, you will be asked to conduct research, to interpret a primary source, or to use your historical imagination to think about how you would have dealt with a situation in the past. Some of these primary sources are challenging to understand. Many of them are closely related to specific Georgia Standards of Excellence.

Introduction

Each chapter ends with a *Georgia Milestones Checklist*, a concept map, and a series of *What Do You Know?* practice questions:

1. The *Georgia Milestones Checklist* tells you exactly what information in the chapter will be tested on the Georgia Milestones EOC Assessment. This detailed checklist asks you to think about what you have learned to see what you can recall about each of the tested Georgia Standards of Excellence in the chapter.

2. The concept map provides a visual representation of the information in the chapter. It will help you to see important relationships and to better remember what is in the chapter.

3. The *What Do You Know?* practice questions are similar in format to the multiple-choice and technology-enhanced items on the actual Georgia Milestones EOC Assessment.

There are many ways to use this book. You may want to use this book as your main resource throughout the school year. It covers everything you need to know for the test. You may also use it alongside another textbook. After you complete each unit in your other textbook, you can review the same topic using one or more chapters in *A Nation Conceived in Liberty*.

Finally, you may want to use this book for a final review in the weeks just before the test. You can focus on each chapter's *Georgia "Peaches" of Wisdom*, *Georgia Milestones Checklist*, concept map, and *What Do You Know?* end-of-chapter practice questions. With its lively text and special learning features, reading through this book provides an outstanding way for you to review everything you have studied this school year to prepare for the test.

Test-Taking Skills: How to Answer EOC Questions

Besides having the knowledge and skills that are being tested, you have to be a good test-taker to perform your best on the Georgia Milestones EOC Assessment or any other test. There are three basic steps that we recommend for answering multiple-choice and technology-enhanced questions. These same steps can be used to answer questions on almost any test.

Step 1: Understand the Question

First, make sure you read the question carefully. Be sure to understand exactly what the question asks. Examine any documentary excerpt, map, chart, or diagram that is included in the question.

Step 2: Think about What You Know

Here comes the hardest part! Many students wish to rush ahead: they want to finish the test early. To do your best, however, you have to take your time. Once you have read and understood the question, take a moment to think about the topic that it asks about. For example, if the question asks about the causes of the Civil War, think about all that you can remember about its causes. You might think about sectionalism, states' rights, slavery, abolitionism, the compromises in Congress over the extension of slavery, the Dred Scott decision, the election of Abraham Lincoln, and the secession of Southern states.

Questions on the Georgia Milestones United States History EOC Assessment will most likely ask you:

1. To identify the cause of something: why did it happen?
2. To identify the effect or impact of something: what were its consequences?
3. To complete a diagram that is missing related information.
4. To explain or describe something.
5. To identify or define something.
6. To compare two or more items.
7. To put events in a sequence or identify an event that is missing from a sequence.
8. To interpret an excerpt from a primary source, a cartoon, a map, a table, or a graph.
9. To provide an example of something.
10. To make an inference or reach a conclusion.
11. To make a prediction: what is most likely to happen next?

Step 3: Answer the Question

Now at last you are ready to answer the question. Review the question itself. You might even think about how you would answer the question based on what you can recall, without looking at the answer choices.

Next, look carefully at each answer choice. Eliminate any choices that are obviously wrong or irrelevant (not related to the question or its topic).

Finally, choose the best of the remaining answer choices based on your knowledge and understanding.

If you have extra time after you have finished the test, be sure to check your work again to eliminate any careless mistakes.

Technology-enhanced questions on the Georgia Milestones United States History EOC Assessment are very similar to multiple-choice questions, except that they ask you to choose two answers out of six choices, or they consist of two parts, each of which is a multiple-choice question.

Special Types of EOC Questions

Many questions on the Georgia Milestones EOC Assessment will ask about a diagram, excerpt, map, graph, political cartoon, or photograph that is included as part of the question.

Each of these is actually just another way of presenting or displaying information. Such questions may ask you what an illustration shows, or to make an inference or draw a conclusion from information in the question. You might be asked to identify causes or effects of a situation or event described in a quotation or shown in a photograph.

Besides interpreting the information presented in the question, you will have to apply your knowledge of United States history to answer the question correctly.

Let's look more closely at six question types that may appear on the test.

Diagrams

A simple line diagram can be used to show the relationship of ideas or things.

For example, the following diagram shows some of the different flavors of ice cream:

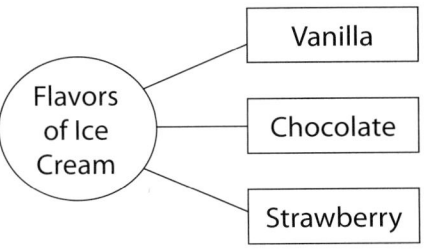

A question on the Georgia Milestones EOC might leave out one of the flavors and ask you to identify what is missing from the diagram.

The same type of diagram can be used to illustrate more complex ideas:

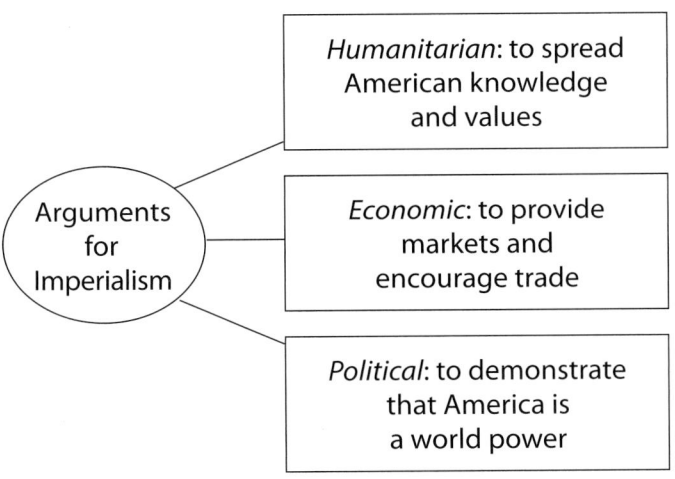

Again, a question on the EOC Assessment might have one empty box and ask you to identify the missing information from the answer choices.

Simple diagrams can also be used to illustrate a sequence of events:

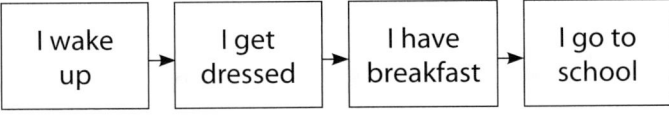

A question on the Georgia Milestones EOC might leave out one of these events and ask you to identify what is missing from the diagram.

The same type of diagram can be used to show a more complex sequence of events:

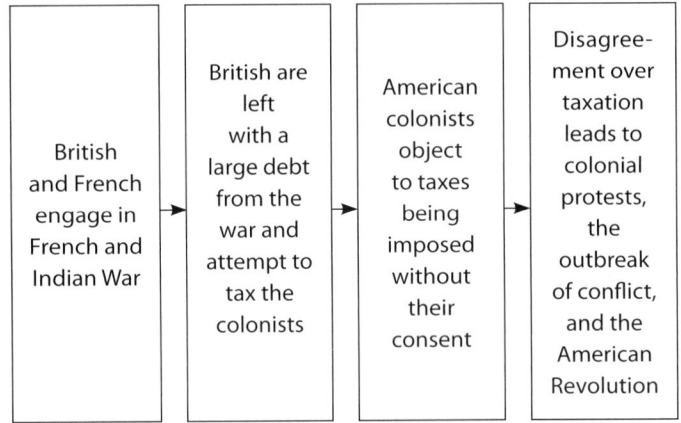

Again, a question on the Georgia Milestones EOC might leave out one of the events in this sequence and ask you to identify what is missing from the diagram. It also might ask you to identify what the diagram shows, or an impact of the events described in the diagram.

Excerpts from Primary Sources

Another common type of question on the Georgia Milestones EOC Assessment asks you to interpret an excerpt from a primary source. The excerpt will appear as the first part of the question. Below the excerpt, the test will usually identify the author, date, and source of the excerpt.

The question may ask you what the excerpt states or shows. You could be asked about the conditions that led to this statement, or about the impact of the statement or its ideas. You might also be asked what other ideas or actions the author of the excerpt would have been likely to approve.

Introduction

Photographs and Pictures

A photograph, drawing, or painting gives us a snapshot into the past. Historians use these sources to understand what the past was really like. To interpret a picture, you have to be a good detective. What details does the picture show? Consider the faces and clothing of the people in the picture. Also, consider the setting or background. What can you learn from it?

Think of the photograph or picture as a piece of evidence. A photograph might be used, for example, to show conditions for workers in an early twentieth-century coal mine. From the photograph, you could see what equipment was used, how crowded the mine was, how much space each worker had, and how safe conditions were. You might also judge how energetic or tired the workers seem, their ages, and their gender and racial background. Questions on a photograph or picture may ask you what it shows or what conclusions you can draw from it.

1. How old are the workers in this coal mine?
2. What equipment are they using?
3. Why do you think this photograph was taken?
4. What conclusions can you draw from this photograph?

Welcome to the American Story

The title of this book is *A Nation Conceived in Liberty*. The title is borrowed from a phrase in Abraham Lincoln's famous "Gettysburg Address." As the Civil War raged around him, President Lincoln asked a critical question: could a nation based on the principles of personal liberty and democratic government survive? Less than a century earlier, the American republic had been founded on the basis of these twin principles at a time when the rest of the world was still ruled by all-powerful kings and queens. Could such a democratic system, in which ordinary citizens held sovereign power, actually work? Or would it eventually break down from disputes between groups of citizens who could not agree? Would "government of the people, by the people, and for the people" perish from the Earth?

This year you will study the history of the United States from its colonial origins until the present. You will find that it is an inspiring story, full of struggle, defeat, and triumph. Several themes stand out: (1) the creation of our system of democratic and limited government, born out of our colonial heritage, revolution against Great Britain, Declaration of Independence, Constitution and Bill of Rights; (2) the territorial expansion of our nation, from the Atlantic coastline to the Pacific and beyond, and the consequences this expansion had on other peoples; (3) the struggle to live up to the promise of equality in our Declaration of Independence by expanding our civil and political rights to all Americans; (4) our technological innovations and accelerated economic growth, which have brought material comfort and prosperity not only to Americans but to the rest of the world; (5) the evolving relationship between our industrial economy and government regulation; and finally (6) America's increasing role in world affairs.

You will learn how Americans at one time were deeply divided by bigotry and racism. Gradually, they overcame slavery, segregation, and the denial of civil rights to minorities. You will see how American women only won the right to vote less than a century ago and the right to equal opportunities in education and employment in recent decades. You will learn how what was once a rural society of isolated communities was totally transformed by the forces of industrialization and urbanization. You will see how modern society was forged by a series of American inventions: the telegraph, the telephone, the electric light bulb, the automobile, the assembly line, radio, television and the computer. Great entrepreneurs turned America into a modern industrial society, based on steel, oil, electricity, and automobiles.

You will see how, throughout our history, people have held differing opinions about how our government should obtain its money—from tariff duties, income taxes, or selling bonds that increase our national debt—as well as on what the role of the government should be in our daily lives.

In the century before the Civil War, America was relatively isolated from the powers of Europe. But after expanding their frontiers to the Pacific and engaging in a great Civil War, Americans were ready to expand outward. They acquired overseas colonies in 1898, and afterward became drawn into two world wars, a "Cold War," and military interventions in the Middle East in defense of democracy and American values. You will consider how these commitments have had enormous costs, and how new weapon technologies, terrorism, and the threat of cyberwar have made modern wars vastly more destructive than conflicts in the past.

What else would you like to know about American history? Identify one thing you would like to learn more about this year on a separate sheet of paper and keep it in a safe place. When you have completed this course, return to the page you have written to see if you have met your objective.

Welcome to the American story. As a young American, it will be up to you to write the next chapter!

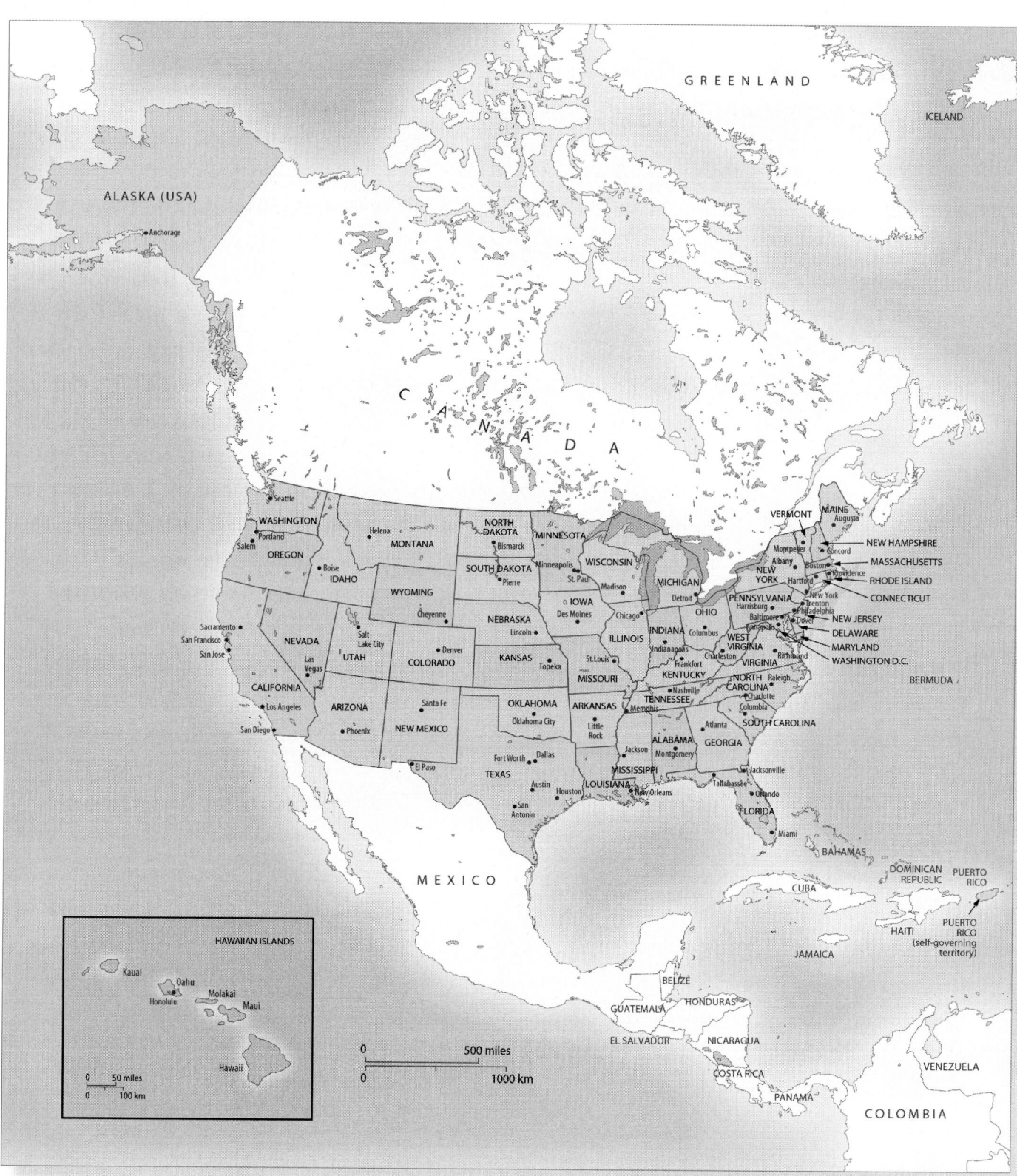

CHAPTER 1 | Colonial Foundations

SSUSH1 How did English settlement and colonization develop during the 17th Century?
  a. How did mercantilism and trans-Atlantic trade lead to the development of colonies?
  b. How did the Southern Colonies develop, including the reasons why they were established, the impact of location and place, their relations with American Indians, and their economic development?
  c. How did the New England Colonies develop, including the reasons why they were established, the impact of location and place, their relations with American Indians, and their economic development?
  d. How did the Mid-Atlantic Colonies develop, including the reasons why they were established, the impact of location and place, their relations with American Indians, and their economic development?

SSUSH2 What was early English colonial society like?
  a. How was colonial society culturally diverse, and what were the contributions of different ethnic and religious groups to colonial society?
  b. What was the Middle Passage? How did the African population in the colonies grow, and what were their contributions to architecture, agriculture, and foodways?
  c. What were the different methods of colonial self-governance in the period of Salutary Neglect?
  d. How did the Great Awakening help unify the colonies and challenge traditional authority?

Names and Terms You Should Know

Mercantilism	James Oglethorpe	"Middle Passage"
House of Burgesses	Debtors	Indentured servants
Mayflower Compact	Southern Colonies	Triangular trades
Puritans	New England Colonies	Salutary Neglect
Religious toleration	Mid-Atlantic Colonies	Great Awakening
William Penn	Trans-Atlantic Slave Trade	

Georgia "Peaches" of Wisdom

1. Mercantilists encouraged European rulers to establish colonies to obtain wealth.

2. In 1607, the first permanent English colony in North America was started at Jamestown. Colonists came to Jamestown to make their fortune.

3. Pilgrims and Puritans came to America for religious reasons. The Pilgrims landed in Plymouth. Before they left their ship, the men signed the **Mayflower Compact** in which they pledged to form their own community and obey its laws. In 1630, the Puritans landed in Massachusetts Bay.

4. Other English colonies were also established. Lord Baltimore started the colony of Maryland as a home for England's Catholics. King Charles II gave eight nobles land for the colony of Carolina. James Oglethorpe started Georgia in 1733 as a home for debtors and as a buffer between the Carolina colonies and the Spanish in Florida.

5. In New England, Roger Williams established the colony of Rhode Island based on religious toleration.

6. In 1664, England took over the Dutch colony of New Netherland and divided it into the colonies of New York, Delaware, and New Jersey. William Penn created a colony for Quakers in Pennsylvania.

7. **Colonial Regions**
The **Southern Colonies** were the warmest and had the longest growing season. Most of their settlers lived spread out on farms. A few Southern landowners owned large plantations that grew cash crops—tobacco, cotton, rice, indigo. They used enslaved African Americans for labor. The slaves were captives from Africa, brought across the Atlantic in cramped slave ships in the brutal "Middle Passage."

The **Mid-Atlantic Colonies** had a milder climate than New England. Their farmers grew wheat, oats, and other grains. People engaged in trade and made goods. This region had the greatest diversity in colonial America.

New England was rocky and cold with a short growing season. New Englanders lived in towns. They grew crops, raised animals, wove cloth, gathered lumber, fished, and engaged in sailing and shipbuilding. New Englanders were active in triangular trades. Their ships carried sugar from the West Indies (Caribbean) to New England, where it was made into rum. The rum was taken to Africa and traded for enslaved Africans. The slaves were taken to the West Indies. New Englanders were religious because of Pilgrim and Puritan influences. Education was important and most people could read and write.

8. Colonists inherited English traditions, including rights under Magna Carta (1215). The colonists also established their own forms of self-government. The British policy of "Salutary Neglect" encouraged colonial self-governance.

9. During the Great Awakening, popular preachers like George Whitefield addressed large numbers of colonists in mass meetings and encouraged them to think for themselves.

The Rise of European Colonial Empires

Before 1492, the peoples of the Eastern and Western Hemispheres had no knowledge of each other (except for the Vikings). This changed when Christopher Columbus, an Italian sea captain, believed he could reach Asia by sailing westwards.

Columbus and his crew crossed the Atlantic Ocean and landed on an island in North America in October. Columbus wrongly thought he had reached Asia.

Columbus made several later voyages, while soon other explorers also began crossing the Atlantic Ocean. Some of these explorers were sent by the rulers of other countries in Western Europe, including Portugal, France, the Netherlands (Holland), and England.

The Spanish conquered the Aztec Empire in Mexico and the Inca Empire of Peru. They took massive amounts of gold and silver from these American empires, making Spain the richest country in Europe. Other Western European nations sent colonists to the Americas to set up their own overseas empires.

The establishment of European colonies in the Americas was greatly influenced by the theory of **mercantilism**. Mercantilists urged European rulers to collect as much gold and silver as possible. These precious metals would enable rulers to pay for large armies and increase their power. Mercantilists believed that the world's wealth was limited. They thought the only way to obtain more wealth was to take it from others through conquest or trade.

Mercantilists believed that overseas colonies were especially useful for their precious metals and raw materials, such as tobacco, sugar, indigo, rice, and lumber. Raw materials from the colonies could be used to make finished goods in Europe. Colonists would then send gold and silver to Europe to pay for expensive finished goods, such as furniture and cloth.

As trade across the Atlantic between the Americas and Europe increased, colonies became more and more attractive.

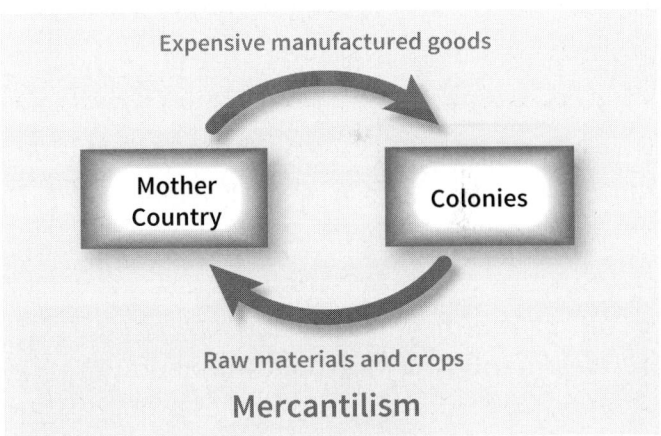
Mercantilism

The Historian's Apprentice

In 1584, Richard Hakluyt wrote a private paper, "Discourse Concerning Western Planting," urging England's Queen Elizabeth to acquire colonies in North America. Hakluyt made the following arguments:

> **1.** That this western discovery will be greatly for the enlargement of the gospel [*teachings*] of Christ whereunto the princes of the reformed religion [*Protestants*] are chiefly bound among whom her Majesty is principal. . . .

Continued ▶

3. That this western voyage will yield unto us all the commodities [*goods; products*] of Europe, Africa, and Asia as far as we were want to travel . . .

13. That hereby the revenues [*income*] and customs [*taxes*] of her Majesty both outwards and inwards shall mightily be enlarged by the toll excises, and other duties [*taxes*] which . . . may be raised. . . .

14. That this action will be for the great increase maintenance and safety of our navy, and especially of great shipping which is the strength of our Realm [*kingdom*], and for the support of all those occupations that depend upon the same. . . .

15. That speedy planting in divers[e] fit places is most necessary upon these last lucky western discoveries for fear of the danger of being prevented by other nations which have the like intention. . . .

20. By the great plenty of those regions the merchants . . . shall lie there cheap, and shall return at pleasure . . . and so he shall be rich and not subject to many hazards [*dangers*], but shall be able to afford [*provide*] the commodities [*products; goods*] for cheap prices to all subjects of the Realm [*kingdom*] . . . .

1. Which of these arguments do you think were most persuasive to Queen Elizabeth of England?
2. Which of these arguments show the influence of mercantilist ideas?

First Southern Colony: Jamestown

The English eventually established colonies along the eastern coast of North America in the South, New England, and the Mid-Atlantic.

> For the Georgia Milestones EOC Assessment, you will not have to know details about individual colonies. You will need to know why each of the three main colonial regions—the Southern, New England, and Mid-Atlantic Colonies—was established and its main characteristics.

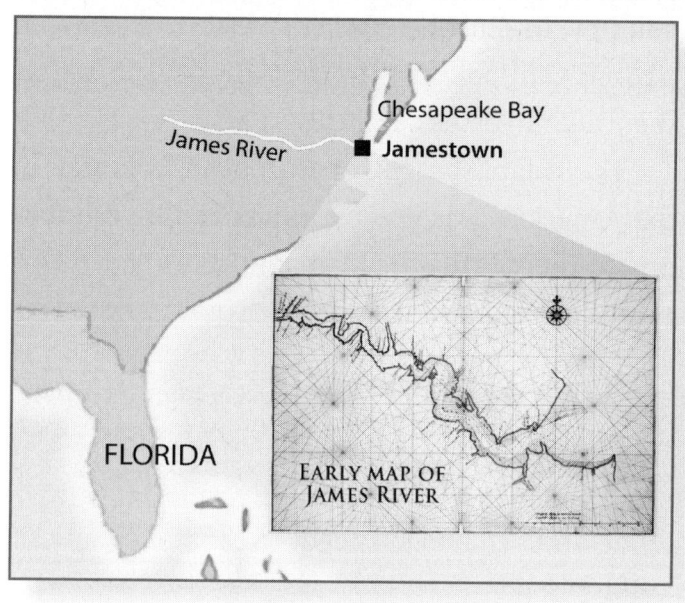

The Southern Colonies (Virginia, North and South Carolina, and Georgia) were mainly founded by investors and speculators who hoped to make money.

The first attempt to establish an English colony in North America in the Outer Banks of North Carolina (1586–1587) failed. The first permanent English colony in North America was established twenty years later at **Jamestown**.

4   Chapter 1 | Colonial Foundations

The **London Company** was formed by English investors who wanted to start a colony. The goal of these investors was to make money. King James, the ruler of England, approved their plan so that England would have its own colony.

The London Company sent three ships across the Atlantic in 1607. They carried just over a hundred colonists, all men. The expedition landed in present-day **Virginia** (named after Queen Elizabeth). The colonists chose to settle on a marshy place on the James River. The river was narrow enough to defend against any future attacks by Spanish ships. But the area was also full of mosquitoes, which carried diseases like malaria.

The colonists at Jamestown built simple cabins. They surrounded their settlement with a stockade of sharpened tree trunks to protect themselves from animals and Indian attacks. Half the newcomers at Jamestown were "gentlemen" who had no intention of working. Instead, they spent their time searching for gold—even though there was none to be found. Soon the settlers started running out of food. Others became sick. More than half of the colonists died.

Despite these losses, the colony survived. New colonists from England kept coming. One colonist, **John Rolfe**, planted tobacco seeds and began growing tobacco. Conditions in Virginia were perfect for this crop, which was already in great demand in Europe. By growing and selling tobacco, the colonists at Jamestown soon prospered.

In 1614, Rolfe married Pocahontas, the daughter of the local Indian chief. This began a period of friendly relations between the colonists and Indians.

The London Company began offering free land to heads of families coming to Virginia, as well as paying for the passage of workers who came as "indentured servants."

In 1619, the first captive Africans arrived. That same year, the colony established its own representative assembly, the **House of Burgesses**. Each district of the colony sent two representatives.

Pilgrims and Puritans in New England

The colony at Jamestown was established by private investors hoping to make money. Its colonists came seeking wealth. The next two groups of English colonists to arrive in North America came for a very different reason: to worship God in their own way. They settled in New England.

The Pilgrims at Plymouth

The **Separatists** were Protestants who disagreed with the teachings of the Church of England—the official Protestant church. Their church leaders decided to start their own colony in North America.

Chapter 1 | Colonial Foundations

About fifty Separatists boarded the ship known as the **Mayflower**. The Separatists were joined by an equal number of other colonists eager to move to the New World. **William Bradford**, one of the leaders of the group, called the colonists "**Pilgrims**." A pilgrim is a person who makes a journey for religious reasons. Unlike the colonists who first went to Jamestown, the passengers on the Mayflower included men, women, and children. They arrived in late November during chilly weather at **Plymouth** (in present-day Massachusetts).

At Plymouth, the Pilgrim colonists faced hardships just as difficult as those at Jamestown. Half of them died from illness in just the first few months.

The Pilgrims were also helped by friendly Indians, who showed them how to plant corn and fertilize the soil with fish.

The Puritans at Massachusetts Bay

Ten years after the Pilgrims landed, a second group of English Protestants arrived. These colonists were known as the **Puritans**. They wanted to "purify" the Church of England. Unlike the Separatists, the Puritans were a very large group—perhaps even a majority of the people in England at the time. But England's new ruler, King Charles I, wanted to take the Church of England in a different direction. Charles disliked the Puritans, who did not respect his authority. Fearing persecution, some Puritans decided to move overseas. In North America, they could establish a community based on their own beliefs without royal interference.

An expedition of 700 Puritan colonists set sail in 1630. They landed in **Massachusetts Bay**, just north of the Pilgrim settlement at Plymouth. Their main settlement was established in Boston.

William Bradford

Like the Pilgrims, the Puritans were very strict. They required attendance in church. They banned gambling, wearing fancy clothing, and watching plays. Life in Puritan Massachusetts centered on avoiding sin and obeying God's commands. The new colony was governed by a group of elected officials known as the **General Court**. Only members of a Puritan congregation could vote in elections or serve on the General Court. To become members of a congregation, colonists had to persuade church leaders that they sincerely held Puritan beliefs.

How the Other English Colonies Were Established

The success of the first three colonies led to the establishment of others. In general, the Southern Colonies were established for economic reasons: for investors, to earn profits, and for the colonists to obtain their own farmland. For example, the Carolinas were established when King Charles I granted land to a few noble friends. The Carolinas then divided into North and South Carolina in 1712. Some Southern Colonies, however, were founded for other reasons: Maryland was established as a home for England's Catholics, while Georgia was founded as a home for debtors and

1607 Jamestown founded

1612 John Rolfe plants tobacco

1619 English women and Africans arrive in Jamestown; House of Burgesses founded

1614 John Rolfe marries Pocahontas

1620 Pilgrims land at Plymouth; Mayflower Compact

to protect the Carolinas. Despite their origins, Maryland and Georgia became largely populated by English settlers who simply hoped to make their fortunes by farming their own land. So many Protestants occupied Maryland that its proprietor, Lord Baltimore, proposed an Edict of Toleration to protect its Catholics. This edict was passed by the colony's assembly in 1649.

In New England, Roger Williams was a minister who believed in religious toleration. He was expelled from Puritan Massachusetts and founded the colony of Rhode Island as a place of religious freedom. Three of the New England Colonies were thus founded for religious reasons—Plymouth, Massachusetts Bay, and Rhode Island. Not all New England Colonies, however, were formed on this basis. Connecticut was founded by a group of settlers from Massachusetts seeking new land. New Hampshire was founded by English investors.

Between the New England and the Southern Colonies lay the Mid-Atlantic Colonies. The Netherlands had established the colony of New Netherland in this region in the early seventeenth century. But the English did not wish to see their colonies to the north and south separated by the Dutch. They therefore conquered New Netherland in 1664. The former Dutch colony was divided into the English colonies of New York, New Jersey, and Delaware. A fourth Mid-Atlantic Colony, Pennsylvania, was founded by William Penn as a home for Quakers. Like several other English colonies founded for religious reasons, Penn's colony was soon filled with English and foreign settlers who were not Quakers. The Mid-Atlantic Colonies displayed greater ethnic and religious diversity than elsewhere because of their Dutch background and the efforts of Penn to recruit settlers from Germany and the rest of Europe.

The Historian's Apprentice

1. Which colonies were founded for religious reasons?
2. What generalizations can you make about why each of the three groups of colonies was established—the New England Colonies, the Mid-Atlantic Colonies, and the Southern Colonies?

Georgia

The construction of "Charles Town" (later known as Charleston) in Carolina in 1670 led to increased tensions between Spain and England. In 1680, the English and their Indian allies attacked Spanish missions on islands in present-day Georgia.

The English government wanted to establish a new colony as a barrier or buffer between Spanish Florida and the English colonies. At this time **James Oglethorpe,** a young military engineer, headed a parliamentary committee investigating conditions in England's debtors' prisons. **Debtors** are people who owe money, but they cannot pay it. In those days, debtors were often sent to prison. Oglethorpe believed that many debtors would do better if provided with a second chance at life. He proposed that these debtors be permitted to move to a new colony in North America. Oglethorpe persuaded others to invest in a new company. These "Georgia Trustees" obtained a charter to start a colony just below South Carolina.

In November 1732, Oglethorpe set sail with 114 settlers. They landed first in Charlestown. The royal governor of South Carolina then went with Oglethorpe and the other colonists to pick a suitable location for the new colony. They chose the mouth of the Savannah River, where a settlement was laid out and built according to Oglethorpe's precise instructions. Oglethorpe signed friendly agreements with the local Indians and invited Highland Scots, known to be skilled fighters, to settle at the southern end of the colony.

Oglethorpe and the other Georgia Trustees limited the size of farms and prohibited slavery and rum in the new colony. They wanted to create a colony of independent farmers made up of former debtors. Oglethorpe directed the colonists in building fortifications, and even led an unsuccessful attack on the Spanish fort at St. Augustine in 1740.

Because of the restrictions placed on Georgia by the Trustees, the colony was not as successful as neighboring South Carolina, where landowners used slave labor to grow rice and indigo on large plantations.

The number of debtors who arrived in Georgia was never great. They were soon outnumbered by other colonists, especially those coming from the Carolinas. Oglethorpe finally returned to England in 1743. In 1750, the ban on slavery in Georgia was lifted. Soon the wealthier colonists began importing slaves and creating large plantations for growing rice and indigo, similar to those in South Carolina. The Georgia Trustees gave up control, and Georgia became a royal colony in 1752.

James Oglethorpe

Relations between the Colonists and Indians

The building of English settlements had harmful effects on local American Indian tribes. The Indians had occupied these lands for thousands of years. They used them for hunting, fishing, and growing corn, squash, and beans. The English had very different ideas of land ownership. They believed in **exclusive ownership**: when an Englishman owned a piece of land, no one else

8   Chapter 1 | Colonial Foundations

1635
Roger Williams banished from Massachusetts

1664
England takes New Netherland and changes its name to "New York"

1712
Carolina divides into North and South Carolina

| 1635 | 1650 | 1700 |

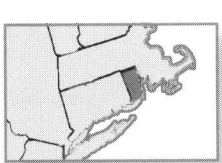

1636
Roger Williams establishes Rhode Island; Connecticut Colony founded

had the right to use it. English settlers cleared the land by cutting down trees, building wooden houses, plowing the soil, and planting crops.

The spread of English settlements reduced the amount of land that Indian tribes living along the Atlantic Coast could use. This led to conflicts between those tribes and other tribes farther west. The introduction of guns and other new weapons made Indian warfare more dangerous. The Indians became dependent on European goods and neglected their own traditional ways. Indian populations were also reduced by the introduction of European diseases such as smallpox.

Relations between Indians and colonists were often friendly at first. But as the size of English settlements grew, especially in the Southern Colonies and New England, relations grew hostile. In Virginia, after the death of Chief Powhatan (the father of Pocahontas), Indians launched a series of attacks on Jamestown. In New England, the son of the Indian chief who had once welcomed the Pilgrims led other tribes in attacking local colonial settlements. They took hundreds of settlers' lives in **King Philip's War** (1675–1676), although they were eventually defeated. Farther south, the Tuscarora Indians started a war against English settlers in North Carolina in 1711. This conflict lasted several years until the Tuscarora were defeated.

Colonists fighting Indians

The Historian's Apprentice

1. Make your own chart identifying some of the effects that the arrival of English colonists had on local American Indian nations.
2. Pretend that you are at a meeting of Indian leaders. Write a speech about how you think they should respond to the increasing numbers of English colonists.

Chapter 1 | Colonial Foundations

The Three Regions of Colonial America

By the early 1700s, English colonies lined the Atlantic Coast. They formed three separate regions: the Southern Colonies, the New England Colonies, and the Mid-Atlantic Colonies.

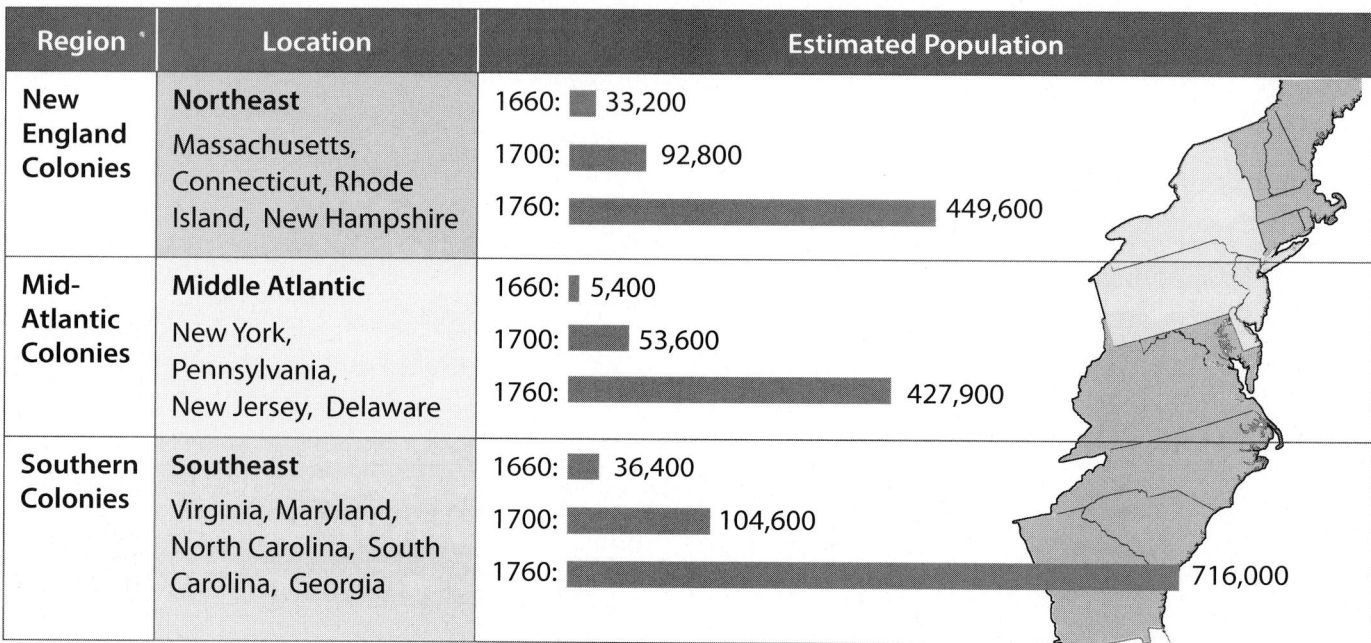

Region	Location	Estimated Population
New England Colonies	**Northeast** Massachusetts, Connecticut, Rhode Island, New Hampshire	1660: 33,200 1700: 92,800 1760: 449,600
Mid-Atlantic Colonies	**Middle Atlantic** New York, Pennsylvania, New Jersey, Delaware	1660: 5,400 1700: 53,600 1760: 427,900
Southern Colonies	**Southeast** Virginia, Maryland, North Carolina, South Carolina, Georgia	1660: 36,400 1700: 104,600 1760: 716,000

The colonies in each of these regions shared important characteristics.

The Southern Colonies

The Impact of Location and Place

Because of their southern location, the Southern Colonies had warmer weather and a longer growing season than either of the other regions.

Most Southern colonists could trace their roots to England, Scotland, or Ireland. A majority were Anglicans (members of the Church of England). People usually came to these colonies for economic reasons, especially to obtain their own land.

Economic Development

In the Southern Colonies, people were spread out on farms. A few wealthy landowners owned **plantations** (*very large farms that grew just a few crops*). Plantations were found along the major water routes (*rivers and streams*) of the wide coastal plain. They benefited from the region's deep rivers. Plantation owners enjoyed privileged lifestyles. They bought English clothes, furniture, glass, and other luxury products. They used slaves as their house servants. Their children had private tutors. Some even sent their children back to England to study. Others sent their children to study at the College of William and Mary in Virginia, the second oldest college in the United States.

Southern plantations grew **cash crops** for sale in England—tobacco, cotton, rice, and indigo (*a plant producing a blue dye*). It was hard for the early Southern landowners to keep workers. With plenty of available land, many workers just wanted to leave and get farms of their own. Southern

10   Chapter 1 | Colonial Foundations

The "Middle Passage"

New slaves were people first captured in Africa by members of a different tribe. Then they were marched to stone fortresses along the coast of West Africa, where they were sold to European slave traders. The slave traders bound them together in chains and crammed them into ships, which carried them across the Atlantic. Slavers called this the **"Middle Passage"** because it was the middle voyage in the triangular trades connecting Africa, England and the colonies. Often the captives were chained down and could barely move throughout the long passage. One fifth of them died during the voyage. Those who survived arrived in the West Indies, Brazil, or the English colonies where they were sold to landowners at slave auctions. Most of them were used as field workers where they were subjected to brutal conditions.

Slavery in the British Colonies

Year	1650	1700	1750	1780
Enslaved Population	1,600	27,817	236,420	575,420
Total Population	50,368	250,888	1,170,760	2,780,369

Source: U.S. Census Bureau

A slave auction in 1655

The Historian's Apprentice

Olaudah Equiano was born in West Africa. He was kidnapped and sold into slavery at the age of 11. He later saved enough money to purchase his freedom and move to England, where he published a book telling of his experiences. Here he writes of his arrival at the ship that will carry him across the Atlantic on the "Middle Passage":

> The first object which saluted my eyes when I arrived on the coast was the sea, and a slave-ship, which was then riding at anchor, and waiting for its cargo. These filled me with astonishment, which was soon converted into terror, which I am yet at a loss to describe, nor the then feelings of my mind. When I was carried on board I was immediately handled, and tossed up, to see if I were sound, by some of the crew; and I was now persuaded that I was got into a world of bad spirits, and that they were

Continued ▶

Chapter 1 | Colonial Foundations

going to kill me. Their complexions too differing so much from ours, their long hair, and the language they spoke, which was very different from any I had ever heard, united to confirm me in this belief. . . . I now saw myself deprived of all chance of returning to my native country, or even the least glimpse of hope of gaining the shore, which I now considered as friendly: and I even wished for my former slavery in preference to my present situation, which was filled with horrors of every kind, still heightened by my ignorance of what I was to undergo. I was not long suffered to indulge my grief; I was soon put down under the decks, and there I received such a salutation in my nostrils as I had never experienced in my life; so that with the loathsomeness of the stench, and crying together, I became so sick and low that I was not able to eat, nor had I the least desire to taste any thing. I now wished for the last friend, Death, to relieve me; but soon, to my grief, two of the white men offered me eatables; and, on refusing to eat, one of them held me fast by the hands, and laid me across, I think, the windlass, and tied my feet, while the other flogged me severely. I had never experienced any thing of this kind before.

Olaudah Equiano, *The Interesting Narrative of the Life of Olaudah Equiano* (1789)

1. What does this tell us about the conditions on the "Middle Passage"?
2. How would you have reacted if you had been a captured African who was brought to a slave ship?
3. What impression do you think Equiano's account had on readers?

landowners at first relied on indentured servants. They paid for servants' passages from England in return for several years of labor on their farms. Southern landowners increasingly relied on enslaved people to work the land and harvest their crops. These slaves were Africans brought to the colonies by force, as well as their **descendants** (*children and later generations*). The first Africans may have been treated as indentured servants, but between 1640 and 1690, Virginia changed its laws by turning African Americans into servants for life. Virginia and other colonies passed **slave codes** (*laws that limited the freedom of enslaved people*).

Most white Southerners were not slave owners. Many settlers first came to the South as indentured servants themselves. In the foothills (above the "fall line") of the Appalachian Mountains, these people became farmers working their own land. Many grew just enough food for their own families, known as **subsistence farming**. They made their own clothes and furniture, and taught their children at home.

The New England Colonies

The Impact of Location and Place

New England had rocky soil, cooler temperatures, and a short growing season. Surprisingly, people often lived longer in New England than in the Southern Colonies because its cold winters killed mosquitoes, which carried disease.

New Englanders generally lived next to each other in towns, where they could worship together. Each town had a village green for public celebrations. Farms were located in fields just outside the town. Lands were divided among the children, so no great landed properties developed as in England. By the early eighteenth century, some of New England's original settlements, such as Boston and Providence, had become bustling port cities.

Religion

New England was influenced by the fact that many of its original colonists came there to worship God in their own way. Church ministers continued to hold great authority. In Massachusetts Bay Colony, only members of Puritan congregations could vote for government officials.

Education

New England was an early center of education. Puritans believed that both men and women should be able to read the Bible. Two-thirds of the men and nearly half of the women in New England could read. The fact that New Englanders lived together in towns made it easier for them to build schoolhouses. In 1647, Massachusetts Bay Colony decided that every town with fifty or more families should have its own public school. The first American universities also opened in New England. Harvard, the oldest college in the United States, was founded in Boston in 1636.

Economic Development

Many colonists in New England grew crops and raised animals for their own use. Others worked in skilled crafts as blacksmiths, weavers, and printers. A large number of New Englanders worked by cutting trees for lumber, as fishermen, by building ships, or by carrying cargo over the ocean.

The Mid-Atlantic Colonies

The Impact of Location and Place

Winters in the Mid-Atlantic Colonies were not as harsh as in New England. The growing season was longer and the land was less rocky and more fertile. Much of the region was still forest that had to be cleared to make farms and towns.

Economic Development

The Mid-Atlantic Colonies produced much of the food that was eaten in the colonies. Its farmers grew wheat, corn, oats, and other grains. They raised cattle, pigs, and other animals. Wheat from the Mid-Atlantic Colonies was sent to the West Indies and Britain.

People in the Mid-Atlantic Colonies engaged in trade and making goods, as well as farming. **Philadelphia**, the capital of Pennsylvania, became the largest city of colonial America by 1760. Another important city in this region was **New York City**.

There was greater **diversity** (*variety*) in the Mid-Atlantic Colonies than elsewhere in British America. In addition to the English, many of its residents were Dutch, German, French, or Scottish. Enslaved Africans were also found in

Massachusetts Hall—Harvard's oldest building

Chapter 1 | Colonial Foundations

The Triangular Trades

New Englanders were especially active in the **triangular trades**. A triangular trade takes place when three places trade together. English ships carried sugar from the islands of the Caribbean (known as the West Indies) to New England. There it was made into rum. The rum might be shipped to Africa, where it was traded for enslaved people. New England merchants also sold fish and lumber to plantation owners in the West Indies. The same ships then carried sugar from the West Indies to England, where the sugar was sold and the ships were filled with English manufactured goods. In yet another triangular trade, ships filled with sugar, tobacco, flour, indigo, lumber, and rum sailed from New England to England. These ships then carried cloth, manufactured goods, and rum to Africa. These goods were then exchanged for captured Africans, who were taken across the Atlantic to the Americas as slaves.

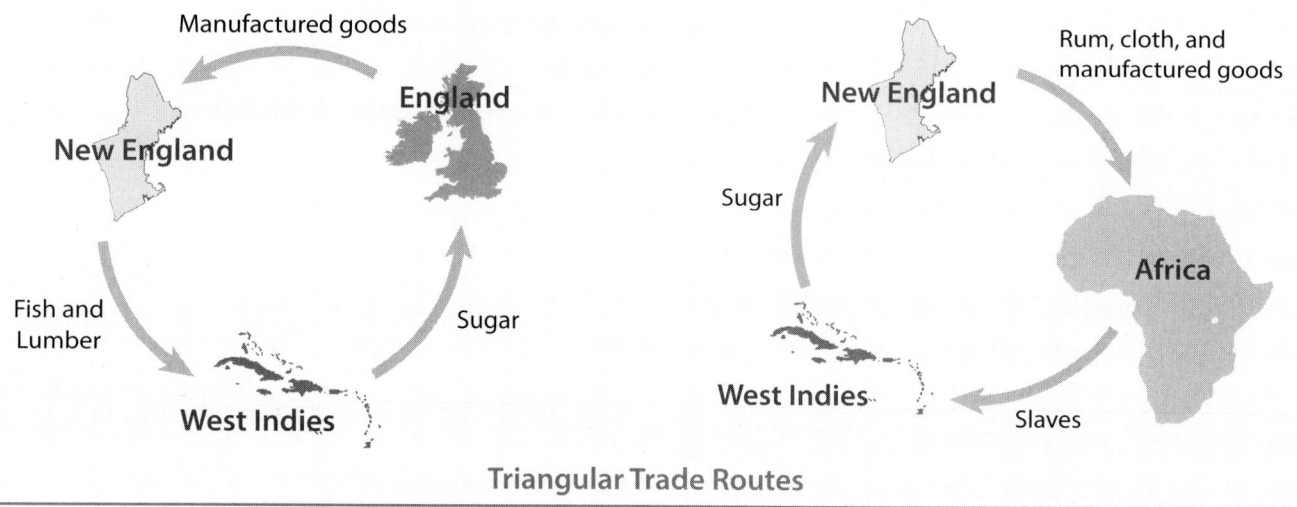

Triangular Trade Routes

The English government controlled this trade across the Atlantic through a series of laws known as the **Navigation Acts**, passed in the mid-1600s. The Navigation Acts stated that all goods shipped to or from the colonies had to be carried on English (and English colonial) ships. Goods from other parts of Europe could only be sent to the colonies from an English port. Finally, goods from the colonies could only be exported to England and not to other parts of Europe. These laws promoted the mercantilist goal of enriching England, the "mother country."

Indentured Servants

Many settlers in the colonies came as **indentured servants**. An indentured servant was a person who signed a contract (*written agreement*) in England with a sponsor. The sponsor paid the expenses for the person to come to America. The indentured servant agreed, in return, to work for the sponsor for four to seven years. After that, the indentured servant was free to do whatever he or she wished.

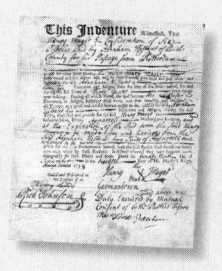

the Mid-Atlantic Colonies, where they served as farm workers and skilled craftsmen. Because of the diversity of its religions, **religious toleration** was introduced. Dutch Reformed Protestants, Anglicans (*members of the Church of England*), Catholics, Quakers, Lutherans, and Jews all lived peacefully side-by-side.

The Historian's Apprentice

What reasons led to the greater diversity of the Mid-Atlantic Colonies? Discuss the answer to this question with a partner.

Complete this map by identifying each colony on the blank line.

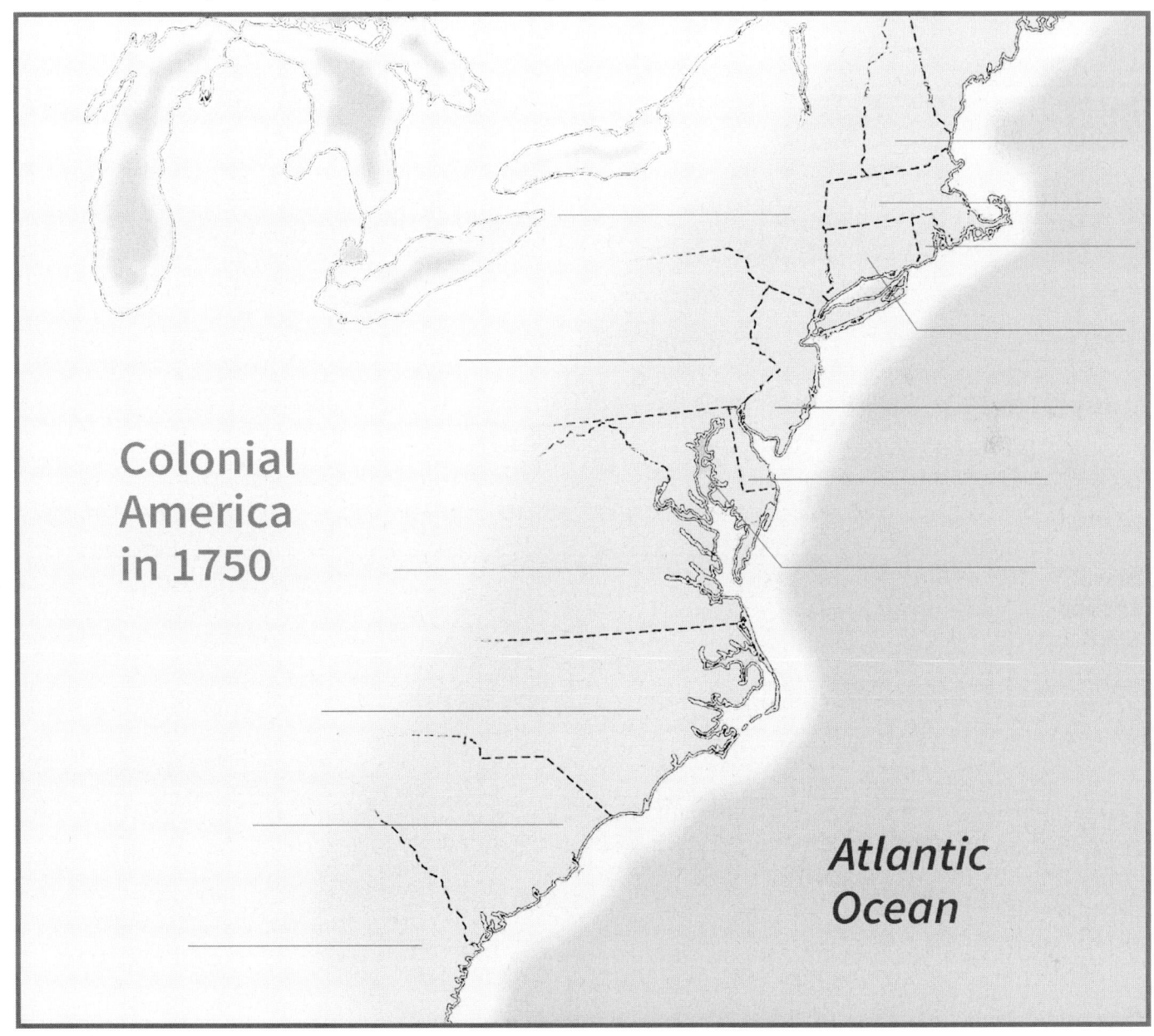

Colonial America in 1750

Atlantic Ocean

Chapter 1 | Colonial Foundations

Fill in the chart below about England's colonies.

Region	Reasons Established	Impact of Location and Place	Relations with American Indians	Economic Development
Southern Colonies				
Mid-Atlantic Colonies				
New England Colonies				

The Contributions of Key Groups

All three colonial regions displayed great cultural diversity. Many different groups made contributions to the development of colonial America.

American Indians 	Relations between settlers and Indians were often peaceful at first. Friendly Indians showed the early colonists how to grow crops in local conditions. They traded furs and foods with the colonists in exchange for guns and other European goods. However, the colonists kept taking more and more land. This led to conflicts between settlers and Indians, especially in New England and the Southern Colonies. In the Mid-Atlantic Colonies, there were fewer conflicts and colonists continued to trade with the Indians for furs and other goods.
Africans 	Africans were brought to the colonies by force. The earliest Africans may have been brought as indentured servants. Later, they were brought as enslaved persons. Slaves did most of the work on Southern plantations. They also worked as craftsmen in all the colonies. Some brought special expertise from Africa to the Americas. For example, traditional African ways of growing rice were successfully adopted in South Carolina. Africans taught the settlers how to successfully plant, harvest, and hull rice. Traditional African foods were also brought to the colonies, such as okra. Africans brought their own forms of music, dance, storytelling, basket weaving, and pottery making. Africans who arrived in the Americas actually represented hundreds of different cultures, each with its own language and customs. Eventually, a new African-American culture was born, based on the shared experience of slavery. New blended languages developed, such as Creole and Gullah. Over time, some enslaved Africans were freed, creating important communities of free African Americans.
Women 	In colonial times, women worked in the home, on farms, and in businesses. They helped plant and harvest crops, cooked food, and sewed clothes. They acted as nurses to other family members. Women had the primary responsibility for raising and teaching their children. At the same time, they did not enjoy the same rights as men. For example, women could not vote or hold public office.
English 	The largest groups of settlers in the thirteen colonies were from England. The English contributed their language and literature, their ways of growing food and building houses, their clothing styles, their music and art, their scientific and medical knowledge, their laws, and their form of government.

Chapter 1 | Colonial Foundations

Scots and Scots-Irish 	People from Scotland, known as Scots, arrived with the earliest colonists. A group of Highland Scots, known for their fierce fighting skills, founded the settlement of Darien in southern Georgia. The Scots-Irish were Protestant Scottish families who moved from Scotland to Northern Ireland in the 1600s. They became one of the largest groups coming to the colonies in the 1700s. Many of the Scots-Irish went to the "backcountry" of the Southern Colonies—the foothills of the Appalachian Mountains. They established their own churches and kept their unique speech patterns and folk songs, enriching American English.
Germans and Dutch 	William Penn made a special effort to attract German settlers to Pennsylvania. His advertisements claimed that abundant farmland, good soil, and plenty of food could be found there. Penn also promised religious freedom and no requirements for military service. Some Germans migrated to Pennsylvania in response to Penn's appeal. They soon invited their relatives and friends to join them, leading to a steady flow of settlers from the German states to the English colonies. Germans later came to escape warfare in Europe and for better economic opportunities. They brought traditions of craftsmanship, such as furniture making, and often lived in their own communities where they could speak in German. Dutch settlers in New York contributed Dutch foods and customs, such as pancakes and bowling, Dutch words, and traditions of religious tolerance and diversity.
Diverse Religious Groups 	Anglicans (members of the Church of England), Puritans, Catholics, Jews, German Lutherans, Dutch Reformed Protestants, Quakers, and other Protestant groups were all found in colonial America. Each made its own contributions to colonial society. The Quakers, for example, promoted a belief in equality and condemned war. The diversity of religions in the colonies encouraged a spirit of toleration and the separation of church and state.

How the English Colonies Were Governed

English Political and Legal Traditions

English colonists benefited from centuries-old traditions they brought from England. Four hundred years earlier, English subjects had won important rights. In 1215, King John had granted his subjects a "Great Charter," better known by its Latin name, **Magna Carta**.

In Magna Carta, John agreed not to collect new taxes without the approval of a council of nobles.

A copy of Magna Carta

He also promised not to put individuals in prison or take away their property without following the laws of the land and giving them a trial by jury.

Magna Carta gave the English people rights unknown in the rest of Europe. The charter also led to the later creation of **Parliament**—an assembly that the king called together whenever he wanted to get the support of his subjects or collect new taxes. **Parliament** consisted of all the nobles, who made up the House of Lords, and representatives elected by the common people, who sat in the House of Commons.

Colonial Government

The colonies were thousands of miles from England. In those days, a ship could take more than a month to sail across the Atlantic. From the beginning, the colonists therefore needed some form of local government to deal with immediate problems as they arose.

- The Virginia Company created the **House of Burgesses**—a representative assembly—in 1619.

- The Pilgrims pledged to create their own form of government and to obey it in the **Mayflower Compact** of 1620.

- In Massachusetts Bay Colony, Puritan communities held **town meetings**. Members of Puritan congregations voted to elect members of the **General Court**, which acted as an assembly for the entire colony.

- When Thomas Hooker took colonists from Massachusetts to Connecticut, he gave them the "**Fundamental Orders of Connecticut**." This document gave all adult men in the colony the right to vote. Hooker's Fundamental Orders was an early type of **constitution** (*a plan of government*).

- In 1682, **William Penn** gave the colonists of Pennsylvania a "**Frame of Government**." Like the Fundamental Orders of Connecticut, Penn's Frame was an early type of constitution.

The Historian's Apprentice

The following excerpts are from William Penn's "Frame of Government." After reading these excerpts, write a paragraph explaining how the colonists of Pennsylvania benefited from these arrangements.

Frame of Government of Pennsylvania, May 5, 1682

That the government of this province shall . . . consist of the Governor and freemen of the said province, in form of a Provincial Council and General Assembly, by whom all laws shall be made, officers chosen, and public affairs transacted . . .

II. That the freemen of the said province shall . . . ch[oo]se out of themselves 72 persons of most note for their wisdom, virtue and ability, who shall meet, on the tenth day of the first month next . . . and act as the Provincial Council . . . .

Continued ▶

Chapter 1 | Colonial Foundations

VII. That the Governor and Provincial Council shall prepare and propose to the General Assembly . . . all bills, which they shall, at any time, think fit to be passed into laws . . .

IX. That the Governor and Provincial Council shall, at all times, have the care of the peace and safety of the province . . .

X. That the Governor and Provincial Council shall, at all times, settle and order the situation of all cities, ports, and market towns in every county, modeling therein all public buildings, streets, and market places, and shall appoint all necessary roads, and highways in the province. . . .

XII. That the Governor and Provincial Council shall [establish] all public schools, and encourage and reward the authors of useful sciences and . . . inventions in the said province. . . .

1. How did the Provincial Council and General Assembly differ?
2. In Penn's Frame of Government, which branch represented the citizens of the colony?
3. What evidence is there in this document that William Penn valued education?
4. Do you think this was a good plan for the colony's government? Why or why not?

By 1700, a similar pattern of government could be found in all the British colonies. Each colony had a governor, a governor's council, and a colonial assembly. The colonial government managed local issues, such as relations with the Indians. The royal government in England handled overseas trade and relations with foreign governments.

The "Glorious Revolution"

New England was made up of five separate colonies. In 1685, King James II of England decided to join them all together into a single colony. The new colony was named the "Dominion of New England." It had only one royal governor. The King was trying to tighten royal control over the colonies.

James II also tried to increase his power in England. He had converted to Catholicism and became very unpopular. The English Parliament finally overthrew James during the "**Glorious**

English or British?

Just as the United States is made up of different states, the United Kingdom is made up of different kingdoms. At one time, England, Wales, Scotland, and Ireland were all separate countries. Together they make up the British Isles. Great Britain is the main island, consisting of England in the east, Wales in the west, and Scotland to the north. In the Middle Ages, Prince Edward conquered Wales and joined it to England. In 1603, the King of Scotland became the King of England. At first, the two countries remained separate. They were finally joined together by the Act of Union in 1707. Historians thus refer to the original American colonies as "English." After the Act of Union in 1707, the colonies became "British."

Colonial Governments in 1700

	The **governor** acted as an **executive**—an official who enforced the laws.
	The **governor's council** was appointed to advise the governor. The council also acted as the "supreme court" for the colony. It looked at appeals from the decisions of judges. Thus it acted as a judicial branch.
	The **colonial assembly** was made up of elected representatives. It acted as a **legislature**—a law-making body. By 1700, all free white adult male property owners in most colonies could vote.

The main difference between the colonies was in how their governors were chosen.

	In **royal colonies**, the king chose the governor. This meant the British government in London appointed the governor.
	In **proprietary colonies**, the king gave a charter to one or more proprietors. For example, Charles II granted his brother, the Duke of York, a charter for New York. He also granted charters to William Penn, Lord Baltimore, the Lords Proprietors for the Carolinas, and two Lords Proprietors for New Jersey. In these colonies, the proprietors chose the governor.
	In **self-governing colonies**, such as Connecticut and Rhode Island, the colonial assembly chose the governor.

Over time, a colony's form of government could change. Many proprietary colonies later became royal colonies.

Chapter 1 | Colonial Foundations

Revolution" of 1688. The King was replaced by his daughter Mary and her husband William, who also ruled the Netherlands.

The following year, Parliament passed the **English Bill of Rights**—a list of rights that were guaranteed to all English subjects. These included freedom of religion for Protestants, a ban on cruel and unusual punishment, and freedom of speech in Parliament.

Writers like **John Locke** justified the Glorious Revolution. Locke argued that the king's power did not come from God but was the result of a "**social contract**." The people had given the king his power in order to protect their individual rights. The people had the right to overthrow their king when he violated the terms of this contract.

John Locke

In New England, the colonists rebelled against the single colony created by James II. They locked up its governor. After James II was overthrown, New England was again divided into the same separate colonies as before. There was one exception: Massachusetts Bay Colony and Plymouth Colony were combined into a single colony known as Massachusetts.

The Period of Salutary Neglect

From the 1720s onwards, the British government did not actively interfere in the government of the colonies. It left most decisions up to the local governors and colonial legislatures. This policy is sometimes known as "**Salutary Neglect.**" "Salutary" means helpful or beneficial. During this period, even the Navigation Acts were not strictly enforced, allowing the colonists to prosper. So long as the colonists were providing trade and helping the British to meet their mercantilist goal of accumulating riches, the British did not interfere with the colonists very much. In this way, the colonists became used to governing themselves. British leaders decided the colonies would be more profitable to Britain if they were less regulated.

During the period of Salutary Neglect, the colonists developed greater confidence in their ability to govern themselves and a separate colonial identity began to emerge. This development would later play a role in the American Revolution.

The Great Awakening

By the 1730s, many Protestants in England and America believed that in order to go to Heaven it was not enough to attend church and participate in religious ceremonies. They believed a good Christian must have strong religious feelings.

In England, several preachers tried to stir up those religious feelings with emotional sermons. Earlier ministers had used their sermons to discuss Bible passages in a dry and scholarly way. Now some preachers became much more emotional. They warned their listeners to look into their very souls to see if they were sinners. Then they told them to put all their faith in Jesus Christ to find salvation; if not, they would face the fires of damnation. This movement became known as the "**Great Awakening.**" In some ways, it was a reaction to the Enlightenment, which had emphasized logic and reason over emotion.

During the Great Awakening, **George Whitefield**, an English preacher, visited the colonies. He held large open-air meetings, which thousands of people would attend. In Boston, **Jonathan Edwards** also spread the message of the Great Awakening in his sermons.

During the Great Awakening, people participated actively in religious services instead of just listening to their minister. **Salvation** (*going to Heaven*) became an individual act. This created a new equality among all believers. Puritans had believed that only a chosen few would go to Heaven. Now, preachers taught that all those who put their faith in God and repented for their sins could go there.

The Great Awakening led people to think more for themselves. It questioned the authority of ministers and church officials. It inspired African slaves to accept Christianity, while urging better treatment from their masters. The Great Awakening appealed to women and encouraged them to be more independent. It brought large numbers of colonists together in mass meetings. It prepared the colonists to speak more openly. It united people across the thirteen colonies in a common cause. These qualities would be important in the future when colonists had disagreements with the British government.

George Whitefield preaching

The Historian's Apprentice

Jonathan Edwards was born in Connecticut in 1703. His father was a Protestant minister. Edwards went to college at Yale, studied Locke and Newton, and became a minister himself. He concluded that the colonists had become too concerned with worldly pleasures and material gain. They had lost their interest in God.

A **sermon** is a short talk that a minister gives during a church service, explaining a passage from the Bible. Edwards preached a series of sermons that became part of the Great Awakening. The following sermon, delivered in Connecticut in July 1741, was his most famous. He described the torments of hell and warned his listeners that they might die and be sent there at any moment. But Edwards also told his listeners that all of them had an opportunity to escape hell if they would just awaken themselves and accept Christian teachings.

Sinners in the Hands of an Angry God

It is no security to wicked men for one moment that there are no visible means of death at hand. It is no security to a natural man that he is now in health and that he does not see which way he should now immediately go out of the world by any accident... The unseen, unthought of ways

Continued ▶

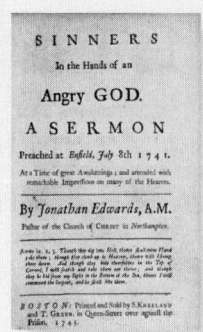 and means of persons going suddenly out of the world are innumerable and inconceivable. Unconverted men walk over the pit of hell on a rotten covering, and there are innumerable places in this covering so weak that they will not bear their weight, and these places are not seen. The arrows of death fly unseen at noon-day; the sharpest sight cannot discern them. . . .

Your wickedness makes you as it were heavy as lead, and to tend downwards with great weight and pressure towards hell; and if God should let you go, you would immediately sink and swiftly descend and plunge into the bottomless gulf. God . . . holds you over the pit of hell, much as one holds a spider, or some loathsome insect over the fire . . .

O sinner! Consider the fearful danger you are in: it is a great furnace of wrath, a wide and bottomless pit, full of the fire of wrath, that you are held over in the hand of that God, whose wrath is provoked and incensed as much against you, as against many of the damned in hell. You hang by a slender thread, with the flames of divine wrath flashing about it, and ready every moment to singe it, and burn it asunder. . .

And now you have an extraordinary opportunity, a day wherein Christ has thrown the door of mercy wide open, and stands in calling and crying with a loud voice to poor sinners; a day wherein many are flocking to him, and pressing into the kingdom of God. Many are daily coming from the east, west, north and south; many that were very lately in the same miserable condition that you are in, are now in a happy state, with their hearts filled with love to him who has loved them, and washed them from their sins in his own blood, and rejoicing in hope of the glory of God. How awful is it to be left behind at such a day! How can you rest one moment in such a condition? . . .

Are there not many here who have lived long in the world, and are not to this day born again? . . . You had need to consider yourselves, and awake thoroughly out of sleep. . . You especially have now an extraordinary opportunity; but if you neglect it, it will soon be with you as with those persons who spent all the precious days of youth in sin, and are now come to such a dreadful pass in blindness and hardness.

Therefore, let every one that is out of Christ, now awake and fly from the wrath to come.

Word Helper

innumerable = many; without number

inconceivable = impossible to think of

unconverted = not converted to Christian belief

discern = see; recognize; make out

loathsome = repulsive; disgusting

incensed = very angry; enraged

slender = narrow

divine wrath = God's wrath

asunder = apart

flocking = coming in groups

---

1. Examine the first paragraph. What does Edwards mean by go "suddenly out of the world"? Why does he emphasize that this could happen at any time?
2. What are the dangers of hell that Edwards speaks of? According to Edwards, what keeps the unconverted from plunging into hell?

3. How does Edwards engage the attention of his listeners? If you had been listening to this sermon, what emotions might you have felt?
4. What is the "extraordinary opportunity" that Edwards mentions at the end of his sermon?
5. What does Edwards mean when he tells his listeners that they "need to consider yourselves, and awake thoroughly out of sleep," or when he tells them: "now awake"?
6. How did this sermon promote a greater sense of equality among all believers, including people of different social classes and races?
7. How did this and similar sermons during the Great Awakening contribute to colonial opposition to British policies just a few decades later at the time of the American Revolution?

For the Georgia Milestones EOC Assessment, you need to know that:

- ☐ Mercantilism was a theory based on the belief that rulers should accumulate as much gold and silver as possible. Mercantilists encouraged European rulers to acquire colonies in the Americas as a source of precious metals and for favorable terms of trade.

- ☐ The rise of trans-Atlantic trade encouraged the development of colonies.

- ☐ Most of England's Southern Colonies (Virginia, Maryland, North and South Carolina, Georgia) began as commercial ventures. Investors hoped to make money and colonists sought their own land. The Southern Colonies had a long growing season and a warm climate. Colonists became successful by planting tobacco, cotton, and indigo, and exporting these crops to England.

- ☐ Several New England Colonies were founded for religious reasons (the Pilgrims at Plymouth, the Puritans in Massachusetts Bay, and Roger Williams in Rhode Island). Connecticut and New Hampshire were settled by colonists from Massachusetts. New England had harsh winters and a short growing season. New Englanders became especially active in shipbuilding, fishing, and trade.

- ☐ Several of the Mid-Atlantic Colonies (New York, New Jersey, and Delaware) were captured by the English from the Netherlands. Another Mid-Atlantic Colony, Pennsylvania, was founded by William Penn as a home for Quakers. The Mid-Atlantic Colonies showed greater diversity than elsewhere. Their climate was milder than farther north or south, and they became the "bread basket" of the thirteen colonies.

- ☐ Different groups of Africans were captured by rival tribes, marched to the coast of West Africa, and sold to Europeans engaged in the **Trans-Atlantic slave trade**. The captives were chained together and crammed into ships for the "Middle Passage"—the crossing of the Atlantic to the West Indies or the thirteen colonies. Enslaved Africans were harshly treated, sold at auctions, and forced to labor on plantations as house servants and at other tasks. Southern planters relied increasingly on enslaved Africans to grow the crops they exported to England.

Continued ▶

- ☐ The thirteen colonies displayed great ethnic diversity with English, African, Scots, Scots-Irish, Dutch, and German settlers. Each group made contributions to colonial society, including foods, furniture and housing styles, clothing and words that were adapted to the English language.

- ☐ The thirteen colonies also displayed great religious diversity, with different Protestant groups, Catholics, and Jews.

- ☐ Colonial merchants, especially from New England, engaged in triangular trades—for example, their ships carried rum and manufactured goods to Africa, enslaved Africans from Africa to the West Indies (Caribbean), and sugar from the West Indies to New England.

- ☐ The colonists enjoyed the traditional rights of English subjects, including the right to trial by jury guaranteed in Magna Carta in 1215. Because England was so far away, the colonists also developed their own forms of self-government: the House of Burgesses (1619); the Mayflower Compact (1620); the Fundamental Orders of Connecticut (1639); and William Penn's Frame of Government (1682). By 1750, all the colonies had a colonial assembly and a governor (usually chosen by the British government). During the period of Salutary Neglect, the British let the colonists largely govern themselves.

- ☐ The Great Awakening was an outburst of religious feelings in the colonies in the mid-18th century. Preachers urged their listeners to seek salvation. The Great Awakening challenged traditional authority, brought colonists together in large assemblies, encouraged people to think for themselves, and helped to unify the colonies.

Name _____

Complete the following chart.

Term	Identify/Describe
Middle Passage	
Contributions of Africans	
Contributions of English	
Contributions of Scots and Scots-Irish	
Contributions of Germans and Dutch	
Methods of Colonial Self-Government	
The Great Awakening	

Name _____

Complete the paragraph frame below.

In the seventeenth and eighteenth centuries, mercantilists believed that a nation's wealth was based on its possession of gold and silver. They further believed that the world's supply of these precious metals was _____. Therefore a country could only obtain wealth through conquest or a favorable balance of _____. They believed that colonies were especially because _____
_____.

Because of their mercantilist beliefs, several rulers of Western Europe established colonial empires across the Atlantic.

The English colonies developed in three separate regions: the Southern Colonies, New England Colonies and Mid-Atlantic Colonies. The reason why most of the Southern Colonies were founded was _____.

These colonies were located _____.

Relations between the Southern colonists and local Native American tribes were generally _____
_____.

Because of their warm climate and long growing season, economic life in the Southern Colonies was focused on _____
_____.

The use of enslaved individuals as a work force became especially common in the Southern Colonies. Enslaved people _____
_____.

The New England Colonies were located _____.
The main reason most of these colonies were founded was _____
_____.

Relations between the New England colonists and local Native American tribes were generally _____
_____.

Because of their cooler climate and shorter growing season, much of the economic life in the New England Colonies was focused on _____.

The Mid-Atlantic Colonies were located _____.
The main reason most of these colonies were founded was _____.
Relations between the Mid-Atlantic colonists and local Native American tribes were generally _____
_____.

Because of their favorable climate and fertile soil, much of the economic life in the Mid-Atlantic Colonies became focused on _____.

The Mid-Atlantic Colonies were especially known for their ethnic and religious diversity.

Chapter 1 | Colonial Foundations

Colonial Foundations

The First English Colonies

Jamestown, Virginia
- Founded in 1607
- Growing tobacco brought profit
- 1619—Women and enslaved persons arrive; House of Burgesses

Plymouth
- Founded by Pilgrims in 1620
- Mayflower Compact (1620)—Self-government

Massachusetts Bay
- Founded by Puritans in 1630 who wanted to "purify" the Church

Impact of Colonists on American Indians
- General impact was harmful
- English colonists took over land—exclusive ownership
- Introduced guns
- Brought European diseases like smallpox
- Defeated Indians in wars

The Regions of Colonial America

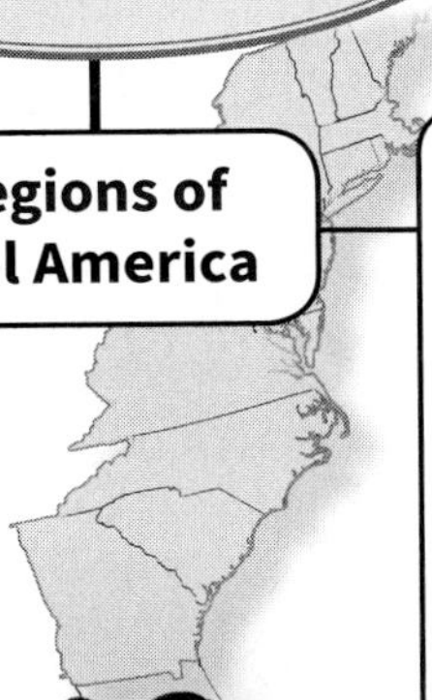

Southern Colonies
- Warmest weather and longest growing season
- People lived on their own farms
- Wealthy landowners had plantations with slaves and grew cash crops
- Farmers above fall line often engaged in subsistence farming

New England
- Rocky soil, short growing season, cold winters
- Farming, fishing, lumber, shipbuilding, sailing
- Merchants active in triangular trades: sugar-rum-slaves
- People lived in towns, participated in town meetings, most were literate, had oldest university

Mid-Atlantic Colonies
- Good soil, climate less harsh than New England
- Great diversity of people

Georgia
- James Oglethorpe
- Home for debtors

Pennsylvania
- William Penn
- Home to Quakers
- Frame of Government (1682)

Rhode Island 
- Roger Williams
- Religious toleration

Maryland
- Lord Baltimore
- Home to Catholics

New York, Delaware and New Jersey
- Taken from Dutch in 1664
- Greater diversity than elsewhere

Connecticut
- Thomas Hooker
- Fundamental Orders of Connecticut (1639)

North and South Carolina
- Divided in 1712
- South Carolina grew rice and indigo

New Hampshire
- Governed by Massachusetts

Government

English Traditions 
- Magna Carta
- Parliament

Colonial Government
- Virginia: House of Burgesses
- Plymouth: Mayflower Compact
- Connecticut: Fundamental Orders
- Pennsylvania: Frame of Government
- New England: town meetings

Religion

Many colonies founded by religious groups

Religious Toleration
- Rhode Island—Roger Williams
- Pennsylvania—Frame of Government
- Maryland—Toleration Act

The Great Awakening (1730s–1740s)
- Emotional sermons
- Everyone had a chance to be saved
- Challenged authority of ministers
- George Whitefield and Jonathan Edwards

Chapter 1 | Colonial Foundations

What Do You Know?

SSUSH1a

1. How did mercantilism encourage the development of colonies?
   A. Mercantilists advised that colonies would promote trade.
   B. Mercantilists believed colonies increased security in wartime.
   C. Mercantilists argued that European rulers must spread their culture.
   D. Mercantilists believed countries with colonies would never go to war.

SSUSH1c

2. Use the chart to answer the question.

Region	Main Reasons for Establishment
Southern Colonies	To make profits for investors and to give land to colonists
New England Colonies	?
Mid-Atlantic Colonies	Taken from Dutch for greater security of other colonies; Pennsylvania as a home for Quakers

   Which phrase BEST completes this chart?
   A. To make profits and provide land
   B. To increase the security of other colonies
   C. To produce wealth for England's rulers
   D. To allow colonists to worship their own way

SSUSH1c

3. Use this list to answer the question.

   - Plymouth
   - Massachusetts Bay
   - Rhode Island
   - Connecticut
   - New Hampshire

   What do the elements in the list have in common?
   A. Counties in England
   B. New England Colonies
   C. Mid-Atlantic Colonies
   D. Southern Colonies

SSUSH2d

4. Use this excerpt from a sermon to answer the question.

   Now you have an extraordinary opportunity, a day where in Christ has thrown the door of mercy open . . . you need to consider yourselves, and awaken thoroughly out of sleep . . .
   —Jonathan Edwards, 1741

   With which movement was this sermon associated?

   A. Mercantilism
   B. Great Awakening
   C. Puritanism
   D. Enlightenment

SSUSH1d

5. Use this list to answer the question.

   - Produced much of the wheat in the colonies
   - Engaged in friendly trade with Indian tribes
   - Greater ethnic and religious diversity than elsewhere
   - Promoted religious toleration
   - Some of the colonies taken from the Netherlands

   What do the elements in the list have in common?

   A. French Colonies
   B. Southern Colonies
   C. Mid-Atlantic Colonies
   D. New England Colonies

SSUSH2d

6. **Which statement describes an impact of the Great Awakening?**

   A. Colonists felt a need to bring more enslaved workers from Africa.
   B. Colonists felt greater loyalty to the Church of England.
   C. Colonists felt a greater sense of unity with one another.
   D. Colonists felt more willing to obey British authorities.

Chapter 1 | Colonial Foundations

SSUSH2b

7. Use the diagram to answer the question.

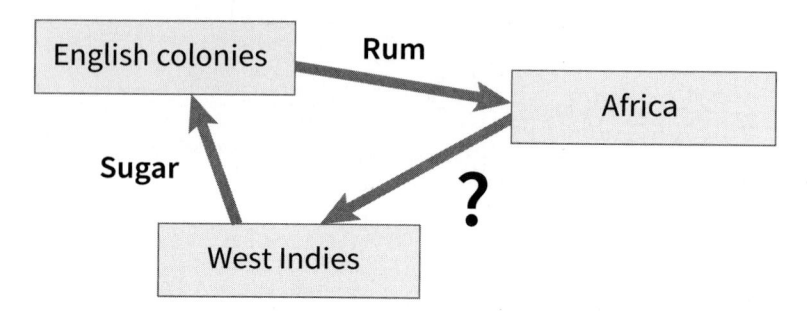

```
English colonies  --Rum-->  Africa
     ^                        |
     |Sugar                   | ?
     |                        v
   West Indies <--------------
```

Which word or phrase BEST completes the diagram?

A. Ironwares
B. Tropical fruits
C. Gold and silver
D. Enslaved individuals

SSUSH1a

8. Use the diagram below to answer the question.

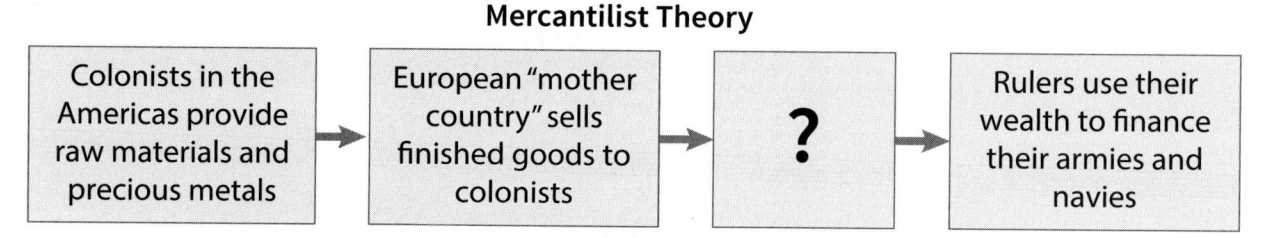

Mercantilist Theory

| Colonists in the Americas provide raw materials and precious metals | → | European "mother country" sells finished goods to colonists | → | ? | → | Rulers use their wealth to finance their armies and navies |

Which sentence BEST completes the diagram?

A. Rulers subsidize the colonists' costs.
B. Rulers move their capital cities to the "New World."
C. Rulers purchase shares in joint-stock companies.
D. Rulers accumulate supplies of gold and silver.

SSUSH2c

9. What was an important consequence of the British policy of "Salutary Neglect"?

A. French merchants took over the colonial carrying trade.
B. British colonists became accustomed to self-government.
C. The British government strictly enforced the Navigation Acts.
D. Britain collected more taxes from the colonists than those living in Britain.

CHAPTER 2 | The American Revolution

SSUSH3 What were the causes of the American Revolution?

    a. How did the French and Indian War and the 1763 Treaty of Paris lay the groundwork for the American Revolution?

    b. What were the colonial responses to the Proclamation of 1763, the Stamp Act, and the Intolerable Acts, as seen in actions of the Sons and Daughters of Liberty and the Committees of Correspondence?

    c. What was the importance of Thomas Paine's *Common Sense* to the movement for independence?

SSUSH4 What were the ideological, military, social, and diplomatic aspects of the American Revolution?

    a. What were the intellectual sources for the Declaration of Independence, how was the Declaration organized, and what was its argument? What was the role of Thomas Jefferson and the Committee of Five in writing the Declaration?

    b. What were the reasons for and what was the significance of the French alliance and other foreign assistance? How successful was the diplomacy of Benjamin Franklin and John Adams?

    c. How successful was George Washington as a military leader? What was the influence of Baron von Steuben and the Marquis de LaFayette, and what was the significance of Valley Forge in the creation of a professional military?

    d. What role did geography play in the Battles of Trenton, Saratoga, and Yorktown?

Continued ▶

New Revenue Policies: Taxation and Protest

After the French and Indian War, the most important issue dividing the colonists and the British government was **taxation**.

People living in Britain were already paying more in taxes than the colonists in North America. The British government therefore decided that the colonists should pay more towards their own defense. Parliament passed a series of laws to tax the colonists. Since the colonies were so far from London, no attempt was made to obtain their prior **consent** (*agreement*) to these new taxes.

The Stamp Act

The first of these laws was the **Stamp Act**, passed in 1765. This act required every official document, newspaper, or pamphlet in the colonies to have an expensive government stamp.

The colonists were greatly angered by the Stamp Act. Colonists held marches and rallies against it. Colonial assemblies sent **petitions** (*formal requests*) to Parliament to change the law. Colonists **boycotted** (*refused to buy*) British goods.

In the Virginia House of Burgesses, **Patrick Henry**, a young lawyer, introduced a series of **resolutions** against the Stamp Act. One of the resolutions declared that only the Virginia House of Burgesses could place new taxes on Virginians. In Massachusetts, colonists declared that "taxation without representation is tyranny." (A **tyranny** is a government that is cruel and unreasonable.)

The colonial assembly of Massachusetts proposed that each of the colonies send representatives to a special "congress." Nine colonies sent representatives to a "**Stamp Act Congress**," which was held in New York City in October. The Stamp Act Congress sent a strongly worded protest against the Stamp Act to the British Parliament in London.

In Boston, **Samuel Adams** and others also formed a secret society called the "**Sons of Liberty**." The Sons of Liberty set the building of the local Stamp Tax distributor in Boston on fire and attacked the house of the colony's Lieutenant Governor. Members of the Sons of Liberty seized tax collectors and put hot tar and feathers on them. Colonists against the Stamp Act also organized "**Committees of Correspondence**." These committees sent information to other colonies about their anti-British activities and helped coordinate the boycott of British goods.

The Stamp Act, 1765

"[T]here shall be raised, levied, collected and paid unto His Majesty . . . [f]or every skin or piece of . . . parchment, or sheet or piece of paper, on which shall be . . . written or printed any declaration, plea . . . or other pleading, or any copy thereof, in any court of law, within the British colonies and plantations in America, a stamp duty of 3 pence."

An excerpt from the Stamp Act, March 22, 1765

1. His Majesty's subjects in these colonies owe the same allegiance [*loyalty*] to the Crown of Great Britain that is owing from his subjects born within the Realm....
2. His Majesty's... subjects in these colonies are entitled to all of the... rights and liberties of his... subjects within the Kingdom of Great Britain.
3. It is... essential to the freedom of a people, and the undoubted right of Englishmen, that no taxes be imposed on them but by their own consent....
4. The people of these colonies cannot... be represented in the House of Commons in Great Britain.

Resolutions of the Stamp Act Congress, October 19, 1765

Repeal of the Stamp Act

The British government was taken by surprise by the many protests against the Stamp Act. British merchants complained that the law was actually hurting their businesses. Parliament acted quickly to **repeal** (*cancel; withdraw*) the law.

The Townshend Duties

The British government still needed to collect money from the colonists. Parliament therefore passed a new series of taxes, known as the **Townshend duties**. These placed taxes on paper, paint, glass, lead, and tea. These were common household goods that were usually shipped to the colonies from Britain.

Once again, Parliament passed these new duties without first obtaining the consent of the colonists. Members of Parliament still felt that the colonists were too far away to consult with them.

The **Daughters of Liberty** had been established in 1765, just after the Sons of Liberty. After the passage of the Townshend duties, these women helped the colonists boycott British goods by making cloth and other products that could be used in their place. They also refused to drink British tea.

More British Troops Arrive

To enforce the Townshend Acts and to prevent further unrest, the British government sent more troops to North America. Four thousand new soldiers landed in Boston in October 1768. The government quartered some of these troops on colonists' properties. To "**quarter**" means to send soldiers to live in public and private buildings.

Could the colonists have had their own representatives in Parliament?

At a time when crossing the Atlantic was slow, any colonial representatives in London would soon have been out of touch with the colonists they represented. Most colonial leaders did not really want to be represented in Parliament. What they wanted was to make their own laws, including those on taxation, in their own colonial assemblies.

Chapter 2 | The American Revolution

May 28, 1754 George Washington fires on French soldiers

July 13, 1755 General Braddock killed in Ohio River Valley

September 13, 1759 General Wolfe takes Quebec

|1750|1755|1760|

May 17, 1756 Start of Seven Years' War in Europe

October 25, 1760 George III becomes King

The Boston Massacre

Colonial resentment against the British troops grew. Tensions reached their peak in Boston in early March 1770. An argument between a colonist and a soldier led a crowd of dockworkers and others to gather in the square in front of the Customs House. A British officer came with several men to the soldier's assistance. With all the noise and excitement, one of the soldiers actually thought he heard the word "fire." The soldiers began firing and soon three of the colonists were dead.

The soldiers were put on trial for murder. They were defended by **John Adams**, a young lawyer from Boston who was also a cousin to Sam Adams. Adams argued that the troops had acted in self-defense and won the case.

His cousin, Sam Adams, saw the event differently. He saw it as another opportunity for attacking British rule. In **broadsides** (*one-sided sheets*) and other printed materials, he described the shooting as a deliberate "massacre" (*the murder of many innocent people*). Paul Revere, a silversmith and artist, drew a famous cartoon that was shown throughout the colonies.

Paul Revere's illustration of the Boston Massacre

The Historian's Apprentice

1. Do you think the soldiers should have been convicted for murder? Write a paragraph explaining your point of view.
2. Do you think Revere's drawing was an accurate representation of the Boston Massacre? Use visual evidence from the drawing to explain your answer.

February 10, 1763
End of the French and Indian War

June 29, 1767
King George III approves Townshend duties

1765

October 9, 1763
Proclamation Line

March 25, 1765
Stamp Act

October 7, 1765
Stamp Act Congress meets

March 18, 1766
Parliament repeals Stamp Act

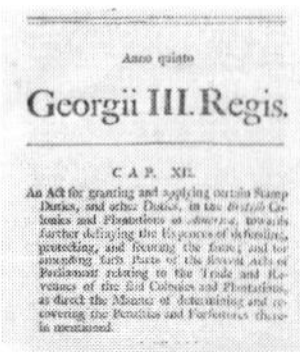

The Tea Act

By 1773, Parliament had finally repealed the hated Townshend duties. However, it passed a new tax on tea in place of the duties. Parliament gave the East India Company, which was in financial difficulties, the right to sell its tea directly to the colonists in North America. This brought down the price of tea, which no longer had to be sold in England. Parliamentary leaders felt that by lowering the cost of tea, they could collect the tea duty without protest. Even so, the colonists were still dissatisfied.

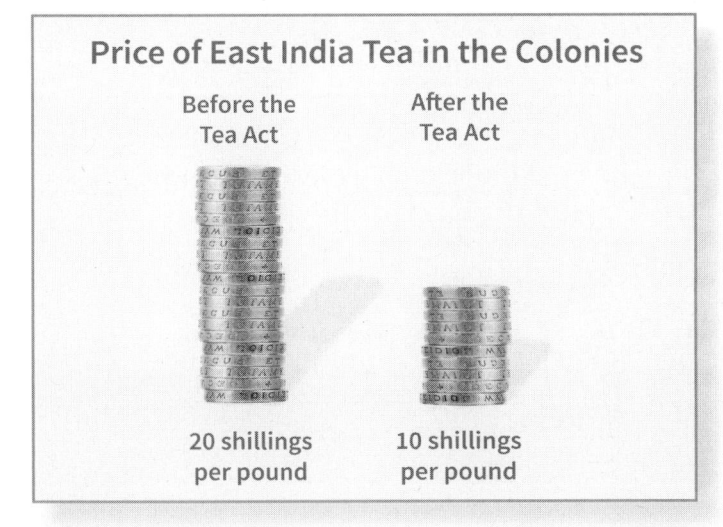

Price of East India Tea in the Colonies

Before the Tea Act: 20 shillings per pound

After the Tea Act: 10 shillings per pound

The Boston Tea Party

British ships carrying tea from the East India Company arrived in Boston Harbor in December 1773. A group of colonists disguised as American Indians boarded three ships at night and threw 342 chests of tea into the harbor in protest. This event became known as the "**Boston Tea Party.**"

The Intolerable Acts (1774)

The British government was outraged when it received news of this destruction of property. Parliament passed a series of laws in March and June 1774 known as the **Coercive Acts**. The colonists called these the "**Intolerable Acts.**"

These British policies eventually led to the writing of the Declaration of Independence.

▶ Boston Harbor was closed until the tea was paid for. Warships blockaded the harbor.

Paul Revere's illustration of the Boston Tea Party

Chapter 2 | The American Revolution   43

| October 1, 1768 British troops land in Boston | March 5, 1770 Boston Massacre | May 10, 1773 Parliament passes the Tea Act | March-May 1774 Coercive Acts |

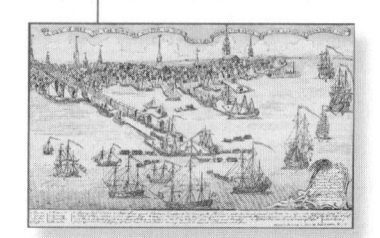

December 16, 1773 Boston Tea Party

- Even ferryboats were not permitted to carry food across the harbor.
- The Massachusetts legislature was suspended (*temporarily closed*).
- The British government was given the power to appoint all officials in Massachusetts until the tea was paid for.
- Royal officials would no longer be tried for crimes in the colonies, but in Great Britain.
- A harsher Quartering Act, requiring colonists to provide shelter to British soldiers, was passed.

The Historian's Apprentice

1. Why did the colonists find British actions to be unreasonable? Pretend you are a colonist from Boston or Philadelphia writing a letter to your cousin in England. Explain your point of view.
2. Imagine that your class is the British Parliament in London. Each member of your class is a member of Parliament. Your class should debate how to treat the colonists after the "Boston Tea Party" and whether to approve the Intolerable Acts.
3. Make your own online timeline of the events leading to the American Revolution. Include a brief description of each event and its significance on your timeline.

Georgians React: The Tondee's Tavern Resolutions

Georgia was the youngest colony and the one farthest from Boston. In the 1770s, many residents of Georgia remained loyal to the King and relied on Britain for protection from neighboring Indian tribes. But others, such as merchants subject to new taxes and settlers from South Carolina, were determined to resist British policies. When South Carolina elected delegates to the First Continental Congress, "Patriots" in Georgia called for a meeting to be held at Peter Tondee's tavern in Savannah. A second meeting was held there in August 1774, with representatives from all of Georgia's parishes [*local districts*]. These Patriots passed several resolutions in response to the Intolerable Acts:

> "Resolved, [unanimously], That an Act of Parliament lately passed, for blockading the port and harbour of Boston, is contrary to our idea of the British Constitution: First, for that in effect deprives good and lawful men of the use of their property without judgment of their peers; and secondly, for that it is in nature of an ex post facto law, and indiscriminately blends as objects of punishment the innocent with the guilty . . .
>
> Resolved, [unanimously], That the Act for abolishing the Charter of Massachusetts Bay tends to the subversion of American rights. . .
>
> Resolved, [unanimously], That we apprehend the Parliament of Great Britain hath not, nor ever had, any right to tax his Majesty's American subjects; for it is evident beyond contradiction, the constitution admits of no taxation without representation . . .
>
> Resolved, [unanimously], That we concur [*agree*] with our sister colonies in every constitutional measure to obtain redress of American grievances, and will by every lawful means in our power, maintain those inestimable blessings for which we are indebted to God and the Constitution of our country—a Constitution founded upon reason and justice, and the indelible rights of mankind."

Despite these resolutions, Georgia became the only colony not to send representatives to the First Continental Congress.

1. Why did these representatives feel that Georgians should protest events happening hundreds of miles away in Massachusetts?
2. Why did these "Patriots" feel that the colonists should not be taxed?

The Enlightenment and Colonial Ideas on Government

The views of the colonists were greatly influenced by new ways of thinking in Europe. These views were known as the **Enlightenment**. Europeans had discovered that science could explain many of the things they observed in nature.

Many writers believed that they could apply human reason to better understand people and society—and to make things better. Because they thought reason brought light to the world, their movement became known as the Enlightenment.

In Europe, Enlightenment thinkers challenged religious prejudice and intolerance. They questioned the inherited privileges of nobles (*Europe's highest social class*).

Enlightenment thinkers did not believe that kings and queens received their powers directly from God. Instead, they accepted the view of **John Locke** that each government was created as part of a **social contract** between people and their rulers. If rulers did not respect the rights of their subjects, then the social contract was broken and the people had the right to overthrow them.

Chapter 2 | The American Revolution

The Fighting Begins

In the spring of 1775, Boston Harbor was closed and the city was filled with British "redcoats" (soldiers in bright red uniforms). The Massachusetts colonial assembly had been shut down. People were tense. Would the situation end in violence? Or would wise leaders be able to work out a skillful compromise?

The First Continental Congress

Because of all the troubles with Britain, the colonies decided to send representatives to Philadelphia for a "**Continental Congress**." Each colony sent delegates except Georgia.

The First Continental Congress met in September 1774. Its members were still loyal to King George III, but they wanted to resolve their **grievances** (*complaints*). They sent a **petition** (*a written plea asking for change*) to the King. It demanded that the Intolerable Acts be repealed. The delegates also made plans for a future boycott of British goods. Finally, they decided that another Continental Congress should be held in May if the King rejected their petition. Then they went home.

King George III never answered the colonists' petition. Instead, he gave a speech to the British Parliament condemning the colonists for their actions.

The Battles of Lexington and Concord—the "Shot Heard Round the World"

Meanwhile, colonists opposed to British policies were organizing in Boston. They called themselves "**Patriots**." The Patriots formed groups of **militia** (*citizens in temporary military service*). Because they claimed to be ready on a minute's notice, these volunteers were also called "**minutemen**." The Patriots secretly collected guns and ammunition for the day when they might have to defend their liberties.

John Hancock was one of the wealthiest merchants in Boston. He was also an important Patriot leader. In April 1775, the royal governor of Massachusetts learned that Hancock and Samuel Adams were in Lexington, a small town just outside Boston. The governor sent a force of 700 soldiers to arrest them and to capture the arms that the Patriots were storing in the nearby town of Concord.

When Patriot leaders in Boston learned that British soldiers were about to march, they sent Paul Revere and other riders on horseback to warn the countryside. The first British troops arrived in Lexington early the next day, April 19th. They were surprised to find 70 Patriots with muskets standing on the village green. After some hesitation, the colonists and British redcoats both fired. Several Patriots lay dead. The first blood of the American Revolution had been spilled. Then the British charged and the colonial volunteers fled.

The British soldiers next marched to Concord. Patriot militia attacked them on a local

Fighting at Lexington

bridge. News of the fighting spread to neighboring towns and villages. Soon hundreds of militia joined the minutemen along the road. They fired at the British soldiers as they marched back to Boston. More than 70 British soldiers and almost 50 colonists lost their lives that day.

The Historian's Apprentice

1. Would you have been willing to risk your life in the Patriot militia?
2. Why did the poet Ralph Waldo Emerson later call this "the shot heard round the world"?

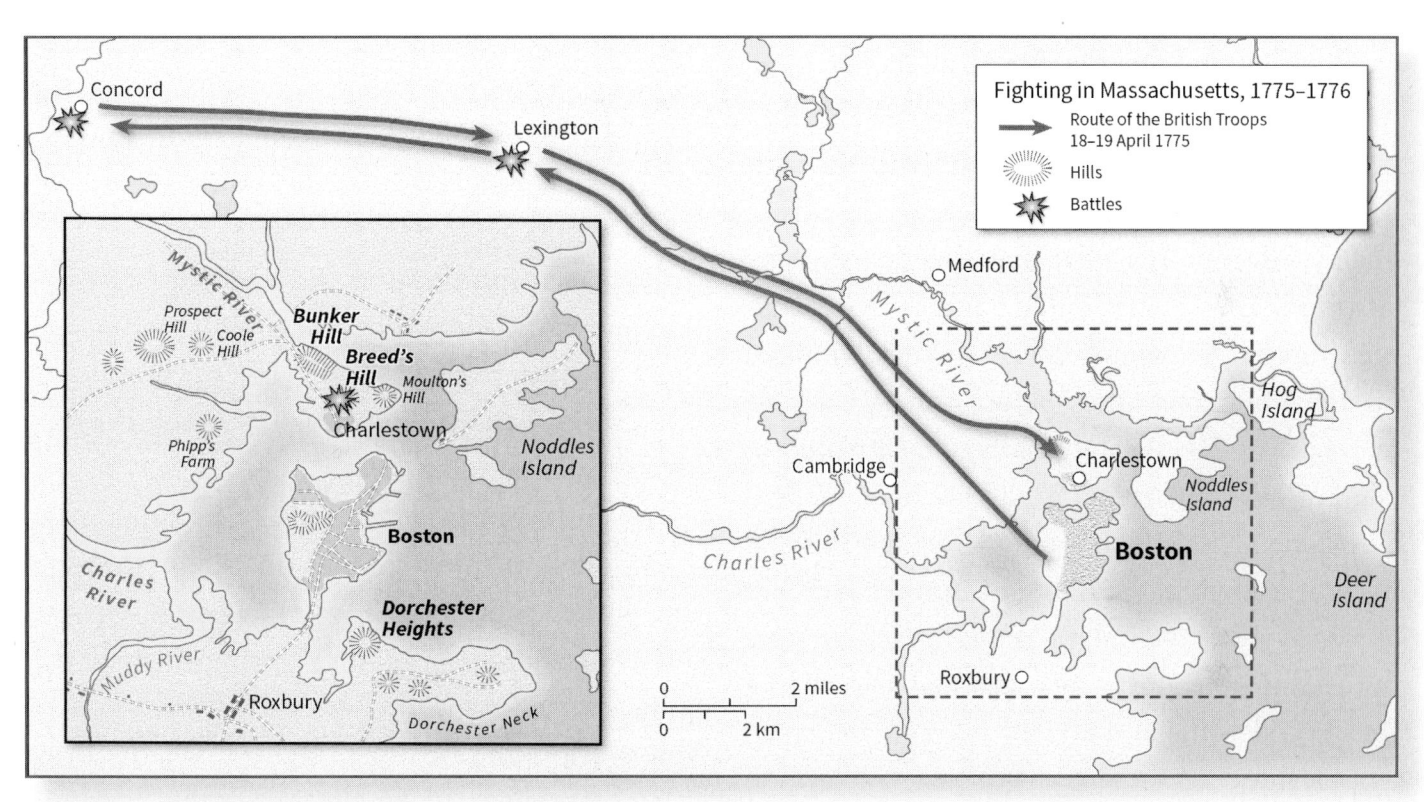

Fighting in Massachusetts from 1775 to 1776

The Conflict Spreads

The Second Continental Congress

George III refused to consider the colonists' petition, so the colonists held a **Second Continental Congress**. Many of its delegates were on their way to Philadelphia when they received news of the shots fired at Lexington and Concord.

The new Congress began its meetings early in May 1775. John Hancock was elected as its President. Other important members included John Adams, Samuel Adams, Benjamin Franklin, Thomas Jefferson, and John Dickinson.

Chapter 2 | The American Revolution 47

The delegates agreed to support the colonists in Massachusetts. If the British government could take away the rights of Massachusetts, it could take away the rights of every colony. The defense of Massachusetts had become the cause of all the colonists.

The Battle of Bunker Hill (June 17, 1775)

After the Battles of Lexington and Concord, colonial militia from all over New England gathered around Boston. On a quiet night in June, they took Breed's Hill, one of the hills overlooking the city. Overnight, the Patriots built walls of earth to protect themselves from enemy gunfire. The next day, the British were surprised to see that Patriot forces had occupied this high ground. British soldiers charged up the hill three times before they were able to retake it. The Patriot volunteers retreated to Bunker Hill and across a narrow neck of land to escape. The British were victorious in what became known as the **Battle of Bunker Hill**, but at a heavy cost—almost half the attackers were injured or killed. The colonists had shown that they could withstand attacks by regular British troops.

Washington Appointed as Commander in Chief

In Philadelphia, the Continental Congress adopted the New England militia as the core of its own new army. They called their force the "**Continental Army**."

George Washington, now 43 years old, was appointed to command it. Washington had valuable military experience from the French and Indian War. It was hoped his appointment would encourage Virginia to support the Patriot cause. Appointed the day before the Battle of Bunker Hill, Washington left immediately for Boston.

The Guns of Ticonderoga

Less than a month after the Battles of Lexington and Concord, a group of colonists atttacked **Fort Ticonderoga**—a British fort on the southern end of Lake Champlain. They took the fort by surprise at night.

A few months later, 59 heavy cannons from Ticonderoga were pulled on sleds through the winter snow all the way to Boston. On the night of March 4, 1776, Washington had the guns carried up Dorchester Heights, another hill overlooking Boston. The next day, the British commander woke up to see the cannons overlooking the harbor. Two weeks later, he marched his troops onto ships and sailed away. Boston was freed from British occupation and remained so for the rest of the war.

The Battle for New York City

Washington thought that the British might move their main army to New York City, so he marched his army southward. His instincts proved right.

The Battle of Bunker Hill

Colonial and British Forces

By August 1776, George Washington had about 20,000 troops under his command. The members of the Continental Army were all volunteers who had enlisted (*signed up for military service*). Most enlisted for only six months. Washington often complained about the shrinking of his forces, as men returned to their families and farms at the end of their enlistment period. At the beginning of the war, soldiers in the Continental Army had little or no experience in fighting. Washington grumbled that they needed more discipline. A few key units were made up of men with longer service. These soldiers formed the backbone of the Continental Army.

In the same month of August 1776, the British landed 32,000 troops in New York Harbor. Their troops consisted of both British soldiers and Hessian **mercenaries** (*troops for hire*). British soldiers usually came from the lowest classes and were "pressed" (*forced*) into service, often for life. Despite their backgrounds, they were trained to become highly disciplined, professional soldiers. British officers came from the upper classes of British society. Officers were often chosen for their social connections rather than their actual talents. "**Hessians**" were paid troops from the German state of Hesse-Cassel. About half the German troops who fought in the Revolutionary War came from this part of Germany.

After 1777, Washington was also helped by a handful of volunteers from Europe. These included the **Marquis de Lafayette,** a young French nobleman, and **Baron von Steuben**, an experienced Prussian officer. In 1780, France contributed 7,000 of its regular troops.

At the time of the American Revolution, soldiers used a type of gun known as a musket. Soldiers had to insert a bullet, push it with a ramrod, add gunpowder from a cartridge, and fire the musket with a spark that came from a flintlock. Muskets were not accurate except at close range. In Europe, soldiers were taught to load, fire, and reload their muskets while standing in a line, creating a deadly wall of gunfire. Highly disciplined troops could load and fire several rounds a minute.

The British landed their troops on Long Island, just south of Washington's own forces. The Continental Army was outnumbered, and the British moved some of their troops behind Washington's army so that they could attack from two sides. Washington lost the **Battle of Long Island**. However, he skillfully retreated across the East River to Manhattan at night. He fought a second battle against the British from the heights of Harlem. Again, his forces were defeated. Washington retreated farther north and fought a final battle on White Plains before crossing the Hudson

Chapter 2 | The American Revolution

River to safety. The British occupied New York City for the rest of the war.

The Battles of Trenton and Princeton

Soldiers in the Continental Army were greatly discouraged by these defeats. Washington decided on a daring attack to boost morale. Geography played an important role in the battle. A large body of Hessian soldiers were encamped at Trenton, New Jersey. They felt safe because Washington and his troops were on the other side of the Delaware River and weather conditions were poor. On Christmas Day of 1775, Washington crossed the Delaware River to surprise the Hessian mercenaries camped at Trenton. The Hessians did not expect to be attacked at Christmas time in such cold weather. They were defeated and captured at the **Battle of Trenton**. Washington followed this with a second victory against several units of British troops in the **Battle of Princeton**.

Patriots versus Loyalists

People in the colonies were greatly divided during the Revolutionary War. Many colonists actually sided with the British. They had British relatives, admired British culture, and valued the trade they enjoyed as members of the British Empire. They did not want to leave the empire but hoped that King George III might be persuaded to change his policies. These British sympathizers were known as **Loyalists**. They were also called **Tories**, after a political party in Britain that was very loyal to the King.

Patriots thought that the colonists should govern themselves. At the beginning of the war, many

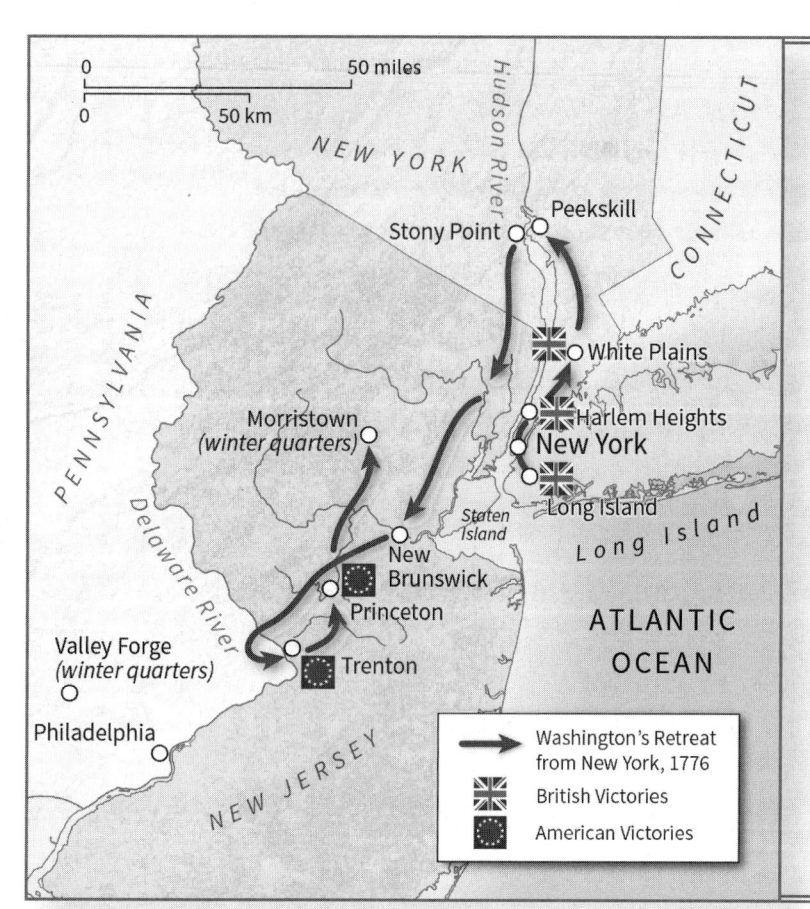

Battles in New York and New Jersey, 1776

We think of the Civil War (1861–1865) as a war of brother against brother, but the same was true of the American Revolution. Benjamin Franklin's son William, for example, was the last royal governor of New Jersey and an active Loyalist. The Revolution led to a breaking of relations between father and son. **Thomas Gage**, the royal governor who sent British troops to Lexington and Concord, had once marched alongside George Washington and Horatio Gates in the French and Indian War.

Thomas Gage

50   Chapter 2 | The American Revolution

Patriots thought this could still be done without leaving the British Empire. As the war dragged on, this became less and less likely. Most Patriots began to look forward to the day when the colonies would be free and independent.

The Historian's Apprentice

1. At the end of 1775, would you have been a Loyalist, a Patriot, or an undecided? Pretend you were living at the time and write a letter to a friend explaining your point of view.
2. What role did geography play at the Battle of Trenton?

Americans Declare Their Independence

Thomas Paine's *Common Sense*

Thomas Paine was an English visitor to the colonies. In January 1776, he published an influential pamphlet entitled *Common Sense*.

Paine wrote in simple and persuasive language that everyone could understand. He argued that it was "common sense" that the thirteen colonies should not be governed by the tiny island of Great Britain, many thousands of miles away. Paine wrote that the costs to the colonists of their connection to Britain were greater than the benefits they received. Based on Enlightenment ideas, Paine argued that the time had come for the colonists to become independent and govern themselves.

Paine also attacked the system of government known as "monarchy." In a **monarchy**, a king or queen inherits power from a parent or other family member. Paine thought this was wrong. He called on the colonists to create a **democracy**—a system in which the people are the source of all political power. He wanted a government based on elected representatives instead of a king.

> I have heard it stated by some that America has prospered from her connection with Great Britain, and that this connection is necessary for her future happiness. We may as well say that because a child has had milk, that it is never to have meat. I challenge the warmest supporter of Britain to show a single advantage that this Continent can gain by being connected with Great Britain....
>
> —Thomas Paine, *Common Sense*

The Desire for Independence Grows

More and more colonists agreed with Paine that the colonies should end their connection with Great Britain. Patriot leaders also knew that they could not have **allies** (*countries that agree to act together*) in the war as long as they remained the King's subjects. Only by becoming independent could they conclude alliances

Chapter 2 | The American Revolution

Richard Henry Lee Proposes Independence

> *Resolved, That these United Colonies are, and of right ought to be, free and independent States, that they are absolved from all allegiance to the British Crown, and that all political connection between them and the State of Great Britain is, and ought to be, totally dissolved.*

Word Helper
absolve = to release or set free
allegiance = loyalty to a superior
British Crown = the King
connection = a link or formal association
dissolved = ended or eliminated

with foreign powers such as France and Spain. They needed the support of these foreign powers to win the war.

The Second Continental Congress therefore began debating the question of American independence early in 1776. John Adams was one of the loudest voices in its favor. Back in Virginia, Patrick Henry, James Madison, and George Mason also urged the Continental Congress to declare independence.

Richard Henry Lee Proposes Independence

Richard Henry Lee, one of Virginia's delegates to the Congress, finally introduced a **resolution** (*formal proposal*) for independence in early June.

The "Committee of Five"

The Continental Congress appointed a special committee, the **Committee of Five**, to draft a declaration explaining the colonists' reasons for declaring independence. John Adams, Benjamin Franklin, and **Thomas Jefferson** were among its members. Jefferson was given the tough job of writing the first draft. The other members of the committee were so pleased with Jefferson's text that they made very few changes to it.

After much debate, the Continental Congress approved Lee's resolution for independence on July 2nd. The **Declaration of Independence** was signed by the members of the Congress two days later. That date, July 4th, is now our national holiday.

The Declaration of Independence actually did several things at once:

1. It declared American independence. It boldly stated that the colonies were no longer part of the British Empire and the former colonists were no longer subjects of King George III.

2. It announced a new theory of government based on the concept of natural rights. Governments, it said, are created to protect individual rights. These rights are not just the rights of British subjects, but the natural rights of all human beings.

3. It listed the grievances (complaints) that the colonists had against King George III and the British government.

4. It justified the conduct of the colonists, both to their fellow countrymen and to the rest of the world.

5. It announced the arrival of the United States as an independent member of the

The Main Ideas of the Declaration of Independence

The Declaration of Independence begins by announcing that it sometimes becomes necessary for a people to end the ties that once joined them to another people. When they do, they should explain their reasons for doing so to the rest of the world.

The next section may be the most famous part of the Declaration. It sets forth the American theory of government. This theory is based on a belief in natural rights and John Locke's social contract. It begins by stating that all people are created equal. They enjoy certain **unalienable rights** under natural law. These are God-given rights that cannot be taken away. Among these rights are **life, liberty, and the pursuit of happiness**.

The Declaration then explains that people have created governments to protect these rights. When a government acts to destroy these rights, its citizens have the right to end that government and create a new one.

The Declaration recognizes that people should not change their government lightly. Disagreement with a few government decisions does not justify changing an entire system of government. But when there has been a long pattern of abuses showing that the government has become **despotic** (*oppressive and dictatorial*), then the people clearly have the right to change their government. Such has been the case, the Declaration argues, for the American colonists.

The British King and his government had committed repeated injuries against them. The Declaration lists many of these abuses. This list of grievances is the longest part of the Declaration. It includes abuses that violated the colonists' rights under Magna Carta as well as their natural rights. These abuses include:

- refusing to approve necessary laws
- imposing taxes without the colonists' consent
- quartering troops in colonists' homes
- making judges dependent on the King's will
- trying royal officials and colonists in Britain instead of in the colonies
- suspending or dissolving colonial legislatures

The Declaration works up to the most serious grievances at the very end of the list. The King:

- has cut off their trade
- has made war on the colonists
- has hired foreign mercenaries against them
- has ordered the burning down of towns
- has even stirred up neighboring Indians to attack them

The final paragraphs of the Declaration explain that the colonists have tried to settle their disagreements with Britain peacefully, but all their attempts have failed. The time has therefore come for the colonies to declare their independence. The very last paragraph contains the wording of Richard Henry Lee's famous resolution: the former colonies "are, and of right ought to be, free and independent states."

Chapter 2 | The American Revolution

international community. This cleared the way for the former colonies to conclude military alliances with France and Spain.

The Historian's Apprentice

1. How important was Thomas Paine's pamphlet *Common Sense* to the movement for independence?
2. Pretend that your class is the Second Continental Congress in early 1776. Debate whether the colonies should declare their independence from Great Britain and George III.
3. What did Jefferson mean by "all men are created equal" and endowed with "certain unalienable rights"?
4. Make a chart summarizing the main ideas of the Declaration of Independence.
5. What were the intellectual sources of the Declaration of Independence?

Did you know that Thomas Jefferson originally had a paragraph in the Declaration condemning George III for promoting the slave trade? This paragraph was taken out of the Declaration to win the support of South Carolina and other slave-holding states.

6. Was it wrong for slave-holding states to support a declaration in the name of freedom and equality?
7. Can we hold earlier Americans to the same standards we have today?
8. How might American history have been different if Jefferson's paragraph against the slave trade had been left in the Declaration?

Reading from the Declaration of Independence

In CONGRESS, July 4, 1776.

The unanimous Declaration of the thirteen United States of America . . .

We hold these truths to be self-evident, that all men are created equal, that they are endowed by their Creator with certain unalienable Rights, that among these are Life, Liberty and the pursuit of Happiness.

Word Helper

self-evident = obvious, clear

endowed = given

Creator = God

unalienable = not capable of being taken away

- What is meant by the phrase "unalienable rights"?
- What examples are given of "unalienable rights"?

Chapter 2 | The American Revolution

That to secure these rights, Governments are instituted among Men, deriving their just powers from the consent of the governed. That whenever any Form of Government becomes destructive of these ends, it is the Right of the People to alter or to abolish it, and to institute new Government . . . organizing its powers in such form, as to them shall seem most likely to effect their Safety and Happiness. Prudence, indeed, will dictate that Governments long established should not be changed for light and transient causes . . . But when a long train of abuses and usurpations, pursuing invariably the same object evinces a design to reduce them under absolute Despotism, it is their right, it is their duty, to throw off such Government, and to provide new Guards for their future security.

Word Helper

secure = to obtain
instituted = created
derive = to obtain from; to come from
consent = agreement
alter = to change
abolish = to end; to get rid of
organize = arrange in order
institute = to start; to create
effect = to bring about
prudence = cautious and careful judgment
dictate = to demand; to determine
transient = temporary; not permanent
long train = long chain or series of events
usurpation = a wrongful taking of someone else's rights
pursue = to chase after something in order to obtain it
object = goal
invariably = always, without change
evince = to provide evidence of
despotism = an oppressive and arbitrary power

Summarize the argument of this excerpt of the Declaration in your own words.

....
....
....
....
....
....

Chapter 2 | The American Revolution

The War Continues

The British Capture Philadelphia

Meanwhile, the fighting continued. The commander of the British forces, General William Howe, thought he might end the war quickly if he could defeat Washington in one great battle. He sailed with most of his troops from New York to Chesapeake Bay in order to attack Philadelphia from the southwest. Howe defeated Washington's army in September 1777 and marched into Philadelphia. The Continental Congress had to flee to western Pennsylvania.

Howe's victory and the flight of the Continental Congress did not end the war as Howe had hoped. And Howe paid a great price for his victory. He did not leave enough troops behind in New York to help in an ambitious new British plan for dividing the rebellious colonies in two.

The Battle of Saratoga: The Turning Point of the War

Earlier in 1777, the British government had come up with a new strategy for winning the war. Three British armies would march from different places to the middle of New York, separating the colonies into two parts.

- The first army would march south from Quebec to Lake Champlain, Lake George, and finally the Hudson River. Americans had used the reverse route earlier in the war in an unsuccessful attempt to invade Canada.
- A second army would march from New York City north along the Hudson River.
- A third army from western New York would travel east along the Mohawk River Valley. It would consist largely of Britain's Indian allies, especially the Iroquois.

The three British armies planned to meet in Albany. Their movement would cut New England off from the rest of the colonies.

From the beginning, things went wrong. General Howe went to attack the Continental Congress in Philadelphia. He did not leave enough soldiers behind in New York to allow many to march north to Albany. A few soldiers were finally sent, but only after it was too late.

Secondly, **General John Burgoyne**, who took command of the British force from Canada, marched too slowly and missed short cuts that might have reduced his march. Geography played a key role in slowing his advance. His men marched through wilderness and faced attacks from hostile colonists and Indian tribes. His heavy baggage train, with tents, wine, and food, was difficult to carry. The Continental Army had pulled down trees to block his path.

Finally, the army from the west never appeared. The American general Benedict Arnold sent messages to the Indians in the British camp misleading them into believing that the Americans had many more troops than they did. The Indians deserted the British, so the army from the west never reached Albany.

General Burgoyne was left on his own. Militia from nearby New England and New York kept joining the Continental Army, whose numbers swelled. Washington had also sent some additional troops. Burgoyne found himself facing forces much larger than those he commanded.

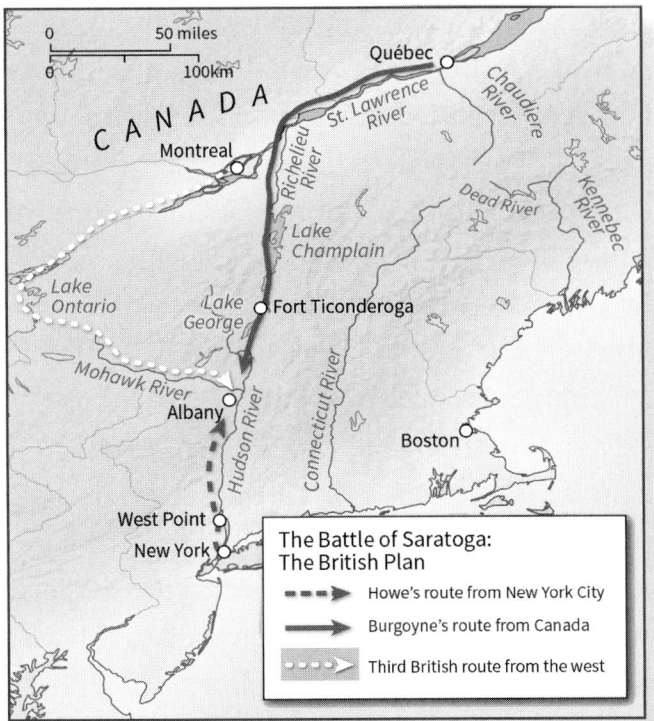

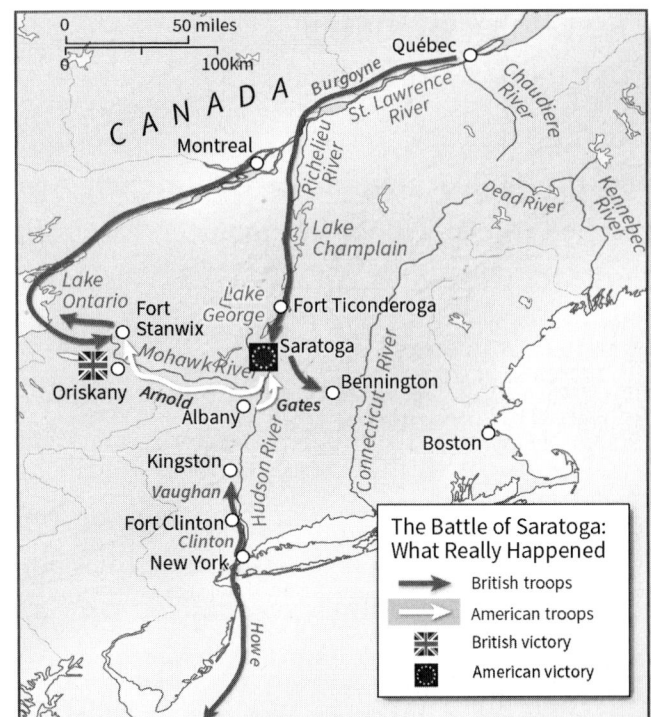

While his troops had been slowly marching southward, the Americans had fortified the high ground around Saratoga. They placed cannons on Bemis Heights, overlooking the approach of the British. Burgoyne's troops fought two short battles in September and October, but they failed to break through. Surrounded and without any hope of reinforcement, Burgoyne finally surrendered 6,000 men and supplies to General Horatio Gates on October 17, 1777. It was a great victory for the Americans.

The French Alliance

The French were still angry at the loss of their North American colonies in 1763. The Continental Congress sent Benjamin Franklin to France to negotiate an alliance with France. John Adams was sent later to help Franklin. The Americans needed French help because they lacked their own naval power, did not have a professional army, and were short of funds. France, in contrast, was the largest country in Europe—a "great power" like Britain. Franklin and Adams understood that securing a French alliance was crucial for American success. News of the victory at Saratoga helped persuade King Louis XVI and his ministers to step in. In February 1778, the French signed a treaty of alliance with the new United States. The treaty was actually concluded by Franklin before Adams arrived.

The British had feared just such an alliance between the Americans and the French. In the same month that the alliance was signed, the British Parliament repealed all its taxes on the colonists and gave up its right to tax them. A special commission was sent to negotiate with the Continental Congress, but it was all too late.

Above all, the British feared that the French might attack their "sugar islands" in the Caribbean. They withdrew 5,000 soldiers from the thirteen colonies and moved them to the West Indies. For the rest of the war, British commanders in North America could no longer count on fresh troops from Britain. General Howe was even ordered to leave Philadelphia.

Chapter 2 | The American Revolution

The Winter at Valley Forge (1777–1778)

Conditions were terrible when Washington and the 12,000 men of the Continental Army reached their winter headquarters at **Valley Forge** for the winter of 1777–1778. Washington chose this grim, windy location because it was 20 miles northwest of Philadelphia, which the British still occupied at the time.

Only a third of Washington's men still had shoes. The rest wrapped their feet in rags. Their shoes had been destroyed by their long marches. Their clothes were also torn and blankets were scarce. Food was just as scarce. The men ate a tasteless mixture of flour and water, and occasional broth. At first they had no shelter and had to build their own rough cabins out of logs and mud. Even their horses were undernourished, and 700 of them died. Many farmers refused to sell their crops to the Continental Army, which paid in paper money that was almost worthless.

Hunger, disease, and cold took the lives of 2,500 of Washington's men that winter. Many of his men deserted. **Alexander Hamilton**, who served as Washington's assistant, sent a stream of complaints to the Continental Congress. Five members of the Continental Congress finally came to view the shocking conditions of the army in late January. Afterwards, the Continental Congress increased its payments.

Despite the terrible conditions, Washington made use of the time in Valley Forge to train his troops. **Baron von Steuben**, a volunteer from the German kingdom of Prussia, drilled the soldiers, taught them how to use their firearms and bayonets, and created a more disciplined army. News of the French alliance also lifted the men's spirits. At Valley Forge, colonial troops were finally trained and became a united and professional fighting force.

The Continental Army stayed at Valley Forge until spring. In June 1778, British forces left Philadelphia to return to New York City. Washington decided to attack them. At Monmouth,

Washington and Lafayette at Valley Forge

> "Unless some great... change suddenly takes place,... this army must... starve, dissolve or disperse, in order to obtain subsistence (*food*) in the best manner that they can."
>
> —General George Washington

58   Chapter 2 | The American Revolution

a force of 6,000 Americans attacked the rear of the retreating British army. However, the British troops turned around and almost defeated their attackers. Only Washington's arrival on the scene helped to turn the situation around.

By nightfall, the battle was inconclusive. There was no clear victor. The British continued their march to New York. It was the last time the two main armies in the war faced one another.

The Historian's Apprentice

1. What role did geography play at the Battle of Saratoga?
2. What was the reason for the French alliance? Why was it significant?
3. What was the significance of the creation of a more professional army at Valley Forge?

The Final Phase of the War

After the failure at Saratoga, the British government came up with a new plan for winning the war. This time it was the "Southern strategy." The British believed there were more Loyalists in the South than in the North. Therefore, they would send a large army to the South, where they could count on Loyalist volunteers.

The War in the South

The plan began well. The British fleet sailed to Savannah, Georgia. British troops took the city in December 1778. Later attempts by American Patriots to recapture the city failed. In May 1780, the British also took **Charleston**, the largest city in South Carolina. The British captured 5,000 American soldiers as prisoners—almost as many men as Burgoyne had surrendered at Saratoga. The loss of Charleston was one of the worst defeats for the Americans in the course of the war.

From Charleston, Lord Cornwallis, the British general in charge of the Southern campaign, marched inland. He defeated Horatio Gates, the hero of the Battle of Saratoga, at the Battle of Camden (August 1780). But Patriot resistance to the British nonetheless remained strong in the hills of South Carolina. Continental forces defeated a group of British troops at the **Battle of Cowpens** (January 1781). Shortly afterwards, Cornwallis marched north to Virginia.

The Surrender at Yorktown

Cornwallis took his soldiers to a peninsula alongside Chesapeake Bay, only a few miles from where the first English colonists had once settled in Jamestown. From this location, Cornwallis hoped to receive help from the British fleet. Learning this, Washington and his French allies decided to lay a trap.

At first, Cornwallis' forces were just opposed by a smaller force commanded by Lafayette. However, the French navy under Admiral de Grasse sailed into Chesapeake Bay, blocking Cornwallis' escape. At the same time, Washington marched his army from New York southward. Another army was brought to Yorktown by the French general, Count Rochambeau.

Cornwallis did not know that the troops against him were being reinforced. Once he

The Impact of the War

The Loyalists

One of the most important effects of the Revolution was that 100,000 Loyalists left the United States for Canada, the West Indies, and Great Britain.

African Americans, American Indians, and Women

The Declaration of Independence loudly proclaimed that "all men are created equal." Three important groups were obviously left out: African Americans, American Indians, and women. Perhaps it is not surprising that white men at that time did not consider members of these groups as equals, and we should not judge people in the past by our own standards. Yet even in the 1770s, there were already some voices demanding rights for all: "Liberty is equally as precious," wrote African-American minister Lemuel Haynes, "to a black man as to a white one."

> "If there be an object truly ridiculous in nature, it is an American patriot, signing resolutions of independence with the one hand, and with the other brandishing a whip over his [frightened] slaves."
>
> —A London pamphlet, 1776

Lemuel Haynes was an African-American minister who served in the Massachusetts militia after the fighting at Lexington and Concord. He served at Fort Ticonderoga in 1776. After the Revolution, Haynes became a popular preacher in Vermont.

African Americans. British critics made fun of American slaveholders who claimed to be fighting for freedom. Thomas Jefferson, for example, owned more than 100 slaves.

At the beginning of the Revolutionary War, the British promised freedom to all enslaved people who enlisted in the British army. Some slaves did so and left the United States at the end of the war with other Loyalists.

During the Revolutionary period, many states in the North began to think about **abolishing** (*ending*) slavery. Vermont became the first place to abolish slavery in 1777. Pennsylvania abolished slavery for the children of slaves in 1780. Massachusetts ended slavery in 1783. Three other New England states began the gradual abolition of slavery in 1783–1784. Even Southerners like George Washington could see the contradiction in having slaves. Washington's private letters show his conscience bothered him about slavery, which he thought was very wrong. In his will, he freed his slaves on his wife's death.

American Indians. The rights of Indian tribes were also ignored by the signers of the Declaration. In general, the American Revolution was a disaster for them. The American victory meant that pioneers would soon be seizing their lands.

Most Indian tribes sided with the British during the Revolutionary War. The six Iroquois nations, for example, had sided with the British during the French and Indian War, and four of the nations did so again during the Revolution.

Many Indians allied with the British

Farther South, the Cherokee were also divided, with some taking each side in the war. In general, the Indians feared that American Patriots would take their lands to make new farms. The British had promised the Indians they could keep their hunting grounds behind the Proclamation Line of 1763. Unfortunately for the American Indians, the British lost the war. After the Revolution, several tribes moved north to Canada along with other Loyalists. Those tribes that remained in the United States were gradually pushed westward.

Women. Women played an important role in the American victory in the Revolution. Many had been active Patriots as Daughters of Liberty. Once fighting broke out, they made homespun cloth for the coats and shirts needed by the soldiers of the Continental Army. They took care of family farms when their men left to fight. Benjamin Franklin's daughter helped raise money to buy clothes for soldiers. Others became "camp followers"—women who followed the army and cooked for the soldiers, sewed torn clothes, and helped nurse the wounded. Deborah Sampson Gannett even dressed herself as a man so that she could enlist in the Continental Army.

Despite their contributions to the war effort, women had few rights. The property of a married woman, for example, belonged to her husband. Women had no right to vote or to hold public office. No woman had the opportunity to sign the Declaration of Independence. Abigail Adams, the wife of John Adams, begged her husband to consider the rights of women.

"Remember the ladies, and be more generous and favorable to them than your ancestors. Do not put such unlimited power into the hands of the husbands."

—Abigail Adams to her husband John Adams

The Historian's Apprentice

1. A **revolution** is a major turning point in history. The term often refers to the violent overthrow of a government by force. Do you think it is correct to describe the events of 1775–1783 as "revolutionary"?
2. Who belongs in the American Revolution Hall of Fame? Select three nominees based on individuals in this chapter. Write a paragraph in support of each of your nominees.

Chapter 2 | The American Revolution

For the Georgia Milestones EOC Assessment, you need to know that:

- ☐ Britain and France fought in the French and Indian War (1754–1763). Britain won the war, and France was forced to surrender control of Canada to the British. The war laid the groundwork for future conflict by leaving the British with a large debt.

- ☐ King George III issued the Proclamation of 1763 prohibiting the colonists from settling west of the Appalachians in order to prevent conflict with the Indians. This angered many colonists.

- ☐ Parliament tried to impose new taxes on the colonists without their consent. Parliament passed the Stamp Act (1765), requiring the colonists to use revenue stamps on newspapers and legal documents. Colonists responded with speeches, protests, petitions, hostile attacks on revenue officials, and boycotts of British goods.

- ☐ Samuel Adams started the "Sons of Liberty," which organized protests and boycotts of British goods. The "Daughters of Liberty," a group of patriotic women colonists, was also established. "Committees of Correspondence" were formed so that "Patriots" from different colonies could inform each other of their anti-British activities.

- ☐ Parliament repealed the Stamp Act but passed new taxes on common household goods, also without the colonists' consent. This led to further protests, and these taxes were also repealed.

- ☐ Parliament imposed a new tax on tea. In December 1773, colonists disguised as Indians threw tea into Boston Harbor in the "Boston Tea Party." Parliament passed the "Intolerable Acts" (1774), closing Boston Harbor and suspending the Massachusetts legislature until the tea was paid for.

- ☐ The American Revolution began in April 1775, when British troops were sent to arrest colonial leaders and recover arms in Lexington and Concord. Patriotic "minutemen" and British redcoats fired on each other.

- ☐ Representatives from the colonies met in Philadelphia for the Second Continental Congress. They created the Continental Army and appointed George Washington, a Virginian, as its commander.

- ☐ Washington was able to force the British out of Boston but was defeated in New York City and forced to retreat. To boost sagging morale, he crossed the Delaware River to defeat Hessian mercenary troops at the Battle of Trenton.

- ☐ Thomas Paine published an influential pamphlet, *Common Sense*, arguing that the colonies should declare their independence. His arguments were persuasive to many.

- ☐ The Second Continental Congress appointed a "Committee of Five," which included Thomas Jefferson, John Adams, and Benjamin Franklin, to draft a "Declaration of Independence."

- ☐ Thomas Jefferson was the main author of the Declaration. He borrowed much of his reasoning from John Locke's writings on natural rights and the social contract. The Declaration argued that: (1) men have "unalienable rights"—the "right to life, liberty and the pursuit of happiness"—which cannot be taken away; (2) governments are created to protect these rights; and (3) when a government tries to destroy these rights, the people have the right to change their government, by force if necessary. Jefferson listed all of the colonial grievances against George III and argued that the King's actions were so despotic that the colonists had no choice but to declare their independence.

- ☐ The Continental Congress voted in favor of independence on July 2, 1776. Its members signed the Declaration of Independence on July 4, 1776.

- ☐ The British planned to divide the rebellious colonies in two by cutting a line through New York. Three British armies were supposed to meet near Albany, but two of the armies never came and the third surrendered at the Battle of Saratoga (1777).

- ☐ Benjamin Franklin and John Adams were sent to negotiate an alliance with France. The French finally signed a treaty of alliance when they received news of the British defeat at Saratoga.

- ☐ During a harsh winter at Valley Forge (1777–1778), the Continental Army was short of supplies. Two volunteers from Europe, Baron von Steuben and the Marquis de Lafayette, helped Washington to train and drill his troops.

- ☐ The British took the war to the South. In 1781, their troops were trapped at Yorktown by American and French forces. Cornwallis surrendered a large British force. The British Parliament decided not to pursue the war any longer.

- ☐ Geography played a crucial role in many battles of the Revolution. At Trenton, the Hessians were surprised that the colonists had re-crossed the Delaware River and could reach them in such cold weather. At Saratoga, the wilderness slowed the British advance. At Yorktown, control of Chesapeake Bay by the French navy blocked a British retreat and forced Cornwallis to surrender. In general, the colonists benefited from the fact that they were fighting on their own soil while the British were fighting a war thousands of miles away from their homeland.

- ☐ During the Revolution, many women were active in promoting the Patriot cause. They raised money, sewed clothes, and kept family farms. Many African Americans also helped the revolutionaries, although others were attracted to the British, who offered freedom from slavery. Some Northern states began abolishing slavery in the aftermath of the Revolution. Most Indian tribes sided with the British, who appeared less likely to seize their lands, but a few tribes sided with the colonists.

- ☐ In the Treaty of Paris (1783), the British recognized the independence of the United States and its control of lands east of the Mississippi River.

Chapter 2 | The American Revolution

Name _____

Complete the following chart.

Term	Identify/Describe
French and Indian War	
Treaty of Paris (1763)	
Proclamation of 1763	
Stamp Act	
Intolerable Acts	
Thomas Paine, *Common Sense*	
Declaration of Independence	
Battle of Trenton	
Battle of Saratoga	
French Alliance	
Battle of Yorktown	
Treaty of Paris (1783)	

Name _____

Complete the Revolutionary "Hall of Fame" below by describing the role of each of the following leaders to the American Revolution.

Thomas Paine	
Thomas Jefferson	
George Washington	
Benjamin Franklin	
John Adams	
Baron von Steuben	
Marquis de Lafayette	

Chapter 2 | The American Revolution

The American Revolution

Causes

French and Indian War
- British and French clash in Ohio River Valley
- Seven Years' War in Europe
- Treaty of Paris (1763): France surrenders Canada to Britain
- Lays groundwork for later Revolution

British Policies Create Discontent

Proclamation Line of 1763
- Prohibits western settlement

Stamp Act (1765)
- Colonial protests
- Sons/Daughters of Liberty
- Parliament repeals Stamp Act

Townshend Duties (1767)
- Taxes on glass, lead, tea, and other items
- Colonial protests
- Committees of Correspondence
- Parliament repeals duties except on tea

Arrival of more British troops (1768)
- Boston Massacre (1770)

Tea Act (1773)
- Boston Tea Party (December 1773)
- Intolerable Acts (1774)

The Fighting Begins
- Shots fired at Lexington and Concord 
- Second Continental Congress appoints Washington
- British Leave Boston
- Washington's retreat from New York City
- Washington surprises Hessians at Trenton

The War Continues

Battle of Saratoga (1777)
- Turning point of the war

Alliance with France

Winter at Valley Forge (1777–1778)
- Training by Steuben and Lafayette

Battle of Yorktown (1781)

Treaty of Paris (1783)
- Ends the war
- Britain recognizes American independence
- United States gains territory up to the Mississippi River

Declaration of Independence (1776)
- Written by Thomas Jefferson
- Based on concept of natural rights
- Governments are created to protect citizens' inalienable rights to life, liberty, and the pursuit of happiness. When governments attack these rights, people have the right to overthrow the government
- Grievances of the colonists against Great Britain
- Colonists declare their independence

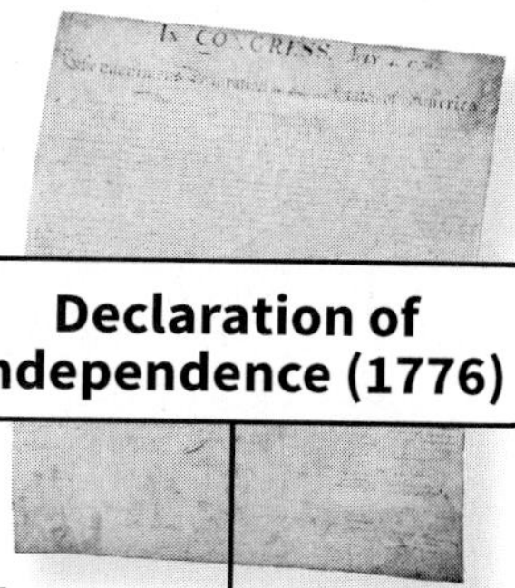

Chapter 2 | The American Revolution

What Do You Know?

SSUSH3a

1. Why did the British government decide to start taxing the colonists in the 1760s?
   A. to build new roads and make other improvements in the colonies
   B. to raise money after the costs of the French and Indian War
   C. to increase the powers of royal governors in the colonies
   D. to encourage more colonists to return to Great Britain

SSUSH3b

2. Why did the Proclamation Line of 1763 anger many American colonists?
   A. It prohibited colonists from settling in the Ohio River Valley.
   B. It promoted peaceful relations with Indian tribes in the west.
   C. It increased the taxes that the colonists paid to Britain.
   D. It gave too much land away to Canada.

SSUSH3b

3. Use the timeline below to answer the question.

   Townshend Duties — 1767
   Coercive Acts — 1774
   1765 — Stamp Act
   1773 — Tea Act

   Which would be the best title for this timeline?
   A. Colonial Reactions to British Taxes
   B. Examples of British Navigation Laws
   C. Abuses of Power by Colonial Legislatures
   D. British Policies Leading to Colonial Protests

SSUSH3b

4. How were the Committees of Correspondence, Sons of Liberty, and Daughters of Liberty similar?
   A. They were all Loyalist organizations.
   B. They were limited to the New England colonies.
   C. They all invited the participation of both men and women.
   D. They were organizations formed in opposition to British policies.

Chapter 2 | The American Revolution

SSUSH4a

5. **Read the passage to answer the question.**

   That to secure these rights, Governments are instituted [created] among Men, deriving [obtaining] their just powers from the consent of the governed, that whenever any Form of Government becomes destructive of these ends, it is the Right of the People to alter or to abolish it, and to institute new Government, laying its foundations on such principles and organizing its powers in such form, as to them shall seem most likely to effect their Safety and Happiness.

   —Declaration of Independence (1776)

   Which theory of government led directly to the views expressed in this passage?
   - A. the Mayflower Compact
   - B. the Divine Right of Kings
   - C. John Locke's social contract
   - D. Baron de Montesquieu's separation of powers

SSUSH4a

6. **What was the main purpose for writing the Declaration of Independence?**
   - A. to create a framework for a new democratic government in America
   - B. to explain the colonists' reasons for separating from Great Britain
   - C. to offer King George III a compromise that would end the conflict
   - D. to persuade the Loyalists to move to Canada

SSUSH4a

7. **Which argument is found in the Declaration of Independence?**
   - A. The British government has failed to respect the rights of the Native Americans.
   - B. The colonists have a right to change their government because it has violated the very rights it is supposed to protect.
   - C. The colonists have the right to declare independence because the British government is too far away to govern effectively.
   - D. The colonists should be able to elect their own representatives to Parliament before the British government imposes any more taxes.

SSUSH4f

8. **How was the signing of the Treaty of Paris in 1783 a victory for the United States?**
   - A. Great Britain was forced to form an alliance with France.
   - B. Great Britain recognized the United States as an independent nation.
   - C. The French and Indian War was over and colonists could move west.
   - D. American Patriots signed an alliance with France to help them win the American Revolution.

SSUSH4d

9. Use the maps below to answer the question.

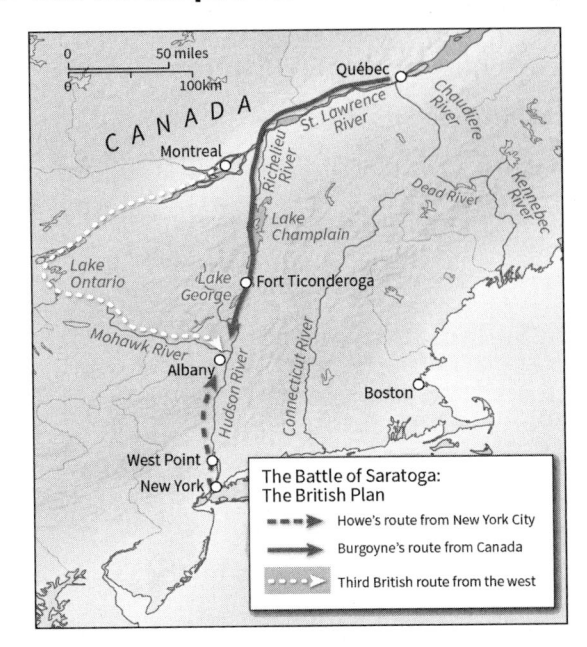

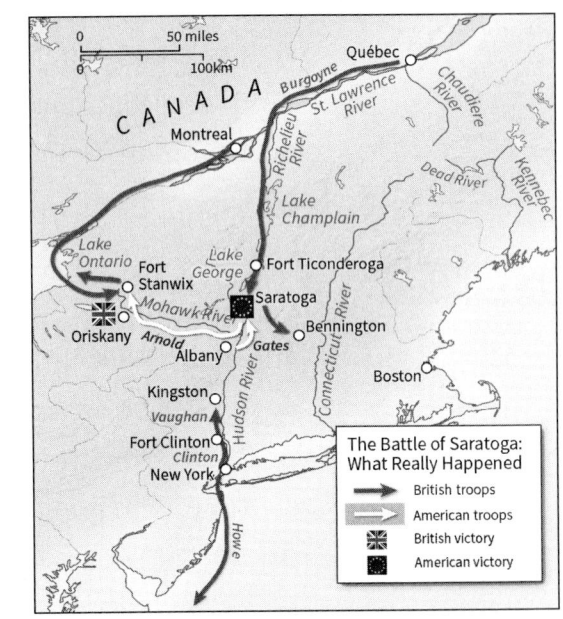

Based on a comparison of these maps, why did the British plan to divide the colonies in two fail?

A. The British plan was impossible to carry out.

B. Not all the British generals followed their plan.

C. Too many American Indians had sided with the colonists.

D. The Continental Army had many more regular troops than the British had.

SSUSH4b

10. What was the significance of the Battle of Saratoga in 1777?

A. The Continental Army ended the British threat in the South.

B. The British decided to grant the colonists their independence.

C. The British were able to divide the colonies into two separate parts.

D. The French were persuaded to enter the war as an ally of the colonists.

SSUSH4a

11. How did Thomas Jefferson MOST contribute to the outcome of the American Revolution?

A. by serving as a U.S. Senator from Virginia

B. by writing the Declaration of Independence

C. by being elected as President of the United States

D. by serving as a general in the Continental Army

Chapter 2 | The American Revolution

SSUSH4d

12. **Which factor MOST contributed to the American victory in the Battle of Yorktown (1781)?**

    A. the support of the French navy and of French troops

    B. George Washington's victory at the Battle of Trenton

    C. the orders of King George III, which confused General Cornwallis

    D. support from the German mercenaries who surrendered at Trenton

SSUSH4e

13. **Why did so many American Indian tribes support the British during the American Revolution?**

    A. They felt a sense of loyalty to King George III.

    B. They feared the colonists would take away their lands.

    C. They felt regret for supporting the French in the French and Indian War.

    D. They did not believe in the equality promised by the Declaration of Independence.

SSUSH4d

14. **Use the list below to answer the question.**

    > - American Patriots fought on their own land.
    > - The British had to ship supplies across the ocean.
    > - American Patriots knew the local land and could lay ambushes.
    > - Thick forests slowed the British advance before the Battle of Saratoga.
    > - The British could capture coastal cities, but could not control the interior.
    > - Control of Chesapeake Bay helped the Americans and French to trap Cornwallis at Yorktown.

    What do these details have in common?

    A. They tell the ways in which American Loyalists influenced the war's outcome.

    B. They describe the effects of geographic factors on the American Revolutionary War.

    C. They identify the advantages of the British army in the American Revolution.

    D. They explain why the French and Spanish decided to support the American Revolutionaries.

CHAPTER 3: The Story of Our Constitution

SSUSH5 How did specific events and key ideas bring about the adoption and implementation of the United States Constitution?

a. What were the strengths of the Articles of Confederation, including the passage of the Land Ordinance of 1785 and the Northwest Ordinance of 1787, and their influence on westward migration, slavery, public education, and the admission of new states?

b. How did the weaknesses in the Articles of Confederation, combined with Shays' Rebellion, lead to a call for a stronger central government?

c. What were the key features of the U.S. Constitution, including the Great Compromise, limited government, and the Three-Fifths Compromise?

d. What were the major main arguments of the Anti-Federalists and Federalists during the debate over ratification of the Constitution, including those arguments expressed in *The Federalist Papers* by Alexander Hamilton and James Madison?

e. How were objections to the ratification of the Constitution addressed in the Bill of Rights?

Names and Terms You Should Know

Government	Limited government	Judiciary
State constitutions	Preamble	Checks and balances
Articles of Confederation	"We the People"	Federalism
Confederation Congress	Congress	Ratification
Land Ordinance of 1785	Senate	Federalists
Northwest Ordinance of 1787	House of Representatives	Anti-Federalists
Daniel Shays	President	Alexander Hamilton
Shays' Rebellion	Electoral College	*The Federalist Papers*
Constitutional Convention	Supreme Court	Bill of Rights
James Madison	Separation of powers	First Amendment
Great Compromise	Legislature	Freedom of religion
Three-Fifths Compromise	Executive	

Georgia "Peaches" of Wisdom

1. After declaring independence, each colony became a separate state. Each state wrote its own constitution.

2. The new states also had to establish some form of national government. The Second Continental Congress approved the Articles of Confederation, which created a very weak central government— a simple "league of friendship" between the thirteen states.

3. The Congress of the Confederation was the only branch of national government. Each state had one vote in the Congress. There was no national executive or judicial branch. The Confederation Congress could not raise its own troops or tax citizens or states. It relied on the states to raise troops and contribute funds.

4. The Confederation Congress passed the Land Ordinance (1785) and the Northwest Ordinance (1787). These ordinances (*laws*) established rules for the Northwest Territory. It was divided up into smaller territories that would be admitted as new states on an equal footing with the original states. The ordinances also set aside land to support public schools, prohibited slavery throughout the Northwest Territory, and guaranteed freedom of religion and the right to a trial by jury.

5. Because the central government was so weak, foreign nations posed a threat. Shays' Rebellion of poor farmers and debtors also frightened many Americans and made them desire a stronger central government.

6. In May 1787, delegates gathered in Philadelphia to revise the Articles of Confederation. Instead, they set about writing a new constitution altogether.

7. The delegates agreed to create a national government with three branches: a legislature (Congress), an executive (the President), and a judiciary (the Supreme Court).

8. The delegates could not agree on representation in Congress. Virginia, a large state, proposed two houses based on proportional representation—larger states would have more members. New Jersey, a small state, proposed each state have equal representation. The delegates adopted the "Great Compromise": each state would have two Senators in the Senate and a number of members in the House of Representatives proportional to its size.

9. Delegates from slave and non-slave states disagreed on how slaves should be counted. They reached the "Three-Fifths Compromise": slaves would be counted as three-fifths of their actual number for purposes of both representation and taxation.

10. The delegates struggled with one main problem: they wanted a central government strong enough to protect the country but not so strong that it would oppress citizens. To prevent this, the delegates introduced four key principles: limited government, federalism, separation of powers, and checks and balances.

11. Article VII stated that the new Constitution would only go into effect if nine states ratified (*approved*) it. During the ratification debates, Anti-Federalists opposed the Constitution. They especially complained that there was no bill of rights. Federalists argued a stronger government was needed and that constitutional principles like federalism and the separation of powers would prevent it from becoming too strong. Federalist arguments were best expressed in *The Federalist Papers* by Hamilton, Madison, and Jay. By June 1788, the Constitution was ratified.

12. The first ten amendments, added in 1791, are known as the Bill of Rights. The First Amendment guarantees freedom of speech, of the press, of religion, and of assembly, and the right to petition the government.

Chapter 3 | The Story of Our Constitution

The years just after the American Revolution were critical for the new republic. No group of colonies had ever declared independence before. No large country had ever governed itself as a representative democracy. In Europe, every large country was a monarchy ruled by a king or queen. The United States was a great experiment. It was unclear whether the former colonies would survive as free and independent states.

> *The establishment of our new government seemed to be the last great experiment for promoting human happiness.*
> —George Washington, January 9, 1790

The New State Governments

Once the Declaration of Independence was signed, each colony became a free and independent state. A **state** is an area with its own government. A **government** is an organization that helps people cooperate, resolve disputes, defend themselves, punish criminals, and achieve things they could not do as individuals. The colonies had once relied on the British government to do all these things. But without British rule, each state needed to establish its own government.

Americans already had some experience in self-government with their colonial assemblies. Special conventions were now held in each state to write a **constitution**, or plan of government. These new state constitutions replaced earlier colonial charters.

Each new state constitution established a republican form of government (based on elected representatives). Seven of these state constitutions included a bill of rights. Every state except Pennsylvania created a legislature with two houses. The new state constitutions were adopted while the Revolutionary War was still being fought. By July 1777, nine states had already adopted new constitutions.

The Articles of Confederation

The thirteen new states no longer had the British government to hold them together. They therefore needed some new form of association. They required some authority to settle disputes. They also needed a way to cooperate in facing foreign nations or defending themselves against American Indian tribes.

The same day that the Second Continental Congress appointed Jefferson and others to write the Declaration of Independence, it appointed a separate committee to decide how the thirteen new states would cooperate. This committee wrote the **Articles of Confederation**.

After their struggle with Great Britain, many Americans were afraid of giving too much power to the central government. They wanted to be sure to preserve those liberties they had claimed under the Declaration of Independence. Could they design a national government that was not too weak and not too strong, but just right?

Americans' first attempt at forming a national government was in the Articles of

Major Provisions of the Articles of Confederation

1. The new Confederation was known as the "United States of America."
2. Each state remained **sovereign** (*had final authority*). The states kept all governing powers except those given exclusively (*only*) to the Confederation Congress.
3. The Congress of the Confederation was to meet every year. Each state could send two to seven delegates to the Congress. Each state delegation had one vote in Congress. All states, whatever their size, had equal representation.
4. Congress was given the exclusive (*sole*) power to declare war, to exchange ambassadors with foreign states, to enter into treaties and alliances, to set weights and measurements, to resolve disputes between states, to establish post offices, and to handle relations with Indian tribes living in several states. These powers could only be exercised by Congress and not by the states.
5. Congress could borrow money, and could build and equip a navy.
6. Congress had the power to direct its own army. However, it could not raise its own troops: these were contributed by the states.
7. All the expenses of the Confederation were paid from a general fund. State legislatures contributed to this fund. Congress could not directly tax citizens on its own.
8. The approval of nine states was needed to pass any new law in Congress.
9. All thirteen states had to agree to any change in the Articles of Confederation.

Confederation. The Articles created a simple "league of friendship" to which all thirteen states belonged. Most governmental powers were left in the hands of the states.

In this loose association, all thirteen states could cooperate, especially in dealing with **foreign affairs** (*relations with other countries*). This association had a "**Congress.**" It was the only branch of the national government. There was no national executive or national court system under the Articles. The **Confederation Congress** was actually a council made up of the representatives of thirteen powerful, independent states. Each state had **one vote** in Congress.

The Articles were debated for almost a year in the Continental Congress. Then they were sent to the state legislatures. The Articles of Confederation were finally approved by all thirteen states in 1781. The individual states did not hold special elections or even send new representatives to the Confederation Congress. Instead, once the Articles were approved, the Second Continental

The Historian's Apprentice

Your class should divide into small groups. Now imagine it is 1776. Each group should consider this question: What kind of national government should the former colonies create? Make a plan for some form of national government. Then have a reporter from your group share your ideas with the rest of your class.

Chapter 3 | The Story of Our Constitution

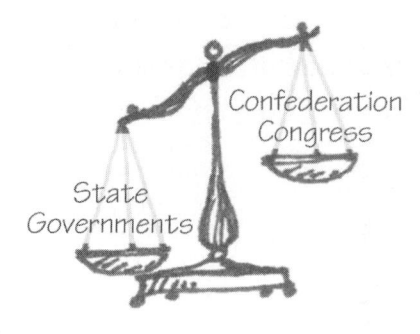

The balance of power under the Articles of Confederation

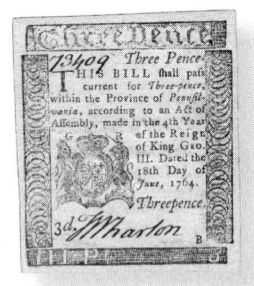

Congress became the Congress of the Confederation. All the members stayed the same.

Under the Articles, individual state governments remained more powerful than the central government. For example, states could print their own money. They could tax goods brought in from other states. Only the state governments could collect taxes and raise troops. The Congress of the Confederation relied on contributions from the states to pay its expenses, yet had no power to force states to contribute. Each state government had its own executive and courts, while the Confederation lacked both of these. Could such a government work?

These weaknesses led to the later writing of the U.S. Constitution

1. Congress had no power to tax.
2. Congress had no power to raise its own troops.
3. Congress had no power to regulate trade.
4. Congress had no power to enforce its laws.
5. There was no national court system.
6. There was no national executive to provide leadership.

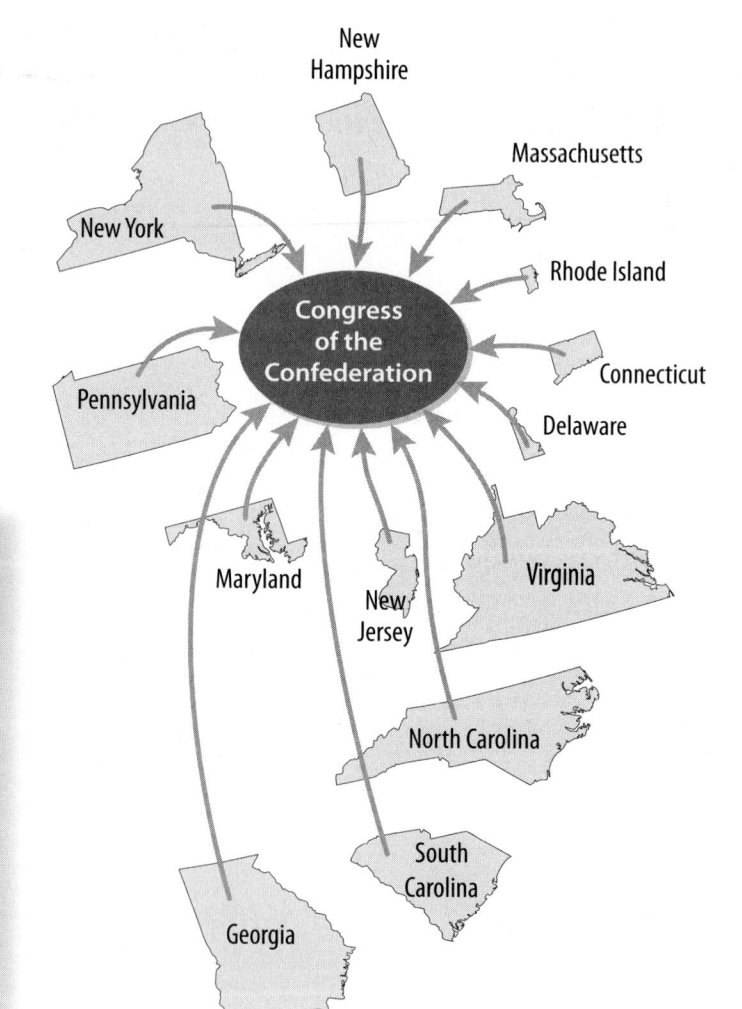

Each state had one vote in the Confederation Congress

Chapter 3 | The Story of Our Constitution

The Historian's Apprentice

1. Why was it necessary to create the Articles of Confederation? What would have happened if the new states had not created any form of association at all?
2. How did the experience of British rule influence John Dickinson and the other authors of the Articles of Confederation?
3. Imagine that the Continental Congress has hired you to design a poster in favor of the new Articles of Confederation. The purpose of your poster is to sway public opinion. What would it say?
4. You have just read about some of the weaknesses of the Articles of Confederation. What do you think were its major strengths?
5. Do you think the authors of the Articles of Confederation succeeded in creating a national government that was "just right"? Or was the new government too strong or too weak? Pretend you are a citizen in 1781. Write an editorial for a local newspaper giving your opinion on this question. An editorial is a short article in which the writer expresses his or her own opinions.

The "Critical Period": America under the Articles of Confederation

The new Confederation Congress had two major achievements. The first of these was that the Congress approved the peace treaty with Great Britain that ended the American Revolution. The second achievement was in the treatment of frontier lands. The Confederation Congress passed the **Land Ordinance** (1785) and the **Northwest Ordinance** (1787).

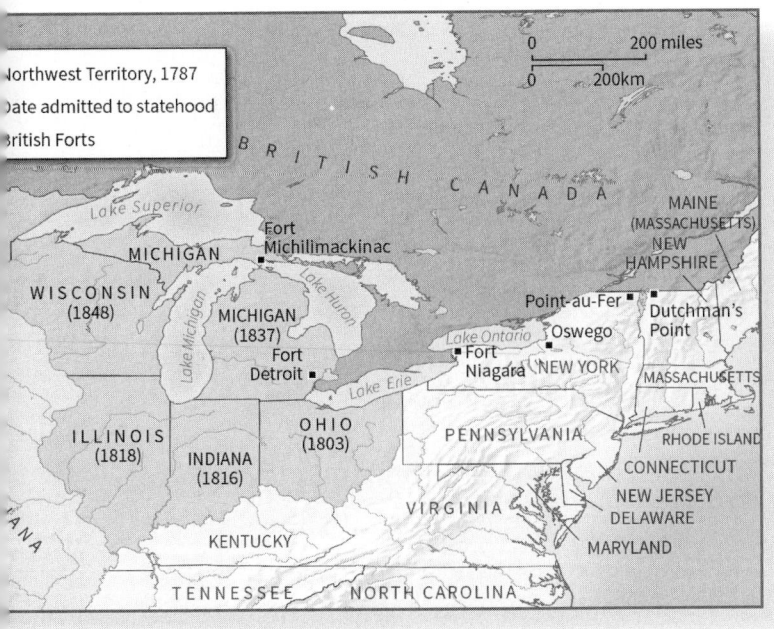

The Northwest Territory

Settlers moving into the Northwest Territory

Chapter 3 | The Story of Our Constitution

Two Important Ordinances

The thirteen colonies had become separate new states with their own constitutions and governments. But what about the frontier lands that the United States had gained by the Treaty of Paris—all of the lands between the Appalachian Mountains and the Mississippi River? What would happen to these territories? Should they be divided up and handed over to the original thirteen states? Or should something else be done?

The Historian's Apprentice

Select a partner. Imagine you are both members of the Confederation Congress. Discuss how you would treat the frontier territories that belong to the United States. Then share your ideas with the rest of the class.

To solve this problem, the Confederation Congress passed a series of **ordinances**, or laws. The frontier lands north of the Ohio River became known as the **Northwest Territory**. The **Land Ordinance** of 1785 divided the Northwest Territory into townships six miles on each side. Each township was further divided into 36 smaller sections. One square mile in each township was set aside to support a public school. This showed support for public education. The rest of the sections were to be sold. The ordinance thus established a process for settlers and investors to buy government land and turn it into private property. This also provided a source of revenue for the national government. Some of the land was to be given to veterans who had fought in the Revolutionary War. A purchaser had to buy at least one section (640 acres), so most of the original purchasers were speculators who later resold the land to farmers.

A second ordinance, known as the **Northwest Ordinance**, was passed in 1787. The Northwest Ordinance divided the Northwest Territory into several smaller territories. It then set up a procedure for each of them to be admitted to

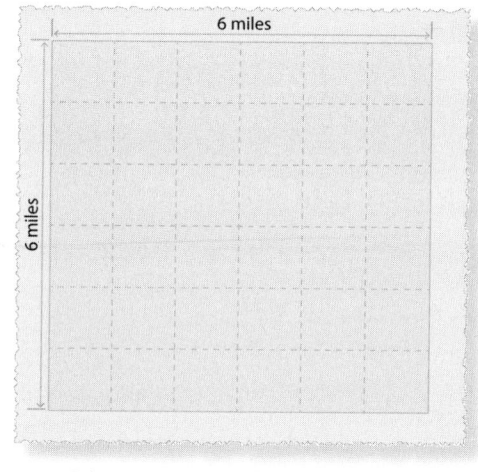

Dimensions of a Township

the United States as a new state once its population reached a certain size.

1. At first, Congress would appoint a governor and judges to run the territory.

2. When 5,000 free adult males were living in the territory, they could elect their own representatives to govern the territory.

3. When 60,000 "free inhabitants" (people) were living in the territory, they could write a constitution and be admitted to statehood "on an equal footing with the original states."

The Northwest Ordinance also prohibited slavery throughout the Northwest Territory. The ordinance guaranteed freedom of religion and the right to a trial by jury in the Northwest Territory. Any male adult who owned fifty acres of land had the right to vote.

The Northwest Ordinance (July 13, 1787)

Article I
No person . . . shall ever be molested [*disturbed*] on account of his mode of worship or religious sentiments.

Article II
All persons shall be bailable [*temporarily released until trial with the payment of bail money*], unless for capital offenses . . . [N]o cruel or unusual punishment shall be inflicted. No man shall be deprived of his liberty or property but by judgment of his peers or by the law of the land . . .

Article V
. . . And whenever any of the said states shall have 60,000 free inhabitants therein, such state shall be admitted by its delegates into the Congress of the United States on an equal footing with the original states in all respects . . .

Article VI
There shall be neither slavery nor involuntary servitude in the said territory. . .

What was the significance of Article I and Article VI above?

Problems under the Confederation Grow

Despite these achievements, serious problems quickly arose.

First, there were problems with foreign nations. The British refused to hand over several forts in the Northwest even though they had promised to do so. Spain challenged the borders of the new United States to the Southwest. In far away North Africa, pirates attacked American ships that were once protected by the British navy. Without a strong national government, there was no one to watch over American interests.

Second, there were growing economic difficulties at home. Despite winning the Revolution, many Americans faced hard times. To raise revenues, states taxed each other's goods. This hurt trade. So did the fact that the British refused to sign a trade agreement with the United States because trade was supposed to be handled by the individual states.

Third, there was a general shortage of money. Some state governments refused to honor their debts from the Revolution or to repay overseas lenders. The Confederation Congress could not raise its own money and had no way to force states to give it revenue, but it owed back pay to veterans who had fought in the American Revolution. Retired army officers and public creditors feared they would never get paid.

A growing number of Americans believed that the state governments were becoming tyrannical and corrupt. George Washington feared that the jealousies and divisions of the states would prevent the development of a genuine national spirit. James Madison feared the "tyranny of the majority"—that state governments would not respect the rights of minorities, including property owners.

Chapter 3 | The Story of Our Constitution

[Can] thirteen states ... be said to be united in government when each state reserves to itself the sole powers of legislation? ... If the states propose to form and preserve a confederacy, there must be a supreme head in which the power of all the states is united.... Without such a head, the states cannot be united and all attempts to conduct the measures of the continent will prove governmental farces. So long as any individual state has the power to defeat the measures of the other twelve, our pretended union is but a name and our confederation a cobweb.

—Noah Webster, *Sketches of American Policy* (1785)

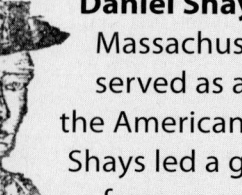

Daniel Shays, a Massachusetts farmer, had served as a captain during the American Revolution. Shays led a group of angry farmers and debtors in an attack on one of the state's courthouses. They demanded freedom for debtors, cheap paper money, and lower taxes.

Shays' Rebellion

In Massachusetts, an economic crisis led the state government to raise taxes and to increase its efforts to collect debts. It **foreclosed** (*took back ownership*) on farms and sent some debtors to prison. Many of these farmers had fought as soldiers in the Revolution. Poor farmers protested. They shut down courts trying to collect taxes and debts. They demanded that Massachusetts print cheap paper money as nearby Rhode Island had done. This would have raised prices and made farmers' debts easier to repay.

Shays' Rebellion created a wave of fear among wealthy landowners and merchants across the country. There was no national army to put down the rebellion if Massachusetts was unable to stop its spread to other states.

In the end, the Massachusetts militia (*citizens' military force*) was able to crush Shays' Rebellion. But with all the other problems facing the country under the Articles of Confederation, many Americans began to think that it was time for a change. Merchants feared the loss of trade, army officers feared the loss of their back pay, and lenders feared the loss of their loans to the government.

The Annapolis Convention: A Call for Action

In 1786, a meeting was held in Annapolis, Maryland. The purpose of the meeting was to discuss trade between the states. Five states sent representatives, including James Madison and Alexander Hamilton. The members could see that the country was in trouble. They called for a new meeting to be held in Philadelphia the following year. Its purpose would be to revise the Articles of Confederation. All thirteen states were invited to send representatives.

We have probably had too good an opinion of human nature in forming our confederation. Experience has taught us that men will not adopt and carry into execution measures the best calculated for their own good without the intervention of a coercive power [*power based on force*]. I do not conceive [*think*] we can exist long as a nation without having lodged [*put*] somewhere a power which will pervade [*fill*] the whole Union . . .

—George Washington to John Jay, August 1, 1786

Meetings of Representatives of the Colonies or States

Meeting	Date	Location	Purpose/Accomplishments
Albany Congress	1754	Albany	Met to discuss cooperation of the colonies just as the French and Indian War was beginning; approved the Albany Plan of Franklin and Hutchinson, which proposed a President-General and a Grand Council.
Stamp Act Congress	1765	New York City	Sent a petition to King George III to repeal the Stamp Act.
First Continental Congress	1774	Philadelphia	Sent a petition to King George III to repeal the Coercive Acts; planned a colonial boycott of British goods.
Second Continental Congress	1775–1781	Philadelphia (except during the British occupation)	Met to discuss a response to the Coercive Acts and other British policies; created Continental Army; appointed George Washington; signed Declaration of Independence; approved Articles of Confederation.
Confederation Congress	1781–1788	Philadelphia, Princeton, Annapolis, Trenton, and New York City (had no fixed capital and moved from place to place)	Had the same members as the Second Continental Congress but acted as the national government under the Articles of Confederation; approved the Treaty of Paris (1783) and passed the Land Ordinance (1785) and the Northwest Ordinance (1787).
Annapolis Convention	1786	Annapolis	Met to discuss trade between the states; called for meeting of delegates to revise the Articles of Confederation.
Constitutional Convention	1787	Philadelphia	Met in Philadelphia to revise the Articles of Confederation, but wrote a whole new constitution instead.

The Historian's Apprentice

1. Which of the representatives' meetings shown in the table was most important? Why?
2. Can you see any patterns in the degree of cooperation between the colonies/states? Explain your answer.

Chapter 3 | The Story of Our Constitution

Name: _____

Complete the concept ladder below by adding your own descriptions and explanations.

The Articles of Confederation (1781)

Shays' Rebellion

Northwest Ordinance

Land Ordinance

Weaknesses of the Confederation

The Confederation Congress

Powers of the Confederation

Chapter 3 | The Story of Our Constitution

The "Miracle at Philadelphia": The Constitutional Convention

In response to the call from Annapolis for a revision of the Articles of Confederation, twelve of the thirteen states sent fifty-five delegates to the state house in Philadelphia in May 1787. It was the same building where eight of them had signed the Declaration of Independence eleven years before.

Back in 1776, the colonists had cut their ties to Britain in the name of liberty. The challenge now was to make a central government that was strong enough to defend the nation and promote its citizens' well-being, but not so strong that it would threaten individual liberties. The Continental Congress had tried to do this with the Articles of Confederation but many Americans felt they had not succeeded. Now it was time to try again.

Every state except Rhode Island sent representatives to this new meeting. All of the delegates were men who owned property. More than half of them were trained lawyers. One third of these men had fought in the Revolution.

The delegates immediately elected George Washington to preside over their proceedings. Just as quickly, they voted to keep their discussions secret from the public to encourage a freer exchange of ideas.

Next, the delegates took a surprising step. They had been asked to revise the Articles of Confederation. Instead, they decided to replace the Articles altogether. The delegates set about writing a new **constitution**—a plan of basic rules for government. Their assembly became known as the **Constitutional Convention**.

What the Delegates Agreed On

The delegates who gathered in Philadelphia in 1787 were in general agreement on a number of important issues. Most agreed, for example, that the national government was too weak.

The Historian's Apprentice

In his opening address, Governor Edmund Randolph of Virginia pointed to these weaknesses in the present system of government:

"(1) the Confederation produced no security against foreign invasion...

(2) the [Confederate] government could not check the quarrels between states nor a rebellion in any...

(3) there were many advantages which the United States might acquire [*get*], which were not attainable under the Confederation, such as a productive impost [*a tax on goods coming from other countries*]—counteraction of the commercial regulations of other nations—pushing of commerce...

Edmund Randolph

Continued ▶

Chapter 3 | The Story of Our Constitution

(4) the [Confederate] government could not defend itself against the encroachments [*improper interference*] from the states . . ."

—James Madison's *Notes of the Constitutional Convention,* May 29, 1787

James Madison

1. Which of the weaknesses identified by Governor Randolph do you feel were most important? Explain your answer.
2. Imagine that you are a delegate at the Constitutional Convention. Write a private letter to a friend explaining how the weaknesses of the Articles of Confederation have led the delegates to decide to write a whole new constitution.

Only a few days after Governor Randolph's opening speech, the delegates passed this resolution:

> *"That a national government ought to be established consisting of a supreme legislative, executive, and judiciary."*

In other words, they agreed to form a new national government with three separate branches, just as their state governments already had.

The Signing of the United States Constitution by Louis S. Glanzman, 1987

In a government, the **legislature** is the body that makes the laws. The **executive** "executes," or carries out, the laws. The **judiciary** (or court system) applies the laws to particular cases.

The legislature makes the law:

The city council passes a law setting the speed limit on Main Street at 30 miles per hour.

The executive enforces the law:

A police officer stops a driver on Main Street who is going 40 miles an hour and gives her a speeding ticket.

The judiciary applies the law:

The driver claims she drove faster to avoid an accident when a truck crossed over onto her lane. A court must decide whether she broke the law and should pay a penalty in this particular situation.

The Legislature

The members of the Constitutional Convention also seemed to agree, at least at first, that the new legislature should have two houses, just like the British Parliament:

- The first house would be known as the **House of Representatives**. It would represent the people. Its members would be elected directly by the people.

- The second house would be the **Senate**. It would represent the wisdom, wealth, and property of America. Senators would serve for longer terms than members of the House of Representatives. This way, they would not be as subject to pressures from the public.

The Executive

All the delegates recognized the need for a **national executive** to provide leadership and to carry out the laws. This had been missing from the Articles of Confederation. The delegates were not sure, however, if this new executive should be a single person or a small group.

After some debate, the members of the Constitutional Convention decided that the national executive should be a single individual, known as the **President**. They further decided that the President should be given the power to **veto** (*deny or refuse*) new laws passed by Congress. However, to make sure the President was not too powerful, the delegates also decided that two-thirds of both houses of Congress should be able to override the President's veto.

The Historian's Apprentice

1. Alexander Hamilton greatly admired the British monarchy. He said that the king identified with his people's interests as a whole, rather than with any special group. Hamilton proposed that the delegates create a powerful executive for life: "The English model was the only good one on this subject. . . . [W]e ought to go as far in order to attain stability . . . as republican principles will admit . . . Let one executive be appointed [for life] who dares execute his powers." The other delegates rejected Hamilton's idea. If you had been present, would you have supported or opposed Hamilton? Write your answer in your journal or on a separate sheet of paper.

2. Do you think it is better to have a single person or a committee as the head of the executive branch of government? Explain your opinion to a partner and then share your ideas with the class. Be sure to consider the advantages and disadvantages of each.

Disagreement and Compromise

Although the delegates generally agreed on the need for a stronger national government, they disagreed on a number of other issues.

Large against Small

The most important disagreement was about representation in Congress. Here, the larger states opposed the smaller ones.

- The larger states argued they should have more representatives because they had more people. They felt it would be unfair for small states with fewer people to have an equal voice in Congress. This would violate republican principles.

- The smaller states feared that the larger states would abuse their power if they were given more representatives. They wanted each state to have equal representation in Congress, just as they had under the Articles of Confederation.

The Virginia Plan

Virginia was still the most populous state in the nation. Its delegates proposed that the representation of each state in Congress should be **in proportion** to its population. That is, the number of each state's representatives should be based on the size of its population. The delegates from Virginia wished to apply this principle to *both* houses of Congress. They suggested that the members of the House of Representatives would select the members of the Senate. Since Virginia, Massachusetts, and Pennsylvania had the largest populations, they would be given the most seats in both the House of Representatives and the Senate. This was known as the "**Virginia Plan**."

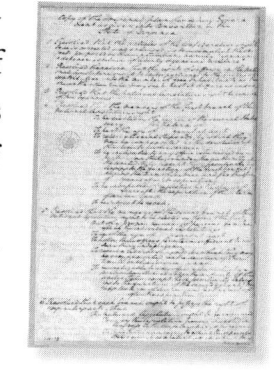

The New Jersey Plan

New Jersey was one of the smallest states. Its delegates opposed the Virginia Plan. They even turned against the idea of a legislature with two houses. Instead, they argued that representation in the legislature should remain as it had been under the Articles of Confederation. They proposed that the legislature have only one house and that each state continue to have **equal** representation in that house. This became known as the "**New Jersey Plan**."

The Historian's Apprentice

Mr. William Paterson (*New Jersey*): "Give the large states an influence in proportion to their [size], and what will be the consequence? Their ambition will be proportionally increased, and the small states will have everything to fear. New Jersey will never [agree]. She would be swallowed up. He had rather submit to a monarch, to a despot, than submit to such a fate...."

Mr. James Wilson (*Pennsylvania*): "[A]s all authority was derived from the people, equal numbers of people ought to have an equal number of representatives, and different numbers of people different numbers of representatives. This principle had been improperly violated in the Confederation, owing to the urgent circumstances of the time... If small states will not [agree] to this plan, Pennsylvania... would not [agree] to any other..."

—James Madison's *Notes of the Constitutional Convention*, June 9, 1787

Dr. Benjamin Franklin (*Pennsylvania*): "The diversity of opinions turns on two points. If a proportional representation takes place, the small states [argue] that their liberties will be in danger. If an equality of votes is to be put in its place, the large states say their money will be in danger..."

—James Madison's *Notes of the Constitutional Convention*, June 30, 1787

1. What was meant by proportional representation?
2. Why did larger states want proportional representation?
3. Why did smaller states want equal representation?
4. Imagine that you are a delegate to the Constitutional Convention in 1787. Would you have agreed with Mr. Paterson or Mr. Wilson? Prepare a short speech to the other delegates at the Constitutional Convention in which you respond to their arguments.

The "Great Compromise"

A **compromise** occurs when each side to a dispute gives up something in order to reach a solution that both sides can accept.

In 1787, the delegates from Connecticut proposed a compromise to end the dispute:

- States should enjoy **proportional representation** in the **House of Representatives**. States with larger populations would have more representatives. This benefited the larger states.
- States should enjoy **equal representation** in the **Senate**. Each state should have the same number of Senators. This benefited the smaller states.

After two months of debate, a revised version of the Connecticut plan was finally adopted. The delegates agreed that each state would have **two Senators** in the Senate. Each state would have a number of representatives in the House of Representatives **proportional** to its size. This solution became known as the **Great Compromise**. It explains the organization of Congress that we still have today.

The Electoral College

The delegates also disagreed over how to choose the President. Most of the delegates did not trust the people enough to let them elect the President directly. James Madison of Virginia, for example, thought that Congress should actually select the President. The Virginia and New Jersey Plans both proposed that Congress should choose the President.

Chapter 3 | The Story of Our Constitution

The Historian's Apprentice

Mr. Elbridge Gerry (*Massachusetts*): The evils we experience flow from the excess of democracy. The people do not [lack] virtue but are the dupes [*fools*] of pretended patriots. In Massachusetts . . . they are daily misled into the most baleful [*harmful*] measures and opinions by the false reports [spread] by [evil] men . . .

—James Madison's *Notes of the Constitutional Convention*, May 31, 1787

Based on this quotation, why do you think Elbridge Gerry opposed the direct election of the President by the people?

The delegates eventually decided that the President should be chosen by a group of special "electors" known together as the **Electoral College**. Each state would have a number of electors equal to the total number of its representatives in both houses of Congress.

To become President, a candidate would need to win the support of a majority of these electors. If no candidate won a majority, then the election would be decided by the House of Representatives, where each state would have one vote.

The "Three-Fifths Compromise"

In 1787, Southern states had large slave populations. They wanted to count their slaves as part of their populations when calculating how many seats they had in the House of Representatives. But they didn't want their slaves to count for purposes of taxation.

Citizens in Northern states had few slaves or none at all. Several Northern states had already outlawed slavery or were in the process of doing so. The delegates from these states thought that slave populations should not be counted as part of a state's population for Congressional representation since slaves were not free citizens. However, they thought the slaves should be counted for purposes of taxation.

In the end, the delegates struck a compromise. Slave populations would be counted at three-fifths of their actual number. In other words, every five slaves would be counted as three persons. The same rule would apply for purposes of both representation and taxation.

The Historian's Apprentice

1. A Southern state has a population of 600,000 free citizens and 500,000 slaves. What is this state's population for purposes of both Congressional representation and taxation under the "Three-Fifths Compromise"?
2. Some historians have described the Constitution as a "bundle of compromises." Which compromise do you think was most important? Why?
3. Create a foldable describing the two main compromises at the Constitutional Convention: the "Great Compromise" and the "Three-Fifths Compromise."

Three Leading Individuals at the Constitutional Convention

Individual	Background	Role at the Convention
George Washington (1732–1799) 	A wealthy Virginia landowner, Washington commanded the Continental Army and won the American Revolution. After the Revolution, he stepped down from his position as the head of the army in order to return to civilian life.	Washington served as the President of the Constitutional Convention. His prestige gave the Convention greater respect and authority.
James Madison (1751–1836) 	Another wealthy landowner, Madison owned a plantation in Virginia with hundreds of slaves. He studied in New Jersey and learned Latin, Greek, and Hebrew. Because of poor health, he was unable to fight in the Revolution. He fought for religious freedom in the Virginia state legislature. Madison was disappointed by the conduct of the legislature and turned against what he considered excessive democracy.	Madison was 36 years old when he attended the Constitutional Convention. He was the author of the Virginia Plan, which became the basis for the Constitution, and is known as the "Father of the Constitution." Madison spoke more than 200 times in the Convention's debates. His notes of the Constitutional Convention are still used by historians today. Madison was one of the three authors of *The Federalist Papers*. Madison led the effort in favor of the Constitution at the Virginia ratifying convention, where he was opposed by the Anti-Federalist Patrick Henry.
Alexander Hamilton (1755–1804) 	Hamilton was born in the Caribbean and came to New York City to study. During the Revolution he was a senior aide to Washington. After the war, Hamilton became a successful lawyer in New York. Hamilton was a leader of the Annapolis Convention, which invited states to send representatives to Philadelphia to amend the Articles of Confederation.	Hamilton believed that a much stronger central government was needed. At the Constitutional Convention, he told the other delegates that he admired the British system of monarchy and thought the President should be chosen for life. Hamilton wrote most of the essays in *The Federalist Papers*, and led the ratification effort in New York.

Chapter 3 | The Story of Our Constitution

A Summary of the U.S. Constitution

By August 1787, a committee of delegates had completed the first draft of the new constitution. Remaining issues were handed over to several smaller committees while a committee on "style"—which had Gouverneur Morris, James Madison, and Alexander Hamilton among its members—wrote the final draft. The final document was approved by the Constitutional Convention one month later. It consisted of a preamble and seven articles and blended the parliamentary traditions of England, the ideals of civic republicanism, and classical liberal principles. The same document still governs us more than two hundred years later.

The Preamble

The first part of the Constitution is the Preamble. A **preamble** is an introductory statement. The Preamble to the U.S. Constitution announces that the new government is the creation of the American people. The rest of the Preamble then explains the goals of the people in establishing this government.

We the People of the United States, in order to form a more perfect Union, establish justice, insure domestic tranquility, provide for the common defense, promote the general welfare, and secure the blessings of liberty to ourselves and our posterity, do ordain and establish this Constitution for the United States of America.

Word Helper

"We the People" = the individual citizens of the United States

union = a group of states united together under one government

establish justice = to administer laws fairly; to treat fairly and reasonably; to punish crimes and reward good deeds

tranquility = peacefulness and calm (also often spelled "tranquillity")

domestic tranquility = peacefulness and calm inside a country

common defense = the defense of the entire community

general welfare = the well-being (happiness, health, and prosperity) of the entire community

posterity = all future generations; those who will live after us

ordain = to order or make official

The Historian's Apprentice

1. Why did the Preamble begin with the words "We the People"?
2. Explain what the Preamble says in your own words.

How Our National Government Is Organized

The first three articles of the Constitution establish the basic structure of our national government, known as the "**federal government**." These articles define three separate branches of government with different powers and responsibilities.

- Article I — Congress
- Article II — The President
- Article III — The Supreme Court

Article I: The Legislative Branch: Congress

- The first article establishes the legislative branch, known as **Congress.**
- Congress has two houses: the **Senate** and the **House of Representatives**.
- In the Senate, each state is represented by two Senators.
- In the House of Representatives, each state is represented by a number of members in proportion to its population.
- Members of the House of Representatives are elected by the people for two-year terms.
- Senators are appointed for six-year terms by their state legislatures. (This method of selecting Senators was changed in 1913.)
- Article I gives Congress very specific powers. These powers are known as the "**enumerated powers**" because they are precisely spelled out. They include the power to declare war, to lay and collect taxes, to raise and support an army and navy, to coin money, to borrow money, to regulate interstate commerce, to establish post offices, and to create lower courts.
- Congress also has the power to pass any law "necessary and proper" for carrying out the powers listed above. These are called the "**implied powers**."
- A **bill** must pass both houses of Congress and be signed by the President in order to become a law. A two-thirds majority in each house can pass a bill without the President's signature (known as "**overriding a veto**").

The Historian's Apprentice

List two important rules about Congress found in Article I of the Constitution.

Chapter 3 | The Story of Our Constitution

Article II: The Executive Branch: the Presidency

- The second article establishes the offices of **President** and **Vice President**.

- The President must be a natural-born citizen who is at least thirty-five years old. The President is chosen by the **Electoral College**. After being elected, the President serves for a four-year term.

- The President enforces federal laws, serves as commander-in-chief of the armed forces, appoints and receives ambassadors, negotiates treaties, gives a "State of the Union" address, and appoints judges and other officials.

- Congress can remove the President from office for misconduct by **impeachment**.

The Historian's Apprentice

List two important rules about the President found in Article II of the Constitution.

Article III: The Judicial Branch: the Supreme Court

- The third article establishes the **Supreme Court** as the highest court in the land.

- The Supreme Court decides all disputes between states or concerning foreign ambassadors. The Supreme Court can also hear appeals of other cases.

- Federal judges hold office for life (unless they commit some crime or other bad behavior).

- The Constitution did not create any lower federal courts, but it gave Congress the power to create lower federal courts in the future.

The Historian's Apprentice

List two important rules about the judicial branch found in Article III of the Constitution.

The Constitution also has a number of other important provisions.

Article IV: The States

- Citizens of every state enjoy the same rights and privileges in all other states.
- Congress can admit new states into the "Union" (*our nation*).
- Every state is guaranteed the **republican** form of government (*a government of representatives elected by the people*).

Article V: The Amending Process

- The Constitution can be **amended** (*added to or changed*).
- An amendment must be proposed by two-thirds (2/3) of each house of Congress and **ratified** (*approved*) by three-fourths (3/4) of the states.

Article VI: The Supreme Law of the Land

- The Constitution and all federal laws are the "supreme law of the land." They are superior to state laws.

Article VII: Ratification

- This last article established a procedure for adopting the Constitution. It stated that the new Constitution would go into effect once nine of the thirteen states **ratified** (*approved*) it.

Constitutional Principles

The delegates to the Constitutional Convention struggled with one central problem. They wanted to create a central government that would be strong enough to protect the country and promote greater cooperation while not becoming so strong that it would oppress them.

The system of government they introduced to solve this problem rested on several key principles. Four of the most important were limited government, federalism, separation of powers, and checks and balances.

Limited Government

Under the Constitution, our federal government has limited power. It only has those powers specifically listed in the Constitution itself. For example, the Constitution gives our federal government the power to take steps in our national defense, but not to decide what children should learn in school. This power is left to state and local governments. The main purpose of limited government is to protect individual rights and to prevent the government from becoming tyrannical.

Federalism

The Constitution divided powers and responsibilities between our national government, known as the **federal government**, and the state governments.

The federal government is responsible for affairs affecting the nation as a whole, such as national defense. Only the federal government has the power to appoint ambassadors,

Chapter 3 | The Story of Our Constitution

negotiate treaties, and declare war. State governments cannot do these things.

Local matters, such as keeping up local roads and running schools, are left to the states. Congress has no power to say what children should learn in school, or what speed people can drive their cars on local roads. This division of power and responsibility between our national and state governments is known as **federalism**.

The authors of the Constitution believed that this division of powers between the federal and state governments would prevent the federal government from becoming too strong.

Separation of Powers

Within the federal government, power is further divided by the separation of powers. The Constitutional Convention gave our federal government three separate branches: legislative, executive, and judicial. Each branch exercises its own separate power:

- **Legislative Power**—the power to make federal laws—is exercised by Congress.
- **Executive Power**—the power to carry out and enforce federal laws—is exercised by the President.
- **Judicial Power**—the power to hear and decide cases applying federal law to specific situations—is exercised by the Supreme Court.

This separation of powers was based on the ideas of a Frenchman, **Baron de Montesquieu**, who wrote during the Enlightenment. By 1787, each state already had a separation of powers in its own state constitution.

The authors of the Constitution saw the separation of powers as another way of making sure that the federal government did not become too strong. In an absolute monarchy, a king or queen has all of the powers of government. The monarch makes the laws, enforces

96   Chapter 3 | The Story of Our Constitution

the laws, and decides if the laws are applied correctly. It is impossible for ordinary citizens to challenge anything that such an all-powerful king or queen has done.

With the separation of powers, it becomes more difficult for the government to commit arbitrary and unfair acts. Each branch acts as a watchdog over the other. "Ambition," James Madison later wrote, "counteracts ambition."

Checks and Balances

Closely related to the separation of powers was the creation of a system of **checks and balances**. Each branch was given specific powers to "**check**"—or *stop*—the other two. This would prevent any single branch of the central government from becoming too powerful. It also created an incentive for the different branches to cooperate.

Checks on Congress

- Each house of Congress checks the other house. The approval of both houses is needed to pass any new law.
- To pass a bill into law, Congress requires the signature of the President. The President can check Congress by **vetoing** its proposed legislation (refusing to sign the bill).
- The Supreme Court can check Congress by ruling that a federal law is unconstitutional (*violates some aspect of the Constitution*).

Checks on the President

- The President appoints Justices to the Supreme Court, ambassadors, and other officials, but these appointments must be approved by the Senate.
- The President negotiates treaties with foreign nations, but these treaties must be approved by two-thirds of the Senate.
- The President controls foreign policy and acts as commander-in-chief of the armed forces, but only Congress can declare war.
- The President establishes programs, but Congress can refuse to provide money for these programs.

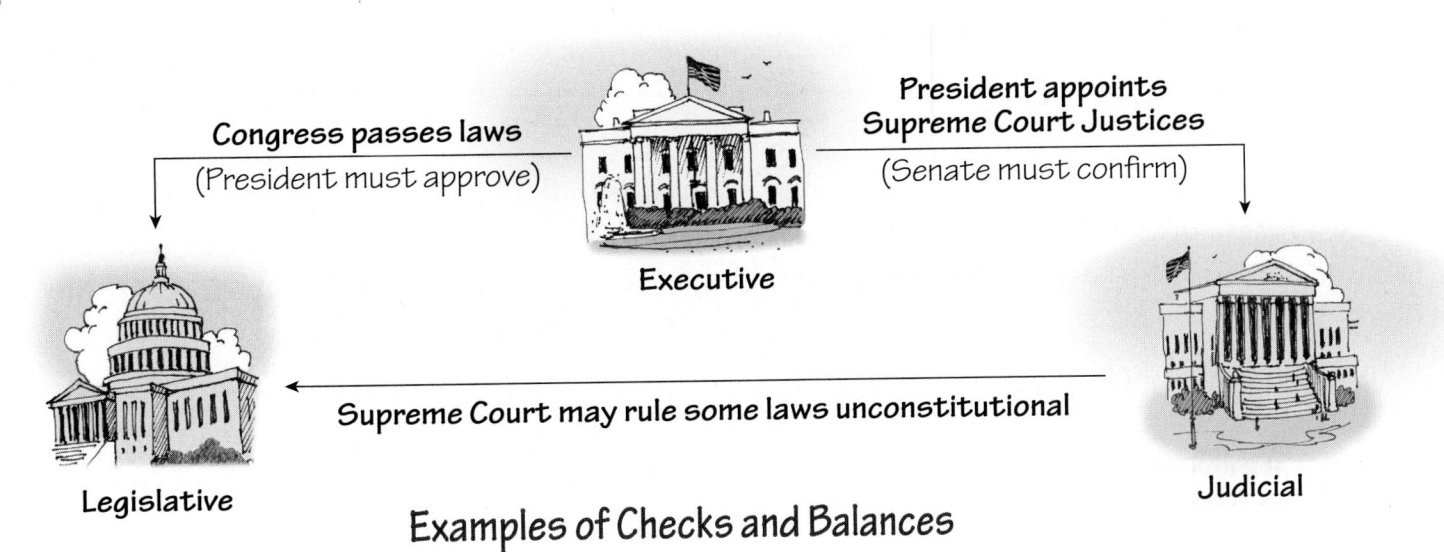

Congress passes laws (President must approve)

President appoints Supreme Court Justices (Senate must confirm)

Executive

Supreme Court may rule some laws unconstitutional

Legislative

Judicial

Examples of Checks and Balances

Chapter 3 | The Story of Our Constitution

- Congress can **impeach** (*remove from office*) the President.
- The Supreme Court can check the President by ruling that an executive order or Presidential action is unconstitutional.

Checks on the Supreme Court

- Congress can override decisions of the Supreme Court on federal law by passing a new law.
- Congress and the states can override the Supreme Court's interpretation of the Constitution by amending the Constitution.
- The President can influence the composition of the Supreme Court through judicial appointments.
- Congress can impeach federal judges for wrongdoing.
- The President can grant a pardon to someone convicted of a crime.

The Historian's Apprentice

1. How do the principles of limited government, the separation of powers, and the system of checks and balances prevent our federal government from growing too strong?
2. Make your own chart showing how the Constitution corrected the most important weaknesses of the Articles of Confederation.

The Debate over Ratification

The Constitution began with these words: "We the People." But did the American people truly support the new Constitution?

Article VII of the Constitution set up a procedure for its adoption. The Constitution would come into force only if it was **ratified** (*officially approved*) by nine states. To decide on ratification, states held special ratifying conventions.

Federalists against Anti-Federalists

Debates now sprang up in all thirteen states to decide whether or not the Constitution should be ratified. Those who favored the new constitution called themselves **Federalists**. Opponents of the new constitution became known as **Anti-Federalists**.

Many of the Anti-Federalists had been leading Patriots during the American Revolution. They feared that the proposed Constitution would establish a central government that was just as oppressive as the British government had been. The Anti-Federalists were convinced that the new government would rob the states of their powers and threaten personal liberties.

The Federalists warned that if a stronger central government were not soon adopted, the country might split apart or be invaded by foreign powers. They also argued that the proposed new government would never become despotic or oppressive. This was because of several safeguards found in the Constitution itself:

1. **The division of power between the federal government and the states**
2. **The separation of powers within the federal government**
3. **The system of checks and balances**

The most important Federalist arguments were published by Alexander Hamilton, James Madison, and John Jay in a series of 85 articles that have become known as *The Federalist Papers*. The purpose of *The Federalist Papers* was to persuade the ratifying convention of New York to approve the Constitution. *The Federalist Papers* argued that a stronger government was badly needed, while the principles of federalism, the separation of powers, and checks and balances would protect the liberty of every citizen.

The Historian's Apprentice

"[How can we maintain] in practice the necessary [separation] of power among the several departments, as laid down in the Constitution? The only answer that can be given is .. by so contriving [designing] the interior structure of the government as that its several ... parts may, by their mutual relations, be the means of keeping each other in their proper places ... [T]he great security against a gradual concentration of the several powers in [one] department consists in giving to those who administer [conduct; manage] each department the necessary constitutional means and personal motives to resist encroachments of the others.... In the ... republic of America, ... power ... is first divided between two distinct governments [federal and state]. Hence a double security arises to the rights of the people. The different governments will control each other, at the same time that each will be controlled by itself."

—James Madison, *The Federalist Papers*, No. 51, February 6, 1788

1. In what two ways, according to Madison, does the Constitution prevent potential abuses of power?

2. Imagine that the students in your class are the members of a state convention in 1788, deciding whether or not to ratify the new Constitution. Some members of the class should pretend to be Federalists. Others should pretend to be Anti-Federalists. The "convention" should debate the question of ratification. Be sure to consider the absence of a bill of rights. After the debate is over, the class should take a vote on whether the Constitution should be ratified.

3. Imagine it is 1788. Write your own newspaper article, make your own political flyer, or make your own political cartoon either for or against ratification of the Constitution.

4. Federalists and Anti-Federalists held beliefs in common even though they disagreed on whether to adopt the new Constitution. Make your own Venn diagram comparing the views of Federalists and Anti-Federalists, showing their similarities as well as their differences.

Chapter 3 | The Story of Our Constitution

The Bill of Rights

During the ratification debates, Anti-Federalists complained that there was no bill of rights in the Constitution. They said this showed that the authors of the Constitution secretly planned to rob the people of their liberties.

A **bill of rights** is a list of rights guaranteed to individuals, such as freedom of religion or freedom of speech. Parliament had issued the English Bill of Rights in 1689. Most states included a bill of rights in their state constitutions.

However, the idea of a bill of rights was hardly discussed at all at the Constitutional Convention and quickly dismissed. To win popular support for the new Constitution, the Federalists promised they would add a bill of rights in the future.

In a spirit of compromise, several states ratified the Constitution with the understanding that the Federalists would quickly introduce a bill of rights.

The Bill of Rights: The First Ten Amendments

The Federalists kept their word. After the Constitution was adopted, the first Congress proposed a bill of rights in the form of twelve amendments in 1789. Ten of these amendments were quickly ratified by the states and became part of the Constitution in 1791. They established individual rights that Congress has no power to take away.

The First Amendment

Congress shall make no law respecting an establishment of religion, or prohibiting the free exercise thereof; or abridging the freedom of speech, or of the press; or the right of the people peaceably to assemble, and to petition the government for a redress of grievances.

The First Amendment set the tone for the Bill of Rights. It was a constitutional command telling Congress what it could **not** do. This amendment placed a limit on the new government's exercise of power. The amendment actually establishes *five freedoms*:

1. Congress cannot establish a state religion.
   At a time when England and other countries in Europe had established churches, this was interpreted to mean that there could be no law creating a national religion.

2. Congress also cannot prohibit the free exercise of religion by individual citizens. Americans are free to worship any faith or religion, or to have no religion at all. These provisions established a separation between church and state.

3. Congress cannot **abridge** (*cut short*) freedom of speech or freedom of the press. People may express themselves in any manner they choose: by speaking, making signs, or putting words in print. However, there are limits to free speech where public safety and civil disorder are involved. Speech is limited whenever it poses a clear and present danger to others. Freedom of the press is especially important for the success of a democracy. A free press informs citizens what is happening in their government and acts as a watchdog making

sure that government officials do not commit wrongdoing.

4. Congress cannot prevent people from exercising their right to **assemble** peaceably.

5. Government cannot deny people the right to **petition** to seek a **redress** (*remedy*) of their grievances.

A Summary of the Bill of Rights

First Amendment The right to freedom of speech, freedom of the press, freedom of religion, freedom of assembly, and freedom to petition the government.

Second Amendment The right to bear arms.

Third Amendment The right not to have troops quartered without permission in one's home in peacetime.

Fourth Amendment No unreasonable search or seizure (*arrest*); these normally require a warrant (*an order signed by a judge*).

Fifth Amendment No accusation for a "capital" offense without indictment by a grand jury; no double jeopardy (*being tried twice for the same crime*); no self-incrimination (*being forced to testify against ourselves*); no taking away of "life, liberty, or property" without "due process of law" (*fair and impartial procedures*); and no taking of property by eminent domain (*taking for a necessary public use*) without just compensation.

Sixth Amendment The right to a speedy and public trial by an impartial jury for a criminal offense; the right to be informed of all criminal charges; the right to face and question witnesses; and the right to have legal counsel (*a lawyer*).

Seventh Amendment The right to a trial by jury in some civil matters.

Eighth Amendment No excessive **bail** (*money paid as security for release of an accused person awaiting trial*); no excessive fines; and no "cruel and unusual punishments."

Ninth Amendment People may have other rights that are not mentioned in the Constitution or the Bill of Rights. Just because individuals are given several specific rights does not mean that they do not also enjoy other unlisted rights.

Tenth Amendment Powers not given to the federal government by the Constitution are reserved for the states and the people.

The Historian's Apprentice

1. Select one of the amendments in the Bill of Rights and create a poster about it.

Continued ▶

2. How well did the Bill of Rights answer the objections of the Anti-Federalists to the ratification of the Constitution?

3. Eileen has written an article about the government. It points out that her representative in Congress has taken a bribe. She includes persuasive evidence. Police go to her home and seize her computer and arrest her. They cannot explain what they are looking for but keep her locked up in the police department for five days. She is not allowed to speak to anyone and is not given a chance to see a lawyer. Next she is brought before a judge, who tells her she is guilty of a serious crime for writing the story and sentences her to three years' imprisonment. Select a partner and discuss which of Eileen's rights in the Bill of Rights have been denied. Make a list of those rights and share your results with the rest of the class.

For the Georgia Milestones EOC Assessment, you need to know that:

- ☐ The Articles of Confederation created a weak central government— a "league of friendship" between the states. Each state had one vote in the Confederation Congress. There was no national executive or judicial branch. The Confederation Congress could not raise its own troops or tax citizens or states directly.

- ☐ The Confederation Congress passed the Land Ordinance (1785) and the Northwest Ordinance (1787). These ordinances (laws) established rules for the Northwest Territory. The Land Ordinance divided the territory into townships of 36 sections, with one section set aside to support public schools. The Northwest Ordinance established a procedure for the admission of territories as new states on an equal footing with existing states; it also prohibited slavery and guaranteed freedom of religion and the right to a trial by jury throughout the Northwest Territory.

- ☐ Because the national government was so weak, many Americans feared their country could not stand up to foreign nations.

- ☐ Daniel Shays led a rebellion of poor farmers and debtors in Massachusetts. Shays' Rebellion was suppressed but there was no national army to stop it if it had spread. This led many Americans to call for a stronger national government.

- ☐ In May 1787, delegates gathered in Philadelphia to revise the Articles of Confederation. Instead, they set about writing a new constitution altogether. The delegates quickly agreed to create a national government with three separate branches: a legislature (Congress), an executive (the President), and a judiciary (the Supreme Court).

- ☐ Delegates disagreed over representation in Congress. Virginia, a large state, proposed two houses based on proportional representation—larger states would have more members. New Jersey, a small state, proposed each state have equal representation. The delegates finally

- adopted the "Great Compromise": each state would have two Senators in the Senate and a number of members in the House of Representatives proportional to its size.
- Delegates from slave and non-slave states also disagreed on whether slaves should be counted in calculating a state's representation. They reached the "Three-Fifths Compromise": three-fifths of a state's enslaved population would be counted for purposes of both representation and taxation.
- A key feature of the new Constitution was the principle of "limited government"—the new federal government could only exercise those powers given to it by the Constitution.
- Other key constitutional principles were federalism (division of power between the federal and state governments), the separation of powers (division of power between the legislative, executive and judicial branches), and checks and balances (ability of one branch to stop others).
- Anti-Federalists opposed ratification (*approval*) of the Constitution because they feared the new government would threaten individual liberties. Anti-Federalists also objected that it contained no bill of rights.
- Federalists argued that a stronger government was needed and that constitutional principles like federalism and the separation of powers would prevent the new government from becoming too strong. Federalist arguments were best expressed in *The Federalist Papers* by Hamilton, Madison, and Jay.
- The first ten amendments, added in 1791, are known as the Bill of Rights. The First Amendment guarantees freedom of speech, of the press, of religion, and of assembly, and the right to petition the government.

Name _____

Complete the following chart.

	Description	Significance/Impact
Strengths of the Articles of Confederation		
Weaknesses of the Articles of Confederation		
Impact of the Land and Northwest Ordinances on westward migration		
Impact of the Land and Northwest Ordinances on slavery		
Impact of the Land and Northwest Ordinances on public education		
Impact of the Land and Northwest Ordinances on the addition of new states		

Name _____

Complete the following chart.

	Description	Significance/Impact
The Great Compromise		
Limited Government		
The Three-Fifths Compromise		
Arguments of the Federalists in favor of ratification		
Arguments of the Anti-Federalists against ratification		
How Anti-Federalist objections were addressed in the Bill of Rights		

Chapter 3 | The Story of Our Constitution

Name _____

Complete the following letter written from one delegate at the Constitutional Convention to another.

To Mr. _____, Representative from the State of _____

My dear Sir,

In my humble view, the main weaknesses of our Articles of the Confederation have been _____
_____
_____

Therefore, I think we made the right decision in writing a whole new Constitution rather than revising the Articles.

It is very clear to me, as it was to most of our fellow delegates, that our national government needs to have separate executive, legislative, and judicial branches. You may recall that some delegates could not decide whether the head of our new national executive should be one person or a small group. I believe the answer is obvious. The head of the executive must be a single person because _____
_____.

I do not believe that the common people can know our leaders well enough or watch them closely enough to actually decide directly which ones should be chosen as President. Therefore, I support the decision to have our President chosen by _____.

As you know, we have had plenty of debate over our new legislature, known as Congress. Should each state have the same number of representatives, or should larger states have more representatives? I believe _____
_____.

This is because _____
_____.

Whether slaves should be represented in the new Congress is another difficult question. Some delegates have proposed a "Three-Fifths Compromise." Under this compromise, _____
_____.

I support/oppose this compromise because _____
_____.

There are those who fear that our new government will be too strong. They say it might abuse and oppress ordinary citizens. But I say that we needed a stronger government to protect us from foreign countries and unrest at home. I believe the Constitution can establish a strong and stable government while also protecting our individual liberties. The principles of _____,
_____, and _____ will prevent our new federal government from becoming too strong.

Yours sincerely with utmost respect,

Your very humble servant,

_____

106 Chapter 3 | The Story of Our Constitution

The Story of Our Constitution

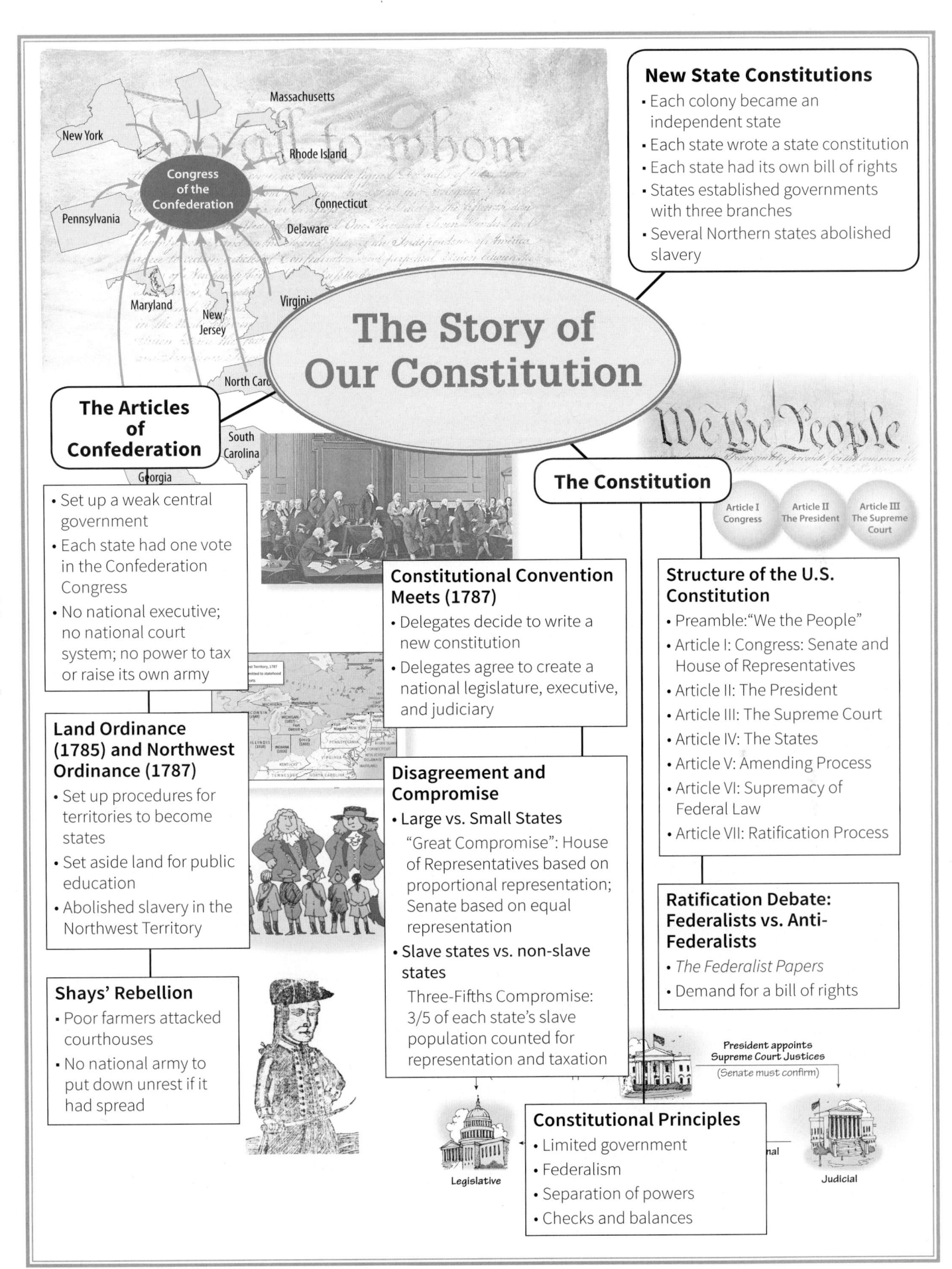

New State Constitutions
- Each colony became an independent state
- Each state wrote a state constitution
- Each state had its own bill of rights
- States established governments with three branches
- Several Northern states abolished slavery

The Articles of Confederation
- Set up a weak central government
- Each state had one vote in the Confederation Congress
- No national executive; no national court system; no power to tax or raise its own army

Land Ordinance (1785) and Northwest Ordinance (1787)
- Set up procedures for territories to become states
- Set aside land for public education
- Abolished slavery in the Northwest Territory

Shays' Rebellion
- Poor farmers attacked courthouses
- No national army to put down unrest if it had spread

The Constitution

Constitutional Convention Meets (1787)
- Delegates decide to write a new constitution
- Delegates agree to create a national legislature, executive, and judiciary

Disagreement and Compromise
- Large vs. Small States
  - "Great Compromise": House of Representatives based on proportional representation; Senate based on equal representation
- Slave states vs. non-slave states
  - Three-Fifths Compromise: 3/5 of each state's slave population counted for representation and taxation

Structure of the U.S. Constitution
- Preamble: "We the People"
- Article I: Congress: Senate and House of Representatives
- Article II: The President
- Article III: The Supreme Court
- Article IV: The States
- Article V: Amending Process
- Article VI: Supremacy of Federal Law
- Article VII: Ratification Process

Ratification Debate: Federalists vs. Anti-Federalists
- *The Federalist Papers*
- Demand for a bill of rights

Constitutional Principles
- Limited government
- Federalism
- Separation of powers
- Checks and balances

President appoints Supreme Court Justices (Senate must confirm)

Legislative — Judicial

Chapter 3 | The Story of Our Constitution

What Do You Know?

SSUSH5a

1. **Which statement identifies an important strength of the Articles of Confederation?**
   A. The Articles created a powerful national executive.
   B. The Articles established a single national currency.
   C. The Articles established a central government during the American Revolution.
   D. The Articles announced the reasons why the colonists had separated from England in 1776.

SSUSH5b

2. **Use the list to answer the question.**

   - No power to collect taxes
   - No national court system
   - No national currency
   - No taxing authority

   How did these weaknesses affect the delegates to the Annapolis Convention in 1786?
   A. They decided to give greater power to state governments.
   B. They asked the states to send representatives to revise the Articles.
   C. They drafted a bill of rights to protect the liberties of individual citizens.
   D. They encouraged groups of states to enter into their own separate arrangements.

SSUSH5b

3. **How did Shays' Rebellion contribute to the desire to revise the Articles of Confederation?**
   A. Poor farmers felt they were not being treated fairly by the states.
   B. Debtors wanted a stronger national government that would create a stable currency.
   C. Property owners feared the national government was not strong enough to put down a rebellion.
   D. Veterans from the Continental Army wanted a stronger national government that could pay their back pay.

SSUSH5c

4. **Which of the following is the BEST example of limited government?**
   A. The approval of the Senate is needed to ratify treaties
   B. The federal government has three separate branches.
   C. Two-thirds of Congress can override a Presidential veto.
   D. Congress cannot impose any taxes on exports.

SSUSH5b

5. **Why did many Americans feel a need to revise the Articles of Confederation in 1787?**

   A. They wanted to give more power to the upper classes.

   B. They wanted to provide the right to vote to all citizens.

   C. They wanted to provide better safeguards for individual rights of life, liberty, and property.

   D. They wanted to create a stronger national government to protect Americans from invasion or domestic unrest.

SSUSH5a

6. **Why did the Continental Congress create a weak central government in the Articles of Confederation?**

   A. Former Loyalists demanded a weak government to protect their property.

   B. Wealthy former colonists wanted a weak government that they could control.

   C. The Treaty of Paris of 1783 had defined the structures of a new national government.

   D. Its members feared that a strong central government would threaten individual rights.

SSUSH5a

7. **How did passage of the Northwest Ordinance of 1787 demonstrate a strength of the Articles of Confederation?**

   A. It showed that the Confederation Congress could sometimes act to meet national needs.

   B. It showed that the Confederation Congress had the power to resist British demands.

   C. It showed that several of the original states would be able to make claims on western lands.

   D. It showed that the Confederation Congress had the power to extend slavery to settlements in the west.

SSUSH5b

8. **Read the excerpt below to answer the question.**

   Each State retains its sovereignty, freedom and independence, and every power and right . . . not expressly granted to the United States, in Congress assembled.

   Which conclusion can be drawn from this excerpt?

   A. The Articles of Confederation gave Congress the power to tax the states.

   B. The Articles of Confederation kept the states totally independent of Congress.

   C. The Articles of Confederation left most governing power with the state governments.

   D. The Articles of Confederation gave most governing power to the national government.

Chapter 3 | The Story of Our Constitution

SSUSH5d

9. **Read the excerpt below to answer the question.**

> *In framing a government which is to be administered by men over men, the great difficulty lies in this: you must first enable the government to control the governed; and in the next place oblige it to control itself.*
>
> —James Madison, *The Federalist Papers*, No. 51 (1788)

How did the proposed Constitution address the problem identified in the excerpt?

A. It included a bill of rights to protect individual liberties.
B. It allowed the slave trade to continue for twenty more years.
C. It included checks and balances to prevent abuses of power by government.
D. It prevented the federal government from waging war without the support of the states.

SSUSH5c

10. **Use the 1787 headlines below to answer the question.**

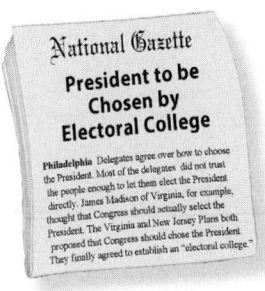

National Gazette — **Proposed Congress to Have Two Houses**
Philadelphia. The first house would be known as the House of Representatives. It would represent the members would be elected directly by the people. The second house would be the Senate. It would represent the wisdom, wealth, and property of America. As one delegate put it, the Senate should have "the most distinguished characters by rank and property." Senators would serve for longer terms than members of the House of Representatives. This way, they would not be as subject to pressures from the

National Gazette — **Each Slave to Count as Three-Fifths of a Person**
Delegates strike a compromise.
Philadelphia. Slave populations will be counted at three-fifths of their actual number. In other words, every five slaves would be counted as three persons. The same rule would apply for purposes of both representation and taxation.

National Gazette — **President to be Chosen by Electoral College**
Philadelphia. Delegates agree over how to choose the President. Most of the delegates did not trust the people enough to let them elect the President directly. James Madison of Virginia, for example, thought that Congress should actually select the President. The Virginia and New Jersey Plans both proposed that Congress should chose the President. They finally agreed to establish an "electoral college."

Which conclusion about the Constitutional Convention is supported by these headlines?

A. It was controlled by states with large enslaved populations.
B. Its members were able to compromise on important issues.
C. Most of its members wanted the President to be chosen directly by the people.
D. It gave states that were small in population the most power in the new Constitution.

SSUSH5e

11. **Which BEST explains why Anti-Federalists insisted a bill of rights be added to the Constitution?**

A. They feared in a democracy the majority would threaten minority rights.
B. They were used to the English Bill of Rights, enacted by Parliament.
C. They feared a strong government would trample on individual rights.
D. They did not want to pay any new taxes to the federal government.

SSUSH5c

12. Use the excerpts below to answer the question.

> ### Article I Section 1
> All legislative powers . . . shall be vested in a Congress of the United States, which shall consist of a Senate and House of Representatives.
> ### Article II Section 1
> The executive power shall be vested in a President of the United States of America . . .
> ### Article III Section 1
> The judicial power of the United States, shall be vested in one Supreme Court, and in [other lower] courts as the Congress may from time to time ordain and establish . . .
> —Constitution of the United States (1787)

Which constitutional principle is illustrated by these excerpts?

A. federalism
B. individual rights
C. popular sovereignty
D. separation of powers

SSUSH5d

13. Which statement BEST summarizes the debate between the Federalists and Anti-Federalists over ratification of the Constitution?

A. They argued over the question of establishing a national bank.
B. They disagreed over whether slavery should continue in the new nation.
C. They disagreed over whether the national executive should be a single person or a group.
D. They disagreed over the distribution of power between the federal and state governments.

SSUSH5b

14. Use the list below to answer the question.

- No power to collect taxes
- No national court system
- No national currency

How did the delegates to the Constitutional Convention attempt to correct these weaknesses in the Articles of Confederation?

A. They gave greater power to state governments.
B. They drafted a plan for a stronger national government.
C. They drafted a bill of rights to protect individual liberties.
D. They encouraged states to enter into their own agreements.

Chapter 3 | The Story of Our Constitution

SSUSH5c

15. Which disagreement led to the "Three-Fifths Compromise"?

A. Delegates at the Constitutional Convention argued over whether to tax trade.

B. Delegates at the Constitutional Convention discussed whether to include women in determining a state's representation in Congress.

C. Delegates at the Constitutional Convention debated whether to count enslaved people in calculating a state's representation in Congress.

D. Delegates at the Constitutional Convention discussed how each state should be represented in Congress.

SSUSH5d

16. Read the excerpt below to answer the question.

> *Let us inquire whether the thirteen states should be reduced to one republic or not? Is it realistic for a country so numerous to elect representatives to speak [for them] . . . A free republic cannot exist in such a large territory . . . citizens will have little [familiarity] with those chosen to represent them . . .*
>
> —Brutus, an Anti-Federalist, 1788

In this passage, which argument does Brutus make against ratification of the proposed Constitution?

A. Citizens do not need to have a direct contact with their representatives in government.

B. Having people elect representatives to govern the whole nation is impractical in a country with such a large size and population.

C. The geographic size and population of the country should not be considered when debating the benefits of a representative government.

D. The proposed Constitution will place the thirteen states under the direction of a single government that is incapable of carrying out the business of the country.

SSUSH5a

17. Use the diagram below to answer the question.

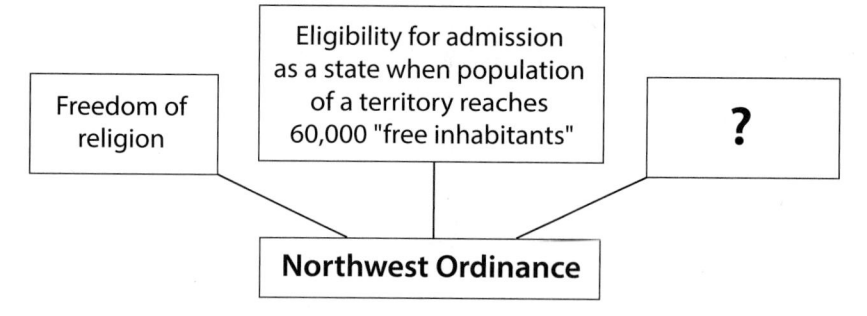

Freedom of religion — Eligibility for admission as a state when population of a territory reaches 60,000 "free inhabitants" — ? → Northwest Ordinance

Which phrase BEST completes the diagram?

A. Prohibition of slavery
B. Checks and balances
C. Freedom of the press
D. Voting rights for women

CHAPTER 4: The First Presidents of the New Republic

SSUSH6 What challenges were faced by our nation's first five Presidents and how did they respond?

    a. What events occurred during the Presidency of Washington and what precedents did he set?

    b. What events occurred during the Presidency of John Adams, and how did the Alien and Sedition Acts influence the outcome of the election of 1800?

    c. How did President Jefferson expand presidential power and how was the Louisiana Territory purchased and explored?

    d. How did President James Madison conduct the War of 1812 and what was the war's significance to the development of our national identity?

    e. Why did President James Monroe issue the Monroe Doctrine?

Names and Terms You Should Know

George Washington

John Adams

Alexander Hamilton

Thomas Jefferson

Cabinet

Hamilton's financial plan

Protective tariff

James Madison

Political party

Federalists

Democratic-Republicans

French Revolution

Whiskey Rebellion

Washington's Farewell Address

Alien and Sedition Acts

Virginia and Kentucky Resolutions

"Revolution of 1800"

Napoleon Bonaparte

New Orleans

Louisiana Territory

Louisiana Purchase

Lewis and Clark

Blockade

Impressment

James Madison

War of 1812

"The Star-Spangled Banner"

Battle of New Orleans

James Monroe

Latin America

Monroe Doctrine

Georgia "Peaches" of Wisdom

1. In 1788, George Washington was elected as the nation's first President. He faced many challenges. Many of his actions would establish precedents—ways of doing things that would be copied in the future.

2. Washington established the Cabinet, made up of the appointed heads of government departments. The Cabinet held regular meetings, discussed issues, and gave advice.

3. Alexander Hamilton, Secretary of the Treasury, proposed a plan for dealing with the nation's finances. He recommended the government issue interest-paying bonds to pay off its debts as well as those of the states. He further proposed that Congress create the Bank of the United States and impose tariffs on imported manufactured goods. Hamilton wanted to protect infant Northern industries from British competition. Finally, Hamilton proposed a tax on whiskey.

4. Jefferson and Madison opposed Hamilton's plan, leading to the rise of the first American political parties. Federalists supported Hamilton's plan. Jefferson and Madison led the Democratic-Republicans, who opposed it.

5. To avoid involvement in the war between Britain and France during the French Revolution, President Washington issued a "Proclamation of Neutrality."

6. Farmers in western Pennsylvania rebelled against the whiskey tax. Washington and Hamilton led an army of 13,000 men against the "Whiskey Rebellion." The rebels avoided a fight and returned home.

7. In his "Farewell Address," Washington advised against political parties and warned about the dangers of entering into entangling alliances in Europe.

8. John Adams, a Federalist, was elected as our second President in 1796. Adams worried about potential spies. Congress passed the Alien and Sedition Acts, which gave him the power to send any foreigner out of the country, to imprison foreigners whose country was at war with the United States, and to fine or imprison anyone who spoke or wrote against the government. Madison and Jefferson believed these acts were unconstitutional.

9. The Alien and Sedition Acts made Adams unpopular and cost him the next Presidential election. Jefferson considered his election victory the "**Revolution of 1800**" because power peacefully passed between opposing political parties.

10. Jefferson purchased the Louisiana Territory from France in 1803. He was unsure if the Constitution gave him the power to do so, but he went ahead anyway. The purchase almost doubled the size of the United States. Jefferson sent Meriwether Lewis and William Clark to explore the Louisiana Territory.

11. Economic warfare between France and Britain placed American merchants in a difficult situation. Jefferson did not want war and pushed the Embargo Act of 1807 through Congress. This law prohibited Americans from exporting goods to foreign countries until Britain and France lifted their restrictions on neutral shipping. It hurt Americans more than foreigners and was unpopular.

12. James Madison was elected President in 1808. Tensions with Britain were high. British officers were supplying guns to Indian tribes in the Northwest, who attacked American settlers. The British navy was stopping American ships on the high seas to search for British deserters. The "war hawks" in Congress pushed for war so that Americans could seize Canada. Congress finally declared war on Britain, starting the War of 1812.

13. American attempts to invade Canada failed. A British force landed in Chesapeake Bay, occupied Washington, D.C., and burned public buildings, including the White House. British ships bombarded Fort McHenry in Baltimore but could not take the fort. Francis Scott Key wrote "The Star-Spangled Banner," our national anthem. American manufacturers benefited when Americans could no longer buy British goods.

14. America and Britain signed a treaty ending the war in December 1814. News of the treaty had not reached America when British troops attacked New Orleans. Andrew Jackson became a hero after defeating the attack. The war contributed to Americans' sense of national identity.

15. Federalists had criticized the war. When peace was signed, the Federalists were branded as unpatriotic. Their party dissolved, leaving a one-party America.

16. James Monroe was elected President in 1816. He issued the Monroe Doctrine in 1823. This announced that the United States would not allow European powers to start new colonies or to restore rule over former ones that had achieved independence.

Chapter 4 | The First Presidents of the New Republic

The Presidency of George Washington (1789–1797)

The members of the Constitutional Convention already had **George Washington** in mind when they created the office of President. It was therefore no surprise when all the members of the Electoral College cast their votes for him in 1788. No one else could better unite the country.

As the nation's first President, Washington faced a number of challenges. First, he had to set up procedures for the new government. Second, he had to decide how to pay the debts left from the Revolutionary War. Third, he had to stop Indian attacks on settlers in the Northwest. Finally, he had to deal with foreign powers.

Establishing Precedents in the New Government

Washington knew that everything he did in office would create a **precedent**—something that was being done for the first time and would be copied by others in the future. Even whether he should be called "Mr. President" became a subject for debate.

The Cabinet The first thing Washington did was to appoint the heads of government departments. He appointed **Thomas Jefferson** as Secretary of State and Alexander Hamilton as Secretary of the Treasury. These heads of department met together regularly with Washington as his Cabinet. The **Cabinet** is the group of top officials who advise the President. The Cabinet is not mentioned in the Constitution. However, Cabinet meetings were held by Washington and have continued under every other President ever since. The creation of the Cabinet was one of Washington's most important precedents.

The Judiciary The next task was to set up the country's judicial branch. Washington appointed John Jay as the first Chief Justice of the Supreme Court. The Constitution had established the Supreme Court, but did not create any courts below it. This important job was left to Congress.

The first Congress passed the **Judiciary Act of 1789**. This law created a system of federal courts below the U.S. Supreme Court. These included both district courts and courts of appeal.

The Bill of Rights Federalists had promised a bill of rights to get the Constitution ratified.

James Madison introduced the **Bill of Rights** to the first Congress. This became the first ten amendments to the Constitution, which you read about in the last chapter. These were ratified by the states and added to the Constitution in 1791.

Hamilton's Financial Plan

The next challenge Washington faced was how to pay the debts left by the Revolutionary War. During the war, the Continental Congress and states had printed paper money. They had also sold war bonds (called "bills of credit"). Each bond was like a government IOU ("I owe you"). The government promised to repay the holder of the bond at a later date. The government had also borrowed money from French and Dutch bankers. **Alexander Hamilton**, the Secretary of the Treasury, came up with a plan to deal with the nation's financial problems.

- Hamilton argued that the nation needed good credit so that it would be able to borrow money in future emergencies. He therefore told Congress that the federal government should pay off all of the nation's debts as well as those of the states from the Revolutionary War. In order to do this, Hamilton proposed that the federal government issue new interest-paying bonds.

- To pay the interest on the bonds, Hamilton further proposed a tariff on manufactured goods. A **tariff** is a special tax on goods coming into the United States from other countries. Hamilton argued that a tariff would not only raise money for the government but that it would also protect America's infant industries from foreign competition.

- To help the government manage its revenues, Hamilton also proposed the creation of a **national bank**. The bank would provide a place where the government could hold the money it collected, and also a place where it could turn to obtain loans in emergencies.

- Finally, to raise additional funds for the federal government, Hamilton proposed a tax on whiskey. This tax would be collected from Western farmers who turned their grain into whiskey to carry across the Appalachian Mountains to sell to people in the East.

How a Tariff Works

Imagine that cotton cloth from Britain costs $10 a yard. The same cloth from an American manufacturer costs $12 a yard. The British cloth is less expensive. But if a tariff of $5 a yard is added to the British cloth, it will cost $15 a yard. The American cloth is now cheaper.

The Historian's Apprentice

1. Make a poster or advertisement either for or against Hamilton's financial plan.
2. Would you have supported Hamilton's financial plan? Why or why not?

The First Political Parties

Thomas Jefferson and James Madison opposed Hamilton's financial plan. They thought it unfairly favored the interests of Northeastern merchants and manufacturers over those of farmers in the South and West. The tariff would make goods more expensive for ordinary farmers. The whiskey tax would also hurt farmers.

Jefferson and Madison further believed that the Constitution did not give Congress the power to create a national bank. They were "strict" constructionists: nowhere in the Constitution did it say that Congress had this power. Hamilton thought the Constitution should be interpreted loosely. Although the Constitution did not say anything directly about creating a national bank, it gave Congress the ability to do whatever was "necessary and proper" to meet its other responsibilities. Hamilton argued that Congress could therefore establish a national bank because the bank would help it to meet its other responsibilities. In the end, President Washington and Congress agreed with Hamilton. The first Bank of the United States was established in Philadelphia in February 1791.

A **political party** is a group of people who share similar views. Members of a political party cooperate to elect their candidates to public office. Political parties had existed for a long time in Britain. President Washington greatly disliked them. He believed that party members put the interests of their party above those of the country. Washington preferred to think of himself as an American, not as a party member.

The disagreement over Hamilton's plan led to the rise of the first American political parties.

Those who supported Hamilton became known as **Federalists**. They took their name from the earlier supporters of the Constitution. They favored financial, commercial, and manufacturing interests. Supporters of Jefferson and Madison, who opposed Hamilton's plan, became known as **Democratic-Republicans**. They favored an agrarian economy of independent, self-reliant farmers, and feared that the Federalists were trying to create a society controlled by a wealthy and corrupt elite.

Federalists	Democratic-Republicans
★ Wanted a strong national government.	★ Favored strong state governments and a weak national government.
★ Favored a "loose construction" of the Constitution.	★ Favored a "strict construction" of the Constitution.
★ Wanted to promote manufacturing and trade. They favored merchants and bankers.	★ Favored independent farmers.
★ Thought that the wealthy and best-educated Americans should control the government.	★ Were friendly to France.
★ Were friendly to Great Britain.	★ Were strongest in the South and West.
★ Were strongest in the Northeast.	

Hamilton

Jefferson

The French Revolution

Federalists and Democratic-Republicans moved farther apart because of events in France. The American Revolution had placed the King of France in debt. In 1788, he called on his nobles for help. They insisted that he summon an assembly representing all the social classes of France. Influenced by Enlightenment ideas and the example of America, middle-class members of this national assembly began demanding sweeping reforms. Poorer citizens in Paris also became involved. In July 1789, they attacked an old fortress in the center of Paris that served as a prison.

Thomas Jefferson was living in Paris when the revolution first began. He looked with pride on these early events, which he believed were inspired by the American Revolution. Jefferson even helped to write the "Declaration of the Rights of Man and the Citizen," a key document defining the rights of French citizens during the French Revolution.

By 1793, the French Revolution had turned violent. Many French citizens were arrested and killed. The King of France was executed in front of a crowd of thousands. A few months later, France and Britain went to war. Despite the violence, Jefferson remained sympathetic to the French Republic. But John Adams and Alexander Hamilton took a different view. They were shocked at French mob violence. They preferred the calm stability of England.

The Proclamation of Neutrality

Once France and Britain were at war, some Americans felt the United States should help France. After all, just a few years earlier the French had helped Americans against Britain. However, President Washington wanted to stay out of European wars. In 1793, he declared that the United States would remain neutral (*not take either side*) in his Proclamation of Neutrality.

He announced: "The duty and interest of the United States require that they should with sincerity and good faith adopt and pursue a conduct friendly and impartial towards the belligerent powers (*the countries at war*)."

The Whiskey Rebellion

Farmers in western Pennsylvania were especially hard hit by Hamilton's new whiskey tax. They held several conventions outside Pittsburgh in protest. They attacked tax collectors and refused to pay the tax. In August 1794, a large number of armed farmers gathered in protest. They threatened resistance and carried banners with the famous slogan of the French Revolution: "Liberty, Equality, and Fraternity (*brotherhood*)."

Washington and Hamilton decided to use armed force to put down the rebellion. They hoped this would strengthen the authority of the federal government. Washington collected a force made up of various state militia. Rather than fight, the rebel army simply dissolved. The farmers returned to their homes. The power and authority of the federal government had been successfully upheld.

The Historian's Apprentice

Make your own Venn diagram comparing Shays' Rebellion and the Whiskey Rebellion. Show both similarities and differences.

Washington's Farewell Address

By 1796, Washington had served two terms as President. Many wanted him to serve for a third term, but Washington refused. Before leaving office, he put a message in the newspapers with parting advice for the new nation. It is known as his "**Farewell Address**." Washington's address attacked the rising party spirit and geographic differences that were dividing Americans. "The name of American," Washington wrote, should

Chapter 4 | The First Presidents of the New Republic

bring greater pride than membership in any particular region or group. "Your union," he reminded Americans, should be the "main prop (*support*) of your liberty."

Washington also wrote of the dangers to America from foreign powers. He urged his countrymen to avoid alliances in Europe and to focus on their own hemisphere. Europeans had entered a long war, and Washington was sure it would be better for Americans to stay out of it. A portion of Washington's address is on the right.

> "The great rule of conduct for us in regard to foreign nations is in extending [stretching] our commercial relations, to have with them as little political connection as possible.... Europe has a set of primary [main] interests which to us have none; or a very remote relation. Hence she must be engaged in frequent controversies, the causes of which are essentially foreign to our concerns... It is our true policy to steer clear of permanent alliances with any portion [part] of the foreign world..."

The Historian's Apprentice

1. What was the significance of Washington's Farewell Address?
2. Why was Washington so suspicious of political parties?
3. Why did Washington advise his countrymen to "steer clear of permanent alliances" with other countries?
4. What advice would you have given to Americans in 1796? Imagine that you are George Washington. Write a paragraph that you think he should have included in his "Farewell Address."
5. Make a chart summarizing the main events of Washington's presidency.

The Presidency of John Adams (1797–1800)

John Adams served two terms as Vice President under Washington. In the election of 1796, he narrowly defeated Thomas Jefferson to become the second President of the United States. The biggest challenge that Adams faced as he began his term was the continuing war between Britain and France. Although friendly to Britain, Adams preferred Washington's policy of avoiding any direct involvement in the conflict.

The Alien and Sedition Acts

Many immigrants were coming to America from Britain, Ireland, and France. Some of the newcomers became active in American politics. Adams feared that some of them might actually be spies. In addition, most of these immigrants favored Jefferson's Democratic-Republican Party over President Adams and the Federalists.

Because of the threats posed by the French Revolution and by the continuing war between Britain and France, Congress passed the Alien and Sedition Acts, which Adams signed into law early in 1798.

An **alien** is a foreigner living in the United States. **Sedition** is any speech, writing, or act that encourages people to rebel against their government.

- The **Alien Acts** increased the length of time that a foreigner had to live in the United States before becoming a citizen from five to fourteen years. They gave the President the power to send any foreigner out of the country. They also gave the President the power to put in jail or send out of the country any foreigner whose country was at war with the United States.

- The **Sedition Act** permitted President Adams to fine or send to jail anyone who spoke or wrote against the government. The act prohibited writing, publishing, or saying anything of "a false, scandalous, and malicious nature" about the government or its elected officials. Several writers were actually thrown into jail based on the new law.

The Historian's Apprentice

[I]t shall be lawful for the President of the United States . . . to order all such aliens as he shall judge dangerous to the peace and safety of the United States, or shall have reasonable grounds to suspect are concerned in any treasonable or secret machinations against the government thereof, to depart out of the territory of the United States . . .

—An Act Concerning Aliens, Section 1 (November 13, 1797)

[I]f any person shall write, print, utter or publish . . . any false, scandalous and malicious writing or writings against the government of the United States, or either house of the Congress of the United States, or the President of the United States . . . then such person, being thereof convicted before any court of the United States having [authority] thereof, shall be punished by a fine not exceeding two thousand dollars, and by imprisonment not exceeding two years.

—The Sedition Act, Section 2 (November 13, 1797)

Read the excerpts above from the Alien and Sedition Acts and discuss the following questions with a partner. Then share your responses with your class.

1. Did Section 1 of this Alien Act give too much power to the President?
2. Did Section 2 of the Sedition Act violate (*go against*) the rights of free speech and free press in the First Amendment?

The Virginia and Kentucky Resolutions

Jefferson and Madison believed that the Alien and Sedition Acts violated the Bill of Rights. They wrote resolutions that were passed by the state legislatures of Kentucky and Virginia in 1798 and 1799.

These resolutions argued that the federal union was a "compact"—an association by agreement—of states. If the federal government exercised powers that did not belong to it, the states had the right to reject those actions. Based on this reasoning, the Kentucky and Virginia legislatures declared that the Alien and Sedition Acts would not be enforced in their states because Congress had no power to limit free speech.

The Historian's Apprentice

1. Discuss the following questions with a partner:
   - Were the Alien and Sedition Acts constitutional?
   - Should individual states have the power to declare federal laws invalid (not enforceable) within their own borders? What is your view?
2. Imagine you are living in Virginia in 1798. Write a letter to the editor of your local newspaper either for or against the Kentucky and Virginia Resolutions.

The Presidency of Thomas Jefferson (1801–1808) and the Louisiana Purchase

The Election of 1800

The Presidential election of 1800 was a bitterly fought contest between John Adams and Thomas Jefferson. Adams had served only one term so far. The Alien and Sedition Acts had made him very unpopular. Some historians believe these acts cost him the election.

Jefferson and the Democratic-Republicans won a great victory, making Jefferson the next President. His political party won a majority (*more than half the members*) in each house of Congress. This was the first time that power peacefully changed hands from one party to their opponents. Jefferson considered this peaceful transfer of power to be a "revolution."

Jefferson hoped that the United States would become a democracy of self-reliant citizens—people who do not need to rely on others. His ideal was the independent farmer who worked his own land. Jefferson wanted a smaller government, not a larger one. He disliked the bankers and merchants whom Hamilton had so favored.

In his Inaugural Address, Jefferson made an appeal to all Americans. He reminded them that, despite party differences, they all shared common principles. Jefferson called for "a wise and frugal government" that left citizens free to follow their own pursuits. "This," he concluded, "is the sum of good government." He wanted to maintain peace, avoid "permanent alliances" with foreign countries, encourage agriculture

122   Chapter 4 | The First Presidents of the New Republic

and commerce, and promote freedom of religion, speech, and the press.

Cutting Down the Size of Government

Jefferson was lucky when his first term began. The worst crisis in France appeared to be over. A successful general named **Napoleon Bonaparte** had seized power and brought stability. Bonaparte made himself dictator and signed a peace treaty with Britain. With peace in Europe, Jefferson was able to cut spending on the army and navy. He ended the hated whiskey tax and reduced the national debt.

The Louisiana Purchase

The **Louisiana Territory** had belonged to Spain since the end of the French and Indian War. In 1800, Napoleon forced Spain to give the territory back to France. Napoleon had plans to create a new French empire in North America. France would control Haiti and other islands in the Caribbean Sea, the port of New Orleans on the Gulf of Mexico, and all lands west of the Mississippi.

In those days, American farmers in the Midwest sent their crops in flatboats down the Mississippi River. The crops were then loaded onto ships in New Orleans, where the Mississippi River empties into the Gulf of Mexico. The rights of Americans to use the port had been guaranteed by Spain. The return of Louisiana to France threatened this right. Jefferson was alarmed and sent negotiators to Paris to see if the United States could purchase **New Orleans** from France.

Meanwhile, Napoleon had decided he could not retake Haiti, where former slaves had established an independent republic. This led him to give up his plans for creating a French empire in North America. He surprisingly offered to sell the whole Louisiana Territory to the United States for the bargain price of $15 million.

Jefferson snapped up the offer. Nothing in the Constitution gave him the power to make such a purchase, yet Jefferson put all his doubts aside. The Louisiana Purchase was just too good to turn down. The Louisiana Purchase doubled the size of the United States. It ended French claims to North America and gave the United States control over the Mississippi River and New Orleans. It put the United States on the road to further westward expansion. Finally, with the purchase Jefferson had expanded Presidential power.

The Louisiana Territory

Chapter 4 | The First Presidents of the New Republic

The Historian's Apprentice

The French offer of the Louisiana Territory posed a special problem for President Jefferson: was the federal government permitted to buy new territory? There was nothing in the Constitution saying that the government could purchase new territories outside the United States.

Jefferson proposed that a new treaty be presented to the Senate for ratification and to the House of Representatives to obtain the funds needed for the purchase. He also thought that the Constitution itself might need to be amended. As he explained in a letter to his friend, John Breckinridge:

Thomas Jefferson

> "This treaty must of course be laid [*put*] before both Houses, because both have important functions to exercise respecting it. They, I presume, will see their duty to their country in ratifying and paying for it, so as to secure a good which would otherwise probably be never again in their power. But I suppose they must then appeal to the nation for an additional article to the Constitution, approving and confirming an act which the nation had not previously authorized. The Constitution has made no provision for our holding foreign territory, still less for incorporating foreign nations into our Union. The Executive in seizing the fugitive [*momentary, shortlived*] occurrence which so much advances the good of their own country, have done an act beyond the Constitution. The Legislature . . . like faithful servants, must ratify and pay for it, and throw themselves on their country for doing for them unauthorized what we know they would have done for themselves had they been in a situation to do it. . . [W]e shall not be disavowed [*rejected; renounced*] by the nation, and their act of indemnity [*exemption; release*] will confirm and not weaken the Constitution by more strongly marking out its lines."
>
> —President Thomas Jefferson to John Breckinridge, August 12, 1803

John Breckinridge

One month later, Jefferson wrote to Senator Nicholas, another friend and ally:

> "I had rather ask an enlargement of power from the nation, where it is found necessary, than to assume it by a construction which would make our powers boundless [*without limit*]. Our peculiar security is in possession of a written Constitution. Let us not make it a blank paper by construction . . .
>
> I confess, then, I think it important in the present case to set an example against broad construction by appealing for new power to the people. If, however, our friends shall think differently, certainly I shall acquiesce [*give in*] with satisfaction; confiding, that the good sense of our country will correct the evil of construction when it shall produce ill effects."
>
> —President Thomas Jefferson to Senator Wilson C. Nicholas, September 7, 1803

Wilson C. Nicholas

1. What were the main ideas expressed in Jefferson's letter to Breckinridge in August 1803? Why did Jefferson feel that the purchase of Louisiana had to be approved by both the Senate and the House of Representatives?
2. Why did Jefferson feel there was a constitutional issue involved in the purchase? What did he mean when he wrote to Senator Nicholas that he did not wish to make the Constitution "a blank paper by construction"?
3. Pretend it is 1803 and hold a class debate on the following:
    - "*Resolved*: that the purchase of Louisiana must be authorized by an amendment to the Constitution."

The Lewis and Clark Expedition (1804–1806)

Jefferson was a scientist as well as a government official. He wanted to learn as much as he could about America's new territories. Most of this land was still unknown to Americans. Jefferson sent **Meriwether Lewis** and **William Clark** to explore the new territory. He asked them to collect information about its geography, Indian tribes, and plant and wildlife. Lewis, Clark, and their "Corps of Discovery" (about 50 men) set out from St. Louis in May 1804. They crossed the Mississippi River, went up the Missouri River, crossed the Rocky Mountains, and traveled through the Oregon Territory to reach the Pacific Ocean in November 1805. Then they turned around to make the trip back. It took more than two years to make the entire journey of 7,000 miles.

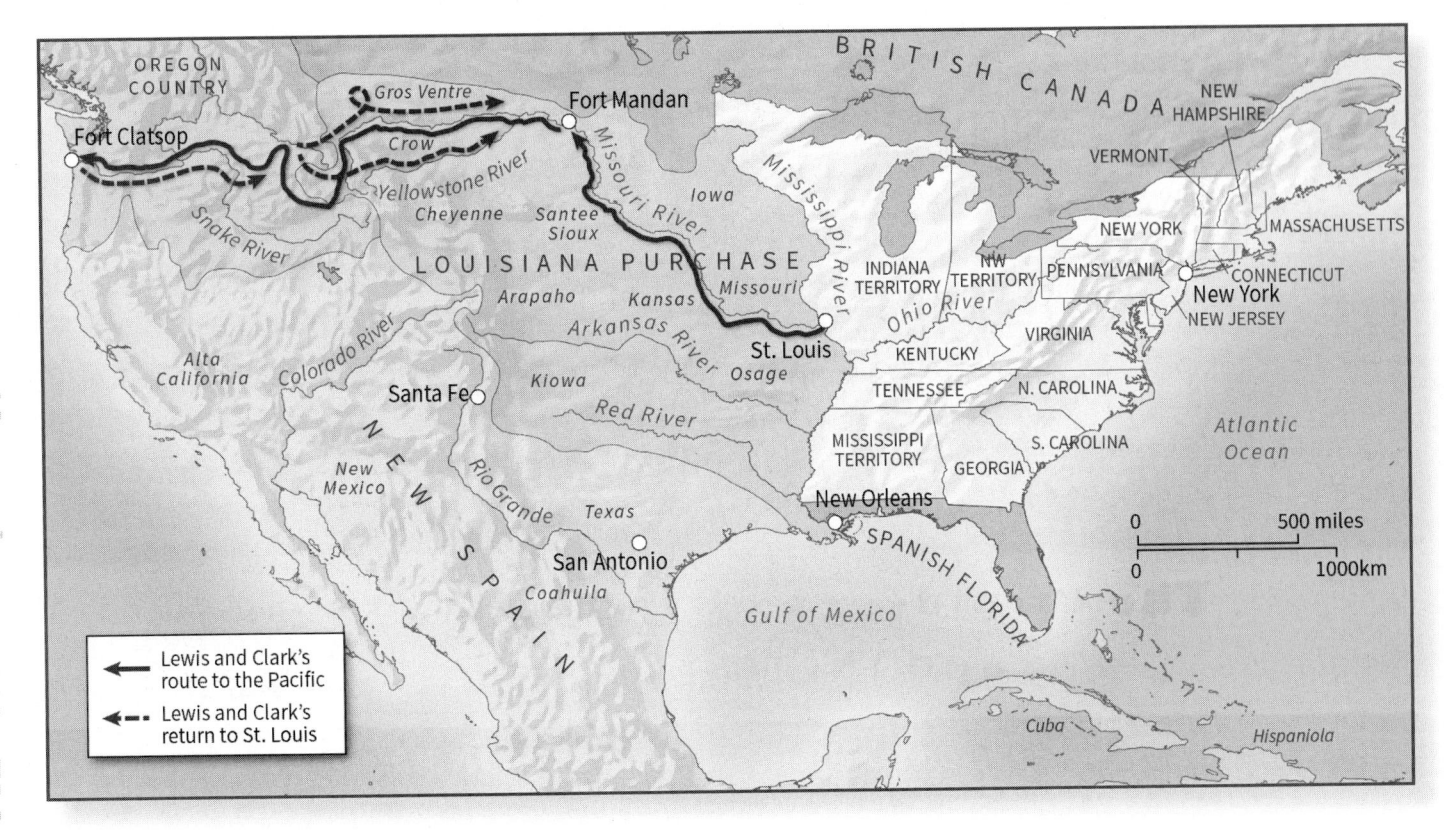

Chapter 4 | The First Presidents of the New Republic

Jefferson's Second Term: Economic Warfare in Europe

Jefferson was re-elected in 1804. He spent most of his second term dealing with foreign affairs. In Europe, the peace made by Napoleon did not last long. By 1803, the other European powers were already forming a new alliance against him. Napoleon crowned himself Emperor of the French at the end of 1804. He defeated the other powers in an astounding victory in 1805. This brought much of the continent of Europe under Napoleon's control. While the French were supreme on land, the British remained supreme at sea. The British Royal Navy defeated the French fleet, giving the British command of the world's seas.

Napoleon had no way to attack Britain, so he decided to use trade as a weapon. This was a new idea at the time. The French Emperor announced that the people of France could no longer trade with Britain. The British reacted by using their powerful navy to set up a **blockade** of Napoleonic Europe. They sealed off the French-controlled continent. No one could sail in or out without their permission. Neutral American ships could still go to France, but only if they first stopped in British ports. There, British officials would inspect them to see if they carried any prohibited war goods. Napoleon threatened, in turn, to seize any neutral ships that stopped in British ports.

These conflicting demands put American merchants in a difficult position. Jefferson responded with the Embargo of 1807, which prohibited U.S. merchants from engaging in foreign trade until the restrictions were lifted. The embargo actually hurt Americans more than foreigners.

Not only were the British attempting to control American trade, but their warships were also stopping American ships at sea. The British boarded American ships to look for deserters from the Royal Navy. If any were found, they could be forced back into service. This practice was known as **impressment**. Even worse, such sailors might be hanged for desertion. In fact, many British sailors had deserted to escape the harsh conditions and discipline of the Royal Navy. Some deserters found work on American ships, but the British were also taking innocent American sailors as well as actual deserters.

The Presidency of James Madison and the War of 1812

Thomas Jefferson followed George Washington's example by serving only two terms. Nevertheless his political party, the Democratic-Republicans, remained in power. Jefferson's close friend **James Madison** became the next President in 1809. Madison was a fellow Virginian, the "Father of the Constitution," and one of the authors of *The Federalist Papers*. He had served as Jefferson's Secretary of State.

James Madison

Trouble in the Northwest

In the Northwest Territory, British officers in Canada were supplying guns to Indian tribes. A Shawnee chief named Tecumseh and his brother, known as "the Prophet," tried to unite all the tribes. The Prophet urged all Indians to give up their guns, European-style clothes and alcohol and to return to their traditional ways. Tecumseh and the Prophet argued that Indian lands belonged to all the tribes. No single tribe had the right to give any of this land away.

While Tecumseh was trying to unite the tribes, Governor Harrison of the Indiana Territory signed a new treaty with other tribal leaders giving two million acres of Indian land to the United States. Tecumseh spoke loudly against the new treaty. He tried to persuade other tribal leaders to reject it. Believing that Tecumseh had plans to attack, Governor Harrison approached Tecumseh's village on the Tippecanoe River with a force of a thousand men. Tecumseh was away visiting other tribal leaders. His brother, the Prophet, decided to attack Harrison's camp in order to surprise the soldiers. The Indians were defeated and fled. After the battle, Harrison burned down the Indian settlement. Harrison was especially annoyed to find that the Indians had crates of brand new British guns.

Outbreak of the War of 1812

The troubles in the Northwest Territory led several young Congressmen to conclude that Britain stood in the way of the United States. They blamed Britain for the Indian attacks. These "**war hawks**" (people who favor war) believed that the United States should invade and take Canada. Only then would the Northwest Territory be safe. The war hawks included John C. Calhoun from South Carolina and Henry Clay from Kentucky.

Meanwhile, officers of the British navy were continuing to board American ships on the high seas in their search for deserters and impressing American sailors. The British were also still interfering with American shipping.

Main Causes of the War of 1812

1. British ships were stopping American ships on the high seas. The British boarded these ships to look for deserters from the British navy. Some American sailors were, in fact, British deserters. But the British also took sailors from American ships who were not deserters at all. This practice was called the *impressment* of sailors because the men were "pressed" into service.
2. After the Battle of Tippecanoe (1811), Chief Tecumseh fled to Canada where he allied with the British. Americans blamed the British for Indian attacks along the Northwest Frontier.
3. Some Americans, especially the "war hawks" in Congress, thought this would be a good time to seize Canada from Great Britain. Since Spain was allied to Britain, they wanted to take Florida from Spain as well.

For all these reasons, President Madison finally asked Congress for a declaration of war against Britain. The conflict became known as the **War of 1812**, although it lasted until 1815.

The Course of the War

The War of 1812 was fought along the Canadian border, in the Great Lakes, and at sea. Americans never attacked Britain itself—it was too far away. Instead, their focus was on Canada. They even thought that French Canadians might welcome joining the United States.

British strategy during the war was based on the defense of Canada and using British naval power. The British were already engaged in a war for survival against Napoleon in Europe. They could not spare many troops for North America. They had fewer than 7,000 regular troops in Canada. The United States did not have many more, but could rely on its militia.

In the first year of the war, American forces tried three different invasion routes into Canada—across the Niagara River, across the Detroit River, and along Lake Champlain. Each attempt failed.

The British Royal Navy established a blockade of American ports. Nevertheless American ships defeated the British in several small battles in which one ship fought another. In 1813, both sides began building new warships on Lake Erie. The U.S. Navy defeated the British in the Battle of Lake Erie, forcing British soldiers to withdraw from nearby Fort Detroit. American troops then crossed Lake Erie into Canada, where they fought the retreating British. Tecumseh, who was allied with the British, was killed in battle.

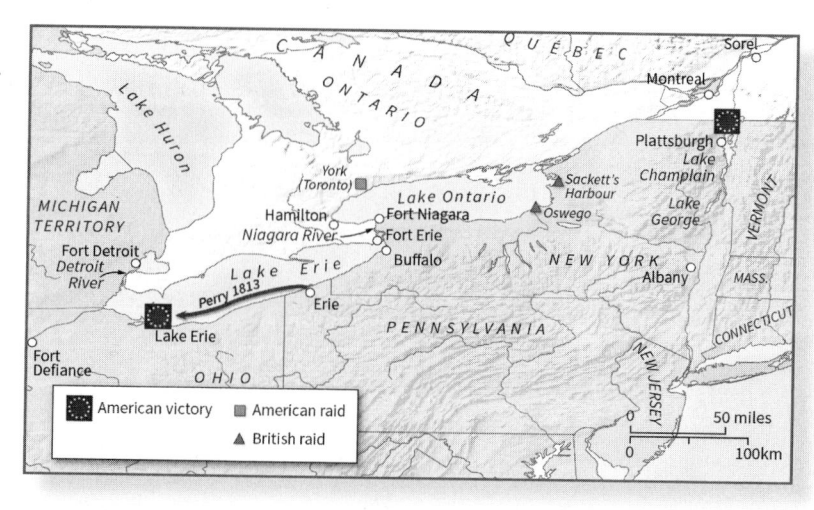

In April 1814, Napoleon surrendered and the war in Europe ended. The British sent thousands of their best soldiers to North America to help in the war effort. In August 1814, a British fleet carrying 4,500 soldiers sailed into Chesapeake Bay. The soldiers landed and marched towards Washington, D.C. American troops were unable to stop their advance. President Madison and members of Congress fled the capital city. President Madison's wife, **Dolley Madison,** took charge of removing government documents, paintings, and other valuables from the White House. British troops arrived just in time to finish President Madison's dinner. Then they set the White House, the Capitol, and other public buildings aflame.

The British left Washington soon afterwards to attack nearby Baltimore. Their ships, however, were unable to take Fort McHenry, which guarded Baltimore's harbor. Francis Scott Key, an American prisoner on a British ship, witnessed the British failure and wrote the poem **"The Star-Spangled Banner,"** which later became our national anthem.

Chapter 4 | The First Presidents of the New Republic

The Historian's Apprentice

The Star-Spangled Banner

O! say can you see, by the dawn's early light,

What so proudly we hailed at the twilight's last gleaming,

Whose broad stripes and bright stars through the perilous fight,

O'er the ramparts we watched, were so gallantly streaming?

And the rockets' red glare, the bombs bursting in air,

Gave proof through the night that our flag was still there;

O! say does that star-spangled banner yet wave

O'er the land of the free and the home of the brave?

How did Key's poem demonstrate a spirit of patriotism?

While the British were attacking Washington and Baltimore, they sent another force from Canada into the United States. The safety of this invasion force depended on British control of Lake Champlain. When Americans defeated a British naval force on the lake in the Battle of Plattsburgh, the British were forced to retreat.

During the war, Americans could no longer buy manufactured goods from Britain. Instead, they relied on using goods manufactured in the Northeast of the United States. The war thus provided a great stimulus to American industry.

The War Comes to an End

British and American representatives began discussing peace terms in Ghent, a town in Europe. A peace treaty was finally signed in December 1814. Both sides gave up their strongest demands and recognized their borders just as they had been before the war. The issue of Britain's right to impress American sailors was left out of the treaty. This was not a current problem since France and Britain were no longer at war.

Even though the peace treaty was signed in December, the most important battle of the war was in fact fought in New Orleans in January 1815. People still had no news of the peace treaty and a British army threatened the city. General Andrew Jackson, who had been fighting Creek Indians in Georgia, arrived in New Orleans and immediately took charge of its defense. Jackson was helped by city residents, including free African Americans and the pirate Jean Lafitte. A British charge was soundly defeated by the city's defenders. Jackson became a national hero, and Americans had the feeling they had won the war.

Battle of New Orleans

Chapter 4 | The First Presidents of the New Republic

Consequences of the War of 1812

1. American nationalism rose. People took pride in their country. The victory over Britain at the Battle of New Orleans made Americans especially proud.
2. American Indian power in the Northwest Territory was destroyed.
3. Both the United States and Canada had successfully defended themselves. Americans considered the War of 1812 a "Second War of Independence."
4. The Federalist Party was disgraced. Its members had opposed the war. Their actions appeared to be unpatriotic, and the party collapsed.
5. American manufacturers benefited. When people could not get British goods, they bought American manufactured products instead.

The Presidency of James Monroe and the Monroe Doctrine

With the end of the war, Americans rejoiced and put their party differences aside. Congress passed a new tariff to protect American manufacturers and approved a charter for a new national bank. In 1816, **James Monroe** was elected as the country's next President. Monroe was the last to become President of the wealthy Virginia landowners who had fought in the American Revolution. It was Monroe who had negotiated the purchase of the Louisiana Territory in France.

During Monroe's Presidency, the United States acquired Florida from Spain. Kentucky Congressman Henry Clay put forward his "American System," proposing that the federal government impose a tariff to protect Northeastern manufacturers and use the revenues from the tariff to finance roads and other internal improvements in the West. Americans dealt with controversial issues, like the admission of Missouri as a new slave-holding state, through compromise.

The Monroe Doctrine

In the early 1800s, the spirit of the American and French Revolutions spread to Mexico and South America. Spanish colonists demanded independence, while Spain was weakened by the Napoleonic Wars. Spain's attempts to put down the rebellions in its colonies failed. A revolution then broke out in Spain itself. A French army marched into Spain and restored the absolute power of the King of Spain.

Americans feared that France might next help Spain to restore its rule in **Latin America**. There was also a threat to American interests in the Far West. Russia, which already owned Alaska, was planning new settlements along the Pacific Coast of Oregon. The Russian Emperor announced that other countries would not be permitted to land their ships or bring merchants to this coast. President Monroe and his Secretary of State, John Quincy Adams, had to deal with both of these problems.

They did not want to annoy Spain before the United States had gained Florida. So, they delayed recognizing Spain's former colonies as independent. In March 1822, President Monroe finally informed Congress that independent states had been established in Mexico, Colombia, Chile, Peru, and Argentina.

Just over a year later, Monroe made another bold statement to Congress. This became known as the "**Monroe Doctrine**." Monroe announced that the United States would oppose any attempt by a European power to establish new colonies or to restore its rule over colonies that had achieved their independence.

The main points of the "Monroe Doctrine" were these:

1. The Western Hemisphere was no longer open to new colonies.

2. The United States would not interfere in European affairs.

3. Any attempt by European powers to establish new colonies or to restore their control over former ones in the Western Hemisphere would be viewed as an "unfriendly act" by the United States.

Monroe's message was a warning to Spain and France not to restore Spain's rule over its former colonies in Latin America. It was likewise a warning to Russia not to create new colonies along the Pacific Coast.

> "The American continents... are henceforth not to be considered as subjects for further colonization by any European powers... [W]e should consider any attempt on their part to extend their system to any portion of this hemisphere as dangerous to our peace and safety."
>
> —President James Monroe, December 2, 1823

Latin America - dates of independence

- GUYANA (1966)
- SURINAME (1975)
- VENEZUELA (1811)
- FRENCH GUIANA
- COLOMBIA (1821)
- EQUADOR (1822)
- BRAZIL (1822)
- PERU (1821)
- BOLIVIA (1825)
- PARAGUAY (1811)
- CHILE (1818)
- ARGENTINA (1816)
- URUGUAY (1828)
- FALKLAND ISLANDS (BRITAIN)

Chapter 4 | The First Presidents of the New Republic

Name _____

Complete the following chart.

Term	Identify/Describe
Cabinet	
Hamilton's Financial Plan	
Tariff	
Whiskey Rebellion	
Federalist Party	
Democratic-Republicans	
French Revolution	
Washington's Farewell Address	
Alien and Sedition Acts	
Presidential Election of 1800	
Napoleon Bonaparte	

Term	Identify/Describe
Louisiana Purchase	
War of 1812	
Monroe Doctrine	

Complete the paragraph frame.

George Washington, the hero of the Revolutionary War, was elected as our nation's first _____ in 1788. Many of his actions established _____, or ways of doing things that would be followed in the future. One of the most important of these was his decision to consult the heads of government departments as a group, known as the _____.

Washington's Secretary of the Treasury, Alexander Hamilton, proposed a bold financial plan. Hamilton said the federal government should pay both state and national debts from the Revolutionary War. To raise the funds to pay these debts, Hamilton proposed _____. He also proposed _____.

Thomas Jefferson and James Madison bitterly opposed Hamilton's plan, giving rise to the first American political parties. Hamilton's followers became known as the _____ and the followers of Jefferson and Madison became known as the _____.

The French Revolution began while Washington was in office. In 1791, French citizens executed their _____. War broke out in Europe. For most of the next 25 years, Europeans remained at war.

Washington's policy was to _____. After two terms in office, Washington decided not to serve again. He published his "Farewell Address," in which he advised Americans _____.

The nation's second President, John Adams, made himself unpopular by supporting the Alien and Sedition Acts. These laws _____.

Some historians believe that Adams lost the election of 1800 because of these acts.

Thomas Jefferson was our nation's third President. As President, Jefferson nearly doubled the size of the United States by making the _____ Purchase from Napoleon of France. Jefferson was unsure whether the Constitution authorized the acquisition, but Napoleon's offer was just too good to turn down.

Chapter 4 | The First Presidents of the New Republic

The First Presidents of the New Republic

Presidency of George Washington

Hamilton's Financial Plan
- Federal government to pay its debts and those of states
- Protective tariff
- National bank
- Whiskey tax

First Political Parties
- Jefferson and Madison oppose Hamilton's financial plan
- Hamilton's supporters known as Federalists

Washington's Farewell Address (1796)
- Attacks political parties
- Advises Americans to avoid alliances with Europe

Setting up a New Government
- Precedent: The first time something is done
- Cabinet

Impact of the French Revolution
- France and Britain go to war in 1793
- Federalists favor Britain; Democratic-Republicans favor France
- Washington's "Proclamation of Neutrality"

Presidency of John Adams

Alien and Sedition Acts
- Gave President power to send foreigners away and to fine or jail those speaking or writing against the government
- Jefferson and Madison attacked acts as unconstitutional
- Made Adams unpopular: may have cost him election of 1800

Presidency of Thomas Jefferson

Jefferson's Election
- "Revolution of 1800"

Louisiana Purchase (1803)
- Napoleon decided to sell all of the Louisiana Territory
- Jefferson unsure if the Constitution gave him power to make purchase
- Doubled size of the United States
- With purchase, Jefferson expanded Presidential power
- Lewis and Clark were sent to explore the Louisiana Territory

Embargo of 1807
- Britain and France blockaded each other
- Jefferson imposed embargo, which hurt Americans

Presidency of James Madison and War of 1812 (1812–1814)

Causes
- British impressment of American sailors
- Americans blame British for Indian attacks
- American "war hawks" want to invade Canada

Course of the War
- Fought on Great Lakes, along border with Canada, and along Atlantic Coast
- Burning of Washington by British
- Francis Scott Key's "The Star-Spangled Banner"
- British attack on New Orleans stopped by General Andrew Jackson
- War ends in December 1814

Consequences of the War
- American independence upheld
- Northern manufacturers benefit
- Collapse of Federalist Party

Monroe Doctrine (1823) 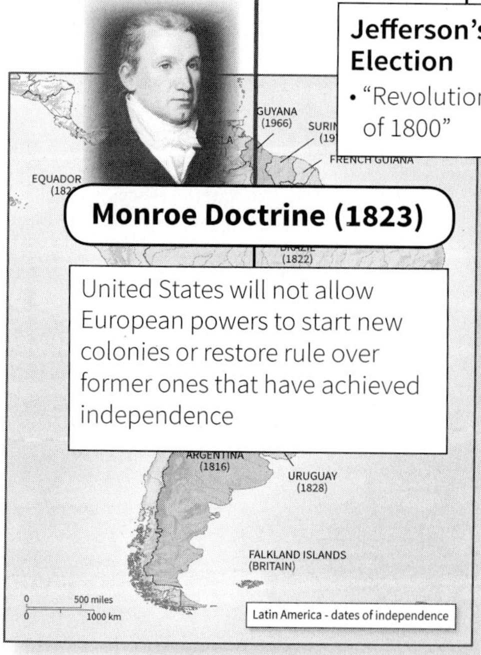
United States will not allow European powers to start new colonies or restore rule over former ones that have achieved independence

Latin America - dates of independence

136 Chapter 4 | The First Presidents of the New Republic

What Do You Know?

SSUSH6a

1. Which action of President George Washington had the MOST lasting influence as a precedent for the federal government?

   A. signing treaties with Britain and Spain
   B. using the army to enforce the Whiskey Tax
   C. creating the First National Bank of the United States
   D. establishing a Cabinet of department heads to advise the President

SSUSH6a

2. Use the excerpt to answer the question.

   > The great rule of conduct for us in regard to foreign nations is, in extending our commercial [business] relations, to have with them as little political connection as possible. So far as we have already formed engagements let them be fulfilled with perfect good faith. Here let us stop.... It is our true policy to steer clear of permanent alliances with any portion of the foreign world.
   >
   > —George Washington, "Farewell Address" (1796)

   Based on the excerpt, with which statement would President Washington have MOST LIKELY agreed?

   A. There are no threats to the security of the United States.
   B. Permanent alliances with foreign nations should be avoided.
   C. Foreign nations profit too much by importing American goods.
   D. Permanent alliances should be a part of every nation's foreign policy.

SSUSH6a

3. Use the list to answer the question.

   - The federal government should not pay the debts of states because this would be unfair to those states that had already paid their debts.
   - The federal government should not place a protective tariff on imported manufactured goods because this would hurt American farmers.
   - The Constitution should be interpreted strictly.

   Which pair of leaders MOST agreed with these views?

   A. John Marshall and John Adams
   B. Thomas Jefferson and James Madison
   C. Benjamin Franklin and Thomas Jefferson
   D. Alexander Hamilton and George Washington

Chapter 4 | The First Presidents of the New Republic

SSUSH6a

4. Use this list to answer the questions below.

> - The United States should pay its debts from the war.
> - The federal government should pay the war debts of the states.
> - The federal government should issue new government bonds to cover these debts. These bonds should pay interest. People will be able to rely on these bonds as a form of money.

Part A
What were the three elements on this list a part of?

A. Articles of Confederation
B. U.S. Constitution
C. Hamilton's financial plan
D. Washington's Farewell Address

Part B
What was an important consequence of these elements?

A. They helped the new nation establish good public credit.
B. They made it difficult for Americans to trade with other countries.
C. They benefited farmers who had borrowed money during the war.
D. They helped shopkeepers and farmers who had supplied the Continental Army.

SSUSH6a

5. Use the diagram to answer the question.

Federalists:
- Favored Hamilton's financial plan.
- Friendly to Britain.

Democratic-Republicans:
- Opposed Hamilton's financial plan.
- Friendly to France.

Center (?):

Which phrase best completes the Venn diagram?

A. Emerged as the first political parties
B. Believed in strong government
C. Opposed ratification of the Constitution
D. Believed manufacturing was more important than farming

138   Chapter 4 | The First Presidents of the New Republic

SSUSH6a

6. Use the excerpt to answer the question.

> The duty and interest of the United States require that they should adopt a conduct friendly and impartial toward the [warring] powers. I have thought fit to declare the position of the United States to observe a conduct towards those powers respectfully; and warn our citizens to avoid all acts which may in any manner tend to [go against] *this position.*
>
> —President George Washington, Proclamation of Neutrality, 1793

Why did President Washington make this proclamation?

A. He believed the United States should avoid involvement in European wars.

B. He thought the United States was required by treaty to defend France.

C. He wanted to respond to those demanding revenge for the execution of the King of France.

D. He knew the British Royal Navy was stopping American merchant ships in its search for deserters.

SSUSH6a

7. Use this drawing of the execution of King Louis XVI to answer the question.

What impact did this event in France have on Americans?

A. Americans decided they should make George Washington their king.

B. Federalists were shocked while Democratic-Republicans remained friendly to France.

C. Federalists turned against Hamilton's financial plan because they feared instability in troubled times.

D. More Americans wanted to ally with the French, who had helped them during the American Revolution.

Chapter 4 | The First Presidents of the New Republic

SSUSH6a

8. Which statement BEST describes the impact of President Washington's handling of the Whiskey Rebellion?

   A. It proved to foreign nations that the U.S. government was still weak.
   B. It reduced Alexander Hamilton's influence over the national economy.
   C. It increased the powers of state governments over new taxes.
   D. It demonstrated the power of the federal government to enforce its policies.

SSUSH6b

9. Use the excerpt to answer the question.

   > [I]f any person shall write, print... or publish... any false, scandalous and malicious writing... against the government of the United States... [then] such person, being thereof convicted... shall be punished by a fine ... and by imprisonment not exceeding two years.
   >
   > —Sedition Act, Section 2 (1797)

   Which conclusion can BEST be inferred from the excerpt?

   A. The Sedition Act violated the right to a trial by jury.
   B. The Sedition Act denied citizens the right to obtain a writ of *habeas corpus*.
   C. The Sedition Act restricted the First Amendment's guarantee of freedom of the press.
   D. Many people were unjustly deported from the United States based on the Sedition Act.

SSUSH6b

10. What impact did the Alien and Sedition Acts have on the Presidential election of 1800?

    A. More voters supported Adams to ensure stability.
    B. Fewer voters supported Adams because they felt he had overextended his power.
    C. More voters supported Adams because they feared foreigners.
    D. French agents interfered with the election in order to repeal these acts.

SSUSH6c

11. Which statement BEST describes the significance of the election of 1800?

    A. John Adams refused to run for another term.
    B. States threatened to secede if John Adams were re-elected.
    C. The Jefferson administration established many new precedents.
    D. There was a peaceful transfer of power to an opposing political party.

SSUSH6c

12. Why did President Thomas Jefferson hesitate to purchase the Louisiana Territory in 1803?

    A. He thought it was too expensive.

    B. He didn't believe Americans needed so much new territory.

    C. He didn't want to bribe French officials.

    D. He didn't think the Constitution gave him the power to do so.

SSUSH6d

13. Use the painting to answer the question.

    The painting shows French and British ships fighting one another during the Napoleonic Wars. What problem did Americans face because of this conflict?

    A. The British navy stopped American ships to search for deserters.

    B. Americans attempted to invade Canada.

    C. The British refused to protect American ships from attacks by the Barbary States.

    D. The British attempted to take over the carrying trade between Europe and America.

SSUSH6d

14. Why did many Americans consider the War of 1812 the "Second War for American Independence"?

    A. American citizens continued to protest against British taxes.

    B. American "war hawks" thought the United States might be able to conquer Canada.

    C. The United States and Great Britain never previously signed a treaty ending the Revolutionary War.

    D. The British had been showing disrespect for the United States by stopping American ships and arming hostile Indians.

Chapter 4 | The First Presidents of the New Republic

SSUSH6d

15. Use the cartoon below to answer the question.

With which statement would the cartoonist have MOST LIKELY agreed?

A. The United States and Britain should find a way to end the War of 1812.

B. British officers have been responsible for Indian attacks on Americans.

C. An independent Indian nation should be created between Canada and the United States.

D. The "war hawks" in Congress have exaggerated the involvement of Britain in Indian attacks.

SSUSH6e

16. Which statement BEST summarizes the main idea of the Monroe Doctrine (1823)?

A. Foreign nations cannot form alliances with the United States.

B. There is a barrier between European nations and the United States.

C. The United States will protect the continents of Europe and Africa.

D. The United States will protect the Western Hemisphere from further European colonization.

SSUSH6e

17. Why did President James Monroe issue his doctrine in 1823?

A. He wished to purchase Alaska from Russia.

B. He wanted to help Americans recover from the War of 1812.

C. He feared France would help Spain recover its colonies.

D. He wanted to promote trade with Great Britain.

142   Chapter 4 | The First Presidents of the New Republic

CHAPTER 5 The Age of Jackson

SSUSH7 What political, economic, and social developments occurred during the Age of Jackson?

  a. What were the characteristics of Jacksonian Democracy, including an expanded suffrage, the Nullification Crisis and states' rights, and the Indian Removal Act?

  b. How were the North, South, and West linked through industrial and economic expansion, and how did Henry Clay's proposed "American System" attempt to unite the country?

  c. What was the influence of the Second Great Awakening on social reform movements, including temperance, public education, and women's efforts to gain suffrage?

  d. How did slavery become a major issue in American politics, and how did slave rebellions and the rise of abolitionism contribute to its growing importance?

Chapter 5 | The Age of Jackson

Names and Terms You Should Know

Andrew Jackson

"Jacksonian Democracy"

Suffrage

Property qualifications

Nominating convention

"Spoils System"

Indian Removal Act

Cherokee Indians

"Trail of Tears"

John C. Calhoun

Tariff

Nullification Crisis

States' rights

Henry Clay

Clay's "American System"

Canal

Steamboat

Telegraph

Eli Whitney

Cotton gin

Second Great Awakening

Temperance

Public education

Women's suffrage

Seneca Falls Convention

Abolitionism

Slave rebellion

Nat Turner

Georgia "Peaches" of Wisdom

1. During the period of "Jacksonian Democracy," America became more democratic. States abolished their property qualifications for voting. All adult white males gained the right to vote. New campaign methods were developed. Party nominating conventions began selecting candidates. Jackson, who worked his way up from poverty, saw himself as the representative of the "common man."

2. Jackson favored rotating officeholders to give ordinary citizens experience in government and to prevent corruption. He dismissed many top government officials and appointed his own supporters. Some people called this the "spoils system."

3. In 1830, Jackson proposed the Indian Removal Act, requiring all Indian tribes to relocate west of the Mississippi. Georgia passed laws requiring the Cherokee Indians to leave. The Cherokee appealed to the federal courts for assistance. The Supreme Court ruled that state officials had no right to enter Cherokee lands. Jackson, however, entered into a treaty with a minority of Cherokee leaders. In 1838, federal troops forced the Cherokee from their homes. They migrated in the fall and winter. About 4,000 Cherokee died on the "Trail of Tears."

4. John C. Calhoun thought the 1828 tariff unfairly favored the North over the South. He also believed the federal union was a "compact" of states and that each state had the right to nullify (*cancel*) federal laws within its borders or to secede. In 1832, Congress passed a new tariff. South Carolina objected and passed the Ordinance of Nullification. It refused to enforce the tariff and threatened to secede. Congress authorized Jackson to use force against the state. The crisis ended when South Carolina withdrew its ordinance.

5. During the Industrial Revolution, new machines used water and steam power to make thread and cloth. During the War of 1812, Americans began buying more goods manufactured in the United States.

6. Americans also experienced a "Transportation Revolution," based on new roads and canals and the invention of the steamboat, railroad, and telegraph. These linked different parts of the country more closely together. The Northeast became a center of manufacturing; the West grew food crops; and the South grew cotton and other raw materials for Northeastern factories.

7. Henry Clay's "American System" favored a tariff to protect Northern industries and provide money for internal improvements in the West. Clay also favored having a national bank.

8. The Second Great Awakening encouraged greater emotion in religion and promoted reform. Ministers saw some of the abuses of American society, such as drunkenness and slavery, as sinful. The American Temperance Society was formed against alcoholic beverages. Horace Mann spread the "Common School" movement, which promoted state-tax funded public schools with trained teachers for children of all backgrounds.

9. In early nineteenth-century America, women did not have the same rights as men. They could not vote, obtain a higher education, or enter the professions. A woman's property became her husband's when she married. In 1848, reformers held the Seneca Falls Convention for women's rights. Their movement came to focus on women's demand for suffrage—the right to vote.

10. In 1793, Eli Whitney invented the cotton gin, which increased the demand for Southern cotton and caused slavery to spread.

11. Enslaved African Americans had virtually no rights. They were treated as property and bought and sold by others in auctions. The threat of whipping and other punishments forced them to work.

12. Slaves themselves resisted. They often did not work as hard as they could; they preserved their traditional culture; they learned to read and write; and they might strike an overseer or try to escape, although punishments for such actions were severe.

13. Enslaved people sometimes rebelled. In 1831, Nat Turner led an unsuccessful rebellion of slaves in Virginia. Turner's rebellion failed but created a wave of fear among slaveholders.

Chapter 5 | The Age of Jackson

In this chapter you will learn about the "Age of Jackson"—the time when Andrew Jackson was President, American democracy expanded to include all adult white males, the textile industry grew, slavery spread, different sections of America became more linked economically, and many Americans demanded reform.

Jacksonian Democracy

The Election of Andrew Jackson

In the Presidential election of 1828, General Andrew Jackson, the hero of the Battle of New Orleans, ran against President John Quincy Adams, the son of John Adams. Jackson's supporters organized clubs, public meetings, and torchlight parades. They printed thousands of pictures of General Jackson on his horse. His troops had once called Jackson "Old Hickory" because they said he was as tough as old hickory wood. His supporters formed "Hickory Clubs" across the nation. Jackson's supporters also created a new political party, known as the Democratic Party. It is the direct ancestor to the Democratic Party we have today.

The same two candidates had faced one another back in 1824, when Jackson had won the popular vote but the outcome in the Electoral

Who Was Andrew Jackson?

Andrew Jackson's father died before he was born. As a boy, he carried papers for the Patriot army during the American Revolution. Both he and his brother were captured and held as prisoners. When Andrew refused to clean the boots of a British officer, his hand was slashed by the swing of a British sword. Andrew and his brother caught smallpox while being held by the British. His brother died. His other brother died in battle. His mother caught cholera while caring for American prisoners-of-war on British ships. She also died, leaving young Andrew an orphan. His entire family was wiped out by the Revolution. Young Jackson worked at odd jobs before studying law and becoming a lawyer on the frontier. He attended the Tennessee state convention in 1796 and became the state's first member in the U.S. House of Representatives. Later, Jackson became one of Tennessee's U.S. Senators as well as a member of the Tennessee Supreme Court. Jackson bought former Indian lands and became one of the founders of the city of Memphis. He also bought a large plantation for himself near Nashville. Jackson became the owner of dozens of enslaved people. In 1804, when one of them ran away, Jackson advertised in local newspapers to recover him. He offered a $50 reward and "ten dollars extra for every hundred lashes any person will give him, to the amount of three hundred." Jackson also became commander of the Tennessee militia. When the War of 1812 broke out, Jackson led militia forces against the Creek Indians. At the Battle of Horseshoe Bend, Jackson's soldiers killed hundreds of Creeks. Jackson forced the Creeks to give over millions of acres of land. In 1815, he became the hero of New Orleans. In 1818, Jackson's march into Spanish Florida created the crisis that led Spain to give Florida to the United States.

Jackson's Inauguration

College had been disputed. Far more people voted in 1828 than four years earlier, and this time Jackson won a clear majority of both the popular vote and the Electoral College.

Jackson took the oath of office as President in front of the U.S. Capitol in March 1829. He was surrounded by a crowd of more than 20,000 people. Jackson left the Capitol riding on a white horse. He trotted up Pennsylvania Avenue until he reached the White House. His new home was already filled with a bustling crowd. People entered the White House wearing dirty boots. Some guests accidentally knocked into the furniture and broke the White House china. Jackson's election was seen as a victory for the "common man." By inviting the public to the White House, Jackson was emphasizing that the Presidency belonged to the people.

The Characteristics of Jacksonian Democracy

During Jackson's two terms in office, the United States became more democratic. Historians often refer to these developments as "**Jacksonian Democracy**." In these years, state governments were changing their requirements for voting. When the United States had been founded, states had **property qualifications**. Only adult white male citizens who owned a certain amount of property could vote. In the 1820s, states were ending these requirements. By 1828, all adult white males could vote in ten states. This meant ordinary workers and farmers could influence state and national elections.

With ordinary working people voting, the nature of politics itself changed. Candidates had to rely on newspaper articles, pamphlets, rallies, and meetings to get their message across. As methods of transportation and communication improved, it became possible to get more people involved in the political process.

Andrew Jackson tried to appeal to these new voters—farmers with small holdings, workers, craftsmen, and middle-class businessmen, such as shop owners. Jackson saw himself as the champion of the "common man." Although he was in fact a rich slaveholder, he had worked his way up from poverty.

Up until this time, party leaders in Congress had chosen their party's candidates for President. During the 1830s, the first party **nominating conventions** were held to select candidates. Ordinary party members participated in these public conventions. The Democratic Party held its first national convention in Baltimore in May 1832. Andrew Jackson was chosen as its candidate.

The "Spoils System"

Jackson felt that many officeholders stayed too long in government. They either became corrupt—using their power to benefit themselves—or they ignored public needs. Jackson favored the rotation (*changing*) of officeholders. He believed ordinary people should be able to fill the offices of government for a time. Then a new group of citizens should take their place. This would give more citizens actual experience participating in government. It would also make government more responsive to public needs. Finally, it would prevent the rise of a group of permanent government officials who were out of touch with the American people.

After Jackson was elected, he dismissed several top officials. Some of them had been in office for many years. Jackson appointed his own supporters in their place. Some called this the "spoils system" because it treated public offices as spoils.

The War on the Bank

Jackson opposed the Second Bank of the United States because he felt it represented the interests of wealthy, privileged people in the Northeast against the interests of other Americans. He made the renewal of the bank's charter a key issue in the 1832 election. Jackson refused to sign a renewal of the charter, and withdrew all federal funds from the bank.

The Indian Removal Act

Jackson had grown up on the frontier. He had commanded troops against the Creek and Seminole Indians. He especially feared that Indian tribes might cooperate with a foreign power like Britain or Spain. While Indians had already been forced off the Northwest Territory, many tribes still remained in the Southeast. Jackson wanted to move all these Indian tribes to west of the Mississippi River in order to give their lands to white settlers.

In 1830, Jackson proposed the Indian Removal Act to Congress. By this act, the Cherokee, Creeks, Choctaws, Chickasaws, Seminoles and all other tribes still in the East were forced to relocate to lands reserved for them west of the Mississippi.

Most of the tribes agreed to move west, including the Choctaw, Creek, and Chickasaw.

General Jackson slaying the National Bank—a many headed monster

A small group of Indians led by Chief Black Hawk resisted, but they were defeated by 1832.

The Cherokee and the "Trail of Tears"

The **Cherokee Indians** also resisted removal. They relied on the American system of law rather than armed resistance. The Cherokee lived in Georgia, North Carolina, Tennessee, and South Carolina. They considered themselves a "civilized" tribe. One of their chiefs, Sequoyah, had even created a special alphabet for their language. The Cherokee had their own written constitution, elected their own officials, and published their own newspaper. They could not believe that their towns would be torn down and their people uprooted.

The State of Georgia passed laws requiring the Cherokee Indians to leave the state. It gave away Cherokee lands to white settlers in a special state lottery. The settlers were especially eager to claim these lands after gold was discovered on them in 1829.

The Cherokee Indians challenged Georgia's removal order in the U.S. Supreme Court. The Cherokee claimed they were protected by several treaties. In one case, Chief Justice John Marshall ruled that the Cherokee tribe was a "dependent"

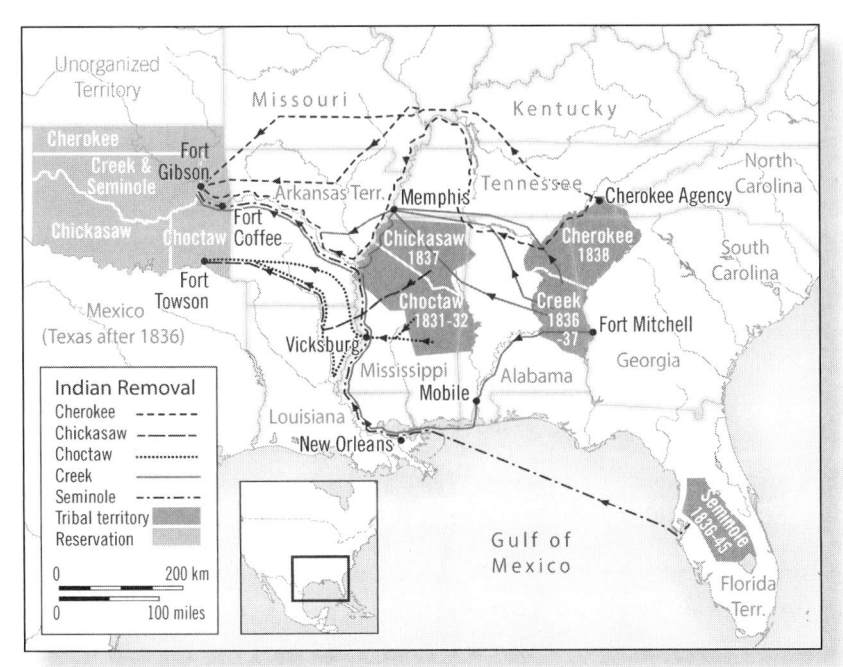

Locations of Indians in the Southeast before the Indian Removal Act

nation. As a "dependent" nation, the tribe had a special relationship with the federal government. In a second case, Marshall held that state officials did not have the right to enter Cherokee lands without tribal permission.

Despite Marshall's decisions, Jackson still wanted to move the Cherokee tribe west of the Mississippi. He concluded a treaty with a minority of Cherokee leaders in 1835. The new treaty gave the Cherokee two years to leave their homes to move to Oklahoma. Cherokee leaders representing three-quarters of the tribe rejected the treaty, but they were ignored by Jackson and Congress. Jackson simply

The Historian's Apprentice

In presenting the Indian Removal Act to Congress, Jackson listed these benefits:

> "It will place a dense and civilized population in large tracts [areas] of country now occupied by a few savage hunters. By opening the whole territory between Tennessee on the north and Louisiana on the south to the settlement of whites it will incalculably strengthen the southwestern frontier.... It will relieve the whole state of Mississippi and the western part of Alabama of Indian occupancy, and enable those states to advance rapidly in population, wealth, and power.
>
> It will separate the Indians from immediate contact with settlements of whites; free them from the power of the states; enable them to pursue happiness in their own way and under their own rude institutions; will retard [slow down] the progress of decay, which is lessening their numbers, and perhaps cause them gradually, under the protection of the government, and through the influence of good counsels, to cast off their savage habits and become an interesting, civilized and Christian community."
>
> —Andrew Jackson, Address to Congress, December 6, 1830

1. Which of the reasons listed above was most important to Jackson? How did Indian removal favor the interests of the white "common man"?

2. Jackson wrote the following to the Creeks: "Where you are now, you and my white children are too near to each other to live in harmony and peace ... Beyond the great River Mississippi ... your father has provided a country large enough for all of you, and he advises you to remove to it." How, according to Jackson, would the proposed act benefit the Indians?

Chapter 5 | The Age of Jackson

did not see Indians as fellow citizens entitled to the benefits of "Jacksonian Democracy."

Cherokee efforts to avoid relocation eventually ended in tragedy. In the late spring of 1838, federal troops appeared on Cherokee lands to take them to "Indian" territory (Oklahoma). They were first taken to guarded camps. Then groups of about a thousand each were forced to make the long journey westward in the fall and winter. About a fourth of the Cherokee died from hunger and cold on the tragic march known as the **Trail of Tears**.

The Nullification Crisis and States' Rights

Another important problem that Jackson faced was the **tariff** issue. A few months before the election of 1828, a bill for a new tariff came before Congress. It raised rates above 60%. Southerners called the new law the "Tariff of Abominations"—an abomination is something that disgusts us.

Jackson's Vice President was **John C. Calhoun** from South Carolina. Calhoun was very concerned about the future of the South. He felt that the tariff unfairly favored the North. He even decided that the tariff was unconstitutional because it so clearly favored one section of the country over another.

Calhoun became the leading spokesman for **states' rights**. These rights are the powers that belong to the states rather than the federal government. Calhoun secretly published an essay that argued that the federal union was simply a "compact" of states. Each state therefore had the right to **nullify**, or cancel, any federal law within its borders that it thought was unconstitutional. According to Calhoun, each state also had the right to **secede**, or break away, from the union.

Others disagreed. In a Senate debate in January 1830, Senator Daniel Webster of Massachusetts argued that the federal union was not a "compact" of states but the "union" of the American people. Individual states therefore did not have the right to nullify a law or to leave the union. Moreover, it was not the role of states to decide if a federal law was constitutional. That job, Webster said, belonged to the U.S. Supreme Court. Webster ended his Senate speech with a striking declaration. He called for "Liberty and Union, now and forever, one and inseparable." Americans could not have one without the other.

Andrew Jackson was a Southerner and a known supporter of states' rights. Calhoun therefore hoped that Jackson would support his views. In April 1830, Jackson, Calhoun, and other important leaders attended a dinner in honor of Thomas Jefferson's birthday. Calhoun made a series of toasts. Finally, it was Jackson's turn to make one of his own. All the guests fell silent and turned their eyes towards the President. "The federal union," Jackson said as he raised his glass, "It must be preserved!" With these words, everyone knew that Jackson opposed Calhoun's ideas on nullification.

South Carolina's Ordinance of Nullification

In 1832, Congress revised the tariff. The new rates were lower than those of the Tariff of Abominations, but South Carolina still objected to it. The citizens of South Carolina held a special state convention. The convention passed an **Ordinance of Nullification**. This ordinance, or law, declared that the Tariff of 1832 was unconstitutional. Therefore, the state would not enforce it. South Carolina further threatened to secede from the union if the federal government tried to make it collect the tariff duties. Meanwhile Calhoun resigned as Vice President in December 1832.

Jackson responded to the crisis at once. He called South Carolina's Ordinance of Nullification an act of treason (*the crime of betraying one's country*). Jackson sent warships to the harbor of Charleston, the principal city of South Carolina. Congress passed a Force Bill authorizing Jackson to use military force against the state. Jackson also published a "Proclamation to the People of South Carolina." He warned its citizens that the nullification power they claimed was "incompatible with the existence of the Union" and that he was prepared to use force.

Faced with this threat, South Carolina quickly stepped down. The state withdrew its ordinance. Henry Clay suggested a compromise in which tariffs were gradually reduced over the next ten years. Congress quickly approved his proposal. In this way, bloodshed was avoided.

The Historian's Apprentice

1. President Jackson had lost his family in the American Revolution and had been a national hero during the War of 1812. He therefore stood by the Union. Jackson told the people of South Carolina the following about their threat of secession:

   "The Constitution of the United States . . . forms a government, not a league; and whether it be formed by a compact between the States or in any other manner, its character is the same. It is a Government in which all the people are represented, which operates directly on the people individually, not upon the States; they retained [*kept*] all the power they did not grant. But each State, having expressly parted with so many powers as to constitute, jointly with other States, a single nation, can not, from that period, possess any right to secede, because secession does not break a league, but destroys the unity of the nation . . . Secession, like any other revolutionary act may be morally justified by the extremity of oppression; but to call it a constitutional right is confounding [*confusing; mistaking*] the meaning of terms . . . [C]ompared to disunion all other evils are light . . ."

   In your own words, explain why Jackson rejected South Carolina's right to secede. Do you agree with his reasoning?

2. Discuss your answers to the following two questions with a partner. Then share your ideas with your class.
   - Do you think Jackson handled the Nullification Crisis effectively?
   - Are there any lessons in how Jackson dealt with the Nullification Crisis for leaders today?

3. Would you consider Jackson a "good" or a "bad" President? Make a chart or graphic organizer showing both his accomplishments and drawbacks. Consider Jacksonian Democracy, Indian removal, and his handling of the Nullification Crisis.

4. Andrew Jackson believed in the political and legal equality of white adult males of all backgrounds and incomes. He was the hero of the "common man." This was a great step forward in the march towards equality. Yet Jackson had no respect at all for Native Americans or African Americans. He also did not look on women as equals. Was he advanced in his views if we judge him by the standards of his time? Or could he have done more to reform society and promote equality? Discuss your views with a partner and share your ideas with the class.

Chapter 5 | The Age of Jackson

Industrial and Economic Expansion Links the North, West, and South

The Industrial Revolution Comes to America

The **Industrial Revolution** began in Britain in the 1700s. People invented new machines to make it easier to spin thread and weave thread into cloth. People began making thread and cloth in factories instead of at home. Many of these factories used running water, or "water power," to turn their machines. The invention of the steam engine made it even easier to power these machines.

In 1793, an English immigrant built the first modern textile factory in America in Rhode Island. By 1810, there were 50 factories in the United States making cotton thread. American textile manufacturers received a boost during the War of 1812. Americans could no longer buy English textiles, so they had to buy American textiles instead. After the war, a group of Americans built a large textile factory in Massachusetts that placed all the operations to turn raw cotton into finished cloth under one roof. Young women from nearby farms were hired as its factory workers.

Henry Clay's "American System"

At the time of the American Revolution, Americans were connected by trails and dirt roads. During spring rains, these roads often became impossible to pass. In summer, they were dry and dusty. They had holes and stones. Travelling by horse, stagecoach, or wagon was often uncomfortable.

The federal government began construction of the National Road in 1811. It extended the road after the War of 1812, which went westward from Maryland.

Congressman **Henry Clay** proposed his **"American System"** to tie the different parts of the country more closely together. He believed the federal government should play an active role in promoting economic growth and national unity. Clay favored a tariff to protect American manufacturers in the Northeast. He proposed using the money gained from the tariff to pay for roads and other internal improvements needed in the West. The South would also benefit because its cotton was needed by Northern factories. Finally, Clay wanted to keep the national bank to promote growth and keep the economy stable. Clay believed that under his plan, all sections of the country would benefit. Clay's plan was challenged by Andrew Jackson. Jackson favored states' rights. He opposed federal financing of internal improvements and equally opposed the national bank.

The Transportation Revolution

In the early nineteenth century, it was much cheaper to transport goods by water than by land. State governments began building **canals** (*human-made waterways*) to help merchants transport their goods. The most successful of these was the **Erie Canal**, which opened in 1825. The Erie Canal connected the Hudson River to Lake Erie, making it possible for farmers in the Midwest to ship their crops to the Great Lakes, then along the Erie Canal to the Hudson River, and finally down the Hudson River to New York

152   Chapter 5 | The Age of Jackson

City and the Atlantic Ocean. This made it much cheaper for Midwestern farmers to ship their goods and led to the spectacular growth of New York City and towns along the canal.

Meanwhile, the invention of the steam engine led to the invention of the **steamboat**. The new steamboat used a steam engine to turn a large wheel with paddles. The turning of the paddlewheel pushed the boat forward in the water. Steamboats did not depend on the wind and could move upstream against the current.

Next, inventors placed a steam engine on a wagon with wheels in order to move it along iron rails held in place by planks of wood—giving birth to the **railroad**. The first railroad in the United States opened in 1830, while Andrew Jackson was President. The spread of railroads was slow at first because they were so expensive to build. But unlike canals and boats, railroads could be built almost anywhere.

Trains kept getting faster and more efficient as engineers improved the design of their locomotives. Train travel was also more comfortable than other forms of travel. Trains were large enough for passengers to move around. The federal and state governments began giving land grants to railroad companies that laid down new tracks. Between 1850 and 1860, the amount of railroad track tripled in the United States.

Miles of Railroad Track in the United States

Year	Miles
1830	23
1835	1,098
1840	2,818
1845	4,633
1850	9,021
1855	18,374
1860	30,626

Along with these improvements in transportation came the **telegraph**. This invention used electromagnetism to send messages instantly across wires over long distances. In the 1840s, Samuel Morse developed a better telegraph and a special code using dots and dashes. Using "Morse Code," operators could send messages along telegraph wires. People could immediately find out election results or the prices of goods in other parts of the country. They could learn if a train or boat had arrived or if it had been delayed.

Industry Links Different Sections Together

With canals, railroads, steamboats, and telegraphs, Americans were better connected than they had ever been before. They developed a national market, where goods produced in one part of the country could be sold in another. This had a great impact on the economic activities of each section.

The Industrial Northeast

The rise of industry and improvements in transportation increased the number of people living in Northern cities. Farm workers moved to towns and cities to find work in factories or to provide services to other people living there.

Northern factories produced textiles and other manufactured goods used throughout America.

The Food-Growing West

Independent farmers and their children kept pushing farther to the West to farm new lands. The West became an important region for growing grain and other food crops, which were sold in the Northeast and South.

Raw Materials from the South

The Industrial Revolution affected the South just as much as it affected the North and West. Northern factories needed raw materials. Textile mills turned raw cotton into finished cloth. But where did all this raw cotton come from? The answer was the South, where cotton was planted, grown, harvested, cleaned, packed, and shipped by the forced labor of enslaved African Americans.

The Spread of Slavery in the South

In 1792, the inventor **Eli Whitney** had just graduated college. He was visiting a plantation in Georgia when he noticed slaves picking seeds from cotton by hand. Whitney thought he had a better idea. He designed a box with a handle that turned. Around the handle were spikes. The spikes pulled the cotton through the teeth of a comb attached to the opposite side of the box. The cotton was pulled through the comb while the seeds were blocked by the comb's teeth and dropped out. Whitney applied for a patent in 1793. He called his machine a "cotton engine." It became known as the **cotton gin**. With a cotton gin, workers could clean cotton fifty times faster than they could by hand.

Whitney's invention of the cotton gin caused the system of slavery to spread. The kind of cotton that could be grown in most of the South had short fibers with many seeds. With the cotton gin, this short-staple cotton could now easily be cleaned and prepared. Soon most of the factories in Britain and the United States were using cotton from Southern plantations. The warm climate and rich fertile soil, especially in the states of Mississippi and Alabama in the Lower South, were perfect for growing cotton. By 1860, three-quarters of the world's supply of cotton came from the Southern United States.

Eli Whitney's cotton gin

154   Chapter 5 | The Age of Jackson

The Second Great Awakening and the Age of Reform

Religious Fervor

The "**Second Great Awakening**" began in the early 1800s and reached its peak in the 1830s. Like the First Great Awakening, it encouraged greater emotion and enthusiasm in religion. People examined their own lives to see if they would be "saved" and go to Heaven.

During the Second Great Awakening, Protestant "revival" meetings took place in frontier areas such as Tennessee, Kentucky, Ohio, and upstate New York. In many of these areas, there were no permanent preachers or churches. Traveling preachers went from place to place. They attracted large audiences from many nearby communities. Women were especially active in the Second Great Awakening.

Hundreds of people gathered outside in the open air at special "camp meetings." They listened to preachers and sang hymns. Different ministers preached and sang until late into the night. As the meeting continued, the sermons became more emotional and the audience grew more excited.

Those who participated in the Second Great Awakening tried to apply Christian values to social issues. Preachers emphasized that each individual had a personal responsibility to help end sinful practices and promote God's will.

> Note: You will not have to know about Finney for the Georgia Milestones EOC Assessment, but his career illustrates the influence of the Second Great Awakening on social reform movements.

Charles Grandison Finney (1792–1875) was a leading preacher during the Second Great Awakening. He taught that people could save themselves if they had the will to do so. Finney introduced "New Measures" in his preaching. He asked women to pray aloud in prayer meetings. He asked listeners to stand up and make public pledges when they felt ready to become born-again Christians. Finney used informal, common language in his prayers and sermons. His "free church movement" had an open-door policy in which anyone could come into his church. Finney's preaching had a radical impact. In 1830, he gave a series of 98 sermons in Rochester, New York—a boomtown along the Erie Canal. His sermons were so popular that half the shops in the town were closed.

In 1835, some of Finney's students took him to Oberlin College in Ohio. This was the first American college to offer education to women and African Americans on equal terms with white men. Finney became a professor and later the president of Oberlin. He was a prominent **abolitionist** (*someone working to abolish slavery*). He encouraged his wife to help with his activities and he also promoted women's rights.

Chapter 5 | The Age of Jackson

They saw reform as an important part of God's plan. Some hoped to make the world a better place in order to bring the return of Jesus (the "Second Coming") sooner. These Christians believed that slaveholding and drinking strong alcoholic beverages were serious sins. Many of them became active in reform movements.

Social Reform Movements

Influenced by the fervor of the Second Great Awakening, reformers wanted to solve social problems and raise the nation's morals. In the 1820s and 1830s, many Americans believed needed reforms could be achieved through private and voluntary efforts. During these years, a large number of reform societies appeared.

The Temperance Movement

In the early 1800s, the average American drank almost three times as much alcohol as today. Cheap whiskey made from corn was very popular. Reformers believed that heavy drinking was bad for health and morals. They blamed heavy drinkers for ruining their families' lives and for committing crimes.

In 1826, the American Temperance Society was founded. Within five years, it had almost 200,000 members. Members made a pledge not to drink strong alcoholic beverages like whiskey.

Temperance groups spread quickly across the West and South. In the 1840s, they began asking states to pass laws against alcoholic beverages. In 1846, Maine became the first state to limit alcoholic drinks. In 1851, it banned them altogether.

Public Education

The rise of industry and the growing number of Americans living in cities created an urgent need for a better system of American education. There was very little uniformity. In some states, children received no formal schooling at all. In others, they went to school but children of all ages were placed together in the same classroom.

In Massachusetts, **Horace Mann** argued that the state should have free and compulsory (*required*) elementary education for all children—both boys and girls. In 1837, Mann was appointed as the secretary to the state's new Board of Education. He reorganized the state's entire educational system. Mann began training teachers. He believed that all children should attend the same common schools. Mann felt that children from all social classes

Horace Mann

Principles of Mann's "Common School" Movement

1. The state should use tax money to pay for elementary schools. School should be free for all families.
2. School should be compulsory for younger children.
3. Children of all backgrounds should be in the same common schools.
4. Schools should not be religious.
5. Teachers should receive professional training.

and backgrounds would benefit from being mixed together. Mann's program became known as the "Common School" movement and was soon adopted in other states as well as Massachusetts.

Women's Suffrage

In the early nineteenth century, American women did not enjoy the same rights as men. They could not vote. They could not get a higher education. They could not have a professional career in medicine, law, or religion. Often a woman had no choice in selecting her husband. Once a woman did marry, her property and any money she earned belonged to her husband, not herself.

Lucretia Mott and **Elizabeth Cady Stanton** were two women **abolitionists** (*people fighting to abolish slavery*). Mott and Stanton organized a convention for women's rights at Seneca Falls in upstate New York in 1848. This was the town where Stanton lived.

Several hundred people attended the **Seneca Falls Convention**. The famous abolitionist Frederick Douglass was one of many speakers. Stanton wrote a "Declaration of Sentiments," which she read aloud at the convention. She based much of it on the Declaration of Independence. Her Declaration of Sentiments included a list of women's grievances. One of the most important demands was that women should have the right to vote. A hundred people at the convention signed the Declaration. The demand for the right to vote—known as **suffrage**—would become the main focus of the women's rights movement in the coming years. But in 1848, many women reformers were willing to put their grievances aside for a time while they put all their efforts into the slavery question.

> We hold these truths to be self-evident: that all men and women are created equal; that they are endowed by their Creator with certain inalienable rights; that among these are life, liberty, and the pursuit of happiness; that to secure these rights governments are instituted, deriving their powers from the consent of the governed . . .
>
> The history of mankind is a history of repeated injuries and usurpation on the part of man toward woman, having in direct object the establishment of an absolute tyranny over her. To prove this, let facts be submitted to a candid world.
>
> —*The Declaration of Sentiments* (1848)

The Slavery Question

Andrew Jackson was a slaveholder. Like many Americans at the time, he saw nothing wrong with the practice of slavery, which was even in the Bible. But during the Age of Reform, many Americans began questioning the ownership of other human beings.

Conditions of the Enslaved

Most of the slaves on Southern plantations worked as field hands. Their lives were extremely hard. The plantation bell sounded before the sun rose. Slaves had to rise early and work all day in

Chapter 5 | The Age of Jackson   157

the fields until sunset. After dark they still had other chores. Many worked up to 18 hours a day for six days a week. Their only days off were Sundays, when slaves enjoyed recreation and went to church.

Workers were controlled by the threat of brutal physical punishment. Overseers carried rawhide leather whips. They cracked their whips as slaves worked in gangs or individually picking cotton. Any violation, like taking a rest or not picking enough cotton, could be punished with a severe whipping. Slaves could be branded, chained, or worse. Overseers were usually paid by how much they made their slaves produce.

Most slaves lived in simple wooden cabins of one or two rooms, often with dirt floors. They had no furniture and usually slept on piles of rags or straw. Each week, slaves were usually given some bacon, molasses, and corn meal for making hominy grits or corn bread. Some were permitted to grow their own vegetables. They were responsible for making their own meals in the few hours when they were not working for the plantation owner. Twice a year, they might be given linen clothes, or clothes of coarse cloth made in Northern factories especially for slaves.

Enslaved people had no rights. They were treated as property, not human beings. They were bought and sold by others in **slave auctions**, where they were often stripped and inspected as merchandise. In most Southern states, it was even against the law to teach a slave to read and write. Slaves could not marry without the permission of their masters. A slave owner could break up families by selling members of the same family to other owners.

The Historian's Apprentice

Solomon Northup was a free African American who was kidnapped and sold into slavery. He described plantation life in his book *Twelve Years a Slave*. His story was later made into a movie, which received the Academy Award for Best Picture in 2013. In the passage below, a "hand" is an enslaved field worker.

> "When a new hand . . . is sent for the first time to the field, he is whipped up smartly and made for that day to pick as fast as he can possibly. At night it is weighed, so that his capability in cotton picking is known. He must bring in the same weight each night following. If it falls short, it is considered evidence that he has been laggard [*slow*], and a greater or less number of lashes is the penalty. An ordinary day's work is two hundred pounds [of cotton]. A slave who is accustomed to picking is punished if he or she brings in a less quantity than that. . . .

> "The hands are required to be in the cotton field as soon as it is light in the morning, and, with the exception of ten or fifteen minutes, which is given them at noon to swallow their allowance of cold bacon, they are not permitted to be a moment idle [*at rest*] until it is too dark to see, and when the moon is full, they often times labor till the middle of the night. They do not dare to stop even at dinner time, nor return to the quarters, however late it be, until the order to halt is given by the driver [*overseer*]. The day's work over in the field, the baskets are "toted," or in other words, carried to the ginhouse, where the cotton is weighed. . . . This done, the labor

of the day is not yet ended, by any means. Each one must then attend to his respective chores. One feeds the mules, another the swine [*pigs*], another cuts the wood, and so forth; besides, the packing is all done by candlelight. Finally, at a late hour, they reach the quarters, sleepy and overcome with the long day's toil. . . ."

Read the passage above and discuss your answers to the following questions with a partner. Then share your answers with the class.

1. If you had been a slave, do you think you would have been able to survive such hard manual work?
2. If you had been an overseer, do you think you would have been able to treat other people so cruelly?
3. Do conditions like this still exist anywhere in the world today? If they do, do we have any responsibility to do something about it? Explain your opinion.
4. How were the conditions of slaves in the South described in this passage related to the rapid expansion of the textile industry in the Northeast and in Great Britain?

The Abolitionist Movement

During the Second Great Awakening, many Christian preachers taught that slavery was a sin. These preachers became early leaders of the **abolitionist movement**—the movement to abolish, or end, slavery. Free African Americans also became prominent abolitionists.

In 1831, William Lloyd Garrison began publishing an abolitionist journal, *The Liberator*, in Boston. Garrison called for an immediate end to slavery and its horrors. In December 1833, Garrison met with other abolitionists in Philadelphia to form the Anti-Slavery Society. A third of its founders were Quakers.

New anti-slavery societies soon sprang up across the North. They mailed pamphlets, printed articles, and sent petitions to Congress against slavery. In the 1830s, abolitionists also mailed anti-slavery flyers to the South. Southern post offices refused to deliver them, fearing they might lead to a **slave rebellion**.

One of the most important abolitionists was a former slave. **Frederick Douglass** escaped from slavery in Maryland. He began speaking at abolitionist meetings to tell about his former life as a slave. William Lloyd Garrison published his autobiography, which became an overnight sensation.

The Underground Railroad

Abolitionists helped organize escape routes for slaves. These routes were known as the "Underground Railroad." This was not a real railroad at all but a group of secret meeting points, escape routes, and safe places known as "stations." The Underground Railroad took enslaved people to free states or north to Canada. The stations were often barns, church cellars, or caves. Slaves

Chapter 5 | The Age of Jackson

The Historian's Apprentice

What arguments did abolitionists use in the struggle against slavery?

Read the following two excerpts with a partner or in a small group. Discuss the arguments they make. Fanny Kemble was an English actress who married a plantation owner from Georgia:

> "The Southern newspapers, with their advertisements of [African-American] sales and personal descriptions of fugitive slaves, supply details of misery that it would be difficult for imagination to exceed. Scorn [*contempt; looking down on someone*], derision [*mockery*], insult, menace—the handcuff, the lash [*whip*]—the tearing away of children from parents, of husbands from wives—the weary trudging [*walking slowly*] in droves [*large groups*] along the common highways, the labor of body, the despair of mind, the sickness of heart—these are the realities which belong to the system, and form the rule, rather than the exception, in the slave's experience. And this system exists here in this country of yours, which boasts itself the asylum [*shelter*] of the oppressed, the home of freedom, the one place in all the world where all men may find enfranchisement [*freedom*] from all thralldoms [*oppressions; subjections*] of mind, soul, or body—the land elect of liberty."
>
> —Fanny Kemble, *Journal of Residence on a Georgia Plantation*

1. What are the main ideas in this excerpt?
2. What impact would her description have had on readers?

---

usually travelled at night in small groups from station to station. "Stationmasters" gave them food. Those who led the escaping slaves were known as "conductors."

Because of the problem of runaway slaves, Congress passed a series of fugitive slave laws. These gave slave owners the right to have their "property"—the escaped slaves—returned. Slave catchers went to Northern states to track down and capture runaway slaves so that they could claim a reward.

This practice was greatly resented by Northerners. It was one of the targets of Harriet Beecher Stowe in her popular abolitionist novel *Uncle Tom's Cabin* (1852).

Resistance and Rebellion

Enslaved African Americans in the South also resisted slavery in a number of ways. The most common was by simply not working as hard as they could. Slaves might be uncooperative or feign ignorance. They could pretend to be sick or break their tools. They also resisted by preserving their own culture and traditions through story-telling, music, and dance. Another way of resisting slavery was by secretly learning to read and write. Less often, slaves might strike back at their overseer or owner, or even try to escape. The punishments for such actions could be very severe.

Chapter 5 | The Age of Jackson

In 1852, Frederick Douglass was invited to speak on the Fourth of July. Here is part of his speech:

"What to the Slave is the Fourth of July?"

"Fellow-citizens, pardon me, allow me to ask, why am I called upon to speak here today? What have I, or those I represent, to do with your national independence? Are the great principles of political freedom and of natural justice, embodied in that Declaration of Independence, extended to us? . . . But, such is not the state of the case. I say it with a sad sense of the disparity [*difference*] between us. I am not included [in] this glorious anniversary . . .

What, to the American slave, is your 4th of July? I answer: a day that reveals to him, more than all other days in the year, the gross injustice and cruelty to which he is the constant victim. To him, your celebration is a sham [*fake*]; your boasted liberty, an unholy license; your national greatness, swelling vanity; . . .your shouts of liberty and equality, hollow mockery . . . and hypocrisy—a thin veil to cover up crimes which would disgrace a nation of savages. There is not a nation on the earth guilty of practices, more shocking and bloody, than are the people of these United States, at this very hour."

—Frederick Douglass, Speech in Rochester, New York, July 4, 1852

1. What are the main ideas in this excerpt?
2. How are these ideas similar to those expressed by Fanny Kemble?
3. Why did Fanny Kemble and Frederick Douglass believe that Americans should abolish slavery?

The strongest form of resistance was rebellion. In August 1831, a slave named **Nat Turner** led a group of seventy slaves in a revolt in Virginia. Turner knew how to read and write, and he believed that he was receiving visions from God. After seeing a solar eclipse, he began preparing for an uprising to end slavery across the South. With a group of about seventy other slaves, Turner went from house to house freeing slaves and killing any white people they

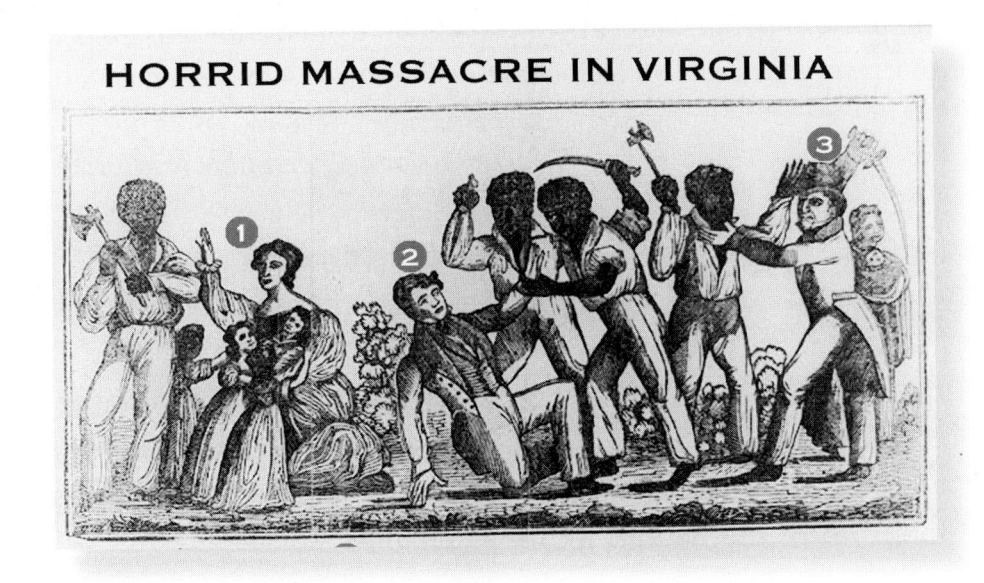

HORRID MASSACRE IN VIRGINIA

Chapter 5 | The Age of Jackson

came across. Turner's group killed about sixty whites, including women and children.

Eventually they were stopped by a militia force. More than fifty of the rebels were caught and hanged. Several hundred other slaves were killed in acts of violence. Nat Turner was captured two months later. Turner was tried and hanged. Nonetheless his rebellion caused a wave of fear among Southern slaveholders.

The Historian's Apprentice

Before Turner was executed, he gave a "confession" that was later published by a lawyer who spoke to him in jail. Read the excerpts below from Nat Turner's confession and from his conviction by the trial court.

> "I began to direct my attention to this great object, to fulfill the purpose for which, by this time, I felt assured I was intended. Knowing the influence I had obtained over the minds of my fellow servants, . . . by the communion of the Spirit whose revelations I often communicated to them, and they believed and said my wisdom came from God. I now began to prepare them for my purpose by telling them something was about to happen that would terminate [end] in fulfilling the great promise that had been made to me. About this time I was placed under an overseer, from whom I ran away, and after remaining in the woods thirty days, I returned, to the astonishment of the [African Americans] on the plantation . . . But the reason of my return was that the Spirit appeared to me and said I had my wishes directed to the things of this world, and not to the kingdom of heaven, and that I should return to the service of my earthly master . . . And about this time I had a vision and I saw white spirits and black spirits engaged in battle, and the sun was darkened, the thunder rolled in the heavens, and blood flowed in streams . . ."
>
> —Nat Turner, *The Confessions of Nat Turner*

> "You have been [accused] and tried before this court, and convicted of one of the highest crimes in our criminal code. You have been convicted of plotting in cold blood the indiscriminate destruction of men, of helpless women, and of infant children. The evidence before us leaves not a shadow of doubt, but that your hands were often imbrued [stained] in the blood of the innocent; and your own confession tells us that they were stained with the blood of a master . . ."
>
> —*Commonwealth v. Nat Turner*

1. Compare the different points of view expressed in these excerpts.
2. How did Turner see his actions? How were these acts interpreted by the court?

The rise of the abolitionist movement, the fear of slave rebellion, and the enforcement of fugitive slave laws brought the question of slavery to the forefront of the nation. By the 1850s, the future of slavery had become the leading question in American politics. You will learn more about the effects of this in the next chapter.

For the Georgia Milestones EOC Assessment, you should know that:

- ☐ Jacksonian Democracy expanded suffrage to all adult white males when states dropped their property qualifications. Political parties began holding nominating conventions to pick their candidates.

- ☐ President Jackson saw himself as the champion of the "common man"; however, Jacksonian Democracy did not extend to enslaved African Americans, Indians, or women.

- ☐ The Nullification Crisis took place when South Carolina claimed the right to nullify the Tariff of 1832 and seemed likely to secede, until President Jackson threatened the use of force to uphold the Union.

- ☐ President Jackson asked Congress to pass the Indian Removal Act, requiring all Indian nations, including the Cherokee, to move west of the Mississippi River.

- ☐ The North, South, and West were all affected by the rise of industry: The North became a center of commerce and manufacturing, the West grew food for the rest of the country, and the South grew cotton and other cash crops for factory production.

- ☐ Different sections of the country became linked together by the "Transportation Revolution" (roads, canals, steamboats, railroads, and telegraphs). Their economies grew more interdependent.

- ☐ Henry Clay proposed his "American System" to unite the country: a tariff would protect Northern industries and yield revenues to finance internal improvements in the West, the South would benefit by selling its cotton to Northern manufacturers, and the National Bank would continue to promote stability and growth. Clay's plans were opposed by President Jackson, who thought Clay's system gave powers to the federal government that belonged to the states.

- ☐ The Second Great Awakening encouraged social reform movements, including temperance (the campaign to prohibit alcoholic beverages), tax-payer supported public education, voting rights for women (women's suffrage), and abolitionism (the movement to end slavery).

- ☐ The invention of the cotton gin and the demand of factories for raw cotton led to the spread of slavery in the South, where slaves lived in terrible conditions.

- ☐ With the rise of abolitionism, slavery become a major issue in American politics.

- ☐ Slave rebellions created a wave of fear among white Southern landholders.

Chapter 5 | The Age of Jackson

Name _____

Complete the following chart.

Name or Term	Description/Significance
Jacksonian Democracy	
Nullification Crisis	
Indian Removal Act	
Henry Clay's "American System"	
Second Great Awakening	
Industrial Revolution	
Transportation Revolution	

Name or Term	Description/Significance
Telegraph	
Cotton Gin	
Temperance Movement	
"Common School" Movement	
Women's Suffrage	
Abolitionist Movement	
Nat Turner's Rebellion	

Name _____

The chart below lists some of the main events during the Presidency of Andrew Jackson and the Age of Reform. Create your own illustrated timeline using some of these events. First, decide on the theme of your timeline and create a title. Then, choose those events that relate to your theme. Finally, make your own illustrations.

May 1828	"Tariff of Abominations"
Nov 1828	Jackson elected as President
March 1829	Inauguration of Jackson
April 1830	Toasts at Jefferson Day Dinner
May 1830	Jackson signs Indian Removal Act; B&O Railroad begins operation
Sept 1830	Charles Grandison Finney's Rochester Revival
Jan 1831	William Lloyd Garrison starts *The Liberator*
March 1831	*Cherokee Nation v. Georgia*
March 1832	*Worcester v. Georgia*
August 1831	Nat Turner's Rebellion
July 1832	Congress passes bill to renew bank charter; Jackson vetoes bank bill
July 1832	Jackson signs Tariff of 1832
Nov 1832	Jackson re-elected; South Carolina passes Ordinance of Nullification
March 1833	Jackson signs Force Bill; Compromise Tariff of 1833; South Carolina repeals Ordinance of Nullification
June 1833	Jackson removes federal funds from Second Bank of the US
Dec 1835	A group of Cherokees sign treaty with Jackson
March 1837	Jackson leaves Washington; Martin Van Buren becomes President
June 1837	Horace Mann becomes Secretary of Board of Education
Summer 1838	US Army begins rounding up Cherokee Indians, starting the "Trail of Tears"; they begin their march that winter
Sept 1838	Frederick Douglass escapes from slavery
March 1841	Dorothea Dix visits women's prison in Massachusetts
July 1848	Seneca Falls Convention for Women's Rights

The Age of Jackson

Conditions of the Enslaved
- Eli Whitney's "cotton gin" leads to an expansion of slavery in the South
- Threat of whipping and other punishments used to force the enslaved to work
- The enslaved live in bare cottages and eat restricted diet; not permitted to learn to read or write or conduct lawful marriages
- Abolitionists wanted to abolish (*end*) slavery
- The enslaved resisted by preserving their traditions, by not working as hard as they might, by learning to read and write; sometimes slaves, like Nat Turner, even rebelled

The Second Great Awakening
- Increased religious fervor
- Participants saw many abuses, like drinking and slavery, as sinful

Social Reform Movements
- Promoted by the Second Great Awakening
- **Temperance:** Goal to prohibit alcoholic beverages
- **Public Education:** Goal to provide free public education by trained teachers to all elementary school children
- **Women's suffrage:** Goal was to give women the right to vote
- "Declaration of Sentiments" at the Seneca Falls Convention (1848)

Slavery Question

Nullification Crisis

John C. Calhoun sees the nation as a "compact" of states: states have the right to nullify laws or secede from the union

South Carolina passes the Ordinance of Nullification, nullifying the Tariff of 1832

Jackson threatens force and South Carolina backs down

Indian Removal Act (1830)

Requires all Indian tribes to move west of the Mississippi River

The Cherokee resist through the courts
- Cherokee win court cases against Georgia
- Jackson signs treaty with a minority of Cherokee leaders
- Cherokee forced to move in fall and winter of 1838, resulting in the "Trail of Tears"

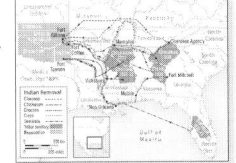

Linking the Nation Together

Industrial Revolution—affected all three sections of the nation
- The North became a manufacturing center
- The West became the nation's bread basket—growing food
- The South grew cotton and other raw materials for factories

Transportation Revolution
Better roads, canals, steamboats, trains, and the telegraph linked different sections more closely

Henry Clay's "American System": Favored the tariff to protect Northern industries and to provide revenue for internal improvements in the West; also supported the National Bank

Presidency of Andrew Jackson (1829–1837)

"Jacksonian Democracy"

States end property qualifications: Expanded suffrage to all adult white males

Party nominating conventions and new campaigning techniques

Rotation of officeholders ("spoils system")

Appeal to the "common man"

Jackson's war against the National Bank

Chapter 5 | The Age of Jackson

What Do You Know?

SSUSH7a

1. In 1828, Andrew Jackson was elected President by a large majority of voters. Which change in American politics contributed to his victory?

    A. The Federalist Party had dissolved.

    B. The Electoral College had been abolished.

    C. Political candidates refused to campaign actively for office.

    D. Many states had recently ended their property qualifications for voting.

SSUSH7a

2. Examine the excerpt to answer the question.

    > It is to be regretted that the rich and powerful too often bend the acts of government to their selfish purposes.....[W]hen the laws ... grant ... exclusive privileges, to make the rich richer and the potent more powerful, the humble members of society—the farmers, mechanics and laborers—who have neither the time nor the means of securing like favors to themselves, have a right to complain of the injustice of their Government.
    >
    > —President Andrew Jackson to the Senate, July 1832

    What action did President Jackson take in support of the beliefs expressed in this excerpt?

    A. Relocating Indians to territories west of the Mississippi River

    B. Opposing Vice President John C. Calhoun's doctrine of nullification

    C. Eliminating all property requirements for voting in elections

    D. Refusing to renew the charter of the Second Bank of the United States

SSUSH7b

3. Which statement BEST describes how American society was affected by Eli Whitney's cotton gin?

    A. It led Northern factories to move to Southern states.

    B. It made Americans less dependent on imports from Great Britain.

    C. It encouraged Southern farmers to grow a larger variety of crops to feed the West.

    D. It encouraged the spread of slavery in much of the South to supply Northern factories.

SSUSH7a

4. Use the cartoon on the right to answer the question.

   Part A

   Which legacy of President Jackson is addressed in the cartoon?

   A. the rotation of officeholders in government
   B. the removal of the Cherokee Indians to Oklahoma
   C. the preservation of the Union in the Nullification Crisis
   D. the destruction of the Second Bank of the United States

   —Thomas Nast, 1877

   Part B

   How did President Jackson defend the system shown in the cartoon?

   A. He explained that this system would increase the power of the federal government.
   B. He argued that ordinary citizens should be able to participate in government by holding public office.
   C. He stated that those who had worked hard to elect a candidate deserved to receive some payback.
   D. He claimed he needed to reward his supporters with public offices in order to hold his political party together.

SSUSH7a

5. Use the excerpt below to answer the question.

   > The . . . speedy removal [of the Indians] . . . will place a dense and civilized population in large tracts of land now occupied by a few savage hunters . . . What good man would [not] prefer a country . . . filled with all the blessings of liberty, civilization, and religion?

   Based on the statement, what conclusion can be made about President Jackson's view of lands occupied by Indians?

   A. He believed white settlers and Indians could successfully use these lands together.
   B. He believed the Indians had destroyed the soils of these lands, which were of little value.
   C. He believed white settlers would make better use of these lands than the Indians had done.
   D. He believed Indian lands were not useful to white settlers and the Indians should be left alone.

Chapter 5 | The Age of Jackson

SSUSH7a

6. Use the table below to answer the question.

May 1828	Tariff of Abominations
December 1828	John C. Calhoun's Exposition and Protest
January 1830	Webster-Hayne Debate
May 1830	President Jackson's Toast to the Union
July 1832	Tariff of 1832
November 1832	South Carolina's "Ordinance of Nullification"
December 1832	President Jackson's "Proclamation to the People of South Carolina"
March 1833	Force Bill
March 1833	South Carolina repeals Ordinance of Nullification

Which conflict did these events MAINLY concern?

A. Large vs. small states
B. Congress vs. the President
C. States' rights vs. federal supremacy
D. Northern bankers and merchants vs. the "common man"

SSUSH7b

7. Which statement BEST describes the impact of canals on the United States in the early 1800s?

A. They led to a decline in American exports to European countries.
B. They caused New York City to lose its position as a manufacturing center.
C. They helped the Midwest to become a major center of American textile production.
D. They made it easier for Midwestern farmers to ship their crops to cities in the Northeast.

SSUSH7c

8. How did the "Second Great Awakening" promote social reform?

A. Participants believed that conditions on Earth could not be improved.
B. Participants grew tired of religion and turned to social reform instead.
C. Participants wanted to apply Christian ethics to important social issues.
D. Participants were no longer concerned with their own personal salvation.

SSUSH7c

9. Which statement identifies the goal of the temperance movement?

A. The sale of alcoholic beverages should be outlawed.
B. African Americans should no longer be held in slavery.
C. Conditions in prisons and hospitals should be improved.
D. Factory workers should receive better pay for shorter hours.

SSUSH7c

10. Use the excerpt to answer the question.

> *Resolved, that all laws which prevent woman from occupying such a station in society as her conscience shall dictate, or which place her in a position inferior to that of man, are contrary to the great precept of nature and therefore of no force or authority.*
> —Seneca Falls Convention, "Declaration of Sentiments" (1848)

Based on this excerpt, to which laws did the signers of the Declaration of Sentiments specifically object?

A. laws giving rights to men but not to women
B. laws forcing the migration of the American Indians
C. laws requiring the return of "fugitive slaves" to the South
D. laws making it difficult for workers to organize into unions

SSUSH7c

11. Examine the excerpt to answer the question.

> *Education . . . is a great equalizer of the conditions of men . . . [I]t prevents being poor.*
> —Horace Mann, 1848

Based on the excerpt, what goal did Mann believe public education should achieve?

A. a society in which poor as well as rich children enjoy opportunities
B. a society in which there are no cultural differences between ethnic groups
C. a society in which slavery is preserved in the South without spreading to the North
D. a society in which the wealthiest and best educated citizens maintain control over government

SSUSH7c

12. Use the table to answer the question.

1817	Thomas Galludet establishes the first school teaching deaf children to read and write.
1821	Emma Willard opens one of the first academies offering advanced education to women.
1833	Oberlin College starts the first coeducational classes.
1837	Horace Mann is appointed Secretary to the Massachusetts Board of Education.
1839	Horace Mann starts the first teacher-training institute.

What inference can BEST be made from this table?

A. Most teachers were well educated in 1839.
B. Every American citizen could read and write by 1839.
C. Few educational changes took place in the early 1800s.
D. Educational opportunities for Americans expanded in the 1820s and 1830s.

Chapter 5 | The Age of Jackson 171

SSUSH7d

13. How did the Second Great Awakening encourage the abolitionist movement?

    A. Most participants decided to give up drinking alcoholic beverages.

    B. Protestant preachers declared that the practice of slavery was sinful.

    C. Defenders of slavery pointed to numerous examples of slavery in the Bible.

    D. Ministers argued that slaves were better treated than factory workers in the North.

SSUSH7b

14. Use the diagram to answer the questions.

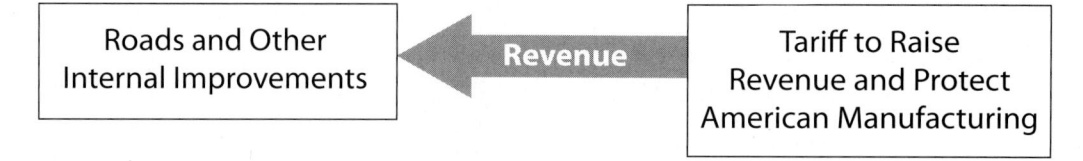

    [Roads and Other Internal Improvements] ← Revenue — [Tariff to Raise Revenue and Protect American Manufacturing]

    ### Part A

    What would be the BEST title for this diagram?

    A. Alexander Hamilton's Financial Plan

    B. Jacksonian Democracy

    C. Henry Clay's "American System"

    D. Monroe Doctrine

    ### Part B

    Which two sections of the United States would have MOST gained from this program?

    A. North and South

    B. South and West

    C. North and West

    D. Northwest and Southeast

SSUSH7d

15. How did the rise of abolitionism and slave rebellions make slavery into a major issue in American politics?

    A. Poor white farmers feared they would be sold into slavery.

    B. Northern workers feared that slaves would take their jobs.

    C. Southern slaveholders feared that slavery would be abolished.

    D. Freed slaves living in the North demanded reparations from Southern state governments.

CHAPTER 6 The Civil War

SSUSH8 How did slavery, increasing North-South divisions, and westward expansion lead to the outbreak of the Civil War?

- a. What was the impact of the Missouri Compromise on the admission of states from the Louisiana Territory?

- b. How did James K. Polk's Presidency fulfill the goal of Manifest Destiny, including the annexation of Texas and the division of the Oregon Territory?

- c. What was the impact of the Mexican War on growing sectionalism?

- d. How did the Compromise of 1850 arise out of territorial expansion and population growth?

- e. What were the roles of the Kansas-Nebraska Act, the failure of popular sovereignty, the Supreme Court decision of *Scott v. Sandford,* John Brown's raid on Harpers Ferry, and the election of 1860 in leading to the Civil War?

SSUSH9 What were the roles of key events, issues, and individuals in the Civil War?

- a. What was the importance of the growing economic disparity between the North and the South, taking into account population, railroad lines, and industrial output?

- b. What were President Lincoln's purposes in using emergency powers to suspend *habeas corpus,* in issuing the Emancipation Proclamation, and in delivering the Gettysburg Address and his Second Inaugural Address?

- c. What were the influences of Ulysses S. Grant, Robert E. Lee, Thomas "Stonewall" Jackson, William T. Sherman, and Jefferson Davis on the course and outcome of the Civil War?

- d. What was the importance of Fort Sumter, Antietam, Vicksburg, Gettysburg, and the destruction of Atlanta to the course of the Civil War, and what was the impact of geography on these battles?

Names and Terms You Should Know

Missouri Compromise
James K. Polk
Manifest Destiny
Annexation
Texas
Oregon Territory
Mexican War
Compromise of 1850
Kansas-Nebraska Act
Popular sovereignty
Dred Scott
Scott v. Sandford
John Brown
Harpers Ferry
Abraham Lincoln
Election of 1860

Habeas corpus
Jefferson Davis
Fort Sumter
Robert E. Lee
Thomas "Stonewall" Jackson
Battle of Antietam
Emancipation Proclamation
Battle of Gettysburg
Gettysburg Address
Vicksburg
Ulysses S. Grant
William T. Sherman
Atlanta
Sherman's March to the Sea
Lincoln's Second Inaugural Address

Georgia "Peaches" of Wisdom

1. Under the Missouri Compromise (1820), Missouri was admitted as a slave state, Maine was admitted as a free state, and slavery was prohibited in the lands of the Louisiana Purchase above the southern border of Missouri, except in Missouri itself.

2. In 1844, James Polk made the annexation of Texas the focus of his election campaign. Polk believed in "Manifest Destiny—that it was the fate of the United States to extend across the continent, from the Atlantic to the Pacific. After Polk was elected, Congress invited Texas to join the nation. In addition, the Oregon Territory was divided between Britain and the United States.

3. A dispute over the border of Texas led to the outbreak of the Mexican War in 1846. The war lasted two years. The Treaty of Guadalupe Hidalgo gave the United States almost half of Mexico's existing territory.

4. Sectionalism describes the loyalty many Americans felt towards their own region—the North, South or West—rather than to the country as a whole. The acquisition of new territories from Mexico increased sectional differences by raising a new issue: should these territories permit slavery?

5. In the Compromise of 1850, California was admitted as a free state, the system of "popular sovereignty" was applied to other new lands taken from Mexico, and a stricter fugitive slave law was enacted.

6. The Kansas-Nebraska Act (1854) overturned the Missouri Compromise by applying the system of popular sovereignty to all the remaining territories of the Louisiana Purchase. The Republican Party was founded to oppose the extension of slavery. Pro-slavery and abolitionist groups sent settlers into Kansas to influence the vote, leading to the violence of "Bleeding Kansas" (1855–1856). In the case of *Dred Scott v. Sandford* (1857), the Supreme Court ruled that African Americans were not citizens and had no rights, and that Congress could not limit the property rights of slaveholders. The abolitionist John Brown attempted to trigger slave revolts across the South by seizing arms at the federal arsenal at Harpers Ferry, but his effort failed.

7. In the Presidential election of 1860, Republican candidate Abraham Lincoln won the election with 39% of the popular vote. South Carolina and six other Southern states immediately seceded and formed the Confederate States of America. Jefferson Davis became the President of the Confederacy.

8. When Lincoln sent supplies to Fort Sumter, South Carolina fired on the fort, beginning the Civil War. Rather than fight fellow Southerners, four more states seceded.

9. The North had many advantages: a larger population, more railroad lines, greater industrial output, and naval power. The South had skilled military leaders, such as Robert E. Lee and Thomas "Stonewall" Jackson, and the fact that white Southerners were fighting to preserve their way of life.

10. In the early campaigns, the South stopped attempted Northern invasions. Lincoln suspended rights to *habeas corpus*. When General Robert E. Lee attempted to advance into Maryland, he was stopped at the Battle of Antietam. The North imposed a naval blockade of the South and gradually took control of the Mississippi River.

11. In September 1862, Lincoln issued the Emancipation Proclamation, which announced the freeing of slaves in states still in rebellion on January 1, 1863.

12. The turning point of the war was reached in 1863, when the North stopped Southern forces at Gettysburg and General Ulysses S. Grant captured Vicksburg, giving the Union full control of the Mississippi River. Lincoln soon put Grant in command of Union forces. General William T. Sherman's destruction of Atlanta and "March to the Sea" helped Lincoln win re-election, further divided the South, and destroyed Southern farms, towns, and railroad lines.

13. In April 1865, Lee surrendered to Grant, ending the war. Less than a week later, President Lincoln was assassinated. The Civil War ended slavery, preserved the Union, and strengthened the federal government.

Chapter 6 | The Civil War

The Civil War was the most divisive conflict in American history. More Americans died in this war than in any other. The wounds left by the Civil War took decades to heal. In this chapter, you will examine both the events preceding the conflict and as well as the course of the war itself.

Roots of the Conflict

What factors could have led citizens of the same nation to take up arms against one another as enemies? Historians often look at three factors as contributing to the outbreak of the Civil War: sectionalism, slavery, and westward expansion.

As you learned in the last chapter, the three main sections of the country—the North, South, and West—were linked but developed quite different economies and societies. The existence of slavery was challenged by abolitionists and slave rebellions just as the practice of slavery was expanding in the South to produce more raw cotton for factories. The western expansion of the United States then posed a crucial question to all Americans: should new territories become "free" or "slave" states? Southerners and Northerners gave different answers to this question, sparking controversy.

At first, American leaders were able to achieve skillful compromises to keep the nation together. The Missouri Compromise in 1820 and the Compromise of 1850 were two dazzling achievements in keeping the different sections of the country united. But starting with the Kansas-Nebraska Act in 1854, the system of compromise started falling apart.

The Missouri Compromise (1820)

In 1819, Missouri applied for admission as a slave state, which would have upset the balance of free and slave states in the Senate.

Henry Clay, the "Great Compromiser," came up with an ingenious solution. At this time, Maine was part of Massachusetts, but it was separated from Massachusetts by other states. Clay proposed that Maine should be admitted

The Missouri Compromise of 1820

Slave and Free States in the U.S. Senate

Year	1789	1800	1812	1817	Dec 1819
Free States	5	8	9	10	11
Slave States	8	9	9	10	11

as an independent, free state while Missouri was admitted as a slave state. This would preserve the existing balance in the Senate between the free and slave states.

Clay further proposed that slavery should be prohibited in the lands of the Louisiana Territory above the latitude line 36° 30' North, except for in the State of Missouri itself. This latitude, the southern border of Missouri, became known as the "Missouri Compromise" line. Congress approved Clay's plan and the "Missouri Compromise" kept the country at peace.

The Texas Republic

The following year, Mexico achieved its independence from Spain. The Mexican government invited American settlers to live in its northern province of Texas, which was underpopulated. When these settlers failed to convert to Catholicism and their numbers began to grow too quickly, the Mexican government prohibited further immigration from the United States. Americans in Texas protested. They demanded greater self-government and rose up in rebellion in 1835. Mexico sent an army, commanded by General Santa Anna, to defeat the defiant Texans. Santa Anna captured the Alamo, a mission in San Antonio that was defended by a small force of almost 200 Texans. Nearly all of the defenders perished in the fighting. In nearby Goliad, a group of Texans surrendered to Santa Anna's troops and were shot in captivity.

Infuriated by the reports from San Antonio and Goliad, Texans declared their independence in 1836. They appointed Sam Houston, a former Governor of Tennessee and a friend of Andrew Jackson's, to command their army. Houston spent the winter and early spring training Texan troops. He then surprised Santa Anna while Mexican troops were having a midday rest. Santa Anna was captured and agreed to recognize the independence of Texas to secure his own release.

Once Texans obtained their independence from Mexico, they asked to join the United States. Surprisingly, Congress refused their request. Many Congressmen feared that if the United States annexed Texas, it might lead to war with Mexico. Congressmen from Northern states did not wish to see a new slave state added to the union. Texas remained an independent republic for the next eight years.

James Polk and Manifest Destiny

The question of the **annexation** of Texas came up again in the 1844 Presidential election. Candidate **James Polk** believed in the concept of "**Manifest Destiny**"—that it was the obvious "destiny," or fate, of the United States to extend from the Atlantic to the Pacific.

> Supporters of "Manifest Destiny" urged westward expansion for a variety of reasons: they believed it was God's will that America should spread from coast to coast; expansion would make the United States more secure against foreign attack; Americans felt they had a responsibility to spread Christianity and democracy; and finally, Americans would gain access to valuable land and natural resources, helping their economy to grow.

Columbia, a personification of the United States' westward expansion

Polk won a landslide victory in the election of 1844. Soon after his election, Congress invited Texas to join the United States. Texans quickly accepted and Texas was admitted as the 28th state in December 1845.

Polk also settled an important disagreement with Great Britain over the control of the **Oregon Territory**. This territory was being occupied jointly by both Britain and the United States. Under the new agreement, the territory was divided at the 49° N. latitude. This extended the existing border between Canada and the United States westward to the Pacific Ocean. It gave Americans the future states of Washington, Oregon, and Idaho, while Britain kept British Columbia. It meant that in the north, the United States now extended from the Atlantic to the Pacific, fulfilling part of what many saw as its "Manifest Destiny."

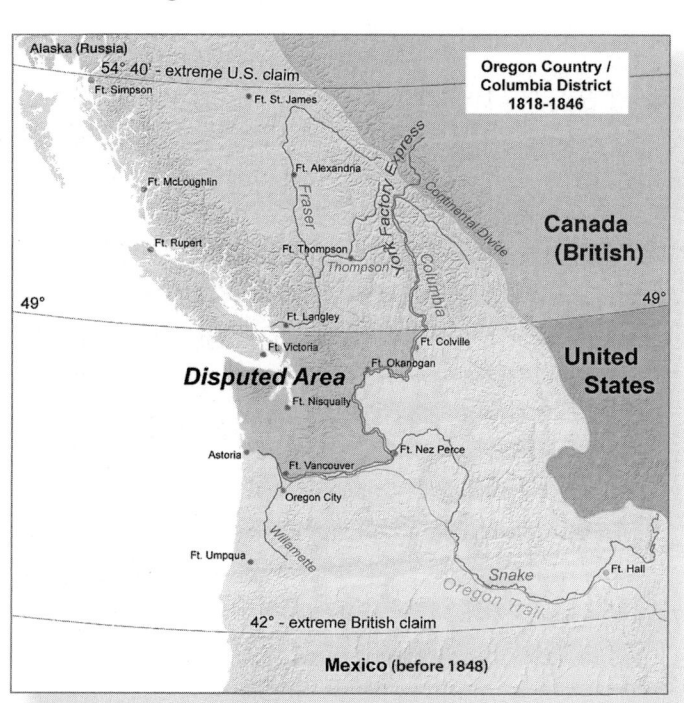

The Mexican War

President Polk was already thinking of other ways to add more territory to the United States. He had his eyes on the Mexican provinces of Upper California and New Mexico. He knew these northern borderlands were under-populated, as Texas had been, and were far from the center of Mexican national life in Mexico City.

There was also a dispute over the border between Texas and Mexico. Now that Texas was part of the United States, this border had to be clearly defined. Mexicans believed their border with Texas was at the Nueces River. Americans claimed that it was farther south at the Rio Grande. Polk sent troops into the contested area between the two rivers. From the Mexican point of view, Americans had entered Mexican soil. When Mexicans fired on American troops, Polk persuaded Congress to declare war.

American troops quickly occupied Mexico's northern border provinces, while the U.S. Navy captured towns in California on the West Coast. But the Mexican government still refused to surrender any of its territory to the United States. Polk therefore ordered an invasion force to march straight into the heart of Mexico. American forces landed at Vera Cruz and marched west towards the capital city. Mexican forces were commanded by General Santa Anna, who made a number of strategic mistakes. When American troops entered Mexico

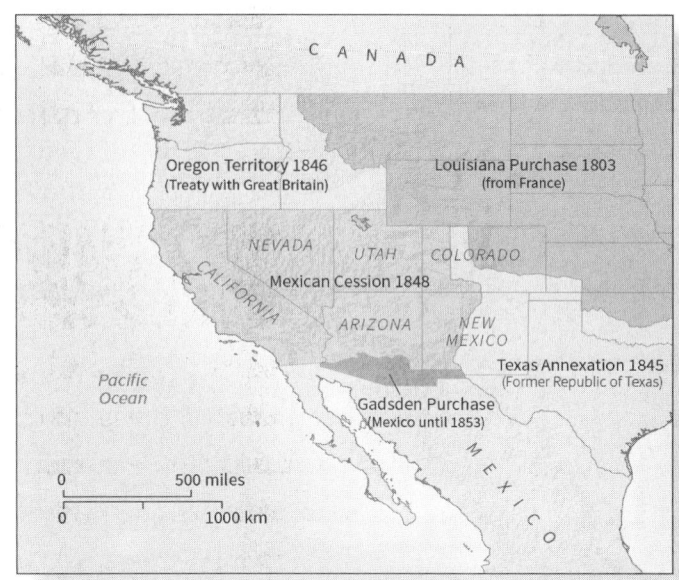

City, the Mexican government finally surrendered. The Treaty of Guadalupe Hidalgo, ending the war, was signed in February 1848. The United States paid Mexico $15 million for the territories known as the "Mexican Cession." These included the present states of California, Utah, Arizona, and Nevada, and parts of Colorado and New Mexico. The annexation of these territories raised an important new question: would these territories permit slavery and later be admitted as free or slave states?

The Growth of Sectionalism

"Sectionalism" refers to the fact that by the 1850s, many Americans were feeling a greater pride in and loyalty to their own "section" (or region) of the country than they did towards the nation as a whole.

Each section had its own interests and ways of life:

- The **South** had slavery—its "peculiar (unusual) institution"—long after slavery had ended in the other two sections. The invention of the cotton gin and the increased demand for raw cotton from factories led to an expansion of slavery in the South. As many as four million people—about one-third of the entire population of the South— were enslaved African Americans. Most of them worked on the large plantations of the wealthiest Southern landowners.

- The **West** (or Northwest) was made up of small, independent farmers. It had become the "bread basket" of the United States. Its farmers grew grain that was shipped by river and canal to the Northeast and the South.

- The **North** (or Northeast) was the center of American manufacturing and trade. It was also the home to the nation's largest cities.

People in each section of the country wanted policies favorable to their own interests. Northerners wanted tariffs to protect their manufactured goods from British competition. They opposed the extension of slavery to the West. Southerners opposed high tariffs and favored the westward extension of their system of slave labor. They were strong supporters of states' rights.

Chapter 6 | The Civil War

The United States in early 1850

As we have seen, the favorable outcome of the Mexican War raised the new question of whether slavery should be extended to the new lands the United States had gained. Bitter feelings over this issue contributed to the further growth of sectionalism.

The Compromise of 1850

Shortly after the Mexican War, gold was discovered in California. People came flooding into the area. By 1850, the population of California reached 93,000 and the territory applied for admission as a state.

The admission of California as a free state would again have upset the balance between free and slave states in the Senate. Once more, a careful compromise was worked out. Both Henry Clay and Illinois Senator Stephen Douglas helped to arrange it:

- California was admitted as a free state.
- The rest of the Mexican Cession was divided into two territories: New Mexico and Utah. The system of "**popular sovereignty**" was to be applied to them. "Popular sovereignty" means letting the people decide. It is a basic principle of our democratic system of government. Senator Stephen Douglas from Illinois came up with the idea of applying popular sovereignty to the slave question in the Mexican Cession. He said that the people living in a particular territory should decide for themselves whether or not to permit slavery. Douglas felt this would restore calm by taking the slave question out of the hands of Congress and placing it back in the hands of the people.
- The boundaries of Texas were settled.
- Slavery was permitted to continue in Washington, D.C. This meant that Southern Congressmen could continue to bring their slaves to the capital as servants. The slave trade, however, was prohibited there: enslaved people could no longer be bought and sold like merchandise in the nation's capital.

180   Chapter 6 | The Civil War

The Compromise of 1850

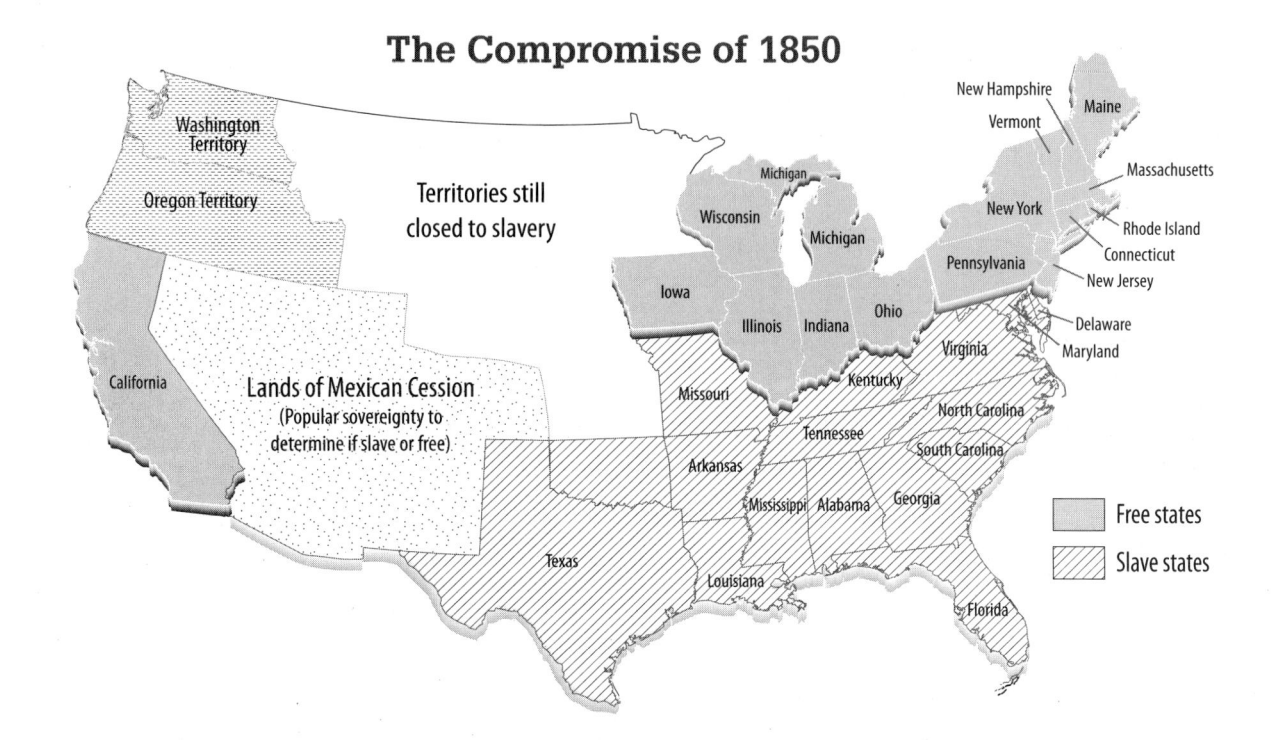

Map showing free states, slave states, Lands of Mexican Cession (Popular sovereignty to determine if slave or free), and Territories still closed to slavery.

▶ As the final part of the compromise, a stricter fugitive slave law was enacted. The new law required states in the North to provide greater help to Southerners trying to recover their runaway slaves.

The admission of California as a free state did upset the balance of free and slave states in the Senate. However, the fact that popular sovereignty would be applied to the rest of the Mexican Cession meant that there was hope among Southerners that the balance would be restored in the future. In the meantime, Southerners had gained other advantages from the compromise, especially the stricter fugitive slave law. This new fugitive slave law was greatly resented in the North.

The Road to War

The peaceful relations between the different sections of the country achieved by the Compromise of 1850 did not last. Over the next decade, a series of events pushed Americans increasingly apart, ending in the Civil War.

The Kansas-Nebraska Act

In 1854, Senator Stephen Douglas from Illinois introduced the **Kansas-Nebraska Act**. Douglas wanted to win Southern support for a railroad line from the Midwest to California. He could only win the support he needed in a crucial Senate committee by overturning the Missouri Compromise.

The Kansas-Nebraska Act divided the Nebraska Territory, a part of the Louisiana Purchase, into two smaller territories: Nebraska and Kansas. The act then repealed the Missouri Compromise by applying the principle of "popular sovereignty" to both of these territories. This meant that slavery might again be possible in the Louisiana Purchase above the "Missouri Compromise" line, where it had been forbidden

Chapter 6 | The Civil War

for more than thirty years. Senator Douglas again argued that "**popular sovereignty**" offered the most democratic way of resolving the slavery question. He continued to think it would remove the issue from national politics. Instead of Congress deciding which territories would permit slavery, residents in the territories would decide for themselves. Many Northerners were shocked at this turn of events.

Birth of the Republican Party

A new political party, the **Republican Party**, was formed in 1854 in reaction to the Kansas-Nebraska Act. Republicans opposed the extension (*spread*) of slavery to any new territories. They could accept slavery where it was, but they could not stand to see it spread any further.

"Bleeding Kansas"

Because of the Kansas-Nebraska Act, the question of whether Kansas would have slavery was to be decided by popular vote. Both pro-slavery and anti-slavery forces tried to influence the outcome. Each side brought its own group of settlers to Kansas. By 1855, two rival state governments had formed. One was pro-slavery and the other was against it. The federal government eventually had to send in troops to restore order.

The *Dred Scott* Decision

In 1857, the U.S. Supreme Court tried to resolve the slavery question with its decision in the case of *Dred Scott v. Sandford*.

Dred Scott was a Missouri slave. Scott lived with his owner, an army officer, for several years in Illinois, a free state. They had also been in a Northern territory where slavery was prohibited. During this time, Scott married another slave and had two children. After the Scotts returned with their owner to Missouri, they sued for their freedom. They claimed that since they had lived in a free state, they were no longer slaves. The Scotts were actually freed in 1850, but the Missouri Supreme Court reversed the decision. The Scotts then appealed their case to the United States Supreme Court. Scott's wife dropped out of the suit to make the case easier.

Dred Scott

Five years later, the Supreme Court reached its decision. Chief Justice Roger Taney ruled that because Dred Scott was an African American, he was not a U.S. citizen. Therefore, he had no right to sue in federal court. According to Taney, a slave was not a person at all but a piece of property that belonged to someone else.

> "[African Americans] had no rights which the white man was bound to respect; and [an African American] might justly and lawfully be reduced to slavery for his benefit. He was bought and sold and treated as an ordinary article of merchandise, whenever profit could be made by it.
>
> [Concerning the Declaration of Independence,] it is too clear for dispute, that the enslaved African race were not intended to be included, and formed no part of the people who framed and adopted this declaration...."
>
> —Chief Justice Roger Taney,
> *Dred Scott v. Sandford* (1857)

A slaveholder, on the other hand, was a citizen and therefore enjoyed certain rights. These rights included the right to own property. On these grounds, the Supreme Court held that the prohibition of slavery in Northern territories by the Missouri Compromise had been unconstitutional. Congress did not have the right to take away a slaveholder's property or to limit his property rights. The decision equally implied that a slaveholder's rights could not be restricted by "popular sovereignty."

This ruling by U.S. Supreme Court Justices, most of whom came from the South, raised a storm of protest across the North. Fortunately for Dred Scott, his owners freed him two months after the decision was announced.

Abraham Lincoln, a successful frontier lawyer, debated the impact of the *Dred Scott* decision with Stephen Douglas in the 1858 election contest for U.S. Senator from Illinois. Lincoln argued that the Supreme Court's decision threatened to permit slavery to spread throughout the nation. Douglas argued in favor of his system of "popular sovereignty" and won re-election to the Senate.

The Historian's Apprentice

What were the roles of the Kansas-Nebraska Act and the *Dred Scott* decision in the breaking down of earlier compromises on the slavery question? Discuss the answer to this question with a partner and share your ideas with the class.

John Brown's Raid on Harpers Ferry

John Brown was a white abolitionist. He believed that he had been chosen by God to end slavery. Brown moved to "Bleeding Kansas," where he fought and killed pro-slavery agitators. Later, Brown drew up plans for launching slave revolts across the South. In 1859, he captured a federal arsenal (*a place where weapons are kept*) in Harpers Ferry as the first step in a general revolt. Brown seized weapons to give to slaves, but no other uprisings joined his. Brown was captured by federal troops commanded by Colonel Robert E. Lee. Brown was tried for treason and hanged, but many abolitionists saw him as a martyr in the struggle against slavery.

The Election of Abraham Lincoln

In the Presidential election of 1860, the Republican Party nominated **Abraham Lincoln**. Democrats were divided. Southern Democrats nominated Vice President John C. Breckinridge and Northern Democrats nominated Stephen Douglas. Another new party, the Constitutional Union, was made up of Southerners who supported the Union. They nominated John Bell.

With all of these candidates, the national vote was greatly divided. Lincoln was able to win the election with only 39% of the popular vote. Not a single Southern state gave its electoral votes to Lincoln.

Popular vote in the Presidential Election of 1860

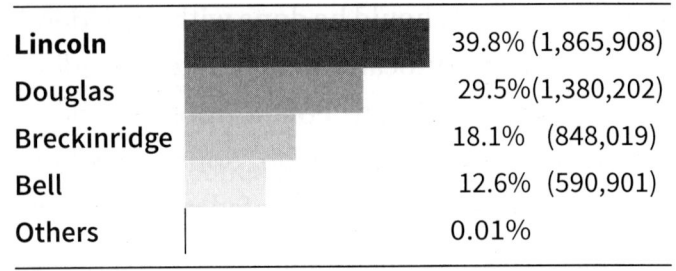

Candidate	Percentage (Votes)
Lincoln	39.8% (1,865,908)
Douglas	29.5% (1,380,202)
Breckinridge	18.1% (848,019)
Bell	12.6% (590,901)
Others	0.01%

Secession of the South

As soon as Lincoln was elected, South Carolina announced its secession from the Union. Six other Southern states, all from the "Deep South"—including Georgia—quickly followed.

Chapter 6 | The Civil War

Name _____

Complete the following chart.

Name or term	Description/Significance
Sectionalism	Restriction of interest. Loyalty to one's own region or section.
Missouri Compromise (1820)	It balanced desires of northern states to prevent expansion of slavery. Admitted Missouri as a slave state.
Manifest Destiny	Idea that the U.S is destined by god
Annexation of Texas	Entered the U.S as a slave state. In 1844, texas was annexed by U.S.
Mexican War	Started as a disputed boundary between U.S and Texas.
Compromise of 1850	5 bills that attempted to resolve disputes over slavery in new territories.
Kansas-Nebraska Act (1854)	Created Nebraska and Kansas. Allowed settlers to decide whether slavery would be allowed.
Popular sovereignty	Authority of a state being sustained by the consent of it's people.
Scott v. Sandford (1857), also known as the Dred Scott decision	Supreme court ruled that American of African descent, were not American citizens.
John Brown's Raid on Harpers Ferry (1859)	John brown's raids was a raid against a federal armory.
Presidential Election of 1860	A election that led to many kinds of problems.
Abraham Lincoln	16th president of the U.S
Secession of Southern states	Withdrawl of the southern states from the Union

198   Chapter 6 | The Civil War

Name _____

Complete the following chart.

Name or term	Description/Significance
Confederacy	The seven south slave states
Jefferson Davis	He was president of the American confederate states.
Fort Sumter	First site of the first battle of the American civil war.
General Robert E. Lee	Confederate general of the confederate states.
Battle of Antietam (1862)	Was a battle of the Civil war. Was a turning point
Emancipation Proclamation (1862)	A proclamation that freed many slaves in the south.
Battle of Gettysburg (1863)	A battle that led to a crushing defeat for the Confederacy.
Gettysburg Address (1863)	A speech over the civil war and about struggle for freedom
Siege of Vicksburg (1863)	Gave control of the Mississippi River a critical supply line to the union.
General Ulysses S. Grant	Led the Union Army to victory. Was also the 18th president.
Destruction of Atlanta (1864)	A mob that protested in which is now Atlanta.
Sherman's March to the Sea (1864)	
Surrender at Appomattox (1865)	

Chapter 6 | The Civil War

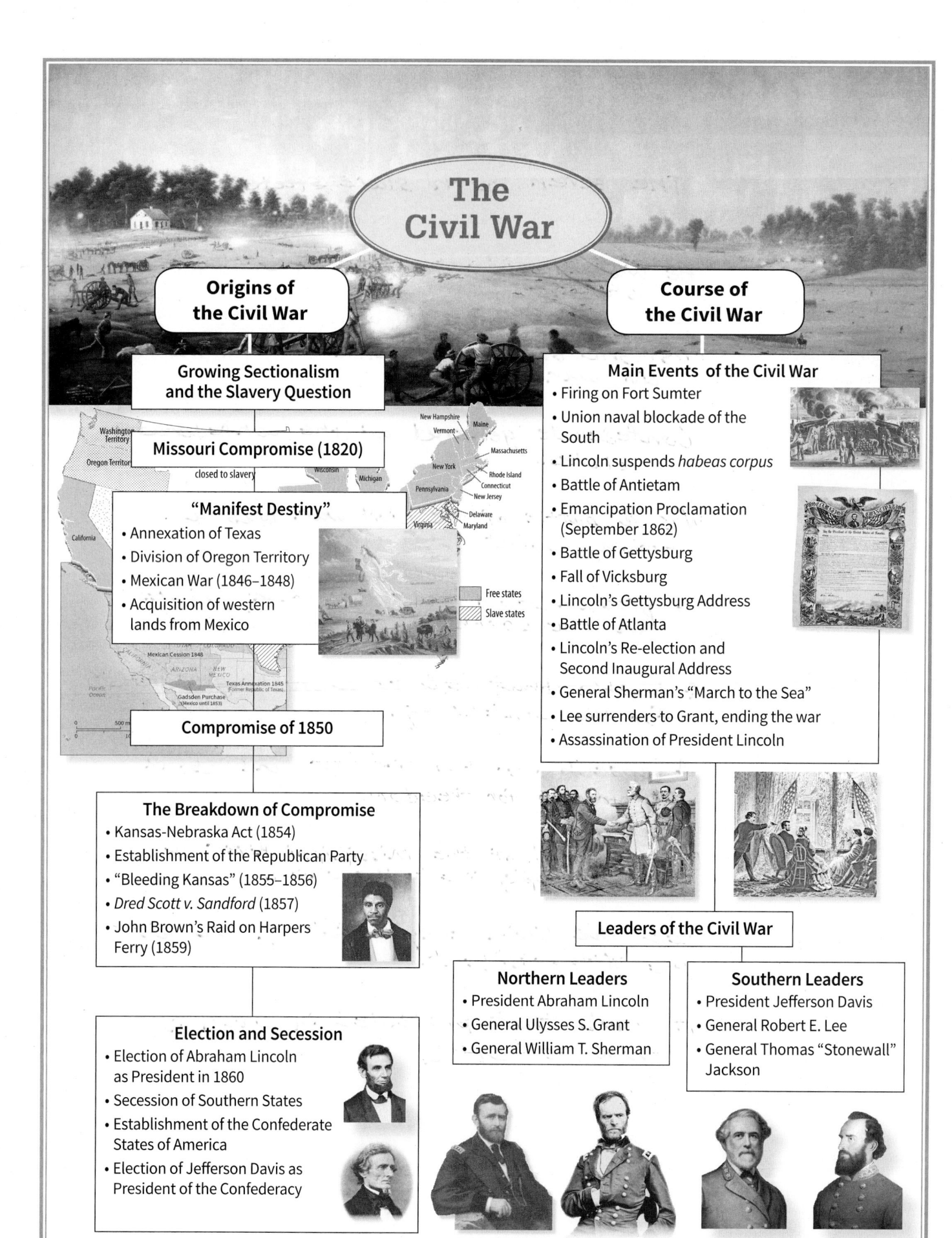

The Civil War

Origins of the Civil War

Growing Sectionalism and the Slavery Question

Missouri Compromise (1820)

"Manifest Destiny"
- Annexation of Texas
- Division of Oregon Territory
- Mexican War (1846–1848)
- Acquisition of western lands from Mexico

Compromise of 1850

The Breakdown of Compromise
- Kansas-Nebraska Act (1854)
- Establishment of the Republican Party
- "Bleeding Kansas" (1855–1856)
- *Dred Scott v. Sandford* (1857)
- John Brown's Raid on Harpers Ferry (1859)

Election and Secession
- Election of Abraham Lincoln as President in 1860
- Secession of Southern States
- Establishment of the Confederate States of America
- Election of Jefferson Davis as President of the Confederacy

Course of the Civil War

Main Events of the Civil War
- Firing on Fort Sumter
- Union naval blockade of the South
- Lincoln suspends *habeas corpus*
- Battle of Antietam
- Emancipation Proclamation (September 1862)
- Battle of Gettysburg
- Fall of Vicksburg
- Lincoln's Gettysburg Address
- Battle of Atlanta
- Lincoln's Re-election and Second Inaugural Address
- General Sherman's "March to the Sea"
- Lee surrenders to Grant, ending the war
- Assassination of President Lincoln

Leaders of the Civil War

Northern Leaders
- President Abraham Lincoln
- General Ulysses S. Grant
- General William T. Sherman

Southern Leaders
- President Jefferson Davis
- General Robert E. Lee
- General Thomas "Stonewall" Jackson

200   Chapter 6 | The Civil War

What Do You Know?

SSUSH8a

1. Which statement BEST describes the Missouri Compromise?
   A. Slavery was prohibited throughout the Louisiana Territory.
   B. The issue of slavery was left to be decided by local residents.
   C. Missouri was admitted as a slave state and Maine as a free state.
   D. A harsher fugitive slave law was enacted and the slave trade was prohibited.

SSUSH8b

2. Use the excerpt to answer the question.

   > The whole continent of North America appears to be [meant] by Divine Providence to be peopled by one nation, speaking one language, professing one general system of religious and political principles, and accustomed to [the same] social usages and customs.
   > —John Quincy Adams, 1811

   Which view is expressed in this excerpt?
   A. support for freedom of the seas
   B. opposition to the extension of slavery
   C. belief in America's Manifest Destiny
   D. resistance to Indian attacks in the Northwest Territory

SSUSH8b

3. In the 1840s, how did the United States and Great Britain resolve their disagreement over control of the Oregon Territory?
   A. The United States sent troops to occupy the disputed territory.
   B. They resolved the dispute peacefully by dividing up the territory.
   C. They created a new territory for Indians to occupy the disputed area.
   D. Americans had a "Second War for Independence" against the British.

SSUSH8d

4. Use this list to answer the question.

   - California admitted as free state
   - Popular sovereignty applied to rest of the Mexican Cession
   - Harsher fugitive slave law

   Which law is described by this list?
   A. Missouri Compromise
   B. Compromise of 1850
   C. Kansas-Nebraska Act
   D. Pacific Railway Act

Chapter 6 | The Civil War   201

SSUSH6c

5. Use the excerpt below to answer the question.

   > We have tried every effort at restoring harmony. The cup of tolerance had been exhausted even before the recent information from the frontier of the Del Norte. But now, after repeated menaces, they have passed the boundary of the United States, have invaded our territory and have shed American blood upon American soil. [They have] proclaimed that hostilities have begun, and that the two nations are now at war.
   >
   > —President James Polk, Message to Congress, 1846

   What was one consequence of the conflict that resulted from this message?

   A. The United States took over the government of Mexico.
   B. The United States acquired territories that contributed to growing sectionalism.
   C. The United States forcibly expelled its Mexican-American residents.
   D. The United States agreed to return Texas to Mexico.

SSUSH8b

6. Use the diagram to answer the question.

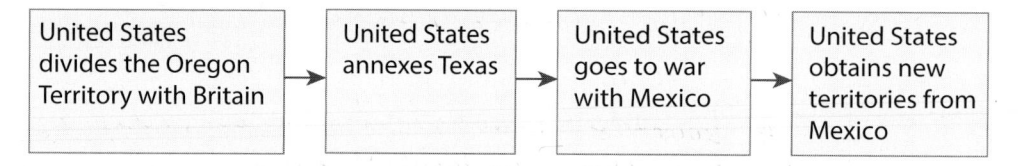

   | United States divides the Oregon Territory with Britain | → | United States annexes Texas | → | United States goes to war with Mexico | → | United States obtains new territories from Mexico |

   Which belief was a motive for the events in the diagram?

   A. Popular Sovereignty
   B. Jacksonian Democracy
   C. Manifest Destiny
   D. Abolitionism

SSUSH8e

7. What was one major effect of the Kansas-Nebraska Act (1854)?

   A. It created the same number of slave and free states.
   B. It closed the New Mexico and Utah Territories to future slavery.
   C. It made slavery possible in territories previously closed to slavery.
   D. It rejected the use of popular sovereignty to resolve the slavery issue.

SSUSH8e

8. Use the diagram to answer the question.

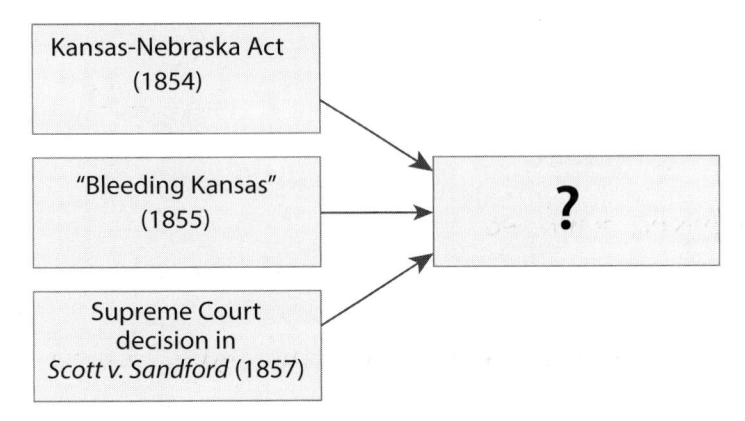

```
Kansas-Nebraska Act (1854) ──┐
                             │
"Bleeding Kansas" (1855) ────┼──▶  ?
                             │
Supreme Court decision in    │
Scott v. Sandford (1857) ────┘
```

Which phrase correctly completes the diagram?

A. Fulfillment of Manifest Destiny
B. Overturning of the Missouri Compromise
C. Admission of California as a Free State
D. Secession of the Lower South

SSUSH8e

9. Use the excerpt to answer the question.

> *Our present condition . . . illustrates the American idea that governments rest upon the consent of the governed, and that it is the right of the people to alter or abolish governments . . . [A] peaceful appeal to the ballot-box declared that so far as [Southerners] were concerned, the government created by [the Constitution] should cease to exist [come to an end].*
>
> —Jefferson Davis, Inaugural Address (1861)

How did Jefferson Davis justify the secession of the Southern states in this excerpt?

A. states' rights and popular sovereignty
B. the continuation of slavery
C. enforcement of the Fugitive Slave Act
D. the balance of power between slave and free states

SSUSH9d

10. Which Civil War battle was a turning point because Confederate losses were so high that General Robert E. Lee never advanced into the North again?

A. Bull Run
B. Antietam
C. Vicksburg
D. Gettysburg

Chapter 6 | The Civil War

SSUSH9b

11. Use the diagram to answer the question.

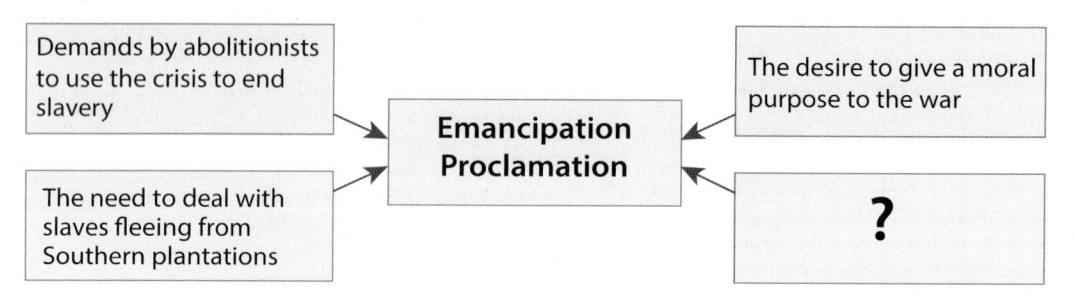

```
[Demands by abolitionists to use the crisis to end slavery] →
[The need to deal with slaves fleeing from Southern plantations] →
    [Emancipation Proclamation]
← [The desire to give a moral purpose to the war]
← [ ? ]
```

Which phrase BEST completes the diagram?

A. The need to end slavery in the border states
B. The need to prevent Britain from helping the South
C. The need to strengthen the powers of the President
D. The need to lift the naval blockade for humanitarian reasons

SSUSH9c

12. Which Civil War general pursued a strategy of "total war" in the South, destroying towns, factories and railroad lines to deprive the Confederate army of its sources of supply?

A. George Meade
B. Robert E. Lee
C. Thomas "Stonewall" Jackson
D. William T. Sherman

SSUSH9d

13. How did geography affect the outcome of the Battle of Gettysburg?

A. The Union victory at Gettysburg divided the Confederacy into two parts.
B. General Lee used the wilderness to hide the fact that he had fewer troops.
C. Union troops occupied higher ground, making it difficult for Confederate troops to attack.
D. Union forces relied on naval power to surround and starve Gettysburg into submission.

SSUSH9b

14. Which was an important purpose of President Lincoln in delivering his Second Inaugural Address in March 1865?

A. to explain that the war had not been fought over the question of slavery
B. to demand the severe punishment of the South for causing the Civil War
C. to admit his personal responsibility for the destruction of the Civil War
D. to start the process of healing the wounds caused by the Civil War

SSUSH9d

15. Use this list to answer the question.

> - Confederate leaders believed many residents in this border state would welcome their army.
> - A Confederate victory in the North might have led to an end of the war.
> - A Confederate victory here might have brought alliances with Britain and France.
> - President Abraham Lincoln issued the Emancipation Proclamation shortly after this battle.

Which battle is BEST described by this list?

A. Bull Run
B. Antietam
C. Gettysburg
D. Atlanta

SSUSH9a

16. Use this table to answer the questions.

Economic Resources of the South and North, 1860

	South	North
Percentage of Miles of U.S. Railroad Track	29%	71%
Percentage of U.S. Banks	13%	87%
Percentage of U.S. Manufacturing Output	10%	90%

Source: Benjamin Arrington, "Industry and Economy during the Civil War," National Park Service

Part A

Which statement BEST explains the differences in the table?

A. Southerners had greater respect for the environment.
B. The first American factories had been built in the South.
C. Southerners invested more in land and slaves than in industry.
D. The North had the most fertile soil and the longest growing season.

Part B

How did the disparities shown on the table affect the course of the Civil War?

A. The British allied with the North to protect their investments in U.S. banks.
B. Most of the major battles were fought in the North, which was more accessible by railroad.
C. The North was able to win the war quickly and easily because the South lacked manufacturing output.
D. The North was eventually able to overpower the South because of its superior economic resources.

Chapter 6 | The Civil War

When the Civil War ended, much of the South had been destroyed. White Southerners had fought for years but had lost. Slavery was abolished. There was no way for Southerners to return to the way things had been before the war.

The Challenges of Reconstruction

The next twelve years were known as the **Reconstruction Era**. To "reconstruct" means to rebuild. During Reconstruction, Americans had to face several political, economic, and social challenges.

Many historians believe the Reconstruction Era was a time of great promise. Unfortunately, America's leaders failed to bring the former slaves into American society on a fair and equal basis.

Challenges

1. How should the Southern states be readmitted into the Union?
2. Does the President or Congress have the power to readmit them?
3. How can the freedmen be helped?
4. How can the economy of the South be rebuilt?

The Freedmen's Bureau

Even before the war had ended, people started thinking about Reconstruction. A special agency was created by Congress in March 1865 as a branch of the War Department. An **agency** is a government office or department that deals with specific problems or provides specific services. The official name of this new agency was the **Bureau of Refugees, Freedmen and Abandoned Lands**. It became known as the Freedmen's Bureau. The "freedmen" were the former slaves. The "refugees" were displaced white Southerners who had lost their homes during the war. "Abandoned lands" were lands that were deserted or that had been taken away from their former owners.

The main goal of this federal agency was to help the former slaves adjust to freedom. The Bureau also had control of abandoned and confiscated lands in Confederate states. It had the power to distribute these lands to the freedmen and refugees. Its commissioner and assistant commissioners were all army officers.

The Bureau gave out food, water and clothes to the freedmen as the war was ending. It also gave food rations to poor white Southerners and Indians. It helped freedmen find lost relatives and performed marriages for couples that had not been permitted to marry under conditions of slavery. The Bureau encouraged former masters and slaves to cooperate as employers and employees. It helped draft employment contracts for the freedmen and made sure their terms were fair. In 1866, Congress extended the life of the Freedmen's Bureau and increased its powers. President Andrew Johnson had vetoed the extension but Congress overrode his veto with a two-thirds majority. Agents of the Bureau kept records and represented freedmen in courts or removed cases to its own court system. The Bureau had its own surgeons and hospital attendants to provide

An office of the Freedmen's Bureau

Lincoln's Plans for Reconstruction

In November 1863, President Lincoln announced his plans for Reconstruction. He did not want to treat the South harshly. As he stated later in his Second Inaugural Address, he intended to act with kindness—"with malice (*bitterness, bad feelings*) toward none, with charity for all." Once 10 percent of the voters of a Southern state pledged allegiance to the Union and agreed to the Emancipation Proclamation, Lincoln planned to readmit that state back into the Union.

medical care. It built more than 40 new hospitals in the South. Most important of all, the Bureau took charge of the education of millions of freedmen who had been previously prohibited from learning to read and write. Congress gave the Bureau the power to use confiscated Confederate property to pay for schools. Volunteers from the North came to teach the freedmen. By the end of 1865, there were 90,000 freedmen enrolled in the Bureau's schools. The Bureau also played a role in establishing new colleges for African Americans.

The Freedmen's Bureau continued its operations until 1872, when Congress ended its funding. Its commissioner, General Howard, and many of its leading agents moved to the West, where they began helping the federal agency looking after Indian affairs.

The Thirteenth Amendment

In April 1864, the Senate proposed the **Thirteenth Amendment**, which prohibited slavery. Lincoln's Emancipation Proclamation had ended slavery, but not in all states. It also was unclear whether the President actually had the authority to end slavery. The Thirteenth Amendment made the abolition of slavery clear and absolute. The proposed amendment passed the House in January 1865. It was ratified (*approved*) by the states before the end of the year.

The Thirteenth Amendment

Neither slavery nor involuntary servitude, except as a punishment for crime whereof the party shall have been duly convicted, shall exist within the United States, or any place subject to their jurisdiction.

The Historian's Apprentice

1. What were the most important accomplishments of the Freedmen's Bureau?
2. Why was the Thirteenth Amendment necessary when Lincoln had already issued the Emancipation Proclamation?
3. What is meant by "involuntary servitude" in the Thirteenth Amendment?

Chapter 7 | The Reconstruction Era

Presidential Reconstruction

President Lincoln was assassinated in April 1865. His Vice President, **Andrew Johnson**, now became President. Johnson was a former slaveholder from Tennessee, a Southern state that had joined the Confederacy. Johnson came from a poor family. He had always resented the wealthiest slaveholders.

In the months before the new Congress assembled, Johnson had complete control over Reconstruction. Many thought Johnson might impose harsh conditions on Southern states. He refused, for example, to give a general pardon to all former Confederate leaders.

However, Johnson soon began giving thousands of individual pardons. He let former Confederates regain their properties as well as their rights of citizenship.

President Andrew Johnson

> Under the U.S. Constitution, the President has the power to **pardon** (*release from punishment*) people who have committed federal crimes.

Johnson hoped that relations between the North and the South would improve quickly. He recognized new Southern state governments run by former Confederate leaders. As a Southerner, Johnson came under the suspicion of many Northerners. They thought he was being too sympathetic to the South.

The Black Codes

With Johnson as President, white Southerners became more daring. In new elections, they elected their former Confederate leaders, including several generals and colonels, to represent them in Congress. Southern states also passed new "**Black Codes.**" These codes were based on the slave codes of the past. Each Southern state wrote its own code, but they all had some things in common. They prevented "persons of color" from exercising the **rights and duties of citizenship**, including voting, serving on juries, holding office, and serving in the state militia. The freedmen were not able to exercise any of these rights and duties. The Black Codes also had rules for freedmen's marriages and labor contracts (*agreements*). "Such persons are *not* entitled to social and political equality with white persons," announced the South Carolina Black Code of 1865.

Finally, the Black Codes made it illegal for freedmen to travel freely or to leave their jobs. Each freedman had to show that he or she had work during the current year. This forced former slaves to remain on the same plantations. Black workers could even be whipped for showing disrespect to their employers—usually their former owners. African-American children were "apprenticed" to white employers, and black convicts were turned over to white employers for hard labor. The whole aim of the Black Codes was to keep Southern society as it had been before the war, despite the abolition of slavery.

Congressional Reconstruction

People in the North were furious when former rebel leaders were elected in Southern states. They were equally shocked at the Black Codes. The victory in the Civil War itself seemed to be in danger. Congress refused to accept former Confederate leaders as members. Moderate Republicans joined hands with the "**Radical Republicans.**"

The Radical Republicans believed that African Americans should be given full political and civil equality. Radical Republicans soon became the most powerful group in Congress.

The Radical Republicans passed the **Civil Rights Bill of 1866**. It made freedmen U.S. citizens. It also outlawed discrimination based on race. President Johnson vetoed this bill, but the Radical Republicans were able to override his veto. The Radical Republicans also passed their own bill for Reconstruction in the South. They divided the South into five districts. Each district was governed by the U.S. Army and placed under **martial law**.

The Fourteenth Amendment

Congress passed the Civil Rights Act of 1866 over President Johnson's veto. But what if the U.S. Supreme Court decided that the act was unconstitutional? To protect the law against this threat, Congress rewrote it as a new amendment. Congress then proposed this amendment—the **Fourteenth Amendment**—to the states for ratification.

CIVIL RIGHTS BILL PASSES • 1866

The Fourteenth Amendment prevented state governments from denying African Americans and other minorities the rights of citizenship. These rights included the right to a fair trial and to the "equal protection of the laws."

The Fourteenth Amendment overturned the earlier *Dred Scott* decision. The amendment begins by defining what a citizen is. It states that anyone who is born in the United States is an American citizen. Because Dred Scott was born in the United States, he would have been a citizen under this amendment.

The Fourteenth Amendment

Section 1.
All persons born or naturalized in the United States, and subject to the jurisdiction thereof, are citizens of the United States and of the State wherein they reside. No State shall make or enforce any law which shall abridge the privileges or immunities of citizens of the United States; nor shall any State deprive any person of life, liberty, or property, without due process of law; nor deny to any person within its jurisdiction the equal protection of the laws.

Word Helper

jurisdiction = authority

reside = live

abridge = limit

privileges = benefits, rights

immunities = freedoms

deprive = take away

due process of law = fair procedures

equal protection of the laws = equal treatment under the law

Chapter 7 | The Reconstruction Era

The Fourteenth Amendment also provided for "**naturalized** citizens." These are immigrants in the United States who become citizens. The amendment did not set up the steps of the naturalization process. That was left for Congress to do.

Finally, the Fourteenth Amendment defined the rights of citizens. These included the right to "due process" and to "the equal protection of the laws." This means no state government can imprison us or take away our property without fair, just, and open procedures. It also means that we are all treated as equals under the law.

To be readmitted to the Union, each Southern state had to ratify the Fourteenth Amendment. The right of former Confederate leaders to hold elected office was also taken away. These changes had a great impact on the make-up of Southern state governments.

The Impeachment of President Andrew Johnson

President Johnson opposed the policies of the Radical Republicans. But in the 1866 Congressional elections, Northern voters supported them. In fact, the Radical Republicans increased the number of seats they had in Congress.

The Radical Republicans next passed a law that limited the President's power to dismiss his own Cabinet members. President Johnson refused to obey this law. He saw it as a clear violation of the separation of powers.

When the President refused to obey this law, Congressional leaders attempted to remove him from office through the process of **impeachment**.

A majority of the House of Representatives successfully impeached President Johnson in February 1868. When he was tried in the Senate, however, the Radical Republicans failed to get enough votes to remove him. Johnson was the first President ever to be impeached. Later that year, General Ulysses S. Grant was elected as the next President of the United States.

The Fifteenth Amendment

Shortly after Grant's election, the Radical Republicans proposed the Fifteenth Amendment to protect the rights of African-American voters. The amendment was ratified in 1870. It guaranteed the right to vote to adult males of all races.

The impeachment trial of President Andrew Johnson

Impeachment of the President

The U.S. Constitution has a two-step process for removing the President from office. First, the President must be "impeached" in the House of Representatives. Second, the President is tried by the Senate. If two-thirds of the Senate approve, then the President is removed.

> **The Fifteenth Amendment**
>
> The right of citizens of the United States to vote shall not be denied or abridged by the United States or by any State on account of race, color, or previous condition of servitude.

Radical Reconstruction in the South

During Radical Reconstruction, state governments in the South came under the control of new groups. These included new arrivals from the North known as "**carpetbaggers**." This was a term of abuse used by Southern newspapers. It meant that the Northerners were able to fit all of their belongings into a few bags made of carpet, and that they came to exploit (*take advantage of*) the South. In reality, many Northerners came for idealistic reasons, especially to help the freedmen. The new Reconstruction governments in the South also included "**scalawags**"—white Southerners who had opposed the Confederacy. Finally, much of the Southern electorate in the Reconstruction Era was made up of new African-American voters.

For the first time, African Americans had the opportunity to participate as citizens in Southern state governments. Over six hundred freedmen

The chart below compares Presidential and Congressional Reconstructions.

	Presidential Reconstruction	Congressional Reconstruction
Who should control the readmission of Southern states?	The President	The U.S. Congress
When should Southern states be readmitted?	President Lincoln said he was prepared to let them enter once 10 percent of the voters pledged allegiance to the Union and agreed to the Emancipation Proclamation. President Johnson similarly thought they should be able to enter immediately, so long as they support the Union and the end of slavery.	Only when most citizens in the state agreed to support the Union and African-American citizens were given their full civil and political rights.
Should former Confederate leaders be punished?		The Radical Republicans in Congress thought that Confederate leaders should be punished and all who served in the Confederacy should lose their political rights.
Should the freedmen be allowed to vote?	President Johnson recommended that state governments give voting rights to educated freedmen and African-American veterans, but he refused to force them to do so.	Yes. During Reconstruction, freedmen, scalawags, and carpetbaggers controlled representation in Southern states.

Chapter 7 | The Reconstruction Era

The Historian's Apprentice

1. Make an illustrated timeline showing the evolution of Presidential and Congressional policies for Reconstruction.
2. Write a paragraph on whether you think President Johnson's impeachment was justified. Examine the grounds for impeachment in the U.S. Constitution. For what reasons do you believe a President should be impeached?

served as state legislators during the Reconstruction Era (1865–1877). **Hiram Revels** became the first African American to sit in the U.S. Congress when he took Jefferson Davis' former seat as Senator from Mississippi in 1870. African Americans also filled many posts in state governments.

Reconstruction governments had many accomplishments. They created new systems of public schools in Southern states. They passed laws against racial discrimination. They encouraged investment in railroads.

Reconstruction governments also had some weaknesses. They had financial difficulties. Some were guilty of the corruption typical of the time, such as taking bribes. They never won the support of most white Southerners. White Southerners resented Northern interference. They refused to see their former slaves as social equals.

Without providing black Southerners with economic security and without changing the attitudes of white Southerners, Reconstruction policies may have been doomed to fail.

The Economics of Reconstruction: The "New South"

One of the main challenges of Reconstruction was to repair the economy of the South. Without slave labor, the old plantation system could not be restored. Some plantation owners were forced to sell off part of their lands. Most plantation owners entered into **sharecropping** arrangements with their former slaves. The landowner provided a cabin, a mule, tools, and a plot of land to farm. In return, the "sharecropper" gave a share of his crop to the landowner. Most freedmen became sharecroppers. A few became tenant farmers. Tenant farmers rented land from the landowner but provided their own tools and provisions. Very few freedmen became landowners themselves.

Some Southerners saw the end of slavery as beneficial to the South. They thought the South could now develop a stronger economy. It could start growing different types of crops and carry out more of its own manufacturing. They called this the "New South." The farming of new crops like fruits and vegetables was added to the

Sharecroppers

216   Chapter 7 | The Reconstruction Era

growth of traditional cash crops like cotton, tobacco, rice, and sugar. Most important of all, more railroads, cotton mills, and steel furnaces were built in the South. More people moved into Southern cities. Although manufacturing in the South was still not as much as in the North, it became much greater than in pre-Civil War times. Most people, however, continued to work at growing cash crops for export such as cotton. Immense quantities of raw cotton and other raw materials were still needed by the factories of the Northeast and Britain.

The Ku Klux Klan

Many white Southerners were unhappy with the changes of the Reconstruction Era. As early as December 1865, six former Confederate officers established the first branch of the **Ku Klux Klan**. The name was taken from a Greek word for "circle." Klans quickly sprang up across the South. Large numbers of former Confederate soldiers were determined to restore white supremacy. Members swore oaths to maintain secrecy. They wore masks and robes and acted at night to hide their identities and inspire fear. Klan members attacked African Americans and agents of the Freedmen's Bureau. They assassinated Southern Republicans and launched a wave of terror across the South. In 1867, they took steps to form a national organization with local chapters. In 1868, Klan members threatened and killed Republican voters in order to win in elections. Klan activities filled the reports of the Freedmen's Bureau. Eventually Klan violence became so extreme that it drew national attention. Congress held hearings and passed a new law to end Klan violence. The Civil Rights Act of 1871 gave President Grant the power to suppress disorders and to suspend *habeas corpus*. Federal troops were used to arrest Klan members. Members were tried in federal rather than state courts, and often faced African-American juries. The Klan was destroyed by 1872 but similar organizations arose to take its place.

The Presidential Election of 1876 Brings Reconstruction to an End

As time passed, Northerners gradually lost interest in what was happening in the South. In 1872, Congress passed the Amnesty Act. This act restored voting rights to most former Confederates. In the same year, Congress suddenly ended the Freedmen's Bureau.

The Reconstruction Era finally came to a sudden end in a surprising way. It was the outcome of a disputed Presidential election. In 1876, the election contest was between Republican candidate **Rutherford B. Hayes** and Democratic candidate Samuel Tilden. Tilden won the popular vote but did not have quite enough votes in the Electoral College.

The election results were disputed in Oregon and three Southern states: Florida, Louisiana, and South Carolina. If all twenty disputed votes went to Hayes, he would win the election.

Tilden needed only one more vote to win. A special Congressional commission was formed to decide the disputed votes. In the end, a compromise was worked out. The Congressmen gave all of the disputed electoral votes to Hayes. In return, Hayes promised to withdraw Northern troops from the South, ending Reconstruction.

President Hayes removed all Northern troops from the South in 1877. Local governments then came back under white Southern rule. Former Confederate leaders began voting and running for office. Southern state legislatures took steps to prevent African-American citizens from voting or enjoying the other rights of citizenship. Many of the gains African Americans had made during Reconstruction were taken away. You will learn more about these developments in Chapter 10.

Reasons for the Failure of Reconstruction

There were several reasons why Reconstruction failed to achieve equality for African Americans.

A Legacy of Racism
White Americans in the North as well as the South failed to recognize African Americans as equals. Centuries of prejudice stood in the way.

The Economic Dependence of African Americans
Reconstruction governments failed to divide up plantations and give freedmen their own plots of land. This meant black Southerners remained dependent on their former owners. Sharecroppers and tenants needed to use the landowner's land to survive. Many tenants quickly fell into debt to their landlords, creating a system of **debt peonage** (*they owed the landlord their labor until they paid off their debt*). To protect their economic livelihoods, most African Americans in the South stopped defending their political rights.

Freedmen Lacked Education and Political Experience
Before the Civil War, it had been against the law to teach slaves to read and write. Most of the freedmen had no formal education. This weakened their ability to compete with whites.

White Terrorism
The **Ku Klux Klan** was a secret society of Southern whites, formed after the Civil War. Klan members terrorized African Americans who attempted to stand up for their rights. Klan members disguised themselves with white hoods at night. They visited the homes of African Americans and beat them or killed them. Other secret societies arose when the Ku Klux Klan was suppressed by the federal government. A "**lynching**" was a brutal hanging by a crowd of people. African Americans who tried to vote might be lynched. Most of the white Southerners who committed these crimes were never charged. Southern sheriffs, judges, and juries were all white.

Loss of Northern Interest
Reconstruction governments were established right after the Civil War. Northerners wanted to assert their control of the South after a hard-fought conflict. After the twelve years of Reconstruction, most Northerners lost interest in events in the South. They also needed the raw cotton and other crops grown in the South for their factories.

For the Georgia Milestones EOC Assessment, you need to know that:

- [ ] The Reconstruction Era refers to the period of rebuilding the South after the Civil War.
- [ ] President Lincoln proposed a lenient treatment of the South; after ten percent of a Southern state's population took an oath of loyalty, the state would be readmitted into the Union. However, Lincoln was assassinated in 1865.
- [ ] Andrew Johnson became the next President. He was from Tennessee and Congress suspected he was too friendly to white Southerners. He pardoned Confederate leaders and let Southern states elect former Confederates and pass "Black Codes," restricting the movement and activities of the former slaves.
- [ ] Southern states at first passed Black Codes to keep the freedmen in conditions close to slavery, but these codes were repealed by Congress with the Civil Rights Act of 1866 and the Fourteenth Amendment.
- [ ] Radical Republicans took control of Congress. They granted full civil and political rights to the freedmen, divided the South into occupation zones, and imposed martial law on the South.
- [ ] The House of Representatives impeached President Johnson but the Senate failed to remove him from office.
- [ ] The Bureau of Refugees, Freedmen, and Abandoned Lands, better known as the Freedmen's Bureau, gave support to former slaves, poor whites and American Indians. It gave out rations at the end of the war, and later provided schooling to the freedmen.
- [ ] The Thirteenth Amendment ended slavery; the Fourteenth Amendment defined citizenship and guaranteed all citizens equal rights from state governments; and the Fifteenth Amendment guaranteed qualified citizens the right to vote regardless of race.
- [ ] During Reconstruction, African Americans participated fully in political life in Southern states. They were elected to Congress and to offices in state and local government. Carpetbaggers from the North and scalawags also joined Reconstruction governments.
- [ ] White Southerners joined the Ku Klux Klan and similar groups. They committed acts of terror to resist racial equality during the Reconstruction Era.
- [ ] The Presidential election of 1876 led to the end of Reconstruction. Samuel Tilden won the popular vote but there were 20 disputed votes in the Electoral College. Republican candidate Rutherford B. Hayes won all 20 disputed votes by promising to end Reconstruction in the South. After his election, the U.S. Army was withdrawn from the South and Reconstruction ended.

Name _____

Complete the following chart.

Term	Description
Reconstruction	
Presidential Reconstruction	
Assassination of Abraham Lincoln	
Radical Republicans	
Congressional Reconstruction	
Impeachment of President Andrew Johnson	
Freedmen's Bureau	
Thirteenth Amendment	
Fourteenth Amendment	
Fifteenth Amendment	
Black Codes	
Ku Klux Klan	
Presidential Election of 1876	

Identify the names and terms in the concept circles below and explain how they fit together.

Name:_____

Circle 1 (quadrants):
- Freedmen's Bureau
- Former slaves
- American Indians
- Poor whites

_____
_____
_____
_____
_____
_____
_____

Circle 2 (quadrants):
- Presidential Reconstruction
- Impeachment of Andrew Johnson
- Radical Republicans
- Congressional Reconstruction

_____
_____
_____
_____
_____
_____
_____

Chapter 7 | The Reconstruction Era   221

Name:_____

| Thirteenth Amendment | Fourteenth Amendment |
| Fifteenth Amendment | Citizenship rights |

| Black Codes | Ku Klux Klan |
| Election of 1876 | End of Reconstruction |

Chapter 7 | The Reconstruction Era

Reconstruction

Presidential Reconstruction
- Lincoln's "Ten-percent" solution
- Johnson pardons Confederates

Constitutional Amendments

13th Amendment
- Abolished slavery

14th Amendment
- Guaranteed citizenship rights

15th Amendment
- Guaranteed voting rights

Congressional Reconstruction
- Radical Republicans
- Civil Rights Bill—rights for freedmen
- Reconstruction Act—Military occupation of South
- Impeachment of President Johnson

Southern States
- "Black Codes" restrict freedom
- Confederate leaders elected

Reconstruction Problems
- How to readmit Southern states?
- How to help freedmen?
- How to rebuild South?

Ku Klux Klan
- Use of violence to terrorize African Americans and restore white supremacy

The South

- Freedmen
- Carpetbaggers
- Scalawags

Reconstruction Governments

Freedmen's Bureau
- Federal agency established to help the freedmen and their families
- The agency set up schools and took charge of educating millions of freedmen
- The agency also gave rations and help to poor whites and Cherokee Indians after the war

- Participation of freedmen in government
- Public schools, investment in railroads
- Some corruption

Economy
- Sharecroppers
- Tenant farmers

End of Reconstruction
- Disputed Election of 1876
- "Compromise of 1877"—North withdraws
- Southern Democrats resume power

Chapter 7 | The Reconstruction Era

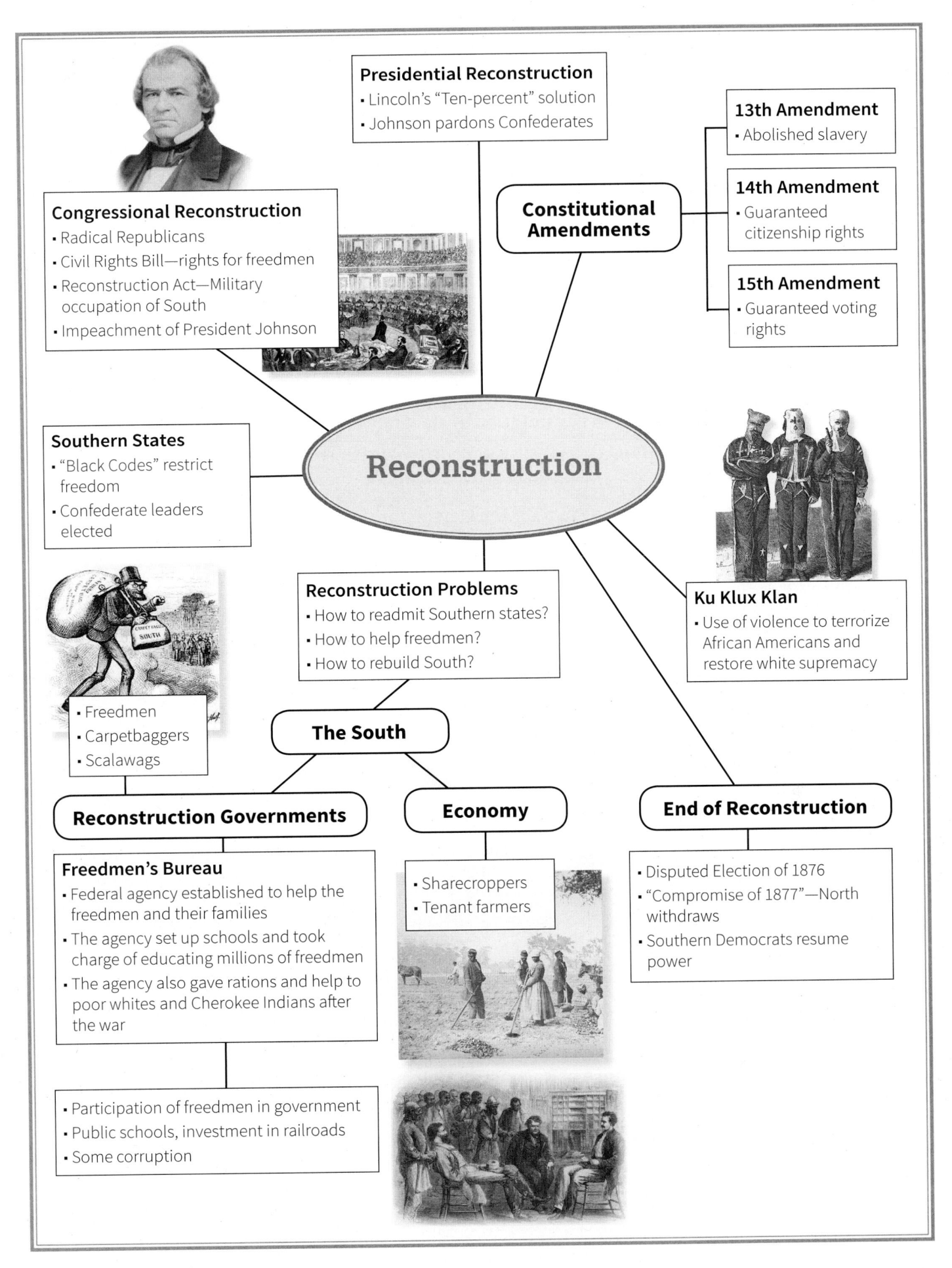

What Do You Know?

SSUSH10a

1. How were Abraham Lincoln and Andrew Johnson similar?
   A. They were both impeached.
   B. They were once slave owners.
   C. Their election resulted in a Civil War.
   D. They favored a lenient treatment of the South.

SSUSH10c

2. Why were many Northerners upset when Southern legislatures passed "Black Codes"?
   A. They preferred a restoration of slavery.
   B. They wanted to pass similar codes in the North.
   C. They feared African Americans might move out of the South.
   D. They felt white Southerners were ignoring the outcome of the war.

SSUSH10a

3. During Reconstruction, how did the Radical Republicans in Congress threaten the separation of powers?
   A. by proposing three constitutional amendments
   B. by giving the full rights of citizenship to former slaves
   C. by interfering with the actions of Southern state governments
   D. by impeaching the President because they disagreed with his policies

SSUSH10c

4. Use the illustration below to answer the question.

   Which consequence of Reconstruction is shown in this drawing?
   A. Freedmen left farming to find work in industry.
   B. Northerners took control of Southern life for more than ten years.
   C. For the first time, African Americans in the South exercised political rights.
   D. Southern whites and African Americans in the South mixed freely without prejudice.

SSUSH10c

5. Which amendment abolished slavery?
   A. Thirteenth Amendment
   B. Fourteenth Amendment
   C. Fifteenth Amendment
   D. Nineteenth Amendment

SSUSH10a

6. Use the list to answer the question.

   > - State governments passed Black Codes.
   > - Southern states elected former Confederate leaders.

   How did the Radical Republicans in Congress respond to the events mentioned above?

   A. They welcomed former Confederate leaders back into Congress.
   B. They voted to give extra federal money to help rebuild the South.
   C. They passed the Civil Rights Act of 1866 and imposed martial law.
   D. They gave extraordinary powers to President Johnson to deal with Southern leaders.

SSUSH10b

7. The statement below is from an interview recorded by the Freedmen's Bureau.

   I work on my former master's land. He gives us our tools and seeds to plant. We give him some of our crop.

   Who is being interviewed?

   A. a scalawag
   B. a carpetbagger
   C. a sharecropper
   D. a tenant farmer

SSUSH10d

8. What was the main purpose of the Ku Klux Klan during the Reconstruction Era?

   A. to make freedmen afraid to exercise their rights
   B. to create a new political party in the South
   C. to teach the freedmen how to read and write
   D. to assist Southerners who had lost their savings in the war

SSUSH10c

9. Which amendment to the Constitution guaranteed the right to vote to African Americans?

   A. Fifteenth Amendment
   B. Nineteenth Amendment
   C. Twenty-fourth Amendment
   D. Twenty-sixth Amendment

Chapter 7 | The Reconstruction Era

SSUSH10a

10. Examine the excerpt.

   > *With malice [resentment, bad feeling] toward none, with charity for all, . . . let us strive on [make efforts] to finish the work we are in, to bind up the nation's wounds . . . to do all which may achieve and cherish a just and lasting peace among ourselves and with all nations.*
   >
   > —Abraham Lincoln, Second Inaugural Address, March 4, 1865

   How did the Radical Republicans in Congress disagree with the views expressed in this passage?

   A. They wanted former Confederate leaders to return to local public office.

   B. They believed the South should be punished for causing the war.

   C. They thought Southern states should be immediately readmitted to the Union.

   D. They did not think the freedmen were able to exercise full civil and political rights.

SSUSH10c

11. The passage below is from the 14th Amendment.

    > *All persons born or naturalized in the United States, and subject to the jurisdiction [legal authority] thereof, are citizens of the United States and of the State wherein they reside [live]. No State shall . . . deny to any person within its jurisdiction the equal protection of the laws…*

    Based on the passage, which conclusion can be drawn about the 14th Amendment?

    A. It gave citizenship to former slaves born in the United States.

    B. It denied citizenship to the freedmen but gave it to their children.

    C. It only permitted people born in the United States to become citizens.

    D. It gave different rights to citizens born in the United States and naturalized citizens.

SSUSH10e

12. How did the Presidential Election of 1876 lead to the end of Reconstruction?

    A. African-American voters refused to support Rutherford B. Hayes, the Republican candidate.

    B. In the election, Southern Democrats regained control of the Senate and voted to end Reconstruction.

    C. The Republican candidate promised to end Reconstruction to obtain Southern support for disputed electoral votes.

    D. Once elected, the new President appointed Supreme Court Justices who declared that Reconstruction was unconstitutional.

CHAPTER 8: The Rise of Industrial America

SSUSH11 What were the connections between the rise of big business, the growth of labor unions, and technological innovations?

  a. What were the effects of railroads on other industries, including steel and oil?
  b. What was the significance of John D. Rockefeller and Andrew Carnegie in the rise of trusts and monopolies?
  c. What was the influence of key inventions on U.S. infrastructure, including the telegraph, telephone, and electric light bulb?
  d. What were the roles of Ellis and Angel Islands in immigration, and how did changes in the origins of immigrants affect their impact on the economy, politics, and culture of the United States?
  e. What were the origins, growth, influence, and tactics of labor unions, including those of the American Federation of Labor?

In 1860, most Americans were farmers living in the countryside. They made most things for themselves—from clothes to furniture—and bought only a few small luxuries or scarce items in the local general store or from a traveling peddler. People depended on candles, torches, or whale oil lamps once the sun went down. American manufacturing consisted mainly in making textiles and ironwares, and in processing foods. Railroads and canals linked together Northeastern cities but much of the American West was still unsettled. Many Americans had only limited contact with the world outside their own community in the course of a lifetime.

By 1920, the United States had changed dramatically. Half of all Americans now lived in cities. Large corporations produced goods for the entire nation. Railroads and telephone lines spanned the country from coast to coast. Americans bought their goods in department stores, chain stores, specialty shops, or from mail-order catalogs. Electric lights illuminated the evening hours, and a large number of factories were driven by electricity. People went to motion picture shows for entertainment. The use of the automobile was spreading. America had become the world's leading industrial power. How did all these great changes come about?

The Foundations for Economic Growth

The Legacy of the First Industrial Revolution

In the late eighteenth century, the "Industrial Revolution" in Great Britain introduced the use of steam power and the mass production of goods in factories. The United States became the first nation to follow Britain's lead. By the 1850s, the use of steam power was firmly established in the United States. Northeastern states became the main centers of American manufacturing. Steamboats and railroads began linking together distant regions of the country. In the South, railroads and steamboats led to an expansion of the "Cotton Belt," producing raw cotton for export to British and American factories. The Midwest produced livestock and wheat for both the Northeast and the South.

The Economic Stimulus Provided by the Civil War

The value of Northern manufacturing doubled in the decade of the Civil War. Wartime needs for uniforms, guns, processed foods, and other goods greatly stimulated production. Huge wartime profits were re-invested in manufacturing. The abolition of slavery at the end of the war united the North and South in a giant free-labor, free-market economy.

At the same time, the secession of the South temporarily freed Northern Congressmen to enact new federal laws favorable to the growth of Northern industry.

State governments also tried to stimulate economic growth. They offered land grants and rights of way to railroad companies.

230   Chapter 8 | The Rise of Industrial America

Civil War Legislation Encouraging Economic Growth

The Morrill Tariff (1861) was enacted to protect American manufacturing from European competition.

National Banking Acts (1863 and 1864) created a national banking system through nationally chartered banks and introduced a national currency through the regulation of bank notes.

The Homestead Act (1862) offered free land to settlers occupying farms in the West.

The Morrill Act (1862) gave land grants to states to support technical and agricultural colleges.

The Pacific Railway Act (1862) gave federal loans and land grants to railroad companies to complete a transcontinental railroad.

Note: You will not need to know the names of these laws for the Georgia Milestones EOC Assessment. You should, however, know the impact of the spread of railroads on other industries, including steel and oil (in the section below).

Emergence of the Modern Industrial Economy

The conditions described above set the stage for America's spectacular economic growth in the decades after the Civil War. The spread of railroads created a tremendous demand for steel and coal. Americans became united by new railroad lines, making possible a truly national market for the first time. Manufacturers were able to produce and sell goods more easily across the entire nation. New forms of business organization enabled producers to raise the vast sums of money needed to cover their larger production and distribution costs. These developments transformed how goods were made and used. New inventions—the Bessemer process, telephones, better sewing machines, and electric light bulbs—further stimulated the economy. On top of this, America had a growing population. Historians sometimes refer to this new burst of economic growth as America's "Second Industrial Revolution." Let's examine each of these developments more closely.

The Spread of the Railways

By the end of the Civil War, the United States had 35,000 miles of railroad track. Only 25 years later, it had more than five times that mileage—in fact, more than all of Europe. Railroad lines were most concentrated between the Northeast and the Midwest. The most new track in this period was laid in the West. The first transcontinental railroad was completed in 1869; four additional transcontinental lines were built by 1893. Soon other lines were extended from these

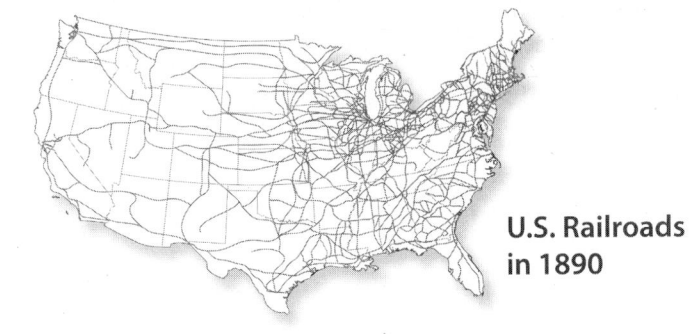

U.S. Railroads in 1870

U.S. Railroads in 1890

Chapter 8 | The Rise of Industrial America

Pullman railroad cars allowed passengers to travel in luxury and even provided sleeping berths

first trunk lines. Federal and state governments encouraged railroad construction by granting rights over vast tracts of land to railroad companies. Steel rails replaced iron ones. A uniform track width (or "gauge") was adopted, making it possible to travel on the tracks of different railroad companies without disruption.

Railroads were made safer and more comfortable by laying double tracks. **George Pullman** invented the sleeping car. **George Westinghouse** invented the air brake, which stopped all the cars of a train at the same time. Gustavus Swift developed the first **refrigerated railroad cars**. Meat was stored in the bottom of a heavily insulated railroad car, while chunks of ice were placed at the top.

Railroads affected just about every aspect of American life. Railroad schedules created the need for uniform time zones across the country. The construction of the railroads provided a tremendous stimulus to the steel, iron, and coal industries. The railroads brought settlers to the Great Plains and connected them with urban markets in the Northeast. Railroads encouraged the growth of cities by enabling workers to commute and allowing farmers to ship their crops and livestock over longer distances. It became possible to slaughter cattle, hogs, and sheep in the stockyards of Chicago, and then to pack and ship the cuts of meat to urban markets in the Northeast. Railroads connected raw materials to factories, and factories to consumers across the nation. They transported oil. Railroad hubs like Chicago and Atlanta mushroomed into major urban centers. Railroads transformed America into a nation on the move as never before.

The Role of Technological Innovation

Just as the "First Industrial Revolution" had depended upon new inventions and innovations, such as the steam engine and its use in factories, the "Second Industrial Revolution" was also based on the twin processes of invention and innovation. Some of the most striking advances occurred in the fields of steel, communications, electricity, oil, and transportation.

Steel and the Bessemer Process

In Britain, Henry Bessemer invented the "**Bessemer process**" in 1855, making the production of steel much more economical. Bessemer blew air through molten pig iron (created by heating iron ore with carbon) to remove impurities before it turned into steel.

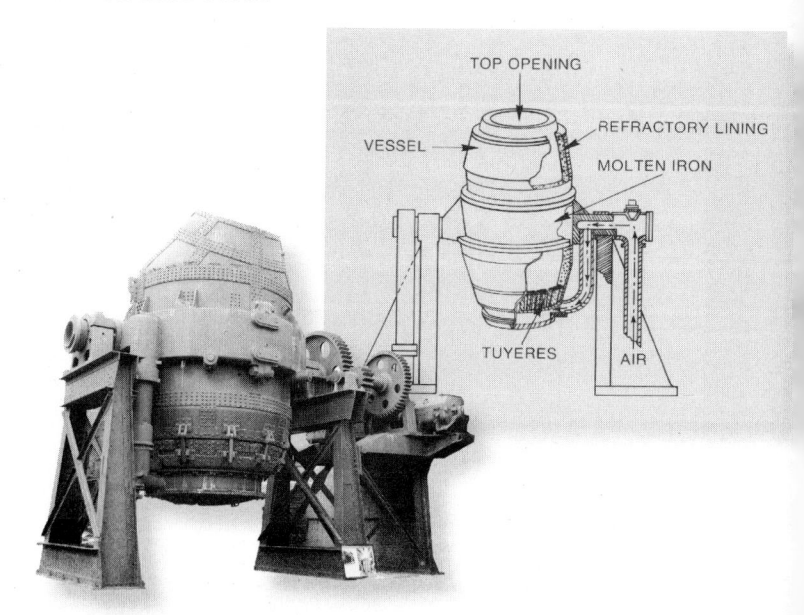

232   Chapter 8 | The Rise of Industrial America

His new process took place in a lined "Bessemer converter." Hot pig iron was poured into the mouth of the converter and air was blown in through the sides. Impurities burned off the top as gas or dropped to the bottom of the converter as "slag."

The Bessemer process reduced the cost of making steel by more than 80%. Cheaper steel made it possible for Americans to produce thousands of miles of railroad track and to build giant steamships, towering steel suspension bridges over rivers, massive turbines and engines, and tall skyscrapers made with steel beams.

Communications

A series of exciting new inventions, most coming from America, completely revolutionized the field of communications.

Samuel Morse (1791–1872): Morse's wife suddenly fell ill and died while she and Morse were apart. The heart-stricken painter then began a search for a faster means of long distance communication. Morse developed the **telegraph** using electromagnetism. He also invented a code of long and short spaces (dots and dashes) capable of transmitting the alphabet. By breaking and closing the circuit, the telegraph operator could move a distant telegraph device on the same circuit. Morse's telegraph made instant communications possible, even over long distances.

Alexander Graham Bell (1847–1922): The mother and wife of this Scottish immigrant were both deaf, while his father and grandfather had both been teachers of speech. Bell began investigating how to reproduce the sounds of speech electronically to help the deaf. He patented the **telephone** in 1875, which carries a variable current to a receiver capable of reproducing the human voice. Bell's invention made it possible to communicate over long distances using natural speech instead of Morse code.

Invention or Innovation?

Invention is the process of developing something for the first time, especially new machines, methods and products. **Innovation** refers to the process of putting these new ideas and methods into practice. An inventor might design and build the first refrigerator; an innovator is the first to build a factory that manufactures them.

Chapter 8 | The Rise of Industrial America

Electricity

Both the telegraph and telephone made use of electrical current. A young telegraph operator, **Thomas Alva Edison**, invented a new "stock-ticker" machine for following the prices of stocks; he also invented an improved telegraph machine. With the money he earned from these first inventions, Edison hired a team of researchers to work in his laboratory in Menlo Park, New Jersey. In 1877, Edison patented the **phonograph** (*record player*). After testing various carbon filaments (*wires*) and gases, Thomas Edison invented a practical **electric light bulb** in 1879, which could burn brightly for many hours.

Edison and his team of researchers developed a whole series of other inventions, including motion pictures, an improved battery, and the first electric power station. In his lifetime, Edison filed more than a thousand patents.

Electricity was also used to run the new **electric motor**, based on the application of electromagnetism to create motion. Electric motors proved to be more adaptable to different uses than steam engines. By the end of the nineteenth century, electricity was being used to power factories and to operate electric streetcars and subway trains.

Nicola Tesla was a Serbian immigrant who came to the United States in 1884 to work for Edison. Two years later, Tesla started his own company. Tesla challenged Edison's reliance on direct current and developed a motor for producing alternating current ("AC"), which could travel longer distances. George Westinghouse, the inventor of the air brake, became Tesla's financial backer. In 1893, they used their high-voltage alternating current to light up the Chicago World's Fair.

Oil

In the early nineteenth century, people had used the blubber (or fat) of whales to make oil for lubrication and lighting. The first oil well was drilled by **Edwin Drake** in Pennsylvania in 1859.

Improvements in refining allowed products from **petroleum**—a liquid hydrocarbon formed over millions of years from the decayed remains of sea organisms—to be used for lighting and machine lubrication. Kerosene was used in lamps in millions of homes. By the end of the century, **gasoline,** also a petroleum derivative, was being used to run another new invention, the internal combustion engine. These developments in steel, electricity, and oil greatly improved the nation's **infrastructure**—the basic facilities and structures on which a society depends, such as roads and water systems.

An internal combustion engine

Other inventions

Other important American inventions in these decades included the typewriter, cash register, and an improved sewing machine.

234   Chapter 8 | The Rise of Industrial America

The Historian's Apprentice

1. Make your own chart or timeline showing the most important inventions of this period and how each invention changed the ways that people lived.
2. Write a short essay on the effects of two key inventions on the nation's infrastructure, such as the Bessemer process, the telegraph, the telephone, or the electric light bulb.

The Emergence of a National Market

The spread of railroads and innovations in communications and manufacturing led to the replacement of separate regional markets by a single national market. Railroads made it cheaper to transport goods to other parts of the country; the telegraph and telephone improved communications; the nation's population expanded; and new methods of advertising and selling were developed. More of the population became concentrated in large cities, where goods were easier to sell. Large corporations developed specialized marketing and advertising departments. New types of retailers—department stores, chain stores (Woolworths), mail-order houses (Sears & Roebuck), and specialty shops—bought items in large quantities from producers at a discount, in order to sell to consumers at a profit.

While the growing population needed consumer goods, expanding industries needed steel, coal, oil, and machinery. National producers could make and ship these capital goods more cheaply than local producers. The high investment costs of modern mass production required a large market to be profitable.

	1860	1920
Total U.S. population	31,443,321	106,021,557
U.S. labor force	7,442,705	42,918,000
Foreign-born population	4,138,697	13,920,692

The spread of railroads helped create a national market.

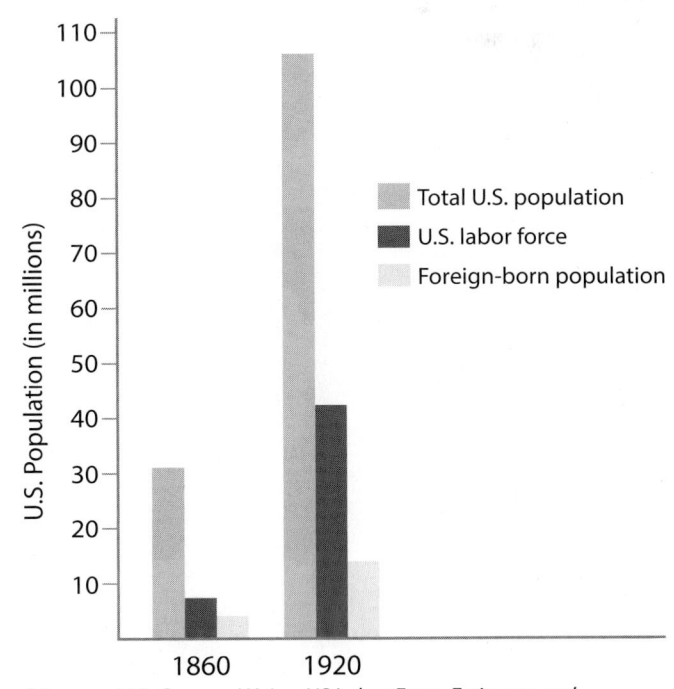

Source: U.S. Census; Weiss, *US Labor Force Estimate and Economic Growth*

Chapter 8 | The Rise of Industrial America

New Business Practices: The Rise of the Corporation

Before the Civil War, most American businesses had been owned either by an individual or by a group of partners. Owners were personally **liable** (*responsible*) for the debts of their company. When the owners died, their business usually dissolved.

In the years following the Civil War, a new form of enterprise became more common. A **corporation** is a company chartered by a state and recognized in law as a separate "person." The corporation issues **stocks,** or shares of ownership in the corporation, to investors.

Each stockholder is a partial owner of the corporation and receives a share of its profits in the form of dividends. Stockholders elect a board of directors, who in turn appoint a general manager (or "CEO") to run the company.

Shareholders

elect | a Board of Directors

which appoints | General Managers

who hire | Company Employees

Corporate stocks are transferable and can be inherited or sold. The death of a stockholder does not affect the survival of the corporation, which can continue indefinitely. Nor are individual shareholders personally responsible for the debts of the company, although they do risk losing their investment.

Building railroads, producing steel, refining petroleum, laying telegraph and telephone wires, and building factories required enormous amounts of money. By issuing stocks, corporations were able to raise greater sums of money than ever before. Individuals were able to pool their money together by investing in a corporation. The corporate form of business organization thus allowed the creation of larger businesses. Large-scale enterprises enjoyed many advantages over smaller competitors:

▶ **Economies of Scale in Production** Larger businesses could build larger production facilities and modernize more rapidly. Such facilities were often more efficient because they could introduce a greater division and specialization of labor, more mechanization, and an increased use of water, steam, or electrical power. They could also invest more money in developing a superior factory design. Increased mechanization—the use of machines—reduced labor costs and expanded productive capacity. Manufacturers were able to produce more goods at lower cost.

▶ **Cheaper Sources of Supply** Giant corporations could obtain raw materials more cheaply from suppliers because the large size of their bulk purchases gave them greater bargaining power and the ability to obtain discounts.

236 Chapter 8 | The Rise of Industrial America

Eventually some large corporations even acquired their own sources of supply.

- **More Efficient Management** The larger size of corporations allowed them to develop better management. Large corporations generally had specialized departments headed by expert managers—accounting, purchasing, processing, marketing, and research and development. They adopted the practice of **cost-accounting**—determining the exact cost of each step in the production and distribution process—to guide their decisions. Corporations could afford to hire engineers, chemists, and scientists to conduct continuous research to improve their existing products and develop new products.

The Great Entrepreneurs

The creation of the modern industrial economy would not have taken place without the guiding hand of the great entrepreneurs. **Entrepreneurs** are those who take risks by engaging in business to make a profit. The leading entrepreneurs considered themselves to be "captains of industry" who adopted new technologies and took advantage of new forms of corporate organization to make cheaper and better products. They had the vision to see the possibilities created by the latest advances in transportation, technology, and corporate finance. They used the same initiative to set up monopolies and trusts.

Critics called them "robber barons" who exploited workers, used dishonest tactics, and exercised their monopoly control over individual industries to overcharge the public. They amassed legendary personal fortunes and frequently turned to **philanthropy** in their old age.

A Portrait Gallery of the Great Entrepreneurs

Andrew Carnegie (1835–1919): At the age of 13, Carnegie came to America from Scotland as a penniless immigrant. He worked as a factory worker, messenger boy, and telegraph operator. He worked his way up to a managerial position in a railroad company and became friends with the owner, who helped him make some investments. During the Civil War, Carnegie helped manage Union railroad lines.

After the war, Carnegie left the railroad industry to start the Keystone Bridge Company. He hoped to build bridges of iron instead of wood. His company became the subcontractor that built much of the first bridge carrying trains across the Mississippi River. To span this long distance, he had to build a structure of steel. Carnegie became a steel producer. He was one of the first to adopt the Bessemer process. He used the corporate form of enterprise to raise additional capital and bought out competing local steel companies in the 1870s.

He joined with Henry Clay Frick to gain access to Frick's coke operations, since coke (*carbon made by heating coal in a furnace without air*) was needed to make pig iron, an essential ingredient for making steel. Carnegie began producing steel girders for building construction, as well as steel rails for railroad tracks.

Carnegie hired chemists to improve his production. He also introduced cost-accounting. He eliminated middlemen and made use of immigrant labor at low wages. Carnegie's workers

Chapter 8 | The Rise of Industrial America

worked 12-hour shifts, and his mills operated all day and all night.

Carnegie pretended to be a friend to labor, and so he hid in Scotland while Frick broke the back of the steelworkers' unions during the Homestead Strike. Carnegie opposed all attempts at worker organization during the strike.

Meanwhile, he bought iron ore mines, a coke works, a limestone company, railroads, and a fleet of ore boats in the Great Lakes. This gave him complete control over all stages of the production and distribution process, known as **vertical integration.**

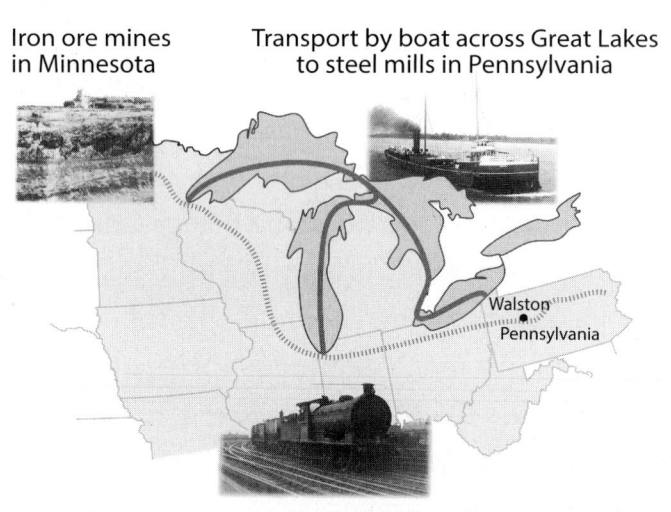

Iron ore mines in Minnesota
Transport by boat across Great Lakes to steel mills in Pennsylvania
Walston Pennsylvania
Transport by train to steel mills in Pennsylvania

By the end of the century, Carnegie was producing one-quarter of all the steel made in the United States. He sold his company to J. P. Morgan in 1901 for $480 million. His personal share was $225 million. He spent the rest of his life giving his money away in acts of philanthropy (*charitable giving*), including millions to establish public libraries throughout the country and Carnegie Hall in New York City.

Andrew Carnegie in 1878, age 43

Carnegie expressed his views on philanthropy in his book *The Gospel of Wealth*. He believed that a rich man should not die with his wealth but should give it away in his lifetime, especially to institutions that promoted self-improvement.

John D. Rockefeller (1839–1937): Rockefeller made profits during the Civil War by investing in oil refineries in Ohio. In 1870, he formed the Standard Oil Company, taking advantage of the corporate form of enterprise.

Rockefeller purchased local rivals in the 1870s and expanded to other Northeastern states. He entered into agreements with railroad companies to give him secret rebates for shipping his oil, while they charged higher prices to his competitors. Later, he started building pipelines to transport his oil, bypassing the railroads altogether. In 1882, Rockefeller formed the Standard Oil Trust, the first great industrial **trust**. It brought 90% of all oil refining in the United States under his control, a form of **horizontal integration** (*when one owner controls all companies and facilities at one stage of production of a good or commodity*).

A Standard Oil Company refinery

Chapter 8 | The Rise of Industrial America

"King" Rockefeller

At the same time, Rockefeller lowered the price of kerosene and other oil products by more than 80%. This made it possible for ordinary people to afford to light their homes at night. The demand for kerosene soared. Just when the invention of the electric light bulb threatened to make Rockefeller's oil less valuable, the invention of the automobile required gasoline, another product made from oil. Like Carnegie, Rockefeller introduced cost-accounting, hired chemists, eliminated middlemen, used cheap labor, and bought out rivals. Also, like Carnegie, he turned to philanthropy in his old age, giving funds to both education and science. He founded the University of Chicago, Rockefeller University, and the Rockefeller Foundation.

John Pierpont ("J. P.") Morgan (1837–1913) was the son of a banker and gifted financier. Much of his early career was spent reorganizing and consolidating failing railroad companies. But Morgan wanted to start his own industry. In 1892, Morgan helped Thomas Edison to form the Edison Electric Company. Edison opposed the use of alternating current, which he thought was too dangerous. When Edison proved to be wrong, Morgan pushed him out of the company. He renamed it as General Electric, and adopted Tesla's system of alternating current. In 1895, Morgan formed J. P. Morgan & Company, a commercial and investment banking institution. In 1901, Morgan bought Carnegie's steelworks and joined them with other steel companies to form U.S. Steel, the first billion-dollar company in the United States.

Note: You will not need to know about J. P. Morgan for the Georgia Milestones EOC Assessment.

J. P. Morgan and the "Gilded Age" mansion he had built for his sister

The Historian's Apprentice

1. Were these leaders of American businesses "Captains of Industry" or "Robber Barons"? Select one of the three great entrepreneurs above. Then present your findings to classmates by pretending to be that entrepreneur. In a short speech to your classmates, justify the actions you took to ensure the success of your business.
2. How did Andrew Carnegie and John D. Rockefeller establish near monopolies through horizontal and vertical integration?

Chapter 8 | The Rise of Industrial America

The Consolidation of Big Business and the Government Response

The mania for laying new railroad lines led first to speculation and then to financial collapse in 1873. In the **depression** (*a prolonged business downturn with high unemployment*) that followed, successful entrepreneurs like Carnegie and Rockefeller drove many smaller competitors out of business and bought up their companies or facilities.

The Dangers of Monopoly

The aim of all these steps was to eliminate competition and to establish a **monopoly**—complete control over the production of a good or service. Monopolies had important disadvantages for the general public:

▶ Monopolists had less incentive to improve their products since they faced no competition.

▶ Monopolists could raise their prices to earn excessive profits. Consumers had no choice but to pay because of the lack of alternative products.

The Government Response

The federal government took few steps to curb the power of "Big Business." In general, government helped business by its absence of regulations or corporate taxes, and its failure to protect either workers or consumers. Under the *laissez faire* ideology of the time, government was not supposed to interfere in relations between producers and buyers, or between employers and employees. The operation of the free market was expected to eliminate inefficient businesses, leading to the best and cheapest goods. A series of Supreme Court decisions affirmed that government had no right to interfere in the relationship between employers and their free employees.

Meanwhile, business leaders often gave hefty campaign contributions to influence government policies. For example, Rockefeller's Standard Oil Company made a large contribution to William McKinley in the 1896 Presidential election. Some businessmen even secretly bribed government officials. They used government support to break up unions and prevent strikes, at the very same time that they argued that government should not interfere in business.

Business consolidations took a variety of forms, from informal agreements to divide markets to complete monopolies. **Trusts** became popular because various state laws placed restrictions on companies operating in more than one state. To get around these restrictions, the stockholders of several related companies gave their stocks to the board of directors of a "trust" in exchange for "trust certificates." These certificates gave their holders dividends based on the profits of the entire trust. The trustees (*directors of the trust*) exercised control over the different companies in the trust and managed them as a single enterprise.

Reformers demanded that the government take measures to regulate "Big Business" and to prevent the formation of monopolies. The abuses of some businesses were so glaring that lawmakers finally recognized that monopolies posed a greater danger to free enterprise than government interference. The first **antitrust laws** (*laws against monopolies*) were weakly enforced, but they established the fundamental principle that Congress could regulate business in some circumstances.

Early Government Regulation of Business

Munn v. Illinois (1877)	In this case, the U.S. Supreme Court ruled that states could regulate businesses affecting the public "interest," such as railroads.
Wabash v. Illinois (1886)	Here, the U.S. Supreme Court ruled that states could not regulate railroads running through several states since this was "interstate commerce." Only Congress could regulate interstate commerce.
Interstate Commerce Act (1887)	In response to *Wabash v. Illinois*, Congress passed this law against unfair practices by railroads. Railroads were prohibited from reaching agreements to divide up territories or giving rebates. All customers were required to pay the same rates, which were to be "reasonable and just." Finally, a special regulatory commission was established to enforce the act.
Sherman Antitrust Act (1890)	In this law, Congress forbade all trusts, combinations, and conspiracies that limited or restricted interstate trade. The act simply stated: "Every contract, combination in the form of trust or otherwise, or conspiracy, in restraint of trade or commerce among the several States, or with foreign nations, is declared to be illegal." The language of the act was extremely vague, weakening its effect. In the 1890s, it was even used against labor unions instead of against "Big Business."
U.S. v. E.C. Knight Company (1895)	In this case, the U.S. Supreme Court ruled that the Sherman Antitrust Act could not be used to break up a monopoly controlling over 90% of all U.S. sugar refining. The Court held that this was a manufacturing monopoly and therefore not within the congressional power to control "interstate trade." This decision greatly weakened the reach of the Sherman Antitrust Act over "Big Business."

The Historian's Apprentice

1. Write a newspaper editorial agreeing or disagreeing with the Supreme Court's decision in *U.S. v. E.C. Knight Company*. Be sure to interpret the Sherman Antitrust Act in your editorial.
2. Write an outline for an essay on the causes or the consequences of the industrialization of the United States in the period 1865–1900.
3. Write a three-paragraph essay on the rise of corporations and the effects of trusts and monopolies on the United States economy in the late nineteenth century.

Chapter 8 | The Rise of Industrial America

Workers Face New Problems

One of the principal factors behind America's rapid economic growth was the increasing exploitation of the industrial worker. Gains in industrial productivity were often achieved at terrible human costs. Some critics complained that industrial workers were treated no better than "wage-slaves":

- **Impersonal Conditions** As factories and workplaces grew larger, individual workers lost personal contact with their actual employers and all influence over their own personal working conditions.

- **Long Hours** Workday hours were long by today's standards. Workers faced a six or seven-day workweek of ten to fourteen hours labor each day. Most steel workers in Carnegie's mills, for example, worked 12-hour shifts either six or seven days per week.

- **Boring, Repetitive Tasks** Skilled workers, like carpenters or mechanics, have extensive training and perform a wide range of specialized tasks. But as industrialists broke up manufacturing into a series of simple tasks to achieve greater speed and efficiency, each worker became nothing more than a human cog in a vast machine. Industrial work became less skilled, more repetitive, monotonous, and boring. There was little pleasure or job satisfaction in repeating the same task for hours on end.

- **Low Wages** Wages were so low that many workers could not afford minimal requirements for food, shelter, and clothing. Every member of the family had to work to make ends meet, even though women and children were especially low paid. Immigrants from overseas and migrants from the countryside flooded the labor market with workers willing to work for very low wages.

- **Dangerous Conditions** Conditions at work in the late nineteenth and early twentieth centuries were often extremely hazardous. There were insufficient safeguards around machinery and overworked employees were often extremely tired. Hundreds of thousands of workers were injured or killed in accidents each year, especially on the railroads or in the coal mines. Others suffered serious illnesses from unhealthy working conditions.

- **Child Labor** Textile mills and coal mines made use of child laborers to perform special tasks and because they were paid less than adults. Children also worked on farms, in canneries and glass factories, and as newsboys and messengers. Almost one-fifth of the American workforce was made up of children at the end of the century. As many as one out of every five children under 15 years old was working outside the home. Many of these workers were immigrant children or worked in factories in the South.

- **Periodic Unemployment** When there was a downturn in business, many employers fired part of their workforce. Employers did not provide health insurance or contribute to a pension for an employee's old age. There was no unemployment insurance when a worker lost his or her job.

- **Lack of Opportunity for Advancement** It was difficult to move from an unskilled to a skilled position or to find a new job with higher wages. There were generally no promotions or automatic increases in pay for being at a job a long time. In times of recession or intense competition with rival companies, pay might even be cut or workers could be laid off.

- **Unpleasant Living Conditions** Most workers lived in crowded, inner-city slums or in company towns. With their low wages, they could not afford better housing. In company towns like Pullman, the company controlled not only the workers' wages, but what workers paid in rent and for food and other supplies in the company store. The company also controlled town officials and the police, making it almost impossible for workers to complain or to organize against the company.

Workers Organize

With the rise of large corporations, individual workers lost all of their bargaining power with employers. Since most work was unskilled, workers could be easily replaced. The only way to achieve better conditions seemed to be through better worker organization. Therefore, industrial workers began to organize. Such organizations, known as **labor unions**, generally had three main goals:

- **To Obtain Higher Wages and Better Working Conditions** By joining together, workers felt they could demand better pay, shorter hours and better working conditions. If an employer refused their demands, all the workers at a factory, steel mill, mine, or other workplace might strike (walk off their jobs at the same time). The business owner's operations would halt, forcing the owner to come to terms with the striking workers to get things going again.

- **"Mutual Aid" Societies** Members of unions regularly contributed to special funds to provide pensions and insurance benefits in times of need, such as injury, illness, strike, or death.

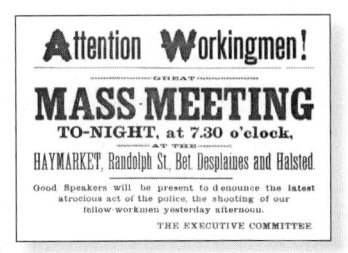

- **To Place Pressure on Government** Unions acted as "pressure groups" on government. Union leaders tried to coordinate workers' votes to influence politicians in favor of their demands. Unions also contributed directly to campaign funds and lobbied in legislatures. Some labor leaders wished to go further and use unions to create a new political party that would represent workers.

The Historian's Apprentice

1. Imagine you are an industrial worker in the late 1870s. Write a letter to a friend describing your conditions at work and how organizing a union might help to improve those conditions.
2. Pretend you are a labor union organizer entering a factory in 1875. Give a speech explaining to the workers there why they should form a union.

Chapter 8 | The Rise of Industrial America

The American Federation of Labor

In the decades after the Civil War, worker organizations were generally weak. To oppose national corporations, labor leaders reasoned they needed to form their own national unions.

One of the first of these, the Knights of Labor, attempted to include all workers—skilled and unskilled, men and women. It sought political and social reform. However, it collapsed due to poor organization and a series of unsuccessful strikes. A different nationwide labor organization was founded in 1881. In 1886, this organization renamed itself as the **American Federation of Labor**, or AFL. The AFL was actually a federation of several national craft unions, including those of carpenters, cigar-makers, and shoemakers. Its membership was restricted to skilled workers.

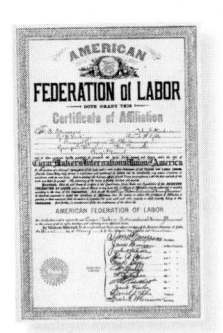

Samuel Gompers, a Jewish immigrant from England, quickly became its leader. Gompers began making cigars at the age of 10, moved with his family to America at the age of 13, joined a local cigar-makers' union at 14, and was elected as the head of his local union at the age of 24 in 1874.

Gompers limited the goals of the AFL to obtaining immediate benefits for its members—higher pay, an 8-hour workday, better conditions in the work place, and a "closed shop" policy (in which the employer promised to hire only union members). Gompers believed that the worker's interests were best served, not by resisting industrial capitalism, but by bargaining for a greater share of its profits. To counter the concentration of industry in the hands of a few owners, Gompers believed workers had to band together to speak in a single voice. While Gompers favored peaceful bargaining with employers, he was willing to use strikes and boycotts when necessary. He also supported political candidates who backed union demands.

Except for a brief period of time, the AFL did not admit women. Gompers had at first insisted that the affiliated craft unions admit African-American workers, but when several refused to do so, Gompers backed down. As a result, only the United Mine Workers and a few other AFL unions admitted African Americans in these years. African-American leaders complained that the unions were holding African Americans back, especially by refusing to admit young African Americans as apprentices. Gompers also failed to counteract ethnic prejudice against different nationalities within particular craft unions.

The American Federation of Labor soon became the leading voice of organized labor. It grew quickly in size. By 1900, it had more than half a million members. It was weakened, however, by the fact that in its early years it excluded unskilled workers. These continued to constitute the bulk of the American labor force. Fewer than 5% of U.S. workers were unionized in 1900.

The Historian's Apprentice

1. Write two paragraphs explaining why workers felt the need to organize in this period.
2. Write two paragraphs explaining the successes and failures of the American Federation of Labor (AFL).

Tactics of Labor and Management

Organized labor had a number of **tactics** (*actions taken to reach a goal*) at its disposal. The first of these tactics was **collective bargaining**—the ability of the union to represent all of the workers at a workplace in negotiations with the employer. The next most important tactic was the ability to **strike**—to walk out of the workplace and refuse to work. While on strike, union workers carried signs outside their place of employment—known as the **"picket line"**—to win public support and prevent the use of **strike-breakers** (*temporary workers hired by management to operate the factory, mine, or mill while the regular workers were out on strike*). To support themselves during a strike, union members made contributions while they were working to a **strike fund**.

In the early days of unions, employers had many more weapons at their disposal than today:

- The company's **managers**—those people running the company—could simply fire striking workers and hire new ones.
- If management did not agree to worker demands, they could close the factory to keep the workers from their jobs. This was known as a **lockout**.
- When workers went on strike, management often brought in temporary workers known as **"strike-breakers"** (or **"scabs"**). These worked in factories or mines until the dispute with the striking workers was settled. Often the strike-breakers were African-American workers or immigrant workers with different ethnic backgrounds than the strikers.
- Employers might force their employees to sign agreements, known as **"Yellow Dog" Contracts**, promising that they would not join a union. (Such agreements were later made illegal.)
- Union leaders and members were often fired. Their names might be circulated to other employers so that they could not get another job. This practice was known as **"blacklisting."**
- Employers hired private detectives, known as *Pinkertons*, to spy on union leaders and to break up strikes, often with violence and sometimes even murder.
- Finally, employers might seek a court order prohibiting a strike. Once such an **injunction** (court order) was issued, employers could count on the government to break up the strike. Police or even state troops might be used to break up the strike.

Violence erupts as troops intervene in the Pullman Railroad strike

Chapter 8 | The Rise of Industrial America

The Influence of Early Labor Unions

The attitudes of government and the public were critical to the fortunes of the early labor movement. In the late nineteenth century, both were often partial towards business. They took a hostile view of unions for several reasons:

- Government leaders saw their proper role as providing protection to private property. Strikers seemed to threaten the security of property.
- The public believed that union demands would raise prices.
- Union activity was associated in the public mind with violence, anarchism, socialism, and ideas brought over by recent European immigrants.
- Businesses contributed to politicians' campaign funds, while business and government leaders often shared the same general outlook. Government officials believed America owed much of its economic success to its business leaders.
- *Laissez faire* attitudes gave businessmen the power to hire or fire employees as they pleased.

As a result of these factors, the impact of labor unions was limited in the late nineteenth century. It was only later that labor unions began improving conditions and raising wages for American workers.

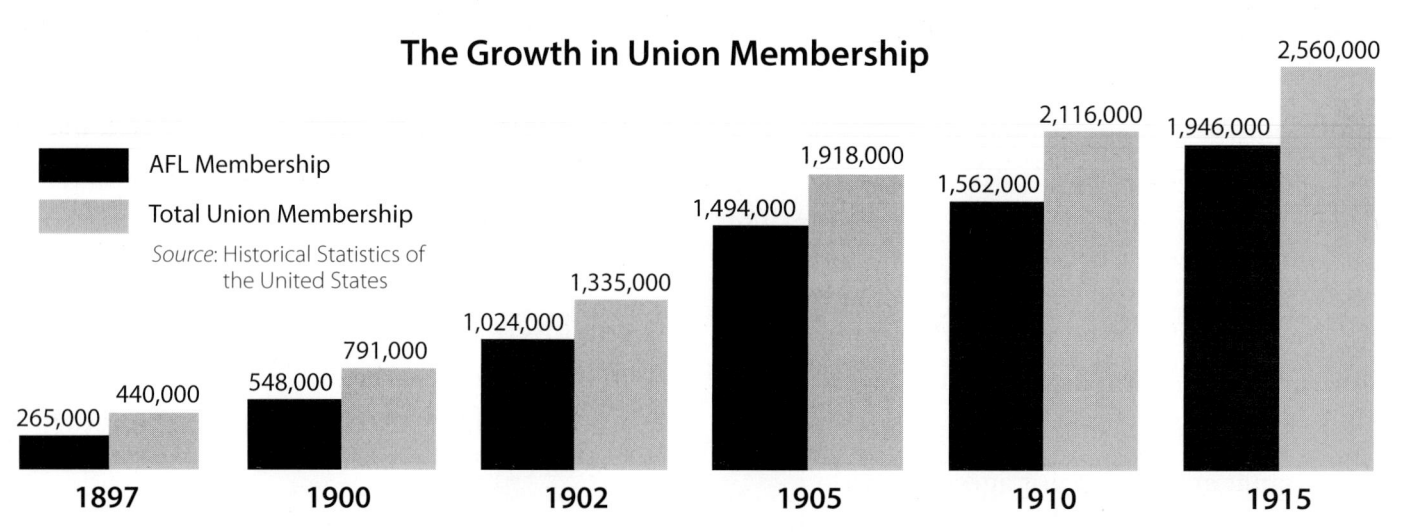

The Growth in Union Membership

Year	AFL Membership	Total Union Membership
1897	265,000	440,000
1900	548,000	791,000
1902	1,024,000	1,335,000
1905	1,494,000	1,918,000
1910	1,562,000	2,116,000
1915	1,946,000	2,560,000

Source: Historical Statistics of the United States

1. When in these years was the growth in union membership the greatest?
2. What factors contributed to the growth in union membership?

The Historian's Apprentice

Pretend you are an early organizer for the American Federation of Labor. Your role is to visit various craft unions and try to persuade them to join the AFL. Write a speech you might give to a local union describing the AFL and its benefits. Be sure to include a discussion of the tactics that AFL members use in labor disputes with management.

Immigrants

The industrialization of America was greatly spurred by a flood of immigration to American shores.

Shifting Patterns of Immigration

Historically, the migration of people to the United States has resulted from a combination of **"push"** and **"pull"** factors: conditions in immigrants' home countries propelled them to leave, while conditions in the United States attracted them to come here.

The "Old Immigrants" (before 1880)

The "Old Immigrants" generally came from Britain, Ireland, or Germany to find new economic opportunities. Most spoke English. Often they came to escape great hardships. For example, the Irish potato famine led to a mass exodus from Ireland to America in the 1840s.

The "New Immigrants" (1880–1924)

Existing patterns of immigration changed in the 1880s. Conditions in Western Europe improved, while lower transportation costs brought migration to America within the grasp of other Europeans. The "New Immigrants" came chiefly from Southern and Eastern Europe. Italians, Poles, Jews, and Greeks came in large numbers. The "New Immigrants" were generally Catholic, Jewish, or Orthodox Christian rather than Protestant. They spoke little or no English and had different appearances and habits from most Americans. Many were extremely poor and uneducated. Many of the "New Immigrants" came to escape religious or political persecution. Jews from Russia, for example, came to escape "*pogroms*" (violent mob attacks on Jewish communities, generally supported by government authorities, in which property was destroyed and community members were often killed).

Most "New Immigrants," however, simply came to escape grinding poverty. In their own countries, land and wealth were controlled by small elites and most people were desperately poor. Because of cheaper steamship travel, many could now afford the voyage to the United States. There were no legal restrictions on European immigration to America at that time. Letters from relatives and accounts in newspapers spread optimistic reports of the benefits of American life. Advertisements from steamship companies selling tickets, railroads selling land grants, and

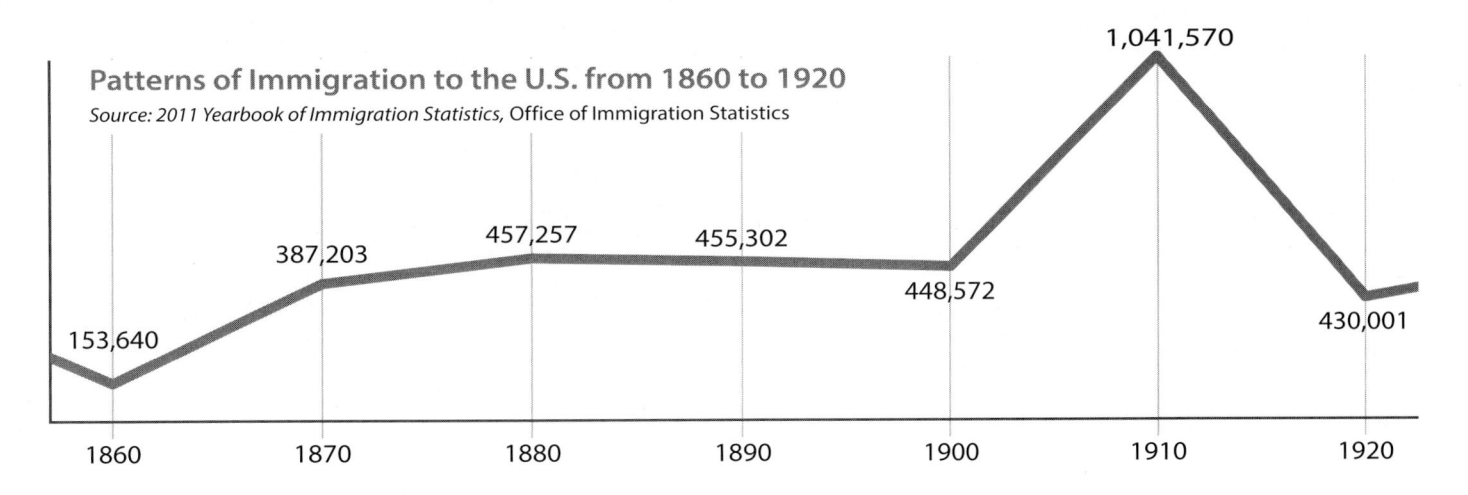

Patterns of Immigration to the U.S. from 1860 to 1920
Source: 2011 Yearbook of Immigration Statistics, Office of Immigration Statistics

Year	Immigrants
1860	153,640
1870	387,203
1880	457,257
1890	455,302
1900	448,572
1910	1,041,570
1920	430,001

Chapter 8 | The Rise of Industrial America

industrialists recruiting labor also attracted newcomers.

Immigrants were drawn by the promise of greater freedom, higher standards of living, and economic opportunity. By 1900, more than 13% of those living in the United States were foreign-born.

The Historian's Apprentice

Make a Venn diagram comparing the characteristics of the "Old" and "New" Immigrants.

Establishing a New Life

The Voyage Across

Usually the "New Immigrants" traveled by train to a port in Europe. Then they crossed the Atlantic in the cheapest class (known as "steerage"). They slept in spaces without windows below the water level. Many carried their belongings in a single bag. Most landed in New York Harbor, where they passed the Statue of Liberty, a gift from France that came to symbolize America's willingness to accept the downtrodden. At the statue's base is a poem by the Jewish-American poet Emma Lazarus, welcoming the "tired" and "poor . . . huddled masses" of other lands, "yearning to breathe free."

After 1892, most immigrants arriving in New York City landed at **Ellis Island** for medical examinations and to be processed for admission to the United States. They could be sent back to Europe for poor health, especially signs of tuberculosis (TB), or for other reasons, such as a criminal history, but most were admitted to the United States. Many immigrants were given new names by officials who could not pronounce their old ones. Once admitted, a large number of the immigrants remained in New York City. Others took trains to join relatives and friends in towns and cities across America.

Challenges in the New Land

The vast majority of the "New Immigrants" settled in the cities of the Northeast and Midwest, where they took unskilled jobs. A few, especially those coming from Scandinavia and Germany,

Thousands of immigrants arrived at Ellis Island every week

248   Chapter 8 | The Rise of Industrial America

went to farms on the Great Plains. They all faced similar challenges:

- ▶ They were unfamiliar with American customs and ways—from foods and kitchen implements to voting in elections.
- ▶ They could only find employment at unskilled jobs for long hours with low pay.

To cope with these problems, immigrants usually settled down in urban neighborhoods with other immigrants of the same nationality, known as "**ghettos**." Different parts of the Lower East Side of New York City, for example, were Jewish or German (*Kleindeuschland*), while Chinatown and Little Italy sprang up on opposite sides of Canal Street. In these ethnic neighborhoods, immigrants could converse with one another in their native language. Here they found churches and synagogues they could attend, and they helped one another to find housing and work. Often they had friends and relatives from the "Old Country" in the same neighborhood. They had groceries with ethnic foods, clothing stores with their traditional garments, and their own banks and insurance companies. There might even be one or more community newspapers printed in their native language. The immigrants felt comfortable surrounded by those who spoke the same language, followed the same customs, and shared the same experiences. But the fact that they lived in these ethnic ghettos also meant that they were cut off from the American mainstream.

The Process of "Americanization"

Only gradually did the immigrants become "**Americanized**"—*assimilated into mainstream American society by learning its values and behaviors*. Often it was the children of the immigrants, and not the immigrants themselves, who were the first to become "Americanized."

Immigrants from Asia

Chinese Americans

Very few Chinese immigrated to the United States before the discovery of gold in California in 1848. "Pushed" by warfare and economic hard times in China, and "pulled" by the lure of gold, Chinese immigrants began arriving in "Gold Mountain"—California—shortly thereafter. At first, most of the arrivals worked panning for gold. Just as the gold was running out, Chinese

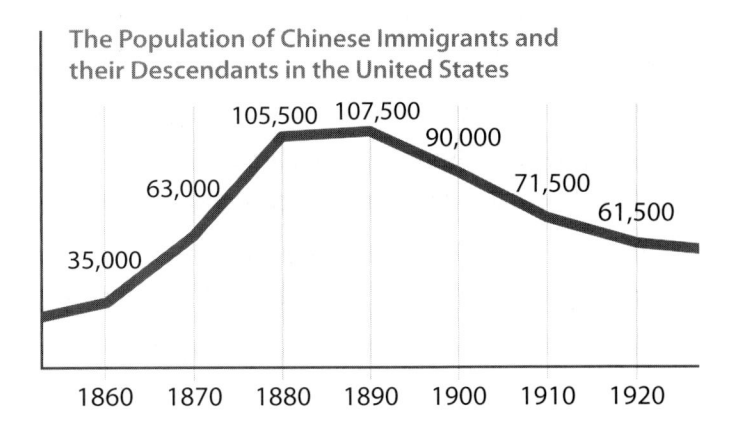

Chinese workers on the Central Pacific, part of the transcontinental railroad

The Population of Chinese Immigrants and their Descendants in the United States

Year	Population
1860	35,000
1870	63,000
1880	105,500
1890	107,500
1900	90,000
1910	71,500
1920	61,500

Chapter 8 | The Rise of Industrial America

Name _____

Explore the connections between technological innovations, the rise of big business, the growth of labor unions by providing the following explanations.

Connection	Explanation
Explain the effects of railroads on other industres, including steel and oil.	
Explain the influence of key inventions on U.S. infrastructure (transportation, communications and buildings), including the telegraph, telephone, and electric light bulb.	
Explain the significance of John D. Rockefeller and Andrew Carnegie in the rise of trusts and monopolies.	

Name _____

Explore the connections between technological innovations, the rise of big business, the growth of labor unions by providing the following explanations.

Connection	Explanation
Describe the roles of Ellis and Angel Islands in immigration.	
Explain how changes in the origins of immigrants affected their impact on the economy, politics and culture of the United States.	
Explain the origins, growth and influence of labor unions, including the American Federation of Labor (AFL).	
Describe the tactics (actions) used by labor unions to achieve their objectives.	

Chapter 8 | The Rise of Industrial America

Name _____

Immigration and Cities

List pull factors that may have contributed to people's choice to immigrate to the United States.
▶
▶
▶
▶
▶

List some of the assimilation problems faced by immigrants when they arrived in the United States.
▶
▶
▶
▶
▶

The Second Industrial Revolution caused an explosion in the size and number of American cities. Describe some of the negative effects of their rapid growth.

_____
_____
_____

Industrialization and the Progressive Era

This cartoon depicts one of America's most successful entrepreneurs.

1. How is John D. Rockefeller depicted in this illustration?
_____
_____

2. What information is shown on Rockefeller's hat? Explain all of the symbols and images that you can identify.
_____
_____
_____

3. What do you think is the cartoonist's view of Rockefeller? Provide evidence in support of your views.
_____
_____
_____

256   Chapter 8 | The Rise of Industrial America

Name _____

This cartoon shows Theodore Roosevelt, who was President from 1901 to 1909. He was also a big-game hunter. You will learn more about Roosevelt in the next chapter. He believed that some business consolidations were necessary, but that others took unfair advantage of competitors, consumers and other businesses. Roosevelt therefore distinguished between "good trusts" and "bad trusts." During his Presidency, he attempted to use the Sherman Anti-trust Act to break up several "bad trusts."

1. According to the cartoonist, how does this hunter treat good and bad trusts differently?

_____
_____
_____
_____

2. One of the "bad trusts" that Roosevelt tried to break up was John D. Rockefeller's Standard Oil Company. Do you think Roosevelt was justified in this action? Explain your reasoning.

_____
_____
_____
_____

3. In your view, was the overall impact of "Big Business" during America's Second Industrial Revolution good or bad? Use facts and examples to support your view.

_____
_____
_____
_____

Chapter 8 | The Rise of Industrial America

The Rise of Industrial America

Immigration

The "Old Immigrants" (before 1880)
- From Western Europe
- Most were English-speaking Protestants

Political "machines"
- Provide sevices to immigrants in exchange for their votes
- Profit from control of city governments

The "New Immigrants" (1880–1924)
- From Southern and Eastern Europe
- Spoke non-English languages
- Most were Catholic or Jewish
- Most were extremely poor
- Most moved to ethnic "ghettos" in cities
- Took low-paying jobs

Asian Immigrants
- From China, Japan, and the Philippines
- Spoke non-English languages
- Faced discrimination in California and the West
- Chinese Exclusion Act (1882)
- Gentlemen's Agreement (1907)

The Rise of Nativism
- Anti-immigrant organizations
- Ku Klux Klan
- Other white supremacists

Workers

New Problems
- Low wages
- Long hours
- Child labor
- Periodic unemployment

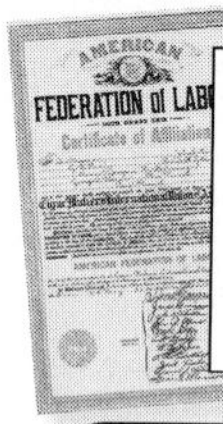

Workers Organize
- Labor unions
- American Federation of Labor

Long-term Causes
- Natural Resources
- Legacy of First Industrial Revolution
- Role of Government
- Stimulus of Civil War

Course

Spread of Railroads

New Inventions
- Morse
- Bell
- Edison
- Tesla

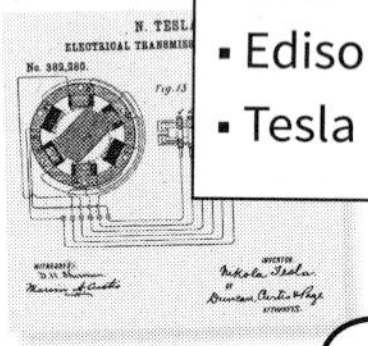

Rise of Corporations

Entrepreneurs
- Carnegie
- Rockefeller
- J. P. Morgan

"Robber Barons"

Philanthropy

Emergence of New Industries

Steel
- Bessemer process

Communications
- Telegraph
- Telephone

Electricity
- Light bulb

Internal Combustion Engine

Consequences

Nationwide Market for Goods

Rise of "Big Business" and Monopolies

Government Regulation
- Sherman Antitrust Act
- Interstate Commerce Act

258 Chapter 8 | The Rise of Industrial America

What Do You Know?

SSUSH11b

1. What was the significance of the passage of the Interstate Commerce Act (1887) and the Sherman Antitrust Act (1890)?
   A. They encouraged Big Business to grow by passing protective tariffs.
   B. They prevented poor quality goods from being shipped across state lines.
   C. They were both used to break up labor unions that interfered with free enterprise.
   D. They established the principle that Congress could regulate business in certain circumstances.

SSUSH11c

2. Which identifies an accomplishment of Thomas Edison and his team of researchers at Menlo Park, New Jersey?
   A. the first telephone
   B. the first steam engine
   C. the first practical light bulb
   D. the first internal combustion engine

SSUSH11a

3. How were Americans influenced by the growth of railroads during the Second Industrial Revolution?
   A. Railroads led to shortages of raw materials for factories and of workers on farms.
   B. Railroads stimulated the construction of steamships to trade up and down rivers.
   C. Railroads created time zones, the growth of cities, and the first truly national market.
   D. Railroads caused cotton, rice, and wheat production to move from the Southeast to the West Coast.

SSUSH11c

4. Which statement BEST describes a major impact of the invention of the telegraph and telephone?
   A. Americans were able to develop a national market for their goods and services.
   B. Americans were able travel more quickly across the North American Continent.
   C. Americans were able to surpass Great Britain and Germany in the production of steel.
   D. The U.S. Army was able to move the Plains Indians onto reservations without bloodshed.

Chapter 8 | The Rise of Industrial America

SSUSH11b

5. Use the cartoon to answer the question.

HOPELESSLY BOUND TO THE STAKE.

Part A

Which issue is addressed in the cartoon?

A. the influence of labor unions

B. the excessive power of Big Business

C. the dangerous conditions of factory labor

D. the corruption of political machines in American cities

Part B

Based on the cartoon above, what conclusion can be reached about the United States in the early 1880s?

A. Most American manufacturing was controlled by business monopolies.

B. Some American critics felt workers were being oppressed by business monopolies.

C. Government leaders were finally taking steps to curb the power of business monopolies.

D. Business monopolies overcharged their customers but were essential to American economic growth.

SSUSH11e

6. Use the illustration to answer the question.

   What was the main goal of the organization that issued this certificate?

   A. to obtain better pay and conditions for skilled workers
   B. to assist in the transition from a capitalist to a socialist society
   C. to help cigar makers obtain better housing and U.S. citizenship
   D. to replace individual unions with a single national union for all

SSUSH11b

7. Which industrialist became wealthy by establishing a virtual monopoly over American oil refining?

   A. John D. Rockefeller
   B. Andrew Carnegie
   C. J. P. Morgan
   D. Henry Clay Frick

SSUSH11e

8. Which TWO tactics were sometimes used by labor unions in disputes with management?

   A. Strike
   B. Lockout
   C. Court injunction
   D. Blacklisting
   E. Use of Pinkertons
   F. Yellow Dog Contracts
   G. Picket line

SSUSH11d

9. Why were immigrants from Southern and Eastern Europe in the late nineteenth century welcomed by industrialists?

   A. The immigrants found it difficult to learn English and assimilate.
   B. The immigrants voted for candidates from the local political machine.
   C. The immigrants lived in ghettos with other people from the same background.
   D. The immigrants were willing to work for lower wages than most other workers.

Chapter 8 | The Rise of Industrial America

SSUSH11d

10. Use the photograph to answer the question.

Ellis Island (1904)

What was the primary purpose of this facility?

A. processing permanent residents applying for U.S. citizenship

B. processing highly skilled workers arriving from China and Japan

C. processing first-class passengers arriving on European steamship lines

D. processing immigrants mainly coming from Southern and Eastern Europe

SSUSH11b

11. Use the cartoon to answer the question.

Source: U.S. Senate

What is the viewpoint of the artist?

A. Trusts mainly compete against one another for profits.

B. Trusts have been subjected to unfair regulation by Congress.

C. Trusts have too much influence over the United States Senate.

D. Trusts play an essential role in promoting American economic growth.

262   Chapter 8 | The Rise of Industrial America

CHAPTER 9 The Last Frontier

SSUSH12 How did the westward expansion of the United States affect the Plains Indians and fulfill "Manifest Destiny"?

  a. How was the first transcontinental railroad constructed, including the role of immigrant labor?

  b. How did the growth in the number of settlers in the West and innovations in farming and ranching affect the Plains Indians?

  c. How did the Plains Indians resist the western expansion of the United States and what were the consequences of their resistance?

Names and Terms You Should Know

Great Plains
Rocky Mountains
Sierra Nevada
Transcontinental railroad
Pacific Railway Act
Central Pacific
Union Pacific
Immigrant labor
Plains Indians
"Indian Wars"

Sioux
Cheyenne
Black Hills
"Indian Wars"
George Armstrong Custer
Chief Joseph
Buffalo soldiers
Reservation
Wounded Knee
Dawes Act

Ranching
Cowboys
"Open range"
"Long drive"
barbed wire
Homestead Act
Sod houses
Groundwater

Georgia "Peaches" of Wisdom

1. The American frontier was the line separating areas of settlement from less densely populated areas. By the end of the Civil War, the frontier was at the Great Plains, Rocky Mountains, and deserts of the Southwest.

2. In 1865, these areas were still occupied by Indian tribes. These tribes had different lifestyles, depending on where they lived. The Plains Indians—such as the Cheyenne, Sioux, and Comanche— rode horses and hunted buffalo. In the Southwest, the Pueblo farmed and lived in adobe houses.

3. During the Civil War, Congress passed the Pacific Railway Act (1862). It authorized construction of the transcontinental railroad using a northern route, from Omaha, Nebraska, to Sacramento, California. The Union Pacific Railroad was built from Omaha westward. Workers were mainly Irish immigrants. The Central Pacific Railroad, financed by four California merchants, was built from Sacramento eastwards, mainly by Chinese laborers. These workers used explosives to create tunnels through the Sierra Nevada. The railroad was completed when the two sides connected in Utah in 1869.

4. The transcontinental railroad led to the destruction of the buffalo on the Plains, the arrival of settlers, and the transformation of the Great Plains into ranches and farms. Ranchers and farmers could now ship their livestock and crops back East.

5. Congress appointed a special commission to negotiate new treaties with the Indians. In 1868, the commission negotiated the Second Treaty of Fort Laramie: Sioux tribes gave up territory for a federal guarantee of their control of South Dakota, which included the sacred Black Hills.

6. In 1874, gold was discovered in the Black Hills. Colonel George Armstrong Custer brought experts and troops to tour the area. In 1876, Sioux and Cheyenne warriors defeated Custer at the Battle of Little Bighorn. The following year, the U.S. Army defeated the Sioux and Cheyenne in several battles. The Sioux were forced to abandon the Black Hills and move to reservations.

7. The Nez Perce in the Northwest were also forced onto a reservation. Chief Joseph and his followers fled towards Canada but were followed and stopped just miles from the border. Chief Joseph made an appeal that he would "fight no more forever."

8. During the "Indian Wars," U.S. troops who had fought in the Civil War used their superior weapons and tactics to defeat the Plains Indians and force them onto reservations—land set aside for Indian tribes.

9. Indian resistance to the westward expansion of the United States thus ended with their confinement on reservations. Reservation lands were unfamiliar and were often inferior to the lands previously occupied by the tribe. Indians enjoyed independence on the reservation, but corrupt federal agents often kept money and provisions intended for the Indians.

10. Reformers wanted Indians to assimilate and become "Americanized." They placed many Indian children in boarding schools, forcing them to speak English and converting them to Christianity. The Dawes Act (1887) allowed each adult male Indian to take some reservation land as private property.

11. Completion of the transcontinental railroad, defeat of the Indians in the "Indian Wars," and the availability of cheap land under the Homestead Act (1862) encouraged settlers and ranchers to come to the Great Plains and Far West.

12. Farmers developed innovative technologies to farm on the dry but fertile Great Plains. They dug wells and built windmills to pump groundwater found deep below the surface. They built sod houses and surrounded their fields with barbed wire to keep livestock in and other animals out. They used steel plows to break up the tough sod.

13. Farmers experienced difficulties when food prices fell even though their costs remained high. The Populist Party was formed in the early 1890s to represent their interests. Populists made many far-reaching proposals that were later adopted: direct election of U.S. Senators, a secret ballot, and federal income tax.

America's Last Frontier

By the end of the Civil War, the United States controlled all of the territory from the Atlantic to the Pacific. Much of this area was settled and divided into states, reaching from Texas to Minnesota. American settlers also occupied lands along the Pacific Coast from California to Oregon. Between these regions lay a vast expanse of territory—equal in size to more than half of the rest of the United States—consisting of the Great Plains, the Rocky Mountains, the Great Basin, the Sierra Nevada Mountains, and the deserts of the Southwest. This was the final "frontier," with sparsely populated territories that had yet to apply for statehood.

The most fertile of these regions, the **Great Plains,** consisted of rolling, treeless plains that stretched from Texas to North Dakota. They received little rainfall, especially on their western side closer to the Rockies. In 1865, the Plains were covered with short, thin grasses and provided a home to millions of American buffalo. The Plains were only vaguely known to most Americans as the "Great American Desert."

Thousands of Indians, originally from eastern states, were then living on the Great Plains in "Indian Territory" (present-day Oklahoma). Thousands of others roamed freely on the rest of the Plains, in the Southwest, and in the Pacific Northwest. These Indians were not one people but many—Cheyenne, Sioux, Comanche, Apache, Navajo, Pueblo, Nez Perce, and many others. Each tribe had its own language, traditions, and culture. The Plains Indians, for example, were superb horsemen who lived off the meat, hides, and bones of the buffalo they hunted. In contrast, the Pueblo Indians grew corn, squash, and beans, and lived in multi-storied dwellings made of stone, logs, and sun-dried adobe bricks.

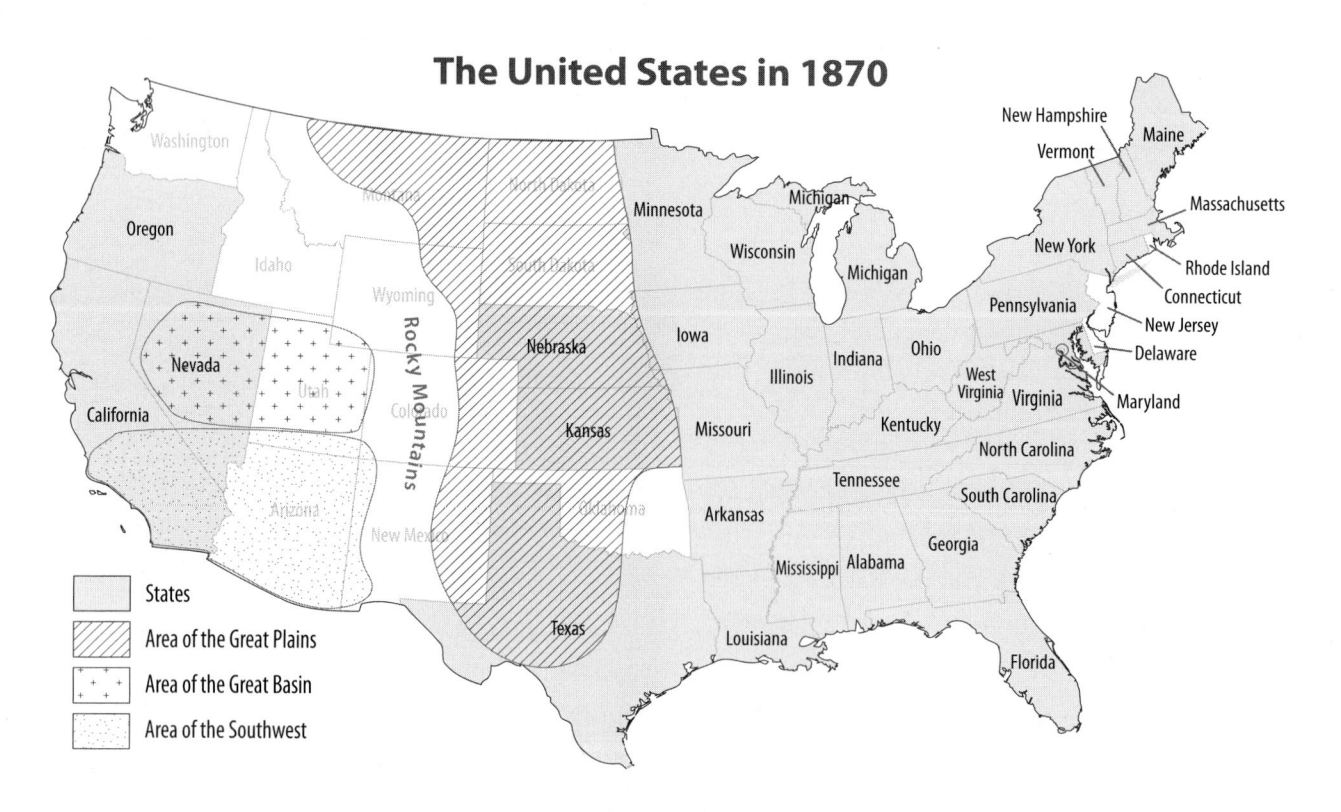

The United States in 1870

The Transformation of the Great Plains and Far West

Four factors combined to transform these lands west of the Mississippi:

1. The discovery of precious metals—such as gold in California.
2. The completion of the first transcontinental railroad (1869) and subsequent railroad lines.
3. The "Indian Wars" and relocation of Indian tribes to reservations.
4. The availability of cheap land to settlers and the development of innovative ranching and farming techniques.

The Transcontinental Railroad

In the days before the Civil War, only a few stagecoach lines, telegraph wires, ships sailing to the Pacific Coast, and, for a brief period, the Pony Express, kept the Far West in contact with the rest of the country. During the Gold Rush (1848-1849), the only ways to reach California were to sail around South America, to make a perilous journey across the Isthmus of Panama, or to join a wagon train crossing the United States. The need for a shorter, quicker and less expensive way to cross the country was easy to see.

In 1855, Congress investigated the possibility of a **transcontinental railroad** (*a railroad crossing the entire continent*). Congress considered several possible routes. Northerners and Southerners could not agree, however, on whether to build the proposed railroad along a Northern or Southern route. For this reason, the project was delayed.

During the Civil War, Southern states were no longer represented in Congress. Northerners took advantage of the situation by passing the **Pacific Railway Act** (1862). This law specified a Northern route for the first transcontinental railroad: it was to run from Omaha, Nebraska, to Sacramento, California.

Two companies were assigned different sections of the railroad to build at the same time. The Union Pacific was to lay down tracks going westward from Omaha. The Central Pacific was to lay down tracks going eastward from Sacramento. The two companies were to meet somewhere in the middle. Each company was promised generous land grants, subsidized loans and other valuable benefits for every mile of track that they laid.

Construction began in 1863, while the Civil War was still raging. Laborers, mainly Irish immigrants, worked on building the Union Pacific line. Meanwhile, crews of Chinese immigrants laid the track for the Central Pacific Railroad from Sacramento. Most of the railroad was thus built by **immigrant labor**. After 1865,

Transcontinental Railroad

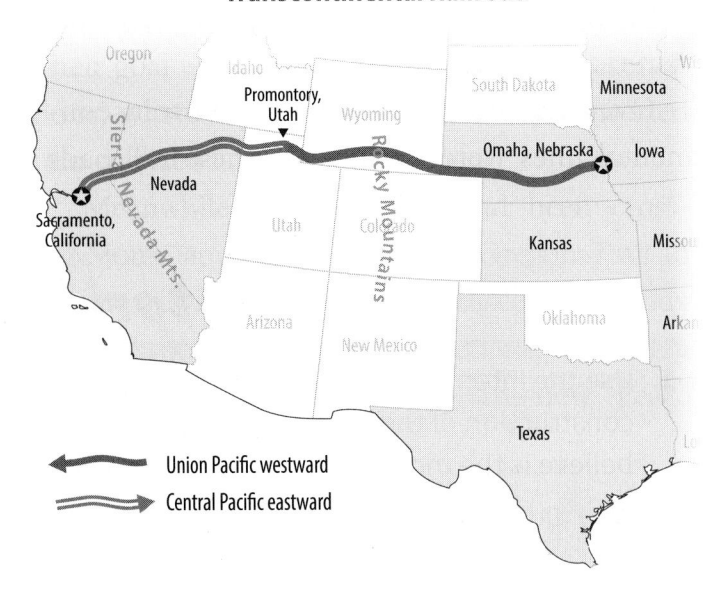

Commission," led by General William Tecumseh Sherman, negotiated the Second Treaty of Fort Laramie in 1868. Ten Sioux tribes agreed to give up their territory in Kansas and Nebraska and not to attack railroad lines. In return, the federal government guaranteed them complete control of South Dakota west of the Missouri River. This territory included the Black Hills, sacred to Sioux tribal beliefs. The treaty stated that no whites could enter these territories without Sioux permission.

When the first transcontinental railroad was completed shortly afterwards, the occupation of more of the Great Plains by settlers suddenly became practical. This greatly increased tensions between settlers and Indians. In the following years, the massacre of millions of buffalo by hunters threatened the Plains Indians' entire way of life. With the Civil War over, career soldiers in the army were sent west to subdue and relocate the Indians.

The "Indian Wars"

In 1874 (only six years after the Second Treaty of Fort Laramie), gold was discovered on Sioux lands in the Black Hills. **Colonel George Armstrong Custer**, a veteran of the Civil War, took troops and mining experts to tour the area, in violation of the Second Treaty of Fort Laramie. Open warfare between settlers and the Sioux finally erupted in 1876. That June, Custer led several hundred of his soldiers onto Sioux lands. By accident, they came across the main Sioux camp with more than 2,000 warriors. Sioux and Cheyenne warriors surrounded and defeated Custer at the **Battle of Little Bighorn**. Custer and all of his men were killed. It was the greatest Indian victory on the Great Plains in history. Afterwards, many of the warriors returned to reservations, while others were defeated once the U.S. Army received reinforcements. The Sioux were forced to surrender the Black Hills.

Similar events occurred on the Southern Plains. Peace Commissioners negotiated a treaty with Comanche tribes in 1867. The Comanche agreed to move to a reservation while the federal government promised to stop hunters from slaughtering buffalo. When the government failed to stop the hunters, Comanche warriors attacked a settlement where many of the buffalo hunters lived. This led the army, in turn, to attack Comanche bands still roaming the Great Plains. They burnt down Comanche shelters, took their horses, and destroyed their supplies of buffalo meat, forcing them to surrender and move onto reservations.

In the Northwest, Chief Joseph of the Nez Perce tribe refused to move onto reservation lands and fled from federal troops. The army chased Joseph and his followers (750 men, women, and children) for 1,500 miles across Oregon, Washington, Idaho, Wyoming, and Montana. Joseph hoped to escape to Canada but his band was stopped just 40 miles from the border. They had no food or blankets in the freezing cold. Chief Joseph finally surrendered in October 1877.

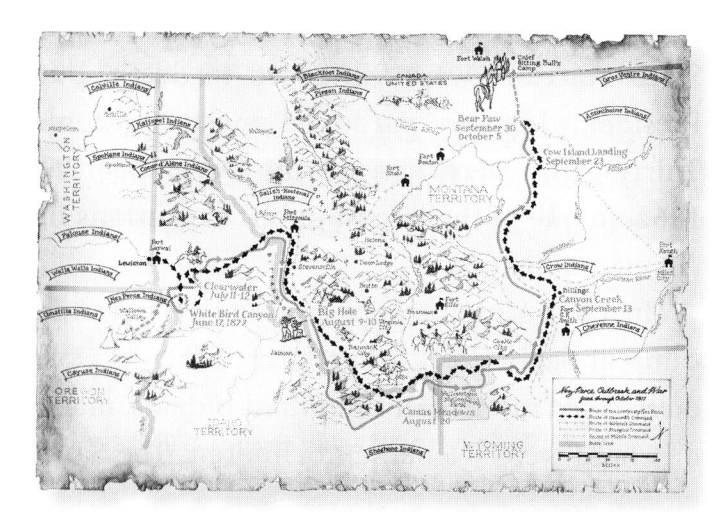

A map of the Nez Perce flight through the Northwest

Chapter 9 | The Last Frontier

The Historian's Apprentice

An American army lieutenant wrote down Chief Joseph's speech of surrender:

> "Tell General Howard I know his heart. What he told me before, I have it in my heart. I am tired of fighting. Our chiefs are killed . . . The old men are all dead. It is the young men who say yes or no. He who led on the young men is dead. It is cold, and we have no blankets; the little children are freezing to death. My people, some of them, have run away to the hills, and have no blankets, no food. No one knows where they are—perhaps freezing to death. I want to have time to look for my children, to see how many I can find. Maybe I shall find them among the dead. Hear me, my chiefs! I am tired; my heart is sick and sad. From where the sun now stands, I will fight no more forever."

1. Do you think the record of this speech was accurate? Or did the U.S. Army translator change some of Chief Joseph's words?
2. This speech is often seen as representing the sorrowful plight of the American Indians. What did Chief Joseph mean by "I will fight no more forever"?
3. Were the Nez Perce treated fairly? What would you have done if you had been Chief Joseph in 1877?

The so-called "Indian Wars" lasted about twenty years. During this period, federal troops were stationed in forts across the West. Some of the soldiers were African Americans, known to the Indians as the "Buffalo Soldiers."

Even the most courageous Indian warriors proved to be no match for federal troops. These troops were battle-hardened soldiers from the Civil War. They also possessed superior weapons. They applied the tactics of "hard war" that had been so successful in defeating the South. The Plains Indians were overwhelmed by both the technological superiority of the U.S. Army and the greater numbers of settlers from the United States.

Life on the Reservation

Once a tribe of Indians submitted to federal authority, its members were moved to a reservation. The government "reserved" particular lands for the tribe. Members of the tribe promised not to go beyond the borders of their lands. Those who did were captured and brought back. Indian tribes generally enjoyed a large degree of independence on their reservations. They were able to follow their own traditions, and tribal leaders regulated daily life.

Reservation lands were usually different from those where the tribe had once lived. They were often located on infertile, undesirable land. While the government wished to encourage peaceful farming, many tribes, such as the Plains Indians, traditionally favored hunting. The federal government usually promised to provide the Indians with food, blankets, seeds, and tools. All too often, the agents who were supposed to deliver these supplies cheated both the government and the Indians. Corrupt agents enriched themselves by pocketing much of the money set aside by Congress for the Indians, leaving the Indians with insufficient food and supplies.

Chapter 9 | The Last Frontier

Many reformers thought that the best hope for the Indians was to **assimilate** (*blend in with other Americans*). They urged Indians to become "civilized." These reformers looked especially to Indian children. The federal government and Christian missionaries established **reservation schools**. Indian children were taught how to be good Christians, how to farm the land, and how to become U.S. citizens.

The federal government also encouraged the creation of boarding schools for Indian children. A **boarding school** is one in which students live away at school instead of at home. Indian children as young as five years old were sent away from their parents. Often these schools were far from home. Most were run by Christian missionaries. Christian ministers and other white teachers taught the children to behave as good Christians and to condemn their own traditions. The children were required to speak in English instead of in their native languages. They were even given new English names. Their hair was cut short and they were forced to wear uniforms or western clothes. Teachers attempted to convert their students to Christianity, while telling them that many traditional tribal beliefs were wrong.

In 1887, reformers succeeded in passing the **Dawes Act**. The aim of this law was to "Americanize" the Indians by turning them into independent farmers. Each adult male Indian was permitted to claim 160 acres of reservation land.

Indian students at boarding school

In fact, the Dawes Act threatened the very survival of traditional Indian culture and actually led to a further sell-off of Indian lands.

While most Indians submitted to their fate, a few still resisted. Geronimo, an Apache warrior, and his followers left their reservation several times. They conducted raids in the Southwest and in Mexico, until they surrendered to U.S. forces in 1886.

In 1890, the sale of some of their reserved lands to settlers combined with a severe drought drove many Sioux to despair. Sioux warriors began performing a "Ghost Dance," alarming white settlers. Fighting broke out briefly in December. An army corps escorted several hundred Sioux to Wounded Knee Creek in South Dakota. When Sioux warriors refused to turn in their guns, the army fired field artillery into the crowd, killing men, women, and children in this final tragedy of the Indian Wars.

The Historian's Apprentice

1. In a short essay, explain how the Plains Indians attempted to resist the western expansion of the United States.
2. What were some of the consequences of their resistance?

Ranchers on the Great Plains

With the construction of railroad lines and the movement of the Plains Indians onto reservations, the Great Plains became profitable for ranching and farming.

By the end of the Civil War, there were several million wild longhorn cattle grazing on the Great Plains in Texas. Some Texans decided to drive these cattle northward to the nearest railroad lines in Kansas. From Kansas, the cattle were shipped by rail to Chicago to be slaughtered. Then the cuts of beef were shipped in refrigerated railroad cars (a recent invention) to cities in the Northeast.

It took almost three months to drive the cattle herds north from Texas to Kansas. On this "long drive," the cattle grazed on the short grasses of the "open range"—public lands not belonging to anyone and not fenced. These lands had abundant grass and water to support the moving herds. Cowboys, who had learned special techniques of riding, roping, branding, and dehorning cattle from the Mexican *vaqueros* ("cowboys"), kept the herds moving together.

In the late 1870s and 1880s, the cattle herds were driven farther north each year before they were ready for slaughter. The cattle fattened themselves by grazing on the northern plains of Montana, Wyoming, and the Dakotas. However, by 1886 such overgrazing had destroyed much of the grass. Meanwhile, sheepherders and farmers had bought up much of the "open range" and enclosed it with barbed wire fences. Hard times in the Northeast meant that prices paid for cattle fell. Two severe winters and an unusually hot and dry summer killed millions of cattle in 1886 and 1887. All of these events finally put an end to the "long drive."

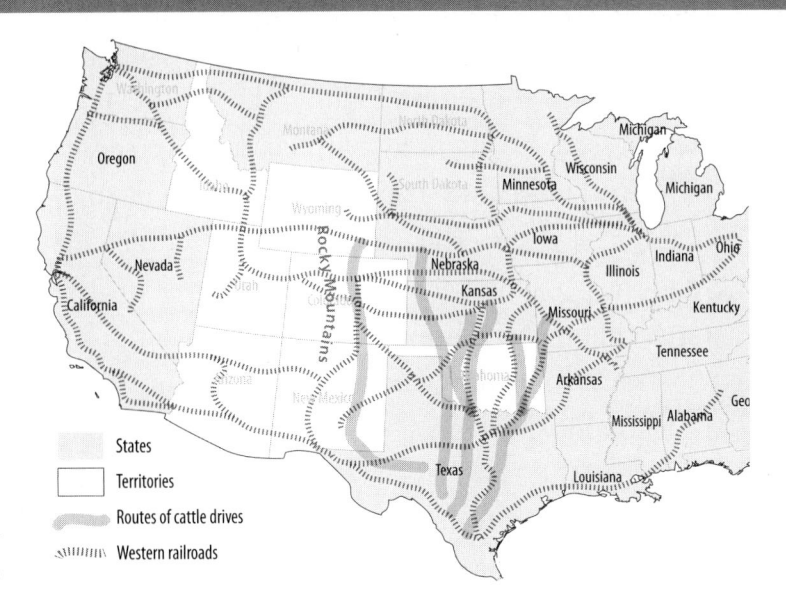

Ranchers nonetheless remained on the Great Plains. They bought their own land, bred cattle on their own fenced-in ranches, and continued to send their cattle by railroad eastwards to be slaughtered.

Pioneer Farmers

Farmers as well as ranchers were attracted to the vast area of the Great Plains. The **Homestead Act**, passed during the Civil War, gave 160 acres of federal land at no cost to settlers who farmed it for five years. The construction of railroads made it possible for farmers to prosper on the Great Plains by selling their produce back East.

The first farming families on the Plains faced the hostility not only of the Indians but also of the cattle ranchers. The cattlemen formed associations to oppose and harass them. Some ranchers cut farmers' barbed wire fences or even hired gunmen to commit acts of violence against them. Eventually, however, farmers won the contest against the ranchers. They arrived on the Plains in greater numbers and began enclosing their properties with barbed wire fences.

Just as serious for the farmers as hostile neighbors were the many natural obstacles they had to overcome. Attracted by railroad advertisements, farmers and their families expected to find amply watered, wooded lands like those in the East. Instead, they were shocked to discover little rainfall, tough soil, few trees, extreme temperatures, plagues of grasshoppers, and a painful sense of isolation caused by the great distances between farms.

Some of the first settlers on the Plains even starved or died of exposure. Large numbers of homesteaders gave up and moved back East. In families that stayed, women and small children were often forced to undertake strenuous physical labor for long hours. During the cold, snowy winters, families might be locked in complete isolation for months at a time.

Nevertheless, with technological ingenuity, the farmers eventually overcame most of the obstacles they faced:

Obstacle: Remoteness of markets

Solution: Farmers on the Plains used the railroads to ship their crops eastwards.

Obstacle: An absence of wood, clay, and stone for homes

Solution: Farmers built "**sod houses**," made from thick clumps of grass and soil cut into bricks.

Obstacle: A lack of wood for fencing

Solution: Farmers used **barbed wire**, first invented in 1874. Wire was twisted together at intervals to create sharp barbs that kept cattle and other animals from jumping over or crawling through the fence.

Obstacle: A lack of rainfall

Solution: Farmers on the Great Plains used drilling equipment to dig wells hundreds of feet deep in order to tap into **groundwater. Windmills** powered pumps that brought this groundwater to the surface.

Obstacle: Tough, dry soil

Solution: Farmers used steel or chilled iron plows. They plowed more deeply to preserve the surface moisture in the soil. These new techniques came to be known as **"dry farming."** Farmers also developed new varieties of wheat that needed less water and were more resistant to cold.

Obstacle: A lack of fuel

Solution: The farmers burned "buffalo chips" (dried buffalo manure) for fuel.

Obstacle: Lack of manpower

Solution: Farmers used machinery, such as horse-drawn harvesters and threshers, to farm more acres with fewer workers. Some of this machinery was actually easier to use on the treeless plains than elsewhere. Farmers were able to turn the Great Plains into productive farmland and the main source of America's wheat.

Obstacle: Loneliness and isolation

Solution: Family members grew close to one another. Social life centered on market days and church services in the nearest small town. Farmers began joining a national association of local social clubs known as the Grange movement. They held meetings to discuss farming techniques and organized social activities like picnics and lectures. Granger clubs also became political, sponsoring candidates and advocating the interests of farmers.

These innovations in ranching and farming, such as the use of barbed wire, "dry farming," and the use of railroads to ship livestock and crops back East made the Great Plains more attractive to settlers. These innovations thus accelerated the relocation of the Plains Indians onto reservations.

The Historian's Apprentice

Willa Cather's *My Antonia* tells about the immigrant experience on the Great Plains. The main character, Jim Burden, remembers his boyhood in Nebraska, where he had Czech and Russian neighbors. Antonia Shimerda was a girl from a Bohemian (Czech) family. The Shimerdas are tricked into buying a homestead without a proper house and have a difficult first winter in Nebraska. Jim and Antonia later follow separate paths because he continues in school while she stays working on the farm, but they stay in touch. In the following passage, Jim describes a typical winter day:

"The basement kitchen seemed heavenly safe and warm in those days—like a tight little boat in a winter sea. The men were out in the fields all day, husking corn, and when they came in at noon, with long caps pulled down over their ears and their feet in red-lined overshoes, I used to think they were like Arctic explorers. In the afternoons, when grandmother sat upstairs darning, or making husking-gloves, I read 'The Swiss Family Robinson' aloud to her, and I felt that the Swiss family had no advantages over us in the way of an adventurous life. I was convinced that man's strongest antagonist is the cold. I admired the cheerful zest with which grandmother went about keeping us warm and comfortable and well-fed. She often reminded me, when she was preparing for the return of the hungry men, that this country was not like Virginia; and that here a cook had, as she said, 'very little to do with.' On Sundays she gave us as much chicken

Continued ▶

as we could eat, and on other days we had ham or bacon or sausage meat. She baked either pies or cake for us every day, unless, for a change, she made my favorite pudding, striped with currants and boiled in a bag. Next to getting warm and keeping warm, dinner and supper were the most interesting things we had to think about. Our lives centered around warmth and food and the return of the men at nightfall. I used to wonder, when they came in tired from the fields, their feet numb and their hands cracked and sore, how they could do all the chores so conscientiously: feed and water and bed the horses, milk the cows, and look after the pigs. When supper was over, it took them a long while to get the cold out of their bones. While grandmother and I washed the dishes and grandfather read his paper upstairs, Jake and Otto sat on the long bench behind the stove, 'easing' their inside boots, or rubbing mutton tallow into their cracked hands. Every Saturday night we popped corn or made taffy, and Otto Fuchs used to sing, 'For I Am a Cowboy and Know I've Done Wrong,' or, 'Bury Me Not on the Lone Prairee.' He had a good baritone voice and always led the singing when we went to church services at the sod schoolhouse."

—Willa Cather, *My Ántonia* (1918), Chapter 9

1. How did life for these immigrant farmers differ from our lives today?
2. What did Jim's grandmother mean when she said that she had "very little to do with" when cooking?
3. Based on the passage, what forms of entertainment were available to farming families on the Great Plains?

Farmers' Problems and the Populist Party

The settlement of the Great Plains and the introduction of better farming techniques created new problems for farmers as the century came to an end. Harvests became more plentiful than ever before, but the large number of crops on the market caused food prices to drop lower and lower. By 1890, the average price of wheat was less than one-third what it had been in 1870. Farmers saw their incomes steadily falling, yet their expenses remained high. They had to pay middlemen like grain elevator operators to store their grain. Railroad companies charged high prices to ship their crops. Many farmers fell into debt. Because of these new problems, farmers formed their own political party in the early 1890s, known as the **Populist Party**. The Populist Party suggested a series of innovative reforms, some of which were later adopted. These included the secret ballot, the direct election of U.S. Senators, and a federal income tax.

In 1896, the Populist candidate, William Jennings Bryan, also won the nomination of the Democratic Party. He only narrowly lost the Presidential election to William McKinley.

For the Georgia Milestones EOC Assessment, you should know that:

- ☐ The first transcontinental railroad was constructed in 1869 by immigrant laborers.
- ☐ It was mainly Chinese immigrants who built the Central Pacific Railway, which went from Sacramento eastward, through the Sierra Nevada Mountains to Utah; Irish immigrants built the Union Pacific Railroad westward from Omaha.
- ☐ The transcontinental railroad shortened the time needed to cross the country, led to the destruction of the buffalo that had lived on the Plains, and opened the Great Plains and Far West to settlement by ranchers and farmers.
- ☐ The Great Plains and Far West were already occupied by Indian tribes. Each Indian tribe had its own customs, traditions, and way of life. The Plains Indians depended on the buffalo for their way of life.
- ☐ The federal government signed treaties with different tribes, obtaining some of their lands but guaranteeing to protect other lands. In 1868, General Sherman signed a treaty with the Sioux guaranteeing their control of the Black Hills of South Dakota.
- ☐ When gold was later found in the Black Hills, Colonel Custer took mining experts and troops into Indian territory. Settlers began arriving in violation of the treaty. Sioux and Cheyenne warriors defeated Custer at the Battle of Little Bighorn in 1876. The following year the U.S. Army defeated the Sioux and forced them onto reservations.
- ☐ Other tribes were also forced onto reservations. The United States defeated those Indians that attempted to resist during the "Indian Wars" (1877–1890). Indian warriors were no match for battle-hardened U.S. troops with superior weapons. The Plains Indians also could not survive without the buffalo on the Plains.
- ☐ Indian resistance to the westward expansion of the United States ended with their confinement on reservations. The growing number of settlers on the Great Plains also put pressure on the Plains Indians to move to reservations.
- ☐ Reservation lands were often unfamiliar and inferior to lands previously controlled by the tribe. Tribes enjoyed relative independence on their reservations. Federal agents often pocketed money and provisions intended for the tribes.
- ☐ Reformers tried to assimilate the Indians into mainstream American life. They sent Indian children to reservation schools and boarding schools, where they became Christians and learned English instead of their own beliefs and traditions.
- ☐ The construction of the transcontinental railroad, the relocation of the Indian tribes onto reservations, and the Homestead Act (1862) led settlers to move to the Great Plains and Far West.
- ☐ Farmers came up with innovative solutions to deal with the dry climate and dense grass of the Plains: they dug wells to get to groundwater and used windmills to pump the water to the surface. They built houses out of sod bricks and made fences of barbed wire. They used steel plows to break up the tough sod and plant seeds. They formed clubs and associations to fight loneliness.

Name:_____

Settlement of the Great Plains

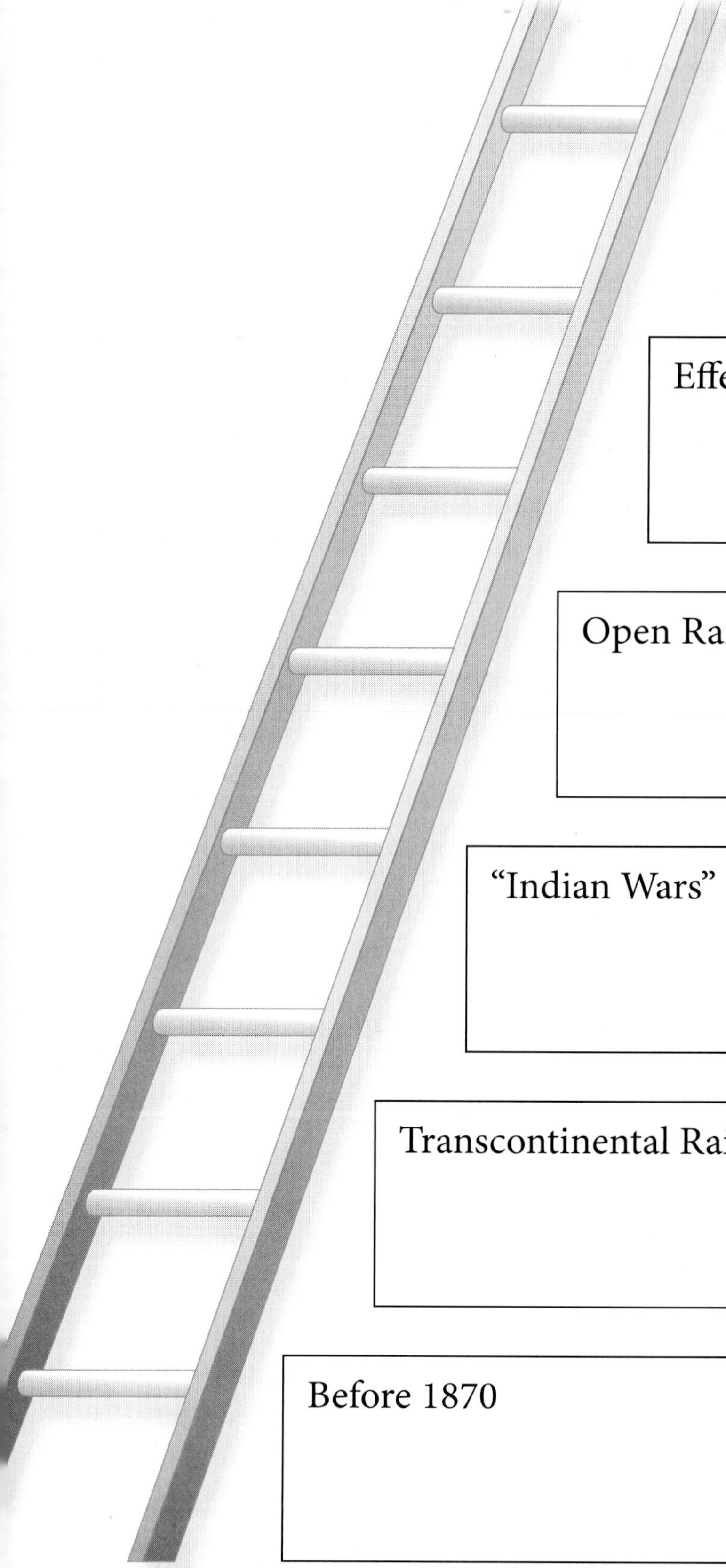

Tribal Life on the Reservation

Effects of Settlement

Open Range

"Indian Wars"

Transcontinental Railroad

Before 1870

Chapter 9 | The Last Frontier

Name:_____

Farming on the Great Plains

Conditions

Barbed Wire

Sod House

Groundwater Wells

Windmills

Steel Plows

Chapter 9 | The Last Frontier 279

SSUSH12a

4. Use the diagram below to answer the question.

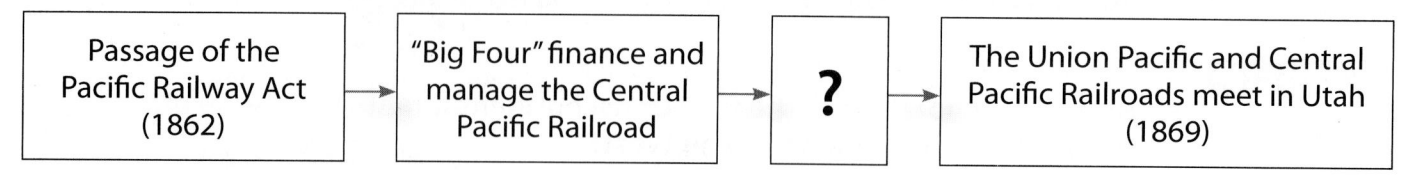

| Passage of the Pacific Railway Act (1862) | → | "Big Four" finance and manage the Central Pacific Railroad | → | ? | → | The Union Pacific and Central Pacific Railroads meet in Utah (1869) |

Which sentence completes the diagram?

- A. Chinese workers blast their way through the Sierra Nevada Mountains.
- B. Railroad workers go on strike.
- C. The federal government buys up the Central Pacific.
- D. The Union Pacific Railway fails to complete its task.

SSUSH12a

5. Use this list to answer the question.

- Built by immigrant labor
- Connected Omaha, Nebraska, to Sacramento, California
- Reduced the time required to cross the country

What do the elements in the list describe?

- A. the Erie Canal
- B. the Missouri River
- C. the Pony Express
- D. the transcontinental railroad

SSUSH12c

6. Which statement BEST describes the result of resistance by the Plains Indians to U.S. settlement of the Great Plains?

- A. Plains Indian tribes were forced onto reservation lands.
- B. Most of the Plains Indians were killed by settlers.
- C. Americans never adequately explored the Great Plains.
- D. Most Indians were assimilated into mainstream American life.

SSUSH12b

7. Which TWO factors led to the growth in the number of settlers on the Great Plains and in the Far West in the late nineteenth century?

- A. rising wheat prices
- B. the availability of cheap land
- C. completion of new railroad lines
- D. the help of friendly Plains Indians
- E. the use of slave labor to farm the land
- F. the demand for cotton from Northern factories

SSUSH12c

8. Use the excerpt below to answer the question.

> *From where the sun now stands, I will fight no more forever.*
> —Chief Joseph of the Nez Perce, October 1877

What circumstances led Chief Joseph to make this statement?

- **A.** The United States signed a treaty promising his tribe thousands of acres.
- **B.** Chief Joseph secretly intended on fighting the United States as long as he lived.
- **C.** Officers of the U.S. Army had tricked Chief Joseph into surrendering to them.
- **D.** Chief Joseph decided his tribe had suffered so much he would accept peace at any price.

SSUSH12c

9. What was the main purpose of the reservation system?

- **A.** to make the new transcontinental railroad safer to operate
- **B.** to clear federal lands for settlement by railroads, ranchers, and farmers
- **C.** to provide employment for Union troops and veterans after the Civil War
- **D.** to make it easier for Indians to assimilate into mainstream American culture

SSUSH12c

10. Which was a negative aspect of the "Americanization" policy of the late 1880s for American Indians?

- **A.** Indians attended reservation schools and learned a trade.
- **B.** Indians could own and farm 160 acres of their own land.
- **C.** Indians learned English and could gain the right to vote.
- **D.** Indians saw the survival of their traditional cultures threatened.

SSUSH12c

11. Use the list to answer the question.

> - Each tribe of Indians was confined to its own reservation lands.
> - Blankets, food and other provisions provided by the federal government were often sold off by corrupt government agents.
> - Indian children were taught in reservation schools and boarding schools to abandon their traditional beliefs and ways.

What do the elements in the list have in common?

- **A.** They describe the major weaknesses of traditional Indian beliefs.
- **B.** They identify reasons why different tribes of Plains Indians were unable to cooperate.
- **C.** They were consequences of the Plains Indians' inability to resist U.S. expansion.
- **D.** They were the result of friendly Indians showing settlers how to farm on the Great Plains.

SSUSH12C

12. Use the cartoon to answer the question.

THE REASON FOR THE INDIAN OUTBREAK
General Miles declares that the Indians are starved into rebellion

What is the main idea of the cartoon?

A. Federal Indian agents assisted Indians in growing crops on reservations.
B. The federal government provided Indians with all the supplies needed.
C. Indians went hungry while federal Indian agents grew wealthy.
D. The livestock raised on most Indian reservations were diseased.

SSUSH12b

13. Use the list to answer the question.

- Built sod houses
- Used dry farming techniques
- Used barbed wire fences
- Burned cow and buffalo chips for fuel
- Windmills pumped water
- Steel plow used for tough soil

What would be the best title for this list?

A. Methods Used by Forty-Niners to Stake Claims
B. Sources of Conflict between Ranchers and Farmers
C. How Farmers Adapted to Conditions on the Great Plains
D. How American Indians and Western Farmers Cooperated

CHAPTER 10 The Progressive Era

SSUSH13 What efforts were taken to reform American society and politics during the Progressive Era?

    a. What was the influence of muckrakers in promoting change by exposing social problems?

    b. What roles did women play in the reform movements of the Progressive Era?

    c. How did the Supreme Court decision in *Plessy v. Ferguson* lead to an expansion of "Jim Crow" laws and, in turn, the formation of the NAACP?

    d. What legislative actions were taken by the Progressives, including steps for the empowerment of voters, new labor laws, and the conservation movement?

Names and Terms You Should Know

- Progressives
- Muckraker
- Ida Tarbell
- Upton Sinclair
- Meat Inspection Act
- Jane Addams
- Settlement house
- Susan B. Anthony
- Florence Kelley
- Ida Wells
- Municipal reform
- Secret ballot
- Referendum
- Recall
- Initiative
- Direct election of U.S. Senators
- Women's suffrage
- Theodore Roosevelt
- Pure Food and Drug Act
- Antitrust laws
- Woodrow Wilson
- Graduated income tax
- Federal Reserve Act
- Triangle Shirtwaist Factory fire
- Child labor laws
- Conservation
- National Conservation Commission
- Disenfranchisement
- Literacy tests
- Poll taxes
- White primaries
- "Jim Crow" laws
- Segregation
- *Plessy v. Ferguson* (1896)
- "Separate but equal"
- W.E.B. Du Bois
- NAACP (National Association for the Advancement of Colored People)

Georgia "Peaches" of Wisdom

1. The Progressive Movement flourished from 1890 until the outbreak of World War I. Its aim was to remedy the political and economic injustices that had resulted from America's rapid industrialization. Progressives were middle-class reformers who believed in using government power to correct these abuses.

2. Progressivism had multiple roots: (1) the appearance of new problems, such as brutal working conditions, urban crowding, the need for more public services, and political corruption; (2) the Populist Party; (3) the "Social Gospel" movement—Protestant ministers who helped the poor out of a sense of moral responsibility based on Christian teachings; (4) "muckrakers"—investigative journalists who exposed the abuses and corruption of industrial society; (5) rising consumer consciousness; and (6) the support of women reformers and organized labor.

3. Through their writings in magazines and newspapers, "muckrakers" like Ida Tarbell and Upton Sinclair exposed evils and stimulated the public outcry for reform. Muckrakers' articles sometimes led to legislative action: for example, Sinclair's description of sausage-making in *The Jungle* led to the Meat Inspection Act (1906).

4. Women reformers like Jane Addams ran settlement houses helping the poor. Other women reformers, like Susan B. Anthony, campaigned for women's suffrage (*the right to vote*). Still other women reformers opposed child labor, inspected factories, and fought to improve conditions for all workers.

5. Municipal reformers attacked the political machines and created new forms of municipal government, such as by city manager, to empower voters. At the state level, Progressives also introduced several reforms to empower voters, including the secret ballot; initiative, referendum, and recall; direct primary elections; direct election of U.S. Senators; and women's suffrage in many states.

6. Progressives also introduced social and economic reforms at the state level, including child labor laws, laws regulating conditions in urban housing, laws regulating safety and health in factories, laws limiting the number of hours that women could work in factories, and workmen's compensation for work-related injuries.

7. Progressive Presidents brought Progressive reform to the federal government. Theodore Roosevelt tried to break up "bad" trusts; introduced federal regulation of meat, food, and drugs; and took steps to conserve the nation's natural resources and wildlife, such as by creating more national parks and monuments and by forming the National Conservation Commission. William Howard Taft followed most of Roosevelt's policies. Democratic President Woodrow Wilson lowered tariffs, introduced a graduated income tax, created the Federal Reserve System, strengthened anti-trust legislation with the Clayton Antitrust Act, and passed a law banning child labor (later held to be unconstitutional).

8. After the end of Reconstruction, Southern state governments introduced literacy tests, poll taxes, and white primaries to keep African Americans from voting. During the Progressive Era, state governments in the South passed "Jim Crow" laws requiring racial segregation (separation of "white" and "colored") in public places. These laws were upheld by the U.S. Supreme Court in *Plessy v. Ferguson* (1896), which held that "separate but equal" facilities were constitutional. Woodrow Wilson, a Southerner, introduced segregation into the departments of the federal government.

9. The NAACP was formed by W.E.B. Du Bois and others to fight racism.

The **Progressive Era** took place in the decades between 1890 and the outbreak of the First World War in 1914. The Progressives were reformers who believed in human "progress." Their primary aim was to remedy the political and economic injustices that had resulted from America's rapid industrialization. They did not oppose industrialization but wanted to use the power of government to correct its abuses. In order to achieve this, they felt they had to reform government itself, which had become corrupted by political "bosses" and "Big Business." Progressives moved the country from a *laissez-faire* economy in which the government kept its hands completely out of private enterprise to one in which government regulations prevented the worst abuses of economic power.

Roots of the Progressive Movement

Why did the Progressive Movement suddenly emerge at the end of the century? Historians see a variety of factors behind the rise of Progressivism.

The Problems of Industrial Society

The rise of industry was accompanied by grave new social problems: brutal working conditions, child labor, political corruption, urban overcrowding, exploitation of the environment, extreme inequalities of wealth, and the sale of misleading, defective, or even dangerous products. The government's "hands off" (*laissez-faire*) policies failed to curb these evils. Progressives believed that some oversight by government was necessary to prevent the worst abuses of the new industrial age while preserving the benefits of free enterprise.

The Legacy of Populism

At the end of the last chapter, you learned how farmers had organized the Populist Party. Progressives borrowed many ideas from the earlier Populists.

A Middle-Class Movement

The Populist movement of the 1890s had been established by farmers and appealed mostly to the South and West. In contrast, Progressivism was mainly urban and middle class. Members of the professional classes—college professors, lawyers, doctors, religious ministers, and writers—provided its core leadership. Members of the lower middle classes—technicians, clerical workers, small business owners, and service personnel—provided its main following. Some historians have argued that Progressives felt challenged by the new industrial age: the rise of industrialists of vast wealth—like Carnegie and Rockefeller—made ordinary professional men and women feel small and insignificant.

As America changed from a nation of small, independent, rural communities to an urban society subject to vast impersonal forces, Progressives called for greater regulation. They believed that professionals of all kinds could help both business and government run more smoothly and efficiently, according to scientific principles.

In general, Progressives felt that the rise of Big Business, organized labor, and political machines had closed the door to individual opportunity. These large concentrations of economic and political power did not engage in fair business practices or permit equal competition. In short, both business and government had become corrupt. Progressives aimed at removing this corruption by regulating business and government practices so that average Americans had more of a chance to compete on a fair basis.

The "Social Gospel" Movement

Progressives often acted out of a sense of moral responsibility based on religion. Many Protestant ministers were alarmed by the plight of the poor in industrial society. They were appalled by living conditions in the slums, by child labor, by poor schools, by the horrendous working conditions of industrial laborers, and by the selfishness of wealthy business owners. These ministers called for reforms, especially safer working conditions, better public schools, and the abolition of child labor. Groups like the Salvation Army emphasized our duty to help the less fortunate.

All of these efforts became known as the "Social Gospel" movement. This movement called on governments, churches, and private charities to work together to help those in need. Members of the "Social Gospel" movement also advocated temperance: they called for a ban on alcoholic drinks, which they saw as one of the chief causes of these social problems.

The Need for Consumer Protection

With the growth of modern industries, many goods were no longer produced locally. Americans began buying mass-produced goods manufactured by large, impersonal companies. There was a need to oversee the market to make sure that these goods were safe and that manufacturers did not misrepresent their products to consumers. Progressives believed that government regulation was needed to protect consumers.

The Historian's Apprentice

1. Create a chart or concept map showing the different influences that came together in the Progressive Movement.
2. Use the Internet or your school library to learn more about the "Social Gospel" movement and make an oral report or PowerPoint presentation to your class.
3. Write a paragraph on the role of the middle classes in the Progressive Movement.

The Muckrakers

With the growth of cities, newspapers and magazines reached larger audiences than ever before. Advertisers were their major source of revenue, but publishers needed to have more readers to attract advertisers. Readers liked human-interest stories, often focusing on the very rich, the very poor, or the very corrupt.

The writers and journalists who exposed the unfair practices of "Big Business" became known as "**muckrakers**" because they "raked" through the muck (*moist dirt or filth*) of American life, exposing some of its worst problems. The muckrakers demonstrated the benefit of a free press. They wrote for magazines like *McClure's* and *American Magazine*. These magazines put money and research assistance at the disposal of journalists, often enabling them to uncover the "inside story." The muckrakers examined the rise of industry and the abuses and corruption that had led to the accumulation of large fortunes. They also examined the lives of the very poor, eliciting sympathy from their readers. Muckrakers wrote in a graphic style that appealed to a wide readership. The muckrakers exposed many evils and stimulated a public outcry for reform. In so doing, they helped launch the Progressive Movement.

"Muckrakers" of the Progressive Era

Writer	Book	What It Did
Jacob Riis	*How the Other Half Lives*	Examined the conditions of the urban poor.
Ida Tarbell	*History of the Standard Oil Company*	Tarbell's investigative journalism revealed how Rockefeller's success was largely based on ruthless business practices.
Lincoln Steffens	*The Shame of the Cities*	Looked at corruption in city governments.
Ray Stannard Baker	*Following the Color Line*	Reported on the conditions of African Americans in both the South and North.
Frank Norris	*The Octopus*	A popular novel that depicted the stranglehold of railroads over California farmers.
Upton Sinclair	*The Jungle*	A novel about poverty-stricken immigrants in Chicago. It included a description of the harmful practices in the meatpacking industry, such as putting dead rats and rat poison in sausage meat.

The Historian's Apprentice

Ida Tarbell was one of the most prominent muckrakers. She studied public documents from court cases and interviewed many of Rockefeller's associates to piece together an accurate history of John D. Rockefeller and his oil company. She then published a series of 19 articles in *McClure's Magazine*, which were eagerly read by a large audience. These articles later became the basis for her book *History of the Standard Oil Company*.

"The strides [*steps forward*] the firm of Rockefeller and Andrews made ... were attributed for three or four years mainly to his extraordinary capacity for bargaining and borrowing. Then its chief competitors began to suspect something. John Rockefeller might get his oil cheaper now and then, they said, but he could not do it often. He might make close contracts for which they had neither the patience nor the stomach. He might have an unusual mechanical and practical genius in his partner. But these things could not explain all. They believed they bought, on the whole, almost as cheaply as he, and they knew they made as good oil and with as great, or nearly as great, economy. He could sell at no better price than they. Where was his advantage? There was but one place where it could be, and that was in transportation. He must be getting better rates from the railroads than they were."

—Ida Tarbell, *History of the Standard Oil Company* (1904)

1. What made the publication of Tarbell's *History of Standard Oil Company* so important?
2. According to Tarbell, what was one of the secret advantages Rockefeller enjoyed against his competitors? What did this show about the relationship between railroads and the early oil industry?
3. Tarbell's father was a small oil producer whose business was ruined by Rockefeller. How might this have shaped her views?

Another important muckraker was **Upton Sinclair**. Sinclair disguised himself in order to work for seven weeks in the meatpacking industry in Chicago to write his novel, *The Jungle*. The novel was first published in serial form in a socialist newspaper and later as a book. It tells the story of Jurgis Rudkus, an immigrant who brings his young wife from Lithuania to Chicago in hopes of a better life. Rudkus finds work in the meatpacking industry, but he and his wife lose their savings when they are tricked into purchasing a run-down house with hidden costs they cannot afford. Rudkus later sprains his ankle at work. He receives no pay when he cannot work for three months and also loses his job. Rudkus attacks his wife's boss when he learns that this employer has sexually assaulted her. For his attack, Rudkus is arrested and sent to jail for a month. Without his wages, his family is evicted from their home. His wife later dies in childbirth because Rudkus cannot afford a doctor. Rudkus begins to drink too much, but conditions improve when he thinks of the future of his oldest son and finds work in a steel mill. Unfortunately, his son drowns in a muddy street. Rudkus becomes a tramp and wanders through the countryside. Later he becomes a beggar and a criminal. Only at the end of the novel is Rudkus saved when he becomes a socialist.

The following passage from *The Jungle* tells how sausages are made. This description shook the conscience of the nation and led directly to the passage of the **Meat Inspection Act** in 1906.

"There was never the least attention paid to what was cut up for sausage . . . There would be meat that had tumbled out on the floor, in the dirt and sawdust, where the workers had trampled and spit uncounted billions of consumption (tuberculosis) germs. There would be meat stored in great piles in rooms; and the water from leaky roofs would drip over it, and thousands of rats would race about on it. It was too dark in these storage places to see well, but a man could run his hand over these piles of meat and sweep off handfuls of the dried dung of rats. These rats were nuisances, and the packers would put poisoned bread out for them; they would die, and then rats, bread, and meat would go into the hoppers together. . . There was no place for the men to wash their hands before they ate their dinner, and so they made a practice of washing them in the water that was to be ladled into the sausage. . . . in the barrels would be dirt and rust and old nails and stale water – and cartload after cartload

Continued ▶

The Progressive Achievement: Legislative Actions by the Progressives

Progressives succeeded in passing new laws and implementing new policies at all three levels of government—local, state, and federal.

Municipal Reform

"**Municipal**" refers to the town or city level of government. Cities had mushroomed so fast in the late nineteenth century that many were incapable of dealing with their problems. Municipal government in many large cities came to be dominated by **political machines**, like Tammany Hall in New York City. The "machine" used its control over city government to make a fortune out of lucrative public contracts. To work for the city, each contractor had to promise to pay a share of its receipts to the political machine. This bribery made city government expensive and inefficient.

Progressives appealed to citizens who were tired of corruption. Muckrakers exposed urban corruption in their magazine articles and books, such as Lincoln Steffens' *The Shame of the Cities*. Progressive reformers replaced "bosses" and political machines with public-minded mayors. Progressives expanded city services to take care of urban overcrowding, fire hazards, inadequate sanitation, and the general lack of public services.

In some cities, Progressives introduced new forms of government, such as government by commission or city manager. Progressives hoped these new arrangements would make city governments more democratic and less open to corruption:

- In the commission form, a city is governed by a panel of experts, each of whom directs a department delivering an essential city service.

- In the city-manager form, an elected board of citizens appoints a specially trained "manager" to run the city. The city manager answers to the elected board.

State Governments

Progressives also elected state officials and legislators to promote reform. These Progressives attacked the power of local political bosses and the influence of railroad companies over state legislatures. They began taxing railroads at the same rates as other property. They also set up commissions to regulate railroad rates and public utilities, and to conserve forests and lakes. Many Progressive measures first adopted by state governments were later copied at the federal level.

State Laws Empowering Voters

Progressives wanted to rid state governments of corruption and the influence of "Big Business." They passed new state laws making government more responsive to the people. Many of these were reforms that had first been proposed by the Populists:

- **Secret Ballot**—Up until this time, voters marked their ballots publicly, making them subject to pressure and intimidation. Progressives passed state laws requiring that voters mark their ballots in private.

- **Initiative**—Many states passed laws giving voters a process for introducing bills directly into their state legislature.

- **Referendum**—States also passed laws that allowed voters to repeal a law passed by the legislature through a special election known as a "referendum."

- **Recall**—Many states passed laws allowing voters to "recall" (*dismiss from office*) an elected official before the end of his or her term in office through a special "recall" election.

- **Direct Primary**—Party members voted in a special election to indicate their preferences for their party's nominees. Up until this time, party leaders generally chose their party's candidates.

- **Direct Election of Senators**—The U.S. Constitution gave state legislatures the power to select U.S. Senators. Progressives insisted that this power be given to the people. The **Seventeenth Amendment** (1913) changed the Constitution by giving voters the power to elect their Senators directly.

- **Women's Suffrage**—"Suffrage" refers to the right to vote in elections. The National Woman Suffrage Association was founded in 1869. It represented millions of women and was active during the Progressive Era in the struggle to achieve voting rights for women. Under the U.S. Constitution, individual states actually controlled the requirements for voting, even in federal elections. During the Progressive Era, several states, especially in the West, gave voting rights to women.

State Laws Protecting Labor and Conserving the Environment

States also enacted new laws to deal with some of the worst social and economic effects of industrialism. These included laws regulating conditions in urban housing, laws against the employment of young children, laws regulating safety and health conditions in factories, laws limiting the number of hours that women could work, laws forcing employers to give compensation to workers injured on the job ("workmen's compensation"), laws regulating railroads and public utilities, laws conserving natural resources and wildlife preserves, and laws prohibiting the sale of alcohol.

> Note: For the Georgia Milestones EOC Assessment, you will not need to know about the Triangle Shirtwaist Factory fire, *Lochner v. New York*, or *Muller v. Oregon*. You should know that, as a result of the Progressive Movement, states passed laws protecting workers and the environment.

For example, in 1911 a fire at the **Triangle Shirtwaist Factory** in New York City led to the deaths of 146 women workers. The factory's doors had been bolted shut and there were no adequate fire escapes. Striking workers had previously protested against these conditions but the owners had refused to make changes. The fire led to widespread public sympathy for

Chapter 10 | The Progressive Era   295

The Historian's Apprentice

◆ What has been the legacy of the Progressive Movement? Complete the following chart showing the legislative actions taken by Progressives at the local, state, and federal levels:

Legislative Action	Description
Municipal government by city commission or city manager	
Secret ballot	
Initiative, Referendum, and Recall	
Seventeenth Amendment (1913): Direct election of U.S. Senators	
Women's suffrage in some states	
State labor laws	
Fire safety codes for factories	
Meat Inspection Act (1906)	
Pure Food and Drug Act (1906)	
Creation of National Conservation Commission (1908)	
Sixteenth Amendment (1913): Graduated income tax	
Underwood Tariff: lower tariff rates (1913)	
Federal Reserve Act (1913)	
Clayton Antitrust Act (1914)	
Prohibition of child labor (1916): later ruled unconstitutional	

Based on this record of legislative achievement, what conclusions can you reach about the Progressives?

The Segregated South

While Progressives were introducing reforms to make American society more democratic, a large group of Americans was being left out. From 1890 to 1917, African Americans living in the South were actually having their political rights being taken away. They were also subjected to an even stricter system of social isolation and racial segregation than before.

African Americans in Southern States Lose Their Voting Rights

The Fifteenth Amendment (1870) guaranteed African Americans the right to vote. During Reconstruction, African Americans participated in politics across the South. When Reconstruction ended, white Southerners regained control of their state legislatures. They used terror and social pressure to prevent African Americans from voting. Starting around 1890, Southern legislators also passed new laws that made it more difficult for African Americans to vote:

- **Literacy Tests** The ability to read (**literacy**) was not a constitutional requirement for voting. However, Southern states started asking voters to pass a literacy test before they could vote. Literacy tests were made especially difficult for African Americans. White citizens were often excused from this requirement.

- **Poll Taxes** These were special taxes that had to be paid before voting. Poor African Americans could not afford to pay them. They often had to be paid long in advance and could not be paid on the day of the election.

- **"Grandfather Clauses"** These laws allowed people qualified to vote at the beginning of 1867, or their descendants, to vote without passing a literacy test or paying a poll tax. Poor whites therefore did not need to meet the new requirements. Only poor African Americans did, because almost no African Americans had been qualified to vote in the South in January 1867. "Grandfather clauses" were finally declared unconstitutional by the U.S. Supreme Court in 1915.

- **"White" Primaries** After white Southerners regained the right to vote, few voted for Republicans. Democratic primary elections became more important in the South than the later general election. Democrats in several Southern states made their primaries open to "white" voters only—effectively disenfranchising their African-American citizens.

As a result of these steps, white Southerners were able to maintain their control of Southern state governments and their representation in Congress.

Racial Segregation: "Jim Crow" Laws and *Plessy v. Ferguson*

In the decades after Reconstruction, Southern states established racially **segregated** (*separate*) public schools and cemeteries, but blacks and whites mixed in many other public places. Starting in the 1890s, Southern state legislatures began passing laws further segregating blacks and whites. African-American and white Southerners attended different schools, rode in separate railway cars, ate in different restaurants, used different public bathrooms and water fountains, and sat on different public benches. These segregation laws became known as **"Jim Crow" laws.**

"Jim Crow" laws denied African-American citizens equal rights and opportunities. They reinforced racial hatred and gave the false message that one race was somehow superior to another.

The Historian's Apprentice

The following are examples of "Jim Crow" laws once passed by the State of Georgia:

> "It shall be unlawful for a white person to marry anyone except a white person. Any marriage in violation of this section shall be void."
>
> "All persons licensed to conduct a restaurant shall serve either white people exclusively or colored people exclusively and shall not sell to the two races within the same room or serve the two races anywhere under the same license."
>
> "The officer in charge shall not bury, or allow to be buried, any colored persons upon ground set apart or used for the burial of white persons."
>
> "It shall be unlawful for colored people to frequent any park owned or maintained by the city for the benefit, use and enjoyment of white persons . . . and unlawful for any white person to frequent any park owned or maintained by the city for the use and benefit of colored persons."
>
> "All persons licensed to conduct the business of selling beer or wine . . . shall serve either white people exclusively or colored people exclusively and shall not sell to the two races within the same room at any time."

What conclusions can you draw about life in Georgia in the early twentieth century based on these laws?

The U.S. Supreme Court upheld these "Jim Crow" laws in 1896 in the case of *Plessy v. Ferguson*. **Homer Plessy** was seven-eighths white and only one-eighth African American. He was supported by a special committee of African-American citizens that was formed to oppose Louisiana's new "Separate Car" Act (1890), which required blacks and whites to ride in separate cars. To test this "Jim Crow" law, Plessy bought a first-class train ticket. He then entered a "whites only" railroad car. Plessy was arrested and tried by the state courts. Plessy claimed that Louisiana's segregation law denied his rights under the Fourteenth Amendment.

The state courts convicted Plessy. Several appeals were filed and the case eventually reached the U.S. Supreme Court. The Supreme Court upheld Louisiana's practice of racial segregation in *Plessy v. Ferguson* (1896). It ruled that racial segregation by a state was permitted so long as the state offered **"separate but equal"** facilities to both races. African-American facilities were supposed to be as good as white ones, but could be separate. So long as this was the case, the Court reasoned, then African-American citizens were not being denied the equal protection of the laws. If African Americans chose to view the use of a separate facility as a badge of their own inferiority, the Court concluded, this was an interpretation they gave to the law but not part of the law itself.

With the Supreme Court's decision in *Plessy v. Ferguson*, the constitutionality of racial segregation was confirmed. In consequence, the system of racial segregation spread even further across the South. President Woodrow Wilson, a Southerner, also introduced racial segregation into the federal government.

A Procedural History of *Plessy v. Ferguson*

The following chronological list of events gives you more details about this famous case.

- In July 1890, Louisiana passed "An act to promote the comfort of passengers on railway trains"(Separate Car Act) which promised "separate but equal" compartments for different races.

- In 1891, a committee of African-American citizens (*Comité des Citoyens*) formed to test the law. In May 1892, the Louisiana Supreme Court ruled that the Louisiana law was unconstitutional with respect to interstate travel.

- On June 7, 1892, **Homer Adolph Plessy**, a 30-year old shoemaker who was seven-eighths white, bought a first class ticket from New Orleans to Covington, Louisiana. He sat in the first class white compartment and was arrested by Chris C. Cain, a private detective hired by the railway.

- Plessy was given a hearing in court. Plessy's attorney, James Walker, argued that Louisiana's "Separate Car Act" violated the Fourteenth Amendment. Judge Ferguson ruled against Plessy on November 18: "There is no pretense that he [Plessy] was not provided with equal accommodations with the white passengers," Judge Ferguson stated. "He was simply deprived of the liberty of doing as he pleased, and of violating a penal statute with impunity . . ."

- Attorneys Albion Tourgée and James Walker next filed a petition on behalf of Plessy against the trial judge, John H. Ferguson, with the Louisiana Supreme Court. They argued that the state's "Separate Car Act" violated the Equal Protection Clause of the Fourteenth Amendment, which forbids states from denying "any person within their jurisdiction the equal protection of the laws."

- The Louisiana Supreme Court upheld Judge Ferguson's ruling.

- The U.S. Supreme Court ruled on the case three and a half years later, on May 18, 1896. It affirmed (*approved*) the decision of the Louisiana Supreme Court:

"We consider the underlying fallacy [*mistake; falsehood*] of the plaintiff's [Plessy's] argument to consist in the assumption that the enforced separation of the two races stamps the colored race with a badge of inferiority. If this be so, it is not by reason of anything found in the act, but solely because the colored race chooses to put that construction upon it . . . The argument also assumes that social prejudice may be overcome by legislation, and that equal rights cannot be secured except by an enforced commingling of the two races . . . If the civil and political rights of both races be equal, one cannot be inferior to the other civilly or politically. If one race be inferior to the other socially, the Constitution of the United States cannot put them upon the same plane."
—Justice Henry Brown, U.S. Supreme Court, *Plessy v. Ferguson* (1896)

- As a result of the U.S. Supreme Court's decision, Plessy returned to the Criminal Court of New Orleans in January 1897, where he pled guilty and paid the $25 fine.

The Historian's Apprentice

1. Imagine that you are an attorney arguing the case of *Plessy v. Ferguson* in the U.S. Supreme Court. Give a five-minute presentation of your ideas, either for Plessy or for the State of Louisiana.
2. Make a slide show showing photographs of daily life in the segregated South between 1890 and 1917.

Formation of the NAACP

African-American leaders responded to conditions in the segregated South in various ways. Booker T. Washington advised them to focus on vocational training rather than on political rights. **W.E.B. Du Bois** was the first African American to obtain a Ph.D. from Harvard University. He believed that African Americans should fight for political rights and equality at all levels. In 1905, Du Bois met with other African-American leaders and white reformers on the Canadian side of Niagara Falls to discuss ways of combatting segregation and the loss of voting rights by African Americans.

Three years later, there was a "race riot" in Springfield, Illinois, the town where Abraham Lincoln was born. African-American leaders decided there was a need for a permanent civil rights organization in the United States. In February 1909, a hundred years after the birth of Lincoln, W.E.B. Du Bois, Ida Wells, other African-American leaders, and white reformers, including Florence Kelley, established a new organization. In 1910, this organization became known as the **National Association for the Advancement of Colored People**, or "**NAACP**." Its goals were to fight for equal rights and to eliminate racial prejudice. Moorefield Storey, a white lawyer, became its first President. W.E.B. Du Bois handled publicity and research. He edited the NAACP's monthly magazine *The Crisis*.

NAACP headquarters were located in New York City. By 1914, the organization had 50 branches and 6,000 members. It began the process of challenging segregation laws in the courts. In 1915, it successfully challenged Oklahoma's "grandfather clause," which was overturned by the U.S. Supreme Court. The NAACP also protested against President Wilson's introduction of racial segregation in federal workplaces. The NAACP further organized demonstrations nationwide against D.W. Griffith's movie *Birth of the Nation*, which glorified the Ku Klux Klan. In addition, the NAACP lobbied Congress for a federal law against lynching. NAACP leaders were determined to fight against racial bias and for equal rights in every way possible.

The Historian's Apprentice

Imagine you are one of the founders of the NAACP. Write a letter to a friend explaining how you feel about "Jim Crow" laws in the South and the decision of *Plessy v. Ferguson*. Then describe the goals you and your colleagues have in founding the NAACP.

The Progressive Era Reaches an End

In 1917, Americans entered World War I. You will learn more about this conflict in Chapter 12. After the war, many Americans became disillusioned. By then, Progressivism had lost much of its appeal. Many of the most important Progressive reforms had already been adopted. You will learn more about the period after the war in Chapter 13 on the "Roaring Twenties."

For the Georgia Milestones EOC Assessment, you should know that:

- Muckrakers were writers and journalists who promoted change by exposing social problems: for example, Ida Tarbell exposed the unfair tactics of John D. Rockefeller's Standard Oil Company, and Upton Sinclair exposed the unhealthy practices of the meat processing industry. Sinclair's book, *The Jungle*, led to the passage of the Meat Inspection Act (1906).

- Women played important roles in the reform movements of the Progressive Era. They ran "settlement houses." They also fought to improve the conditions of workers, to have state inspections of factories, to prohibit child labor, and to obtain women's suffrage (*the right to vote*).

- Progressives were responsible for major legislative actions at the local, state, and federal levels. In general, Progressives were middle-class reformers who wanted to use the power of government to correct the worst abuses of industrial society, to end corruption in government, to limit the influence of "Big Business," and to preserve opportunities for the middle class.

- Progressive legislative actions included: (1) steps for the empowerment of voters (secret ballot; initiative, referendum, and recall; direct election of U.S. Senators; primary elections; women's suffrage in some states); (2) new labor laws (state laws limiting working hours for women; prohibition of child labor that was later found unconstitutional; Clayton Antitrust Act preventing courts from using antitrust laws against labor unions; state fire codes for workplaces after the Triangle Shirtwaist Factory fire); and (3) laws promoting conservation (creation of National Conservation Commission; creation of new national parks; designation of national monuments). Other important Progressive reforms included the Pure Food and Drug Act, lower tariffs, the introduction of graduated income tax, and the creation of the Federal Reserve System.

- Southern states disenfranchised their African-American citizens in the late nineteenth century. They used literacy tests, poll taxes, and white primaries to take away African Americans' voting rights. White citizens preserved their rights through "grandfather" clauses.

Continued ▶

- ☐ Southern state legislatures also established a system of racial segregation in which African Americans and white residents used separate water fountains, public restrooms, park benches, waiting rooms, railway cars, and similar facilities. These segregation laws became known as "Jim Crow" laws.

- ☐ The U.S. Supreme Court upheld these segregation laws in *Plessy v. Ferguson* (1896), so long as states offered African Americans "separate but equal" facilities. This decision led to an expansion of state segregation laws across the South. In addition, President Woodrow Wilson introduced segregation into the federal government.

- ☐ The NAACP (National Association for the Advancement of Colored People) was formed in reaction to the disenfranchisement of African-American citizens and the passage of "Jim Crow" laws in the South. NAACP leaders like W.E.B. Du Bois vowed to fight for African-American rights and equal opportunities.

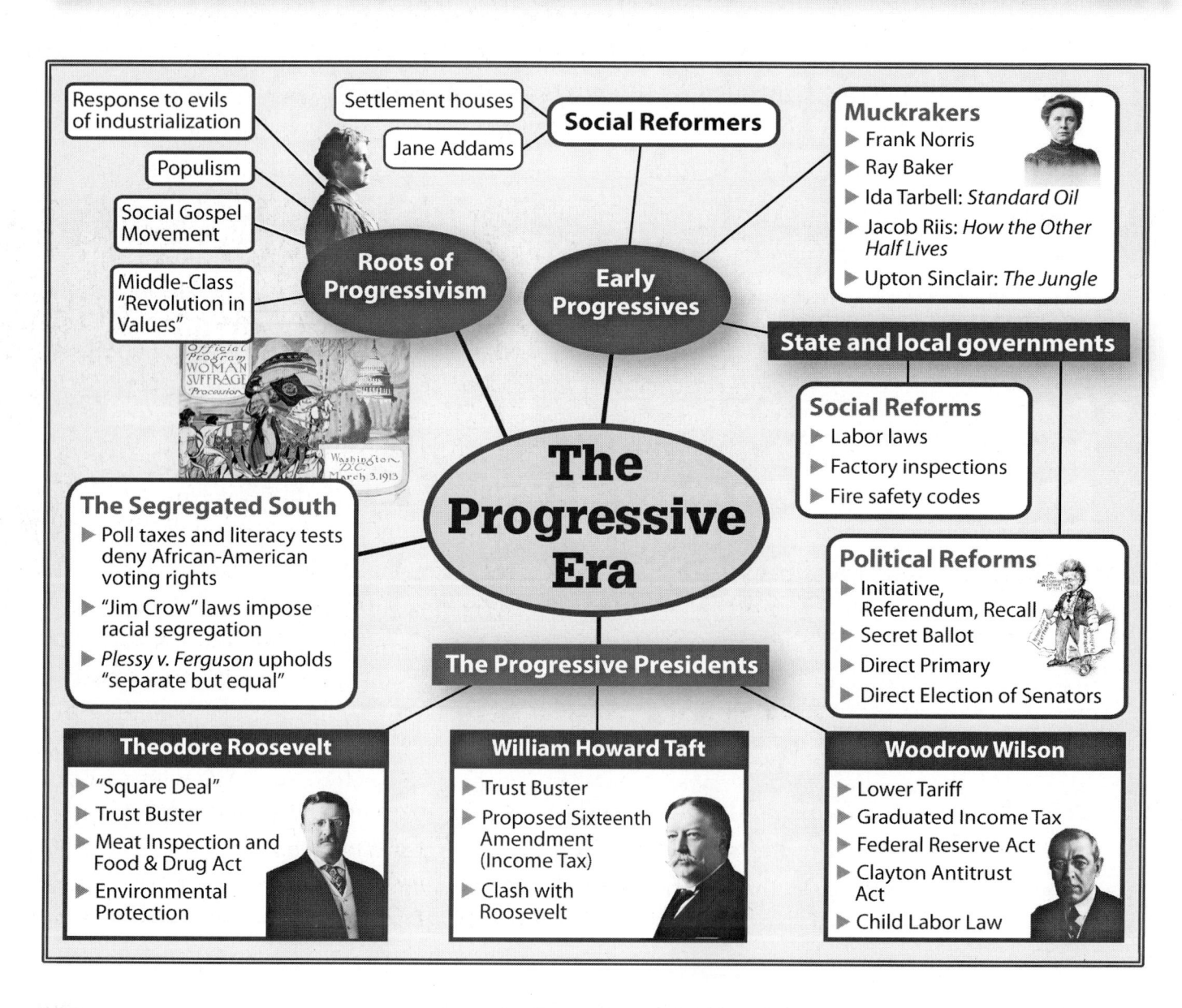

The Progressive Era

Roots of Progressivism
- Response to evils of industrialization
- Populism
- Social Gospel Movement
- Middle-Class "Revolution in Values"

Social Reformers
- Settlement houses
- Jane Addams

Early Progressives / Muckrakers
- Frank Norris
- Ray Baker
- Ida Tarbell: *Standard Oil*
- Jacob Riis: *How the Other Half Lives*
- Upton Sinclair: *The Jungle*

State and local governments

Social Reforms
- Labor laws
- Factory inspections
- Fire safety codes

Political Reforms
- Initiative, Referendum, Recall
- Secret Ballot
- Direct Primary
- Direct Election of Senators

The Segregated South
- Poll taxes and literacy tests deny African-American voting rights
- "Jim Crow" laws impose racial segregation
- *Plessy v. Ferguson* upholds "separate but equal"

The Progressive Presidents

Theodore Roosevelt
- "Square Deal"
- Trust Buster
- Meat Inspection and Food & Drug Act
- Environmental Protection

William Howard Taft
- Trust Buster
- Proposed Sixteenth Amendment (Income Tax)
- Clash with Roosevelt

Woodrow Wilson
- Lower Tariff
- Graduated Income Tax
- Federal Reserve Act
- Clayton Antitrust Act
- Child Labor Law

Chapter 10 | The Progressive Era

Name _____

Fill in the charts below.

Progressives

Define this group:	How did the Progressives differ from other groups?
People who were Progressives:	People who were *not* Progressives:

Muckrakers

Define this group:	How did muckrakers differ from other reformers?
Examples of muckrakers:	Examples of reformers who were *not* muckrakers:

Chapter 10 | The Progressive Era 307

Name _____

Fill in the charts below.

Political Machines

Define the term:	How did political machines differ from other organizations?
Examples of activities undertaken by political machines:	Examples of activities that were *not* undertaken by political machines:

Consumers

Define this group:	How do consumers differ from other groups?
Examples of activities by consumers:	How did Progressives attempt to protect consumers?

308   Chapter 10 | The Progressive Era

What Do You Know?

SSUSH13d

1. Use the list below to answer the question.

   - Meat Inspection act
   - Pure Food and Drug Act
   - Clayton Antitrust Act
   - Federal Reserve Act

   What do these laws demonstrate about the views of Progressives?

   A. They favored a policy in which government did not interfere in the economy.

   B. They believed that states rather than the federal government should regulate the economy.

   C. They favored a socialist approach in which the federal government owned the most important businesses.

   D. They thought some federal regulation was needed to prevent the worst abuses of industrialization.

SSUSH13a

2. Use the diagram below to answer the question.

There was never the least attention paid to what was cut up for sausage . . . [R]ats, bread, and meat would go into the [sausage] together . . . —Upton Sinclair, *The Jungle* (1906)	The purpose of the Act is to prevent . . . the manufacture, sale, or transportation of food or drugs which are either . . . below the standard of quality expected by the purchaser, or are so poisonous . . . as to be injurious to health . . . —Pure Food and Drug Act (1906)

   What inference can be made from the diagram?

   A. The best tasting foods are not always the most healthy ones.

   B. Most Progressive social reforms occurred at the state level.

   C. Muckrakers had an impact in promoting change by exposing problems.

   D. Upton Sinclair used his success as a writer to win election to Congress.

SSUSH13b

3. Which of these was a major goal of women reformers during the Progressive Era?

   A. a reduction of income tax rates on wealthy individuals

   B. a constitutional amendment lowering the voting age

   C. a requirement that all workers join a labor union

   D. a federal law prohibiting child labor

Chapter 10 | The Progressive Era

SSUSH13d

4. Use the list below to answer the question.

   - Setting aside federal land as national parks
   - Protecting other landmarks on federal lands by designating them as national monuments
   - Establishing the National Conservation Commission

   What would be the BEST title for this list?

   A. Steps taken by Progressives to protect the environment
   B. Legislative actions overturned by the U.S. Supreme Court
   C. Actions by Progressives opposed by Southern states
   D. Executive actions approved by Congress during the Civil War

SSUSH13b

5. Use the diagram to answer the question.

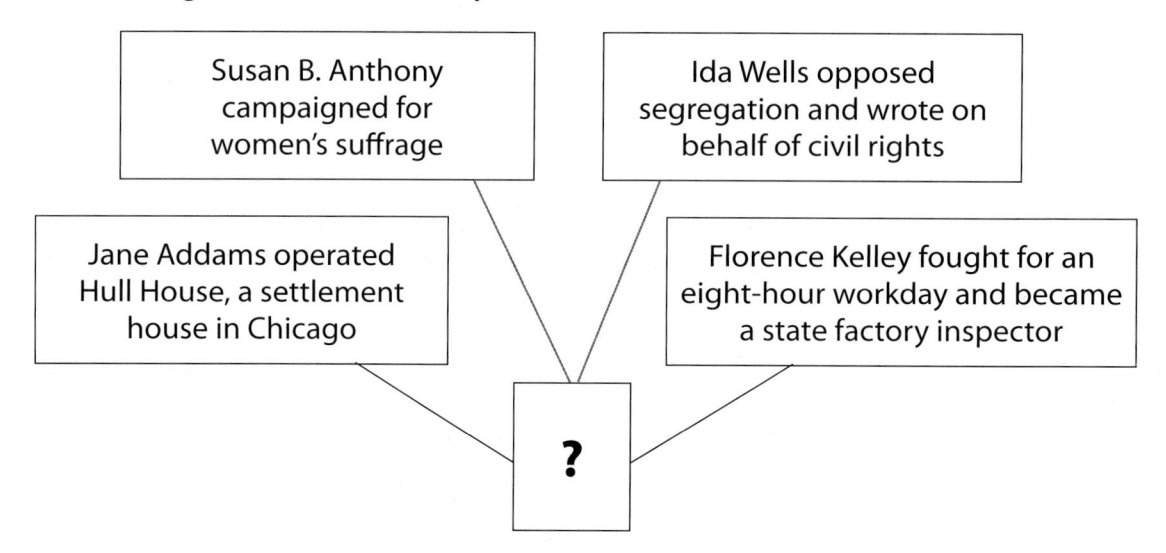

   - Susan B. Anthony campaigned for women's suffrage
   - Ida Wells opposed segregation and wrote on behalf of civil rights
   - Jane Addams operated Hull House, a settlement house in Chicago
   - Florence Kelley fought for an eight-hour workday and became a state factory inspector
   - ?

   Which phrase BEST completes the diagram?

   A. Women encouraging overseas expansion in the Progressive Era
   B. Women supporting "Big Business" in the Progressive Era
   C. Women empowering voters in the Progressive Era
   D. Women promoting social reform in the Progressive Era

SSUSH13c

6. What was the MAIN purpose behind the establishment of the NAACP?

   A. to encourage American expansion overseas
   B. to oppose racial segregation and secure civil rights
   C. to help workers organize and improve their working conditions
   D. to reduce taxes and limit government interference in our private lives

SSUSH13a

7. Use the list below to answer the question.

> - Frank Norris exposed the unfair practices of railroad companies.
> - Ida Tarbell revealed the dishonest business tactics of the Standard Oil Company.
> - Jacob Riis showed the conditions of the urban poor in New York City tenements.

Which statement best describes the influence of these muckrakers?

A. Society changed in response to their promotion of Social Darwinism.
B. Voters agreed to let Big Business owners create more profitable monopolies.
C. Copies of their articles abroad resulted in a decrease in immigration.
D. Public reaction to their writings led to legislation addressing the abuses of industrialization.

SSUSH13d

8. Use the cartoon to answer the question.

Which legislation was directed at remedying the abuses depicted in the cartoon?

A. temperance laws
B. child labor laws
C. Meat Inspection Act
D. workmen's compensation laws

SSUSH13c

9. Which statement BEST describes "Jim Crow" laws?

A. Enslaved persons who escaped to the North had to be returned to their owners.
B. People of different races were not permitted to use the same public facilities.
C. Citizens whose grandfathers were able to vote were also automatically entitled to vote.
D. African Americans in the South were unable to travel to different towns without special passes.

Chapter 10 | The Progressive Era

SSUSH13d

10. Use the list to answer the question.

• Secret Ballot	• Recall
• Initiative	• Primary Elections
• Referendum	• Direct Election of Senators

What was the main aim of these Progressive reforms?

A. to expose social problems
B. to empower voters
C. to protect the environment
D. to improve the conditions of workers

SSUSH13d

11. Read the excerpt to answer the question.

> **Section 2.** That the introduction into any State or Territory or the District of Columbia from any other State or Territory or the District of Columbia, or from any foreign country, or shipment to any foreign country of any article of food or drugs which is adulterated or misbranded, within the meaning of this Act, is hereby prohibited.
>
> —Pure Food and Drug Act (1906)

What conclusion is supported by information in the excerpt?

A. Congress remained under the control of "Big Business" interests.
B. Congress rarely exercised its ability to override a Presidential veto.
C. Congress took on a new role in protecting the health and safety of consumers.
D. Congress obtained the power to interfere in the economic activities of a single state.

SSUSH13c

12. Use the excerpt to answer the question.

> *If the civil and political rights of both races be equal, one cannot be inferior to the other civilly or politically. If one race be inferior to the other socially, the constitution of the United States cannot put them upon the same plane.*
>
> —Plessy v. Ferguson (1896)

What was the impact of the reasoning in this excerpt?

A. Racial segregation in public places continued in the South for another half century.
B. Southern state governments were forced to end their practice of racial segregation.
C. State governments had to ensure the economic and social equality of all individuals.
D. State governments no longer had to provide equal facilities to members of different races.

CHAPTER 11 American Imperialism

SSUSH14 What was America's evolving relationship with the world towards the beginning of the twentieth century?

a. How did the Spanish-American War, the war in the Philippines, and territorial expansion lead to a debate over American imperialism?

b. How did the United States become involved in Latin America, such as by the Roosevelt Corollary to the Monroe Doctrine and by the creation of the Panama Canal?

"A LESSON FOR ANTI-EXPANSIONISTS."
"Showing how Uncle Sam has been an expansionist first, last, and all the time."
Judge, Arkell Publishing Company, New York, 1899 [artist: Victor Gillam]

313

Names and Terms You Should Know

- Spanish-American War
- Cuba
- Yellow journalism
- Humanitarian
- De Lôme letter
- *U.S.S. Maine*
- Philippines
- Imperialism
- Alfred Thayer Mahan
- "White Man's Burden"
- Anti-Imperialist League
- Mark Twain
- Puerto Rico
- Teller Amendment
- Platt Amendment
- Hawaii
- Queen Liliuokalani
- Panama Canal
- Yellow fever
- Monroe Doctrine
- Roosevelt Corollary
- "Big Stick" policy

Georgia "Peaches" of Wisdom

1. In 1895, Cubans launched a war for independence. Spain took harsh measures to suppress the rebellion. Sensationalist reports in the Hearst and Pulitzer newspapers—referred to as "yellow journalism"—fanned the American desire to intervene. Americans were motivated by both humanitarianism and self-interest. De Lôme, the Spanish ambassador, wrote a letter criticizing President McKinley as weak, which was leaked to the press. Shortly afterwards, the *U.S.S. Maine* exploded in Havana Harbor. These events led to a public outcry. Americans blamed Spain for the explosion, and President McKinley asked Congress for a declaration of war.

2. The Spanish-American War lasted only a few months. Theodore Roosevelt organized the "Rough Riders," who fought in Cuba. Commodore Dewey defeated Spanish naval forces in the Philippines. Congress promised not to annex Cuba in the Teller Amendment. Cuba became independent but fell under indirect control. Under the Platt Amendment (1901), Cuba gave the United States the right to intervene in Cuban affairs.

3. A debate arose over American imperial expansion. Anti-imperialists argued that: (1) Americans had once fought against British imperialism and should not become imperialists themselves; (2) imperialism was anti-democratic; and (3) ownership of colonies would bring Americans into international conflicts. Imperialists argued that: (1) colonies were needed to provide natural resources and markets; (2) America had a moral obligation to help colonial peoples; (3) Americans should grab remaining territories before Europeans did; and (4) colonies would provide strategic naval bases, encourage trade, and bring wealth and power.

4. The outcome of the debate was that America annexed the Philippines and Puerto Rico. A Filipino rebellion was put down with some brutality. Fighting against the Filipino rebels lasted for several years—much longer than the Spanish-American War.

5. The United States also expanded to other places. American plantation owners in Hawaii overthrew Queen Liliuokalani in 1893 with the support of U.S. troops. President Cleveland refused to annex Hawaii, but President McKinley and Congress agreed to do so in 1898.

6. Midway, Guam, and Samoa also became U.S. possessions in the Pacific. In the Caribbean, Americans purchased part of the Virgin Islands in 1917.

7. President Roosevelt wanted to build a canal through the Isthmus of Panama to provide easier access between the Atlantic and Pacific Oceans. When talks with Colombia for building a canal stalled, Roosevelt supported Panamanian rebels. In exchange for U.S. recognition and protection, Panama gave control of the canal zone to the United States. The canal took a decade to build and was the most complicated engineering project of its day.

8. The "Roosevelt Corollary to the Monroe Doctrine" asserted that America would act as a policeman in Latin America, leading to repeated U.S. interventions in Central America and the Caribbean.

In the last six chapters, you studied events occurring within the United States. In this chapter and the next, you will study U.S. foreign relations: how Americans have interacted with the rest of the world.

The Spanish-American War

Spain once had the greatest of all colonial empires. But from the eighteenth century onwards, Spanish power was in continual decline. By 1898, all that remained of the once great Spanish empire was Cuba, the Philippines, Puerto Rico, and several smaller possessions. That year, the United States went to war with Spain to liberate Cuba from Spanish rule. Most Americans thought they were fighting to help the oppressed people of Cuba, but as a result of the war, the United States acquired its own overseas empire. The Spanish-American War thus marked a major turning point in the history of American foreign relations.

Origins of the Spanish-American War

Most Cubans were laborers working on the sugar and tobacco plantations of wealthy landlords. Cuban revolutionary **José Marti** organized a rebellion while living in exile in the United States. In April 1895, Marti declared Cuban independence and returned to Cuba. He was killed one month later. Cuban rebels continued to wage guerilla warfare, destroying plantations and sugar mills. General Weyler was sent from Spain to suppress the rebellion. Weyler used brutal methods, forcing Cuban peasants into "concentration camps" surrounded with barbed wire in order to separate them from the rebels. In fact, terrible atrocities were committed by both sides.

Humanitarian Concerns

Many Americans felt they had a moral obligation to intervene in Cuba. The same Progressive impulse that had promoted reform at home now encouraged intervention abroad.

The Impact of "Yellow Journalism"

American humanitarian concerns were deliberately stirred up by "yellow journalism," or the "yellow press." **Yellow journalism** was a new technique for selling more newspapers by sensationalizing and even distorting news events to arouse interest and evoke sympathy. In the 1890s, Joseph Pulitzer's *New York World* and William Randolph Hearst's *New York Journal* deliberately sensationalized news from Cuba to sell more papers. They depicted Spaniards as murderous brutes and Cuban rebels as helpless victims. These newspaper publishers distorted events and even printed false stories of fictitious atrocities. Through such methods, Hearst was able to increase his newspaper circulation substantially, but Americans received an inaccurate picture of the Cuban civil war.

316   Chapter 11 | American Imperialism

Economic Interests

U.S. government and business leaders were concerned to protect American investments in Cuba, which exceeded $50 million. They believed that the Cuban civil war was hurting American trade. Some American businessmen even thought that American intervention in Cuba might lead to new business opportunities after the war.

The Triggering Events: The De Lôme Letter and the Explosion of the Maine

In February 1898, a letter by Enrique Dupuy de Lôme, the Spanish ambassador to the United States, was published in the Hearst press. The letter caused a public outcry for calling President McKinley "weak." It indicated that the Spaniards were not being totally honest in their negotiations with the United States over events in Cuba. This leak was followed almost immediately by the explosion of the American battleship **USS *Maine*** in Havana Harbor in Cuba. The *Maine* had been sent to Havana to protect American lives and property. Historians still do not know why the ship exploded, but the Hearst press immediately blamed Spain for an act of sabotage. The De Lôme letter and sinking of the *Maine* so inflamed public opinion that President McKinley found it hard to resist the outcry for war. The Spanish government agreed to McKinley's demands for a cease-fire with the rebels and even for opening up the camps where they were forcing Cubans from the countryside to go in order to isolate the rebels. However, Spain refused to grant formal independence to Cuba. Given the climate of American public opinion, President McKinley felt he had no other choice but to ask Congress for a declaration of war.

The Course and Consequences of the War

The Spanish-American War lasted only four months. The U.S. Navy blockaded Cuba and destroyed the ships defending the island. American land forces overwhelmed Spanish troops. Theodore Roosevelt, Assistant Secretary of the Navy, resigned his post and gathered a group of volunteers, known as the "**Rough Riders.**" Roosevelt arranged for these volunteers to serve along with regular army units. Most of the Rough Riders were recruited in Texas and the Southwest. From there, they took a train to Tampa, Florida, where they waited for orders to embark for Cuba. About one-third of the Rough Riders remained in Tampa for the course of the war; the rest sailed from Tampa to Cuba, where they fought in several battles. Under Roosevelt's command, they led a famous cavalry charge against Spanish artillery up San Juan Hill. Their victory helped the U.S. Army capture Santiago, the capital of Cuba.

"Rough Riders" take San Juan Hill

On the other side of the globe, the U.S. Navy under **Commodore George Dewey** defeated the Spanish fleet in Manila Bay and occupied the **Philippines**. The American triumph in the Spanish-American War advertised to the world the fact that the United States was now a "great power."

Chapter 11 | American Imperialism

As a result of the war, Spain lost Cuba, the Philippines, Puerto Rico, and Guam. The United States annexed all of these territories except Cuba. It paid Spain $20 million for the Philippines. Cuba became independent in name but fell under the indirect control of the United States. War broke out again in the Philippines when American leaders decided to annex these islands instead of granting the Filipinos their independence.

The Historian's Apprentice

Make your own chart showing the main causes and effects of the Spanish-American War.

The Debate over Imperial Expansion

Imperialism is the rule of one country by another. Most Americans had traditionally opposed imperialism. As citizens of a former colony that had won its independence, they felt they should not impose colonial rule on others. The rule of one country by another was simply seen as a violation of the democratic principles upon which America was based. Democracy, by definition, implied self-government. Many Americans also feared that the acquisition of colonies would drag them into conflicts with other imperial powers. For these reasons, President Cleveland and the U.S. Congress had refused to annex Hawaii in 1894 (you will learn more about this later in this chapter). Anti-imperialist sentiment was still strong in the United States in 1898. For example, in authorizing the Spanish-American War, Congress had passed the **Teller Amendment**. This was an amendment (*or addition*) by Congress to its original declaration of war, promising that the United States would not annex Cuba, even if it won the war. It received overwhelming support in the House of Representatives.

The Motives for Imperialism

In the aftermath of the Spanish-American War, however, the United States became an imperial power. Some Americans opposed ratification of the **Treaty of Paris**, the peace treaty with Spain ending the war, since its terms made the United States an imperial power. But others argued that new factors had made the acquisition of colonies extremely desirable. They pointed to the following.

The Need for Raw Materials and Markets for American Industry

The rise of industry had created new needs. Imperialists argued that colonies could provide raw materials for American factories and guarantee markets for American manufactured goods. The expansion of American industry thus propelled the United States overseas. Farmers hoped to sell their surplus crops to colonial populations. Imperial expansion seemed all the more necessary because high protective tariffs limited trade among the industrialized countries. A colonial

> *[The United States] disclaims any disposition of intention to exercise sovereignty, jurisdiction, or control over said island except for pacification thereof, and asserts its determination, when that is accomplished, to leave the government and control of the island to its people."*
>
> —Teller Amendment, April 1898

empire would provide Americans with a protected market for trade.

New Technological Capabilities

The steamboat, railroad, improved rifle, machine gun, telegraph, and telephone, as well as better medicines, made it possible to colonize many new areas, especially in the Tropics.

The Importance of Naval Power

The most influential imperialist thinker, Captain **Alfred Thayer Mahan**, published his book *The Influence of Sea Power Upon History* in 1890. President of the Naval College at Annapolis, Mahan believed that it was sea power that made a nation truly great. He urged the United States to increase its wealth and power by developing a strong navy.

To provide sailors for the navy and to encourage trade, Mahan argued, the United States also needed a large fleet of merchant ships and overseas colonies. The navy would safeguard ocean-shipping lanes to protect the country's colonies and merchant fleet. "England's naval bases have been in all parts of the world," he observed, "and her fleets have at once protected them, kept open the communications between them, and relied upon them for shelter." He concluded that "colonies attached to the mother-country afford, therefore, the surest means of supporting abroad the sea power of a country."

The key to world power thus lay in overseas colonies, strategic naval bases, a large merchant marine, and a powerful navy. Mahan recommended that the United States build a canal through Panama, annex colonies in the Pacific and Caribbean to serve as naval bases, and develop greater trade with East Asia. Mahan's most famous disciple, Theodore Roosevelt, would put much of Mahan's program into effect during his Presidency.

Competition with the European Powers

In the 1880s and 1890s, European powers were carving up Africa, Asia, and the Pacific into colonies and "spheres of influence." American imperialists urged the United States to follow suit and to grab some territories of its own before nothing was left.

Clipper ships and steamships brought tea and other goods from China and the rest of East Asia to the United States. Colonies in the Pacific like the Philippines and Hawaii could help to protect America's growing trade with Asia.

A Golden Opportunity

Imperialists argued that the final collapse of the Spanish empire had created a "golden opportunity" for the United States by placing these last Spanish possessions in America's lap. President McKinley reasoned in the following way in deciding the fate of the Philippines: he could not return them to Spain or give them to any other European power; at the same time, the Filipinos did not appear to be ready for self-government. McKinley concluded that the United States had no choice but to assume control over the Philippines itself.

The New "Manifest Destiny"

The United States had already expanded from the Atlantic to the Pacific Coast. So the earlier ideal of Manifest Destiny seemed to have been fulfilled. But in the 1890s, "Manifest Destiny" suddenly took on a whole new meaning: it became America's divine mission not simply to reach the shores of the Pacific, but to extend beyond. This notion was also closely tied to feelings of Anglo-Saxon superiority.

The "White Man's Burden"

Many Americans believed in the superiority of "Anglo-Saxons" (those of British ancestry). They thought that white Protestants—especially

Anglo-Saxons—were a superior race that deserved to rule over others. Their conviction in Anglo-Saxon superiority also satisfied deep psychological needs in many Americans. Josiah Strong, a popular Protestant preacher and writer, even predicted that Anglo-Saxons would multiply and eventually take over the Earth.

There was also a strong humanitarian impulse behind these beliefs. Many Americans genuinely wanted to help other peoples around the world. Such humanitarians thought that by spreading American institutions and Protestant Christianity, they were doing native peoples in other parts of the world a great favor.

The Anti-Imperialist Argument

Other Americans opposed imperialism. These **anti-imperialists** felt that imperialism—the rule of one people by another—was immoral and went against the most basic values of American democracy. Some dreaded negative economic repercussions. Labor leader Samuel Gompers feared colonies would become a source of cheap labor, leading to lower wages in the United States. The industrialist Andrew Carnegie was a pacifist and thought that the possession of colonies would lead to rivalry and armed conflict with other imperial powers. In 1898, the same year as the Spanish-American War and the annexation of Hawaii, critics of imperialism formed a new organization called the **Anti-Imperialist League**. In April 1899, ten thousand members gathered in Chicago to merge several local leagues into the **American Anti-Imperialist League**. Former President Grover Cleveland, Andrew Carnegie, Samuel Gompers, Jane Addams, and William Jennings Bryan all became members of this League.

British author Rudyard Kipling wrote a poem about the "White Man's Burden" (1899) regarding the responsibility to help others. Kipling was specifically addressing the American acquisition of the Philippines, and he published his poem in the Progressive magazine, *McClure's*.

The White Man's Burden, by Rudyard Kipling

Take up the White Man's burden—
Send forth the best ye breed—
Go, bind your sons to exile
To serve your captives' need;
To wait, in heavy harness,
On fluttered folk and wild—
Your new-caught sullen peoples,
Half devil and half child. . . .

Take up the White Man's burden—
The savage wars of peace—
Fill full the mouth of Famine,
And bid the sickness cease;
And when your goal is nearest
(The end for others sought)
Watch sloth and heathen folly
Bring all your hope to nought.

▸ According to Kipling, how did imperialism actually help colonial peoples? Use evidence from the poem to support your answer.

▸ What were Kipling's ideas about colonial peoples? Use evidence from the poem to support your answer.

The most famous member of the Anti-Imperialist League was the celebrated writer Mark Twain, a bitter critic of imperialism. Twain had traveled through India and Africa on his speaking tours and had been outraged at the treatment of native peoples by the imperial powers, which reminded him of the treatment of slaves in the South in his boyhood. Originally, Twain had favored American intervention in the Philippines: "I said to myself, here are a people who have suffered for three centuries. We can make them as free as ourselves, give them a government and country of their own, put a miniature of the American constitution afloat in the Pacific, start a brand new republic to take its place among the free nations of the world. It seemed to me a great task to which we had addressed ourselves." But he was shocked when he learned that such liberation was not the true aim of American leaders: "I have seen that we do not intend to free, but to subjugate the people of the Philippines. We have gone there to conquer, not to redeem. We have pledged the power of this country to maintain and protect the abominable system established in the Philippines by the [Spanish monks]. It should, it seems to me, be our pleasure and duty to make those people free, and let them deal with their own domestic questions in their own way. And so I am an anti-imperialist. I am opposed to having the eagle put its talons on any other land."

In 1900, William Jennings Bryan was nominated a second time as the candidate for President of the Democratic Party—this time on an anti-imperialist platform. In his acceptance speech, he summarized the main arguments for imperialism and responded to each one:

Imperialist Argument 1: The United States must enter international politics and become a world power.

Bryan's Response: "The United States is already a world power. Its Declaration of Independence and Constitution are what make it a world power . . . For ten decades it has been the most [powerful] influence in the world."

Imperialist Argument 2: The United States needs to keep the Philippines to further its commercial interests in the Pacific and Asia.

Bryan's Response: America could bargain for a base in the Philippines without establishing a colony there. "It is not necessary to own a people in order to trade with them." Trade can only be profitable when it is voluntarily based on the high quality and cheapness of American goods. The use of force for trade is never profitable when the actual costs of using force are taken into account.

Imperialist Argument 3: The United States must spread the Christian religion.

Bryan's Response: The Filipinos are already Christian, and forcible Christianity goes against the principles of Christianity itself. "Imperialism finds no warrant in the Bible." True Christianity is based on charity and serving others, not using force.

Imperialist Argument 4: There is no honorable retreat for the United States from the Philippines, now that American blood has been shed.

Bryan's Response: The fact that American blood has been shed there does not mean the United States cannot leave. Americans shed blood in Cuba and promised to leave there. "Better a thousand times that our flag in [Asia] give way to a flag representing the idea of self-government than that the flag of this Republic should become the flag of an empire."

The Historian's Apprentice

Imagine it is 1898 after the Spanish-American War. Write your own newspaper editorial explaining either the advantages or the disadvantages for the United States of becoming an imperialist power.

The American Colonial Empire

In the aftermath of the Spanish-American War and a vigorous debate, Americans acquired a colonial empire in the Pacific Ocean and the Caribbean Sea. The United States also asserted informal control over much of the Caribbean area, which became an "American lake."

Possessions in the Pacific

The Philippines

When the Spanish-American War broke out, Filipino rebels were already at war with Spain. They declared their independence in June 1898 and were bitterly disappointed when McKinley decided to annex the Philippines.

Filipino rebels, led by **Emilio Aguinaldo**, rejected annexation by the United States and launched a rebellion against American rule that lasted for another three years. After the United States defeated the Filipinos in the Battle of Manila, the rebels used guerilla warfare against the occupiers. American military commanders ironically used methods similar to those previously used by Spain in Cuba, such as burning villages and torturing prisoners. The atrocities committed on both sides were so severe that the U.S. Senate held special hearings on the conduct of the war. The war against the Filipino rebels actually cost Americans more in money and lives than the shorter Spanish-American War. As many as 200,000 Filipinos died from warfare and disease. Filipino forces were only finally defeated in 1902. Afterwards, the United States built roads, hospitals, and schools in the Philippines. The Jones Act gave Filipinos the right to elect both houses of their own legislature in 1916, and promised eventual independence.

Hawaii

Hawaii is an archipelago (*a chain of islands*) in the Pacific Ocean. It provided a useful coaling station on trips from the United States to East Asia. In the mid-nineteenth century, Hawaiians had welcomed American settlers, who built sugar and pineapple plantations and then imported Chinese and Japanese laborers. By the 1880s, however, native Hawaiians and American plantation owners were coming into increasing conflict. Wealthy American landowners forced the King of Hawaii to accept a constitution that gave only property owners like themselves the right to vote. In 1893, a new ruler, **Queen Liliuokalani**, tried to take back political power. She announced that she would issue a new constitution. In response, the American minister to Hawaii and leading American landowners, with the help of the U.S. Marines, seized power. The Americans formed a provisional government and asked

Queen Liliuokalani

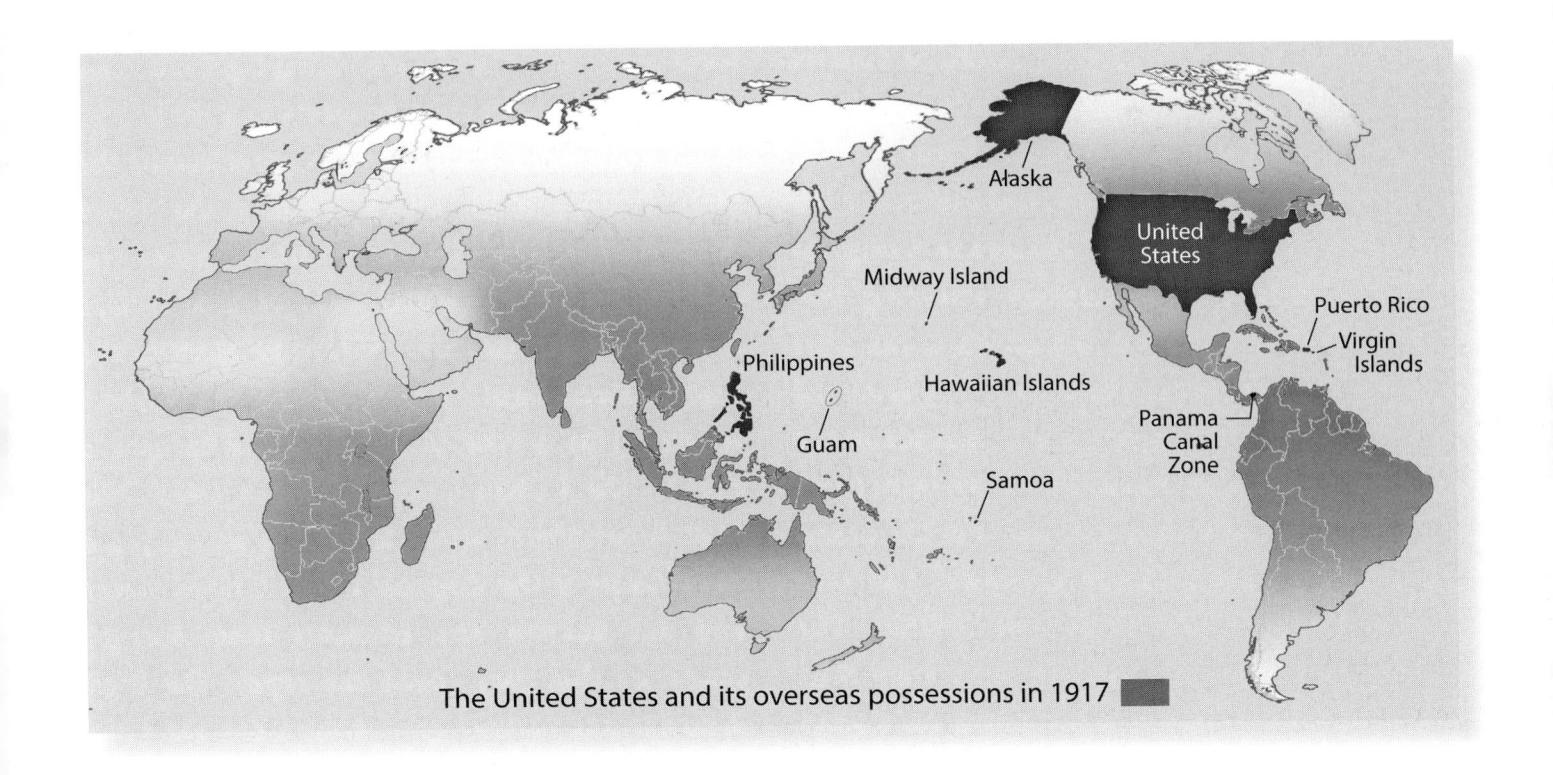

The United States and its overseas possessions in 1917

for Hawaii to be annexed by the United States. President Cleveland, however, refused because the landowners had overthrown the queen by force. Congress also voted not to interfere in Hawaiian affairs in 1894. After the outbreak of the Spanish-American War and the rise of new imperialistic sentiment in the United States, American businessmen in Hawaii petitioned for annexation again in July 1898. This time, Congress voted overwhelmingly in favor of annexation.

Other Pacific Islands: Guam, Samoa, and Midway

In these years, Americans also acquired a number of smaller islands in the Pacific. **Midway** had been an American possession since 1867. **Guam** was taken from Spain following the Spanish-American War. **Samoa** was placed under the joint control of Britain, Germany, and the United States in 1889. In 1899, it was divided between Germany and the United States. These islands provided valuable coaling stations for American ships sailing to Asia, where they could obtain coal, fresh water, food, and other supplies.

New Interests in the Caribbean

Puerto Rico

Puerto Rico also became an American possession after the Spanish-American War. It was not until 1952 that Puerto Rico became a self-governing "Commonwealth." Today, the United States provides for the island's defense and sets its foreign policy. Puerto Ricans are U.S. citizens and enjoy rights of unrestricted immigration to the United States. Many Puerto Ricans would like their island to become the 51st state.

Cuba: An Informal Protectorate

When President McKinley asked Congress for a declaration of war against Spain in 1898, he promised to establish "a stable government" in Cuba. Congress responded with a joint resolution authorizing him to use force against Spain but promising "recognition of the independence of the people of Cuba" when the war was over. Senator Henry Teller proposed a further amendment to this resolution, promising that the United States had no "intention

Chapter 11 | American Imperialism

to exercise sovereignty, jurisdiction, or control over [Cuba] except for pacification thereof," and that when the war was over, the United States would "leave the government and control of the island to its people." Both Houses of Congress passed the **Teller Amendment,** ensuring that the United States would not annex Cuba after the war. Consequently, Cuba was not annexed and Cubans were given their independence once Spain was defeated. However, American influence was so strong in Cuba that the island became a virtual U. S. "protectorate" (*an area under American protection and control*). For three years after the Spanish-American War, American forces actually remained on Cuban soil. They created sanitation systems, trained a local police force, and gave voting rights to male Cubans meeting certain property qualifications.

In 1901, both Houses of Congress passed the **Platt Amendment,** which replaced the Teller Amendment. The Platt Amendment stated the conditions for the withdrawal of U.S. troops from Cuba. Cubans were forced to agree to the Platt Amendment, which passed the Cuban Assembly by a vote of 16 to 11 and became a part of the Cuban Constitution in 1902. The Platt Amendment stated that Cuba would place naval bases at the disposal of the United States and not borrow any amounts from foreign countries that they could not repay. The Platt Amendment further gave Americans the right to intervene in Cuban affairs at any time.

The Platt Amendment, 1901

I. That the government of Cuba shall never enter into any treaty or other compact with any foreign power or powers which will impair or tend to impair the independence of Cuba, nor in any manner authorize or permit any foreign power or powers to obtain by colonization or for military or naval purposes or otherwise, lodgement in or control over any portion of said island.

II. That said government shall not assume or contract any public debt that [they would not have sufficient income to repay].

III. That the government of Cuba consents that the United States may exercise the right to intervene for the preservation of Cuban independence, the maintenance of a government adequate for the protection of life, property, and individual liberty, and for discharging the obligations with respect to Cuba imposed by the Treaty of Paris on the United States, now to be assumed and undertaken by the government of Cuba....

VII. That to enable the United States to maintain the independence of Cuba, and to protect the people thereof, as well as for its own defense, the government of Cuba will sell or lease to the United States lands necessary for coaling or naval stations at certain specified points to be agreed upon with the President of the United States.

---

1. Review these four articles from the Platt Amendment. Which article do you think was the most important? Why?
2. Were Cubans really independent after they accepted the Platt Amendment? Why or why not? Use evidence from the Platt Amendment to support your point of view.

Indeed, American troops were sent back to Cuba as early as 1906. The American occupation did at least benefit Cuba in some ways. Americans established a school system, organized finances, and helped eliminate yellow fever in Cuba. Cubans also benefited from American investment in sugar and tobacco plantations, sugar refineries, electricity, and utilities. Most of Cuba's exports went to the United States.

The Virgin Islands

Americans completed their acquisitions in the Caribbean by purchasing several of the Virgin Islands from Denmark in 1917.

The Historian's Apprentice

Create your own map showing American territorial acquisitions between 1867 and 1917.

American Relations with East Asia and Latin America, 1898–1914

In the years after the Spanish-American War, American foreign policy was mainly focused on developing trade with East Asia and Latin America, strengthening America's hold over its new colonies, and building a canal in Central America.

American Trade with East Asia

The United States was in an advantageous location for trade with East Asia. Only the Pacific Ocean separated this region from the West Coast of the United States. In the late nineteenth century, Americans developed an active trade with China. Other Asian territories, like the Dutch East Indies (present-day Indonesia), became important sources of spices, rubber, and other goods. Control of the Philippines transformed the United States into an important power in the Pacific. Midway, Hawaii, Guam, and Samoa provided naval bases and coaling stations for ships going back and forth to East Asia.

Americans also began trading with Japan. In the 1600s, Japan's rulers had limited their contact with the rest of the world. In July 1853, Commodore Matthew Perry sailed into Tokyo Bay with a small squadron of four ships and forced the Japanese to sign a treaty opening their ports to trade with the United States.

The United States and Latin America

The Panama Canal

The Spanish-American War had demonstrated the importance of building a canal in Central America to connect the Atlantic and Pacific

Early stages of Panama Canal construction

Chapter 11 | American Imperialism

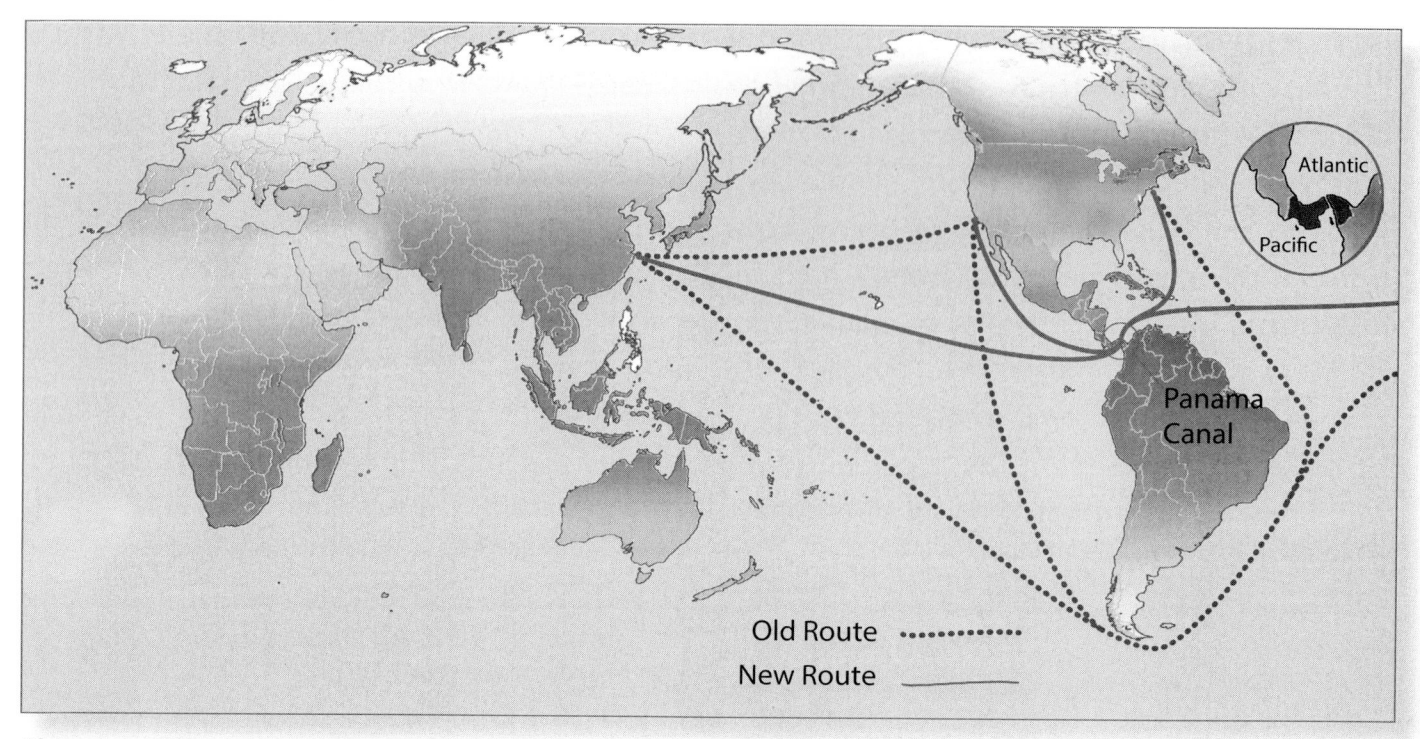

Shipping routes were dramatically shortened by the Panama Canal

Oceans. Without it, the Atlantic fleet would have to sail all around South America to come to the aid of the Pacific fleet. By 1903, President Theodore Roosevelt therefore decided it was essential to build a canal across the Isthmus of Panama, then a part of Colombia. The United States offered $10 million and an annual fee to Colombia for a strip of land on which to build the canal. The Colombian government wanted more money, however, and delayed. Roosevelt then struck a deal with rebels in Colombia who were attempting to establish a new country in Panama. A U.S. warship prevented the Colombian government from suppressing the rebellion in Panama, while Roosevelt immediately

The Panama Canal connected the Pacific to the Atlantic

The Historian's Apprentice

Use the Internet or your school library to conduct research on the construction of the Panama Canal. Describe the problems encountered in building the canal. Then explain the advantages to the United States of building the canal.

326   Chapter 11 | American Imperialism

gave Panama diplomatic recognition. In return, the new nation of Panama agreed to give the United States complete control over a ten-mile strip running through the center of Panama, known as the "Panama Canal Zone," for building the canal. Colombia and other Latin American countries were greatly angered by Roosevelt's high-handed and self-serving policies.

Roosevelt ordered the construction of the canal almost at once. It was a monumental undertaking, requiring engineers and workers to cut through hills and jungle. There were a large number of difficulties. The tropical jungles of Panama were home to mosquitoes carrying malaria and **yellow fever**. American engineers had to drain swamps and spray insecticides. Next, American engineers rebuilt the Panama Railway to carry equipment for constructing the canal. Modern steam shovels and other expensive equipment were used to build a reservoir and locks at each end of the canal to raise ships up to the highlands and lower them back down to sea level. Ships crossing the canal even today sail into a lock, which is then filled with water to raise the ship. At the other end of the canal, locks are drained to lower the ship. The Panama Canal took more than ten years to complete, costing thousands of lives and $400 million.

The "Roosevelt Corollary to the Monroe Doctrine"

Almost a century earlier, President Monroe had announced the **Monroe Doctrine** in 1823. He had stated that the United States would oppose any attempt by European powers to establish new colonies in the Western Hemisphere. In the late nineteenth century, American governments extended the meaning of the Monroe Doctrine. In 1904, when the Dominican Republic owed debts to European countries, President Roosevelt refused to let those countries use force to collect them. Instead, Roosevelt declared that the United States would intervene and collect the debts for them, acting as an "international police power." Roosevelt took over collection of the Dominican Republic's customs, turning more than half the receipts over to foreign creditors. This approach became known as the "**Roosevelt Corollary to the Monroe Doctrine**." Because Roosevelt's motto was to "speak softly and carry a big stick," it also became known as the "**Big Stick**" **policy**. Under this policy, the United States sent troops to the West Indies and Central America so often that the Caribbean became known as an "American lake." Haiti, Nicaragua, Honduras, and the Dominican Republic joined Cuba as virtual American protectorates. The "Roosevelt Corollary" was deeply resented by most Latin American nations.

The Historian's Apprentice

1. What was the difference between the original Monroe Doctrine (1823) and the "Roosevelt Corollary"?
2. Use the Internet to find political cartoons that illustrate President Theodore Roosevelt's "Big Stick" policy toward Latin America. Then write a short analysis of one cartoon. In your analysis, consider these key questions: (1) Who are the characters in the cartoon? (2) What objects or symbols does the cartoonist use and what does each represent? (3) What is the cartoonist's overall message? (4) How would this cartoon have affected views at the time it was created?

Name _____

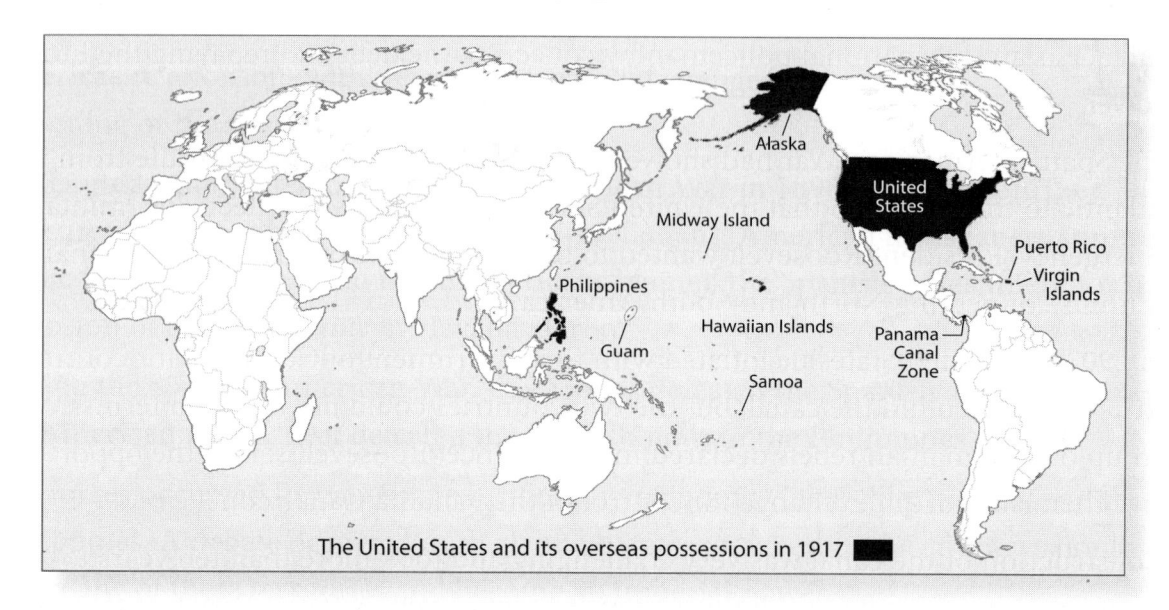

The United States and its overseas possessions in 1917

Based on the map, where did U.S. imperialists acquire overseas territories?

Territory	Reason for Acquisition

THE BIG STICK IN THE CARIBBEAN SEA

1. What is the main idea of this cartoon?

2. What is the cartoonist's view of Roosevelt's policy?

Chapter 11 | American Imperialism

Name _____

Panama Canal

Complete the chart below by describing the motivations for the U.S. to build the Panama Canal.

Economic		Military

Security

Complete the following chart by summarizing the main arguments of American imperialists and anti-imperialists after the Spanish American War.

Arguments of the Imperialists	Arguments of the Anti-imperialists

Chapter 11 | American Imperialism 331

What Do You Know?

SSUSH14a

1. Which action was a direct result of the Spanish-American War?
   A. The United States annexed several former Spanish possessions.
   B. The United States occupied Madrid and other cities in Spain.
   C. The United States helped Portugal win its independence.
   D. The United States took control of the Panama Canal Zone.

SSUSH14a

2. Which TWO statements accurately present arguments used by imperialists to justify American expansion?
   A. Merchants need to have coaling stations on the way to Asia.
   B. Americans can trade overseas without owning other territories.
   C. It is expensive to maintain overseas colonies.
   D. The United States needs to catch up with the European powers.
   E. Possessing overseas colonies will drag Americans into European wars.
   F. Ruling other territories violates American principles of self-government.

SSUSH14a

3. Use the excerpt to answer the questions.

   > [C]olonies attached to the mother country afford . . . the surest means of supporting abroad the sea powers of a country.
   > —Alfred Thayer Mahan, *The Influence of Sea Power on History* (1890)

   ### Part A

   Based on this excerpt, why would Mahan have MOST favored U.S. annexation of Spain's former colonies?

   A. to promote overseas trade
   B. to increase U.S. naval power
   C. to meet America's humanitarian responsibility
   D. to spread America's democratic system of government

   ### Part B

   Which group would have MOST disagreed with Mahan's reasoning?

   A. Populists
   B. Progressives
   C. Suffragettes
   D. Anti-Imperialists

SSUSH14a

4. Which action illustrates an impact of American imperialism?
   A. Americans built railroad lines, hospitals, and schools in Cuba.
   B. Cubans in Florida began making cigars for export to Europe.
   C. The United States placed no restrictions on immigration from Latin America in the nineteenth century.
   D. Most individuals from the Caribbean region migrated to the United States.

SSUSH14a

5. Use this list to answer the question.

   > Puerto Rico
   > Hawaii
   > Guam
   > Samoa
   > Midway
   > Panama Canal Zone

   What do the elements in the list have in common?
   A. They gained independence in 1898.
   B. They became U.S. possessions.
   C. They rebelled against Spain.
   D. They exported manufactured goods.

SSUSH14b

6. Which statement BEST summarizes the "Roosevelt Corollary" to the Monroe Doctrine?
   A. The United States would not exercise sovereignty over any foreign territory.
   B. America would oppose all attempts by European powers to establish new colonies in the Americas.
   C. The United States would act as an international policeman in the Caribbean, collecting debts owed to foreign powers.
   D. The United States would only extend diplomatic recognition to democratically elected governments in the Caribbean region.

SSUSH14a

7. Which argument was used by anti-imperialists?
   A. Colonies can provide useful coaling stations for trade.
   B. Ruling over others violates America's democratic principles.
   C. America needs to acquire some colonies before rival powers grab them all.
   D. Americans should spread their ideals and values to other parts of the world.

Chapter 11 | American Imperialism

SSUSH14a

8. Use the timeline to answer the question.

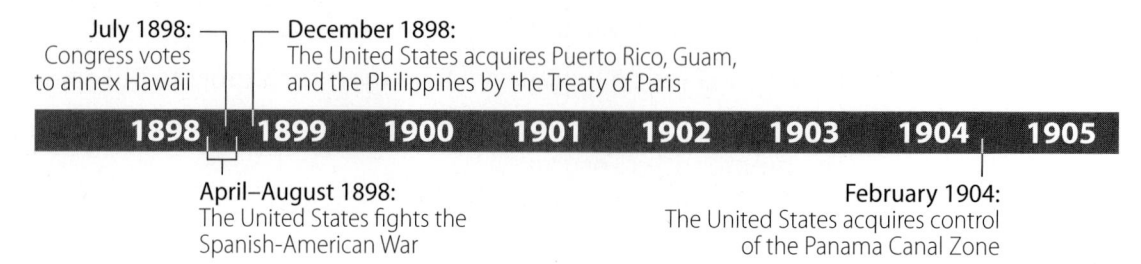

July 1898: Congress votes to annex Hawaii

December 1898: The United States acquires Puerto Rico, Guam, and the Philippines by the Treaty of Paris

| 1898 | 1899 | 1900 | 1901 | 1902 | 1903 | 1904 | 1905 |

April–August 1898: The United States fights the Spanish-American War

February 1904: The United States acquires control of the Panama Canal Zone

What was one of the arguments used in favor of these changes?

A. American industries need raw materials and markets found overseas.

B. The system of imperialism is contrary to American democratic principles.

C. Colonial peoples are inviting American leadership to develop their economies.

D. Imperialist expansion threatens to bring the United States into conflict with European powers.

SSUSH14b

9. Use the political cartoon below to answer the question.

This political cartoon was published in December 1903. The hill in the background says "Bogota," the capital of Colombia. In 1911, former President Theodore Roosevelt stated: "I took the Canal Zone and let Congress debate; and while the debate goes on, the Canal does also."

To what event do the cartoon and President Roosevelt's statement refer?

A. a debate in Congress over whether to appropriate funds to build the Panama Canal

B. the many obstacles that the geography of Panama posed to the construction of a canal

C. the debate over whether construction of the canal would be useful to U.S. national security

D. Roosevelt's decision to help Panamanian rebels against Colombia in exchange for the Canal Zone

SSUSH14a

10. Use the diagram below to answer the question.

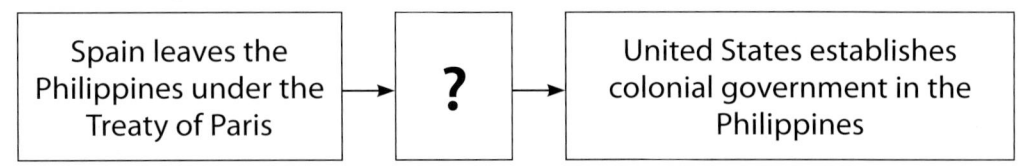

| Spain leaves the Philippines under the Treaty of Paris | → | ? | → | United States establishes colonial government in the Philippines |

Which sentence BEST completes the diagram?

A. U.S. Senate refuses to annex the Philippines.

B. Filipino leaders invite the United States to annex the Philippines.

C. American businessmen overthrow the King of the Philippines.

D. U.S. forces fight a three-year war against Filipino rebels seeking independence.

SSUSH14a

11. Read the excerpt below to answer the question.

> *Mr. President, the times call for* (honesty). *The Philippines are ours forever, "territory belonging to the United States," as the Constitution calls them. And just beyond the Philippines are China's [unlimited] markets. We will not retreat from either. We will not repudiate our duty in the archipelago. We will not abandon our opportunity in the Orient* (Asia).
>
> —Senator Albert J. Beveridge to the U.S. Senate on January 9, 1900

Based on this speech, what conclusion can be inferred about the views of American imperialists in 1900?

A. They intended to spread the democratic form of government to China.

B. They feared the growing economic and naval power of the Japanese Empire.

C. They believed that the Constitution required U.S. acquisition of the Philippines.

D. They saw the Philippines as a useful base for increasing American trade with East Asia.

SSUSH14b

12. Use the diagram to answer the question.

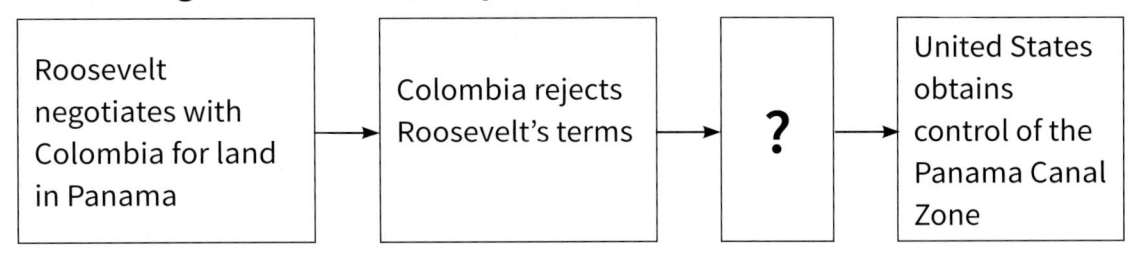

| Roosevelt negotiates with Colombia for land in Panama | → | Colombia rejects Roosevelt's terms | → | ? | → | United States obtains control of the Panama Canal Zone |

Which phrase BEST completes the diagram?

A. Roosevelt helps Panamanian rebels.

B. Roosevelt increases the payment to Colombia.

C. Roosevelt sends the U.S. Navy to seize land in Panama.

D. Roosevelt collects debts from Colombia owed to European powers.

Chapter 11 | American Imperialism   335

SSUSH14a

13. Use the excerpt below to answer the question.

> There is no reason whatever why we cannot administer the Philippines in a manner satisfactory to their people as well as to ourselves.... They are near the center of the great lines of commerce from the East to the West.... The whole world sees in China a splendid market for our native products—our timber, our locomotives, our rails, our coal oil, ... and numberless other articles ... The Philippines are a foothold for us in the Far East. Their possession gives us standing and influence. It gives us also valuable trade both in exports and imports.
> —Charles Denby, "Shall We Keep the Philippines?" in *Forum*, November 1898

Which of these actions is BEST supported by the excerpt?

A. returning control of the Philippines to Spain
B. granting independence to the people of the Philippines
C. holding on to the Philippines as an American possession
D. handing the Philippines over to another European power

SSUSH14a

14. Use the excerpt below to answer the question.

> We took up arms only in obedience to the dictates of humanity and in the fulfillment of high public and moral obligations. We had no design of aggrandizement and no ambition of conquest.
> —President William McKinley, Instruction to U.S. Peace Commissioners, September 16, 1898

Which TWO actions might cause critics to question these statements?

A. Americans fought against the Filipino rebels.
B. The Teller Amendment was passed by Congress.
C. Americans wanted to build a canal across Central America.
D. The United States had already expanded its frontiers to the Pacific Ocean.
E. The United States annexed Puerto Rico, Hawaii, and the Philippines.
F. The Spanish government had brutally suppressed the Cuban Revolution.

THE BIG STICK IN THE CARIBBEAN SEA

Chapter 11 | American Imperialism

CHAPTER 12: The United States in World War I

SSUSH15 What were the causes and consequences of American involvement in World War I?

a. How did the United States move from neutrality to engagement in World War I, including the impact of unrestricted submarine warfare and the Zimmerman Telegram in bringing the United States into the war?

b. What was the domestic impact of World War I, including the beginnings of the Great Migration, the Espionage Act, and the treatment of the Socialist Eugene Debs?

c. What were Wilson's Fourteen Points? Why did the United States refuse to join the League of Nations?

World War I was a global war fought with new destructive technologies that resulted in the deaths of millions of people. Americans managed to stay out of this conflict for almost three years—from its outbreak in Europe in August 1914 until April 1917. American intervention on the side of the Allies brought an end to the war in just over a year. The war changed the face of Europe, toppling empires and creating new states. In the United States, the war led to temporary government controls over the economy, a massive mobilization of manpower in the armed services, a rise in taxation and the national debt, an increased use of women and minorities as workers in American industry, and new limits on freedom of speech and the press. The results of the war disappointed those American idealists who had hoped to make the world "safe for democracy." It led to two decades of relative American isolation from world affairs. The war also turned the United States into the world's preeminent economic power.

Origins of the War in Europe

Note: You will not need to know about the European origins of the war for the Georgia Milestones EOC Assessment.

Archduke Francis Ferdinand, the heir to the throne of **Austria-Hungary**, was assassinated in Sarajevo on June 28, 1914 by Slavic nationalists. The Austrian government decided to teach Serbia a lesson. They sent an ultimatum, making demands that Serbia could not meet. Austria then invaded Serbia (see map on page 351). Because of their alliances, Russia backed Serbia and Germany supported Austria. France was pulled into the war by its alliance with Russia. When Germany marched through neutral Belgium to advance on Paris, Britain also became involved.

What should have been a minor regional crisis thus escalated into a major European war between the **Central powers** (Germany and Austria-Hungary, joined by Ottoman Turkey) and the **Allied powers** (Britain, France, Russia, and, after it changed sides, Italy).

Fighting in Europe

Military leaders thought the contest would be over quickly. They were wrong. In fact, the war became a struggle lasting several years. A host of new and improved weapons were used to fight the war—machine guns, poison gas, submarines, airplanes, and tanks. These new weapons prevented either side from quickly defeating the other.

▶ **Trench Warfare**. The Germans at first advanced through Belgium and northern France. However, their advance was stopped by the use of machine gun fire, which made it difficult to advance any further. Both sides dug **trenches** that soon extended for hundreds of miles. Soldiers in the trenches suffered from loud shelling, rats and lice, dampness, trench foot, and disease. The trenches were separated by an area of barbed wire and land mines known as "no man's land." Anyone advancing into "no man's land" would be fired at by machine guns. **Tanks** were still new and unable to break through. Each side bombarded the other with heavy artillery and even tried using **poison gas**—a form of **chemical warfare**—but neither side could defeat the other.

- **Naval Blockade.** With the stalemate in Western Europe, Great Britain set out to use its naval power to starve Germany into submission. The British established a naval blockade of the North Sea, preventing foreign arms or foodstuffs from reaching Germany. The Germans did not have enough battleships to defeat the British navy. They responded by using their submarines to prevent ships from bringing supplies to Great Britain. The submarines used their torpedoes to sink enemy ships.

- **Airplanes.** Overhead, a new invention, the airplane, dominated the sky. Airplanes were often used for reconnaissance—to see what was happening on the battlefield below. Pilots from opposing sides sometimes engaged in "dogfights"—duels in the sky in which each pilot tried to shoot down the other. However, airplanes were still new and did not play as important a role as they would in later wars.

America Goes to War

While the armies of Europe were locked in ferocious combat, Americans attempted to follow their traditional policy—first announced in Washington's "Farewell Address" more than a century earlier—of avoiding entanglement in European conflicts. The United States was not a member of either European alliance. Americans felt relatively safe, protected by the oceans. President Wilson declared that America would remain neutral. Two years later, Wilson was re-elected President in 1916 with the campaign slogan, "He kept us out of war!" Pacifists, isolationists, and German Americans were especially opposed to being dragged into a war on behalf of the Allies. Despite these efforts at maintaining **neutrality**, Americans did eventually enter the war in April 1917. Why did this happen?

Cultural Ties

Most Americans already favored the Allies in the war. Many Americans traced their ancestry to Britain. A common language and a common history also tied Americans to Britain. The United States, Great Britain, and France further shared the same political system—democracy. Although Germany had a Parliament, its government was controlled by an autocratic **Kaiser** (*Emperor*). Most Americans detested German militarism. On the other hand, a large number of Americans could trace their ancestry to Germany.

German Atrocities and Allied Propaganda

Americans were especially shocked at the German invasion of Belgium. German war plans had called for the German army to march through neutral Belgium as the quickest way to invade France and encircle Paris. Germany went ahead with these plans even though Belgium had not declared war and the invasion was a violation of international law. When the German army encountered unexpected resistance, they shot

Chapter 12 | The United States in World War I   341

civilians without trial and destroyed buildings. Such atrocities were widely reported in the American press. American newspapers even carried exaggerated stories of German soldiers cutting off children's hands and slicing babies with bayonets. Even though these stories were false, American public opinion was horrified.

Isolation of the Central Powers

The British blockade cut off the Central powers from the United States. Americans grew more favorable to the Allies because they heard only their side of the story. While American trade to Germany dropped to almost nothing, American trade to Britain and France increased four-fold between 1914 and 1916. American bankers lent $2 billion to the Allied powers—and only one-tenth of that amount to the Central powers. The United States became the main source of arms, supplies, and food for Britain and France.

German Submarine Warfare and the United States

To break the British blockade, to save their own people from starvation, and to win the war, the German government resorted to submarine warfare. This was the main factor leading to American entry into World War I.

The British Blockade

The British blockade of Germany was in violation of international law. The British put explosive mines in the North Sea. They forced all ships to land in Britain before entering the North Sea. They prevented food as well as arms from going to Germany. They also blockaded neutral countries like Norway, Sweden, and Denmark. President Wilson protested against these violations, but he did not cut off American trade with the Allies. U.S. merchant ships traveled in groups, or **convoys**, escorted by battleships. Meanwhile, hundreds of thousands of Germans were starving to death from the lack of food and fertilizers.

The German Counter-Blockade

The German fleet was not powerful enough to challenge the British navy. However, the Germans did have a strong fleet of submarines ("**U-Boats**"). A few months after the British declared their naval blockade of Germany, Germans retaliated by announcing a submarine blockade of Britain. Germany threatened to sink all Allied merchant ships sailing in the blockaded area. Because their submarines were underwater and so small, the Germans were unable to provide traditional warnings before attack or even to rescue survivors. All this violated international law. The Germans did not intend to attack American ships, but those Americans traveling on Allied ships would be affected. Most Americans felt this violated "freedom of the seas."

Sinking of the Lusitania, May 1915

On May 7, 1915, a German submarine shot a single torpedo at close range at the ***Lusitania***, a British passenger ship that had sailed from New York and was just off the Irish Coast. The ship sank in just 18 minutes, far faster than the *Titanic* had three years earlier. Although there were sufficient lifeboats, people simply did not have time to get in them. More than a thousand passengers

HMS Lusitania

were killed, including 128 Americans and 94 children. American newspapers widely reported this disaster. The sinking of the *Lusitania* had a powerful impact on the American public, stirring up anti-German feelings and creating a desire for revenge. Germans claimed the *Lusitania* had secretly concealed armaments. President Wilson sent a strong protest to Germany, but he refused to declare war over this incident.

The "Sussex Pledge," 1916

After a German submarine attack on an unarmed French passenger ship, the *Sussex*, Wilson threatened to break off diplomatic relations with Germany. The German government then pledged not to sink any more ocean liners or merchant ships without prior warning or making provisions for passengers. However, Germany agreed to these terms only on the condition that the United States persuade the Allies to lift the naval blockade of Germany. Meanwhile the British continued to use convoys—groups of merchant ships traveling together and protected by one or more battleships—to reduce their losses to submarines.

Germany Declares "Unrestricted Submarine Warfare," January 1917

German leaders realized that a resumption of submarine warfare would probably result in war with the United States, but they were suffering desperately from the lack of supplies and food due to the British blockade. Moreover, along the Eastern Front, Russia was almost defeated, while on the Western Front, several French units had mutinied. German military leaders felt that with unrestricted submarine warfare, they could probably defeat Britain and France before the United States could effectively intervene. They therefore took a calculated risk by announcing that they would sink all ships—neutral as well as Allied—traveling in the area of their blockade around Britain. This new policy was a clear violation of the American principle of "freedom of the seas"—the right claimed by the United States, as a neutral country, to ship non-military goods, even to nations at war.

The Zimmerman Telegram, March 1917

Popular feelings against Germany were further inflamed when a secret telegram was discovered and decoded by the British. It was from the German Foreign Minister, Arthur Zimmerman, promising Mexico the return of New Mexico, Arizona and Texas if it allied with Germany against the United States. The telegram was printed in American newspapers on March 1, 1917, and caused public outrage.

German Submarines Sink American Merchant Ships, March 1917

Even after the German announcement of unrestricted submarine warfare and the publication of the Zimmerman telegram, Wilson still hoped to avoid war. He decided he would not ask Congress for a declaration unless Germany actually

German U-boats at anchor at Kiel in Northern Germany. The U-20 on the far right sank the *Lusitania*.

committed "overt acts" against American shipping. In March 1917, German submarines then sank several unarmed American merchant vessels. Wilson addressed Congress and obtained a declaration of war in early April 1917.

American Idealism—Making the World "Safe for Democracy"

An idealistic Progressive, Wilson expanded the American war effort from a defense of "freedom of the seas" to a crusade for democracy. By the time that Americans entered the war in April 1917, Russia had been shaken by the first of two revolutions. In April 1917, Russia was a democracy, and the Allies had become a league of democratic nations. Wilson therefore told Congress that the United States was not going to war against the German people, but against their leaders. America's aim in entering the war was to establish the ultimate peace of the world and to free its peoples: "The world must be made safe for democracy." Most Americans found it inspiring to endure the rigors of the war for such high-minded ideals. With a strong sense of moral superiority, they set out to save and remake the world.

The Historian's Apprentice

Have your class hold a debate on the following:

"Resolved: That American intervention in World War I was justified."

Those in favor of the resolution should show why the United States was right to enter the war. Those opposed should show why Americans should not have become involved.

America at War, 1917–1918

Mobilization

Allied leaders in Europe hoped that the United States would send fresh troops to fill their own ranks. Instead, Wilson announced he would keep American troops together as the million-man **American Expeditionary Force** (AEF). Despite more than three years of conflict across the Atlantic, Americans were not prepared for war in April 1917. The first task ahead was **mobilizing** (*bringing into use*) America's vast resources.

The Selective Service Act

Wilson hesitated between raising a voluntary army or relying on conscription. He finally decided on **conscription** (or compulsory military service, also known as the "draft"). Because the notion of "service" was in the air, Congress called its conscription law the "**Selective Service Act**." Ten million men immediately registered for the "draft." Dates of birthdays were chosen out of a glass jar to determine the order in which men would be called to serve. Eventually, almost three million men were drafted into the armed services, while another two million volunteered.

Some men refused to serve because it violated their religious beliefs to kill others. These men became known as **conscientious**

objectors. Even if they weren't prepared to fight, they were still expected to report to military camp if they were drafted. Many conscientious objectors were sent to France to serve in noncombatant roles, such as driving an ambulance or caring for the wounded. Others were permitted to work on farms in the United States, where there was a shortage of labor, or to serve as fire fighters.

The Committee of Public Information

George Creel was appointed to run the **Committee of Public Information** (CPI). This agency created posters, printed pamphlets, made billboards, offered news releases to newspapers, made short newsreels to be shown in movie theaters, and provided other forms of propaganda in favor of the war effort. **Propaganda** is one-sided information designed to persuade listeners. Creel's "four-minute men" were trained speakers who gave short speeches on behalf of the war during intermissions in movie theaters and at public assemblies. Hollywood helped in the effort by making patriotic, anti-German films.

The War-Time Economy

The United States now had to train and equip a large body of troops as well as continue helping its European allies. American leaders continued to lend money to Britain and France, thinking that this might help reduce the future cost of the war in American lives. Americans also had to manufacture arms and equipment.

In peacetime, Wilson had acted to curb Big Business in favor of free competition. After the outbreak of the war, however, he collaborated with the leaders of Big Business and organized labor in order to coordinate the economy and direct it towards the war effort.

The war saw a vast expansion of the federal government. Wilson was given sweeping powers by Congress to regulate wartime production. For this purpose, he established a number of special agencies:

- The **War Industries Board**, headed by Bernard Baruch, coordinated America's wartime manufacturing. Wilson and Baruch hoped to persuade businesses to take voluntary action. Baruch offered high prices for products, using profits rather than state controls to stimulate wartime industries. The War Industries Board also set standard specifications for all kinds of goods.

- The **Food Administration** oversaw the production and distribution of food. The head of the Food Administration, **Herbert Hoover**, expanded agricultural production by raising food prices. He guaranteed farmers a minimum price for wheat. Hoover wanted to avoid the rationing of food. He preferred voluntary methods, persuading the public to eat less wheat and meat so that these could be sent overseas. Hoover also instructed farmers in more efficient farming methods. Farm incomes rose, food production increased and home consumption fell, creating a surplus of food for American troops and their overseas allies.

Chapter 12 | The United States in World War I

- The **Fuel Administration** regulated coal and gasoline, and called for voluntary conservation.
- Railroads were nationalized and placed under the control of the **Railroad Administration**. Fares were standardized, the facilities of different railroad companies were shared, and railroad workers were paid higher wages.
- Wilson recognized organized labor, supported the eight-hour workday and even addressed the American Federation of Labor (AFL) in November 1917. He created the **War Labor Board**, a new body for resolving disputes between owners and workers. AFL leader Samuel Gompers promised Wilson that workers would not go on strike before the end of the war. During the war, workers' wages went up, and membership in the AFL almost doubled.

Paying for the War

At first, Wilson and his Cabinet thought they would pay for most of the war with the new graduated income tax and special taxes on "war profits" (*extra profits made by companies supplying the government with wartime goods*). This would have placed most of the burden of paying for the war on the wealthy, and was strongly supported by Progressives such as Robert La Follette. The costs of the war turned out to be far greater than anyone had ever expected. William McAdoo, Secretary of the Treasury, gave up all hopes of paying for even half of the war through taxation. In the end, the war cost over $30 billion, an unimaginable sum at that time and more than 30 times the total revenue of the federal government in 1916. Taxes, mainly on the wealthy, paid for about one-third of the war, while war bonds, sold to the public, paid for the rest. The national debt rose from $1 billion in 1916 to $20 billion by the war's end.

The war bonds became widely known as "**Liberty bonds**." They paid low interest rates. The government whipped up enthusiasm for the war effort to encourage people to buy them. Purchasing Liberty bonds became a patriotic act. There were posters, newspaper advertisements, and public drives to sell war bonds. Some Americans, especially German Americans, were pressured into buying war bonds to demonstrate their patriotism.

As much as one-third of the money spent during the war was lent to the Allies. As a result, the United States turned from a *debtor* to a *creditor* nation—instead of owing money to foreign countries for their earlier investments, these countries now owed money to the United States.

A **bond** is a note sold by the government. The government promises to pay interest to the holder of the bond at a fixed rate for a period of time, and then promises to buy the bond back at the end of this period.
A **war bond** is sold by the government in time of war to meet wartime expenses.

---

346 Chapter 12 | The United States in World War I

Civil Rights on the Home Front

In wartime, there are often demands to reduce the scope of individual rights in the interests of national security. In the case of World War I, Wilson and his government became suspicious of critics; other Americans grew distrustful of the nation's large German-American population. As a result, Congress passed emergency measures restricting free speech.

In 1917, Wilson pushed the **Espionage Act** through Congress. This law created procedures for detecting and imprisoning spies. It allowed the federal government to censor the mails and to arrest anyone interfering with the enforcement of the draft.

This was followed the next year by the **Sedition Act of 1918**. This law made it a crime to use "disloyal" or "abusive language" about the government, the flag, or the Constitution.

The government prosecuted more than 2,000 people under these acts. Postmaster General Albert Burleson had his employees read through the mail. Burleson refused to allow socialists and other groups critical of Wilson's policies to mail their newsletters and magazines at the lower rates generally given to periodical publications. He also required advance translation of all foreign periodicals into English for government review. The expense and delay involved in translating and obtaining government approval meant that many foreign language newspapers had to close down.

Socialists viewed the war as a capitalist quarrel using workingmen as cannon fodder. The Socialist Party became the rallying point for those who opposed the war. In June 1918, **Eugene Debs**—the former Socialist candidate for the Presidency—gave an anti-war speech in Ohio and was arrested. Debs claimed that he had a right to exercise his free speech, which was protected by the First Amendment, but he was imprisoned all the same. Other leading socialists against the war were also sent to prison.

Charles Schenck was arrested for violating the Espionage Act of 1917 when he mailed leaflets advising young men to resist the draft. Schenck claimed his arrest violated his free speech rights. In *Schenck v. U.S.* (1919), the Supreme Court upheld limits on free speech whenever "a clear and present danger" is evident.

In the cases of *Debs v. U.S.* (1919) and *Abrams v. U.S.*, the Supreme Court again upheld these restrictions on free speech. Not only the federal government, but also the state governments took steps against those people they suspected of disloyalty.

The Historian's Apprentice

One of the most famous Supreme Court Justices, Justice **Oliver Wendell Holmes**, wrote the unanimous opinion of the Court in *Schenck v. U.S.*:

> "The most stringent [strict] protection of free speech would not protect a man in falsely shouting fire in a theatre and causing a panic. . . . The question in every case is whether the words used are used in such circumstances and are of such a nature as to create a clear and present danger that they will bring about the substantive evils that Congress has a right to prevent."

Continued ▶

1. Was the imprisonment of Eugene Debs justified?
2. Do you think Schenck's actions created a "clear and present danger"?
3. In times of war, which actions should be permitted as forms of free speech and which ones should be prohibited?

The Experiences of Women and Minorities—at Home and Overseas

Women

In January 1917, Jeanette Rankin became the first woman in Congress. When Congress declared war a few months later, many women's rights organizations were actively campaigning for a constitutional amendment guaranteeing women the right to vote. Suffragists were angry at Wilson's failure to support women's rights more actively. Most women's organizations were strongly opposed to U.S. entry into the war. However, once the United States entered the conflict, they wanted to display their patriotism. The National American Woman Suffrage Association (NAWSA) gave strong support to the war effort. A special Woman's Committee was created to coordinate women's efforts. Ida Tarbell, the muckraker, acted as vice-chairman of this group. The National Woman's Party, on the other hand, continued to oppose American involvement in the war.

Women performed every sort of task on the home front. They sold war bonds, knitted socks, cooked meatless dinners, and wore shorter skirts to save cloth for uniforms. Others joined the Red Cross or volunteered as nurses overseas. Because of the labor shortage at home, many women took men's jobs in factories and other places.

African Americans

African Americans had supported Wilson in 1912 but had been very disappointed by his record on race relations. Wilson, who was from Virginia, actually brought racial segregation back to the Post Office and U.S. Treasury Department. He also refused to integrate the armed services. In July 1917, 15,000 African Americans silently marched down Fifth Avenue, New York, to protest "Jim Crow" laws and lynchings in the South.

Thousands of African Americans nonetheless volunteered for service when the war broke out. More than 100,000 of them eventually went to France. African-American leaders encouraged their followers to enlist so that, by fighting for freedom and democracy abroad, they could help to achieve it more rapidly at home. A special segregated facility was set up in Iowa to train African-American officers. Some African-American combat units were assigned directly to French forces. They fought in France and marched into Germany with the French army. The first two Americans to receive the French *Croix de Guerre* for heroism in combat were African Americans: Henry Johnson and Needham Roberts.

African-American soldiers sometimes resisted discrimination. In Houston, Texas, townspeople shouted insults at an African-American regiment, and the soldiers fired back. Seventeen were killed. Thirteen of the soldiers were later executed. After living in France, many African-American soldiers were eager for change in the United States.

The Labor Shortage and the Great Migration

When men left for training and the battlefields of Europe, this created a labor shortage at home. Women, African Americans, and members of other minorities filled much of this gap by taking jobs in factories, farms, and railroads. Labor agents went to the South to recruit workers for Northern factories. This started the flow of African Americans known as the **Great Migration**. Thousands of African Americans left the South, with its "Jim Crow" laws and rural poverty, for cities in the Northeast and Midwest. Southerners sometimes resorted to violence to prevent the loss of more African Americans, whom they needed for their labor.

The Historian's Apprentice

Choose one of the groups above and write a brief report describing their experiences during World War I.

"Over There"—Allied Victory in Europe

The United States entered the war in April 1917. That same spring, German submarines aggressively attacked Allied ships until the use of the convoy system reduced shipping losses in the Atlantic. American troops did not begin arriving in France for several months and at first only in a trickle. In the meantime, Russia dropped out of the war, allowing Germany to concentrate all its efforts on the Western Front. The Germans launched a great offensive in March 1918. But German leaders miscalculated when they thought they could achieve a breakthrough. The German offensive was unable to reach Paris and soon collapsed.

By June 1918, American troops began arriving in large numbers—about 10,000 a day. Almost two million American troops eventually reached Europe. The new American Expeditionary Force gave the Allies overwhelming superiority. The German army finally surrendered in November 1918. An **armistice**, or ceasefire, was signed and all fighting stopped. Although Americans had only been in the war just over a year, they suffered heavy casualties with 117,000 killed.

American soldiers celebrate the announcement of peace

The Peace Settlement: Wilson and the Treaty of Versailles

The Fourteen Points

Even before the war had ended, President Wilson announced America's aims in a famous speech to Congress in January 1918. Wilson enumerated "**Fourteen Points**." These reflected his view that the war should become a crusade for democracy. The Fourteen Points demanded national self-determination for the peoples of Europe. The map of Europe would be redrawn so that each nationality had its own nation-state

Chapter 12 | The United States in World War I

and government. Austria-Hungary would be broken up into smaller states. Poland, divided up by neighboring European monarchs more than a century before, would be reunited.

Wilson called for a "New Diplomacy" to replace the older policies of militarism and balance-of-power politics that had led to the war. He also demanded freedom of the seas, equal trade terms, reduced armaments, an end to secret diplomacy, and the creation of a new international peace-keeping organization, the "League of Nations." Wilson thus hoped to create a world of peaceful democratic states in which future world wars would no longer be possible. Inspired by Wilson's promises and hoping to get better peace terms, Germans overthrew the Kaiser (*the German Emperor*) in November 1918.

Woodrow Wilson

The Historian's Apprentice

The Fourteen Points

1. Open covenants of peace, openly arrived at . . . [D]iplomacy shall proceed always frankly and in the public view.
2. Absolute freedom of navigation upon the seas . . .
3. The removal, so far as possible, of all economic barriers and the establishment of equality of trade conditions among all the nations . . .
4. Adequate guarantees given . . . that national armaments will be reduced . . .
5. A free, open-minded, and absolutely impartial adjustment of all colonial claims . . .
6. The evacuation* of all Russian territory and such a settlement of all questions affecting Russia as will secure the best and freest cooperation of the other nations of the world . . .
7. Belgium, the whole world will agree, must be evacuated and restored . . .
8. All French territory should be freed and the invaded portions restored, and the wrong done to France by Prussia in 1871 in the matter of Alsace-Lorraine, which has unsettled the peace of the world for nearly fifty years, should be righted . . .
9. A readjustment of the frontiers of Italy should be effected along clearly recognizable lines of nationality.
10. The peoples of Austria-Hungary, whose place among the nations we wish to see safeguarded and assured, should be accorded the freest opportunity to autonomous** development.
11. Romania, Serbia, and Montenegro should be evacuated; occupied territories restored . . .
12. The Turkish portion of the present Ottoman Empire should be assured a secure sovereignty, but the other nationalities which are now under Turkish rule should be assured an . . . opportunity of autonomous development
13. An independent Polish state should be erected which should include the territories inhabited by indisputably Polish populations . . .

*evacuate = to leave
**autonomous = independent, self-governing

14. A general association of nations must be formed under specific covenants for the purpose of affording mutual guarantees of political independence and territorial integrity to great and small states alike ...

1. Explain two of Wilson's Fourteen Points in your own words.
2. In what ways did the Fourteen Points represent American values? Use specific evidence from the Fourteen Points to support your answer.

The Paris Peace Conference and the Treaty of Versailles

Even though the armistice was concluded, the Allies and defeated powers still had to arrange a final peace. Wilson personally traveled to Paris to negotiate the peace treaties. Most historians agree that Wilson made a crucial mistake in not inviting influential Senators to accompany him, since the U.S. Senate would eventually have to ratify each treaty. In Paris, Wilson came into conflict with other Allied leaders who wanted to impose a harsher treaty on Germany. Wilson eventually made many concessions to their views in order to win their support for the League of Nations, which was included in the peace treaty at Wilson's insistence.

The final terms of the **Treaty of Versailles** and its related treaties were extremely harsh on Germany and the other defeated Central Powers:

1. Germany lost territory to France and Poland, and lost all of its colonies.

2. Germany lost its navy, while its once powerful army was reduced to the size of a police force.

3. Germans were forced to sign the "**War Guilt**" clause, accepting blame for starting the war. For this reason, they were required to pay huge **reparations** (*payment for damages*) to the Allies.

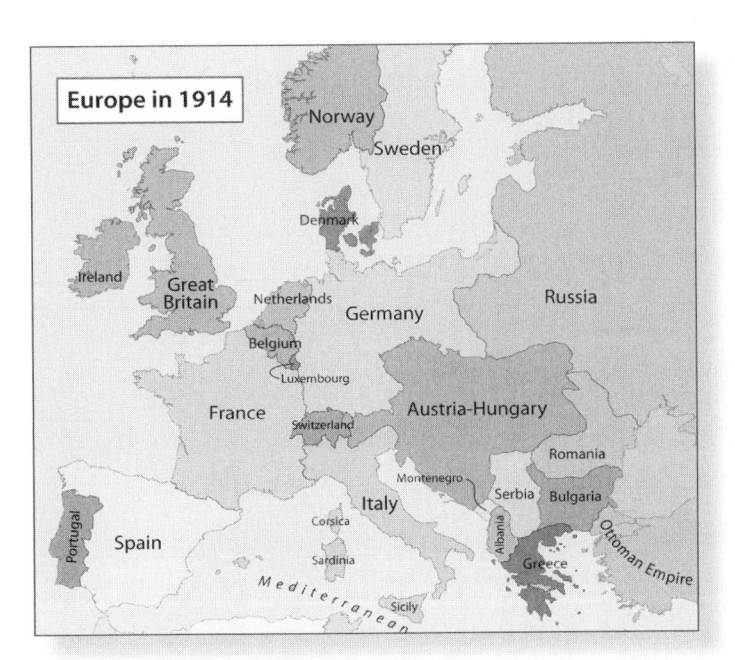

Chapter 12 | The United States in World War I

4. Austria-Hungary was divided into several smaller national states.

5. Like the Tsar and the Kaiser, the Sultan was overthrown and Turkey became a republic. The Ottoman Empire lost most of its territories in the Middle East. Although the Allies had made various promises to local peoples, most of these territories were given to Britain or France to govern as "mandates."

The League of Nations

Just as Wilson had demanded, the Versailles Treaty created the **League of Nations**—an organization of nations that would defend each other against aggressors. It was believed that this new institution could discourage aggression and prevent future wars. Since the League had no army of its own, however, it depended entirely on the good will of its members to stop acts of aggression. **Article X** of the **Covenant of the League of Nations** (*the agreement inserted into the Treaty of Versailles creating the League*) stated that League members would help other League members facing aggression.

The U.S. Senate Rejects the Versailles Treaty

When Wilson returned back home, he needed the support of two-thirds of the U.S. Senate to ratify the treaty. But many Americans were disillusioned with what had been achieved after the heavy costs of the war. Their disillusionment was reflected in the 1918 Congressional elections, in which Republicans gained control of the Senate. Republicans especially objected to Article X.

When the Versailles Treaty was debated in the Senate in 1919, Wilson refused to accept any compromises offered by Senator Henry Cabot Lodge and other leading Republicans. He instructed Democrats to oppose ratification of the Treaty with Lodge's modifications. Wilson decided to appeal directly to voters by giving speeches throughout the country. Three weeks after he began this exhausting campaign to win public support, Wilson suffered a major stroke, which left him partially paralyzed.

The Senate then rejected Wilson's treaty. Republicans won further support in the 1920 Presidential election. In fact, the United States never joined the League of Nations. Instead, it signed a separate peace with Germany in 1921. Americans once again decided to avoid entanglements with Europe. They became more concerned with their well-being at home and less committed to foreign affairs. This approach is sometimes referred to as **isolationism**.

The Historian's Apprentice

Pretend your classroom is the U.S. Senate in 1919. Hold your own debate on the Treaty of Versailles, including the League of Nations. One class member should act as Woodrow Wilson addressing the Senate. Another should act as Henry Cabot Lodge, opposing the treaty and proposing amendments. Other class members should speak as Senators. Then hold a vote on whether to ratify the treaty.

Name _____

1. Review the names and terms below. Then assign each name or term to its proper category.

Alliance System	Convoys	Sedition Act
Militarism	Lusitania	Committee of Public Information
Nationalism	Zimmerman Telegraph	Eugene Debs
Archduke Francis Ferdinand	Unrestricted Submarine Warfare	*Schenck v. United States*
Serbia	Mobilization	Oliver Wendell Holmes
Austria-Hungary	Conscription	Great Migration
Allied Powers	American Expeditionary Force (AEF)	German Americans
Central Powers	Selective Service Act	Conscientious Objectors
Trench Warfare	War Industries Board	Fourteen Points
Airplanes	Herbert Hoover	Treaty of Versailles
Chemical Warfare	War Bonds	League of Nations
Naval Blockade	Espionage Act	

Causes of World War I	New methods of warfare	Reasons for U.S. involvement

U.S. Minorities during the War	Life on the Home Front during the war	Individual rights and World War I	The Peace Settlement

Chapter 12 | The United States in World War I

Name _____

Write a paragraph explaining how the United States became involved in World War I.

_____
_____
_____
_____
_____
_____
_____
_____

The Home Front

Buying U.S. bonds was one way that Americans on the home front participated in World War I. List other ways that ordinary citizens helped in the war effort.

1. _____
2. _____
3. _____
4. _____
5. _____

Complete the chart below describing the experiences of Americans during World War I.

Group/Action	Description
Soldiers of the American Expeditionary Force (AEF)	
Women	
African Americans (including the Great Migration)	
German Americans	
Restrictions on Individual Rights (including the Espionage Act)	

For the Georgia Milestones EOC Assessment, you should know that:

- ☐ World War I broke out in Europe in 1914 between the Allies (Britain, France and Russia) and the Central powers (Germany, Austria-Hungary, and the Ottoman Empire). The countries at war quickly reached a deadlock, with defensive trenches running hundreds of miles across Europe.

- ☐ Britain set up a naval blockade of Germany. Germany, in turn, declared a blockade of Britain. It prohibited the shipping of war supplies to Britain, which it enforced with its submarines. Americans continued, as neutrals, to trade with Britain.

- ☐ In the first three years of the war, the United States followed its traditional policy of neutrality. Publication of the secret Zimmerman Telegram, in which Germany offered Mexico the return of some of its former territory taken by the United States, and unrestricted submarine warfare by Germany led to American entry into the war in April 1917.

- ☐ Entry into the war had important domestic effects. Men volunteered or were conscripted into military service. New government agencies coordinated wartime production, the railways, the use of coal and gasoline, and labor disputes.

- ☐ As men went off to war, women and minorities filled their places in factories, farms, and railroads. African Americans left the South for jobs in Northern factories, beginning the "Great Migration."

- ☐ During the war, individual rights were restricted in the interests of national security. The Espionage Act of 1917 permitted government censorship of the mails and imprisonment of those who interfered with the draft. The Sedition Act of 1918 prohibited the use of "disloyal" language. The socialist and labor leader Eugene Debs was imprisoned for speaking out against the war.

- ☐ The arrival of American troops in Europe broke the deadlock between the Allies and the Central powers. In November 1918, Germany surrendered.

- ☐ President Woodrow Wilson announced American war aims in January 1918 in the "Fourteen Points." These included national self-determination for the peoples of Europe; freedom of the seas; equal trade terms; a reduction in armaments; an end to secret diplomacy; and the creation of the League of Nations.

- ☐ President Wilson traveled to Paris to negotiate the treaties ending the war. The Treaty of Versailles was especially harsh on Germany. The Treaty included a section creating the League of Nations, a new international organization to preserve peace. When Wilson returned to the United States, the U.S. Senate refused to ratify the treaty or to join the League of Nations.

Chapter 12 | The United States in World War I

The U.S. in World War I

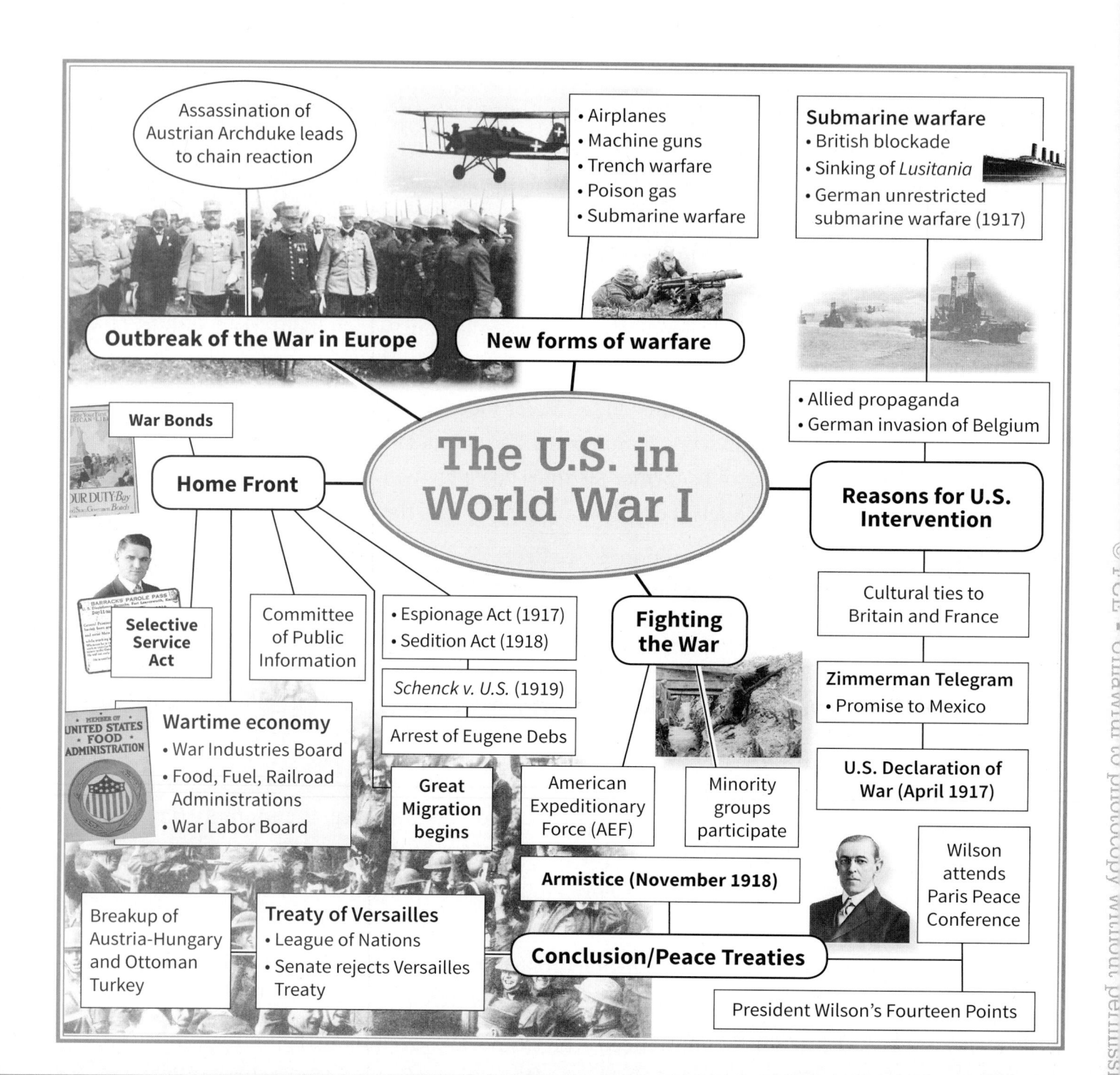

Outbreak of the War in Europe
- Assassination of Austrian Archduke leads to chain reaction

New forms of warfare
- Airplanes
- Machine guns
- Trench warfare
- Poison gas
- Submarine warfare

Submarine warfare
- British blockade
- Sinking of *Lusitania*
- German unrestricted submarine warfare (1917)

Reasons for U.S. Intervention
- Allied propaganda
- German invasion of Belgium
- Cultural ties to Britain and France
- Zimmerman Telegram
  - Promise to Mexico
- U.S. Declaration of War (April 1917)

Home Front
- War Bonds
- Selective Service Act
- Committee of Public Information
- Espionage Act (1917)
- Sedition Act (1918)
- *Schenck v. U.S.* (1919)
- Arrest of Eugene Debs

Wartime economy
- War Industries Board
- Food, Fuel, Railroad Administrations
- War Labor Board

Fighting the War
- Great Migration begins
- American Expeditionary Force (AEF)
- Minority groups participate
- Armistice (November 1918)

Conclusion/Peace Treaties
- Wilson attends Paris Peace Conference
- President Wilson's Fourteen Points
- Breakup of Austria-Hungary and Ottoman Turkey
- Treaty of Versailles
  - League of Nations
  - Senate rejects Versailles Treaty

What Do You Know?

SSUSH15b

1. Which sentence BEST describes the experiences of African-American soldiers during World War I?

    A. They were unable to engage in combat because of racial prejudice.

    B. They successfully persuaded the government to desegregate the army.

    C. They were segregated but many engaged in combat under French command.

    D. They were treated as equals with ample opportunity for advancement through the ranks.

SSUSH15a

2. The cartoon on the left was published on February 1, 1917. The letter from Germany to Uncle Sam reads:

   > *Ruthless warfare at sea. Ships enter blockade zone at their risk. Pledges as to warnings cancelled.*

   What was the impact of the message shown in this cartoon?

   A. The United States declared war after the *U.S.S. Maine* was blown up in Havana Harbor.
   B. The United States declared war after Germany sank American ships in the blockaded zone.
   C. Mexicans allied with Germany after learning of this new policy.
   D. Germany announced it would not attack passenger ships or merchant ships without warning.

SSUSH15a

3. Use the excerpt below to answer the question.

   > *We ... will make a proposal of alliance to Mexico on the following terms: we make war together, we make peace together, we give generous financial support and an understanding that Mexico is to regain the lost territory in Texas, New Mexico, and Arizona. ...*
   >
   > —Foreign Minister of Germany to the German Ambassador to Mexico, Jan 1917 (Secret message discovered by the British government and published in March)

   What was the impact of the publication of this letter?

   A. Mexico allied with Germany in World War I.
   B. American public opinion was outraged against Germany.
   C. The United States Senate immediately declared war on Mexico.
   D. The United States paid Mexico compensation for its lost territories.

SSUSH15c

4. Why did the U.S. Senate refuse to ratify the Treaty of Versailles in 1919?

   A. Senators opposed the severe sanctions that the treaty placed on Germany.
   B. Senators feared the League of Nations would involve the United States in foreign wars.
   C. Senators felt the League of Nations would interfere with American plans in the Philippines.
   D. Senators predicted that membership in the new League of Nations would be too expensive.

Chapter 12 | The United States in World War I

SSUSH15c

5. Which was NOT one of President Woodrow Wilson's Fourteen Points?
   A. creation of an independent Poland
   B. preserving the integrity of the Ottoman Empire
   C. creation of a peace-keeping association of nations
   D. autonomous development for the peoples of Austria-Hungary and the Ottoman Empire

SSUSH15c

6. Read the excerpt below to answer the question.

   > **ARTICLE X**
   > The Members of the League undertake to respect and preserve the territorial integrity and existing political independence of all Members of the League against external aggression. In case of any such aggression or threat of such aggression, the [Executive] Council shall advise on the means by which this obligation shall be fulfilled.
   > —Covenant of the League of Nations, Treaty of Versailles

   Why did many U.S. Senators object to this article?
   A. They had plans to seize new overseas territories for the United States.
   B. They were afraid that the League would be controlled by hostile powers.
   C. They feared Americans would be required to act against aggression in Europe.
   D. They thought it demanded that Americans grant Philippine independence.

SSUSH15b

7. Which BEST describes how American women reacted to U.S. entry into World War I?
   A. Most supported the war effort and many filled men's jobs.
   B. Because of a shortage of enlisted men, many women served in combat for the first time.
   C. Women's continuing protests for women's suffrage dangerously impeded the war effort.
   D. Large numbers of women were forced to move from their homes to meet wartime needs.

SSUSH15b

8. How was the Socialist Eugene Debs treated after giving an anti-war speech in Ohio?
   A. He was elected to the U.S. Senate.
   B. He arrested for violating the Espionage Act.
   C. He was invited to speak with President Wilson at the White House.
   D. He was recruited to work for the Committee of Public Information.

Chapter 12 | The United States in World War I

CHAPTER 13 The Roaring Twenties

SSUSH16 How did political, economic, and cultural developments after WW I lead to a shared national identity?

  a. How did fears of rising communism and socialism in the United States lead to the Red Scare and the restriction of immigration?

  b. What were the effects of the Eighteenth and Nineteenth Amendments?

  c. How did mass production and advertising lead to increasing consumerism, including Henry Ford and the automobile?

  d. How did the radio and movies act as unifying forces in national culture?

  e. How did modern forms of cultural expression emerge in this period, such as jazz and the Harlem Renaissance?

Names and Terms You Should Know

Communism	Organized crime	Advertising agency
Socialism	Nineteenth Amendment	Installment purchasing
"Red Scare"	Women's suffrage	Radio
"Palmer Raids"	Flappers	Motion picture
Immigration	Mass production	Great Migration
Quota	Henry Ford	Harlem Renaissance
Emergency Quota Act (1921)	Assembly line	Langston Hughes
National Origins Act (1924)	Suburbs	Marcus Garvey
Eighteenth Amendment	Consumerism	Jazz
Prohibition	Advertising	Louis Armstrong

Georgia "Peaches" of Wisdom

1. The triumph of communism in Russia, the formation of the Communist Labor Party of America, widespread strikes and a series of bombings in the United States led many Americans to fear communists and socialists during the "Red Scare" of 1919. Thousands of foreign-born radicals were arrested and several hundred were deported in the "Palmer Raids." Two Italian anarchists, Sacco and Vanzetti, were convicted for murder in 1920 on flimsy evidence.

2. Prejudice against immigrants from Southern and Eastern Europe, a desire to preserve America's "Anglo-Saxon" and Protestant heritage, and the "Red Scare" led to the first limits on immigration from Europe. The Emergency Quota Act of 1921 and the National Origins Act of 1924 imposed harsh restrictions on immigration in order to preserve America's existing ethnic composition.

3. The Eighteenth Amendment (1919) outlawed the manufacture and sale of alcoholic beverages. Its passage had long been the goal of the Temperance Movement. Anti-German sentiment against German-sounding brewers of beer helped to secure its ratification. The amendment laid the basis for Prohibition. Foreign-born immigrants and city-dwellers opposed Prohibition, encouraging widespread defiance of the law and the growth of organized crime. Criminals like Al Capone supplied illegal alcohol to consumers. Prohibition led to the unintended consequence of the growth of organized crime. It was considered a failure and repealed in 1933.

4. The Nineteenth Amendment (1920) gave women the right to vote in all states. It was the goal of the women's suffrage movement. Ratification of the amendment symbolized women's equality and encouraged women to become more assertive and independent in the Twenties. More women worked outside the home and a few pursued higher education and professional careers. "Flappers" wore loose clothing and went out without chaperones. Politicians had to pay more attention to women's issues since they could now vote.

5. The spread of the automobile and new electric appliances contributed to the economic prosperity of the decade. Automobile-maker Henry Ford introduced the use of the conveyor belt to his assembly-line production. This method was so efficient that he could raise his workers' wages while lowering the prices of his cars. Ford's Model T changed automobiles from a luxury product to one that many middle-class Americans could afford. Manufacturers followed his example in other industries, bringing down the prices of goods and promoting economic prosperity. The spread in the use of the automobile required steel, oil, roads, and gas stations, propelling the entire economy forward.

6. Mass production required new marketing techniques to reach consumers across the nation. Manufacturers relied on advertising on billboards, in newspapers and magazines, on the radio and in movie theaters to promote their products, while new installment payment plans made buying goods easier. The lower prices of mass-produced goods, advertising, and installment plans promoted mass consumerism.

7. Radio broadcasts and motion pictures with sound were both introduced in the 1920s. They helped to create a shared national identity in which Americans listened to the same radio programs and watched the same movies and newsreels.

8. During the "Great Migration," many African Americans moved from the South to the cities of the Northeast and Midwest. The Harlem Renaissance saw a flourishing of African-American culture, with essays, novels, short stories, and poetry. Its writers and painters produced great works of literature and art based on the African-American experience. Marcus Garvey encouraged African Americans to rely more on themselves and to separate from whites. Jazz music, a fusion of African-American and European musical traditions, became popular among both whites and blacks. Despite these successes, African Americans continued to face Jim Crow laws, lynchings, and economic inequality in the South, and even in Northern cities, they faced racism and violence.

After the reforms of the Progressives and the sacrifices of World War I, many Americans embraced the call of Warren G. Harding, who was elected President in 1920, for a "return to normalcy." America needed a rest. Instead of trying to save the world, Americans would focus on earning money and spending it. But this was a far cry from a simple return to the pre-war days: the Twenties were a period of profound change. Political, economic, and cultural developments in this period helped build a shared national identity. The rise of the "media" (radio and movies), consumerism of mass-produced goods, the greater freedom enjoyed by women, a flourishing of African-American culture, and a fear of foreign influences all contributed to this process.

The "Red Scare"

The Twenties began with a short phase of uncertainty and fear. A group of **communists** seized power in Russia in November 1917, while World War I was still raging. These communists not only pulled Russia out of the war but also opposed private property, religious beliefs, and free enterprise. They were therefore viewed as anti-American.

President Wilson authorized U.S. troops in Russia to intervene on the side of the "Whites," the opponents of the communists (or "Reds") in the Russian Civil War. American troops stayed in Siberia until 1920, but they failed to prevent a communist victory. American leaders refused to extend diplomatic recognition to the new Russian government. Meanwhile, communists threatened to seize power in both Germany and Hungary.

In the United States, workers expressed concern over the future as the war came to an end. A wave of strikes took place across the United States in 1919. In Boston, police went on strike; in Seattle, workers staged a general strike. Workers at U.S. Steel, many of whom were immigrants from Eastern Europe, demanded the right to organize into unions and also went on strike. So did coal workers in Indiana. Meanwhile radical socialists formed the Communist Labor Party of America in August 1919.

The success of communists in Russia, the communist attempts in Central Europe, the wave of strikes across the United States, and the formation of the Communist Labor Party made many Americans fearful of a communist revolution happening here. Because

---

Socialism, communism, and anarchism were ideologies that developed in response to the Industrial Revolution. **Socialists** believe that governments should take over certain basic industries, such as transportation, and should provide basic benefits to all citizens, including education, health care, and retirement pensions. **Communists** believe that all history is the story of class struggle—one social group oppressing another. They think workers can only improve their conditions by seizing power through a violent revolution. Once they obtain power, communists plan to establish social equality by abolishing private property altogether. All citizens in a communist society are supposed to share their talents and help each other out. **Anarchists** believe that all organized governments are harmful. They favor a society without government, in which people can act freely.

communists had adopted the color red as their symbol, this popular fear became known as the "**Red Scare**."

The "Palmer Raids"

Mitchell Palmer, a Pennsylvania Quaker and a Progressive Democrat, was appointed as Attorney General by President Wilson in March 1919. Only a month after his appointment, letter bombs sent by Italian-born anarchists (*people who opposed organized governments*) were found in the U.S. mail. One of these bombs was addressed to Palmer. In June, a bomb actually exploded on Palmer's porch while other bombs exploded in several cities.

Palmer created a new group inside the Justice Department, led by an energetic young lawyer, J. Edgar Hoover. In November, Hoover supervised the arrest of Russian workers suspected of radical activity in twelve cities: more than 200 of them were deported (*sent out of the country*). In January 1920, Hoover directed simultaneous raids without search warrants in 30 cities, known as the "**Palmer Raids**." About 6,000 suspects were arrested. Most of them were foreign-born residents from Russia and Germany, who could be deported after a brief hearing without a jury. Palmer would have deported most of the arrested suspects, but the Department of Labor believed many of the arrests were illegal and refused to deport more than 556. The rest of the suspects were released. Emma Goldman, a prominent radical activist, was one of those deported. Palmer predicted there would be a communist uprising in the United States, but this never happened.

The Historian's Apprentice

"Like a prairie fire, the blaze of revolution was sweeping over every American institution of law and order a year ago. It was eating its way into the homes of the American workmen . . . burning up the foundations of society. Robbery, not war, is the ideal of communism. This has been demonstrated in Russia, Germany, and in America. . . . Obviously, it is the creed of any criminal mind . . . By stealing, murder and lies, [communism] has looted Russia, not only of its material strength but of its moral force . . . My information showed that communism in this country was an organization of thousands of aliens who were direct allies of Trotsky [*a Russian communist leader*] . . . The Government is now sweeping the nation clean of such alien filth . . ."

—A. Mitchell Palmer, "The Case against the Reds" (1920)

"Every human being is entitled to hold any opinion that appeals to her or him without making herself or himself liable to persecution. . . . It requires no great prophetic gift to foresee that this new governmental policy of deportation is but the first step towards the introduction into this country of the old Russian system of exile for the high treason of entertaining new ideas of social life and industrial reconstruction. Today so-called aliens are deported, tomorrow native Americans will be banished."

—Emma Goldman, speaking at her deportation hearing (October 1919)

Imagine that you are a newspaper editor in 1920. First read the excerpts from Palmer's pamphlet and Goldman's speech above. Then write your own editorial on whether the Palmer Raids were justified.

Nicola Sacco   Bartolomeo Vanzetti

Two Italian immigrants, Nicola Sacco and Bartolomeo Vanzetti (a shoemaker and a fish seller) were arrested in 1920 for murders committed during a payroll truck robbery. Not only were they immigrants, Sacco and Vanzetti were also anarchists—radicals who opposed organized government. The trial judge made several statements against the accused outside the court. Although the evidence was unclear, they were convicted and sentenced to death. Despite new evidence and multiple appeals, requests for a retrial were denied. After a legal battle that lasted seven years, Sacco and Vanzetti were finally executed in 1927. There were loud outcries of injustice both at home and abroad. Almost a century later, it remains a subject of controversy whether or not Sacco and Vanzetti were guilty of the robbery, but there is general agreement that their trial was unfair.

Restrictions on Immigration

The Twenties also saw new limits on immigration. **Immigration** from Europe had been unrestricted before World War I. During the war, submarine warfare made it dangerous to cross the Atlantic. The great flood of immigration that had begun in the late nineteenth century was temporarily halted. In 1917, Congress passed a literacy test over President Wilson's veto. The new law required immigrants to read and write in their own language. This was intended to keep out poorer, uneducated, and unskilled immigrants from Southern and Eastern Europe. Even so, about 800,000 newcomers still arrived between June 1920 and June 1921.

Nativist sentiment, agitation by labor unions fearing competition from cheap labor, and popular prejudice against Southern and Eastern Europeans had been growing for decades. Many Americans believed people coming from these other places were inferior. They further wanted to keep traditional American culture the way it had been before World War I—dominated by white, "Anglo-Saxon," Protestants ("WASPs").

The Ku Klux Klan ("KKK") was also revived in the 1920s. The Klan opposed immigration from Southern and Eastern Europe much as it supported racial segregation. The "Red Scare" also contributed to anti-immigrant feeling. These forces now led to the passage of laws restricting immigration from Europe for the first time in our history.

Emergency Quota Act (1921)

During the 1920 election campaign, Harding had called for limits on immigration. Soon after he took office, Congress passed the **Emergency Quota Act of 1921**. A "**quota**" refers to a fixed number of people permitted to do something. The Emergency Quota Act limited the total number of immigrants who could lawfully enter the United States in any one year to 350,000. This was fewer than half the number admitted in 1920.

Under the new law, each foreign country was assigned its own quota, or maximum number of immigrants, based on the number of immigrants from that country living in the United States in 1910. The new quota system was aimed at drastically reducing the number of immigrants from Southern and Eastern Europe. Immigration from most of Asia had already been banned in 1917, except for immigrants from the Philippines. Immigration from Latin America, however, remained unrestricted.

The National Origins Act (1924)

When Harding died in 1923, Calvin Coolidge became President. Coolidge believed that "Nordics" (people from Northern and Western Europe) were superior to other ethnic groups. During his Presidency, restrictions on immigration were further tightened. Experts testified before Congress that people from Eastern and Southern Europe were genetically inferior. The **Immigration Act of 1924** lowered the total number of legal immigrants per year to 150,000 (this was 2% of the number of foreign-born residents living in the United States in 1890).

The quota for each country was also changed. The date on which it was based was pushed back from 1910 to 1890, a time before the large influx of "New Immigrants." The way in which the quota for each country was calculated was changed too. In 1921, this had been based on the percentage of immigrants of each nationality compared to all immigrants living in the United States. In 1924, it was based on the percentage of people of each national origin compared to all Americans. For this reason, the 1924 law is sometimes known as the "**National Origins Act**." Asian immigrants were banned altogether.

The total effect of these changes was to reduce drastically the number of immigrants coming to the United States from Southern and Eastern Europe. For example, before World War I about 200,000 Italians migrated to the United States each year. The Emergency Quota Act of 1921 reduced this number to 40,000. Under the 1924 Immigration Act, a mere 4,000 Italians could be legally admitted into the United States.

The Historian's Apprentice

1. Your class should debate the following resolution:

   Resolved: The United States should have continued to permit unrestricted immigration from Europe.

2. How important was the "Red Scare" to the passage of new laws restricting immigration?

The Eighteenth and Nineteenth Amendments

During the Twenties, two important amendments were shaping American life—the Eighteenth and Nineteenth Amendments. Each amendment introduced a change that had long been sought by Progressive reformers. The two amendments differed, however, in their degree of success. One led to permanent changes in American society, while the other became a social experiment that failed.

Chapter 13 | The Roaring Twenties

The Historian's Apprentice

Eighteenth Amendment (1919)

Section 1. After one year from the ratification of this article the manufacture, sale, or transportation of intoxicating liquors within, the importation thereof into, or the exportation thereof from the United States and all the territory subject to the jurisdiction thereof for beverage purposes is hereby prohibited.

Section 2. The Congress and the several States shall have concurrent power to enforce this article by appropriate legislation . . .

Nineteenth Amendment (1920)

Section 1. The right of citizens of the United States to vote shall not be denied or abridged by the United States or by any State on account of sex.

Section 2. Congress shall have power to enforce this article by appropriate legislation.

* * *

1. Based on the excerpts above, what did each of these amendments do?
2. Why did these changes have to be made by Constitutional amendment rather than by a simple federal law?
3. Why did both amendments give Congress the power to enforce them by "appropriate legislation"?

Prohibition

As you know, the **Temperance Movement** began in the nineteenth century. Supporters believed that alcoholic beverages caused poverty, crime, sinful behavior and the breakdown of families. They called for laws outlawing alcoholic drinks. Protestant church groups and women reformers were especially active in this movement. Temperance also appealed to the residents of small towns. Nineteen states had banned alcohol by the beginning of World War I.

The **Eighteenth Amendment** extended this "noble experiment"—a clear attempt to legislate public morality—to the national level. The amendment was ratified by the states by the beginning of 1919. Anti-German feeling helped win support for ratification, since many breweries (like Pabst and Busch) had German-sounding names. The amendment prohibited "the manufacture, sale, or transportation of intoxicating liquors," including their importation. The amendment gave both Congress and state governments powers of enforcement. In October 1919, Congress passed the Volstead Act, a federal law that defined "intoxicating liquors" to include both wine and beer. The law provided penalties for the manufacture, sale, and transportation of alcoholic beverages, but not for their consumption. It also permitted limited production of alcohol for medical or religious purposes.

Prohibition—the *prohibiting* of alcoholic drinks—proved difficult to enforce. The federal

Authorities disposing of illegal alcohol

government did not set aside enough money for enforcement. There were very few enforcement agents. Most European immigrants and many city-dwellers did not believe it was wrong to drink alcohol and refused to obey the law. "Bootleggers" brought beer and whiskey across from Canada. Others made their own brew in secret stills. Illegal nightclubs— known as "speakeasies"—served liquor in cities. Even President Harding secretly served alcohol to his guests in the White House.

As a result of Prohibition, some people began to lose their respect for the law in general. The manufacture, transportation, and sale of alcohol was largely taken over by criminal gangs. Criminal bosses like Al Capone in Chicago made fortunes selling bootlegged liquor. Organized crime used its increased wealth and power to move into gambling, prostitution, and the collection of money from local businesses. Although Prohibition reduced social drinking, its unintended consequence—the rise of **organized crime**—turned out to be far worse than any of its benefits. The "noble experiment" failed, and Prohibition was repealed by the Twenty-First Amendment in 1933.

Chicago Police Department mug shot of Al Capone

Women's Suffrage

The decade also opened with ratification of the **Nineteenth Amendment** (1920), which guaranteed women the right to vote in federal elections. The amendment was recognition that women were entitled to the same rights of citizenship as men, as well as an acknowledgement of the help that women had given to the war effort.

During the Twenties, women's roles continued to change. More women joined the work force, finding employment outside the home as secretaries, sales clerks, telephone operators, nurses, and factory workers. Some entered occupations traditionally reserved for men. A small number—graduates of women's colleges—became professional "career women." Meanwhile new household appliances—such as the refrigerator, electric washing machine, and vacuum cleaner—gave middle-class women more leisure time.

Manners and morals were also changing. In the 1920s, many women became more assertive. Some smoked and drank in public. They stopped wearing restrictive clothing like petticoats, corsets, broad hats, and long dresses. **"Flappers"** were fashionable young women who wore lipstick, short hair, and straight simple dresses or pleated skirts that only reached to their knees. The name "Flapper" referred to their greater freedom—they were birds "flapping" their wings.

With a greater number of women living in cities and a growing number of cars, many young women began going out without chaperones (*an older person accompanying a younger*

Chapter 13 | The Roaring Twenties

unmarried woman). In general, women not only gained the right to vote in the Twenties but also enjoyed greater freedom of self-expression and independence.

Passage of the Nineteenth Amendment also meant that candidates for public office had to seek the support of women voters and pay more attention to issues of concern to women.

The Historian's Apprentice

Why was women's suffrage (Nineteenth Amendment) more successful than Prohibition (Eighteenth Amendment)?

Boom Times: Economic Prosperity in the Twenties

For most Americans, the 1920s were a period of economic prosperity. More jobs were available and wages increased. Profits and production soared. Republican Presidents encouraged business growth with low taxes, fewer regulations and higher tariffs. Mass production and advertising led to increased **consumerism**. Consumerism, in turn, increased the demand for goods, helping businesses, boosting production, and creating additional jobs.

Mass Production

One of the keys to the prosperity of the 1920s was **mass production**—the use of machines to produce a large number of identical copies of a good. The techniques of mass production greatly increased the efficiency of American industry.

In 1914, the car manufacturer **Henry Ford** introduced electric conveyor belts to his **assembly lines**. Each car chassis moved along the belt to different groups of workers who completed one small portion of the car's assembly. Production time was astonishingly cut to one-sixth of what it had previously taken. Ford was able to lower the prices for his cars, increase his workers' wages, and still make more money than ever before.

In the 1920s, the conveyor belt and other new techniques were adopted not only by the automobile industry but also by other manufacturers, making American workers more productive.

The Spread of the Automobile and Other New Industries

The product that most transformed American life in this period was the automobile. Ford's vision of mass-produced automobiles, built on an assembly line, brought the price of his basic "Model-T" car low enough to become affordable to middle-class purchasers instead of remaining a luxury item just for the very rich. In 1920, there were just over 8 million cars on the road; by 1930, there were three times that number, or one car for every six Americans.

A Ford assembly line

Annual Car Registrations in the United States

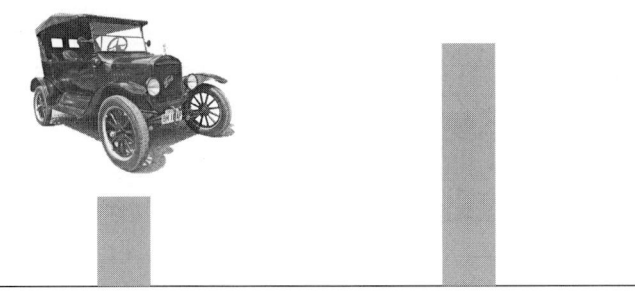

1920: 8.5 million 　　　1929: 23 million

The production of automobiles required vast amounts of steel, glass, and rubber, stimulating those industries. Motorists required paved roads, bridges, garages, gas stations, gasoline, and motor oil. All of this stimulated the economy. By 1929, one out of every nine workers was employed in an auto-related industry. The automobile had other effects as well. School buses allowed the creation of larger schools to serve wider areas. Tractors increased farm production. Trucks could deliver goods to areas not reached by train. Cars gave people greater mobility, allowing farmers to drive into town for shopping or families to drive away on vacation. People could travel and visit other parts of the United States. Automobile travel became a shared experience, reinforcing the development of a more national culture.

The construction of **suburbs**—living areas on the outskirts of cities with more open space—was greatly encouraged by the spread of the car. Real estate values rose. Along with the growth of suburbs was the appearance of the first shopping centers—groups of stores that could only be reached by car. Even "bootlegging" and the rise of organized crime were helped by the presence of cars and trucks, which transported hidden alcohol or helped criminals escape the scene of the crime.

Other industries also contributed to the national prosperity. **Airplanes**, using the same internal combustion engines as cars to drive their propellers, began making commercial flights. The use of **electricity** by Americans more than doubled in the 1920s. New electric household appliances, like the vacuum cleaner, refrigerator, and electric toaster, became generally available for the first time (although the first home refrigerator cost more than a Model T car). The American chemical industry likewise greatly expanded in these years. Commercial broadcasts on radio first began in 1920 and led to the manufacture and sale of millions of radio sets. By the end of the decade, the new motion picture business was also becoming a large industry. The emergence of all of these industries created new jobs, generated profits, and changed the ways in which Americans lived, traveled, communicated, and enjoyed themselves. They contributed to a shared national identity.

New Marketing Practices in an Age of Increasing Consumerism

Mass production required **mass consumption**, which in turn required new ways to **market** (*promote the sale of*) goods. How would millions of consumers know what to buy? The growth of **advertising** informed potential consumers while creating a demand for products and services. New **advertising agencies** studied psychology and specialized in developing slogans and advertisements to attract customers. Advertisements were placed in newspapers and magazines, and on street signs and billboards. Businesses like the Ford Motor Company sponsored radio programs, so that they could have their advertisements read to listeners. Homes received

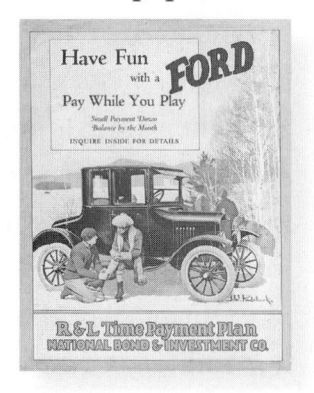

Chapter 13 | The Roaring Twenties

mail-order catalogs, while shoppers in cities visited giant department stores where clothing and household items from different manufacturers were displayed. All this advertising and marketing tied Americans together and again helped forge a new national culture.

Manufacturers and retailers developed special marketing practices to help their customers pay for products, such as **installment buying**. The buyer had only to pay a small down payment to take an item home. The purchaser then paid the balance in small monthly payments (which included interest). Henry Ford was one of the first to introduce installment buying, letting his customers pay for their cars over two years. Consumers also used installment buying to purchase such goods as refrigerators and household appliances.

The Historian's Apprentice

Look online to find advertisements from the 1920s. How are these advertisements similar to, and how are they different from, the advertisements we see today?

Radio and Movies Help Unify National Culture

Greater leisure time gave people more time for entertainment. By 1930, more than half the U.S. population was going to the movies once a week. More than half of all American families owned radios. Radio and motion pictures helped to forge a truly national culture as millions of Americans listened to the same voices on the radio or saw the same scenes in the movie theater.

Radio

In the late nineteenth century, scientists discovered that electromagnetic waves could travel through space. In the early twentieth century, an Italian inventor used these "radio waves" to transmit messages. The same inventor developed new transmitters so that radio waves could travel over longer distances. The invention of the vacuum tube made it possible to reproduce sound from radio waves more accurately.

During World War I, radio waves were used for military communications. Shortly after the war, the Radio Corporation of America (RCA) began making the first regular radio broadcasts. NBC was founded in 1926 and CBS was founded in 1928 to make radio broadcasts.

Americans began buying radios so that they could listen to radio plays, sports events, musical concerts, and the news. Listening to the radio was free because radio programs were paid for by advertisers. For the first time, Americans could listen to the World Series or learn election results almost instantaneously. Families sat around their radio for evening entertainment, just as many families watch television today. Radio made it possible for people across America to listen to the same broadcasts and learn about the same events at the same time—and more quickly than ever before.

Movies

Thomas Edison's company perfected the technology for **motion pictures**, or "movies," at the end of the nineteenth century. Light was shown through a photograph printed on transparent film, projecting an image onto a screen. A shutter closed on each picture or frame, creating a short interval of darkness that the viewer could not see. Instead, the viewer saw a series of images that seemed to move. Edison set up the first film studio in New York and began producing films for the public as early as 1893.

Other companies set up rival film studios in New York, but several decided to move to avoid disputes with Edison over patent rights. In 1910, the director D. W. Griffith took a group of actors to Los Angeles. They settled in Hollywood, then a small village. In 1915, Griffith filmed *Birth of a Nation*, a silent film about the Civil War and Reconstruction, which became one of the most successful films of all time.

Soon other filmmakers, attracted by the warm and sunny weather, also moved to Hollywood. In 1927, *The Jazz Singer*, the first "talkie" film with sound, was released. The following year, Walt Disney introduced viewers to Mickey Mouse in *Steamboat Willie*, an animated film with synchronized sound.

Movie studios like Paramount and Warner Brothers acquired their own movie theaters, where they showed their productions. Writers, directors, actors, and actresses signed contracts with movie studios and received salaries and training, but they were only allowed to make films for the studio they contracted with. Hollywood began producing westerns, comedies, romances, and musicals.

More and more Americans became attracted to the movies as a form of entertainment. Movie stars like Rudolph Valentino, Charlie Chaplin, Mary Pickford, and Greta Garbo became household names. Movie houses often showed newsreels before the main feature, and thus became places where Americans learned more about current affairs.

Like radio, movies brought Americans together. Viewers from around the country shared the same experience. More Americans paid a weekly visit to the local movie theater than attended houses of worship. Films revealed how other people lived. Movie stars served as role models. These were all major steps in creating a shared national identity as Americans.

Modern Forms of Cultural Expression: The Harlem Renaissance and Jazz

The 1920s marked a great break from the more restrictive morals and social rules of the late nineteenth century. Women enjoyed greater freedom. Art became expressionist or abstract. People became more open in expressing their feelings. African-American culture also flourished in these years, making important contributions to modern forms of cultural expression.

The "Great Migration"

By the late nineteenth century, there was a steady flow of African Americans from the South to the cities of the Midwest and Northeast. Their number only increased during World War I. They were escaping segregation and seeking new job opportunities. Many also moved because of the destruction of the cotton crop by the boll weevil. Their movement in this period is called the "**Great Migration**." This migration and the participation of African Americans in the war effort set the stage for the successes of African-American writers, artists, and musicians in the Twenties.

The Harlem Renaissance

During the 1920s, African Americans developed a new sense of pride. There were approximately 15 million African Americans living in the United States. An important concentration of African Americans was located in **Harlem**, a neighborhood in New York City. Because discrimination often prevented them from finding apartments in other parts of the city, African Americans of different occupations and backgrounds mixed together in Harlem, living side by side.

African-American communities in New York and other Northern cities started their own daily newspapers, such as *The Defender* in Chicago, which reached 300,000 subscribers by 1930, and the *Pittsburg Courier* with 100,000 readers. The NAACP published its own monthly magazine, *The Crisis,* while the National Urban League published the magazine *Opportunity.* These magazines not only reported news events and rallied supporters, they also published the work of African-American writers and poets, giving birth to a flourishing of black culture that has become known as the "**Harlem Renaissance**."

The Harlem Renaissance began with the publication of the essay "Enter the New Negro" by Alain Locke, an African-American philosophy professor. Locke's "New Negro" rejected the timidity and subservience of the "Old Negro"—African Americans who had attempted to reconcile themselves to white supremacy. Instead, the "New Negro" took pride in being black. With "renewed self-respect and self-dependence," the New Negro would rise above racism: "[F]rom some inner, desperate resourcefulness," wrote Locke, "has recently sprung up the simple expedient of fighting prejudice by mental passive resistance, in other words by trying to ignore it."

Some of the writers and artists who participated in the Harlem Renaissance were veterans of World War I. After fighting for democracy abroad, they resented second-class citizenship and white supremacy at home. One of their goals was to disprove racial prejudice by showing that African Americans were capable of creating great works of art and literature.

> **Note:** You won't be required to know the names of specific writers, artists, or musicians for the EOC Assessment, but it helps to know their work in order to understand what the Harlem Renaissance was about.

Among these writers was Countee Cullen, a poet who had studied English and French literature and married the daughter of NAACP founder W.E.B. Du Bois. Another participant was Jean Toomer, who wrote *Cane* (1923)—a modern novel consisting of short stories, poems and a play, all of which described

W.E.B. Du Bois

372 Chapter 13 | The Roaring Twenties

African-American experiences in both the South and the North.

The most celebrated poet of the Harlem Renaissance was **Langston Hughes**. Hughes aimed to capture "the spirit of the race" and inspire his people: "Most of my poems are racial in theme and treatment, derived from the life I know." Hughes was fluent in German, Spanish, and French. He had studied engineering at Columbia University and lived in Paris before returning to Harlem. His poems first appeared in the magazines *The Crisis* and *Opportunity*. In 1926, Hughes published his first complete volume of poetry.

Another writer, Claude McKay, came from Jamaica. McKay wrote *Home to Harlem* in 1928, a novel providing a realistic portrayal of African-American life in Harlem. McKay, Hughes, and the other young writers of the Harlem Renaissance believed that they should uncover the terrible consequences of racism in their writings, including the conditions of poor African Americans in the North. Other important writers of the Harlem Renaissance included Zora Neale Hurston, who published short stories. Another writer, Wallace Thurman, believed that black writers should not have a specific agenda other than to express themselves. Thurman, Zora Neale Hurston, and Langston Hughes began publishing a literary journal, *Fire!!!*

The painter Archibald Motley is often considered a member of the Harlem Renaissance, even though he lived in Chicago. Motley is famous for his African-American portraits and scenes of nightlife. Other notable painters were Palmer Hayden and Aaron Douglas.

The most prominent African-American leader in the Twenties was **Marcus Garvey**, another immigrant from Jamaica. Born in Jamaica, Garvey traveled to both Latin America and England. Returning to Jamaica in 1914, he established the Universal Negro Improvement Association. In 1916, Garvey moved to Harlem. He believed that "black is beautiful," and that all people of African heritage should take pride in their race. He emphasized the achievements of African history: "Negroes, teach your children that they are the direct descendants of the greatest and proudest race that ever peopled the earth."

Garvey opposed cooperation with whites in organizations like the NAACP and encouraged African Americans to form their own businesses and act independently. Garvey set up stores, restaurants, a hotel, and even published his own newspaper, *The Negro World*. He also established his own shipping line—the "Black Star Line"—with routes to the Caribbean, and started a "Back to Africa" movement.

Garvey soon had half a million followers. In 1920, he held the "International Convention of the Negro Peoples of the World" in Madison Square Garden, where he had himself proclaimed as "Provisional President" of Africa. However, his shipping venture failed, and he made the mistake of meeting with Ku Klux Klan leaders in the South, enraging other African-American leaders. In 1923, Garvey was tried and convicted for mail fraud. He spent two years in prison and was deported to Jamaica in 1927. His movement never recovered, although some of his ideas would later re-emerge during the Civil Rights Movement.

While the 1920s saw the achievements of the Harlem Renaissance, it was also a period of increasing racial violence. In the South, African Americans suffered from a legal system of racial segregation, the revival of the Ku Klux Klan and repeated lynchings (*mob hangings*). In Northern cities, periodic spurts of violence sometimes ended in rioting and the destruction of African-American neighborhoods.

Jazz Music

With its syncopated (*shifted or unexpected*) rhythms from ragtime, its use of notes from the blues scale, and its emphasis on improvisation, jazz music became popular in the 1920s. Jazz had its roots in old work songs, the ragtime rhythms of pianist-composers like Scott Joplin, blues music from the South, and African-American spirituals. It began in New Orleans as a fusion of European and African music. After the war, many jazz musicians migrated to Chicago and New York. It was a unique African-American musical form.

Langston Hughes tried to capture the pulse of jazz in one of his poems: "In many of them I try to grasp and hold some of the meanings and rhythms of jazz. Jazz to me is one of the inherent expressions of Negro life in America: the eternal tom-tom of revolt against weariness in a white world."

Musicians such as Louis Armstrong, Cab Calloway, and Duke Ellington played jazz music in Harlem nightclubs. Ella Fitzgerald, Billie Holiday, and Bessie Smith became famous as jazz vocalists. Radio stations began playing music and included jazz recordings. Jazz became popular across the country. Although African Americans continued to face prejudice and racism, jazz music was accepted and became part of the national culture. White New Yorkers flocked at night to the Cotton Club in Harlem, where black musicians played to white audiences. White composers like George Gershwin created jazz compositions. F. Scott Fitzgerald popularized jazz in his books. The Twenties has become known as the "Jazz Age."

Louis Armstrong (1901–1971) was born in New Orleans. He became a cornet and trumpet player in New Orleans. In 1922, Armstrong moved with Joe "King" Oliver and his band to Chicago. Later, Armstrong left Oliver's band to move to New York. Armstrong was one of the first jazz musicians to emphasize solo performances. He also became famous for his composing, recording, and singing, including "scat singing" (*singing sounds without words*).

The Historian's Apprentice

1. Look up one of the writers from the Harlem Renaissance on the Internet or in your school library, and read an excerpt from his or her works. Write a short summary of the excerpt to share with your class.
2. Pretend your classroom is a jazz club. Have members of your class impersonate jazz musicians or writers and artists from the Harlem Renaissance. Have each participant tell the rest of the class about his or her work.

3. Write an essay explaining how the 1920s was a period of profound change that helped to shape our shared national culture.

For the Georgia Milestones EOC Assessment, you should know that:

- [ ] Fears of rising communism and socialism in the United States led to the "Red Scare" (1919–1921).
- [ ] The Red Scare, belief in "Anglo-Saxon" superiority, and a dislike of Southern and Eastern Europeans led to the first restrictions on immigration from Europe, with the Emergency Quota Act of 1921 and the even more restrictive Immigration Act of 1924.
- [ ] The Eighteenth Amendment (1919) established Prohibition, forbidding the manufacture and sale of alcoholic drinks; it had the unintended consequence of leading to the rise of organized crime, and was subsequently repealed.
- [ ] The Nineteenth Amendment (1920) gave women the right to vote, encouraging greater self-expression and self-confidence among women, leading women to enter into new occupations, and creating a new influence in elections.
- [ ] The Twenties was a time of economic prosperity for many, when mass production and advertising led to increasing consumerism and helped to create a common national culture.
- [ ] The Twenties saw a great spread in the use of the automobile, which contributed to the period's economic prosperity and a shared national identity.
- [ ] Radio and movies were first introduced in the 1920s and acted as unifying forces in creating a national culture.
- [ ] The Twenties was a period when modern forms of cultural expression emerged, such as jazz music and the Harlem Renaissance.

"Getting Religion" by Archibald Motley, an African-American artist associated with the Harlem Renaissance

Name _____

Complete the following chart.

Term	Description	Importance/Impact on the Twenties
Communism		
Socialism		
Red Scare		
Palmer Raids		
Restriction of Immigration		
Eighteenth Amendment		
Prohibition		
Nineteenth Amendment		
Mass Production		

Name _____

Complete the following chart.

Term	Description	Importance/Impact on the Twenties
Assembly Line		
Advertising and New Marketing Practices		
Henry Ford		
Impact of the Automobile		
Impact of Radio and Movies		
Hollywood		
Jazz		
Harlem Renaissance		

Chapter 13 | The Roaring Twenties

The Roaring Twenties

Restriction of Immigration

Causes
- Prejudice against immigrants from Southern and Eastern Europe
- Belief in superiority of "Anglo-Saxon" Protestants
- Impact of the "Red Scare"

Legislation
- Emergency Quota Act (1921): set up national quotas
- National Origins Act (1924): reduced quotas

Impact
- Drastically reduced immigration from Southern and Eastern Europe; banned Asian immigration

The Red Scare
- Communist takeover of Russia
- Labor strikes in the United States
- Formation of Communist Labor Party
- Bombings in the United States
- "Palmer Raids"
- Trial of Sacco and Vanzetti

Impact of New Constitutional Amendments

Eighteenth Amendment (1919)
- Outlawed manufacture and sale of alcoholic beverages
- Goal of Temperance movement
- Established Prohibition
- Widely evaded—led to rise of organized crime
- Repealed in 1933

Nineteenth Amendment (1920)
- Guaranteed women the right to vote
- Goal of women's suffrage movement
- Recognized that women were entitled to the rights of citizens
- Led women to be more independent and assertive in the Twenties
- More women work outside the home; some pursue higher education

Mass Production and Consumerism
- Henry Ford introduces use of conveyor belt to his assembly-line production
- Ford raises wages and lowers the price of cars
- Automobiles become available to the general public
- Expansion in automobile ownership promotes prosperity
- Other new industries also promote prosperity: electrical appliances, radios
- Manufacturers use advertising and installment buying to promote sales and consumerism

Radio Broadcasts and Motion Pictures
- The first radio broadcasts and motion pictures with sound are in the 1920s
- Millions buy radios and go to local movie theaters each week
- Radios and movies help to create a shared national identity

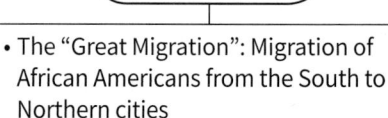

The Harlem Renaissance and Jazz Music
- The "Great Migration": Migration of African Americans from the South to Northern cities
- Harlem: An African-American neighborhood in New York City
- African-American writers and artists realistically portray the African-American experience to combat racism
- Marcus Garvey urges African Americans to be more self-reliant
- Jazz music has African-American origins but becomes popular with whites and as well as blacks

Chapter 13 | The Roaring Twenties

What Do You Know?

SSUSH16a

1. What was a consequence of rising fears of communism and socialism after World War I?

   A. President Wilson invited Soviet leaders to visit the United States.

   B. Americans decided to provide economic aid to Germany and Hungary.

   C. Congress passed laws restricting immigration from Europe.

   D. Most Americans preferred to listen to jazz rather than to music from Europe.

SSUSH16a

2. Use the diagram to answer the question.

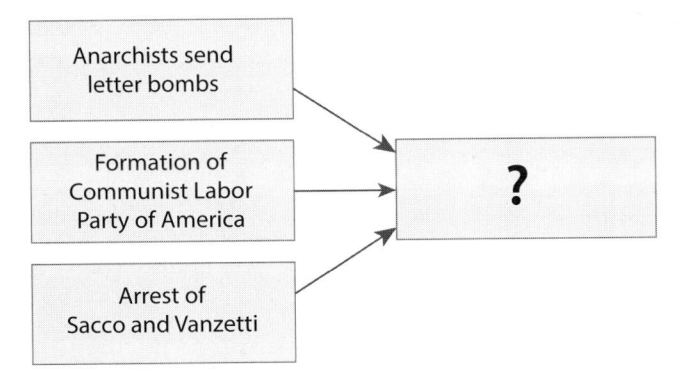

   ```
   [Anarchists send letter bombs]  ─┐
                                    │
   [Formation of Communist Labor    ├──→ [ ? ]
    Party of America]               │
                                    │
   [Arrest of Sacco and Vanzetti]  ─┘
   ```

   Which word or phrase BEST completes the diagram?

   A. Prohibition

   B. Women's suffrage

   C. Cold War

   D. Red Scare

SSUSH16a

3. Use the excerpt to answer the question.

   > My information showed that communism in this country was an organization of thousands of aliens who are direct allies of [Russian communists]. The Government is now sweeping the nation clean of such filth.
   >
   > —Attorney General A. Mitchell Palmer, 1920

   Which event is described in this excerpt?

   A. Progressive Era

   B. Cold War

   C. Red Scare

   D. Civil Rights Movement

Chapter 13 | The Roaring Twenties   379

SSUSH16b

4. Use the diagram to answer the question.

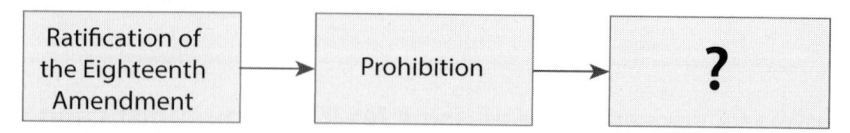

   Ratification of the Eighteenth Amendment → Prohibition → ?

   Which phrase BEST completes the diagram?

   A. Immigrants and city-dwellers abandon drinking
   B. Large-scale migration of Americans to Canada
   C. Widespread support for the law
   D. Rise of organized crime

SSUSH16b

5. Which TWO reasons MOST LIKELY spurred ratification of the Eighteenth Amendment?

   A. Reformers believed that alcoholic drinks caused immorality and crime.
   B. Politicians hoped to raise money by selling expensive exemptions to the law.
   C. Anti-German sentiment during the war viewed beer drinking as unpatriotic.
   D. Immigrants wanted to assimilate more quickly into mainstream traditions.
   E. Scientists had published new evidence of the damaging effects of alcohol.
   F. The cost of importing wine and beer from Europe was hurting the U.S. economy.

SSUSH16a

6. Use the cartoon to answer the question. What is the main idea of this cartoon?

   A. The land of opportunity is not for Russian immigrants.
   B. If an alien is from Latin America, he or she can be deported.
   C. Packing aliens together like sardines violates their human rights.
   D. Dangerous foreign-born socialists and communists should be expelled.

380 Chapter 13 | The Roaring Twenties

SSUSH16a

7. Use this list to answer the question.

> 1917 Literacy Test
>
> 1921 Emergency Quota Act
>
> 1924 National Origins Act

What do the elements in this list demonstrate?

A. By 1924, there were more Catholics than Protestants living in the United States.

B. Most immigrants in the early twentieth century could not speak English.

C. Prejudice against immigrants from Eastern and Southern Europe led to restrictions on immigration.

D. European immigrants faced greater discrimination than African Americans in the South.

SSUSH16b

8. Use the excerpt to answer the question.

> *The right of citizens of the United States to vote shall not be denied or abridged by the United States or by any State on account of sex.*
>
> —19th Amendment, Section 1

Which statement BEST describes an impact of this section?

A. Politicians had to take the views of women voters into account.

B. Women were paid as much as men who performed similar jobs.

C. Women no longer had to work outside the home.

D. Clothes manufacturers continued to make restrictive clothing for women.

SSUSH16c

9. Use the diagram to answer the question.

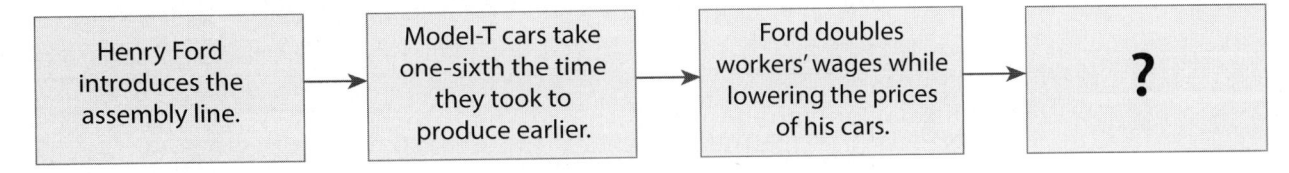

Henry Ford introduces the assembly line. → Model-T cars take one-sixth the time they took to produce earlier. → Ford doubles workers' wages while lowering the prices of his cars. → ?

Which sentence BEST completes the diagram?

A. Most Americans still preferred to take trains to automobiles.

B. More Americans can afford to buy their own car.

C. Cars remain a luxury item for the very rich.

D. Ford Motor Company faces bankruptcy, threatening the U.S. economy.

SSUSH16d

10. Use the list to answer the question.

   - Mass-produced automobiles
   - Radios
   - Motion picturess

   What was an important consequence of the items on the list?

   A. Reinforcement of local traditions

   B. Rapid growth of the national debt

   C. Americans imported more goods than they exported

   D. Development of a shared national identity

SSUSH16c

11. Use the image to answer the question.

    Which phrase BEST describes the aim of this 1920s advertisement?

    A. to help readers overcome the "Red Scare"

    B. to inform readers about Babe Ruth's achievements

    C. to give readers tips for improving their baseball batting averages

    D. to persuade consumers to purchase a mass-produced good

SSUSH16e

12. What was one goal African-American writers and artists hoped to achieve during the Harlem Renaissance?

    A. to display their ability as diligent workers in the workplace

    B. to show that the pursuit of material success often leads to tragedy

    C. to demonstrate that African Americans could produce great works of literature and art

    D. to reveal that conditions for African Americans in the South were almost as bad as in the North

CHAPTER 14 | The Great Depression and the New Deal

SSUSH17 What were the causes and consequences of the Great Depression?

    a. What were the causes of the stock market crash of 1929 and the Great Depression, including overproduction, under-consumption, and stock market speculation?

    b. What factors, such as over-farming and climate, led to the "Dust Bowl," and how did that result in movement and migration west?

    c. What were the social and political effects of widespread unemployment, such as developments like Hoovervilles?

SSUSH18 How effective was Franklin D. Roosevelt's New Deal as a response to the Great Depression and how well did its various programs aid those in need?

    a. How were President Roosevelt's efforts at relief, recovery, and reform reflected in various New Deal programs?

    b. What was the importance of the Social Security Act to the second New Deal?

    c. What were the major political challenges to Roosevelt's leadership and New Deal programs?

    d. How did Eleanor Roosevelt change the role of the First Lady, including her role in the development of New Deal programs for those in need?

Names and Terms You Should Know

- Great Depression
- Boom
- Overproduction
- Under-consumption
- Speculation
- Stock market
- Stockbroker
- "Black Tuesday"
- Stock Market Crash of 1929
- Default
- Unemployment
- "Run" on the bank
- Bank failure
- "Safety net"
- Homelessness
- Shantytown
- Hoboes
- Soup kitchen

- Herbert Hoover
- Laissez-faire economics
- Hooverville
- "Bonus Army"
- Drought
- "Dust Bowl"
- Foreclosure
- "Okies"
- Franklin D. Roosevelt
- Eleanor Roosevelt
- "New Deal"
- Relief
- Recovery
- Reform
- Bank Holiday
- Federal Deposit Insurance Corporation (FDIC)
- "Work-relief"
- Government agency

- Civilian Conservation Corps (CCC)
- Works Progress Administration (WPA)
- National Recovery Administration (NRA)
- Agricultural Adjustment Act (AAA)
- Tennessee Valley Authority (TVA)
- Securities and Exchange Commission (SEC)
- Second New Deal
- Social Security Act
- National Labor Relations Act ("Wagner Act")
- Huey Long
- Supreme Court
- "Court-packing" plan
- First Lady

Georgia "Peaches" of Wisdom

1. The Great Depression was the greatest economic crisis in our nation's history. Production fell by half and one quarter of the work force was unemployed.

2. Mass production had created a surplus of goods. By the end of the Twenties, most people who could afford those goods had already bought them. Practices like buying stocks on margin led to soaring speculation on the New York Stock Market.

3. Overproduction, under-consumption, and stock market speculation combined to bring about an economic collapse. On "Black Tuesday" (October 29, 1929), the stock market crashed. People tried to sell their stocks but few were willing to buy them.

4. The stock market crash set off a "chain reaction." People who lost money on the stock market could no longer invest or buy as many goods. Businesses and consumers stopped making new purchases. Businesses fired workers, creating mass unemployment. Banks failed. Prices and the demand for goods fell. People lost their homes and many even had to beg for food.

5. On the Great Plains, a series of droughts combined with unsuitable plowing techniques and soil erosion led to the disaster known as the "Dust Bowl." This catastrophe had both natural and human causes. Many farmers on the Plains lost their farms and moved west.

6. President Hoover did not think the government should interfere too directly in the economy. He took some steps to fight the Depression, but his actions were too little, too late. Shantytowns of homeless and unemployed Americans became known as "Hoovervilles." Hoover even used the army to break up a peaceful group of veterans and their families demanding a bonus from Congress.

7. Franklin D. Roosevelt won the Presidential election of 1932. His plan to end the Depression, called the "New Deal," had three goals: relief, recovery, and reform. Roosevelt declared a "Bank Holiday" to prevent bank runs and renew public confidence in banks. He created the Federal Deposit Insurance Corporation (FDIC) to insure bank deposits. The Securities and Exchange Commission was created to regulate the stock market. The National Recovery Administration (NRA) encouraged businesses to establish codes that set prices, wages, and working hours. The Agricultural Adjustment Act (AAA) limited production of crops and livestock to prevent surpluses and help farmers. The Civilian Conservation Corps (CCC) provided young men with work on public projects. The Tennessee Valley Authority (TVA) built dams to control floods and provide electricity to one of the country's poorest areas.

8. The "Second New Deal" aimed at reform and security. The Social Security Act created a "safety net" for Americans by establishing unemployment insurance, retirement benefits, and aid to the disabled and orphaned. The National Labor Relations Act ("Wagner Act") gave workers the right to unionize.

9. President Roosevelt's wife, Eleanor Roosevelt, changed the role of "First Lady" by remaining politically active. She championed the needs of women, the poor, the young, and African Americans.

10. Both conservative and liberal critics attacked New Deal programs. The Supreme Court struck down some New Deal legislation. Roosevelt attempted to save the New Deal from the Court with his "court-packing" scheme. His plan was widely condemned and rejected by Congress.

11. John Steinbeck's novel *The Grapes of Wrath* depicted the plight of the "Okies." Dorothea Lange took photographs of poor migrants and sharecroppers. Their works gave a human face to the Depression.

Chapter 14 | The Great Depression and the New Deal

The Great Depression was the worst economic downturn in our nation's history. Production fell by half, one-quarter of the work force was unemployed, and prices plummeted. Behind these statistics was a great deal of suffering and misery. Only America's entry into World War II put a final end to the Depression.

Causes of the Great Depression

What caused the American economy to change from the **boom** (*period of general prosperity*) of the 1920s to the Great Depression of the 1930s? Economic historians have identified a number of factors that led to the collapse. Weaknesses in the economy in the Twenties actually set the process in motion.

Overproduction/Under-consumption

The 1920s saw rapid economic expansion as manufacturers made and sold new products like cars, radios, and home appliances. By the late 1920s, most of those who could afford these products had already purchased them. There was a drop in consumer demand. A large share of the national income went to a small, wealthy group at the top of society. Not enough income went into the paychecks of average wage earners to buy all the consumer goods that were being produced.

Workers' wages rose in the 1920s, but production increased even faster. And many groups—such as farmers, African Americans, coal miners, railroad workers, and the elderly—were already in economic difficulties. They did not share in the general prosperity.

By the late 1920s, inventories of unsold products began to pile up in stores and warehouses. Manufacturers continued to produce more goods than they could sell. With unsold inventory, manufacturers eventually had to cut production and lay off workers, causing unemployment to rise.

High Tariffs Restricted International Trade

American producers might have sold their goods overseas, but they faced problems there as well. Tariffs protected American markets, but made it harder for farmers and manufacturers to sell their goods abroad. Some countries retaliated against the United States by placing high tariffs on American goods. The effect of these tariffs was to restrict international trade. The highest U.S. tariff of all, the Smoot-Hawley Tariff, went into effect in 1930. It raised customs duties on thousands of goods and contributed to a reduction of U.S. trade by more than half.

Speculation and the Over-extension of Credit

Speculation is the practice of buying stocks, real estate (*land or buildings*), or anything else to sell later at a profit. During the 1920s, the government failed to regulate the stock market or banks effectively, and speculation flourished.

Overproduction and under-consumption are two sides of the same coin. **Overproduction** occurs when more is produced than is purchased and consumed. **Under-consumption** occurs when consumers do not purchase and consume enough of what is produced.

A **stockbroker** is someone who earns a commission by buying and selling stocks for others on the **stock market**. In the 1920s, stockbrokers stimulated sales by lending money to their clients. Investors were able to "buy stocks on margin"—putting only 10% down and borrowing 90% from the stockbroker. The stockbroker was often financed by a bank. Investors sold their stocks after they went up in price in order to pay off the loan. This strategy worked well in a "bull market"—a stock market in which stock prices are steadily increasing.

In the bull market of the 1920s, stock prices became vastly inflated, reflecting the results of speculation rather than company earnings. For the first time, middle-class Americans began investing in the stock market, driving stock prices up still further.

In the Twenties, Americans also speculated in real estate, buying properties and hoping to sell them after prices rose. Even ordinary consumers borrowed: they bought consumer goods on credit or obtained mortgages from banks to buy their homes. Widespread speculation and a vast overextension of credit made the entire economy vulnerable. But so long as speculation continued and credit kept expanding, the economy prospered.

> **Buying Stocks "on Margin" in a Bull Market**
> An investor buys 10 shares of a stock at a price of $100 a share. He puts only 10% down, or $100 for all 10 shares. The stockbroker buys the shares, in effect lending the client $900. When the stock reaches a price of $120 per share, the investor sells his shares. He receives $1,200 and pays the $900 he owes the stockbroker. He has made a profit of $200 in a short time on an investment of only $100.

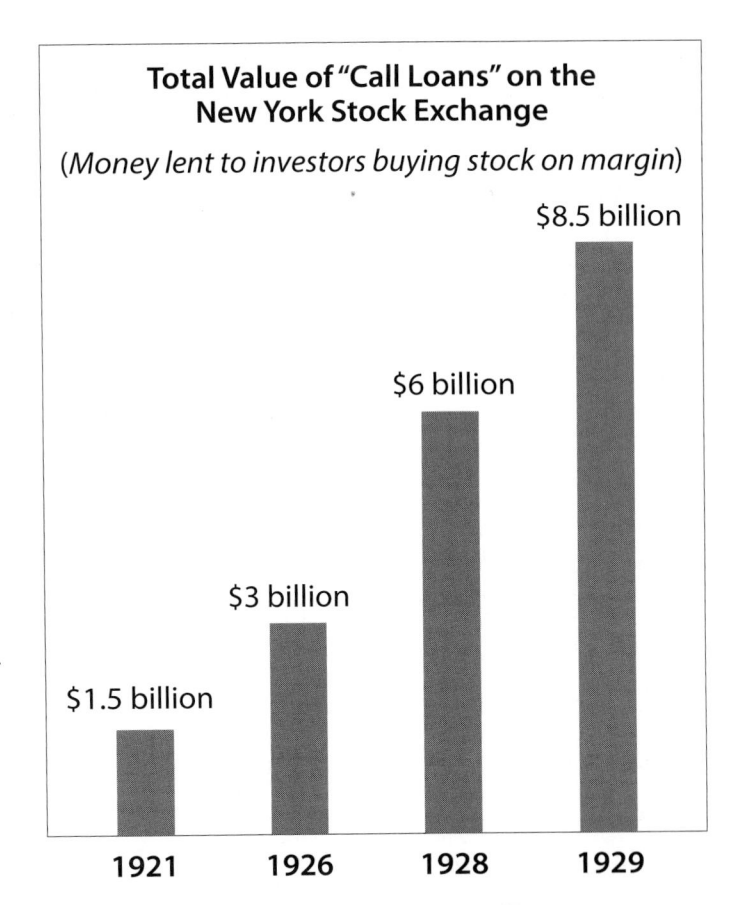

Total Value of "Call Loans" on the New York Stock Exchange
(Money lent to investors buying stock on margin)

- 1921: $1.5 billion
- 1926: $3 billion
- 1928: $6 billion
- 1929: $8.5 billion

The "Crash of 1929" Triggers a Chain Reaction

By 1928 there were signs that the economy was slowing down. Nevertheless the election of Herbert Hoover in that year and the promise of four more years of Republican prosperity unleashed a frenzy of buying on the stock market. As long as people wanted to buy stocks, their prices kept rising and the bull market continued. Stock prices continued to climb for almost another year. In the summer of 1929, the price of a share of stock in the telephone company AT&T rose from $209 to $304. Shares of the automobile manufacturer General Motors similarly rose from $268 to $391 in the same period. The Dow Jones Industrial Average, a measure of the value of stocks, reached a high point of 381.17 on September 3, 1929.

The very next month, the market turned sharply downward. The decline began on

Chapter 14 | The Great Depression and the New Deal

October 24, but a group of wealthy bankers bought stocks at above market prices to halt the slide. Five days later on October 29, known as "Black Tuesday," the market crashed. Corporations and private shareholders all tried to sell their stocks at the same time. Prices kept going lower as people competed to sell and no one was willing to buy. In only three weeks, stocks lost half their value and $30 billion simply disappeared. This was as much as the United States had spent in all of World War I. In the following months, stock prices continued to fall. By 1932, the Dow Jones Industrial Average reached its low point of 41.22 and a share of AT&T stock was worth only $72.

Many historians believe that the stock market crash set off a chain reaction throughout the economy. Corporations could no longer raise funds. Business prospects became gloomy. More than 25,000 businesses failed in 1930. Most important of all, people who lost money in the crash could no longer repay their loans. This led to a series of **bank failures**. There was little regulation of banks and no general insurance of bank deposits. Many people lost their entire life savings.

In this new economic climate, the demand for goods decreased. Consumers, worried about the future, bought less. Prices fell. Manufacturers were forced to close their factories and fire their workers, increasing unemployment. More banks failed. The country became caught in the grip of a vicious downward spiral.

Many historians believe the faulty banking system and the Federal Reserve were as much to blame for the economic collapse as the crash on Wall Street. When banks had to cover losses on the stock market, people grew nervous and withdrew their bank deposits. This reduced banks' ability to meet their own obligations or lend to businesses and farmers. As more depositors withdrew their savings, the banks themselves began to fail. The Federal Reserve refused to make more money available, which might have made it easier for banks to meet their depositors' demands. Americans lost their savings and their faith in the financial system.

Panic-stricken customers trying to withdraw their money from the American Union Bank

The Depression Becomes Worldwide

American banks and investors had invested overseas to help Europeans rebuild their economies after World War I. Now American banks and investors called in their funds from Europe. New loans to Europe were canceled.

In 1929, monetary currencies around the world were still backed by gold. When American

The Historian's Apprentice

Did the stock market crash cause the Great Depression? Historians actually have different views on this question.

Opposing Viewpoints

"'Most academic experts agree on one aspect of the crash: It wiped out billions of dollars of wealth in one day, and immediately depressed consumer buying. If you look at sales of consumer goods, particularly radios or automobiles, you will see they fell dramatically,' said Economics Professor John Galbraith. 'The crash had the impact of glass shattering, and while other more essential factors took over as the Depression wore on—universal fear, the slump in agricultural production because of drought, the decline in business investment—it is hard to argue that the collapse of the market did not start things in motion.'"

—Albert Scardino, "Did the '29 Crash Spark the Great Depression?" (1987)

"Much mythology surrounds these dramatic events in 1929. Perhaps the most [enduring] misconception portrays the Crash as the cause of the Great Depression. The disagreeable truth is that [historians] have been unable to demonstrate an appreciable cause-and-effect link between the Crash and the Great Depression. So, legend to the contrary, the average American—a description that in this case encompasses at least 97.5 percent of the population—owned no stock in 1929. Accordingly, the Crash had little direct economic effect on the typical American. The Depression, however, would be another story."

—David Kennedy, *Freedom from Fear* (1999)

1. How do these views differ?
2. With which historian would you most agree? Why?

---

banks began calling in their debts, gold had to be shipped back across the Atlantic. Germany **defaulted** (*refused to pay*) on its reparation payments to Britain and France. Those countries in turn weren't able to make payments on their debts to America. So the Depression quickly spread from America to Europe.

The Human Experience of the Depression

The Great Depression was a national nightmare. Tens of thousands of businesses failed. Half a million farmers lost their farms. One quarter of American banks failed. More than ten million people were thrown out of work.

What made matters worse was the fact that in those days there was no "**safety net**" as we have today—there was no federal system of unemployment relief, retirement benefits, or bank deposit insurance. People who had been working tirelessly for years could lose their jobs and savings, then lose their homes, and finally find themselves on the street begging for food.

Private charities and local relief agencies were overwhelmed by the scope of the disaster. Many Americans went hungry. Children suffered from malnutrition. Over a million men without work became "**hoboes**" riding railroad freight cars. Others sold apples on the street. **Shantytowns** of **homeless** people, living in canvas tents or shacks made of scrap wood, packing crates, and cardboard, sprang up on the outskirts of cities. Millions of Americans depended on the **soup kitchens** and breadlines provided by local charities for their daily survival. Ironically, this widespread hunger occurred at a time when farmers were unable to sell their food crops and were going bankrupt in the thousands. Minority groups were especially hard-hit because they suffered the highest unemployment rates.

The tremendous human suffering caused by the Great Depression was reflected in the popular culture of the time. Dorothea Lange took photographs of people afflicted by poverty, including sharecroppers and migrant workers. Her photograph, *Migrant Mother*, is one of the most famous photographs in American history.

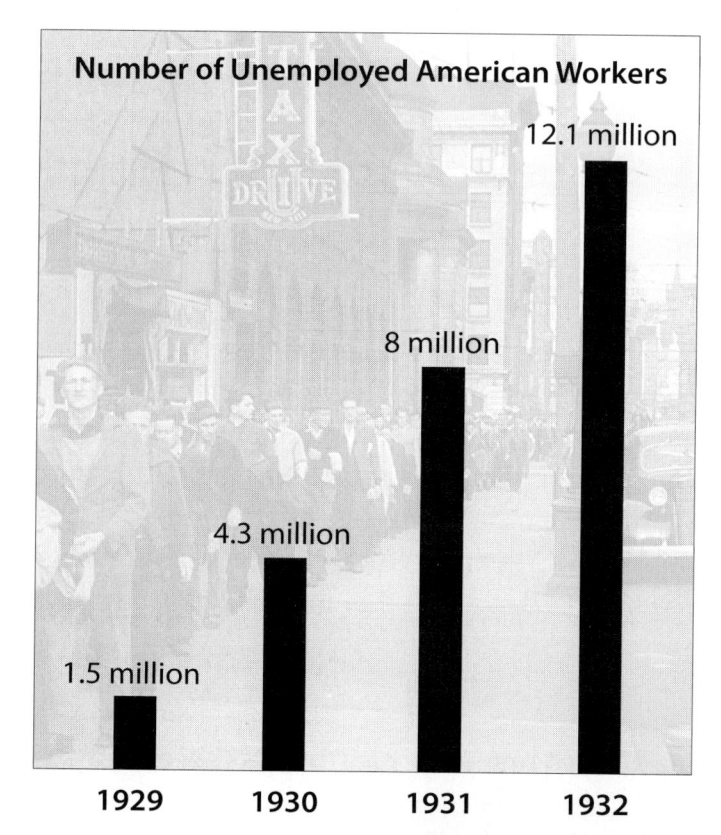

Number of Unemployed American Workers

- 1929: 1.5 million
- 1930: 4.3 million
- 1931: 8 million
- 1932: 12.1 million

Hoover Fails to Halt the Depression

Conservative economists advised Hoover not to interfere directly in the economy. They believed the market just needed time to repair itself. When prices got low enough, people would start buying goods again. Once people resumed buying, manufacturers would start producing again. As production picked up, employment would increase. Unfortunately these predictions turned out to be wrong. Instead, the Depression got worse month by month. More and more people lost their jobs as production was cut back further and further.

Hoover believed in *laissez-faire* economics. He did not think it was the federal government's job to interfere in the economy. Hoover feared that federal aid would weaken individual character. Even so, he eventually took more active steps than any President before him to fight the economic downturn. Hoover held meetings with business leaders asking them not to lay off workers. He cut taxes and increased federal spending on public works projects (like Hoover Dam) by almost $1 billion. He directed a federal agency to buy surplus farm crops. Hoover also approved sending Mexican immigrants back to Mexico, including children born in the United States who were actually U.S. citizens.

Herbert Hoover

Hoover Dam

The problem was that all this was not enough. The scope of the disaster was too great. Hoover rejected the demand that the federal government provide direct payments to the unemployed and the needy. He feared this would create an unmanageable federal bureaucracy. He also believed this would reduce the incentive to work, undermining the "rugged individualism" that he saw as the key to American success. Instead, Hoover believed that emergency relief for the needy should come from local governments and private charities.

By 1932, it was clear that Hoover's commitment to voluntary action was not working. Hoover then established a new government agency—the **Reconstruction Finance Corporation** ("RFC")—to cope with the crisis. This agency gave emergency loans to banks and businesses. Hoover believed that cheap loans to businesses would save them from bankruptcy and help them to grow again. As they expanded, they would hire more workers. The benefits would then "trickle down" to the average American. However, the amount lent by the RFC under Hoover was only $2 billion. Losses on the stock market had reached $40 billion. Hoover's efforts remained inadequate to cope with the magnitude of the problem.

Matters were actually made worse by the Federal Reserve System. The Federal Reserve stood by as banks failed, without lending money or increasing the money supply to save them. In part this was because the currency was tied to the gold standard, so the Federal Reserve was limited in its options. Bankers thought gold was the only safe asset in an unstable economy. The Federal Reserve mistakenly contracted (*shrank*) the money supply, pulling the economy further downward.

Americans found Hoover's lack of leadership frustrating. The shantytowns that sprang up on the outskirts of cities became known as **"Hoovervilles."** Some people demonstrated against the federal government's relative inaction. About 40,000 unemployed veterans and their families—former soldiers who had fought

A "Hooverville"

Chapter 14 | The Great Depression and the New Deal

in the American Expeditionary Force during World War I—camped out in Washington, D.C. in the summer of 1932. They hoped to persuade Congress to grant them a promised bonus they were supposed to receive in 1945. Fearing a possible riot, President Hoover used the army to disperse this "Bonus Expeditionary Force" (or "**Bonus Army**") by force. Many were shocked at this action.

The "Dust Bowl"

Farmers on the Great Plains had to contend with an environmental disaster as well as with the Depression. Both climate and human action contributed to the calamity. In previous decades, farmers had removed the tough, deep-rooted prairie grasses that once protected the soil on the Plains from wind erosion. During World War I, the demand for food increased. Farmers cut the grasses of less fertile land on the Plains to turn into farmland as well. They used a new type of plow that broke up the soil instead of just making ditches through it. Farmers didn't realize that the period from the late 1890s until the 1920s had been "wet years" on the Great Plains, with more rain than usual.

A series of **droughts** (*periods without rainfall*) then began in the early 1930s. Without sufficient rain, farmers' crops failed and the topsoil dried out, turning into dust. There was no longer enough grass holding in moisture and keeping the dry soil in place. The strong winds of the Great Plains swept up the dry soil and carried it into the air and across the Plains. Blizzards of dust fell from the sky, choking farmers and livestock. Dust even reached cities in the Midwest and Northeast.

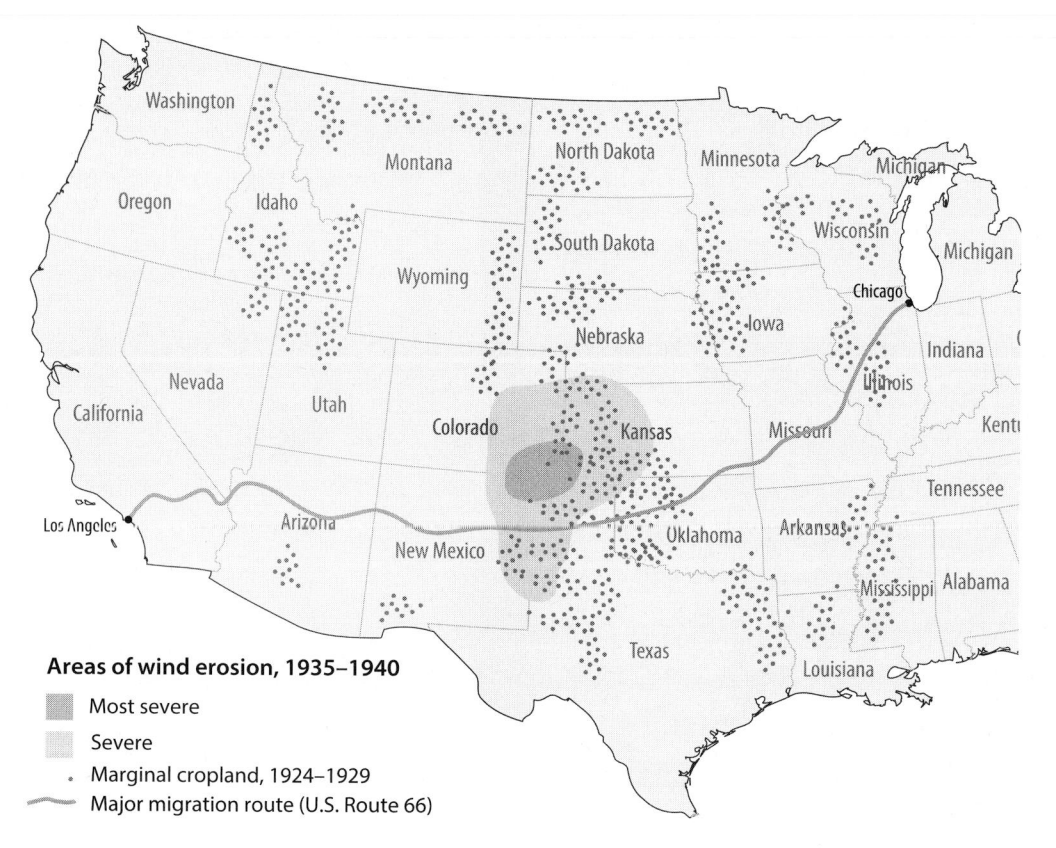

Areas of wind erosion, 1935–1940
- Most severe
- Severe
- Marginal cropland, 1924–1929
- Major migration route (U.S. Route 66)

392   Chapter 14 | The Great Depression and the New Deal

The Historian's Apprentice

Ann Marie Low was 22 years old and living with her family on the Great Plains at the time of the "Dust Bowl." She described the conditions of the Dust Bowl in her diary:

April 25, 1934, Wednesday

> "Last weekend was the worst dust storm we ever had. We've been having quite a bit of blowing dirt every year since the drought started, not only here, but all over the Great Plains. Many days this spring the air is just full of dirt coming, literally, for hundreds of miles. It sifts into everything. After we wash the dishes and put them away, so much dust sifts into the cupboards we must wash them again before the next meal. Clothes in the closets are covered with dust. . . .Newspapers say the deaths of many babies and old people are attributed to breathing in so much dirt."

August 1, 1934, Wednesday

> "Everything is just the same—hot and dry. . . . The drought and dust storms are something fierce. As far as one can see are brown pastures and fields which, in the wind, just rise up and fill the air with dirt. It tortures animals and humans, makes housekeeping an everlasting drudgery, and ruins machinery. The crops are long since ruined. In the spring wheat section of the U.S., a crop of 12 million bushels is expected instead of the usual 170 million. We have had such drought for five years all subsoil moisture is gone. Fifteen feet down the ground is dry as dust. Trees are dying by the thousands. Cattle and horses are dying, some from starvation and some from dirt they eat on the grass."

1. Which information from these diary entries most surprised you?
2. Which do you think was more responsible for the "Dust Bowl"—human actions or forces of nature? Write a paragraph answering this question and giving evidence in support of your point of view.

Unable to grow their crops, many farmers on the Plains could no longer pay their mortgages or property taxes. Banks eventually **foreclosed** on them *(seized their property to sell at an auction for whatever the bank could get)*, forcing the farmers to abandon their farms. About 350,000 farmers and their families took their belongings and moved from the Dust Bowl westward to California, in search of better opportunities for farmers. Because so many of these migrants came from Oklahoma, they became known

Chapter 14 | The Great Depression and the New Deal

Migrant workers

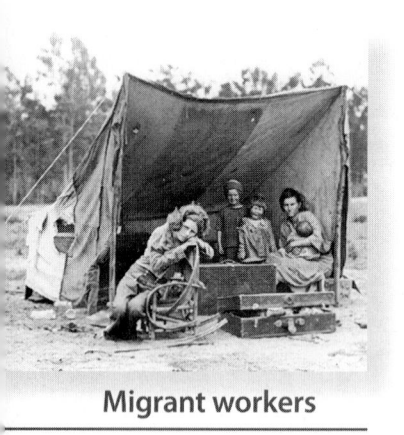

as "**Okies**." The Okies hoped to find work planting or harvesting fruits on farms or in cities, especially because government policies had cut off the influx of migrant workers from Mexico. Nevertheless the Okies were distrusted by local residents, and often had difficulty finding work.

The writer **John Steinbeck** described the "Okies" and their struggles in California in the most famous of all Depression novels, *The Grapes of Wrath* (1939). Steinbeck won the Pulitzer Prize and later won the Nobel Prize for literature. The book was also made into a popular movie. It tells the story of the Joads, a family who lose their farm and are driven from Oklahoma by the Dust Bowl. They move to California where they hope to find work, but they discover conditions are not as promised and become migrant laborers. Steinbeck's aim was to depict the suffering of the Depression and the greed and indifference that, in his eyes, made it even worse.

The New Deal

Under these conditions, it was not surprising that Democratic candidate **Franklin D. Roosevelt** (also known by his initials as "**FDR**") defeated Hoover in a landslide election in November 1932.

Roosevelt promised Americans a "**New Deal**." This "New Deal" was a major turning point in American history. It established the principle that the federal government bears the ultimate responsibility for the smooth running of the American economy and for the protection of ordinary Americans from severe economic distress.

Presidential Election of 1932

Candidate	Political Party	% of Popular Vote	Electoral Vote
Franklin D. Roosevelt	Democrat	57.4%	472
Herbert C. Hoover	Republican	39.7%	59

Problems Facing Americans in 1933

When Roosevelt took office in March 1933, the Great Depression was at its height. Americans faced a series of economic problems of catastrophic dimensions.

Widespread Unemployment

Unemployment was the most serious and immediate problem. Over one-quarter of the nation's workforce was now unemployed. Local governments and private charities did not have enough resources to deal with these problems. There was no "safety net" to provide food and shelter to the unemployed and their families. Many feared the frustrations of the unemployed might boil over into social revolution.

Franklin D. Roosevelt

394   Chapter 14 | The Great Depression and the New Deal

Collapse of the Banking System

For three years, "**runs**" had been occurring in which bank customers attempted to withdraw their deposits from banks. Since banks invest most of their depositors' money and do not have these funds on hand, these bank runs threatened to topple the entire banking system. By March 1933, 9,000 banks had already failed since the Depression had begun. Each bank failure meant thousands of families lost their life savings. By the time Roosevelt took office, many state governors had ordered the banks in their state to close their doors to avert a crisis.

Reduced Production

National production had greatly decreased. Manufacturers no longer made goods because no one would buy them. Industrial production in 1932 was half of what it had been in 1929. Many businesses went bankrupt.

Foreclosures

Across America, people could no longer pay their mortgage payments on their homes or farms. Banks and lenders, also in grave financial difficulties, were forced to foreclose on their properties.

The Historian's Apprentice

The following are excerpts from President Roosevelt's First Inaugural Address:

> "This great Nation will endure as it has endured, will revive and will prosper. So, first of all, let me assert my firm belief that the only thing we have to fear is fear itself—nameless, unreasoning, unjustified terror which paralyzes needed efforts to convert retreat into advance. In every dark hour of our national life a leadership of frankness and vigor has met with that understanding and support of the people themselves which is essential to victory. I am convinced that you will again give that support to leadership in these critical days.
>
> In such a spirit on my part and on yours we face our common difficulties. They concern, thank God, only material things. Values have shrunken to fantastic levels; taxes have risen; our ability to pay has fallen; government of all kinds is faced by serious curtailment of income; the means of exchange are frozen in the currents of trade; the withered leaves of industrial enterprise lie on every side; farmers find no markets for their produce; the savings of many years in thousands of families are gone.
>
> More important, a host of unemployed citizens face the grim problem of existence, and an equally great number toil with little return . . .
>
> This Nation asks for action, and action now. Our greatest primary task is to put people to work. This is no unsolvable problem if we face it wisely and courageously. It can be accomplished in part by direct recruiting by the Government itself, treating the task as we would treat the emergency of a war, but at the same time, through this employment, accomplishing greatly needed projects to stimulate and reorganize the use of our natural resources . . .

Finally, in our progress toward a resumption of work we require two safeguards against a return of the evils of the old order; there must be a strict supervision of all banking and credits and investments; there must be an end to speculation with other people's money, and there must be provision for an adequate but sound currency. . . .

I am prepared under my constitutional duty to recommend the measures that a stricken nation in the midst of a stricken world may require. These measures, or such other measures as the Congress may build out of its experience and wisdom, I shall seek, within my constitutional authority, to bring to speedy adoption."

—Franklin D. Roosevelt, March 4, 1933

1. What did President Roosevelt identify as the greatest problem facing Americans?
2. How important did Roosevelt believe good leadership was to overcoming the crisis?
3. How did Roosevelt promise an approach that was different from Hoover's?
4. How was his speech aimed at restoring public confidence in the economy? Do you think his speech succeeded?
5. Imagine you are an adviser to President-elect Roosevelt in early 1933. Write a letter advising him how to handle the economic crisis facing the country.

The New President and His Advisers

The new President had been born into a wealthy New York family. He was a distant cousin to President Theodore Roosevelt. His wife, **Eleanor Roosevelt**, was Theodore Roosevelt's niece. As a Progressive Democrat, Franklin Roosevelt had served as Woodrow Wilson's Assistant Secretary of the Navy. In 1920, Roosevelt was nominated as the Democratic candidate for Vice-President, but the Democrats had lost the election.

In 1921, tragedy occurred when Roosevelt was struck with polio, a crippling disease. His legs were almost completely paralyzed. Slowly, with Eleanor's support, Roosevelt trained himself to stand with heavy metal braces. He also became a frequent visitor to Warm Springs, Georgia, where he bathed in hot spring water to relieve his aching legs. His experience with polio gave Roosevelt a rare ability to empathize with suffering and the necessary patience and confidence to overcome the difficulties that confronted the nation during the Depression.

Roosevelt returned to politics and was elected as Governor of New York. When the Depression started, Eleanor Roosevelt served as her husband's eyes and ears by traveling around the state. As Governor, Roosevelt tried out many of the programs that he would later apply to the nation as President.

Roosevelt realized the importance of surrounding himself with

Eleanor Roosevelt

capable advisers. After his election as President, he assembled a galaxy of talents to serve in Cabinet posts and as informal advisers. Much of the New Deal program was developed by a team of reform-minded professors. Roosevelt appointed Republicans as well as Democrats to his Cabinet. He also appointed the first woman to a Cabinet post: Frances Perkins, who became Secretary of Labor.

Roosevelt was an excellent speaker and communicator. His optimism and confidence were in striking contrast to Herbert Hoover. Roosevelt's 1932 campaign song was "Happy Days are Here Again." One of the first things he did to improve the public mood was to end Prohibition. In his Inaugural Address, he told Americans that "the only thing we have to fear is fear itself." Part of Roosevelt's purpose was psychological—to restore public confidence—so that people would redeposit their savings in banks, begin buying and investing again, and resume their normal economic activities, bringing the economy back to its feet.

Roosevelt came to the Presidency at a time when new means of communication— radio and movies—made it possible for the President to reach out to more people than ever before. He gave informal radio addresses to millions of listeners, known as "**fireside chats**," in which he explained his policies in simple conversational terms. Roosevelt also held frequent press conferences with newspaper reporters. Americans further learned about New Deal programs from newsreels shown in cinemas.

New Deal Legislation: "Relief, Recovery, Reform"

The New Deal was pragmatic (*realistic, practical*), making choices based on trial and error. Roosevelt was willing to try almost anything that might work. He created so many agencies during his first term in office that Americans referred to these New Deal programs (which used their initials for abbreviations) as "alphabet soup."

Roosevelt explained New Deal measures in terms of three goals: "Relief, Recovery, and Reform."

> **Relief** measures provided temporary support to tide people over until the economy recovered; they included both emergency payments and "work-relief" (employment on government projects).
>
> **Recovery** measures were programs aimed at restoring the country's economy.
>
> **Reform** measures aimed at remedying defects in the economy so that such a severe depression (*economic downturn*) could never occur again.

The First New Deal

The "First New Deal" lasted from 1933 until 1935. It mainly focused on relief and recovery. As soon as Roosevelt took office, he assembled Congress for a special session to cope with the nation's economic problems. Democratic control of both Houses of Congress and the severe economic crisis allowed Roosevelt to push through legislation that would not have been possible in other times.

> You won't be required to know the names of specific New Deal agencies for the EOC Assessment, except for **Social Security**; however, it helps to know something about these programs in order to understand what the New Deal was all about.

The Bank Holiday

When Roosevelt took office, 38 states had already shut their banks. Roosevelt closed all the nation's banks just after his inauguration by declaring a "Bank Holiday." All banks came under federal supervision. Each bank was permitted to reopen only after the government inspected its records and found it was financially sound. This helped banks avoid "runs" in which all their customers tried to withdraw their funds. In his first fireside chat, Roosevelt encouraged the public to redeposit their savings in the reopened banks. Roosevelt succeeded in restoring confidence: when banks reopened, deposits exceeded withdrawals. The Emergency Banking Act authorized the federal government to assist threatened banks with emergency funds. The Homeowners Loan Corporation (1933) gave emergency loans at low interest rates to homeowners facing foreclosure.

Federal Deposit Insurance Corporation (1933)

The Federal Deposit Insurance Corporation (FDIC) was created to insure deposits in banks so that people would no longer have to worry about losing their savings in the event of a bank failure. If a bank failed, the federal government would pay a depositor the value of the deposit up to a specified amount. We still rely on this reform measure today.

Work-Relief: FERA, PWA, CWA, CCC, and WPA

Roosevelt favored "work-relief"—government projects that gave people meaningful work. This preserved their sense of dignity and also improved the nation's infrastructure by providing needed roads and public buildings and conserving natural resources.

The Federal Emergency Relief Act, or "FERA" (1933) gave money to state and local governments to provide emergency relief and to hire millions of unemployed Americans on "make-work" projects. The Public Works Administration (1933) and the Civil Works Administration (1933) built highways, bridges, hospitals, airports, courthouses, and other public facilities. The Rural Electrification Administration gave loans to state and local governments to extend electric power lines to rural areas.

The **Civilian Conservation Corps** (1933), or "CCC," gave outdoor jobs to young men, such as planting trees, draining swamps, and improving national and state parks. Participants in the CCC lived in camps supervised by army officers and received free uniforms and food. They were required to send most of their pay home to their families.

The **Works Progress Administration**, or "WPA," replaced the FERA early in 1935. It also increased employment by creating many new public works projects. The WPA hired workers and paid them directly with federal money, rather than giving money to state and local governments to fund relief efforts. The WPA spent over $11 billion and gave nine million people jobs building public schools, courthouses,

A CCC crew at work in 1933

roads, and bridges. The WPA also hired unemployed artists, architects, writers, and musicians and paid them to paint murals, design buildings, write guidebooks, and produce plays and concerts. This program greatly encouraged the creative arts during this period.

Through its relief programs and public works projects, the government put money into the hands of workers. It was hoped that workers would spend their money, increasing the demand for goods and services. Producers would then start to produce again and hire more workers. Demand, production, and employment would continue to increase until the Depression was over. Economists called this "**pump priming**": putting a little water into a dry pump to get it flowing again.

The National Recovery Administration (1933)

Roosevelt also introduced special legislation to help industry and agriculture recover from the Depression. Recovery measures were meant to restore the national economy to normal health. The **National Industrial Recovery Act** was designed to help industries. The act created another New Deal agency—the **National Recovery Administration, or "NRA."** All businesses and companies in the same industry were asked to cooperate in drawing up a "code of fair practice." Each code set standard prices, limited production, reduced the workweek to 40 hours, and established a minimum wage for the industry.

The law gave federal officials the power to approve the proposed industry code or to suggest changes. Once the code was approved, businesses voluntarily following the code were allowed to display large posters with blue eagles, informing customers that they were NRA members. It was hoped that this would help industries raise their prices and avoid cutthroat competition. The NRA also guaranteed the rights of workers to organize into unions, established a National Labor Board to settle labor–management disputes, and abolished most forms of child labor. Over 95% of all industries eventually adopted NRA "codes of fair practice."

Earlier Progressives had generally opposed business combinations. In the atmosphere of economic crisis, the New Deal actually encouraged competing businesses to cooperate in order to raise prices. Antitrust restrictions on price-fixing and collaboration were ignored. Some critics accused the NRA of favoring Big Business at the expense of smaller ones, since larger businesses were usually more influential in drawing up the new codes.

The NRA came to a sudden end in 1935 when the Supreme Court declared the National Industrial Recovery Act

MORE PRIMING FOR THE PUMP

Chapter 14 | The Great Depression and the New Deal

unconstitutional on the grounds that the federal government had no power to interfere in businesses conducted within a single state. This was a major defeat for the First New Deal.

The Agricultural Adjustment Act (1933)

The **Agricultural Adjustment Act** or "**AAA**," was another recovery measure. Its purpose was to help farmers. To pay their expenses, farmers had kept growing more and more crops each year, but all this had done was to lower crop prices. The AAA provided incentives to farmers to limit their production.

The federal government offered farmers subsidies for planting fewer acres and killing surplus livestock. The money for the subsidies was taken from a special tax on food processors, such as millers. Much of the food taken from the farmers was turned over to relief agencies for distribution to the unemployed. Payments under the AAA helped many farmers save their farms. A separate New Deal agency provided mortgages to farmers at low rates.

The AAA succeeded in raising the prices of crops, as intended; however, in 1936 the Supreme Court declared the AAA unconstitutional on the same grounds that it had invalidated the National Industrial Recovery Act: it said the federal government had no authority to regulate economic activities carried on in a single state.

Tennessee Valley Authority (1933)

The **Tennessee Valley Authority**, or **TVA**, was a major experiment in public ownership. The South was the region hardest hit by the Depression. In many areas of the South, homes still lacked electricity or indoor plumbing. The Tennessee Valley was an impoverished region covering parts of seven Southern states. The TVA

The TVA spurred economic development in seven states.

built and maintained 21 large dams along the Tennessee River. These dams controlled floods, produced hydroelectricity, and manufactured fertilizers. The construction of dams and the introduction of conservation measures like the planting of trees brought greater prosperity to the region. Although the experiment was a success, Congress failed to extend this approach to other parts of the country.

The Securities Exchange Act (1934)

This reform measure created the **Security and Exchange Commission** (SEC), a new federal agency to oversee the operations of the stock market. Its role was to prevent fraud and guard against the conditions that had led to the stock market crash. Companies selling securities were required to provide accurate information to potential investors.

The Second New Deal

The Supreme Court struck down several of the First New Deal's programs, prompting President Roosevelt to modify his approach. The "**Second New Deal**" began in 1935. It was aimed more directly at reform. **Reform** measures aimed at remedying defects in the structure of the American economy, to make sure another severe depression would never occur again. Roosevelt felt that he had to reform the capitalist system in order to save it. The Second New Deal made great strides in labor reform and in creating a "safety net" to protect working Americans and their families.

Social Security Act (1935)

The **Social Security Act** was the single most important law passed by the New Deal. Americans continue to be protected by Social Security today, which now makes up a large part of the federal budget.

One of the reasons the Depression had caused so much human suffering was that Americans had no "safety net" to fall back on when they were struck by unemployment, illness, or a death in the family. Social Security changed all this by adopting measures already in existence in many European countries. It established the following:

(a) **Unemployment insurance**: Workers received unemployment insurance, paid out of a tax on employer payrolls.

(b) **Retirement benefits**: Employees were to receive monthly payments after their retirement, paid for by a special tax on their own wages and contributions made by their employer. The same fund provided benefits to their spouses and children in the event of an early death. Because employees paid in their own contributions to finance the program, it was not based on need and was not considered to be a relief program or form of charity.

(c) **Benefits for the disabled and orphaned**: Orphaned Americans and those with disabilities were eligible to receive special grants from Social Security.

National Labor Relations Act (1935)

This law, known as the "Wagner Act," replaced several provisions of the National Industrial Recovery Act, which had been declared unconstitutional.

The Wagner Act gave workers the right to form unions, to bargain collectively, and to submit their grievances to a new federal agency. Employers could not engage in "unfair" anti-union practices. By allowing workers to organize, Roosevelt hoped to push up wages, increase workers' purchasing power, and create fair working conditions.

Fair Labor Standards Act (1938)

This act set maximum working hours and a minimum wage, while it prohibited child labor in factories.

The Second Agricultural Adjustment Act (1938)

In 1938, Congress passed a second Agricultural Adjustment Act. Under this law, the federal government decided how much of a particular crop should be sold each year. Each farmer was then assigned a specific number of acres for planting that crop. After harvest, farmers' surpluses were stored by the federal government, until crop prices rose to what farmers had received 1909–1914.

Meanwhile, the government gave "loans" to farmers based on the value of their stored crops. Government experts also showed farmers new ways of preventing soil erosion.

The Historian's Apprentice

Complete the following chart of New Deal programs.

Type of Measure	Purpose/Description	Examples of Agencies/Programs
Relief		
Recovery		
Reform		

Challenges to the New Deal

The New Deal did not end the Depression, but the economy gradually began to improve. Roosevelt won a landslide victory in the 1936 Presidential election, with a majority in all but two states. He formed a new Democratic coalition composed of workers, the poor, African Americans and other minority groups, and the Democratic "Solid South."

Although the New Deal was generally popular, it faced criticism from two directions. Conservative critics charged Roosevelt with being a "socialist" and a "traitor to his class." They opposed government intervention in the economy.

On the other side, some liberal critics felt that Roosevelt was not doing enough. One critic, for example, wanted to give all citizens over 65 years old a pension of $200 a month, to be spent within the month. Another popular critic, the Catholic priest Father Coughlin, gave radio addresses demanding the nationalization of banks and utility companies.

Senator **Huey Long**, a former Governor of Louisiana, argued that New Deal agencies were too bureaucratic and confusing. He told audiences that Roosevelt had broken his campaign promise to tax the rich in order to help the poor, and that conditions in 1935 were almost as bad as they had been in 1933. Long proposed to give every American family an income of $5,000 a year, which was to be paid for by seizing the fortunes of the very rich. Long was popular and might have challenged Roosevelt in the 1936 election, but he was assassinated in September 1935.

> In Georgia, Governor Eugene Talmadge at first supported Roosevelt but turned against the New Deal, which he saw as a government "handout" and a challenge to states' rights. Talmadge believed that the New Deal gave too much power to the federal government and promoted socialism. He refused to accept New Deal programs that would have helped struggling Georgians. When Georgia's state legislature passed a bill creating old age pensions, Talmadge vetoed it: "I am opposed to all kinds of pensions, except a soldier's pension. I do not want to see the incentive of the American people to work and to lay up something for their old age destroyed."

The Historian's Apprentice

The following is from a radio broadcast by the liberal critic Huey Long:

> "And now it is with PWA's, CWA's, NRA's, AAA's, J-UG's, G-IN's, and every other flimsy combination that the country finds its affairs and business tangled to where no one can recognize it. More men are now out of work than ever; the debt of the United States has gone up another $10 billion. There is starvation; there is homelessness; there is misery on every hand and corner, but mind you, in the meantime, Mr. Roosevelt has had his way..."

from white Southern Democrats and was not vocal in supporting African Americans. Mrs. Roosevelt tried to make up for this. She felt that many New Deal agencies discriminated against African Americans, who were not receiving enough government help. She invited African Americans as guests to the White House, visited Howard University (an African-American university), visited African-American schools in Washington, and wrote about their conditions in her newspaper columns. In 1936, she spoke at the annual conventions of both the NAACP and Urban League. When a famed African-American singer was denied the use of a hall for a concert by the Daughters of the American Revolution, Mrs. Roosevelt arranged for the singer to give a public concert at the Lincoln Memorial. She also worked for a bill to make lynching a federal crime, although this failed to pass through Congress.

In summary, Eleanor Roosevelt changed the role of First Lady by being more visible in the public eye and by taking a firm stand on many social and political issues, including the defense of women, African Americans, young people, and the poor.

The Historian's Apprentice

Here are two excerpts from Eleanor Roosevelt's written and spoken work.

"What do ten million women want in public life? That question could be answered in ten million different ways. . . .

Frances Perkins as Labor Commissioner in New York [has] done much to make women feel that a really fine woman, well trained in her work, can give as good an account of her stewardship as any man, and eventually women, and perhaps even men, may come to feel that sex should not enter into the question of fitness for office. . . .

When it comes to the matter of having a woman as a member of the President's Cabinet, there are I think, many women who feel that the time has come to recognize the fact that women have practically just as many votes as men and deserve at least a certain amount of recognition.

Take the Department of Labor for instance. Why should not the Secretary of Labor be a woman, and would not a woman's point of view be valuable in the President's Council? There are many other places to which women may aspire, and the time will come when there will be new departments, some of which will undoubtedly need women at their heads. . . .

Do women want to take an active part in framing our laws? I think the answer to that is decidedly yes. There are more and more women elected to legislative bodies every year."

—Eleanor Roosevelt, "What Ten Million Women Want," *Home Magazine*, March 1932

"There was an old family—two old sisters and two old brothers—who had lived on a farm not far from us in the country just as long as I could remember... Well, I did not see them for two or three years. Then, one Election Day, I went to get them and I found one old lady in tears because that day one surviving brother had been taken to the insane asylum because the worry of how they were going to get enough to eat and enough to pay their taxes had finally driven him insane...

Well, I can hardly tell you how I felt. In the first place, I felt I had been such a bad neighbor that I did not know just what to do. I felt so guilty, and then it seemed to me as though the whole community was to blame. They had lived there all their lives; they had done their duty as citizens; they had been kind to the people about them; they had paid their taxes; they had given to the church and to the charities. All their lives they had done what good citizens should do and they simply had never been able to save. There always had been someone in the family who needed help; some young person to start; somebody who had gone to the city and who needed his rent paid. And if I had needed any argument to settle the question for me—that the community owes to its old people their own home as long as they possibly can live at home—these old neighbors would have supplied it....

And that is what an old age security law will do. It will allow the old people to end their days in happiness, and it will take the burden from the younger people who often have all the struggle that they can stand. It will end a bitter situation—bitter for the old people because they hate to be a burden on the young, and bitter for the young because they would like to give gladly but find themselves giving grudgingly and bitterly because it is taking away from what they need for the youth that is coming and is looking to them for support..."

—Eleanor Roosevelt, speech in favor of Social Security, 1934

1. In 1933, Franklin D. Roosevelt appointed Frances Perkins as Secretary of Labor. Perkins became the first female Cabinet member. How would Eleanor Roosevelt have felt about this appointment?
2. How persuasive were Roosevelt's arguments on social security?
3. What do these two excerpts reveal about Eleanor Roosevelt's views of her role as First Lady?

The New Deal Comes to an End

Roosevelt's court-packing plan alienated Southern Democrats, who refused to back further New Deal measures. In 1936, just when the economy seemed to be recovering, Roosevelt therefore cut government spending. The result was an immediate worsening of the Depression. Roosevelt quickly resumed federal spending and the Works Progress Administration began rehiring more of the unemployed. The New Deal itself, however, never returned the country to full employment. This only occurred as America prepared to enter World War II. You will learn more about that in the next chapter.

For the Georgia Milestones EOC Assessment, you should know that:

- The causes of the stock market crash of 1929 and the Great Depression included overproduction, under-consumption, the effects of stock market speculation, and shaky banking.

- The tearing up of prairie grasses and breaking up the top soil through plowing on the Great Plains, when combined with droughts in the early 1930s, led to the "Dust Bowl." The disaster thus had both natural and human causes. This catastrophe led many farmers to lose their farms and migrate westward to California.

- The Great Depression led to widespread unemployment, which had social and political effects, including the loss of savings when banks failed, homelessness, and the rise of shantytowns known as "Hoovervilles."

- Franklin D. Roosevelt won the Presidential election in 1932 by promising Americans a "New Deal." His efforts at relief, recovery, and reform were reflected in various New Deal programs. Relief measures provided temporary support to help people survive the crisis. Recovery measures were to help the economy get moving again. Reform measures were to prevent future depressions.

- The Social Security Act was important to the Second New Deal and provided a federal "safety net" to working Americans by providing old age pensions, unemployment insurance, and benefits for orphans and those with disabilities.

- Major political challenges to the New Deal arose from those who thought it expanded federal power too much, from those who thought it didn't do enough to redistribute income and help the poor, and finally from the Supreme Court, which invalidated several early New Deal programs. Roosevelt's "court-packing" plan aroused opposition across the country, but in its aftermath, the Supreme Court stopped ruling against New Deal programs.

- Eleanor Roosevelt changed the role of the "First Lady" by playing an active role in promoting New Deal programs for those in need, including women, minorities, and young Americans.

Name _____

Read the names and terms below. Then decide in which group each name or term belongs and place it in the proper column.

- Buying on margin
- Stock market speculation
- Overproduction
- Under-consumption
- Black Tuesday
- Herbert Hoover
- "Hoovervilles"
- Bonus Expeditionary Force
- Reconstruction Finance Corporation
- Hoover Dam
- Foreclosures
- Dust Bowl
- Overfarming
- Drought
- Okies
- Franklin D. Roosevelt
- Fireside chats
- Relief, Recovery, Reform
- Bank Holiday
- National Recovery Act
- National Recovery Administration (NRA)
- Agricultural Adjustment Act (AAA)
- Civilian Conservation Corps (CCC)
- Works Progress Administration (WPA)
- Federal Deposit Insurance Corporation (FDIC)
- Social Security Act
- Tennessee Valley Authority (TVA)
- National Labor Relations Act (Wagner Act)
- Court-packing plan
- Dorothea Lange
- First Lady
- *It's Up to the Women*
- Concern for African Americans

Causes of the Great Depression	Conditions during the Great Depression	Presidency of Herbert Hoover	Dust Bowl

First New Deal (1933–1935)	Second New Deal (1935–1937)	Eleanor Roosevelt

Chapter 14 | The Great Depression and the New Deal

Name _____

Complete the following chart.

Event or Policy	Description or Explanation
Reasons for the Stock Market Crash and Great Depression	
Causes of the Dust Bowl	
New Deal: Relief, Recovery and Reform	
Social Security Act	
Impact of Eleanor Roosevelt on the Role of the "First Lady"	
Challenges to the New Deal	

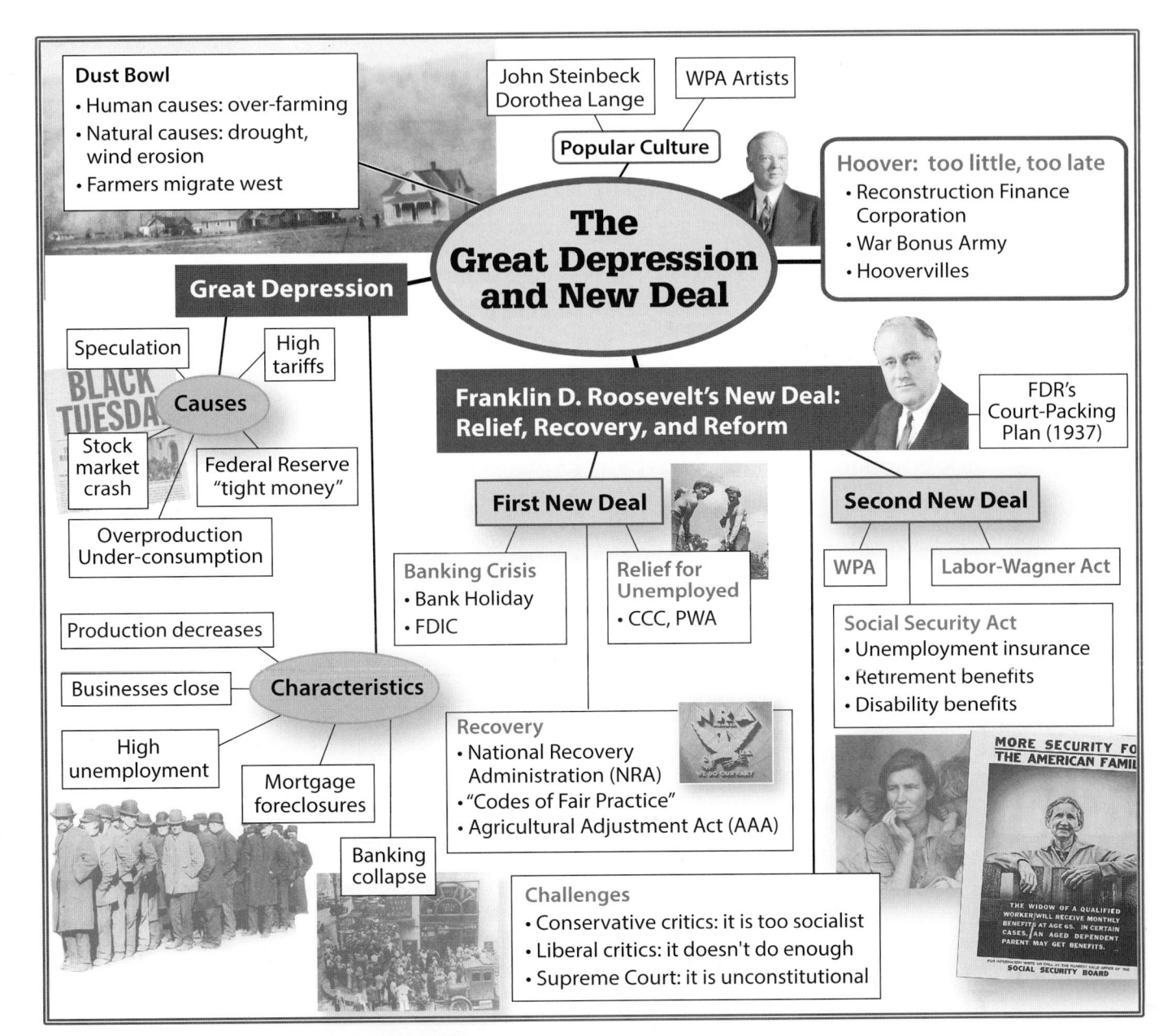

The Great Depression and New Deal

Dust Bowl
- Human causes: over-farming
- Natural causes: drought, wind erosion
- Farmers migrate west

Popular Culture
- John Steinbeck
- Dorothea Lange
- WPA Artists

Hoover: too little, too late
- Reconstruction Finance Corporation
- War Bonus Army
- Hoovervilles

Great Depression

Causes
- Speculation
- High tariffs
- Stock market crash
- Federal Reserve "tight money"
- Overproduction Under-consumption

Characteristics
- Production decreases
- Businesses close
- High unemployment
- Mortgage foreclosures
- Banking collapse

Franklin D. Roosevelt's New Deal: Relief, Recovery, and Reform

FDR's Court-Packing Plan (1937)

First New Deal

Banking Crisis
- Bank Holiday
- FDIC

Relief for Unemployed
- CCC, PWA

Recovery
- National Recovery Administration (NRA)
- "Codes of Fair Practice"
- Agricultural Adjustment Act (AAA)

Challenges
- Conservative critics: it is too socialist
- Liberal critics: it doesn't do enough
- Supreme Court: it is unconstitutional

Second New Deal
- WPA
- Labor-Wagner Act

Social Security Act
- Unemployment insurance
- Retirement benefits
- Disability benefits

Chapter 14 | The Great Depression and the New Deal

What Do You Know?

SSUSH17a

1. Use the diagram to answer the question.

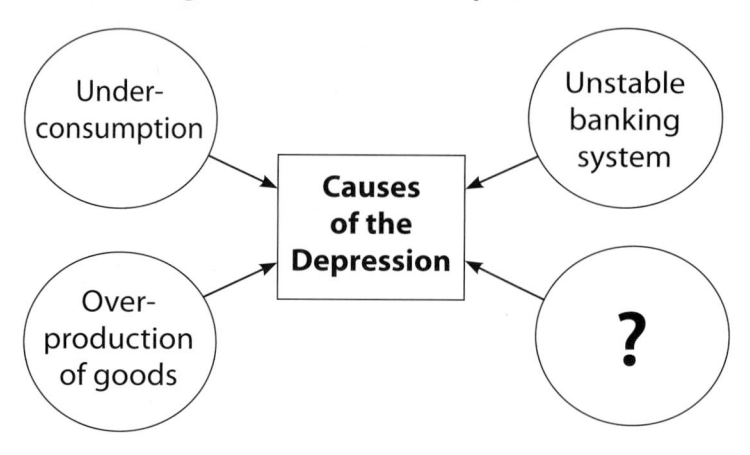

   ```
   Under-consumption ──┐
                        ├─→ Causes of the Depression ←── Unstable banking system
   Over-production ────┘                              ←── ?
   of goods
   ```

   Which phrase BEST completes the diagram?

   A. Conflicts in Europe
   B. Dropping Food Prices
   C. Stock Market Speculation
   D. Creation of New Technologies

SSUSH17c

2. Use the photograph below to answer the question.

   The photograph shows unemployed men waiting at a private "soup kitchen" in Chicago in 1931. Which statement BEST explains this situation?

   A. The prohibition of alcoholic drinks had led to a massive loss of jobs in cities.
   B. Soup kitchens served to help unemployed workers find jobs.
   C. President Hoover gave federal assistance through private soup kitchens.
   D. There were no federal programs providing direct relief to the unemployed before the New Deal.

Chapter 14 | The Great Depression and the New Deal

SSUSH17b

3. Use the diagram to answer the question.

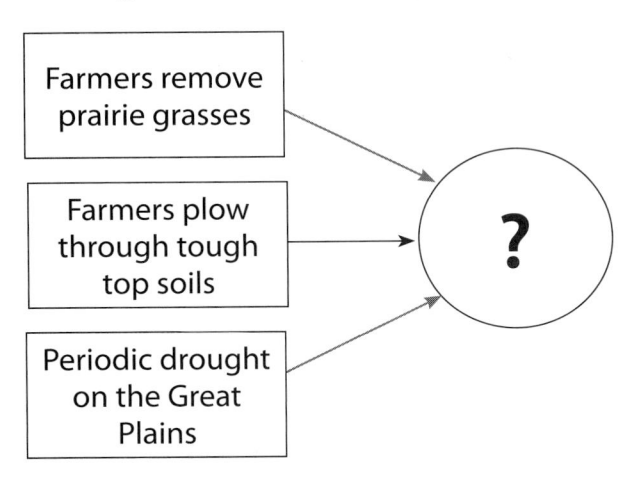

```
[Farmers remove prairie grasses] ──┐
                                    │
[Farmers plow through tough top soils] ──→ ( ? )
                                    │
[Periodic drought on the Great Plains] ──┘
```

Which phrase BEST completes the diagram?

A. Creation of Dust Bowl
B. Birth of the Populist Party
C. Falling prices for farmers' crops
D. Increased competition between farmers and ranchers

SSUSH17b

4. Use the photograph to answer the question.

Stratford, Texas, in 1935

What was one effect of such events on the Great Plains in the 1930s?

A. Local banks profited from farm foreclosures.
B. Many farmers from the Plains migrated to California.
C. The New Deal suspended federal assistance to farmers.
D. Farm production increased because the dust clouds brought fertile soil.

Chapter 14 | The Great Depression and the New Deal

SSUSH18a

5. Use the list to answer the question.

> - Homeowner's Loan Corporation
> - Public Works Administration
> - Civil Works Administration
> - Civilian Conservation Corps
> - Works Progress Administration

What do the elements in the list have in common?

A. They were federal agencies created by Herbert Hoover.

B. They were New Deal agencies primarily aimed at relief.

C. They were New Deal agencies primarily aimed at recovery.

D. They were New Deal agencies primarily aimed at reform.

SSUSH18b

6. Use the excerpt to answer the question.

> Today a hope of many years' standing is in large part fulfilled. The civilization of the past hundred years, with its startling industrial changes, has tended more and more to make life insecure. Young people have come to wonder what would be their lot when they came to old age. The man with a job has wondered how long the job would last. . . .
>
> We can never insure one hundred percent of the population against one hundred percent of the hazards and vicissitudes of life, but we have tried to frame a law which will give some measure of protection to the average citizen and to his family against the loss of a job and against poverty-ridden old age.
>
> —President Franklin D. Roosevelt, August 14, 1935

How does the program referred to in the excerpt above continue to affect Americans today?

A. American investors rely on the Securities and Exchange Commission to prevent fraud on the stock market.

B. Americans rely on the Federal Deposit Insurance Corporation to guarantee their deposits in U.S. banks.

C. Working Americans depend on the Social Security Administration for income after they retire.

D. Residents in several Southern states depend on the Tennessee Valley Authority to prevent floods and generate hydroelectricity.

SSUSH17b

7. Use the photographs to answer the question.

   Which of the following was a major cause of the conditions in the 1930s depicted in the photographs?

   A. tree-felling by logging companies

   B. over-farming on the Great Plains

   C. the massacre of buffalo on the Great Plains

   D. insufficient irrigation in the Southwest

SSUSH18c

8. How did Senator Huey Long's approach to the Depression differ from that of the New Deal?

   A. Long opposed increased federal spending.

   B. Long promised an income of $2,000 to every family to be financed by taxes on the rich.

   C. Long called for the government ownership of banks and utilities.

   D. Long accused Roosevelt of being a "traitor" to his class.

SSUSH18c

9. On what grounds did the U.S. Supreme Court rule that several New Deal programs were unconstitutional?

   A. The federal government had no right to interfere in businesses operating in a single state.

   B. New Deal programs were interfering too much with interstate commerce.

   C. New Deal programs failed to protect the rights of minorities.

   D. The federal government needed to take stronger action to promote the general welfare.

Chapter 14 | The Great Depression and the New Deal

SSUSH18c

10. Examine the cartoon to answer the question.

    Based on the cartoon, what was the reaction to President Roosevelt's 1937 "court-packing" plan?

    A. The public wanted Roosevelt to act more quickly to save New Deal programs.

    B. Congress handed Roosevelt his first major defeat by upholding the separation of powers.

    C. A majority of Americans agreed that many of the Supreme Court Justices were too old.

    D. Most Americans agreed with the Supreme Court that the NRA and AAA were unconstitutional.

SSUSH18a

11. Use the graph below to answer the question.

    U.S. Unemployment Rate, 1930–1945

    What inference can be made from the data on the graph?

    A. President Hoover's policies were more effective than the New Deal in fighting unemployment.

    B. By 1938, the New Deal had successfully brought unemployment down to pre-Depression levels.

    C. New Deal policies failed to improve the economy because of the interference of the Supreme Court.

    D. Despite Roosevelt's New Deal programs, the unemployment rate remained high throughout the 1930s.

SSUSH18d

12. What impact did Eleanor Roosevelt have on the role of "First Lady"?

    A. She preserved the traditional role of First Lady despite attacks by critics.

    B. She turned the position into an office for fund raising and campaigning for her husband.

    C. She made it a position for hosting dinner parties to diplomats to enhance America's status abroad.

    D. She changed its role by using her position to champion those Americans most in need.

Chapter 14 | The Great Depression and the New Deal

CHAPTER 15 America in World War II

SSUSH19 What were the origins, major developments, and the domestic impact of World War II?

   a. What were the origins of U.S. entry in the war, including the Lend-Lease Act and the Japanese attack on Pearl Harbor?

   b. What were the main events of the war in the Pacific Theater, including the difficulties that Americans faced in delivering weapons, food, and medical supplies to troops, the Battle of Midway, the Manhattan Project, and the dropping of two atomic bombs on Japan?

   c. What were the main events of the war in the European Theater, including the difficulties that Americans faced in delivering weapons, food, and medical supplies to their troops, the Allied landing on the beaches of Normandy on D-Day, and the fall of Berlin?

   d. What was the domestic impact of the war, including wartime mobilization, rationing, wartime conversion, and the role of women and African Americans in the war effort?

   e. Was Roosevelt's use of executive powers during the war justified, including his executive orders for the integration of workers in the defense industries and for the relocation and internment of Japanese Americans living along the West Coast?

> Note: For the Georgia Milestones EOC Assessment you will not be required to know most of the details in the next two sections about the origins of World War II in Europe and U.S. neutrality; however, these sections provide important background information about U.S. involvement in World War II. The EOC Assessment will require you to know about: (1) the Lend-Lease Act; and (2) the Japanese attack on Pearl Harbor.

The Origins of World War II in Europe

The Rise of Dictatorships in Europe

In Germany, the **Nazi** (National Socialist) Party was founded shortly after World War I. The Nazis and their leader, **Adolf Hitler**, believed that Germans were a superior race, destined to rule over Europe. Hitler and the Nazis felt a special hatred for Jews, whom they blamed for Germany's defeat in World War I. The Nazi Party also taught the doctrine of absolute personal obedience to the will of the party leader, or *"Führer."* They despised weakness and were determined to use German technological superiority and military strength to achieve mastery of Europe.

Although the Great Depression had begun in the United States, it quickly spread to Europe, where German unemployment reached catastrophic proportions. Membership soared in the Nazi Party. People were looking for radical solutions to their country's problems. In the 1933 elections, the Nazis received more votes than any other party—though they were still not a majority. Hitler was appointed as the head of the German government by conservative politicians who believed they could control him. Only one month after his appointment, the building housing the German legislature, or *Reichstag*, was set on fire by an arsonist. The Nazis themselves may have been responsible for the *Reichstag* fire. The German legislature granted Hitler full dictatorial powers in the emergency—powers that he never surrendered. The Nazis began murdering opponents or imprisoning them in "concentration camps." They also began persecuting Jews, while all German institutions from unions to schools were brought under Nazi control or closed. Opposition newspapers and political parties were banned. In a special ceremony, the German army took an oath of personal allegiance to Hitler.

The Failure of the League of Nations

The League of Nations was charged with responsibility for preventing another war. However, it proved to be powerless before the aggressive acts of Hitler and other dictators. The League was based on the idea of **collective security**—that peaceful nations should band together against aggressors to prevent future wars. Yet the League had no army of its own and depended on its members' actions. The United States and the Soviet Union failed to become members of the League; Germany and Japan were originally members but left the League in 1933. Hitler began to rebuild German military power in open violation of the Treaty of Versailles.

The Failure of Appeasement

In February 1938, Hitler annexed **Austria**, the small German-speaking republic that was left when the Austro-Hungarian Empire dissolved

Chapter 15 | America in World War II

in 1918. Next, Hitler demanded the **Sudetenland**, a part of Czechoslovakia with a large number of German-speaking people. France and Britain promised to protect Czechoslovakia, despite the fact that Hitler threatened war. British and French leaders met with Hitler in the German town of Munich to work out a solution. At the **Munich Conference** in September 1938, British and French leaders, seeking to avoid war, agreed to hand over the western part of Czechoslovakia to Germany. This policy of giving in to the demands of a potential enemy has since become known as "**appeasement**." Neville Chamberlain, the British Prime Minister, returned to London promising his countrymen "peace in our time." However, his policy of appeasement only encouraged Hitler to make further demands. The annexation of the Sudetenland left the rest of Czechoslovakia weak and defenseless. In March 1939, Hitler persuaded the Slovaks in the east to declare their independence. Hitler sent a German army to occupy Prague (*the Czech capital city*) and what was left of the country. Czech leaders surrendered without resistance.

World War II Begins: The German Invasion of Poland

Next, Hitler began making demands on Poland. He claimed the city of **Danzig** (present-day Gdańsk), which contained a large number of German-speaking residents.

By now, British and French leaders had reached the conclusion that Hitler's goal was the mastery of Europe. This time they resisted his demand and pledged to protect Poland against German aggression. Hitler responded by negotiating a secret treaty with the Soviet dictator, **Joseph Stalin**. Under the terms of the

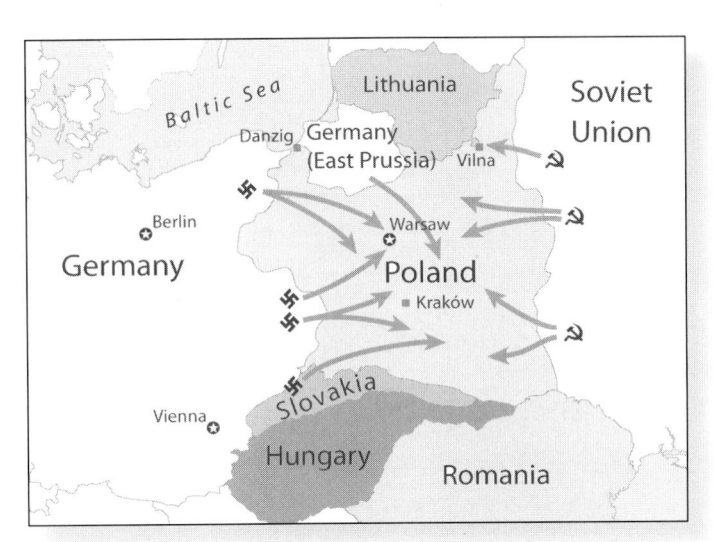

In 1939, Poland was invaded by Germany from the west and the Soviet Union from the east

Nazi-Soviet Pact, signed in August 1939, Hitler and Stalin agreed to divide Poland between themselves. In September 1939, Germany invaded Poland from the west, while the Soviet Union invaded Poland from the east. Britain and France responded by declaring war on Germany, and **World War II** began in Europe.

The German army had developed new tactics for waging warfare. During World War I, troops had remained stationary in trenches, unable to advance without being mowed down by machine-gun fire. In this new type of warfare, planes, tanks, motorized artillery, motorized troop carriers, and radio communications were used together to make rapid advances. German planes bombed Polish cities and troops from the air. German tanks and motorized artillery invaded Polish territory by land, followed by infantry forces. Because of the speed of the German advance, this new form of warfare came to be known as ***Blitzkrieg***, or "lightning warfare."

The Fall of France

During the first months of 1940, Western Europe remained quiet. Then in April, Germany invaded Denmark and Norway; in May, the Germans

Chapter 15 | America in World War II

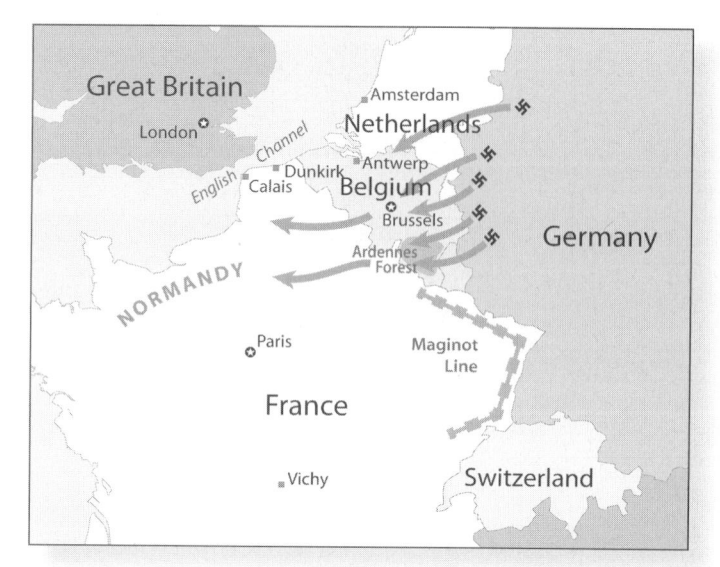

The advance of the German army and the defeat of France in June 1940

attacked the Netherlands, Belgium, Luxembourg, and France. German troops avoided the strong French fortifications built along the border between France and Germany by marching through the Ardennes Forest and across Belgium. By June 1940, the French were forced to surrender.

The French defeat happened so quickly that British forces on the European Continent were trapped at the French coastal town of Dunkirk. **Winston Churchill,** a strong anti-Nazi, replaced Chamberlain as British Prime Minister at the beginning of May. Churchill refused to negotiate with the Nazis. Instead, he sent private merchant ships, fishing boats, and pleasure craft across the English Channel to Dunkirk to ferry British and some French troops onto larger British destroyers (*small warships*) in order to bring them safely home. More than 330,000 troops were eventually ferried across the Channel.

The "Battle of Britain"

Having conquered most of Western Europe, Hitler now attempted to use his air force to bomb the British into submission. German planes bombed London and other British cities to create a sense of terror. However, the fighter planes of the Royal Air Force were able to shoot down many of the attacking German planes, while the civilian population endured these attacks by crowding into bomb shelters or the deep shafts of the London Underground (*subway*). The British also used the new invention of **radar** to detect arriving planes and identify where attacks were likely to occur.

The Historian's Apprentice

1. Make your own illustrated chart or graphic organizer showing the causes of World War II in Europe. Classify each cause as social, political, or economic.

2. Hold a class debate on this topic: "Resolved: World War II could have been prevented." Evaluate the policies of appeasement, the weaknesses of the League of Nations, and U.S. isolationism. Would more active measures have prevented the expansion of Nazi Germany without war? If so, what might the world look like today?

3. Make an illustrated timeline of the events of World War II in Europe from the German invasion of Poland to the Battle of Britain.

America Maintains Neutrality

After World War I, most Americans were deeply disillusioned from their involvement in the war. In the 1920s, they returned to their traditional policy of isolationism—refusing to join the League of Nations, insisting on the collection of war debts from Britain and France, passing high tariffs, and restricting immigration from Europe. In the early 1930s, Americans became too absorbed in the problems of the Great Depression to become very active in world affairs.

The Neutrality Acts of 1935–1937

As the likelihood of war in Europe grew, Congress passed a series of laws designed to keep Americans out of the conflict. The United States had been drawn into World War I in part because Americans had been killed on Allied ships like the *Lusitania*. German submarines had attacked ships carrying supplies to Britain and France. The Neutrality Acts aimed at avoiding a repetition of these events. They were passed before World War II in Europe had even begun.

- **Neutrality Act of 1935**: The first Neutrality Act was passed for a limited period of six months. It prohibited Americans from sending "arms, ammunition, and implements of war" to foreign nations that the President proclaimed were at war. The act also warned Americans traveling on the ships of nations at war that they did so at their own risk.

- **Neutrality Act of 1936**: This act renewed the Neutrality Act of 1935 for another 14 months. Since it did not cover civil wars or prohibit the sale of nonmilitary goods, it permitted American companies to sell trucks and oil to parties in the Spanish Civil War, which was being fought at that time. However, it prohibited American loans to nations at war.

- **Neutrality Act of 1937**: This act extended the prohibition on the sale of arms to parties engaged in civil wars, including the Spanish Civil War. It also prohibited Americans from traveling on the ships of nations at war. However, the new act permitted, at the discretion of the President, the sale of nonmilitary goods to countries at war on a "**cash-and-carry**" basis—in other words, so long as the buyer paid in cash and arranged their transportation. When Japan invaded China in July 1937, Roosevelt refused to apply the terms of the Neutrality Act since war was not officially declared. This allowed Americans to continue sending supplies to China.

The Neutrality Act of 1939

Even after the Nazi invasion of Poland in September 1939, most Americans still opposed involvement in European conflicts. A majority in Congress, however, favored helping Britain and France with all measures short of war. Because the Neutrality Act of 1937 forbade the sales of arms to nations at war, Congress passed a new Neutrality Act in November 1939. This new act prohibited Americans from entering war zones. It also renewed the "cash-and-carry" provision of the 1937 act and extended it to include the sale of arms. Roosevelt's goal was to help the Western Allies as much as possible, while keeping the United States out of war.

America Begins Preparations for War

Americans began making preparations for war, just in case they were drawn into the conflict. Congress increased its spending on the army and navy. Shortly after the German defeat of France, Congress passed the first peacetime draft. All men between the ages of 21 and 35 had to register and became eligible for one year of military service.

The Lend-Lease Act of 1941

> Note: You are required to know about the Lend-Lease Act for the Georgia Milestones EOC Assessment.

In the 1940 Presidential election, Roosevelt broke with tradition by running for a third term. Both Roosevelt and his Republican opponent advocated strong defense measures in their campaigns. By the time of Roosevelt's re-election, the British were desperate for food and arms. In December 1940, Roosevelt proposed in one of his fireside chats that America, as the "**arsenal of democracy**," should supply arms to the British. The British could pay for the arms later, he suggested, or simply return them after the war was over. "There is far less chance of the United States getting into war," the President explained to his listeners, "if we do all we can now to support the nations defending themselves against attack..."

In March 1941, Roosevelt signed the **Lend-Lease Act**. This act repealed parts of the Neutrality Act of 1939 and authorized the United States to sell, lease, or lend war materials to "any country whose defense the President deems vital to the defense of the United States." As Roosevelt had proposed, the law permitted the British to return these supplies ("lend") after the war was over or pay for them at a future date ("lease").

Congress also voted new funds for the production of ships, tanks, planes, and other weapons. American battleships began protecting British merchant ships carrying American supplies across the Atlantic. Critics of the program feared that it might draw the United States into the war. Most Americans, however, supported Roosevelt's view that the United States must help beleaguered Britain. They hoped to keep the United States out of the war by strengthening British resistance to Nazi tyranny.

The Historian's Apprentice

1. How did the Lend-Lease Act differ from the earlier Neutrality Acts?
2. Why did Congress pass the Lend-Lease Act if it wanted to keep Americans out of war?

The Four Freedoms and the Atlantic Charter

In his State of the Union address in 1941, President Roosevelt told Americans that he hoped to establish a world based on **Four Freedoms**:

1. "freedom of speech and expression"
2. "freedom of every person to worship God in his own way"
3. "freedom from want"
4. "freedom from fear," by which he especially meant freedom from the fear of war.

Several months later, Roosevelt secretly met with British Prime Minister **Winston Churchill** aboard a ship in the Atlantic off the coast of Canada. Roosevelt was convinced that American entry into the war was inevitable. Roosevelt and Churchill discussed their long-term objectives for a postwar world. They announced that they sought no territorial gains and wished to restore self-government to conquered peoples. They also favored free trade, freedom of the seas, economic development, social security, and a reduction of armaments. Finally, they agreed that a new international organization should replace the League of Nations.

The Japanese Attack on Pearl Harbor

Roosevelt came to believe that U.S. entry into the war would be necessary to defeat Hitler and save democracy. But he knew that he had to win wider public support before taking the country to war, so he proceeded in small steps. In 1941, armed American merchant ships began carrying supplies directly to Britain while U.S. troops occupied Greenland and Iceland. It appeared as though American involvement in the war was just a matter of time.

Increasing U.S.-Japanese Tensions

Surprisingly, it was events in Asia, not Europe, that finally brought Americans into the war. The military leaders of Imperial Japan, like the German Nazis, believed they belonged to a superior race destined to rule over others. They had occupied Manchuria in 1931 and invaded the rest of China in 1937. Despite these aggressive acts, Roosevelt had not restricted American trade with Japan. In fact, Japan continued to import most of its oil from the United States.

Impressed by Hitler's stunning victories in Europe, the Japanese entered into a defensive alliance with Germany and Italy in September 1940. In June 1941, Hitler suddenly abandoned his pact with Stalin and invaded the Soviet Union. Japanese leaders debated whether to declare war on the Soviet Union or to advance southwards, seizing rice fields and rubber plantations, cutting supply routes to China, and extending their empire in the direction of the oil fields of the Dutch East Indies (present-day Indonesia).

Japanese leaders decided to send their forces into Southern Indochina. Roosevelt reacted by freezing Japanese assets in the United States and placing new restrictions on sales of oil, iron ore, steel, and rubber to Japan. This left Japan with only a limited supply of oil. Roosevelt offered to restore normal trade relations, but only if the Japanese withdrew their forces from China and Indochina. The Japanese refused this demand.

Japan Plans a Surprise Attack

Japanese leaders decided instead to seize the Dutch East Indies so that they would have their own oil fields. They reasoned that such a daring act would first require their control of certain strategic locations—including Hong Kong, Singapore, and the Philippines. Realizing that these actions would bring the United States into the war, they decided to launch a surprise attack on America first. Prime Minister **Hideki**

Tojo and other Japanese leaders believed that an attack on the naval base at Pearl Harbor would catch American forces unprepared and eliminate American naval power in the Pacific for a limited period of time. During this time, Japan could consolidate its conquests and strengthen its position. Japanese leaders believed they would then be able to negotiate a compromise peace with the United States, leaving Japan in control of East Asia.

The Attack at Pearl Harbor

In early December 1941, six aircraft carriers, a fleet of Japanese warships, and 360 airplanes secretly sailed north of the island of Oahu in Hawaii. The ships sailed without radio communication to avoid detection. The commander's ship proudly flew the same flag that had sailed with the Japanese fleet that defeated Russia in 1905. On the morning of December 7, 1941, two separate waves of Japanese airplanes attacked the U.S. Pacific fleet stationed in **Pearl Harbor**, Hawaii. The surprise attack destroyed six ships and 180 aircraft, took the lives of 2,403 Americans, and wounded 1,178 others. Almost half of those killed were on the *U.S.S. Arizona* when it was hit and sunk. The Japanese attackers rejoiced at their success, although they failed to destroy the repair yards or vast storage tanks used to refuel ships, and no aircraft carriers were at Pearl Harbor at the time. American opinion was enraged. The next day, President Roosevelt asked Congress for a declaration of war on Japan.

Japanese airplanes bomb the U.S. naval fleet at Pearl Harbor

426 Chapter 15 | America in World War II

The Historian's Apprentice

President Roosevelt addressed Congress the day after the attack:

> "Yesterday, December 7, 1941—a date which will live in infamy—the United States of America was suddenly and deliberately attacked by naval and air forces of the Empire of Japan.
>
> The United States was at peace with that nation, and, at the solicitation of Japan, was still in conversation with its government and its Emperor looking toward the maintenance of peace in the Pacific. . . .
>
> [T]he distance of Hawaii from Japan makes it obvious that the attack was deliberately planned many days or even weeks ago. During the intervening time the Japanese government has deliberately sought to deceive the United States by false statements and expressions of hope for continued peace.
>
> The attack yesterday on the Hawaiian Islands has caused severe damage to American naval and military forces. I regret to tell you that very many American lives have been lost.
>
> In addition, American ships have been reported torpedoed on the high seas between San Francisco and Honolulu. Yesterday the Japanese government also launched an attack against Malaya. Last night Japanese forces attacked Hong Kong, Guam, the Philippine Islands, and Wake Island. And this morning the Japanese attacked Midway Island.
>
> Japan has, therefore, undertaken a surprise offensive extending throughout the Pacific area. The facts of yesterday and today speak for themselves. I ask that the Congress declare that since the unprovoked and dastardly attack by Japan on Sunday, December seventh, a state of war has existed between the United States and the Japanese Empire."
>
> —Franklin D. Roosevelt before a Joint Session of Congress, December 8, 1941

1. Imagine you are a member of Congress who has just heard President Roosevelt's speech. Write a message to the voters in your district giving your views on the attack and how the country should respond.
2. Why did Japanese leaders decide to launch the attack on Pearl Harbor?
3. In what ways was the attack on Pearl Harbor similar to the more recent attacks of September 11, 2001? How were these attacks different? Prepare your answer in the form of a chart or Venn diagram.

Four days later, Germany and Italy, acting as the allies of Japan, declared war on the United States. Americans were now officially at war on two fronts: the Atlantic and the Pacific.

Chapter 15 | America in World War II

The United States at War: Mobilization on the Home Front

In 1941, Americans faced enemies more ruthless and terrible than at any other time in our history. With their doctrines of racial superiority and glorification of conquest, Nazi Germany, Imperial Japan, and Fascist Italy showed no mercy to the peoples they subdued. Their aim was world conquest and the extermination of many of their enemies through **genocide** (*murder of an entire people*). World War II became a brutal contest to the death between the **Allied powers** (Britain, the Soviet Union, and the United States) and the **Axis powers** (Germany, Japan, and Italy). The U.S. government now had to mobilize American manpower and production to meet enormous wartime needs. (**Mobilization** refers to putting resources to use for a particular purpose, especially getting troops and supplies ready for war.)

The Draft

After Pearl Harbor, the draft was extended to all able-bodied men between the ages of 18 and 45. The **Selective Service System**, with more than 6,000 local draft boards, was set up to oversee this system. One out of every ten Americans ended up in uniform during the war. By the time the war was over, more than 15 million men had voluntarily enlisted or been drafted.

For the first time, women were also permitted to enlist. The **Women's Army Corps**, or "WACs," was established in 1942. WACs received uniforms and underwent basic training, although they did not serve in combat. WACS plotted aircraft paths, operated radios and telephone switchboards, organized supplies, drove army vehicles, and worked as stenographers, typists, and clerks. The Navy established their own women's corps; another 57,000 women served as nurses in the Army Nurse Corps.

Minorities also played an important role in America's fighting forces. A million African Americans served, although they were placed in segregated units and were not sent into combat until late in the war. The **Tuskegee Airmen**, a unit of African-American fighter pilots, flew more than 1,500 missions in Europe. American Indians also played a critical role. **Najavo "code talkers"** used the Navajo language to create secret codes in the Pacific campaign that Japanese code-breakers could not decipher.

Wartime Conversion and Production

Among America's greatest contributions to the Allied war effort was its wartime production. Even before the war, American productive capacity greatly exceeded that of the other powers: U.S. coal production, for example, was double that of Germany. In 1937, Japan had manufactured 26,000 cars and Germany 330,000; in the same year, the United States had produced 4.8 million. During the war, American farms and factories were protected from bombing or invasion by distance and the oceans. America truly became, as Roosevelt had foreseen, the "arsenal of democracy."

Chapter 15 | America in World War II

New federal agencies sprang up to manage the sprawling wartime economy, just as during World War I and the New Deal. The **War Production Board** was set up to ease the **conversion** (*change*) from peacetime to wartime production. A hundred billion dollars in government contracts were awarded to private industry within the first six months of the war. An executive from General Motors was placed in charge of overall production. Shipyards in Richmond, California, built new "Liberty Ships" to carry men and supplies. Before long, a new ship was being rolled out every four and a half days. In Michigan, Henry Ford's plants began turning out thousands of bombers instead of cars. The **Office of War Mobilization** was created in 1943 to oversee the allocation of both materials and manpower. It supervised the War Production Board and other wartime agencies.

The demand for war goods finally brought the Great Depression to an end. The draft, combined with the expansion of production, ended unemployment. Large numbers of workers entered the armed services and were sent overseas. Women, African Americans, and other minority workers stepped in to fill the gaps left by the men in uniform. For the first time, women took jobs in heavy industry. African Americans continued to migrate to Northern cities, where many found work in war industries.

Food was desperately needed by American troops, by the Allies in Europe, and by American consumers. Crop prices rose, helping farmers. Farm production increased based on improved techniques and the cultivation of new areas. Areas of the former Dust Bowl enjoyed a recovery due to greater rainfall, better plowing techniques, and the increased demand.

Rationing

The War Production Board found it necessary to **ration** essential goods like gasoline, heating fuel, metals, and rubber. Eventually, canned, frozen, and processed foods were also rationed to ensure enough food for the soldiers. On the home front, people received **ration booklets** with coupons. Each rationed item was given a point value. Consumers paid money to the seller to cover the purchase of the product, but they also had to give the seller ration coupons to make the purchase. Consumers could buy no more of a good than the coupons in their ration books allowed. Many Americans grew their own fruits and vegetables in "**Victory Gardens**," so that more food would be available for the troops.

Paying for the War

The cost of the war to the United States was over $300 billion—more than eight times that of World War I. Almost half of this was paid for by tax receipts. In 1939, only 4 million Americans filed personal income tax returns. They paid a total of $1 billion in income taxes. By 1945, there were 43 million taxpayers who paid $40 billion in income taxes. The practice of withholding taxes from workers' payrolls, a practice that affects most Americans today, was also introduced during the war.

Expenses not paid for by tax revenues were financed by borrowing. Patriotic Americans bought "war bonds," which were repaid with interest by the government after the war was over. Only a quarter of these war bonds were sold to individuals: most were sold to banks and other financial institutions.

Information and Propaganda

The federal government made efforts to control the flow of information and maintain popular support. The **Office of War Information** (OWI) created posters, censored newsreels and even produced its own radio programs to promote patriotism and boost the war effort. The Office of War Information set up a "Motion Picture Bureau" in Hollywood to review movie scripts. Even children's comic books were recruited in the war effort.

The Historian's Apprentice

1. Make a chart or diagram showing the measures Americans took to mobilize for the war.
2. How were the steps taken to mobilize for war in 1941–1945 similar to and different from the steps taken in 1917–1918?

The Internment of Japanese Americans

Many Americans on the West Coast feared that the 120,000 Japanese Americans living in the United States might commit acts of sabotage. Many of these Japanese Americans were from families that had been living in the United States for generations.

On February 19, 1942, President Roosevelt signed **Executive Order 9066**. This order permitted military commanders to designate "military areas" from which groups of people might be excluded. In May 1942, the Western Defense Commander ordered all persons of Japanese ancestry living in a 100-mile wide zone along the West Coast to move to "relocation centers" farther inland, where they were required to remain until the end of the war. Most of these Japanese Americans were forced to sell their property and belongings on very short notice. Internment camps were established, in which the relocated families lived in wooden barracks surrounded by barbed wire, in primitive and crowded conditions. Roosevelt justified this forced relocation as a military necessity even though there was no actual evidence of acts of disloyalty. In contrast,

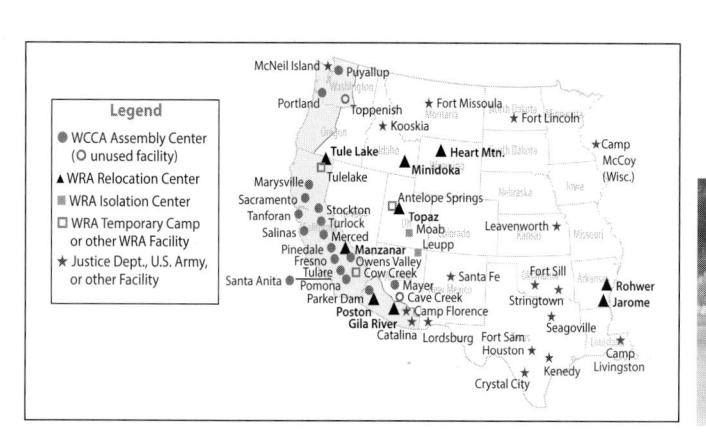

Locations of Japanese-American internment camps

Japanese-American family awaiting internment in a camp shown above

430   Chapter 15 | America in World War II

only a few Italian Americans and German Americans were subject to internment during the war. Nor were any steps taken against the many Japanese Americans living in Hawaii.

Although they were forced into internment camps, young Japanese-American men became eligible to enlist. Some refused to cooperate. Many more saw military service as a way to distinguish themselves and their community, proving that their relocation had been unjust and that they were patriotic Americans. For example, the 442nd Infantry Regiment, a Japanese-American unit, fought with great distinction in Europe with one of the highest casualty rates. Other Japanese-American soldiers acted as interpreters.

Korematsu v. United States

Fred Korematsu, a Japanese American, refused to relocate because he believed Executive Order 9066 was unconstitutional. He was arrested and convicted, but he challenged his conviction. The U.S. Supreme Court upheld his relocation in *Korematsu v. United States* (1944). The Court viewed the government assessment of risk in wartime as reasonable and concluded that the suffering of the Japanese-American community was simply one of the many burdens of the war. Almost fifty years later, Congress apologized and voted to pay compensation to the survivors of the relocated families.

The Historian's Apprentice

In *Korematsu v. United States*, Justice Hugo Black wrote the majority opinion:

"Korematsu was not excluded from the Military Area because of hostility to him or his race. He was excluded because we are at war with the Japanese Empire, because the properly constituted military authorities feared an invasion of our West Coast and felt constrained to take proper security measures, because they decided that the military urgency of the situation demanded that all citizens of Japanese ancestry be segregated from the West Coast temporarily . . ."

Justice Frank Murphy dissented (*disagreed*). Murphy argued that the forced relocations had unfortunately been based on nothing more than racial prejudice:

"I dissent . . . from this legalization of racism. Racial discrimination in any form and in any degree has no justifiable part whatever in our democratic way of life. It is unattractive in any setting, but it is utterly revolting among a free people who have embraced the principles set forth in the Constitution of the United States. All residents of this nation are kin in some way by blood or culture to a foreign land. Yet they are primarily and necessarily a part of the new and distinct civilization of the United States. They must, accordingly, be treated at all times as the heirs of the American experiment, and as entitled to all the rights and freedoms guaranteed by the Constitution."

Was Roosevelt's use of executive power to relocate Japanese Americans justified? Have your class either hold a debate on this question or stage its own mock trial of Fred Korematsu.

Racial Integration of the Defense Industries

During the Great Depression, African Americans had suffered higher levels of unemployment than most other groups. As the nation prepared for war, African-American leaders were concerned that African Americans might be excluded from new jobs. **A. Philip Randolph**, a civil rights leader and former President of the Brotherhood of Sleeping Car Porters, proposed holding a "**March on Washington**" in support of jobs for African Americans. The march was scheduled for July 4, 1941. More than 100,000 participants were expected to attend.

President Roosevelt did not want the spectacle of dissatisfied African Americans marching down Washington's streets just as he was preparing the nation for war. Instead, he negotiated an agreement with Randolph and other African-American leaders. On June 25, President Roosevelt issued **Executive Order 8802**. This order "reaffirmed" that no federal agency would discriminate in its hiring practices on the grounds of race, creed (religion), color or national origin. The order further stated that any private company receiving a federal government contract could not discriminate. This executive order meant that during the war all defense industries had to have an **integrated** work force (they did not have **segregated**, or separate, groups of white and African-American employees). Roosevelt's order also established a new federal agency to oversee enforcement of the order. As a result of Executive Order 8802, thousands of jobs were thrown open to African-American workers. Large numbers of African Americans continued to migrate to the North to fill them. At the same time, the armed services themselves remained segregated.

The Historian's Apprentice

1. Make a Venn diagram or chart comparing Executive Orders 8802 and 9066.
2. Was President Roosevelt acting within his authority in making these orders?

The European Theater: The War against Germany

Note: You will not be required to know about the Holocaust or the German invasion of the Soviet Union for the Georgia Milestones EOC Assessment, but this background will help you to understand the American war effort.

Although it was Japan that had attacked the United States, Roosevelt wanted to focus American energies on defeating Germany first. He saw Nazi Germany as the most dangerous Axis Power and the only one that could threaten the survival of Britain or the Soviet Union. By the time that Americans entered the war, Hitler was already in control of most of Europe and North Africa.

Hitler's Plans and the Holocaust

In his book *Mein Kampf*, Hitler had described his plans to reorganize Europe along racial lines. Germans were to form a new ruling class. Other peoples would be turned into slaves. Jews, Gypsies, Poles, and several other groups were to be eliminated through mass murder. These Nazi plans led to the **Holocaust**—the systematic slaughter of millions of Jews and other peoples.

The Nazi policy of mass extermination evolved gradually. One of the first steps was to spread propaganda, whipping up anti-Semitism (*prejudice against Jews*). In 1935, Germany passed laws depriving German Jews of citizenship, preventing them from holding jobs in the professions, and prohibiting marriages between Jews and non-Jews. In 1938, Jewish shops were closed, Jews were made to pay a large fine, and many Jews were arrested.

With the conquest of Poland in 1939, millions of Polish Jews fell into Nazi hands. They were crowded into **ghettos**—restricted areas of Polish cities, sealed off from the outside, where many died from malnutrition, exposure, and disease. When German troops advanced into Russia in 1941, special firing squads were set up to kill Jewish residents through mass shootings.

At the beginning of 1942, Nazi leaders finally decided on the "**Final Solution**": the complete extermination of all the Jews in Europe. Special extermination camps were constructed, such as Auschwitz in southern Poland. Jews, Gypsies, and other victims across Nazi-occupied Europe were herded into tightly packed cattle cars and carried by train to these special camps. When they arrived, the tired and thirsty victims were shaved and stripped and led into what they were told were "showers," where they were gassed to death. The victims included men, women, and children. Their bodies were then burned in large ovens. Six million Jews and an equal number of others—Poles, Russians, Gypsies, political opponents, prisoners of war, homosexuals, Jehovah's Witnesses—perished under these cruel and barbaric conditions, which many consider to be the worst atrocity in human history.

The Historian's Apprentice

1. Use information from the websites of the U.S. Holocaust Memorial Museum, Yad Vashem, or other sources to research a topic about the Holocaust and present an oral report to your class.
2. Report on an example of genocide that has happened in the past twenty years or that is happening today. What steps should nations take to ensure that acts of ethnic hatred and genocide do not ever occur again?

Nazi Germany Invades the Soviet Union

By mid-1941, Hitler was the master of much of Europe with only Britain opposing him. He then committed his two greatest blunders: first, he invaded the Soviet Union in June 1941; second, he declared war on the United States in December 1941. Hitler had always planned to attack the Soviet Union and believed the German army would quickly defeat the Soviets. At first, the Nazi invasion of the Soviet Union made rapid progress. But by late 1941, the German advance halted just short of Moscow, stopped by the bitter cold of the Russian winter and insufficient supplies of gasoline.

The Battle for the Atlantic

While German tanks and troops were battling the Soviets, German **U-boats** (*submarines*) were causing havoc in the Atlantic Ocean and along the Eastern seaboard of the United States by sinking tankers and other Allied ships. This made it difficult for Americans to send needed weapons, fuel, food and medicines to the European Theater. Keeping the sea lanes across the Atlantic open was of vital concern to the Allies. "Maximum safety of these lines of communication," wrote **General Dwight Eisenhower** in February 1942, "is a 'must' in our military effort, no matter what else we attempt to do."

As soon as the United States had entered the war, Germany sent U-boats across the Atlantic to the East Coast where they torpedoed merchant ships, especially tankers carrying oil to refineries. Valuable cargoes and shipping capacity were lost, and coastal shipping was almost brought to a standstill. In mid-1942, the German submarines moved away from the coast into the middle of the Atlantic. At this time, at least 200 German submarines were active in the Atlantic, and fifteen more were being added every month.

The Allies relied on the **convoy system**, in which a group of merchant ships sailed together, accompanied by an escort of warships and air support. Allied convoys consisted of as many as sixty merchant ships sailing in ten columns, surrounded by a dozen circling warships with airplanes overhead. It took from ten to fifteen days for an Allied convoy to cross the Atlantic.

German submarines travelled in "wolf-packs" of twelve or more submarines to attack these convoys. In the course of 1942, the Allies lost a million tons of shipping capacity to German submarine attacks. In July 1942, German submarines and aircraft were able to sink 23 out of 34 ships in a large convoy bound for Russia, forcing the Allies to temporarily delay further shipments. German submarines also attacked an Allied convoy bringing needed fuel to North Africa, sinking seven of nine tankers. German naval commanders calculated that if they could sink enough Allied ships, they could starve Great Britain and isolate the Soviet Union.

In 1943, newly designed escort and merchant ships with flat tops capable of carrying aircraft, improved radar, and the introduction of longer range aircraft helped the Allies to reduce this threat. German U-boats could not remain underwater for extended periods of time. Improved sonar and radar enabled Allied planes to destroy the German submarines when they surfaced. Forty-three German submarines were destroyed in the month of May 1943 alone. The average life span of a German submarine was sharply reduced to three months. By the end of May 1943, the Germans withdrew most of their submarines from the North Atlantic. The "Battle for the Atlantic" had been won by the Allies. Between June and September 1943, 62 allied convoys with 3,546 merchant ships were able to cross the Atlantic without the loss of a single ship.

North Africa and Italy

Roosevelt and his military advisers were anxious to open up a "Second Front" in Western Europe to relieve German pressure on the Soviet army. Churchill, however, remembered Britain's heavy losses on the battlefields of France during World

The Allied Invasion of Italy, 1943

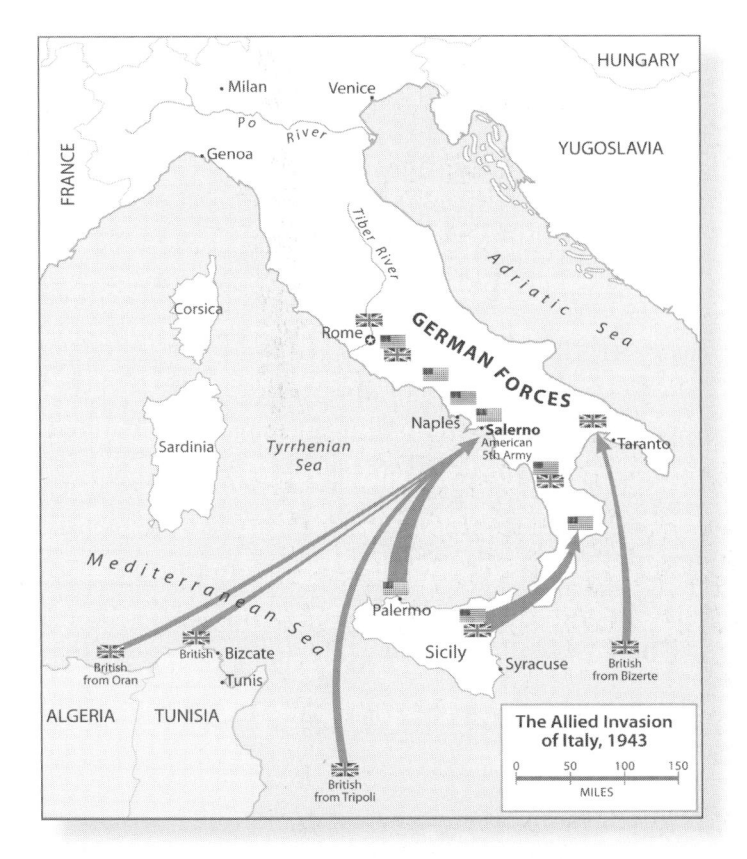

War I. He preferred to wait for the Western Allies to build up more forces, for the Americans to have more combat experience, and for the Germans to exhaust themselves fighting the Soviets before launching an invasion of France.

Churchill therefore proposed postponing the invasion. Instead, he wanted the Americans to help the British in North Africa, where the British were already fighting German and Italian troops. Roosevelt's leading military advisers were outraged and recommended that the United States turn its focus on defeating Japan. But Roosevelt would not stray from his "Germany First" strategy. He agreed with Churchill that American forces were not yet ready for a landing in France. Because it was important for them to engage in combat to maintain public support for the war, Roosevelt accepted Churchill's alternative. Stalin was infuriated, even though Roosevelt promised to open a second front against Germany in France as soon as possible.

In November 1942, U.S. and British troops landed on the coasts of Morocco and Algeria. Much of the fighting in the North African campaign took place between tanks in the desert. Eventually, German and Italian forces were trapped in Tunisia, and 275,000 of them surrendered to the Allies in May 1943.

After defeating German forces in North Africa, American and British forces crossed the Mediterranean Sea to land in **Sicily** in July 1943. Allied success in Sicily led to the overthrow of Italian Fascist dictator Benito Mussolini, who had allied with Hitler. In September 1943, a new Italian anti-Fascist government surrendered to the Allies. By then, however, German troops had taken up most of the positions previously held by the Italian army. The Allies launched an amphibious attack on **Salerno**, on the mainland of Italy, on September 9, 1943. American generals expected the landing to be an easy one, but they met with fierce resistance from German troops and casualties were high.

Stalingrad

Meanwhile, German and Soviet troops had been locked in deadly combat in the city of **Stalingrad** in the Soviet Union (August 1942–January 1943). This battle proved to be the turning point of the war in Europe. By this time, the Soviet army had developed new tactics to counter German *Blitzkrieg* warfare. They fought close to Nazi lines, making German air-power ineffective, or fought from buildings, which could not be easily taken by tanks. The Soviets also had more effective tanks and weaponry. By November 1942, the Soviets had encircled an entire German army at Stalingrad. Hitler ordered his generals not to retreat under any circumstances. After running out of food and ammunition,

A Soviet soldier raising the Red Flag at Stalingrad

the last 100,000 German troops surrendered at the end of January 1943, in violation of Hitler's orders. Only 6,000 of them actually survived the harsh conditions of Soviet imprisonment.

The Tehran Conference

Roosevelt crossed the Atlantic to meet with Churchill and Stalin at **Tehran** in November 1943. Against Churchill's advice, Roosevelt promised Stalin that the Western Allies would launch their long-awaited invasion of France by the spring of 1944. Stalin in turn promised to declare war on Japan once Germany had surrendered.

D-Day

In early 1944, American and British troops began preparing for a massive amphibious invasion of France, known as "Operation Overlord." **General Dwight D. Eisenhower** was placed in supreme command of the Allied invasion. Large numbers of men, tanks, motorized troop carriers, and artillery were assembled in Britain. Ships brought vast quantities of canned meat, candy bars, chewing gum, and cigarettes from America to sustain the Allied troops. The amount of supplies needed for Operation Overlord was so large that the invasion was delayed while provisions were collected. Eventually, five million tons of supplies and munitions, including a thousand motorized vehicles, were stockpiled in Britain.

Before the invasion was launched, Allied airplanes conducted bombing missions night and day to weaken German positions. The Western Allies even took steps to fool the German army into thinking that their main assault would be farther north at Calais. Bad weather delayed the launching of the invasion. Finally, on "**D-Day**," June 6, 1944, thousands of ships and landing craft crossed the English Channel to carry more than 150,000 troops to the beaches of Normandy in northwestern France. Most of these soldiers were Americans. It was the largest amphibious assault in history.

The Western Advance

Once they had established a foothold in France, the Western Allies moved quickly eastward. Paris was liberated just two months later with the help of the French resistance and the "Free French." Allied forces advanced even faster than they had expected. Eventually, they had to slow their advance because of a lack of supplies, especially gasoline. While sufficient supplies were available in Britain, they had to be carried by truck to the Allied front. The forty Allied divisions in France, with each division consisting of 15,000 men, required almost 20,000 tons of supplies a day.

When some of the Allied divisions reached the Ardennes Forest in northeastern France, the Germans launched a surprise counterattack. Hitler hoped he could divide and defeat the American and British armies, forcing each of them to sue for a separate peace. Then Germany would have a free hand to fight the Soviets to the east. The "**Battle of the Bulge**" was fought with great

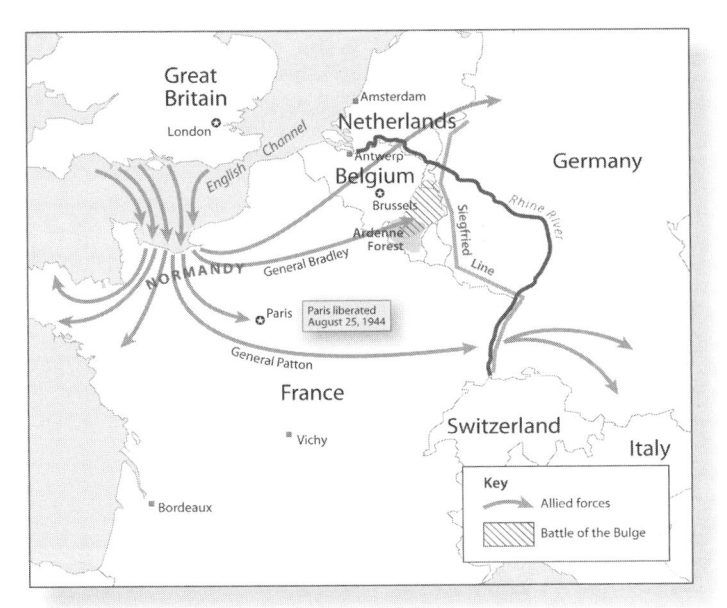

The Allied Advance, 1944–1945

ferocity for six weeks from December 16, 1944, until the end of January 1945. It saw the bloodiest action by U.S. forces in the war, with 19,000 killed, 62,000 wounded, and 26,000 missing. For the first time during World War II, African-American troops were sent into combat.

In the end, vigorous American resistance, bitterly cold weather, Allied reinforcements, and unfavorable terrain caused the German offensive to collapse. Hitler's last attempt to bring the war to a successful conclusion failed. The Western Allies now advanced to the Siegfried Line, a series of defensive fortifications and bunkers along Germany's western frontier. In March 1945, they crossed the Rhine River.

The Collapse of Nazi Germany

While American, British and Free French forces were invading Nazi Germany from the west, Soviet forces continued their advance from the east. By the summer of 1944, the Soviet army had crossed into eastern Poland. Polish patriots rose up in resistance against their Nazi rulers during the Warsaw uprising of August 1944. Their rebellion was savagely repressed. Most of the city was destroyed by the retreating Nazis as Soviet troops, on Stalin's orders, watched passively from a distance. The Soviet army resumed its advance into Poland at the end of January, crossed the German border in February, and occupied Vienna in March.

The Fall of Berlin

Hitler had moved his command to an underground bunker in the center of Berlin, the German capital. He hoped that a successful defense of the capital city would rally the rest of the country. The British proposed a concentrated advance from the west to reach Berlin before the Soviets did. They were overruled by Eisenhower, who preferred a broad sweep through western Germany to find and destroy the German army. This left the conquest of Berlin to the advancing Red Army.

By April 1945, two Soviet armies reached Berlin. The city was bombed relentlessly by airplanes and artillery. German units made a desperate last-ditch effort to defend their city. Hitler saw the contest in mythical terms, and believed that if Germans were unable to defend their capital, they did not deserve to survive. Even young school children and old men were called up in its defense. Many Berliners feared savage treatment at the hands of the Soviet army, while Nazi officials were hanging any residents who refused to assist in the city's defense. Soviet troops had to take the city block-by-block, costing hundreds of thousands of lives and the total destruction of much of the city.

Hitler, now addicted to powerful medications, thought he might still be saved through some miracle, but he was soon disappointed. The German dictator finally committed suicide at his underground bunker on April 30. His body was

Chapter 15 | America in World War II

burned so that his remains would not be found by the Soviets. Meanwhile, in revenge for Nazi acts in the Soviet Union, Soviet troops looted the city of Berlin and raped its women. The army seized machinery, equipment, art works, and currency and shipped these off to the Soviet Union.

The United States insisted on the unconditional surrender of the Axis powers. Germany's military leaders officially surrendered to the Allies at Eisenhower's headquarters in France on May 7 and in Berlin on May 8—known as V-E Day, or "Victory in Europe." The long ordeal in Europe was finally over. President Roosevelt did not live to see the surrender: he died of a stroke in Georgia on April 12, 1945, just two and a half weeks before Hitler's suicide.

The Historian's Apprentice

1. Make an illustrated timeline of the war in Europe, 1939–1945.
2. Was the delay by Britain and the United States in opening a second front justified? Have your class hold a debate on this question.
3. How important was the supply of weapons, fuel, food, and other materials to the course and outcome of the war?

The Pacific Theater: The War against Japan

Unlike the war in Europe, Americans fought most of the war in the Pacific on their own. Distances were vast—the distance across the Pacific was three times that from New York to London—making it difficult to send supplies. Pacific islands lacked landing strips and roads, which often had to be built. The tropical climate meant food supplies spoiled easily. Soldiers faced malaria, dysentery, and other tropical diseases. Finally, Roosevelt's decision to fight Germany first meant that only limited supplies and equipment were available for the Pacific Theater in the first years of the war.

The Fall of the Philippines

Back in December 1941 and early in 1942, the Japanese had made striking gains after their attack on Pearl Harbor. They had successfully conquered Hong Kong, Burma, Malaya, Borneo, the Solomon Islands, Java, and Singapore. Japanese forces had also attacked the Philippines. **General Douglas MacArthur**, the U.S. Commander in the Far East, retreated to **Bataan** (a peninsula near the capital at Manila). MacArthur was personally ordered to leave Manila for Australia. His troops remained in the Philippines, fighting bravely until they finally surrendered in April 1942. The Japanese forced the exhausted and half-starved American and Filipino prisoners-of-war to undertake the 80-mile "**Bataan Death March**" in the heat. Guards beat and bayoneted the prisoners, who were given no food and little water. Several thousand died along the way.

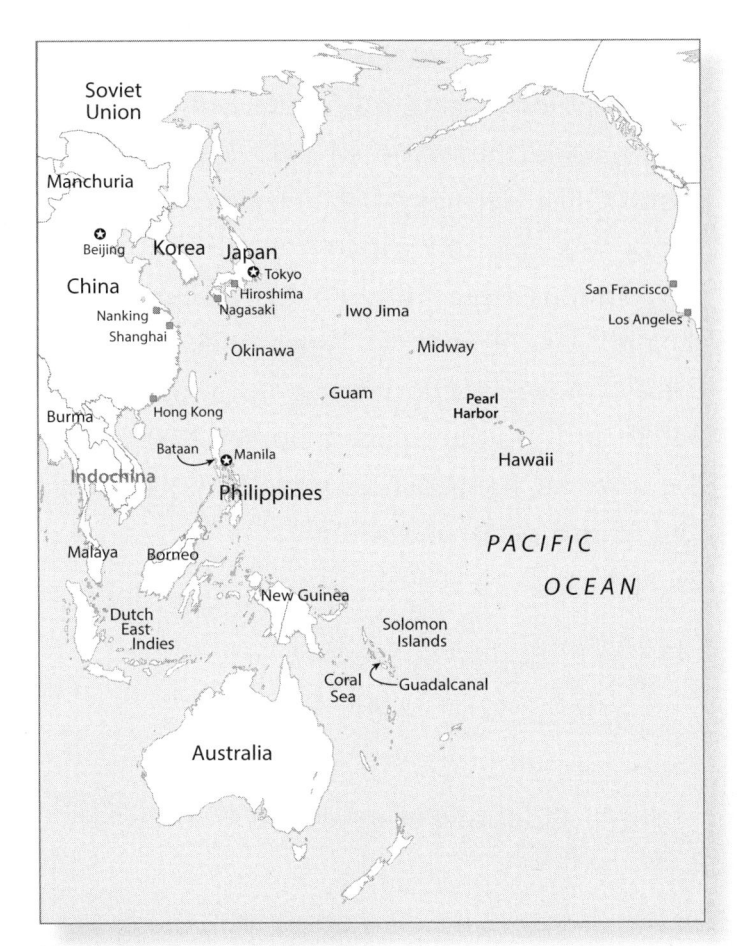

World War II in the Pacific

In the distance below, a Japanese aircraft carrier burns following a U.S. air strike at the Battle of Midway

The Battle of Midway

In May 1942, American and Japanese aircraft carriers fought one another in the **Battle of the Coral Sea**. It was the first time in history that aircraft carriers fought while separated by more than 100 miles of ocean. Planes from each side flew and attacked the other side's ships. Japanese bombers sank one American aircraft carrier and severely damaged a second.

The following month, the Japanese attempted to lure the U.S. Pacific fleet into a trap near the island of **Midway**. Their aim was to destroy all U.S. aircraft carriers operating in the Pacific and to capture the U.S. naval base on Midway. However, the Americans had deciphered part of the Japanese secret naval code and knew that they were planning a major attack on Midway.

Admiral Chester Nimitz, the U.S. naval commander, assembled several aircraft carriers and had rapid repairs made to the carrier that had been damaged at the Battle of the Coral Sea. The American carriers moved into position just northeast of Midway Island without detection. The Japanese began their attack on Midway not knowing that the U.S. Navy was nearby. Just when the Japanese carriers were least defensible, American dive-bombers suddenly appeared in the sky and bombed their decks. The Japanese lost four large aircraft carriers, while the Americans lost only one. The **Battle of Midway** (June 4–7, 1942) was the turning point of the war in the Pacific.

Guadalcanal

The Japanese had occupied islands across the Pacific to create a defensive perimeter around their new empire. In **Guadalcanal**, at the southwestern end of the Solomon Islands, they began building an airfield to protect their bases and enable their planes to threaten Australia. Two months after the Battle of Midway, American

Chapter 15 | America in World War II

Marines landed on the island, which they took by surprise. Despite a series of fierce land and naval attacks, the Japanese failed to retake Guadalcanal.

The Japanese Empire Begins to Crumble

By 1943, the tide had turned in the Pacific. American forces began "island-hopping," liberating some Pacific islands from Japanese control while bypassing others. The need for more landing craft, being collected in Europe, sometimes delayed the American advance. In April 1944, American forces landed in Western New Guinea; early in 1945, they regained control of the Philippines. Once Germany was defeated, the United States was able to turn its full fury on Japan. Preparations began for a massive invasion of Japan's home islands. In April 1945, American forces landed in **Okinawa**, a large island only 340 miles from the Japanese home islands. After the German surrender in May 1945, the Soviet Union also declared war on Japan and invaded Manchuria.

The Historian's Apprentice

1. What role did aircraft carriers play in the Pacific Theater?
2. Imagine that you are an American sailor serving in the Pacific during World War II. Write a letter to your family describing your experiences.

Dawn of the Atomic Age: The Manhattan Project

Just before the Nazi invasion of Poland, the famous scientist **Albert Einstein**—a German-Jewish refugee and a pacifist—had written a personal letter to President Roosevelt recommending that the United States develop an **atomic bomb**. Einstein believed Nazi scientists were already working on one. "A single bomb of this type," wrote Einstein, "carried by boat and exploded in a port, might very well destroy the whole port together with some of the surrounding territory...." Einstein wrote to Roosevelt again in 1940 about signs of Nazi efforts to develop a weapon from uranium based on a nuclear chain reaction.

Shortly after the attack on Pearl Harbor, the U.S. government launched its top-secret "**Manhattan Project**." Its goal was to develop an atomic bomb. Physicist Robert Oppenheimer was placed in charge of the secret weapons laboratory at Los Alamos, New Mexico, where the first atomic bomb was built. A team of scientists was assembled, which included refugee scientists who had fled from Nazi Germany and Fascist Italy. By 1945, 6,000 people were working at the secret laboratories in Los Alamos. After the government invested $2 billion on the project, the first atomic bomb was successfully tested in the New Mexican desert in July 1945.

America Drops Two Atomic Bombs on Japan

The Manhattan Project was so secret that the new President, **Harry S. Truman**, only learned about it after Roosevelt's death. Fighting in the Pacific had been fierce and the Japanese were expected to fight even more tirelessly to defend their home islands. A planned Allied invasion of Japan was expected to cost close to a million American lives. To make such a costly invasion unnecessary, Truman turned to the new atomic bomb. He rejected the idea of exploding the bomb in the ocean, since it was unlikely to persuade the Japanese to surrender. Instead, Truman selected two cities that were centers of Japanese military production as targets. On August 6, the first atomic bomb was exploded over **Hiroshima**. Three days later, a second bomb was exploded over **Nagasaki**. As many as 100,000 people were killed in each explosion. Each city was totally destroyed. Japan surrendered on **V-J Day**, just after the second explosion, once the United States agreed to permit the Japanese Emperor to remain on his throne.

The Historian's Apprentice

In the book *Hiroshima*, reporter John Hersey tells the stories of six survivors from the blast. Here, a survivor runs through the city in search of his family immediately after the explosion:

> "He was the only person making his way into the city; he met hundreds and hundreds who were fleeing, and every one of them seemed to be hurt in some way. The eyebrows of some were burned off and skin hung from their faces and hands. Others, because of pain, held their arms up as if carrying something in both hands. Some were vomiting as they walked. Many were naked or in shreds of clothing. On some undressed bodies, the burns had made patterns—of undershirt straps and suspenders and, on the skin of some women (since white repelled the heat from the bomb and dark clothes absorbed it and conducted it to the skin), the shapes of flowers they had had on their kimonos. Many, although injured themselves, supported relatives who were worse off. Almost all had their heads bowed, looked straight ahead, were silent, and showed no expression whatsoever."
>
> —John Hersey, *Hiroshima* (1946)

1. Imagine you are a military adviser to President Truman at the beginning of August 1945. Write a short paper stating your recommendation on whether or not to use the atomic bomb on Japan. Would its use be justified?
2. Hersey wrote his account in 1946, less than one year after the war ended. Popular feelings against Japan were still high. What impact do you think his account had on American readers?

The Consequences of World War II

World War II had many far-reaching effects. More than 60 million people lost their lives. Much of Europe, Asia, and North Africa lay in ruins. The collapse of European and Japanese power left the United States and the Soviet Union as two superpowers in command of the world. The weakened condition of the older European powers, such as Britain and France, encouraged

Chapter 15 | America in World War II

independence movements in their former colonies. Even the United States granted the Philippines its independence in 1946. The war led to the development of new technologies, such as jet aircraft, missiles, and the atomic bomb.

Increased Power of the Federal Government

Like the New Deal, World War II increased the powers and responsibilities of the federal government.

The Nuremberg Trials

The liberation of the concentration camps by Allied forces at the end of the war added to the evidence of Nazi crimes and revealed the full extent of Nazi brutality. Just over twenty leading Nazis were put on trial before a tribunal of Allied judges in **Nuremberg**, Germany, between 1945 and 1946 for "crimes against humanity." The defendants were charged with starting the war and with committing atrocities such as the extermination of Jewish citizens and the mistreatment of prisoners of war. The accused Nazis tried to defend themselves by claiming that they had only been following orders. Most were convicted and sentenced to be hanged or imprisoned for life.

The Occupation of Germany and Japan

Germany was occupied by the United States, Britain, France, and the Soviet Union. Each Allied Power established its own occupation zone. The capital city of Berlin was similarly divided into separate sectors. The occupying powers introduced re-education programs, explaining the evils of Nazi beliefs to the German public to counter Nazi propaganda.

The United States also occupied Japan. General MacArthur was placed in charge of rebuilding that country. Important changes were imposed to make Japan less aggressive and imperialistic. Japan's overseas empire was taken away, and its military leaders were put on trial. Japan renounced the use of nuclear weapons and the waging of war. Japan was forbidden to have an army or navy, except for peacekeeping purposes. A new constitution went into effect in May 1947, turning Japan into a democracy.

The Birth of the United Nations

One of the most important consequences of the war was the creation of the **United Nations**. Despite the failure of the League of Nations, the victorious Allies were committed to forming a new international peacekeeping organization. Roosevelt, who had served under President Wilson, was determined to ensure that the United States participated in this new body. He therefore strove to avoid all of Wilson's mistakes. For example, Roosevelt kept Republican Congressmen involved at every step. He continually negotiated with Soviet diplomats to make sure that the Soviet Union joined the United Nations, too.

In the autumn of 1944, a conference was held outside of Washington, D.C., where the Allies agreed on the general structure of the United Nations. The United Nations Charter was finally completed at the San Francisco Conference (April–June 1945), in which fifty nations participated. The United States was the first nation to sign the U.N. Charter. The major aims of the United Nations are the maintenance of peace and the encouragement of friendship and cooperation among nations. The United Nations also seeks to eliminate hunger, disease, and ignorance in the world. All member nations belong to the **General**

Assembly. Five nations serve as permanent members of the **Security Council**. These permanent members—the United States, Great Britain, Russia, China, and France—enjoy special powers, including veto power over all U.N. peacekeeping operations. Other important bodies in the United Nations include the International Court of Justice and the Economic and Social Council.

The Universal Declaration of Human Rights

After the barbarities of the Holocaust and World War II, one of the first acts of the new United Nations General Assembly was to draft the **Universal Declaration of Human Rights**. **Eleanor Roosevelt** served as the chairwoman of the committee that drafted the Declaration. The Declaration defined rights to which all human beings are entitled, including the right to life, the prohibition of slavery and torture, freedom of religion, freedom of movement, and freedom of association. It also established social, economic, and cultural rights, such as the right to work, the right to an adequate standard of living, and the right to an education.

For the Georgia Milestones EOC Assessment, you should know that:

- ☐ Hitler came to power in Germany in 1933. Based on his Nazi ideology, Hitler planned to conquer much of Europe. In September 1939, he launched an invasion of Poland, beginning World War II. Germans overran Denmark, the Netherlands, Belgium, and France but were unable to defeat the British. In June 1941, Hitler ordered the invasion of the Soviet Union.

- ☐ Americans attempted to stay out of the war in Europe. Congress passed a series of Neutrality Acts that prohibited shipping munitions to countries at war. When Americans became worried about the collapse of democracy, Congress passed the Lend-Lease Act, which permitted the United States to send arms to Britain, for which the British could pay later.

- ☐ The United States threatened to boycott Japan and cut off its supply of oil, leading the Japanese to launch a surprise attack on the U.S. Navy at Pearl Harbor in Hawaii on December 7, 1941. The attack on Pearl Harbor brought the United States into the war.

- ☐ Hitler declared war on the United States because of Germany's alliance with Japan. President Roosevelt decided to focus the American war effort on defeating Germany first.

- ☐ U.S. involvement in the war led to the mobilization of manpower and resources: men were drafted; after wartime conversion, American factories began producing war goods; women and minorities found jobs in wartime production; essential goods like gasoline, rubber, and aluminum were rationed; and the government began selling war bonds.

Continued ▶

- ☐ President Roosevelt issued executive orders that led to the internment of Japanese Americans on the West Coast and that mandated the integration of workers of all races in defense industries.

- ☐ Women worked in war industries, including heavy industry, and were able to enlist in the army or navy for the first time.

- ☐ Americans faced difficulties in delivering weapons, food, fuel, and medical supplies to their troops in Europe and the Pacific. In sending supplies across the Atlantic, Americans faced attacks from German submarines and aircraft. Americans reduced these dangers by sending merchant ships in convoys with escorts, and by developing escort ships that could carry aircraft that attacked submarines. In sending supplies to the Pacific, Americans faced the challenges of vast distances, the tropical climate, and the fact that the European campaign took priority in receiving supplies. In some cases, the need for supplies delayed Allied advances.

- ☐ Americans and British delayed opening a second major front in Western Europe while the Soviets faced most of the German army; instead Americans and British sent troops to North Africa, Sicily, and Italy.

- ☐ On "D-Day" (June 6, 1944), the Western Allies opened a second front in Western Europe by landing troops on the beaches of Normandy in the largest amphibious operation in history.

- ☐ After D-Day, American and British forces advanced on Germany from the west while Soviet troops advanced from the east. Soviet troops occupied Berlin in April 1945. Germans fought ferociously in the Battle of Berlin, which led to the destruction of much of their city. Hitler committed suicide at the end of April and the German army officially surrendered in early May.

- ☐ The Battle of Midway (June 1942) was the turning point in the war against Japan. In this naval battle, the United States used its superior intelligence to trick the Japanese and destroy several of their aircraft carriers.

- ☐ The United States began a campaign of "island hopping," taking some Pacific islands and passing over others.

- ☐ After the surrender of Germany, the United States put its full efforts into the campaign against Japan; after fierce fighting on several islands, Americans prepared for a full-scale invasion of Japan.

- ☐ The top-secret "Manhattan Project" developed the world's first atomic bombs. Two atomic bombs were dropped on Japan in early August 1945 on the cities of Hiroshima and Nagasaki, leading to the Japanese surrender and the end of World War II.

Name _____

Describe the following developments leading to, or occurring during, World War II.

Development	Description
Rise of Nazism	
Invasion of Poland (1939); Fall of France (1940); and Battle of Britain (1940)	
U.S. Neutrality Acts (1935, 1936, 1937, 1939)	
Lend Lease (1941)	
Attack on Pearl Harbor (December 1941)	
Battle for the Atlantic (1942–1943); difficulties in delivering supplies to Europe	
Battle of Midway (May 1942)	
Difficulties in delivering supplies to the Pacific Theater	
Allied landings in Normandy: D-Day (June 1944)	
Fall of Berlin (May 1945)	
Dropping of atomic bombs on Japan (August 1945)	

Chapter 15 | America in World War II

Name _____

Describe the following developments on the home front during World War II.

Development	Description
Wartime mobilization	
Rationing	
Conversion to Production of War Goods	
Paying for the War	
Role of Women	
Internment of Japanese Americans	
African Americans and Federal Employment	

1. This photograph was taken in Pearl Harbor, Hawaii, on December 7, 1941. Describe what the photograph shows.

_____
_____
_____
_____

2. Identify two effects of this event.

_____
_____
_____
_____
_____

446   Chapter 15 | America in World War II

World War II

Causes

Rise of Fascism

Nazism in Germany—Adolf Hitler
- Nationalistic
- Warlike/Violent
- Obedience to Leader
- Belief in superiority of Aryan race
- Anti-Semitism

- Failure of League of Nations
- Failure of Appeasement
- Munich Conference—1938

Early Years

German Expansion
- Invasion of Poland
- *Blitzkrieg* warfare
- Defeat of France
- "Battle of Britain"

Battle for the Atlantic
- Difficulties in delivering supplies: German U-boats vs. Allied convoys

U.S. Neutrality
- Neutrality Acts of 1935, 1936, 1937, 1939; "Cash-and-Carry"
- Lend-Lease Act of 1941
- "Four Freedoms" & Atlantic Charter

Course of the War

Japanese Attack on Pearl Harbor, December 7, 1941 brings U.S. into the war

War in Europe
- North Africa
- Sicily
- Salerno & Mainland Italy
- Soviets at Stalingrad
- D-Day Invasion
- "Battle of the Bulge"
- V-E Day: May, 1945

War in the Pacific
- Philippines—"Bataan Death March"
- Coral Sea
- Midway
- "Island-hopping"
- Atomic bombs on Hiroshima & Nagasaki
- V-J Day: August 1945

Home Front

Mobilization
- Draft—Selective Service
- Women in WACS and WAVES
- War Production Board
- Rationing
- Higher income taxes and war bonds
- Full Employment—women & minorities fill jobs
- Office of War Information

Minorities
- Internment of Japanese Americans
- *Korematsu v. U.S.*
- Planned "March on Washington" leads FDR to open federal jobs to African Americans
- Tuskegee Airmen
- Navajo "code talkers"

Consequences

Holocaust
- Persecution and murder of 6 million Jews and an equal number of others

Nuremberg Trials
- Nazis tried for "crimes against humanity"

- Loss of 60 million lives
- Atomic Age—development of nuclear weapons
- Germany divided and occupied; Japan occupied by U.S.

United Nations
- Security Council and General Assembly
- Declaration of Human Rights

Chapter 15 | America in World War II

What Do You Know

SSUSH19a

1. Examine the photograph to answer the question.

   Which event caused this explosion?

   A. Japanese attack on Pearl Harbor
   B. aircraft bombing at the Battle of Midway
   C. sabotage by German spies in Honolulu
   D. an accident as the navy prepared to invade Japan

   Explosion of *U.S.S. Shaw* in Hawaii, December 7, 1941

SSUSH19a

2. Read the excerpt to answer the question.

   > From the standpoint of Imperial General Headquarters, based on the assumption that a peaceful solution has not been found and war is inevitable, the Empire's oil supply, as well as the stockpiles of many other important war materials, is decreasing day by day with the result that the national defense power is gradually diminishing. If this deplorable situation is left unchecked, I believe that, after a lapse of some time, the nation's vitality will deteriorate and ultimately fall into dire straits.
   >
   > —Admiral Osami Nagano at the Imperial Conference of September 6, 1941, in Tokyo, Japan

   What step did Japanese leaders take to deal with this problem?

   A. They attacked Pearl Harbor.
   B. They invaded the Soviet Union.
   C. They signed a treaty of alliance with Nazi Germany.
   D. They sent submarines to the West Coast of the United States.

SSUSH19d

3. Which of the following BEST describes the steps taken by President Franklin Roosevelt to mobilize for World War II?

   A. Increase in the production of consumer goods, a reduction of taxes, and the importation of laborers from Mexico
   B. Conscription of men, production of war goods, rationing of essential materials, and sale of war bonds
   C. Ending shipments across the Atlantic, keeping goods in the United States, and refusing to supply the Allies
   D. Permitting criticism of his policies during wartime, relying only on voluntary enlistment to raise troop levels, and depending on private donations to raise funds

448 Chapter 15 | America in World War II

SSUSH19d

4. Use the list to answer the question.

> - High levels of voluntary enlistment in the armed services
> - Widespread purchase of war bonds
> - Few cases of draft evasion
> - General obedience to wartime regulations
> - Cooperation in the rationing of goods

What inference can be made from this list about the domestic impact of World War II?

A. There was little popular support for the war.
B. Many Americans were inspired by a sense of patriotism.
C. Most Americans became afraid of their own government.
D. Most Americans believed the Allies would lose the war.

SSUSH19d

5. Use the poster to answer the question.

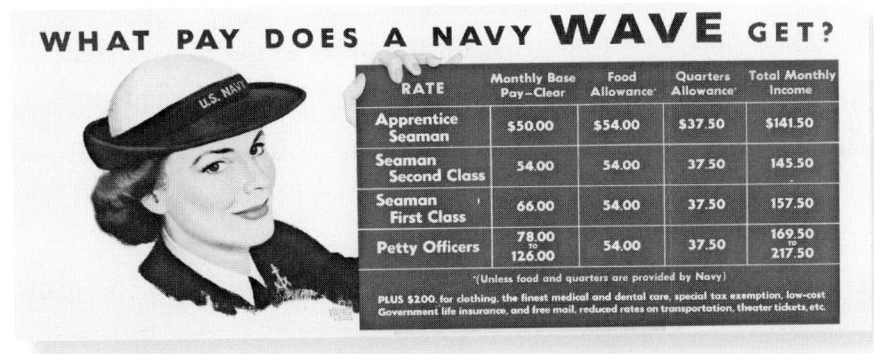

WHAT PAY DOES A NAVY WAVE GET?

RATE	Monthly Base Pay–Clear	Food Allowance*	Quarters Allowance*	Total Monthly Income
Apprentice Seaman	$50.00	$54.00	$37.50	$141.50
Seaman Second Class	54.00	54.00	37.50	145.50
Seaman First Class	66.00	54.00	37.50	157.50
Petty Officers	78.00 TO 126.00	54.00	37.50	169.50 TO 217.50

*(Unless food and quarters are provided by Navy)

PLUS $200 for clothing, the finest medical and dental care, special tax exemption, low-cost Government life insurance, and free mail, reduced rates on transportation, theater tickets, etc.

What conclusion can be drawn from this World War II government poster?

A. Women were needed by the U.S. Navy during the war.
B. Women were conscripted for military service just like men.
C. Women were encouraged to serve in combat roles during the war.
D. Women were valued on the home front but not by the armed forces.

SSUSH19b

6. Examine the photograph to answer the question.

Which evidence BEST supports President Harry Truman's decision to use this weapon against two Japanese cities?

A. After the defeat of Germany, Japanese leaders believed their situation was generally helpless.
B. Many Americans felt that the Japanese should have to pay for their surprise attack on Pearl Harbor.
C. Japan did not immediately surrender, even after the first bomb was dropped on Hiroshima.
D. After the surrender of Germany, the Soviet Union declared war on Japan.

Chapter 15 | America in World War II

SSUSH19e

7. Use the diagram to answer the question.

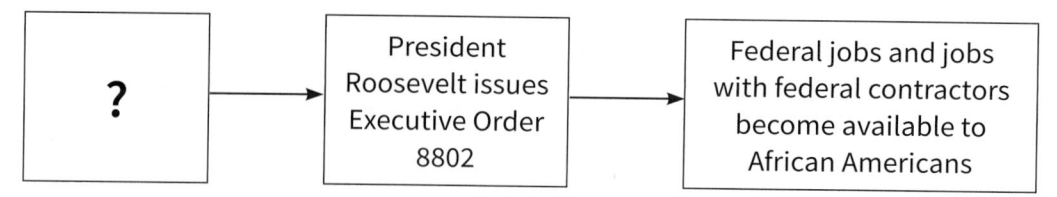

```
[ ? ] → [ President Roosevelt issues Executive Order 8802 ] → [ Federal jobs and jobs with federal contractors become available to African Americans ]
```

Which phrase BEST completes the diagram?

A. Japanese Americans are relocated to internment camps.

B. A. Philip Randolph proposes to hold a "March on Washington."

C. The U.S. Supreme Court declares racial segregation to be unconstitutional.

D. Three-quarters of the states ratify the Fourteenth Amendment.

SSUSH19d

8. What new opportunities did World War II create for women?

A. They were able to enlist in the army or navy for combat.

B. They were able to follow combat units as camp followers.

C. They were able to fill many jobs traditionally held by men.

D. They were able to receive benefits for moving to less populated areas.

SSUSH19c

9. Use the picture to answer the question.

On what day did these American troops land on the beaches of Normandy in the largest amphibious operation in history?

A. D-Day

B. V-E Day

C. V-J Day

D. French Liberation Day

SSUSH19c

10. Use the diagram to answer the question.

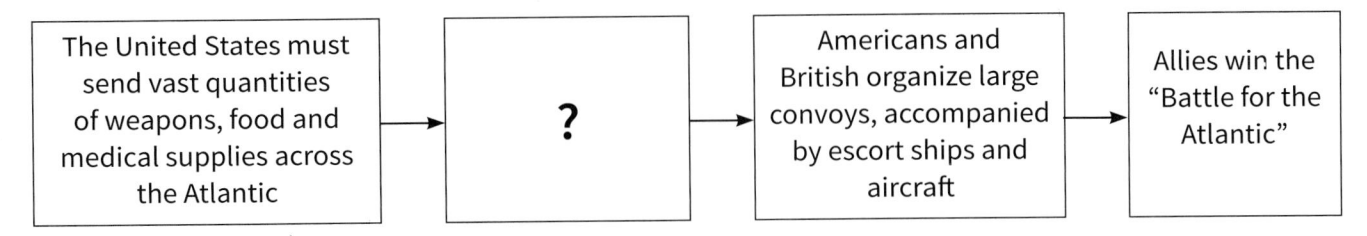

| The United States must send vast quantities of weapons, food and medical supplies across the Atlantic | → | ? | → | Americans and British organize large convoys, accompanied by escort ships and aircraft | → | Allies win the "Battle for the Atlantic" |

Which statement BEST completes the diagram?

A. Rough waters of the Atlantic Ocean prove too difficult to pass.

B. German U-boats sink Allied merchant ships carrying goods.

C. The tropical climate destroys perishable Allied provisions.

D. American merchants refuse to send goods in dangerous waters.

SSUSH19c

11. Which set of events is listed in chronological order?

A.
1. Allied Landing in Normandy
2. Attack on Pearl Harbor
3. Fall of Berlin
4. Battle for the Atlantic

B.
1. Allied Landing in Normandy
2. Fall of Berlin
3. Attack on Pearl Harbor
4. Battle for the Atlantic

C.
1. Attack on Pearl Harbor
2. Battle for the Atlantic
3. Allied Landing in Normandy
4. Fall of Berlin

D.
1. Attack on Pearl Harbor
2. Fall of Berlin
3. Battle for the Atlantic
4. Normandy Landings

SSUSH19e

12. Use the excerpt to answer the question.

> *Korematsu was not excluded from the military area because of hostility to him or his race. He was excluded because we are at war with the Japanese Empire, because the ... authorities feared an invasion of our West Coast and felt constrained to take proper security measures.*
>
> —Justice Hugo Black, U.S. Supreme Court,
> *Korematsu v. United States* (1944)

Based on this excerpt, with which statement would Justice Black have agreed?

A. Individual rights can be restricted in wartime if a "clear and present danger" exists.

B. Only the Supreme Court can legally deprive citizens of civil rights and liberties.

C. Individual rights must be maintained at all costs, even in national emergencies.

D. The Supreme Court lacks the power to block executive orders made during wartime.

SSUSH19e

13. Examine the photograph to answer the question.

Japanese Americans in temporary housing during World War II

Which statement BEST explains the relocation of these citizens?

A. U.S. military leaders feared they might commit acts of sabotage.

B. Japanese Americans had published a declaration of loyalty to Japan.

C. Japanese leaders had threatened to bomb Japanese-Americans' homes.

D. Their homes on the West Coast were needed to shelter American troops.

SSUSH19e

14. Use the excerpt to answer the question.

> [T]he army did not notify each family exactly where they would be going, what kind of weather they would be encountering, or exactly when they would be moving. Efforts within each family started to get rid of, sell, or store their household goods.... It was a hectic, frantic time for all the Japanese families. In our family, my father... destroyed all of his Japanese language books because rumors spread that if the FBI came to your home and found Japanese language books, your father or uncle or mother would be taken away and fear just gripped the community over things like that.
>
> —Ms. Aiko Herzig-Yoshinaga recalling when her family was relocated during World War II (1994 inteview)

What inference can be made from this excerpt about the enforcement of Executive Order 9066?

A. The U.S. Army possessed evidence of actual sabotage by Japanese Americans.

B. The removal of Japanese Americans from coastal areas was necessary for U.S. security.

C. Japanese Americans were given very little time to take care of their personal possessions.

D. The treatment of Japanese Americans was the same as the treatment of Jewish residents in Germany.

452　　Chapter 15 | America in World War II

CHAPTER 16 The Truman and Eisenhower Years: Cold War, Prosperity, and Civil Rights

SSUSH20 What were the major foreign and domestic policies of the Truman and Eisenhower administrations, and what were the effects of those policies, including their impact on technological advancements and social change?

  a. What international policies and actions did U.S. leaders develop in response to the Cold War, including containment, the Marshall Plan, the Truman Doctrine, and the Korean War?

  b. How were major domestic issues connected to their social effects, including the G.I. Bill, Truman's integration policies, McCarthyism, the National Interstate and Defense Highways Act, and *Brown v. Board of Education*?

  c. What was the influence of Sputnik (1957) on U.S. technological innovations and education?

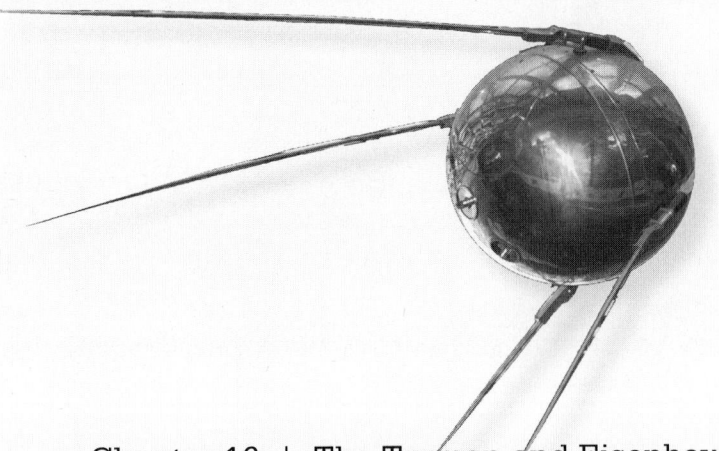

Names and Terms You Should Know

Superpower
Joseph Stalin
Yalta Conference
Cold War
Iron Curtain
Harry S. Truman
Potsdam Conference
Containment
Truman Doctrine
Marshall Plan
NATO

Warsaw Pact
Mao Zedong
Korean War
Douglas MacArthur
Dwight Eisenhower
Senator Joseph McCarthy
McCarthyism
G.I. Bill of Rights
Suburbs
National Interstate and Defense Highways Act

Interstate Highway System
Desegregation
Integration
Brown v. Board of Education (1954)
Dr. Martin Luther King, Jr.
Sputnik
NASA
National Defense Education Act
"Space race"

Georgia "Peaches" of Wisdom

1. The Cold War was rooted in political, economic, and social differences. The Soviet Union was a communist dictatorship with a planned economy, collectivized farming, and state-owned factories. The United States was a capitalist democracy. People enjoyed individual rights and elected their own leaders.

2. Stalin mistrusted the West. He felt the Soviet Union had the right to control Eastern Europe for its own security. American leaders equally mistrusted Stalin. Stalin had promised free elections in Poland at Yalta but failed to honor his pledge. An "Iron Curtain" fell on Eastern Europe. Communications between Eastern and Western Europe were cut off.

3. In 1947, communists threatened the governments of Greece and Turkey. President Truman announced the "Truman Doctrine": the United States would provide assistance to free peoples resisting communism. This was the beginning of U.S. containment policy.

4. In 1948, the United States introduced the Marshall Plan. This program provided U.S. economic aid to the countries of Western Europe to help them rebuild their economies and better resist communism.

5. Stalin cut off land routes to West Berlin in 1948. The United States responded with the "Berlin Airlift." After several months, Stalin reopened the roads.

6. The Western Allies formed NATO in 1949. The Soviet Union and its Eastern European satellites formed the Warsaw Pact in 1955.

7. China was taken over by communists led by Mao Zedong in 1949. Chinese Nationalists retreated to the island of Taiwan. President Truman refused to recognize the communist government of China.

8. Communist North Korea attacked South Korea in 1950. Truman decided to help South Korea resist the attack. General MacArthur chased the North Koreans to the borders of China, bringing China into the war. Truman dismissed General MacArthur when the general publicly pressed for an unlimited war.

9. Many Americans began to fear communist spies at home. Loyalty Review Boards and the House Committee on Un-American Activities interrogated citizens on their political activities. The Rosenbergs were executed for giving atomic secrets to the Soviet Union.

10. Senator Joseph McCarthy claimed to have evidence of communists in government, although he never produced it. People with liberal views became afraid of being accused of being communist. McCarthy remained popular until people realized he had no evidence to support his claims.

11. President Eisenhower announced the Eisenhower Doctrine—that the United States would oppose the spread of communism to the Middle East.

12. The end of World War II led to demobilization and the "Baby Boom." The G.I. Bill of Rights gave returning veterans benefits such as money for education and a low-interest loan to buy a home. The demand for American goods was high. American consumers bought refrigerators, cars, and televisions. Americans experienced a long period of prosperity.

13. President Eisenhower proposed the National Interstate and Defense Highways Act, which created our present system of interstate highways.

14. In 1948, President Truman issued Executive Order 9981, desegregating the armed services.

15. In *Brown v. Board of Education* (1954), the Supreme Court overturned *Plessy v. Ferguson* and unanimously held that in public education segregation has no place.

16. In 1955, Rosa Parks was arrested for refusing to move to the back of a city bus in Montgomery, Alabama. Dr. Martin Luther King, Jr., led a boycott of the city's buses. The boycott ran for almost a year until a federal court ordered the public transit system to desegregate.

17. When the Governor of Arkansas tried to prevent nine black students from attending an all-white school in Little Rock in 1957, President Eisenhower sent in federal troops.

18. The Soviet success in sending Sputnik into space in 1957 surprised most Americans and caused the United States to increase its spending on science education and to start the "space race." President Eisenhower founded NASA, and Congress voted to use federal funds to support math and science education.

Chapter 16 | The Truman and Eisenhower Years

In this chapter, you will learn about events during the Presidencies of Harry Truman and Dwight Eisenhower. The United States abandoned its traditional isolationism to take on a new role as leader of the "free world" in the struggle against communism. Americans also took some of the first steps towards ending racial segregation.

Two Midwestern Presidents: Truman and Eisenhower

Harry S. Truman (1884–1972) grew up on his family's farm in Missouri. He was the last President not to complete college. After high school, Truman took courses and worked at various clerical jobs. He enlisted in the Missouri National Guard and moved up the ranks to become commander of an artillery battery in France during World War I. The war demonstrated his leadership abilities. After the war, Truman and a business partner opened up a men's clothing store, but it failed in the recession of 1921. In 1922, Truman was elected as a county court judge. In 1933, he was chosen to direct the Missouri branch of the federal re-employment program (a New Deal agency). The following year, Truman was elected to the U.S. Senate, where he served for ten years. In 1940, he chaired a committee that investigated wasteful spending in government. His committee saved the government millions of dollars and put Truman's picture on the cover of news magazines like *Time*. In 1944, Roosevelt chose Truman to be his running mate. Truman and Roosevelt rarely met and Truman was not even told about the top-secret Manhattan Project. He had only been Vice President for three months before Roosevelt died, catapulting Truman to the White House.

Dwight David Eisenhower (1890–1969) grew up in Abilene, Kansas. He graduated from the U.S. Military Academy at West Point in 1915. Eisenhower spent World War I training tank crews in the United States, despite his request to go to Europe. He was one of the first strategists to realize that tanks would promote rapid movement in warfare. Eisenhower served under General MacArthur in the Philippines and was promoted to brigadier general by 1941. After the attack at Pearl Harbor, he assisted in the development of U.S. war plans. In 1942, Eisenhower was sent to London and soon placed in charge of U.S. forces stationed there. He became Commander-in-Chief of the Allied forces invading North Africa and Italy, and was later appointed as Supreme Allied Commander in Europe, in charge of the Allied landings on D-Day and the subsequent invasion of France and Germany. Eisenhower excelled at balancing conflicting interests and personalities. After the war, he held a variety of senior military positions as well as becoming President of Columbia University. Truman encouraged Eisenhower to run for President as a Democrat, but Eisenhower announced that he was a Republican.

The Cold War

The end of World War II left two great "**superpowers**" in charge of world affairs: the United States and the Soviet Union. The Soviet Union (or "U.S.S.R.") was formed after the Russian Revolution. It consisted of present-day Russia and neighboring countries that were once part of the Russian empire.

Although the United States and the Soviet Union had been allies during World War II, they quickly became rivals in a "Cold War" that would last for more than four decades. The war was "cold" only in the sense that, because of nuclear weapons, the two superpowers never confronted each other directly in open warfare. However, their global competition led to frequent world crises and regional confrontations on every continent.

Origins of the Cold War

The roots of the Cold War lay in the competing ideological systems of the United States and the Soviet Union, and in their conflicting strategic needs. The United States wanted to spread its democratic, free market system. The Soviet Union wanted to spread its system of communism. It was inevitable that these two superpowers should clash in the pursuit of these objectives.

The Main Ideas of Communism

You may recall that the Soviet Union was the world's first communist nation. The Soviet system was based on the ideas of the nineteenth-century thinker Karl Marx, as interpreted by the Russian revolutionary Vladimir Lenin. Its main ideas are described below.

Class Struggle and Revolution

Communists believe that in noncommunist societies, landowners and businessmen, known as "capitalists," use their wealth and power to exploit workers. Capitalists keep for themselves most of the wealth that workers create. The conflict of interest between capitalists and workers leads to class struggle. The conditions of workers grow increasingly worse until workers are finally driven to overthrow the ruling class of landowners and businessmen in a violent revolution. Soviet communists claimed this was what happened in Russia in 1917.

From "Dictatorship of the Workers" to "Worker's Paradise"

After a successful revolution, communist leaders are supposed to establish a dictatorship to educate the people in the ideas of communism and to look after their true interests. Although this dictatorship is run for the benefit of the workers, communist leaders keep control in their own hands. Ownership of the means of production is taken over by the state. This "dictatorship of the workers" is meant to gradually create a new communist society. In this ideal society, private property will be eliminated, government will wither away, and everyone will work happily for the good of society as a whole.

The Reality of Soviet Communism

In practice, the Soviet Union became a ruthless dictatorship. Under Lenin, communists confiscated wealth and property from Russian nobles, landowners, and businessmen. All free organizations were suppressed, and only communist views could be expressed. Lenin consolidated power after a brutal civil war but died shortly thereafter. His successor, **Joseph Stalin**, murdered political opponents or sent them to *gulags*—concentration-type camps located in the frozen wastelands of Siberia. Stalin used force to confiscate peasant lands to "collectivize" agriculture. In Ukraine, he confiscated all food and left the population to starve. Stalin used a combination of propaganda and coercion to build up basic industries (like steel production) instead of providing for consumer needs. He kept all power in his own hands and was responsible for the deaths of millions of innocent people. Communist ideology became a mere pretext justifying his own absolute power.

A Clash of Systems

The United States had a far different political and economic system. In the United States, people elected leaders democratically. Ordinary citizens enjoyed free speech, freedom of the press, freedom of religious beliefs, and the right to a fair trial when accused of a crime. They were also free to own property and to make whatever they could afford to produce and sell. This system was the exact opposite of the Soviet system under Stalin. Americans hoped the war-torn countries of Europe would adopt their system, while Stalin hoped to spread Soviet-style communism.

The Historian's Apprentice

Create a chart or table comparing the Soviet and American systems in 1945. Consider social, political, and economic differences.

The Cold War begins in Europe

Both the United States and the Soviet Union had tried their best to keep out of World War II. In 1939, Stalin had signed a "Non-Aggression Pact" with Hitler, allowing the German army to march into Poland while Soviet forces invaded Poland from the east. Stalin was hoping for continued peace with Germany, but in June 1941 Hitler ordered the invasion of the Soviet Union. Six months later, Japan attacked Pearl Harbor and Hitler declared war on the United States. The United States and the Soviet Union thus became allies. But Stalin greatly resented the fact that the United States and Great Britain had waited until June 1944 to land their troops in France. All this time, the Soviet army bore the main brunt of Nazi attacks. About 400,000 Americans died in World War II; in sharp contrast, Soviet deaths in the war exceeded 23 million.

Postwar Plans at Yalta (February 1945)

In late 1944 and early 1945, American, British, and French troops marched through France and into Germany from the west while the Soviet

"Red Army" advanced from the east. The Red Army marched across Eastern Europe, liberating Poland, Romania, Czechoslovakia, Bulgaria, and Albania from Nazi rule.

In February 1945, Roosevelt, Churchill, and Stalin met at Yalta in the Soviet Union. At the **Yalta Conference**, these "Big Three" laid plans for the postwar reconstruction of Europe. They agreed that Germany should be divided into four separate occupation zones. They confirmed the structure of the new United Nations organization, which had been negotiated five months earlier. They also agreed that the Soviet Union would keep the area of pre-war Poland it had annexed in 1941, while Poland would be given a slice of Germany. Finally, Stalin made a pledge to allow free elections in Poland when the war ended.

Churchill, Roosevelt, and Stalin

The three powers actually signed a "Declaration of Liberated Europe," which Roosevelt afterwards presented to Congress. This recognized "the right of all people to choose the form of government under which they shall live" and promised "free elections of Governments responsive to the will of the people" in all liberated territories. A separate declaration on Poland stated that the provisional Polish government would hold "free and unfettered elections as soon as possible on the basis of universal suffrage and [a] secret ballot."

The Potsdam Conference

Roosevelt died in April 1945. The new President, **Harry S. Truman**, met with Stalin at **Potsdam**, Germany, in late July and early August to discuss the treatment of Germany, the war against Japan, and the future of Europe. It was during this conference that Truman made the decision to drop the atomic bomb on Japan.

Serious differences between the Soviet Union and the United States quickly arose at Potsdam, especially over the future of Eastern Europe.

The Soviet Point of View

Stalin believed the Soviet Union should have control over Eastern Europe to ensure that it was never invaded again. Just as the United States controlled Latin America through the "Monroe Doctrine," Stalin claimed the right to a Soviet "sphere of influence" in Eastern Europe. He felt the Western powers had no direct interests there and should not interfere. Since the Red Army was already occupying the region, Stalin saw this as a historic opportunity to achieve control. He placed no trust in Western leaders, who had delayed opening a second front in France, resulting in an unparalleled loss of Soviet lives during the war.

The American Point of View

President Truman felt that Stalin had promised free elections in Poland and should keep his word. He further believed that other European countries desired to become democratic, free-market nations like the United States. Most of Truman's advisers agreed that communism was a dangerous system that should not be allowed to spread. They saw Stalin as a brutal dictator, like Hitler, who could not be trusted. Truman's leading advisers felt it would be a dangerous mistake for the United States to turn its back on European affairs as it had done after World War I. They did not want to make the same error with Stalin that European leaders had made with Hitler. They felt it was important to resist Stalin's demands from the beginning, rather than to wait for the Soviet Union to grow ever more powerful.

The Fate of Poland

Although the Soviet army had liberated Poland from Nazi rule, few Poles saw the Soviet Union as their friend. Part of Poland had once been under the rule of the Russian Tsars, and Stalin had cooperated with Hitler in dividing Poland in two. Stalin had ordered the murder of more than 20,000 Polish military officers in the Katyn Forest in 1940, and he refused to return the eastern part of Poland after the war. In 1945, Stalin deliberately let the German army destroy Warsaw, the Polish capital, before ordering Soviet troops to liberate what was left. He also refused to recognize the provisional Polish government-in-exile in London, recognized by most Poles. Instead, he had formed his own puppet Polish government, led by pro-Soviet Polish communists. Stalin even arrested the Poles who had led the heroic resistance against the Nazis. Despite his promises at Yalta, Stalin failed to permit genuinely free elections in Poland. Protected by the Soviet army, Poland's communist government arrested thousands of political opponents, delayed elections until 1947, and falsified the election results.

The Historian's Apprentice

Imagine you are an American journalist at the end of World War II. Write an editorial on how American leaders should respond to the failure to hold "free and unfettered elections" in Poland.

An "Iron Curtain" Descends on Eastern Europe

Once the Soviets failed to permit free elections in Poland, the "Cold War" began in earnest. Local Communists came to power in other countries of Eastern Europe. Trade and communications between Eastern and Western Europe were cut off.

Winston Churchill told Americans in a speech in 1946 that an **"Iron Curtain"** had fallen, closing off Eastern Europe from the West. For the next forty years, travel and contact between the East and West was restricted, and Eastern European governments became **"satellites"** (*dependent states*) of the Soviet Union.

The Historian's Apprentice

Make a Venn diagram comparing the Truman Doctrine and the Marshall Plan. Consider both their goals and the means they used to carry out those goals. How were they similar? How did they differ?

The Division of Germany and the Berlin Airlift, 1948

In May 1948, the French, British, and Americans decided to merge their zones of occupation in Germany into a single state, the Federal Republic of Germany, also known as "West Germany." Berlin, the former capital of Germany, was located deep within the Soviet occupation zone. Because of its importance, the city had been divided into four sectors, each one occupied by one of the four Allied powers—the Soviet Union, the United States, Great Britain, and France. The Soviets reacted to the merging of the western zones of Germany by announcing a blockade of West Berlin (the sectors of the city occupied by the three Western Allies). They closed all highway and railroad links to the city from the West. The Western Allies refused, however, to abandon West Berlin. They began a massive airlift to feed and supply the city. The Berlin Airlift successfully defied Stalin. Within a year, the Berlin blockade was lifted. The Soviets then turned their occupation zone in Germany into a new country, the German Democratic Republic, also known as "East Germany." Germany had been divided in two.

The Birth of NATO and the Warsaw Pact

In response to the tensions of the Cold War, the United States, Canada, and ten Western European countries formed the **North Atlantic Treaty Organization (NATO)** in 1949. Each member of NATO pledged to defend every other member if attacked. Through NATO, the United States extended the protection of its nuclear arsenal to the countries of Western Europe.

When West Germany joined NATO in 1955, the Soviet Union responded by creating the **Warsaw Pact**, an alliance with its Eastern European "satellites." The Warsaw Pact was later used by the Soviet Union to justify armed intervention

Berliners watch as supplies are flown in by Western Allies

Chapter 16 | The Truman and Eisenhower Years

in the affairs of Eastern Europe. Soviet leaders sent troops into the satellite states whenever their communist governments were threatened by local dissent.

Containment in Asia

American statesmen had succeeded in checking the spread of communism in Europe. Could they contain communism in other regions, such as Asia? Since 1927, communist Chinese had been attempting to overthrow the "Nationalist" Chinese government. During World War II, Chinese Nationalists and communists agreed to a temporary truce. After the defeat of Japan, fighting between the Nationalists and communists resumed. The communists, led by **Mao Zedong**, received support from the Soviet Union. In 1949, they succeeded in defeating the Nationalists, who retreated to the island of Taiwan.

Mao Zedong turned China, the world's most populous nation, into a communist state. President Truman refused to extend U.S. diplomatic recognition to China's communist government. Instead, the United States continued to treat the Nationalist government on Taiwan as China's official government of China. The United States was also able to keep the Nationalist government as China's official representative to the United Nations.

The "fall of China" to communism raised new questions for American leaders. Should they try to check the spread of communism around the globe? And did communism hold a special appeal to the impoverished and struggling peoples of Asia, Africa, and Latin America? In many of these countries, leaders were angry at the West for abuses they had suffered under colonial rule. Communism seemed to offer a better path towards economic modernization and social equality.

The Division of Korea (1945–1950)

Korea is a mountainous peninsula jutting out from Manchuria and pointing towards Japan. It is bordered by China and Russia to the west and north, and by Japan across the sea to the east. Korea was ruled by Japan from 1905 until the end of World War II.

Three months before the Japanese surrender in 1945, the Soviet Union declared war on Japan and sent troops to northern Korea. The United States quickly sent its own troops to southern Korea. Korea was placed under joint Soviet and American control. It was then divided into two occupation zones through the middle of the country at the 38th parallel of latitude. Soviet forces remained in the north, and American troops in the south.

Similar to Germany, a communist government was proclaimed in the Soviet zone, led by Kim Il Sung, a Korean communist who had trained in the Soviet Union.

The United Nations ordered national elections to reunify the country, but Kim Il Sung refused to participate. Since the population of the south was greater than the north, he feared he would lose. Elections were held in the south in August 1948. Syngman Rhee—a Korean exile who had spent much of his life in the United States promoting Korean independence—was elected as President of the "Republic of Korea." One month later, North Korea declared its independence as the "Democratic People's Republic." Both governments claimed control over all of Korea, and both

Kim and Rhee took harsh measures against their opponents. Meanwhile, the Soviet Union and the United States withdrew their troops from the peninsula.

The Korean War (1950–1953)

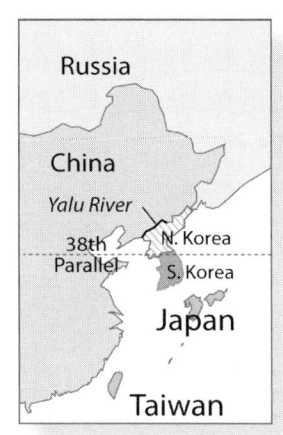

In June 1950, North Korea suddenly invaded South Korea in an attempt to reunify the country under communist rule. The North Koreans were helped by the Soviet Union, which provided them with modern tanks, but the idea for the attack came from Kim. He did not expect the United States to defend a distant country in Asia that seemed to have little to do with U.S. security. However, when Truman heard news of the invasion, it reminded him of Hitler's 1938 annexation of Czechoslovakia. He decided to send U.S. troops to South Korea to resist the invasion.

At this time, the Soviet Union was boycotting the U.N. Security Council for refusing to admit communist China. This coincidence permitted Truman to pass a U.N. resolution condemning the North Korean attack as an act of aggression. Truman was thus able to send U.S. troops to South Korea with U.N. authorization. Thirteen other nations joined the U.N. force.

Only five years after the end of World War II, Americans were again at war. Exercising his powers as Commander-in-Chief, Truman committed these troops in a "police action" rather than asking Congress for an official declaration of war. Members of Congress stood up and cheered at the announcement.

The Course of the War and the Truman–MacArthur Controversy

By then, North Korean forces had overrun most of South Korea and occupied its capital city of Seoul. Truman appointed **General Douglas MacArthur** to command the U.N. forces (mainly made up of Americans and South Koreans). A legendary general, MacArthur had commanded American forces in the Pacific against Japan and had served as the military governor of Japan during the postwar occupation.

U.S. troops from occupied Japan were quickly sent to Korea, but they were not well prepared for war. South Korean and U.S. forces were quickly pushed to the southern tip of the Korean Peninsula.

To save the situation, MacArthur proposed a bold amphibious operation at Inchon Beach, just west of Seoul and north of the main North Korean army. The landing took the North Koreans by complete surprise, enabling U.N. forces to recapture Seoul and trap the North Korean army. In less than two weeks, U.N. forces retook all of South Korea up to the 38th parallel. MacArthur was hailed as a military genius.

The operation was so successful that MacArthur proposed to cross into North Korea and unify the peninsula under Syngman Rhee. Truman's advisers and the American public generally agreed. MacArthur assured Truman that China would not intervene in the war. He was therefore authorized to counterattack by crossing into North Korea. U.N. forces successfully advanced almost up to the Yalu River, the border between North Korea and China. MacArthur confidently predicted that the war would be over by Christmas. His advance, however, brought the communist Chinese directly

General Douglas MacArthur (seated with binoculars) at Inchon Beach

into the war. At the end of November, a Chinese army of 300,000 "volunteers" entered the Korean Peninsula and forced MacArthur to beat a hasty retreat. U.S. casualties were extremely high. The Chinese in turn crossed the 38th parallel in late December 1950 and recaptured Seoul in January 1951.

Rather than accept any blame for his miscalculation, MacArthur proposed to pursue the war more vigorously. He wanted the help of the Chinese Nationalists, and offered to assist them in the recapture of mainland China. MacArthur wanted to blockade China, bomb industrial targets, and even use nuclear weapons if necessary. Truman, on the other hand, wanted to keep the conflict as a "limited war"—limited in geography to the Korean Peninsula and in weaponry to non-nuclear arms.

Public support for Truman was fading and the Democrats did poorly in congressional elections in November 1950. In Tokyo, MacArthur gave interviews to reporters in which he called for an all-out war. He even sent a letter to a Congressman who was critical of Truman. MacArthur's letter, calling for an unlimited war, was read aloud to Congress. Truman finally removed MacArthur from his command and ordered his return to the United States. The President thus successfully asserted civilian control over the military. It was a necessary step but did not diminish MacArthur's popularity. On his return to the United States, MacArthur received a standing ovation from Congress and a ticker-tape parade in New York City. Few Americans, however, wanted to see any expansion of the war.

President Eisenhower Ends the Korean War

By June 1951, the North Koreans and Chinese had again been pushed out of South Korea. The war still dragged on inconclusively for another two years. In November 1952, **Dwight D. Eisenhower** was elected as the next President of the United States. In his election campaign, Eisenhower had promised to end the war. An **armistice** (*cease-fire*) was finally signed in July 1953 at Panmunjom, a village sitting on the demilitarized zone (DMZ) between North and South Korea. 35,000 Americans and four million Koreans had died in the three years of conflict. The armistice left Korea divided at the 38th parallel, exactly as it had been before the North Korean invasion.

The Historian's Apprentice

1. Write a short essay on whether or not American intervention in Korea was justified.
2. Whose approach to fighting the Korean War was better—Truman's or MacArthur's? Imagine you are a journalist writing in 1951. Write an editorial on this question.

Containment Policy under Eisenhower

Although Eisenhower ended the Korean War, he generally continued Truman's containment policy. Americans gave aid to France, then fighting pro-communist nationalists in Indochina. Eisenhower also authorized the Central Intelligence Agency (the CIA) to train exiles to overthrow the socialist government of Guatemala. The United States further pledged to the Nationalist Chinese that it would protect Taiwan from attack. On the other hand, Eisenhower felt unable to do anything when Soviet troops invaded Hungary, a country in Eastern Europe, in 1956. Eisenhower actually preferred to rely more on nuclear weapons and the threat of "massive retaliation" than on having a large standing army.

The "Eisenhower Doctrine"

Eisenhower took a special interest in the Middle East. In 1948, Truman had been a strong supporter of the creation of the new state of Israel. Other countries in the Middle East were gaining their independence from Britain and France. Americans feared that Arab states like Egypt would side with the Soviet Union in the Cold War. In 1956, Eisenhower prevented Britain, Israel, and France from taking over the Suez Canal. The following year, Eisenhower sent U.S. troops briefly to Lebanon and announced that the United States would be "prepared to use armed force . . . [to counter] aggression from any country controlled by international communism." This extension of the Truman Doctrine to the Middle East came to be known as the "**Eisenhower Doctrine**."

Eisenhower and Khrushchev

The Soviets exploded their first atomic bomb in 1949. Americans exploded the first hydrogen bomb in 1952, which was hundreds of times more powerful than an atomic bomb. The Soviets exploded their own hydrogen bomb just a year later in August 1953.

The same year, Stalin died and **Nikita Khrushchev** became leader of the Soviet Union. Although far less brutal than Stalin, Khrushchev still believed in the superiority of the communist system. He also believed that, with nuclear weapons, the United States and Soviet Union could only survive through "peaceful coexistence." Khrushchev visited the United States in 1959. A summit meeting between Khrushchev and Eisenhower in Paris the following year ended abruptly when Khrushchev demanded an apology for an American spy plane, which had been shot down over the Soviet Union just a few days earlier.

The Historian's Apprentice

Fill in the chart below, identifying some of the major policies that U.S. leaders developed in response to the Cold War and describing their impact.

Policy/Action	What it was	Impact
Containment Policy		
Truman Doctrine		
Marshall Plan		
Korean War		

The Cold War at Home

Despite the Cold War, some Americans continued to believe that communism offered the best solution to the problems posed by industrialization. Stalin's worst atrocities were generally unknown, and some Americans remained sympathetic to the Soviet Union. Similar to the "Red Scare" 30 years earlier, the rights of these sympathizers were challenged in the postwar era in the name of national security.

Americans became suspicious of anyone holding communist beliefs. Fearing a communist threat inside the United States, President Truman created **Loyalty Review Boards** to conduct investigations of government employees suspected of "un-American" activities, such as membership in the American Communist Party. Congress also conducted its own investigations in the **House Committee on Un-American Activities (HCUAA)**. This committee interrogated actors, directors, writers, government employees, union leaders, and other individuals about their political beliefs and activities.

Leaders in the entertainment industry were especially targeted because of their influence on American culture. Those questioned by the committee were often asked to report on the activities of others as well as themselves. Many were "blacklisted" and unable to find work because they were suspected of being communist sympathizers or had refused to respond to the committee. The "Hollywood Ten" in 1947, for example, were ten screenwriters and directors who refused to answer the committee's questions. None of them found work in Hollywood again for a decade or more. Hundreds of others were similarly blacklisted.

The fall of China to communism and the Soviet development of nuclear weapons greatly increased American **paranoia** (*exaggerated fear and distrust*). People wondered: had communist sympathizers in the U.S. State Department (*the department of the federal government that conducts foreign relations*) secretly helped the communists in China? Did communist spies in the U.S. Department of Defense provide nuclear secrets to the Soviet Union? J. Edgar Hoover, Director of the F.B.I., began collecting information on suspected communist sympathizers. In 1950, **Julius and Ethel Rosenberg** were charged with handing atomic secrets over to the Soviets. The Rosenbergs were tried and executed, although many historians today believe that Ethel was innocent.

McCarthyism

The anti-communist hysteria only escalated in the early 1950s. In February 1950, **Joseph McCarthy**, U.S. Senator from Wisconsin, shocked Americans by announcing that he had a list of communist spies who had infiltrated the U.S. State Department. McCarthy used different forms of media to spread his message—including newspapers, pamphlets, radio, and television.

The Historian's Apprentice

The following speech was given by Senator Joe McCarthy at Wheeling, West Virginia, on February 9, 1950. McCarthy showed that he held a list of names, but he never made this list public. Later, he reduced the claimed number of names on his list from 205 to 57.

> "Today we are engaged in a final, all-out battle between communistic atheism and Christianity. The modern champions of communism have selected this as the time, and ladies and gentlemen, the chips are down—they are truly down . . .
>
> Six years ago, . . . there was within the Soviet orbit, 180,000,000 people. Lined up on the anti-totalitarian side there were in the world at that time, roughly 1,625,000,000 people. Today, only six years later, there are 800,000,000 people under the absolute domination of Soviet Russia—an increase of over 400 percent. On our side, the figure has shrunk to around 500,000,000. In other words, in less than six years, the odds have changed from 9 to 1 in our favor to 8 to 5 against us . . .
>
> The reason why we find ourselves in a position of impotency is not because our only powerful potential enemy has sent men to invade our shores . . . but rather because of the traitorous actions of those who have been treated so well by this Nation . . .
>
> This is glaringly true in the State Department. There the bright young men who are born with silver spoons in their mouths are the ones who have been most traitorous . . . "

Senator McCarthy

Continued ▶

> I have here in my hand a list of 205 . . . a list of names that were made known to the Secretary of State as being members of the Communist Party and who nevertheless are still working and shaping policy in the State Department . . ."

1. Which factors made McCarthy's speech believable to listeners? Which factors made the claims in McCarthy's speech seem doubtful?
2. Can members of the public distinguish when leaders are truthful or telling falsehoods? How does this remain a problem today?

McCarthy later made accusations about other federal departments. He blamed former Secretary of State George Marshall for losing China to the communists. The public began to fear that communists could be found in every government department.

People of liberal political views became afraid of being accused of communist sympathies. Those who came under suspicion could not work for the government and often could not find jobs in private industry. McCarthy was so popular that he was able to help other Republican candidates get elected. Eisenhower disapproved of McCarthy but refused to criticize him openly.

McCarthy was put in charge of his own congressional subcommittee and continued to hold hearings. He bullied witnesses, disregarded their rights, and sabotaged their careers. In 1953, he even accused the U.S. Army of sheltering communists. The army fought back by accusing McCarthy of using improper influence on behalf of a friend. Extensive hearings were held on television. The American public witnessed McCarthy's bullying tactics first hand. McCarthy was unable to provide evidence for his accusations and was finally condemned for his lack of "decency" in attacking others. A famous journalist denounced McCarthy for failing to distinguish between dissent (*disagreement*) and disloyalty. McCarthy himself was censured (*formally criticized*) by the Senate. Today, the term "McCarthyism" stands both for the anti-communist hysteria of the 1950s and the practice of making unsubstantiated accusations against innocent people.

Postwar Prosperity

The years after World War II were a period of astonishing economic growth in the United States. An unusually favorable combination of political, economic, and social factors lay behind this postwar prosperity.

The "G.I. Bill of Rights"

In 1944, Congress passed the "Servicemen's Readjustment Act," better known as the "**G.I. Bill of Rights**." G.I. stood for "Government Issue"—the term applied to military equipment, like helmets and uniforms, furnished by the government. G.I. came to refer to the soldiers themselves during the war.

The G.I. Bill gave special benefits to returning veterans, including unemployment payments while they were looking for work, mortgages at low rates so that they could buy their own homes, low interest loans so that G.I.s could start businesses, and money to enable them to pursue further education. Every veteran who served at least 90 days was qualified to receive these benefits. More than two million veterans eventually used G.I. benefits to go to college, while another five million used G.I. benefits to receive some other form of training.

The "Baby Boom"

Many war veterans quickly married and had children, leading to a surge in the birth rate known as the "**baby boom**." Between 3.5 and 4.2 million babies were born each year for a period of more than a decade. Those born in these years became known as the "baby boomers."

America—the World's Leading Producer

With much of Europe and Asia in ruins, America became the world's largest producer. Although it had less than 7% of the world's population, the United States produced half of its manufacturing output, including more than half of its oil and steel and 80% of its automobiles.

There was little foreign competition and American crops and manufactured goods were badly needed overseas. The Marshall Plan gave Europeans more purchasing power and expanded the demand for American goods. The demand for consumer goods within the United States was also at an all-time high. With higher incomes and low unemployment, American families bought vast quantities of mass-produced goods, from refrigerators and washing machines to cars and television sets. Fifty million automobiles and fifty million television sets were sold in the decade after World War II. Postwar government spending also remained far above pre-war levels and contributed to economic growth.

New technologies and methods of production contributed to American economic supremacy. During the war, new drugs, new synthetic materials, and new inventions like the jet engine were developed or improved. These innovations were now put to peacetime purposes. Many Americans found jobs in the aircraft, electrical, chemical, automobile, and food-processing industries. With restrictions on immigration, most new jobs went to workers already living in the United States. The **Gross National Product** (or GNP)—the goods and services produced by all Americans in a single year—doubled in the fifteen years between 1945 and 1960. Real incomes rose by 59% between 1950 and 1962, while unemployment remained low.

Housing and the Growth of Suburbs

Home construction also increased employment and contributed to economic growth. The G.I. Bill made it easier than ever before for Americans to obtain loans to buy houses. Between 1945 and 1960, American home ownership increased by a half.

In 1947, William Levitt built Levittown, New York—the first mass-produced tract housing development. Each house had an identical design. Levitt applied the techniques of assembly-line production to build these homes at low cost and at breakneck speed. With their housing benefits, veterans could often buy Levitt's houses for less than it cost them to rent a city apartment. **Suburbs**—residential communities on the outskirts of cities with single-family houses, private lawns, and plenty of fresh air—began to grow faster than the cities they surrounded.

The Historian's Apprentice

1. Which factors most contributed to the postwar prosperity?
2. What lessons from the postwar period might be applied to encourage economic growth today?

The Interstate Highway System

In 1953, Dwight D. Eisenhower became President. Despite being the first Republican President in twenty years, Eisenhower kept most New Deal programs. One of his greatest achievements was another public project. During the war, he had been impressed by the German highway system and its role in moving troops. He believed that Americans needed a similar system—in part for the national defense, to be able to move troops or evacuate cities in case of war.

In 1956, Congress passed the **National Interstate and Defense Highways Act**. This act led to the construction of the interstate highway system—the network of highways across states that still unites our country today. The building of these highways contributed to the general prosperity and further encouraged middle-class Americans to move to the suburbs. New highways gave them better access to urban centers. Suburban residents could drive on the highway to work in the city each morning and return home along the same route each night. Trucks could move goods more easily from one part of the nation to another, and troops could be moved quickly in the event of a national emergency.

The **St. Lawrence Seaway** was also built by the United States and Canada during Eisenhower's Presidency. It connected the Great Lakes to the Atlantic Ocean.

The Social Impact of Suburban Life

The general prosperity, the growth of suburbs, the triumph of mass production, the spread of the mass media, and fear of communism all led to a greater emphasis on conformity in the 1950s. To "conform" is to act like everyone else. At work, many Americans became the employees of large corporations with little room for individuality. At home, a growing number of Americans lived in suburbs in houses that were identical to those of their neighbors. Many suburban communities established their own rules, which residents were expected to obey. They also enforced racial, ethnic, and religious uniformity. White residents in prosperous suburban neighborhoods signed agreements pledging not to sell their houses to people of color. Universities had quotas limiting the number of Jewish applicants they would admit.

Americans purchased similar mass-produced cars, appliances, clothing, and food. The rise of the mass media—newspapers, magazines, movies, radio, and television— helped to forge a new mass culture, which extolled the virtues of middle-class family life. Popular television programs, like "Father Knows Best" and "Leave it to Beaver," depicted what was supposed to be a typical American family—white, middle-class, living in the suburbs, with the father at work, the mother at home, and two or three children. Unusual ideas and behavior were frowned upon. Fear of communism strengthened the general dislike of non-conformist attitudes.

The Civil Rights Movement

The **Civil Rights Movement** was a major turning point in establishing equal rights and transforming our nation into a more diverse and pluralistic society. The postwar years saw great strides forward in civil rights.

The Truman Years, 1945–1953

For centuries, racism had been deeply ingrained in American life. Not only did racial segregation exist in the South, but even the U.S. Army that fought in World War II remained divided into segregated units. National sports like baseball had segregated teams.

In April 1947, Jackie Robinson became the first African-American player to be signed up by a national team—the Brooklyn Dodgers—to play major league baseball. Robinson broke the ground for all future African-American athletes. Just over a year later, President Truman issued Executive Order 9981, **desegregating** the armed forces and ending all racial discrimination in hiring by the federal government. Several Northern states, such as New York, also passed their own state laws prohibiting racial discrimination in housing, employment, and the use of public services.

Jackie Robinson of the Brooklyn Dodgers

The Historian's Apprentice

The following is the text of Truman's desegregation order.

"NOW THEREFORE, by virtue of the authority vested in me as President of the United States, by the Constitution and the statutes of the United States, and as Commander in Chief of the armed services, it is hereby ordered as follows:

1. It is hereby declared to be the policy of the President that there shall be equality of treatment and opportunity for all persons in the armed services without regard to race, color, religion or national origin. This policy shall be put into effect as rapidly as possible, having due regard to the time required to effectuate any necessary changes without impairing efficiency or morale.

2. There shall be created in the National Military Establishment an advisory committee to be known as the President's Committee on Equality of Treatment and Opportunity in the Armed Services, which shall be composed of seven members to be designated by the President.

3. The Committee is authorized on behalf of the President to examine into the rules, procedures and practices of the Armed Services in order to determine in what respect such rules,

Continued ▶

> procedures and practices may be altered or improved with a view to carrying out the policy of this order..."
>
> —President Harry S. Truman, Executive Order 9981 (July 26, 1948)

1. What was the significance of this executive order?
2. Was President Truman acting within his lawful authority?
3. Despite Executive Order 9981, there were still some segregated units fighting in the Korean War. Why did it take some time for this order to be fully implemented?

Brown v. Board of Education of Topeka, Kansas, 1954

In *Plessy v. Ferguson* (1896), the U.S. Supreme Court had upheld the constitutionality of state segregation laws, so long as the facilities offered to each race were of "equal standards." This became known as the "separate-but-equal" doctrine.

Starting in the 1930s, African-American lawyers at the NAACP began challenging the "separate-but-equal" doctrine. They began by questioning the exclusion of African Americans from law schools and graduate programs in state universities across the South. Since there were no separate state law schools for African Americans, these states had failed to meet the "separate-but-equal" requirement. Last minute efforts by several states to set up separate programs for African-American law students failed to be "equal." The U.S. Supreme Court ruled in favor of the NAACP on the grounds that African Americans had not been offered "equal" alternatives by these states.

In the early 1950s, the NAACP was ready to challenge the "separate-but-equal" doctrine more directly. Linda Brown was a schoolgirl from Topeka, Kansas. Her father sued the local school board because his daughter had been forced to attend a "colored" school when a "white" school was closer to their home. In 1953, the NAACP appealed her case with a number of others to the U.S. Supreme Court.

Thurgood Marshall, the NAACP lawyer handling the case, did not argue that the facilities given to African-American children were inferior, even though this was generally the case. Instead, he argued that segregated education sent African-American children the message that they were not "good enough" to be educated alongside white children. The very act of separating children by race thus created inequality. Marshall supported his argument with the findings of a famous African-American psychologist, Kenneth Clark. Clark showed white and black dolls to African-American children and found that they preferred the white dolls to the black ones. Clark concluded that racial segregation had led to this painful sense of inferiority.

Earl Warren, former Governor of California, had only just been appointed as Chief Justice of the Supreme Court. As Attorney General of California in the 1940s, Warren had assisted in the forced relocation of innocent

Japanese Americans during the war. Regretting his earlier actions, he became a committed supporter of civil rights. Warren wanted to avoid a divided decision on the *Brown* case. With great effort, he obtained the support of all his fellow Justices. Warren wrote their unanimous decision, declaring that racial segregation in public schools was unconstitutional. "Separate but equal," he boldly announced, "has no place" in the field of public education.

The Historian's Apprentice

Here is part of Chief Justice Warren's decision:

> "Does segregation of children in public schools solely on the basis of race, even though the physical facilities and other 'tangible' factors may be equal, deprive the children of the minority group of equal educational opportunities? We believe that it does.
>
> ... Segregation of white and colored children in public schools has a detrimental effect upon the colored children. The impact is greater when it has the sanction of the law, for the policy of separating the races is usually interpreted as denoting the inferiority of the negro group. A sense of inferiority affects the motivation of a child to learn.... We conclude that, in the field of public education, the doctrine of 'separate but equal' has no place. Separate educational facilities are inherently unequal."
>
> —U.S. Supreme Court, *Brown v. Board of Education of Topeka, Kansas* (1954)

1. Why did Justice Warren conclude that segregated schools were "inherently" unequal?
2. How was this conclusion important to the Court's judgment?

When the *Brown* decision was announced, Southern Senators in Congress signed a public protest. Local officials across the South swore they would never enforce the Court's ruling. Membership in the Ku Klux Klan increased.

Southern resistance required the Supreme Court to make a separate ruling on how the *Brown* decision was to be implemented (*put into effect*). Enforcement of the *Brown* decision was handed over to the lower federal courts, which were to see that local school districts followed the desegregation order "with all deliberate speed." The *Brown* decision would in fact take several years to carry out. Many Southern public schools preferred to close rather than integrate (*bring people of different races together*). In some cases, courts eventually resorted to busing—requiring districts to send students in school buses to more distant schools in order to achieve a better racial mix.

Note: You will not need to know about the murder of Emmet Till, the Montgomery Bus Boycott, or the "Little Rock Nine" for the Georgia Milestones EOC Assessment, but they were important developments in the Civil Rights Movement. You should be sure to know about the beliefs, actions, and achievements of Dr. Martin Luther King, Jr.

Chapter 16 | The Truman and Eisenhower Years

The Montgomery Bus Boycott, 1955–1956

In the 1950s, the system of segregation in the South extended far beyond education. African Americans were prevented from sharing restaurants, lunch counters, movie theaters, public restrooms, and even water fountains with whites. On public buses, African Americans were forced to sit in the back seats, while the front section of the bus was reserved for whites.

There were also unwritten social rules that African Americans were expected to obey. **Emmet Till**, a 14-year-old African-American boy from Chicago, was visiting his aunt in Mississippi in 1955. He was murdered after he was said to have whistled at a young white woman in a shop. Till's mother brought his mutilated body back to Chicago for a funeral with an open casket, which received widespread publicity. Many were shocked when the murderers were acquitted by an all-white jury in Mississippi, despite overwhelming evidence against them.

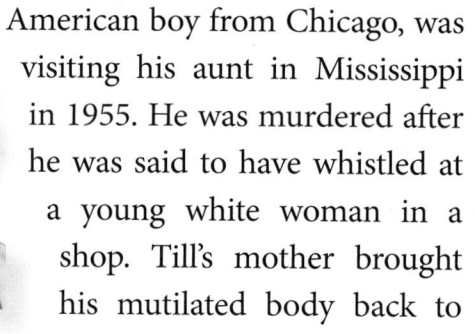

One evening in December 1955, **Rosa Parks** was riding home on a city bus in Montgomery, the state capital of Alabama. The bus became increasingly crowded. When a white passenger entered and there was no room left in the "white" section, the bus driver asked Parks to get up and move to the back of the bus. Parks, an active member of the local branch of the NAACP, refused to do so and was arrested. Later she wrote, "I thought of Emmett Till, and I just couldn't go back."

Local NAACP leaders organized an immediate boycott of Montgomery's city buses to protest her arrest. They demanded courteous treatment, an end to segregation on the bus, and the hiring of African-American bus drivers. They formed the "Montgomery Improvement Organization" and elected an inspiring young Baptist minister as their leader: **Dr. Martin Luther King, Jr.** King had been born and raised in Atlanta. He had studied the writings of David Thoreau and Mahatma Gandhi on non-violence, as well as Christian teachings. He believed that passive resistance to unjust laws could change the attitudes of oppressors.

The organizers arranged car pools and cabs to take the boycotters to work; others walked. City buses sat idle. The boycott, which lasted just over a year, demonstrated that African Americans could act together in their determination to oppose segregation. At the same time, Parks and other bus riders sued in federal court, claiming that segregation on public buses was unconstitutional. In June 1956, the court ruled in their favor.

Five months later, the U.S. Supreme Court refused to review the decision (in effect upholding it). The protestors had won the contest, and Montgomery's city buses were integrated. After the boycott was over, Dr. King and other African-American ministers formed the Southern Christian Leadership Council ("SCLC"). Its goal was to fight for racial equality using non-violent means.

The "Little Rock Nine," 1957

Meanwhile, officials in many Southern states were still delaying implementation of the *Brown* decision. When the school board of Little Rock, Arkansas, admitted nine African-American children to its all-white high school, the Governor of Arkansas ordered the state's National Guard to prevent the children from entering the school. After pressure from President Eisenhower, the Governor removed the National Guard and allowed the children to attend the school, but he took inadequate steps to protect them. The **"Little Rock Nine"** (the nine African-American students) were threatened by an angry white mob. The situation finally forced President Eisenhower to take decisive action: he sent 1,000 federal troops to Little Rock and ordered the Arkansas National Guard to defend the African-American students. Federal troops surrounded the high school, and for the rest of the year the students were provided with military escorts.

The Historian's Apprentice

Imagine you are living in Montgomery in 1955 or Little Rock in 1957. Write a letter to a friend in Georgia describing the bus boycott or the "Little Rock Nine."

The Impact of Sputnik

On October 4, 1957, the Soviets launched **Sputnik** into space, the first man-made satellite to orbit the Earth. Sputnik was relatively small—a shiny aluminum sphere about the size of a beach ball, weighing 184 pounds. The force needed to hurl such a mass into space was far greater than Americans had thought the Soviets were capable of producing. Once in orbit, Sputnik traveled at a speed of 18,000 miles an hour, circling the Earth every 92 minutes. It emitted beep-like sounds that were broadcast on the American news. The following month, the Soviets launched Sputnik II: it weighed over a thousand pounds, carried scientific instruments, and included a dog as a passenger.

Americans were shocked that the Soviets seemed to be so far ahead. They were accustomed to the United States being in the lead. Many Americans believed that totalitarian states, by suppressing free ideas, were incapable of technological innovation. To make matters worse, two months later an attempt by the United States to launch its own Vanguard missile spectacularly failed when the missile exploded on the launch pad.

Not only did the Sputnik launch mark the beginning of the **"space race,"** but it also had great military significance. The same rocket engines that could take a satellite to outer space could also power intercontinental ballistic missiles carrying nuclear warheads to the United States. (An **intercontinental ballistic missile**, or ICBM, is a missile that soars above Earth's atmosphere, glides in space, and then falls back to Earth, hitting a target thousands of miles away.) A special government report responded by calling for massive increases in U.S. military spending and the building of fallout shelters (*shelters thought to protect people from a nuclear attack*).

Despite the clamor, President Eisenhower kept a cool head. The launching of Sputnik revealed that Soviet scientists had made breakthroughs in sending rockets into space, but Eisenhower knew from photographs taken by U.S. spy planes that they still lagged behind in their production of nuclear warheads. While the Soviets had launched the first ICBM, they still lacked a missile system that could effectively strike at the United States. For military purposes, Eisenhower remarked, it was better to have "one good . . . nuclear-armed missile than a rocket that could hit the moon." Eisenhower believed that the United States had actually increased its military superiority over the Soviet Union but he had to keep this information secret because he did not want Soviet leaders to know he was monitoring their progress so closely.

Sputnik also established the principle that outer space was open to all and that each nation had the right to send satellites flying over other nations—two rules that the United States was anxious to establish.

The American public nonetheless remained in a panic. Eisenhower responded by creating a special advisory board of leading scientists. In 1958, he created the **National Aeronautics and Space Administration**, or **NASA**, which would oversee the American space program. The birth of this important agency was thus a direct result of Sputnik.

Because of the shock caused by Sputnik, Congress also passed the **National Defense Education Act** in September 1958. This act provided massive federal funding for math and science education. It was another turning point. Up until this time, the federal government had not provided significant financial support to schools and universities. These generally relied on state and local governments for their

The Historian's Apprentice

Fill in the chart below, describing some of the major events during the Truman and Eisenhower Presidencies, and identifying their effects.

Event	Description	Effects
G.I. Bill		
Truman's Integration Policies		
McCarthyism		
National Interstate Highways Act		
Brown v. Board of Education		
Launch of Sputnik		

478   Chapter 16 | The Truman and Eisenhower Years

funding. Now there appeared to be an urgent need for American education to "catch up" with its Soviet competitor. Education had become a matter of defense, not just of the general welfare.

Finally, the Sputnik launch had an impact on the next Presidential election, three years later. Democratic candidate Senator John F. Kennedy claimed that Republicans had let the United States fall behind the Soviet Union, creating a "missile gap." The successful launch of Sputnik seemed to support Kennedy's claim and may have given him a slight edge in what proved to be the closest election of the century. Soon after becoming President, Kennedy announced that the United States would put the first man on the moon by the end of the decade. Americans succeeded in this goal when Neil Armstrong became the first person to step onto the moon's surface in July 1969.

Satellites turned out to have useful civilian purposes, too. Today, nearly a thousand satellites orbit the Earth. They help us to predict the weather and provide the basis for our global telecommunications and for the Global Positioning System, which is used by GPS receivers around the world. All this began with Sputnik, the first human-made satellite to orbit Earth in outer space.

For the Georgia Milestones EOC Assessment, you should know that:

- [ ] After World War II, the United States and the Soviet Union entered into a "Cold War": the United States promoted democracy and capitalism, while the Soviet Union promoted its system of communism.
- [ ] The Cold War began in response to Stalin's failure to fulfill his agreement at Yalta to allow free elections in Poland. Instead, communist governments were put into place in all those countries occupied by the Red Army, and an "Iron Curtain" fell on Eastern Europe.
- [ ] President Truman decided to oppose any further expansion of communism in Europe with his "containment" policy—the United States would not challenge communism in Eastern Europe, but would not permit communism to spread any further.
- [ ] When Greece and Turkey were threatened by communism in 1947, Truman announced the "Truman Doctrine"—the United States would assist all free peoples resisting communism. Under the Truman Doctrine, the United States sent financial aid, weapons, and military advisers to Greece and Turkey, enabling these countries to resist communism.
- [ ] To help European nations struggling with the economic devastation of World War II, the United States introduced the Marshall Plan in 1948—a program of economic aid from the United States. This program helped Western European nations rebuild their economies, resist communism, and become future trading partners with the United States.
- [ ] When communist North Korea attacked South Korea in 1950, President Truman sent U.S. troops with U.N. authorization to help the South Koreans. Although the North Korean army had almost overrun all of South Korea, General MacArthur was able to

Continued ▶

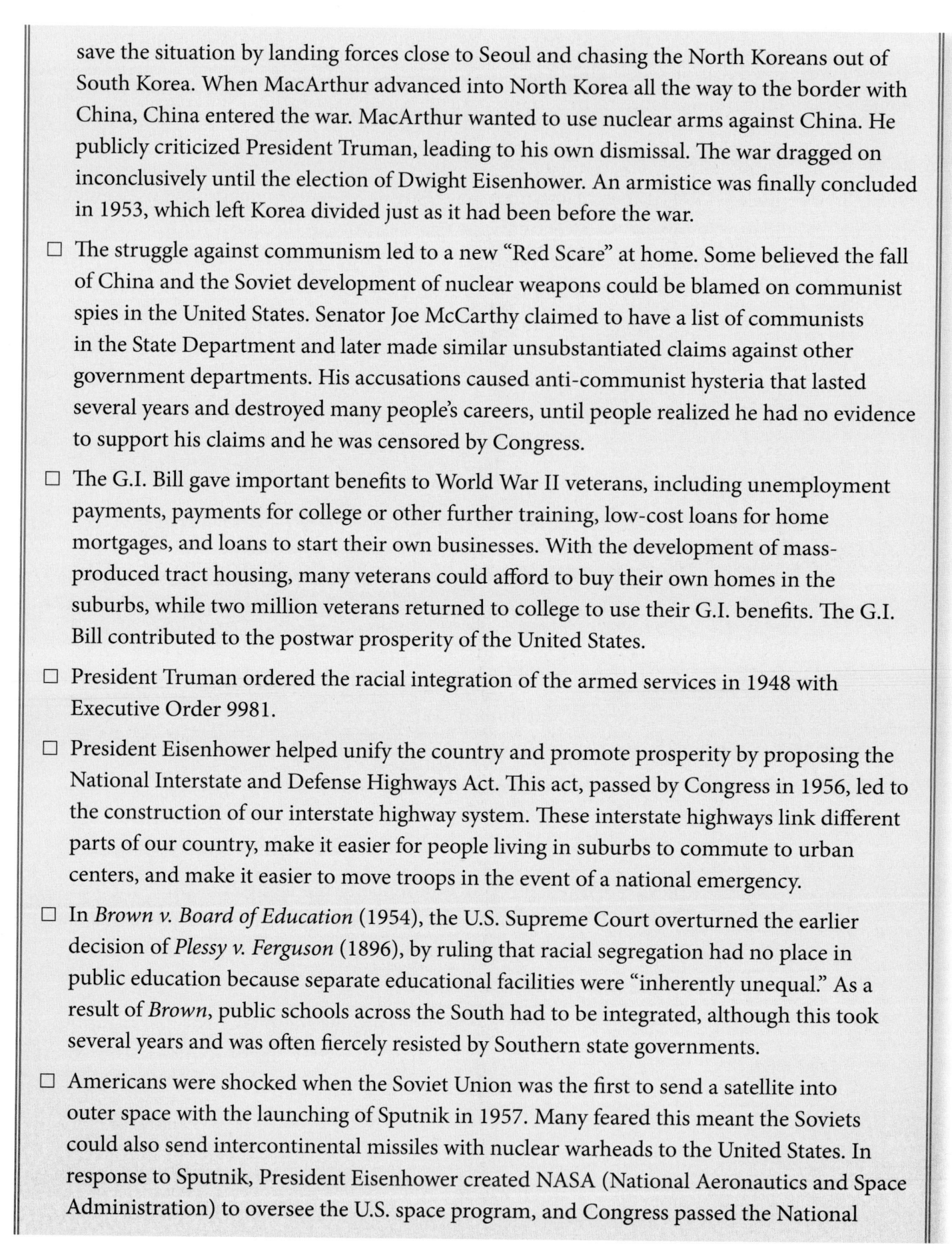

save the situation by landing forces close to Seoul and chasing the North Koreans out of South Korea. When MacArthur advanced into North Korea all the way to the border with China, China entered the war. MacArthur wanted to use nuclear arms against China. He publicly criticized President Truman, leading to his own dismissal. The war dragged on inconclusively until the election of Dwight Eisenhower. An armistice was finally concluded in 1953, which left Korea divided just as it had been before the war.

- [ ] The struggle against communism led to a new "Red Scare" at home. Some believed the fall of China and the Soviet development of nuclear weapons could be blamed on communist spies in the United States. Senator Joe McCarthy claimed to have a list of communists in the State Department and later made similar unsubstantiated claims against other government departments. His accusations caused anti-communist hysteria that lasted several years and destroyed many people's careers, until people realized he had no evidence to support his claims and he was censored by Congress.

- [ ] The G.I. Bill gave important benefits to World War II veterans, including unemployment payments, payments for college or other further training, low-cost loans for home mortgages, and loans to start their own businesses. With the development of mass-produced tract housing, many veterans could afford to buy their own homes in the suburbs, while two million veterans returned to college to use their G.I. benefits. The G.I. Bill contributed to the postwar prosperity of the United States.

- [ ] President Truman ordered the racial integration of the armed services in 1948 with Executive Order 9981.

- [ ] President Eisenhower helped unify the country and promote prosperity by proposing the National Interstate and Defense Highways Act. This act, passed by Congress in 1956, led to the construction of our interstate highway system. These interstate highways link different parts of our country, make it easier for people living in suburbs to commute to urban centers, and make it easier to move troops in the event of a national emergency.

- [ ] In *Brown v. Board of Education* (1954), the U.S. Supreme Court overturned the earlier decision of *Plessy v. Ferguson* (1896), by ruling that racial segregation had no place in public education because separate educational facilities were "inherently unequal." As a result of *Brown*, public schools across the South had to be integrated, although this took several years and was often fiercely resisted by Southern state governments.

- [ ] Americans were shocked when the Soviet Union was the first to send a satellite into outer space with the launching of Sputnik in 1957. Many feared this meant the Soviets could also send intercontinental missiles with nuclear warheads to the United States. In response to Sputnik, President Eisenhower created NASA (National Aeronautics and Space Administration) to oversee the U.S. space program, and Congress passed the National

Defense Education Act to provide federal funding for math and science education. Three years later, President Kennedy announced that Americans would land a man on the moon by the end of the decade, which they succeeded in doing in 1969.

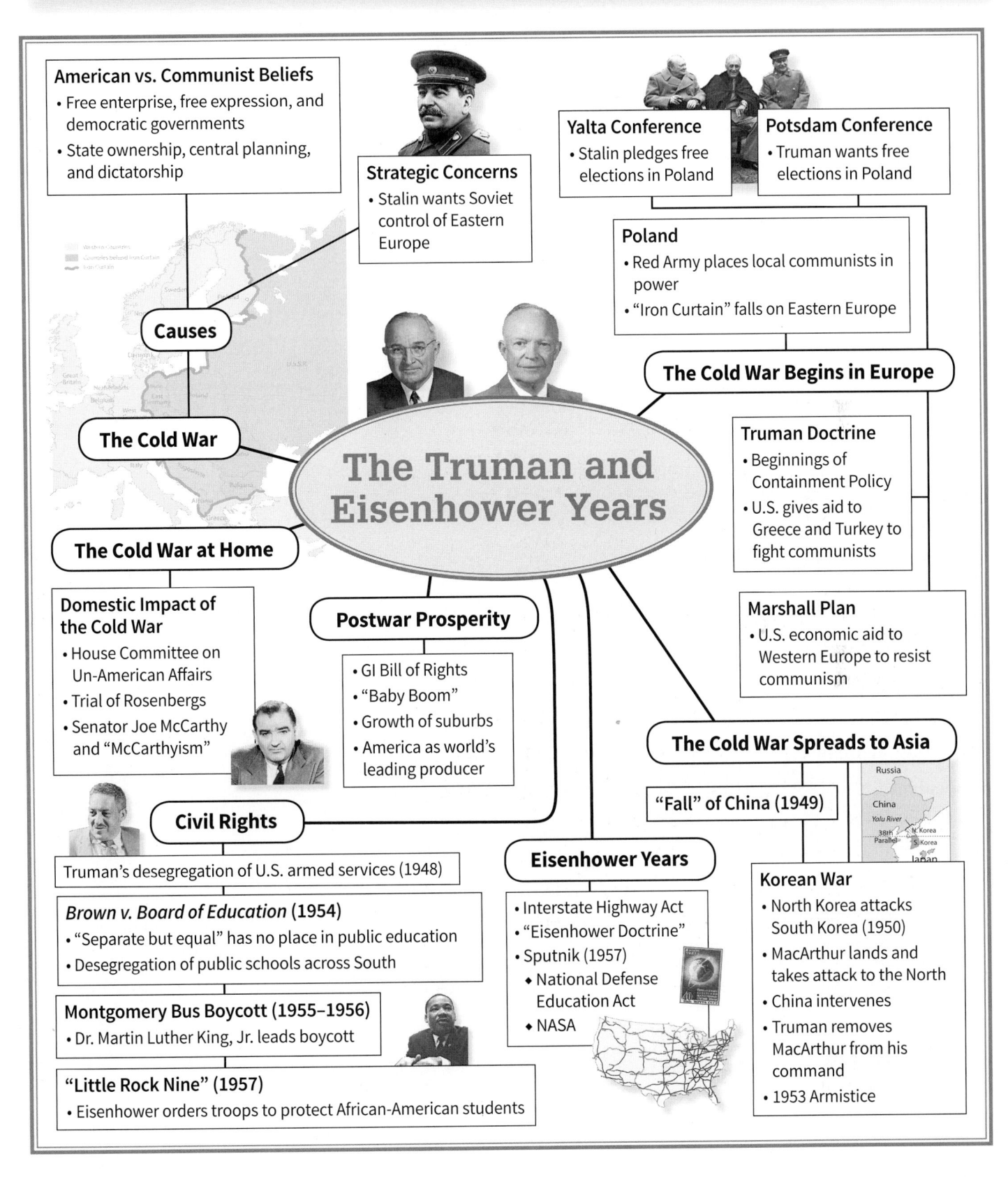

The Truman and Eisenhower Years

Causes

American vs. Communist Beliefs
- Free enterprise, free expression, and democratic governments
- State ownership, central planning, and dictatorship

Strategic Concerns
- Stalin wants Soviet control of Eastern Europe

Yalta Conference
- Stalin pledges free elections in Poland

Potsdam Conference
- Truman wants free elections in Poland

Poland
- Red Army places local communists in power
- "Iron Curtain" falls on Eastern Europe

The Cold War Begins in Europe

Truman Doctrine
- Beginnings of Containment Policy
- U.S. gives aid to Greece and Turkey to fight communists

Marshall Plan
- U.S. economic aid to Western Europe to resist communism

The Cold War Spreads to Asia

"Fall" of China (1949)

Korean War
- North Korea attacks South Korea (1950)
- MacArthur lands and takes attack to the North
- China intervenes
- Truman removes MacArthur from his command
- 1953 Armistice

Eisenhower Years
- Interstate Highway Act
- "Eisenhower Doctrine"
- Sputnik (1957)
- National Defense Education Act
- NASA

Postwar Prosperity
- GI Bill of Rights
- "Baby Boom"
- Growth of suburbs
- America as world's leading producer

The Cold War at Home

Domestic Impact of the Cold War
- House Committee on Un-American Affairs
- Trial of Rosenbergs
- Senator Joe McCarthy and "McCarthyism"

Civil Rights

Truman's desegregation of U.S. armed services (1948)

Brown v. Board of Education (1954)
- "Separate but equal" has no place in public education
- Desegregation of public schools across South

Montgomery Bus Boycott (1955–1956)
- Dr. Martin Luther King, Jr. leads boycott

"Little Rock Nine" (1957)
- Eisenhower orders troops to protect African-American students

Chapter 16 | The Truman and Eisenhower Years

Name _____

The Cold War

Define "Cold War."	How did the Cold War differ from other wars?

Explain how the Truman Doctrine, Marshall Plan, and containment policy were U.S. responses to the development of the Cold War.

Make a question for each of the following clusters of names and terms. Then define or identify any of these names or terms you cannot recall.

Joseph Stalin
Yalta Conference
Harry S. Truman
Potsdam Conference

_____
_____
_____
_____

Iron Curtain
Truman Doctrine
Marshall Plan
Containment

_____
_____
_____

482   Chapter 16 | The Truman and Eisenhower Years

Name: _____

| North and South Korea |
| Korean War |
| General Douglas MacArthur |
| Chinese Intervention |

| House Committee on Un-American Activities |
| Julius and Ethel Rosenberg |
| McCarthyism |

| Dwight Eisenhower |
| Sputnik |
| NASA |
| National Defense and Education Act |

| G.I. Bill of Rights |
| National Interstate and Defense Highways Act |
| Integration of Armed Services |
| *Brown v. Board of Education* |

Chapter 16 | The Truman and Eisenhower Years

483

What Do You Know?

SSUSH20a

1. Examine the excerpt to answer the question.

   > At the present moment in history nearly every nation must choose between alternative ways of life. The choice is too often not a free one. . . .
   >
   > I believe it must be the policy of the United States to support free peoples who are resisting attempted subjugation by armed minorities or by outside pressures. . . . If we falter in our leadership, we may endanger the peace of the world—and we shall surely endanger the welfare of our own nation.
   >
   > —President Harry S. Truman, March 12, 1947

   What threat was President Truman referring to in this speech?

   A. a regional war between India and Pakistan
   B. the spread of communism to Greece and Turkey
   C. Communist infiltration of the U.S. State Department
   D. Vietnamese resistance to French postwar imperialism

SSUSH20a

2. How did the Marshall Plan intend to discourage the spread of communism in Europe?

   A. by joining European nations together into the European Union
   B. by restoring economic stability to the nations of Western Europe
   C. by providing military assistance to France, Great Britain, and Italy
   D. by establishing freely elected governments in Poland and Czechoslovakia

SSUSH20a

3. Use the timeline to answer the question.

   1948 — June: Soviets close roads to Berlin; Berlin Airlift begins | August: Alger Hiss is accused of being a Communist
   1949 — April: Formation of NATO | May: Soviets open roads to Berlin; Berlin Airlift ends | August: Soviet Union explodes its first atomic bomb
   1950 — October: Communists seize power in China | June: Communist North Korea invades South Korea

   Which foreign policy did American leaders follow in response to these events?

   A. imperialism
   B. isolationism
   C. containment
   D. détente

Chapter 16 | The Truman and Eisenhower Years

SSUSH20a

4. Use the diagram to answer the question

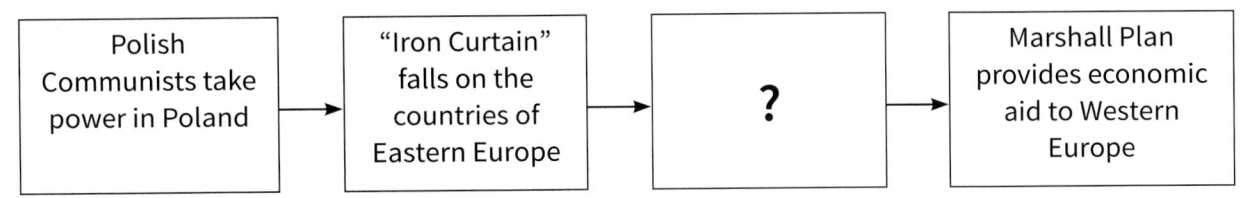

```
[Polish Communists take power in Poland] → ["Iron Curtain" falls on the countries of Eastern Europe] → [?] → [Marshall Plan provides economic aid to Western Europe]
```

Which statement BEST completes the diagram?

A. Stalin withdraws Soviet troops from East Germany.

B. Communist governments are elected by voters in France and Italy.

C. The United States sends its troops to defend South Korea from invasion.

D. Truman announces the U.S. will help Greece and Turkey resist communism.

SSUSH20a

5. Use the document to answer the question.

> NR: DA TT 3426   PAGE 2
> Detailed instructions reference Navy and Air Force follow
>
> All restrictions which have previously prevented the full utilization of the U.S. Far East Air Forces to support and assist the defense of the South Korean territory are lifted for operations below the 38th Parallel. All North Korean tanks, guns, military columns and other targets south of the 38th Parallel are cleared for attack by U.S. Air Forces. The purpose is to clear South Korea of North Korean military forces. Similarly U.S. Naval forces may be used without restriction in coastal waters and sea approaches of Korea south of the 38th Parallel against forces engaged in aggression against South Korea.   (End DA-1)
>
> Washington: DA-2

U.S. Army Teletype Conference, ca. June 1950, Library of Congress

Which foreign policy goal led to the instructions in this document?

A. American leaders wanted to prevent China from taking over North Korea.

B. American leaders wanted to unite North and South Korea into a single republic.

C. American leaders wanted to maintain military bases in both North and South Korea.

D. American leaders wanted to prevent communists from taking over South Korea.

SSUSH20a

6. Which statement BEST describes the outcome of the Korean War (1950–1953)?

A. North Korea made minor gains in the south but lost territory in the north to China.

B. A majority of North Koreans fled southward, causing a collapse of North Korea.

C. North and South Korea remained divided at the 38th parallel, just as they had been before the war.

D. Korea was reunited under a coalition government consisting of both Northerners and Southerners.

Chapter 16 | The Truman and Eisenhower Years

SSUSH20c

7. Use the list to answer the question.

> - The National Aeronautics and Space Administration (NASA) was created.
> - The National Defense Education Act passed.
> - Federal money was provided to improve public schools, especially with mathematics and science programs
> - More money was appropriated by Congress for research and development.

Which event led to the developments on this list?

A. The Soviet Union successfully launched Sputnik into space.
B. Mao Zedong led a successful communist revolution in China.
C. North Koreans crossed the 38th parallel to invade South Korea.
D. Senator Joseph McCarthy announced the discovery of Communist Party members in the U.S. State Department.

SSUSH20b

8. Examine the excerpt to answer the question.

> *We conclude that in the field of public education the doctrine of "separate but equal" has no place. Separate educational facilities are inherently unequal.*
> —Brown v. Board of Education (1954)

What inference can be made from this excerpt about the power of the Supreme Court?

A. It can limit the actions of Congress.
B. It can rule state laws to be unconstitutional.
C. It can dictate new laws to state legislatures.
D. It can provide funding for public education.

SSUSH20b

9. Which of the following was one of the main causes of American economic prosperity in the 1950s?

A. Increased domestic demand for electrical appliances and cars
B. Reconstruction of war-torn areas of the United States
C. Rapid settlement of the Great Plains
D. Increased immigration from Eastern and Southern Europe

SSUSH20b

10. Use the map to answer the question.

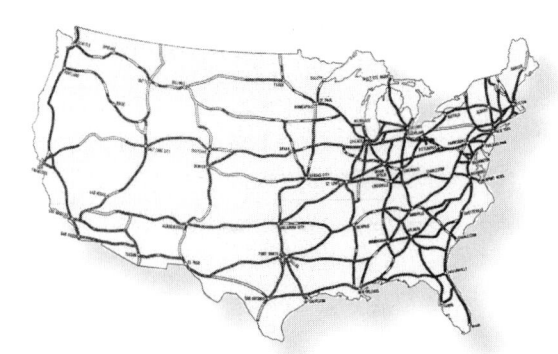

Roads created by the National Interstate and Defense Highways Act

What was an important impact of these roads on the United States?

A. State control of immigration routes has increased.

B. Travel and commerce between states became easier and faster than before.

C. Towns bypassed by the interstate system grew faster than those on the highways.

D. Increased traffic made it more difficult to move troops around the country.

SSUSH20b

11. Which benefits did the G.I. Bill provide to veterans returning from World War II?

A. free medical care and a special retirement plan

B. low-interest mortgages and a bonus payment after five years

C. low-interest mortgages and payments towards high school, vocational school, or higher education

D. a guaranteed job and payments towards high school, vocational school, or higher education

SSUSH20c

12. Why were many Americans alarmed by the launch of Sputnik into space?

A. It demonstrated Soviet missile capabilities.

B. It showed that the Soviets were winning the space race.

C. It enabled the Soviets to spy on everyday Americans.

D. It used advanced technologies taken from the United States.

SSUSH20a

13. Which statement BEST explains the reason for U.S. intervention in the Korean War?

A. The United States wanted to defend South Korea from communist aggression.

B. The United States wanted to overturn the communist government of China.

C. The United States feared another Japanese conquest of the Korean peninsula.

D. The United States wanted to import inexpensive Korean manufactured goods.

Chapter 16 | The Truman and Eisenhower Years

`SSUSH20b`

14. Use this 1947 comic book cover to answer the question.

    Which American leader MOST exploited the fears illustrated by this cover?

    A. President Harry Truman
    B. Julius Rosenberg
    C. Senator Joseph McCarthy
    D. Dr. Martin Luther King, Jr.

`SSUSH20a`

15. Use the excerpt to answer the question.

    > Our concern over the lawless action taken by the forces from North Korea, and our sympathy and support for the people of Korea in this situation, are being demonstrated by the cooperative action of American personnel in Korea, as well as by the steps taken to expedite and augment assistance of the type being furnished under the Mutual Defense Assistance Program.
    >
    > —President Harry S. Truman, June 26, 1950

    Which event led President Truman to make this announcement?

    A. Soviet boycott of the United Nations Security Council
    B. Mao Zedong's victory on mainland China
    C. Japanese evacuation of Korea
    D. North Korean invasion of South Korea

`SSUSH20b`

16. Use the excerpt to answer the question.

    > Segregation of white and colored children in public schools has a detrimental effect upon the colored children. The impact is greater when it has the sanction of the law, for the policy of separating the races is usually interpreted as denoting the inferiority of the [African-American] group. A sense of inferiority affects the motivation of a child to learn.
    >
    > —Brown v. Board of Education (1954)

    What was the impact of the reasoning of the U.S. Supreme Court in the excerpt?

    A. Racial segregation ended in elementary schools but was permitted to continue in higher grades.
    B. Southern states were forced to end racial segregation in all public schools.
    C. Southern states were required to ensure the economic and social equality of members of all races.
    D. Southern states were permitted to maintain separate public schools for African-American children so long as they were as good as other schools.

Chapter 16 | The Truman and Eisenhower Years

Georgia "Peaches" of Wisdom

1. John F. Kennedy was elected President in 1960 after performing well in the first televised debates between candidates—showing the impact of television. He gave an inspiring inaugural address but many of his proposed reforms were stalled in Congress.

2. In 1959, Fidel Castro established a communist state in nearby Cuba. Under Eisenhower, the CIA began training Cuban exiles to overthrow Castro. When Kennedy became President, he approved their invasion of Cuba at the Bay of Pigs. The attempt failed.

3. In October 1962, Americans discovered Cubans were about to install Soviet nuclear missiles. This led to the Cuban Missile Crisis—the closest the world has come to nuclear war. Kennedy blockaded Cuba and threatened to invade. Khrushchev removed the missiles when Kennedy pledged not to invade Cuba.

4. In 1963, Martin Luther King, Jr., led a march on Birmingham, Alabama. King was arrested and wrote his "Letter from Birmingham Jail," in which he explained why African Americans could no longer wait to receive their rights.

5. Alarmed by the police violence, Kennedy proposed a civil rights bill. In August 1963, civil rights leaders held a "March on Washington" in support of the bill. King delivered his "I Have a Dream" speech in which he looked forward to a future without prejudice.

6. In November 1963, Kennedy was assassinated. Lyndon B. Johnson became the next President. Johnson was able to push the Civil Rights Act of 1964 through Congress. It banned racial discrimination in hotels, restaurants, and unions.

7. President Johnson also called for a "War on Poverty." After re-election in 1964, he proposed his "Great Society" programs. Medicare and Medicaid provided health insurance to seniors and others. Project Head Start helped low-income children. The Housing and Urban Development Act gave assistance to cities.

8. In 1965, violence against demonstrators marching from Selma to Montgomery led Johnson to propose the Voting Rights Act of 1965, which increased the powers of the federal government to enforce voting laws.

9. Cesar Chavez helped organize Hispanic migrant farm workers. He started the United Farm Workers (UFW) and launched boycotts of grapes and lettuce to force growers to improve conditions for migrant workers.

10. Vietnam, a nation in Southeast Asia, was divided in 1954: North Vietnam became a communist dictatorship and South Vietnam was placed under a pro-Western Emperor. Prime Minister Ngo Dinh Diem deposed the Emperor but refused to hold promised elections to reunite the country. The Vietcong (South Vietnamese Communists) began a campaign of guerrilla warfare against Diem.

11. Many Americans believed in the "domino theory"—that if Vietnam fell to communism, neighboring nations would fall like a row of dominoes.

12. In August 1964, Congress passed the Gulf of Tonkin Resolution: it authorized Johnson to send in troops. Helicopters, napalm, Agent Orange, and bombing missions were used in support of U.S. troops, but Americans were not used to the environment and often could not detect the enemy.

13. Television had a great impact on politics and culture. It exposed violence against African Americans in the South. When government leaders said the United States was winning the war in Vietnam, television news seemed to show this was not the case.

14. 1968 became a pivotal year. The Vietcong launched the "Tet Offensive," a major assault on cities in South Vietnam. Although the offensive failed, it showed the war was far from over. In April 1968, Dr. King was assassinated in Tennessee. His death was followed by angry riots in America's cities. Three months later, antiwar candidate Robert F. Kennedy was also assassinated. There were student protests throughout the spring and summer, and violence erupted at the Democratic National Convention in Chicago. With Democrats divided, Republican candidate Richard Nixon won the 1968 Presidential election.

Chapter 17 | The Kennedy and Johnson Years

In this chapter, you will learn about the Sixties—a time of promise but also one of turmoil. The decade began on an optimistic note with the election of a young and ambitious President. Americans were enjoying continued postwar prosperity and astounding technological progress—from dishwashers and home air-conditioners to color television and jet travel. Many looked forward to a future end of racial and gender discrimination, the elimination of poverty, and the victory of democracy over communism abroad. By the late Sixties, however, the dream had crumbled. Americans were mired in an unwinnable war in Vietnam while a new generation of young Americans challenged traditional ways of doing things. African-American militants threatened to use violence, antiwar students burned their draft cards, assassinations robbed Americans of their best leaders, and riots erupted on the streets of America's cities as a symptom of popular discontent. How did these changes occur?

The Presidential Election of 1960

The Presidential election of 1960 was contested by two younger politicians: Senator John F. Kennedy ("JFK") and Vice President Richard Nixon. Kennedy was less known than Nixon, President Eisenhower was popular, and the country was prosperous. Moreover, Kennedy was Catholic and Americans had never elected a Catholic as President before.

Nixon might have been expected to win, but Kennedy pulled ahead in the polls after the country's first **televised debates** between Presidential candidates. The candidates held four debates. Kennedy appeared calm, relaxed, and tan. Nixon refused to wear makeup and looked sweaty, unshaven, and nervous. Those who heard the first debate on radio thought Nixon had won but most of those who watched it on television felt that Kennedy was the winner. Kennedy accused Republicans of letting Americans fall behind the Soviet Union, while Eisenhower failed to give strong support to Nixon during the campaign. The election in November was extremely close.

John F. Kennedy and the "New Frontier"

Young, handsome, intelligent and wealthy, Kennedy won the election and set a new tone for the Presidency. In his **Inaugural Address**, he famously challenged Americans to "ask not what your country can do for you; ask what you can do for your country." Kennedy's speech was a bold attempt to ignite the spirit of American idealism.

Kennedy's slogan, the "New Frontier," symbolized the vigor of youth in contrast to what he criticized as the complacency of Eisenhower's later years as President. Kennedy appointed a talented team of leading intellectuals and corporate managers to Cabinet posts. He set to work harnessing the powers of the federal government to solve America's problems:

▶ The "**Space Race**": Kennedy announced that Americans would place a man on the moon by the end of the decade. During Kennedy's administration, Alan Shepard became the first American to travel into space and John Glenn became the first American to orbit the Earth.

- **Help for Americans with intellectual disabilities:** Kennedy brought new attention to the needs of Americans with intellectual disabilities by establishing the President's Council on Mental Retardation and the National Institute of Child Health and Human Development.

- **Rights for women:** Kennedy set up a federal commission to report on the status of women. He appointed **Eleanor Roosevelt** to serve as its chairperson. In 1963, Kennedy signed the **Equal Pay Act**, which guaranteed women the same pay as men for the same job.

Much of Kennedy's "New Frontier" legislation became tied up in Congress, where it was opposed by an alliance of Republicans and Southern Democrats. For example, Kennedy proposed a tax cut to stimulate the economy, a new Cabinet-level Department of Urban Affairs, a civil rights bill, Medicare, housing subsidies, immigration reform, and increased federal aid to education. None of these proposals actually passed through Congress during his Presidency.

Cuba and the Cold War

One of the greatest challenges Kennedy faced as President was the communist presence in Cuba, only 90 miles from Florida.

The Bay of Pigs Invasion, 1961

In January 1959, **Fidel Castro** and his guerilla fighters had overthrown the Cuban dictator Fulgencio Batista. Batista had given control of Cuba's sugar plantations to Americans and had permitted American criminal interests to invest in Havana; at the same time, he had imposed a repressive police state on the Cuban people. Castro promised to establish a democracy in Cuba but he set up a communist dictatorship instead. He nationalized foreign property, most of which was owned by Americans. President Eisenhower was infuriated and cut off trade and diplomatic relations with Cuba. Eisenhower also gave his approval to a secret plan to train and support Cuban exiles who believed they could topple Castro. The exiles were armed and given special training by the CIA in Guatemala. As Eisenhower's second term as President came to an end, the Cuban exiles were still being trained.

When he arrived at the White House, Kennedy faced the crucial question of whether or not to proceed with CIA plans for using these Cuban exiles to expel Castro. Kennedy decided to do so. In April 1961, more than a thousand CIA-trained exiles attempted to invade Cuba by landing at the **Bay of Pigs** on the south side of the island. The night before the attack, CIA planes bombed Cuban airfields, although they failed to destroy all Cuban aircraft. American naval ships staged decoy operations to confuse the Cuban government. Kennedy refused, however, to give air support openly during the invasion the next day, and the rebels were defeated. Some of the

Chapter 17 | The Kennedy and Johnson Years

captured exiles were publicly interrogated in Cuba to demonstrate to the rest of the world that the United States was actually behind the failed invasion attempt. Although the operation had been planned during Eisenhower's Presidency, Kennedy took full blame for its failure. Many thought the CIA was at fault for advising the new President that the operation would succeed.

The "Alliance for Progress," 1961

To meet the challenges posed by communism in Latin America, Kennedy created the "Alliance for Progress," a program offering grants and loans to Latin American nations to promote democratic government, adult literacy, economic progress, and land reform. The program also helped American companies sell their goods in Latin America.

The program had a promising start but was generally unsuccessful because local elites in Latin America were reluctant to make recommended reforms, and the amount of aid offered under the program was insufficient.

The Cuban Missile Crisis, October 1962

The Bay of Pigs invasion led Castro to strengthen his ties with the Soviet Union. He especially feared the United States would try to invade Cuba again. In October 1962, U.S. spy planes discovered that Cubans were secretly building bases for Soviet missiles with nuclear warheads. Once these missiles were installed, the Soviet Union would be able to launch an immediate nuclear attack on the United States with medium range missiles.

Kennedy resolved to prevent the Soviets from setting up the missiles. But how could he do this without triggering a nuclear war? There were no direct telephone communications between Soviet and American leaders at this time. Some of Kennedy's advisers urged him to attack Cuba or at least to strike at the missile sites; others said to rely on the United Nations and diplomatic pressure. After carefully considering all of the options, Kennedy imposed a naval blockade around Cuba and threatened to invade the island if the missiles were not withdrawn. At the same time, he privately offered to withdraw American missiles that were located in Turkey, on the border with the Soviet Union. There were tense moments when Soviet ships approached the U.S. naval blockade, but the Soviets turned back rather than attacking the U.S. ships or attempting to break through the blockade. **Nikita Khrushchev**, the Soviet leader, agreed to withdraw the Soviet missiles from Cuba for a pledge that the United States would not invade Cuba. Kennedy also privately assured Khrushchev that the United States would withdraw its own missiles from Turkey.

The Cuban Missile Crisis is often seen as Kennedy's greatest foreign policy success. Because of his cool handling of the crisis, he was able to persuade the Soviet Union and Cuba to back down. Critics, however, say that Kennedy took the world too close to nuclear war.

A US Navy reconnaissance plane observing a Soviet freighter carrying missiles to Cuba

In the aftermath of the crisis, American and Soviet leaders set up a "hot line"—a special telephone connection so they could address one another in a crisis. They also began negotiations for a partial "test ban" treaty, which they signed the following year. It banned all testing of nuclear weapons except underground.

The Berlin Wall

Meanwhile, the Cold War continued in other parts of the world. In 1961, Khrushchev ordered the construction of the **Berlin Wall**—a wall of concrete and barbed wire, guarded by machine gun towers—in order to separate East and West Berlin. Its purpose was to prevent East Germans from escaping through Berlin to the West. Kennedy visited Berlin and told Berliners, "Ich bin ein Berliner" (I am a Berliner). By this, he meant that the United States would not abandon West Berlin.

New Programs

Kennedy expanded the operations of the **Green Berets**—a special elite corps trained to combat communism in developing nations by using the tactics of guerilla warfare. He also started the **Peace Corps**, a program in which young American volunteers provided economic and social assistance to developing countries.

The Historian's Apprentice

1. Did Kennedy make a mistake in attempting the Bay of Pigs invasion?
2. Did Kennedy handle the Cuban Missile Crisis correctly?

Civil Rights in the Kennedy Years

The Civil Rights movement gained new momentum during the Kennedy and Johnson years. In 1960, a group of African-American students sat at a "whites only" lunch counter in a Woolworth's store in Greensboro, North Carolina. The students refused to get up, even when they were surrounded and harassed by an angry crowd. The students' tactic, known as a "**sit-in**," was widely copied by other African-American and white students across the South. They staged sit-ins at lunch counters, libraries, parks, pools, and other public places, where they were often taunted, beaten, or arrested. Students from thirty states, most of whom had been active in sit-ins, gathered in North Carolina in the spring of 1960. They formed a new civil rights organization named the **Student Nonviolent Coordinating Committee, or "SNCC."**

Kennedy had actively campaigned for African-American support during the Presidential election of 1960. Once in office, however, he was reluctant to push for civil rights because he did not want to lose the support of white Southern Democrats. As violence in the South escalated, Kennedy became more open in his support of civil rights. In 1962, Kennedy proposed a constitutional amendment to ban poll taxes in federal elections, since these taxes were frequently used to prevent African Americans from voting.

"Freedom Rides"

Since 1955, federal laws had prohibited racial segregation on buses traveling through more than one state, but these laws were often difficult to enforce. Civil rights groups organized the first **"Freedom Ride"** in 1961. During a "Freedom Ride," a small interracial group rode on a bus traveling through several Southern states. The Freedom Riders sat together in interracial pairs or in sections reserved for whites.

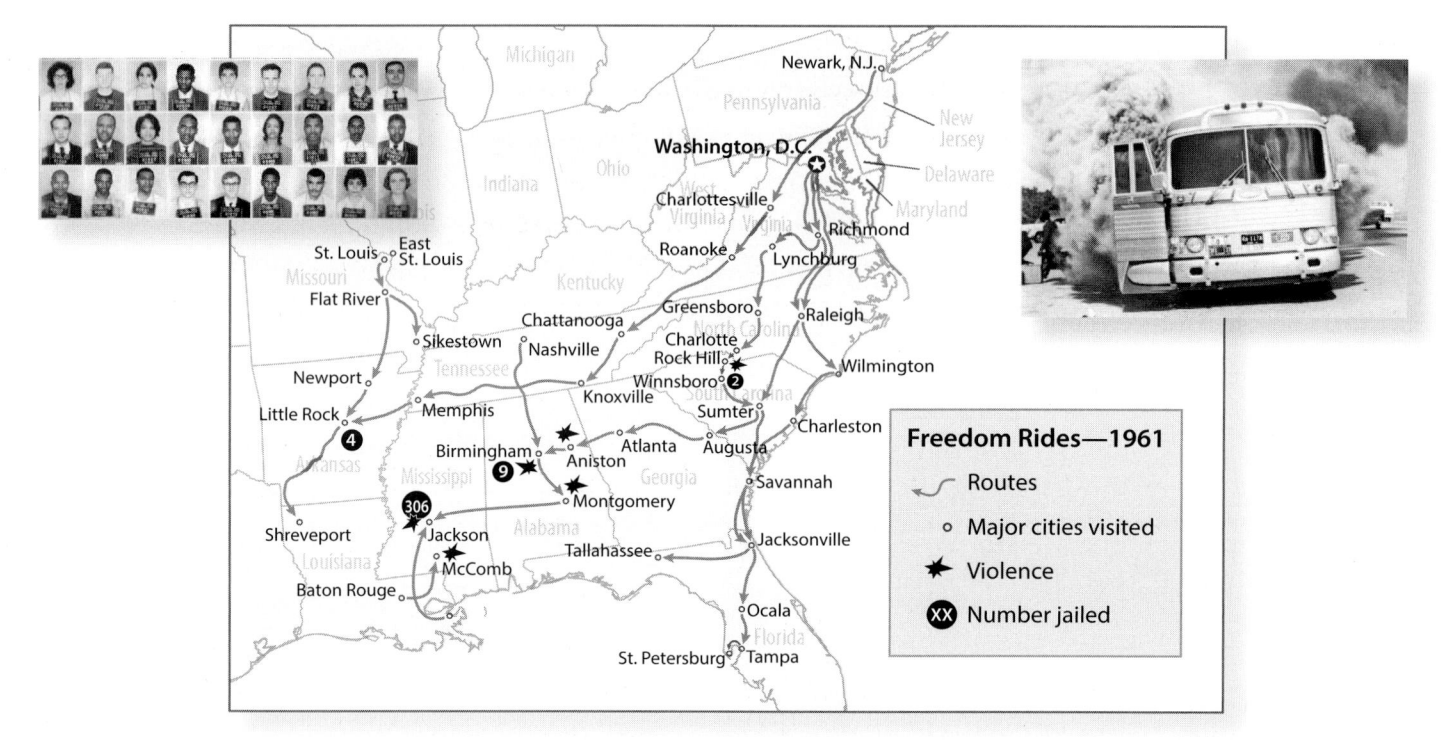

Freedom Riders frequently faced violence: they were attacked by angry mobs, arrested by hostile police, and even bombed. Young white students as well as African Americans proved willing to risk injury and even death. Federal marshals eventually had to be sent to protect them.

Dr. King's "Letter from Birmingham Jail," 1963

In the spring of 1963, Dr. Martin Luther King, Jr. and other prominent civil rights leaders focused their efforts on Birmingham, the largest city in Alabama. King led a march into the city. He was arrested and put in solitary confinement. While a prisoner, he wrote his famous **"Letter from Birmingham Jail,"** explaining why, after 340 years, African Americans could no longer delay in their struggle for equal rights.

The Historian's Apprentice

Read these excerpts from Dr. King's famous letter:

> "For years now I have heard the word 'Wait!' It rings in the ear of every Negro with piercing familiarity. This 'Wait' has almost always meant 'Never.' We must come to see, with one of our distinguished jurists, that 'justice too long delayed is justice denied.'
>
> We have waited for more than 340 years for our constitutional and God-given rights.... Perhaps it is easy for those who have never felt the stinging darts of segregation to say, 'Wait.' But when you have seen vicious mobs lynch your mothers and fathers at will and drown your sisters and brothers at whim; when you have seen hate-filled policemen curse, kick and even kill

> your black brothers and sisters; when you see the vast majority of your twenty million Negro brothers smothering in an airtight cage of poverty in the midst of an affluent society; when you suddenly find your tongue twisted and your speech stammering as you seek to explain to your six-year-old daughter why she can't go to the public amusement park that has just been advertised on television, and see tears welling up in her eyes when she is told that Funtown is closed to colored children, and see ominous clouds of inferiority beginning to form in her little mental sky . . . There comes a time when the cup of endurance runs over, and men are no longer willing to be plunged into the abyss of despair."
>
> —Dr. Martin Luther King, Jr., "Letter from Birmingham Jail," 1963

1. Why did Dr. King argue that African Americans could no longer wait to demand equal rights?
2. Imagine you are the editor of a newspaper in 1963. Write an editorial supporting or criticizing Dr. King's letter.

As more and more demonstrators were arrested, they began to fill the jails of Birmingham. The new medium of television revealed to the rest of the nation the brutal tactics used by the Birmingham police to break up peaceful marches and protests, including the use of fire hoses and police dogs.

To end the violence, the white owners of downtown stores in Birmingham agreed to desegregate their lunch counters and to hire African-American employees. Some residents objected to these concessions, and a large Ku Klux Klan rally was held in Birmingham. Dr. King's home was bombed, and riots broke out. President Kennedy finally had to send in federal troops to restore order.

Kennedy's Civil Rights Bill, 1963

In the aftermath of these events, Kennedy proposed a new civil rights bill to ban racial discrimination in public accommodations and to increase the powers of the federal government for enforcing school desegregation. He was unable, however, to get this bill through Congress.

The "March on Washington," August 1963

In the summer of 1963, Dr. Martin Luther King, A. Philip Randolph, Bayard Rustin and other civil rights leaders organized a "**March on Washington**" in support of Kennedy's civil rights bill. More than a quarter of a million people gathered along the Reflecting Pool in front of the Lincoln Memorial. Dr. King gave his most famous speech ("I Have a Dream") in which he looked forward to the day when Americans of all races and backgrounds would live peacefully together as brothers and sisters.

Chapter 17 | The Kennedy and Johnson Years

The Historian's Apprentice

Dr. King delivered this speech from the Lincoln Memorial during the "March on Washington":

"I have a dream that one day this nation will rise up and live out the true meaning of its creed: 'We hold these truths to be self-evident, that all men are created equal.'

I have a dream that one day on the Red Hills of Georgia, the sons of former slaves and the sons of former slave owners will be able to sit down together at the table of brotherhood.

I have a dream that one day even the State of Mississippi, a state sweltering with the heat of injustice, sweltering with the heat of oppression, will be transformed into an oasis of freedom and justice.

I have a dream that my four little children will one day live in a nation where they will not be judged by the color of their skin but by the content of their character.

I have a dream today! . . .

I have a dream that one day every valley shall be exalted, and every hill and mountain shall be made low, the rough places will be made plain, and the crooked places will be made straight; 'and the glory of the Lord shall be revealed and all flesh shall see it together.'

This is our hope, and this is the faith that I go back to the South with.

And this will be the day—this will be the day when all of God's children will be able to sing with new meaning, 'My country, 'tis of thee, sweet land of liberty, of thee I sing. . .'

And if America is to be a great nation this must become true. So let freedom ring . . . From every mountainside, let freedom ring.

And when this happens, and when we allow freedom to ring—when we let it ring from every village and every hamlet, from every state and every city, we will be able to speed up that day when all of God's children—black men and white men, Jews and Gentiles, Protestants and Catholics—will be able to join hands and sing in the words of the old Negro spiritual: 'Free at last! Free at last! Thank God Almighty, we are free at last!'"

—Dr. Martin Luther King, Jr., August 28, 1963

1. Based on this speech, how did Dr. King's religious beliefs help give him courage?
2. How does this speech compare to his "Letter from Birmingham Jail"?
3. To what extent has Dr. King's dream been realized today?

The Kennedy Assassination

The Kennedy years came to a sudden and tragic end when President Kennedy was assassinated in Dallas on November 22, 1963. The assassin, Lee Harvey Oswald, shot the President in the head from the sixth floor of the Texas Book Depository. Kennedy was riding in a motorcade in an open car without a roof. Oswald, a U.S. military veteran, had lived in the Soviet Union, had a Russian wife, and had attempted to visit Cuba just a few months earlier, but he was apparently acting alone. Various conspiracy theories have been suggested over the years but none has been substantiated. Oswald himself was shot two days later while in police custody.

KENNEDY ASSASSINATED
Johnson Sworn as President;

Johnson's Domestic Policies: Civil Rights and the Great Society

The new President, **Lyndon B. Johnson ("LBJ")**, was a Texan with long experience in the Senate. Skilled at managing Congress, Johnson began his Presidency by calling on legislators to pass the failed civil rights bill as a tribute to Kennedy: "No memorial oration or eulogy could more eloquently honor President Kennedy's memory than the earliest possible passage of the civil rights bill for which he fought so long."

The Civil Rights Act of 1964

The **Civil Rights Act of 1964** was the most important civil rights legislation since Reconstruction. The act protected women and religious minorities as well as African Americans. As a liberal Southern Democrat, Johnson took special pride in its passage.

President Johnson signing the Civil Rights Act of 1964

The Civil Rights Act of 1964

- Prohibited discrimination on the basis of race, color, religion, ethnic origin, or sex (gender) in hotels, motels, restaurants, theaters, trade unions, and any places of employment doing business with the federal government or affecting commerce.
- Prohibited discrimination in the enforcement of voting rights by government officials and increased the power of the federal government to register voters.
- Cut off federal aid to school districts with segregated schools.
- Created the Equal Employment Opportunity Commission to enforce the act's provisions on employment and trade unions.

Chapter 17 | The Kennedy and Johnson Years

The Historian's Apprentice

Read the excerpt below from the Civil Rights Act of 1964:

Title II of the Civil Rights Act: Discrimination in Places of Public Accommodation

(a) All persons shall be entitled to the full and equal enjoyment of the goods, services, facilities, and privileges, advantages, and accommodations of any place of public accommodation, as defined in this section, without discrimination or segregation on the ground of race, color, religion, or national origin.

(b) Each of the following establishments which serves the public is a place of public accommodation within the meaning of this title if its operations affect commerce, or if discrimination or segregation by it is supported by State action:

(1) any inn, hotel, motel, or other establishment which provides lodging to transient guests, other than an establishment located within a building which contains not more than five rooms for rent ... and which is actually occupied by the proprietor [*owner*] of such establishment as his residence;

(2) any restaurant, cafeteria, lunchroom, lunch counter, soda fountain, or other facility principally engaged in selling food for consumption on the premises, including, but not limited to, any such facility located on the premises of any retail establishment; or any gasoline station;

(3) any motion picture house, theater, concert hall, sports arena, stadium or other place of exhibition or entertainment ..."

1. What is meant by "public accommodation" in this act? Can you provide examples of "public accommodations" identified in the section above?
2. Why was the prohibition of discrimination in this act limited to either those accommodations whose operations "affect commerce" or cases where discrimination by a particular public accommodation is "supported by State action"?
3. Where in the act can you find an exception for small business owners who live in their own small hotels, motels, or restaurants? Why do you think this exception was permitted?
4. Why was this federal law so important?

Some people questioned whether the federal government had the power to outlaw discrimination in private business. If the owners of a business were prejudiced, did the federal government have the power to force them to serve people they did not like? The answer was yes—in December 1964, the Supreme Court upheld the constitutionality of the Civil Rights Act based on the power of the federal government to regulate interstate commerce. If business owners are willing to serve people in interstate commerce, then they must do so without racial, sexual, or religious discrimination.

Passage of the Civil Rights Act was a crucial step in the transformation of America into a more diverse, multicultural society. Prior to passage of the act, African Americans could not safely travel to many parts of the country because they were not able to obtain food or find a place to sleep.

The Twenty-fourth Amendment

Despite the Fifteenth Amendment, a majority of African Americans had been denied voting rights in the South ever since the end of Reconstruction. Southern states used poll taxes and literacy tests, as well as fear and ignorance, to withhold these rights.

The **24th Amendment** was introduced by President Kennedy and submitted by Congress to the states in 1962. By the time of Kennedy's assassination, it had been ratified by 36 states. It became part of the Constitution when it was ratified by two more states in January 1964. The amendment prohibited states from denying citizens the right to vote in federal elections for not paying a poll tax.

The "War on Poverty"

As a young man, Lyndon Johnson had taught impoverished students in Texas. After teaching the children of Mexican immigrants, he concluded that the nation could not rest until it provided equal opportunities to all Americans, including the very poor. One of the first steps Johnson took as President was to declare an "unconditional war on poverty in America." The Economic Opportunity Act of 1964 aimed at increasing educational opportunity and vocational training. It created the Office of Economic Opportunity to administer several new programs, including:

- **Job Corps**, which trained underprivileged youths
- **VISTA (Volunteers in Service to America):** a domestic "Peace Corps" made up of volunteers helping to fight poverty in the United States
- **Work-study** programs at colleges
- Grants for adult education programs
- Community action programs

The Presidential Election of 1964

In the 1964 Presidential election, President Johnson had the opportunity to be elected in his own right. He faced a conservative politician, **Senator Barry Goldwater** of Arizona. Goldwater questioned the wisdom of the "welfare state" and criticized the growing influence of the federal government. At the same time, Goldwater wanted to strengthen American military power and even suggested that Americans in battle might use tactical nuclear weapons. Johnson's campaign featured television commercials showing an explosion of an atomic bomb. A narrator asked voters if they thought Goldwater could be trusted with control of America's nuclear arsenal. This television advertising, combined with the achievements of Johnson's first year in office, proved very effective. Johnson won a landslide victory with 61% of the popular vote and control of both houses of Congress.

Johnson's "Great Society"

After the election, Johnson felt confident enough to propose even more comprehensive social legislation. In January 1965, Johnson introduced his **"Great Society"** programs. His aim was to turn the United States into a more egalitarian society by opening up opportunities for all Americans. His "Great Society" was the most ambitious program of social reform since the New Deal.

- **Medicare and Medicaid:** The most enduring part of Johnson's "Great Society" was the introduction of Medicare and Medicaid. **Medicare** provides hospital insurance and inexpensive health

Chapter 17 | The Kennedy and Johnson Years

insurance to those over 65 years of age. **Medicaid** was a new partnership of states with the federal government. It gave federal money to states providing health benefits to people with low incomes, including children, pregnant women, elderly people in nursing homes, and people with disabilities.

▶ **Federal Aid to Education:** The Elementary and Secondary Education Act gave over $1 billion to local school districts. The Higher Education Act provided funds for 140,000 scholarships and created the **National Teacher Corps**. Johnson also introduced **Project Head Start**, a project to help prepare underprivileged children between the ages of three and five for elementary school. All federal aid to education was made conditional on the desegregation of school districts.

▶ **Aid to Cities:** The Housing and Urban Development Act created a new Cabinet post in charge of programs for helping the nation's cities. Billions in aid were appropriated to urban planning, slum clearance, rental subsidies for the poor, and the reconstruction of dilapidated buildings.

▶ **Appalachian Regional Development Act:** This act provided federal funds to create new jobs and industries in **Appalachia**, one of the poorest regions of the United States at this time. The Appalachian Commission defined Appalachia as stretching from Southern New York to Mississippi, with its center in West Virginia.

▶ **The Immigration Act of 1965:** This law ended the discriminatory "national origins" system, which had favored immigrants from Western Europe. In its place, the new act established a more equitable system by giving each country the same maximum number of immigrants it could lawfully send to the United States.

▶ **Other Programs:** Johnson created the National Foundation of the Arts and the Humanities. He raised the minimum wage and increased expenditures for both his "War on Poverty" and the space program. He signed the bill that created public television (PBS). Finally, his administration issued new regulations to reduce smog and water pollution.

The Historian's Apprentice

"In a land of great wealth, families must not live in hopeless poverty. In a land rich in harvest, children just must not go hungry. In a land of healing miracles, neighbors must not suffer and die untended. In a great land of learning and scholars, young people must be taught to read and write."

—Inaugural Address of Lyndon B. Johnson, January 20, 1965

1. How were Johnson's Great Society programs meant to address the problems identified in his Inaugural Address?
2. From the Progressives to President Lyndon B. Johnson, the power of the federal government over American society had been increasing. Make your own timeline showing the major milestones in the growth of federal power from 1900 to 1965.

Despite these efforts, many Americans still remained in poverty. Increasing involvement in Vietnam, discussed later in this chapter, then forced President Johnson to reduce the funding for many Great Society programs.

African-American Voting Rights

In March 1965, Dr. Martin Luther King—who had only just won the Nobel Peace Prize—went to Alabama to lead a march from Selma to Montgomery in support of African-American voting rights. The demonstrators were forced to start out several times because of police violence. On their television sets, Americans across the nation could see peaceful marchers being clubbed and tear-gassed. The demonstrators were only able to continue their march after they received the protection of federal troops.

President Johnson was outraged and summoned a joint session of Congress, where he proposed a new voting rights bill. The President concluded his speech by dramatically including a well-known slogan from the Civil Rights Movement—he told Congress: "We shall overcome."

The **Voting Rights Act of 1965** increased the powers of the federal government to enforce the Fifteenth and Twenty-fourth Amendments. States were prohibited from using any "test or device," such as a literacy test, to prevent their citizens from voting. The law prohibited all poll taxes used to deny African Americans the right to vote. Perhaps most important of all, the act authorized the appointment of special federal examiners to register voters. The Voting Rights Act led to a large increase in the number of African-American voters.

Affirmative Action, 1965

In 1965, President Johnson also issued an executive order requiring employers and institutions with federal contracts to raise the number of their minority and female employees. "**Affirmative action**" programs led to increased numbers of women and minorities in universities and the professions. Minority-owned businesses received a larger share of government contracts. President Johnson appointed Robert Weaver as the first African-American member of the Cabinet, and he nominated **Thurgood Marshall**, the NAACP attorney in the *Brown* case, as the first African-American Justice on the U.S. Supreme Court.

The "Black Power" Movement

Despite the successes of the Civil Rights Movement in fighting segregation in the South, little had been done to improve the economic conditions of African Americans, especially in Northern cities. Many younger African Americans believed that the goals of the civil rights leaders were too narrow and that progress was too slow. They disagreed with Dr. King's policy of non-violent protest in cooperation with sympathetic whites.

In the late 1960s, the Civil Rights Movement splintered when militant African-American leaders took a new direction. These leaders believed in "Black Power." Like the leaders of the Harlem Renaissance, they took great pride in their own history and culture. They wanted to use African-American votes to improve the social and economic conditions of minorities. Many of these leaders thought that African Americans should take control of their own communities, buy goods from their own businesses, and free themselves from the economic, cultural, and political control of whites. "Black Power" leaders were especially influenced by the progress of African nations, many of which had just won their independence.

Note: You will not need to know the names of specific "Black Power" leaders for the Georgia Milestones EOC Assessment.

▶ **Malcolm X** questioned Dr. King's tactics of non-violent resistance. He thought that African Americans should respond to the violence of white racism with their own violence. He sought the separation of whites and blacks and advocated "black nationalism" (*black self-government*).

Malcolm X

▶ In 1966, Bobby Seale and Huey Newton formed the **Black Panthers**. Their original purpose was to patrol black neighborhoods to protect their residents from police violence. Eventually, the Black Panthers called for the arming of African Americans. They wore black pants, black leather jackets, and black berets. Some carried guns. The Black Panthers published their own newspaper and started a free breakfast program to feed poor African-American children. The organization had 10,000 members by 1969. The Black Panthers adopted a ten-point program, which included the demand that the United States pay "reparations" to African Americans for centuries of unjust exploitation. FBI Director J. Edgar Hoover set up a secret program to discredit and break up the Black Panthers and several radical groups. This program resulted in the murder of two Black Panthers.

As a result of the Black Power Movement, there was greater effort to remove racist stereotypes and to eliminate racist language. Greater appreciation of African-American culture led to the introduction of black studies courses and departments at American universities, and to the appointment of more African-American professors.

Cesar Chavez and the Migrant Farm Workers

The achievements of the Civil Rights Movement influenced other groups, such as migrant farm workers. American farmers often relied on the help of Spanish-speaking migrant workers (*workers who move from place to place*). The migrant workers were usually forced to live in temporary housing without basic amenities. Growers paid them very low wages.

Cesar Chavez was born in Arizona in 1927. His grandfather migrated to the United States in the late 1880s. His family lost their store and ranch during the Great Depression and became migrant farm workers in California, where they picked peas, lettuce, cherries, beans, and grapes. They faced discrimination as well as poverty. In 1942, Cesar's father was killed in a car accident. Cesar later served in the navy for two years, but found that he faced prejudice as a Mexican American.

Chavez became a community organizer and helped Mexican Americans register to vote. In 1962, he helped to start the United Farm Workers Association, or "UFW"—a union of migrant farm workers demanding better wages and living conditions.

In 1965, Chavez organized a strike by grape pickers and a march to California's state capital in Sacramento. He also led a nationwide boycott of grapes.

In the 1970s, Chavez led the UFW in another strike for lettuce pickers. The UFW demanded the use of less pesticide, which endangered the health of farm workers. Chavez conducted hunger strikes, once starving himself for 28 days in order to get better conditions. Eventually, Chavez succeeded in gaining recognition for the United Farm Workers and the passage of laws protecting the rights of migrant farm workers.

The Historian's Apprentice

How important is the leadership of individuals like Dr. Martin Luther King, Jr., and Cesar Chavez to the success of reform movements? Support your views with evidence.

The War in Vietnam

The war in Vietnam became the most divisive conflict in American history since the Civil War. Why and how did Americans become involved in this distant country? And why did this engagement become more divisive than either World War II or the Korean War?

Background to the Conflict

Vietnam is located in the eastern part of **Indochina**, a large peninsula directly south of China. Vietnam consists of heavily forested mountains, highlands, and valleys. The Red River Valley to the north and the Mekong Delta in the south provide fertile land for rice production. The country has warm, wet winters and hot, wet summers.

In the nineteenth century, the countries of **Indochina** (Vietnam, Laos, and Cambodia) came under French rule. The Vietnamese Emperor was permitted to remain on his throne, but the French governed Vietnam as a colony for their own benefit. As early as 1900, a Vietnamese nationalist movement emerged. One of the leading Vietnamese nationalists was **Ho Chi Minh**, a dedicated revolutionary. Ho Chi Minh left Vietnam in 1912, joined the French Communist Party in 1920, and served in the communist parties of Russia and China in the 1930s.

> Note: You will not need to know about the background to the Vietnam War, the Geneva Accords, or the Diem government for the Georgia Milestones EOC Assessment, but these sections will help you to understand how Americans became involved in the region.

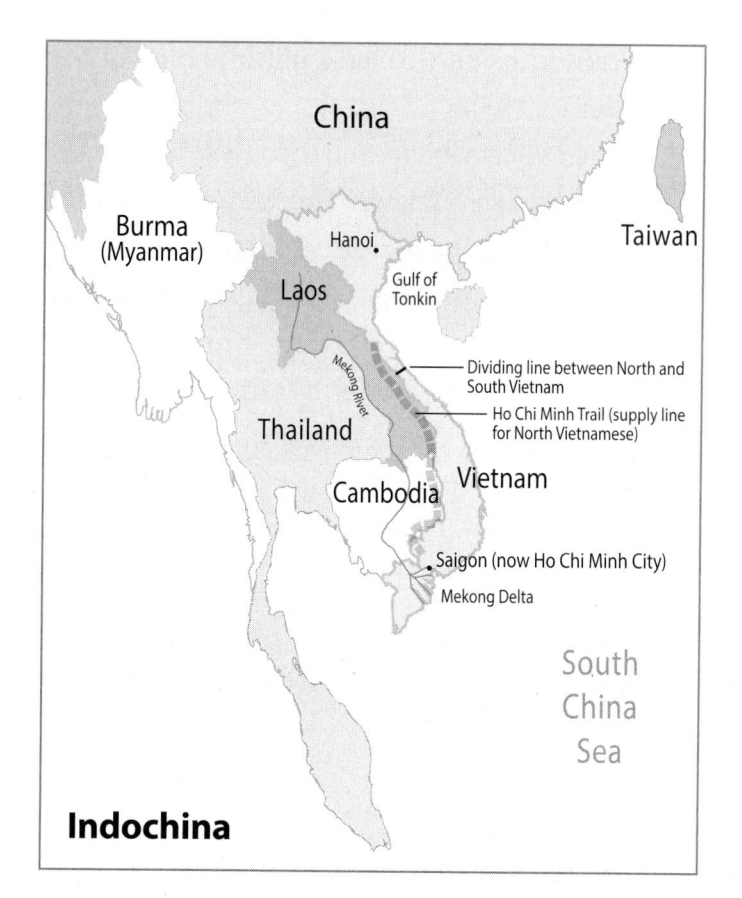

During World War II, Japan seized control of French Indochina. Ho Chi Minh led Vietnamese nationalists in an underground struggle against the Japanese.

After the surrender of Japan, Vietnamese nationalist forces entered Hanoi. Ho Chi Minh declared the independence of Vietnam, and the Vietnamese Emperor abdicated in favor of the new republic. France, however, refused to recognize the independence of Vietnam. Armed conflict between Vietnamese and French forces began in 1946 and lasted for nine years. Ho Chi Minh kept control of the North but was unable to establish his power in the South, where the French restored the Vietnamese Emperor. In 1950, the Soviet Union and communist China recognized Ho Chi Minh's government. American leaders, viewing Ho Chi Minh as a communist, gave assistance to the French. By 1954, the United States was paying for most of the French war effort, although President Eisenhower refused to commit U.S. troops. Vietnamese forces won a decisive victory in 1954, forcing France to withdraw from Indochina.

The Geneva Accords, 1954

In the spring of 1954, representatives from Indochina, France, China, the Soviet Union, Great Britain, and the United States assembled in Geneva, Switzerland, to negotiate a peace settlement. Laos and Cambodia were made into independent neutral states. The country of Vietnam was divided in two: Ho Chi Minh and the Vietnamese communists were left in control of the North, while the Vietnamese Emperor remained in power in the South. The division of Vietnam was meant to be temporary: free elections were supposed to be held and the country was to be re-united in 1956.

Reasons for American Involvement

After the Geneva Conference, the United States replaced France as the chief supporter of South Vietnam. Why did American leaders assume this responsibility?

▶ **Fear of Communism—The "Domino Theory":** As you know, American leaders feared the spread of communism. They saw all the communist nations of the world as part of the same monolithic bloc. Since the end of World War II, communism had spread from the Soviet Union to Eastern Europe, China, North Korea, and North Vietnam. American leaders were afraid that if they did not make a stand, communism would spread even further. They believed that if South Vietnam fell to communism, other Southeast Asian countries—Laos, Cambodia, Thailand, and Malaysia—

would fall next, like a row of dominoes. Communism would continue to spread throughout the world until it posed a direct threat to the United States. These ideas became known as the "**domino theory**."

▶ **Belief in the Benefits of Democracy:** American leaders were also idealistic: they believed strongly in the advantages of democracy and free enterprise. They hoped to introduce political, social, and economic reforms that would benefit the Vietnamese people. They hoped this would provide an alternative to communism. American leaders thought that Vietnam provided an opportunity to build a successful democracy, which would serve as an attractive model for other developing countries in Asia, Africa and Latin America.

▶ **An Example to Allies:** Once they had committed themselves to Vietnam, U.S. leaders felt that America's prestige as the leader of the "Free World" was at stake. If America deserted the government of South Vietnam, they argued, other nations would lose faith in America's ability to protect them.

▶ **Underestimation of the Enemy:** A final reason American leaders became involved in Vietnam was that they misunderstood the nature of the conflict. They believed that the superiority of American democracy, combined with America's advanced technologies and economic resources, would enable South Vietnam to resist communism. They underestimated the strength of Vietnamese nationalism and the determination of Ho Chi Minh and the North Vietnamese to unify their country.

The Diem Government in South Vietnam, 1954–1963

After the Geneva Conference, Vietnam's Emperor remained in France. He appointed a Catholic nationalist, **Ngo Dinh Diem**, as his prime minister. Diem deposed the Emperor the following year. Diem refused to hold elections in 1956, claiming that elections would not be free in the North, where Ho Chi Minh had already established a communist dictatorship. Thousands of North Vietnamese Catholics fled to South Vietnam with tales of communist atrocities.

Diem established his own oppressive regime in the South, executing many political opponents. Diem's brother became the hated head of the secret police. Lands that had been distributed to the peasants were returned to the landlords. Diem, a Catholic, also began a policy of discrimination against Vietnamese Buddhists.

The Vietcong Revolt

When Diem refused to hold the elections required by the Geneva Accords, South Vietnamese communists formed a revolutionary army, known as the **Vietcong**. They began a campaign of **guerilla warfare** (*a form of irregular fighting, in which smaller groups of forces suddenly strike and then disappear*), murdering officials and government sympathizers.

Chapter 17 | The Kennedy and Johnson Years

President Kennedy sent military aid and several thousand military advisers to help Diem fight the Vietcong. However, Diem's policies made him increasingly unpopular. Diem was overthrown and murdered by his own generals in November 1963. President Kennedy was assassinated in Dallas only a few weeks later.

President Johnson Escalates the War, 1964–1968

After the death of Diem, the United States became even more involved in the defense of South Vietnam. In August 1964, President Johnson announced that the North Vietnamese had attacked American ships in international waters in the Gulf of Tonkin. In the "**Gulf of Tonkin Resolution**," Congress voted to give the President extraordinary powers to take all measures necessary to stop North Vietnamese aggression. Johnson saw this Congressional resolution as the legal basis for an **escalation** of the war. Years later it became clear that the American ships had been in North Vietnamese waters and that they were protecting South Vietnamese boats that had been bombing North Vietnamese targets.

The Historian's Apprentice

Gulf of Tonkin Resolution, August 7, 1964

"Whereas naval units of the Communist regime in Vietnam, in violation of the principles of the Charter of the United Nations and of international law, have deliberately and repeatedly attacked United States naval vessels lawfully present in international waters . . .

Whereas these attackers are part of [a] deliberate and systematic campaign of aggression that the Communist regime in North Vietnam has been waging against its neighbors and the nations joined with them in the collective defense of their freedom . . .

Congress approves and supports the determination of the President, as Commander in Chief, to take all necessary measures to repel any armed attack against the forces of the United States and to prevent further aggression. . . .

This resolution shall expire when the President shall determine that the peace and security of the area is reasonably assured . . . except that it may be terminated earlier by concurrent resolution of the Congress."

1. What powers did this resolution give to the President?
2. Based on the resolution, why did Congress grant these powers?
3. When did these powers expire?

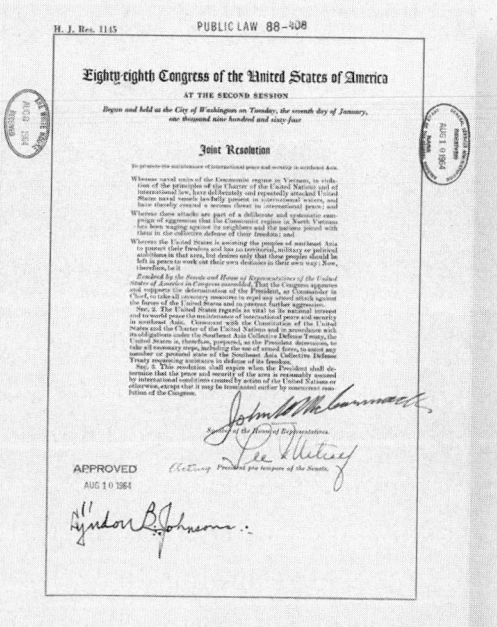

In March 1965, President Johnson sent the first American combat troops to Vietnam. By the end of the year 184,000 American soldiers were active there. Johnson also ordered bombing missions over North Vietnam to wear down North Vietnamese resistance and to destroy supply routes from North to South Vietnam. The missions failed to achieve either objective. Resentment against the United States grew and the Vietcong and North Vietnamese became more determined than ever to achieve their national independence.

The Nature of Combat

President Johnson hoped to use America's technological superiority and an overwhelming number of troops to win the war. Jet planes bombed Vietcong supply routes and enemy forces. New destructive weapons like napalm (*gasoline mixed with a gel that sticks to skin as it burns*) and cluster bombs inflicted terrible damage on their victims. Herbicides, like Agent Orange, destroyed the jungle cover. Vietnam was the first "helicopter" war. Helicopters transported supplies, moved whole American units, and picked up wounded American soldiers.

Helicopters provided mobility for US soldiers

Agent Orange destroyed jungle cover used by North Vietnamese forces

Nevertheless, American soldiers faced immense obstacles in Vietnam. The climate was hot and uncomfortable. The jungles and forests of Vietnam provided cover for enemy movements and supply routes. Booby traps set in rice paddies and jungles could go off at any time. The Vietcong, who were more familiar with the terrain, adopted the tactics of guerilla warfare. They seldom came out in the open. They persuaded or coerced other Vietnamese to cooperate with them. American soldiers were unable to distinguish hostile Vietcong from friendly Vietnamese. Any Vietnamese civilian, including women and children, might be a secret Vietcong. American units occasionally destroyed whole villages in their search for the enemy. Some atrocities even occurred, such as when American forces killed unarmed men, women, and children in the village of My Lai.

American search-and-destroy missions and Vietcong terrorism drove many Vietnamese from the countryside to the cities. Saigon (the capital of South Vietnam) and other cities became clogged with refugees. A massive influx of supplies for American troops subverted the

South Vietnamese economy. These conditions encouraged the spread of bribery and corruption. Meanwhile, the South Vietnamese government never introduced effective land reform. None of the military governments that ruled South Vietnam after Diem's death ever commanded a strong base of popular support. This made it easier for the Vietcong to gain control over much of the countryside.

By the end of 1968, more than half a million American troops were in Vietnam and the war was costing Americans $25 billion a year. Yet there were still no signs of future victory. Critics began calling Vietnam a "quagmire" or swamp.

Why were Americans Unable to Win the War?

Ho Chi Minh and other North Vietnamese leaders had been fighting to achieve control over a unified Vietnam since 1946. They were willing to sustain large losses to obtain their goal. Increasing casualties did not weaken their resolve. As the Americans sent in more troops, so did North Vietnam. The North Vietnamese were also able to obtain supplies from the communist governments of China and the Soviet Union. Supply routes to the South like the Ho Chi Minh Trail were so primitive that they could be quickly rebuilt when they were bombed.

American leaders might have pulled out of a war they felt they could not win, but they were afraid of the effect this might have on their popularity in the United States. Lyndon Johnson did not want to be accused of giving in to communists or of appearing to be weak, so he continued to escalate the war rather than abandon South Vietnam. Since American leaders would not pull out and North Vietnamese leaders would not give in, the war just dragged on and on.

The Historian's Apprentice

1. Hold a class debate on this question:

   Resolved: The United States should never have entered the war in Vietnam.

2. Your class should divide into groups. Using the Internet, find photographs and other primary sources on different aspects of the war in Vietnam between 1964 and 1968. Then make an informative poster or display. Take a "gallery walk" to see the displays of the other groups in your class.

The Impact of Television

In the Kennedy and Johnson years, television had a dramatic impact on American culture and politics. Television was a relatively new invention. The British Broadcasting Company (BBC) actually began making the first public broadcasts in the 1930s, but it wasn't until after World War II that television came into more general use. In 1948, there were about 170,000 television sets in the United States. In 1950, only 10% of American households had a television. But television expanded rapidly after that. By 1954, 25 million American households had television. By 1960, almost 90% of American households had a television set.

Politics

The powerful impact that television could have on American politics was first seen in 1955 when Vice President Nixon was accused of using campaign contributions for private gain. He went on national television to dispel the rumors, explaining to the public how modest his means really were. Nixon also told viewers he would not return "Checkers," a pet dog that had been given to his family as a campaign gift. Americans responded so favorably that Eisenhower kept Nixon on his ticket.

In the 1960 Presidential election, Kennedy's performance in the televised Presidential debates helped him to win the election. As President, Kennedy televised his press conferences, showcasing his intelligence, relaxed manner, and wit. His assassination in November 1963 became another occasion when Americans, in their shock and grief, turned collectively as a nation to their television sets.

Television allowed government leaders, especially the President, to appeal directly to citizens. The role of television in campaigns also meant that politicians suddenly needed larger sums of money to pay for television advertising. Political parties became less important when candidates could reach voters directly through television.

Civil Rights

Television played an equally important role in the Civil Rights Movement. The coverage of civil rights marches by national television networks revealed the extent of the violence faced by civil rights activists and helped them win national support. In 1963, television cameras captured the police of Birmingham, Alabama, using police dogs and fire hoses to attack peaceful protesters. The brutality revealed on American television screens was so shocking that it put public pressure on President Kennedy to take more forceful actions to protect the demonstrators. In March 1965, the pattern was repeated when Dr. King led the **Selma-to-Montgomery march** for voting rights. Television cameras showed state troopers using clubs and tear gas against nonviolent demonstrators. Local civil rights leader Amelia Boynton was beaten unconscious and a picture of her wounded body lying on the ground was carried by television news reports around the world. This televised brutality helped Johnson win support for the Voting Rights Act, which was introduced into Congress immediately afterwards.

Vietnam

The war in Vietnam was equally affected by television news. For the first time, Americans were able to watch the horrors of war on television from their living rooms. These scenes turned many Americans against the war. American leaders realized that they not only had to fight the war but also to manage its public relations. Their concern to impress the public favorably sometimes led to a twisting of the facts and a growing "credibility gap." President Johnson told Americans that the United States was winning the war, but the public received a different impression from nightly television broadcasts. People began to lose faith in the trustworthiness of their government.

Popular Culture

Television affected not only politics but also national culture. Television programs influenced fashion, music, travel, and cooking. On television, Americans could see other parts of the country and the rest of the world. Television disseminated new styles. The clothes worn by television actors affected the clothes other Americans wanted to buy. Television advertisements successfully promoted children's toys, foods, chewing gum, cigarettes, automobiles and other products.

Parents began using television sets as virtual "baby sitters" and children began watching cartoons on television, causing them to play less outdoors. The Public Broadcasting System (PBS) began producing educational children's shows, like "Mr. Rogers' Neighborhood."

Variety programs like the Ed Sullivan Show helped singers and bands to promote their records. When the Beatles, a popular British rock band, played on the Ed Sullivan show in 1964, this became another occasion when television united families across the country in a common activity.

Moon Landing

The unifying effects of television were especially evident in July 1969, when Americans landed the first man on the moon. The entire world watched on live television to see Neil Armstrong take his first steps on the lunar surface and receive a call from President Nixon. In stepping onto the moon's surface, Armstrong declared it to be "one small step for man, one giant leap for mankind."

The Historian's Apprentice

Make a chart comparing the impact of television in the 1960s with the impact of the Internet and social media today.

1968—Year of Turmoil

The Kennedy-Johnson years came to a dramatic end in 1968, another landmark year in American history.

The Tet Offensive

The year began with the **Tet Offensive.** On January 30th, the first day of Tet, the Vietnamese lunar New Year, Vietcong soldiers blasted a hole in the wall of the U.S. Embassy in Saigon. Other Vietcong and North Vietnamese forces launched simultaneous attacks in cities across South Vietnam. North Vietnamese leaders expected soldiers in the South Vietnamese army to defect and the countryside to rise up in revolt against U.S. "imperialism," but this didn't happen.

The worst fighting was in the ancient capital of Hue and lasted for three weeks. American and South Vietnamese soldiers held on to their military headquarters, but the Vietcong and North Vietnamese took over the rest of the city. American and South Vietnamese troops proceeded to remove Vietcong and North Vietnamese forces block by block. They relied heavily on artillery fire, which destroyed most of the city. When the Vietcong finally had to evacuate, they made the decision to murder more than a thousand unarmed, innocent civilians whom they feared would reveal their own hidden identities to South Vietnamese officials.

In the end, the Vietcong and North Vietnamese failed to hold on to any South Vietnamese cities and suffered heavy casualties—as many as 40,000 were killed, lost, or wounded. U.S. generals declared Tet to be an American victory. The American public, however, felt that they had been deceived. Only two months earlier, President Johnson had announced that the war was almost won and that the light could be seen at the "end of the tunnel." After Tet, the public doubted that this was the case.

Although Tet was actually a military victory for the United States, it demonstrated that the war was far from over. After years of fighting, the Vietcong and North Vietnamese were still able to launch massive attacks across all of South Vietnam. From television sets in their living rooms, Americans could watch explosions, hear gunfire, and see injured bodies being carried away. CBS news anchor Walter Cronkite, the most trusted journalist in America, flew to Vietnam to report on the action. On his return, Cronkite told viewers that there was in fact no light at the end of the tunnel. Cronkite believed that both the optimists and pessimists were wrong about the war. It was neither won nor lost: "It seems more certain than ever," he concluded, "that the bloody experience of Vietnam is to end in a stalemate."

U.S. military leaders in South Vietnam asked President Johnson to send another 200,000 troops in addition to the half a million U.S. troops already there. Johnson and his new Secretary of Defense consulted a group of experienced senior statesmen—known as the "wise men." They told the President that the Vietnam War no longer seemed to be winnable. However many troops Americans poured into South Vietnam, the North Vietnamese would match them. Based on this advice, Johnson sent only a few thousand more troops to Vietnam. He also announced a bombing halt on Hanoi and Haiphong Harbor. At the same time, he invited the North Vietnamese to enter into negotiations. To his surprise, the North Vietnamese accepted his offer to hold peace talks in Paris.

By this time, campaigning for the next Presidential election had already begun. In the New Hampshire Democratic primary in early March, Johnson was opposed by **Senator Eugene McCarthy**. McCarthy called for an immediate end to the war and won 42% of the vote. Once these results were known, **Robert ("Bobby") Kennedy**—the younger brother of the deceased President Kennedy—announced that he was also entering the race. On March 31, Johnson appeared on national television to explain the partial bombing halt and to announce that he would not seek re-election for another term. The President appeared to be a broken man.

The Assassination of Dr. King

On April 4, only five days after Johnson's announcement, Dr. Martin Luther King was assassinated by an escaped convict. King was standing on his motel balcony in Memphis, Tennessee, where he had come to help striking African-American sanitation workers win recognition of their union.

Anger at King's assassination led to rioting across the nation lasting for an entire week. In Baltimore, Chicago, Kansas City, Detroit, Pittsburgh, and other cities, angry rioters smashed

Chapter 17 | The Kennedy and Johnson Years

windows, overturned cars, and started fires. Some of the worst rioting took place in Washington, D.C., where the Capitol Building was lit up by the flames of nearby burning buildings. Police and federal troops were needed to stop the riots, in which 43 people died.

A special commission was appointed to investigate the causes of the unrest. It concluded that the lack of job opportunities for African Americans, urban poverty, and racism had all contributed to the disturbances. The riots and report led to the Civil Rights Act of 1968 (also known as the "Fair Housing Act"). This law prohibited racial discrimination in the sale or renting of housing. Its aim was to end the confinement of African Americans to particular neighborhoods or ghettos due to racial discrimination in housing.

Student Protests

In late April 1968, students at Columbia University in New York City occupied five buildings to protest their university's policies. After campus buildings were occupied for six days, the university administration called in police and the students were forced out. Bitter feelings between antiwar protesters and those who supported the war ran high. The students passed through rows of police who struck at them with clubs. Almost 700 students were arrested and nearly a hundred were injured.

By May 1968, the feeling of discontent seemed to have spread worldwide. Student protests took place in Paris, London, Berlin, Bologna, Milan, Mexico City, Tokyo, and other cities. Demonstrations in Paris led to strikes and new elections. In Prague, Czechs demanded greater freedom under communism. Their reform movement was crushed by the intervention of Soviet tanks and troops.

The Democratic Party Convention

Back in the United States, **Robert Kennedy** won several primary contests. He successfully united antiwar protesters, minorities, feminists and blue collar workers in a new Democratic coalition. But on June 5, just as he was celebrating victory in the California primary, Kennedy was shot and killed by a young Palestinian immigrant.

By this time, Vice President Hubert Humphrey had entered the election contest. Humphrey was a liberal from Minnesota who enjoyed the support of labor unions and the Democratic Party organization. He had personal doubts about the war but as Vice President he had kept his feelings private out of loyalty to Johnson. After the assassination of Robert Kennedy, Humphrey was certain to become his party's nominee.

Antiwar demonstrators planned to make a showcase out of the **Democratic National Convention**, which was held in Chicago in August. Antiwar activists Jerry Rubin and Abbie Hoffman formed a new group, the Youth International Party (or "Yippies"). The Yippies used the methods of street theater to support their antiwar protests: for example, Hoffman and Rubin brought a pig to Chicago as their chosen nominee for the Presidency.

Richard Daley, the Mayor of Chicago and a Democratic city boss, was determined not to let the antiwar demonstrators interrupt the convention. He refused to give the protestors permits to march or to sleep at night in the city's public parks. A large police force guarded the convention hall and patrolled Chicago's streets. Chicago police were given wide discretion to use force against the demonstrators, including tear gas, mace, and police clubs. They used tear gas to clear Lincoln Park of protesters. Television news broadcasts switched back and forth

Demonstrators and National Guardsmen at the 1968 Democratic Convention

between speeches at the convention and street battles between demonstrators and the police. Later, eight of the antiwar leaders were put on trial for the violence. They included not only Rubin and Hoffman, but also Tom Hayden, who had helped found the SDS (Students for a Democratic Society), and Bobby Seale, one of the founders of the Black Panthers.

The Presidential Election of 1968

Meanwhile, Republicans nominated **Richard Nixon**—the Vice President who had lost to Kennedy eight years earlier. Nixon emphasized his foreign policy experience. He hired advertising and public relations specialists to manage his campaign and spent large sums on television and radio advertising. Nixon attacked hippies and antiwar protesters, and claimed to have a secret plan for ending the Vietnam War and bringing "peace with honor." He looked to the support of what he called the "Silent Majority" of Americans, who held traditional values.

The Presidential election of 1968 turned out to be three-way race. Former Governor of Alabama George Wallace ran as a third-party candidate. Wallace was supported by Southern segregationists and by those who viewed the antiwar movement as unpatriotic. Wallace also attempted to appeal to working class voters by offering federal job training and other benefits.

While Republicans united around Nixon, Democrats were divided, both by the war and by the violence that had occurred at their convention. Humphrey failed to condemn the war openly until September, when he announced that if elected, he would stop the bombing of North Vietnam in order to accelerate the negotiations in Paris. Nixon's agents secretly urged the South Vietnamese to delay participating in the peace talks until after the election, claiming Nixon would offer them a better deal.

Despite all the problems that Humphrey faced, 1968 still proved to be a very close election.

Nixon did especially well in the South and West. There was "backlash" (*a negative reaction*) against Democrats' liberal social policies, Johnson's handling of the Vietnam War, the antiwar movement, and the summer riots.

In 1968, the antiwar movement, African-American militant groups, and the "counter culture" were challenging traditional values and beliefs. In response, American voters decided, by a slim margin, to take the country in a more conservative direction by electing Richard Nixon.

Candidate	Party	Popular Vote	Percent of Popular Vote
Richard Nixon	Republican	31,785,480	43.4%
Hubert Humphrey	Democrat	31,275,166	42.7%
George Wallace	American Independent	9,906,473	13.5%

For the Georgia "Milestones" EOC Assessment, you should know that:

- ☐ John F. Kennedy's performance in television debates helped him win the 1960 Presidential election.

- ☐ Kennedy authorized the Bay of Pigs invasion hoping to overturn Fidel Castro. The invasion failed and drove Castro closer into the arms of the Soviet Union.

- ☐ In October 1962, U.S. spy planes saw sites in Cuba were being prepared for Soviet missiles with nuclear warheads capable of striking the United States. This triggered the "Cuban Missile Crisis," when the world came dangerously close to nuclear war. Kennedy instituted a naval blockade and threatened to invade Cuba if the missiles were not removed. Soviet leader Khrushchev agreed to remove the missiles for a pledge that the United States would not invade Cuba and would remove its missiles from Turkey.

- ☐ Civil rights groups used marches, demonstrations, "sit-ins," "freedom rides," and other tactics in the struggle for equal rights.

- ☐ Dr. Martin Luther King, Jr., was arrested in Birmingham and wrote his "Letter from Birmingham Jail." He explained why, after 340 years, African Americans could no longer wait patiently for their constitutional rights.

- ☐ Kennedy proposed a civil rights bill. Dr. King and other civil rights leaders held a "March on Washington" in support of the bill. Dr. King gave his "I Have a Dream" speech in which he told of his dream that one day America would honor its creed that "all men are created equal." King dreamt of the day when Americans of all races, colors, and religions would "sit down together at the table of brotherhood."

- ☐ In November 1963, President Kennedy was assassinated. In the aftermath of Kennedy's death, President Lyndon B. Johnson was able to pass the Civil Rights Act of 1964. This act prohibited discrimination on the basis of race, sex, or religion by public accommodations affecting interstate commerce (for example, hotels, motels, and restaurants).

- ☐ President Johnson declared a "War on Poverty." After his re-election in 1964, Johnson introduced his "Great Society" programs to help eliminate poverty. These included Medicare and Medicaid, increased federal aid for education and urban development, and aid to the poverty-stricken region of Appalachia.

- ☐ Cesar Chavez organized migrant farm workers, who demanded better wages and living conditions. Chavez started the United Farm Workers Association and led marches, strikes, and boycotts.

- ☐ The introduction of television had a great impact on American politics and culture. Kennedy's performance in televised debates helped him win the 1960 election. News coverage showing the brutality of the police and state troopers in Birmingham and Selma,

- Alabama, increased nationwide support for the Civil Rights Movement and led to the passage of the Voting Rights Act. Live coverage of the horrors of the war in Vietnam turned many viewers against the war. Television also permitted Americans to share common moments, such as the moon landing in July 1969.

- In 1954, Vietnam was divided into North and South Vietnam. The North came under the rule of a communist government led by Ho Chi Minh. When South Vietnam refused to participate in nationwide elections with the North, Vietcong (Vietnamese Communists) aided by North Vietnam began a rebellion in the South.

- Americans intervened to protect South Vietnam. American leaders believed in the "domino theory"—that if South Vietnam fell to communism, nearby states would follow.

- In August 1964, the U.S. government claimed that North Vietnam had shot at U.S. ships in international waters in the Gulf of Tonkin. Congress passed the Gulf of Tonkin Resolution, giving the President full powers to act in Vietnam against North Vietnamese aggression. In March 1965, President Johnson sent the first American combat troops to Vietnam.

- Americans proved unable to win the war despite their superior technologies and escalation in their troop strength. By 1968, there were half a million American troops in Vietnam.

- 1968 was a year of turmoil. The Tet Offensive showed that the North Vietnamese and Vietcong could launch powerful attacks in South Vietnam and that the war was far from over. The U.S. military requested 200,000 more troops in Vietnam but Johnson's advisers told him the war could not be won. Johnson began a partial bombing halt and invited the North Vietnamese to peace talks. On March 31, President Johnson announced he would not seek re-election as President.

- On April 4, Dr. Martin Luther King, Jr., was assassinated in Tennessee. Dr. King's assassination led to rioting in many American cities, including Washington, D.C. Police and federal troops were needed to stop the rioting.

- Robert F. Kennedy—the younger brother of the deceased President—decided to run for President. Kennedy won the Democratic primary in California but was assassinated at his victory celebration. The nomination of Vice President Hubert Humphrey by Democrats was assured. Antiwar protesters came to demonstrate at the Democratic National Convention in Chicago, where they faced police violence. Television crews showed the violence on the streets of Chicago. Eight of the demonstrators were placed on trial.

- Republicans nominated Richard Nixon, who claimed to have a secret plan to end the war and promised "peace with honor." With the Democrats badly divided, Nixon won the election.

Chapter 17 | The Kennedy and Johnson Years

Name _____

Complete the following chart about the Kennedy-Johnson years.

Event	Description or Explanation
Division of Vietnam at Geneva in 1954	
Fidel Castro seizes power in Cuba	
U.S. Presidential Election of 1960	
Bay of Pigs Invasion	
Cuban Missile Crisis	
Dr. King's "Letter from Birmingham Jail"	
March on Washington: Dr. King's "I have a Dream" speech	
Assassination of President John F. Kennedy	
President Johnson's "Great Society"	
Gulf of Tonkin Resolution	
Civil Rights Act of 1964	
Voting Rights Act of 1965	
Assassinations of Dr. Martin Luther King, Jr., and Robert F. Kennedy	
1968 Democratic National Convention in Chicago	

Fill in the timeline with events from the Kennedy and Johnson years.

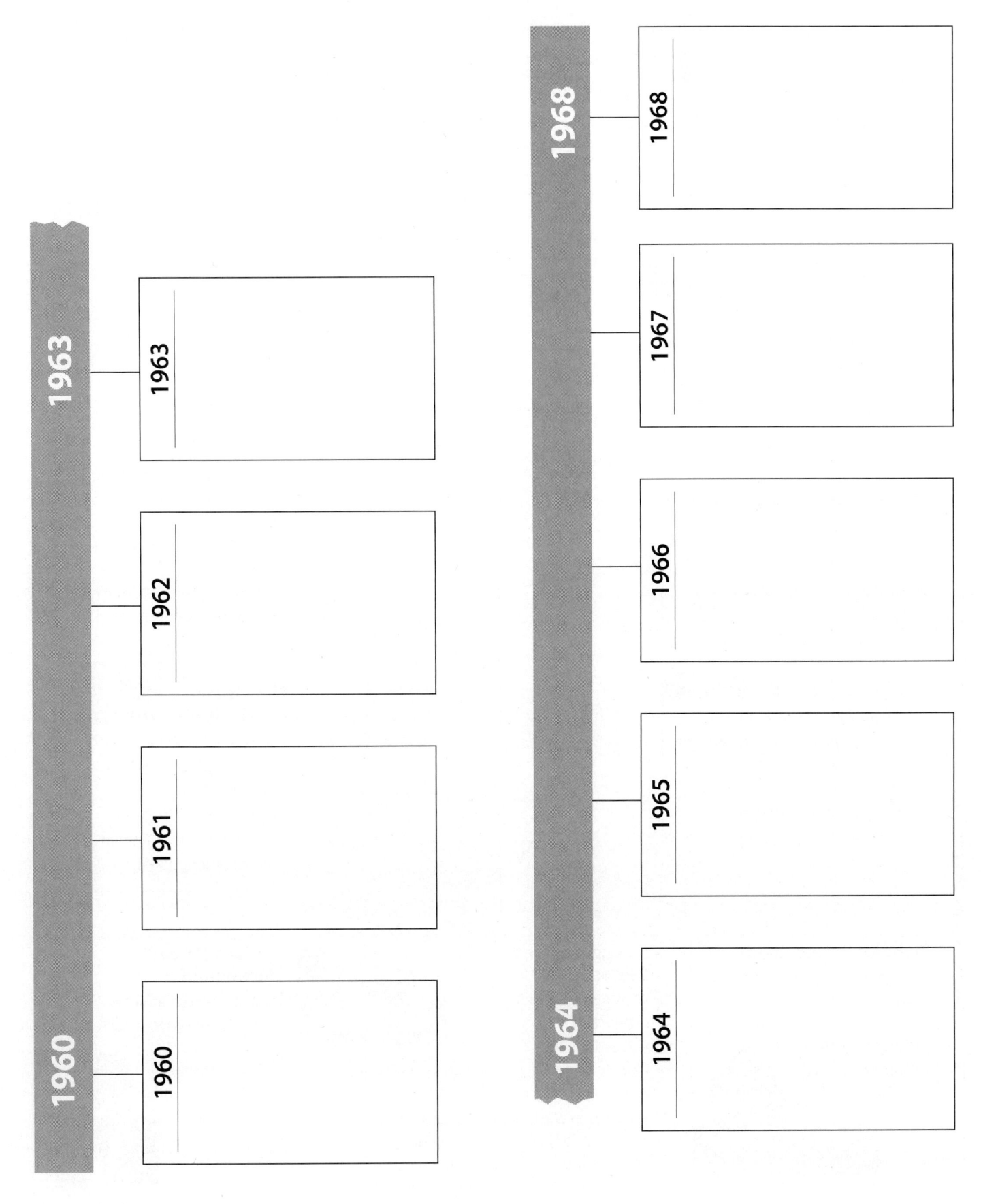

1960
- 1960:
- 1961:
- 1962:
- 1963:

1963

1964
- 1964:
- 1965:
- 1966:
- 1967:
- 1968:

1968

Chapter 17 | The Kennedy and Johnson Years 519

The Kennedy and Johnson Years

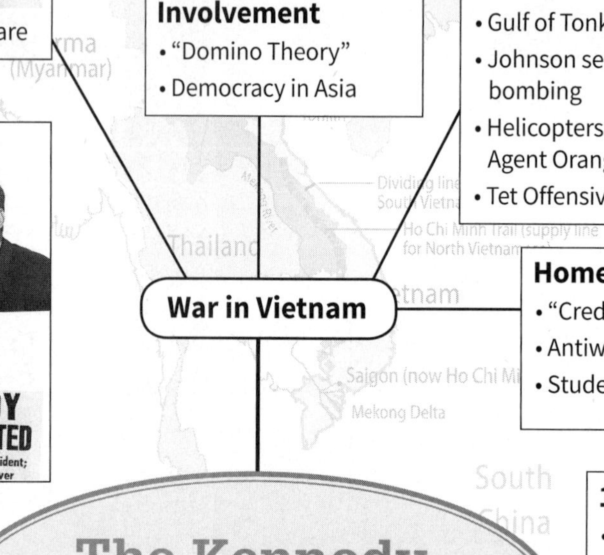

Background
- Geneva Accords (1954): Vietnam divided
- Diem: refused elections
- Vietcong Insurgency—guerilla warfare

President John F. Kennedy
- "New Frontier" programs
- "Bay of Pigs" Invasion
- Khrushchev orders Berlin Wall
- Cuban Missile Crisis (Oct 1962)
- JFK's "Ich bin ein Berliner" speech
- Assassination (1963)

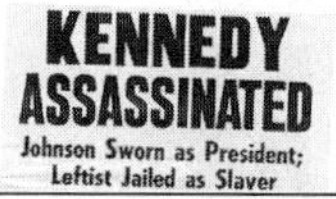

Domestic Policy

President Lyndon Johnson
- "War on Poverty"
- Jobs Corps and VISTA
- "Great Society"
  - Medicare/Medicaid
  - Federal Aid to Education
  - Housing and Urban Development
  - Appalachian Regional Development
  - Immigration Act of 1965

War in Vietnam

Reasons for U.S. Involvement
- "Domino Theory"
- Democracy in Asia

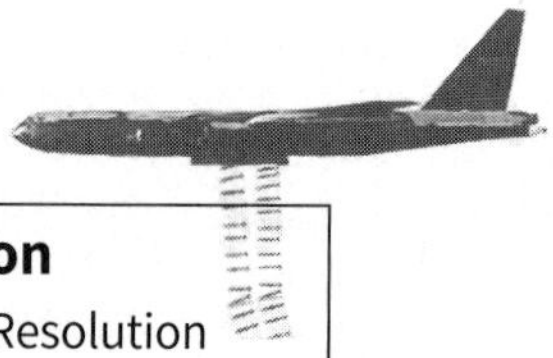

U.S. Escalation
- Gulf of Tonkin Resolution
- Johnson sends troops/bombing
- Helicopters, napalm, Agent Orange
- Tet Offensive

Home Front
- "Credibility gap"
- Antiwar Movement
- Student Protests

1968: Year of Turmoil
- Tet Offensive
- Assassination of Dr. Martin Luther King, Jr.
- Urban riots
- Assassination of Robert Kennedy
- Violence at the Democratic National Convention

The Impact of Television
- Spread of television
- Kennedy-Nixon television debate
- Impact on Civil Rights
- Impact on war in Vietnam
- Moon landing (1969)

Civil Rights

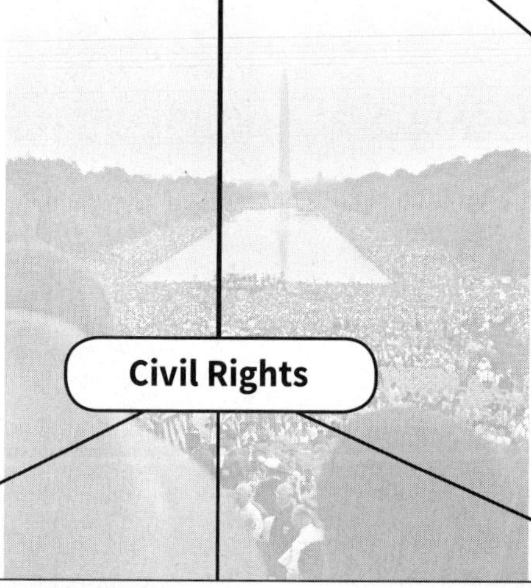

Fight for Voting Rights
- 24th Amendment prohibits poll taxes
- Violence at the Selma to Montgomery March
- Voting Rights Act of 1965

Struggle against Segregation
- "Sit-ins" at lunch counters 
- "Freedom Rides"
- King's "Letter from Birmingham Jail" (April 1963)
- "March on Washington" (August 1963); Dr. King's "I Have a Dream" speech
- Civil Rights Act of 1964: Prohibits racial discrimination by restaurants, hotels, unions

"Black Power" Movement
- Militants disappointed at slow progress of Civil Rights
- Pride in being black

Chapter 17 | The Kennedy and Johnson Years

What Do You Know?

SSUSH21a

1. Use the diagram to answer the question.

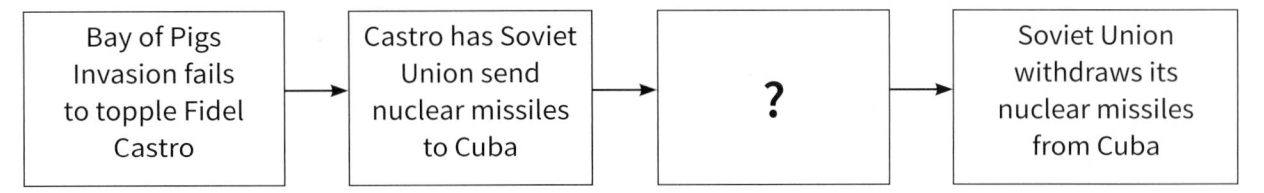

   Bay of Pigs Invasion fails to topple Fidel Castro → Castro has Soviet Union send nuclear missiles to Cuba → ? → Soviet Union withdraws its nuclear missiles from Cuba

   Which statement BEST completes the diagram?

   A. President Kennedy sends U.S. military forces from Florida to Cuba.
   B. President Kennedy uses diplomatic pressure in the U.N. to force the Soviets to retreat.
   C. President Kennedy uses strategic strikes by aircraft against the new missile sites.
   D. President Kennedy blockades Cuba, threatens an invasion, and secretly negotiates with the Soviet Union.

SSUSH21d

2. How were Dr. Martin Luther King, Jr.'s "Letter from Birmingham Jail" and "I Have a Dream" speech similar?

   A. Both argued that the use of violence against repeated acts of racism can be justified.
   B. Both appealed to all citizens based on American principles of liberty and equality.
   C. Both were focused solely on the plight of African Americans in Southern states.
   D. Both urged African Americans to help themselves without the aid of others.

SSUSH21d

3. Read the excerpt to answer the question.

   > We must come to see, with one of our distinguished jurists, that 'justice too long delayed is justice denied.'
   > —Dr. Martin Luther King, Jr. "Letter from Birmingham Jail"

   What aim did Dr. Martin Luther King, Jr. have in publishing this message?

   A. to explain why racial segregation was wrong
   B. to explain why African Americans could no longer wait in demanding equal rights
   C. to explain that conditions for African Americans in Northern states were just as bad as they were in Southern states
   D. to explain that the use of violence to achieve equal rights is sometimes justified

Chapter 17 | The Kennedy and Johnson Years

SSUSH21b

4. Use the chart below to answer the question.

Legislation	Description
Civil Rights Act of 1964	Hotels and restaurants cannot discriminate on the basis of race
24th Amendment	States cannot impose poll taxes, which made it more difficult for African Americans to vote
Voting Rights Act of 1965	?

Which phrase BEST completes the chart?

A. States cannot deny citizens the right to vote on the basis of gender.

B. States cannot deny citizens the right to vote on account of race.

C. States cannot deny citizens over 18 the right to vote on account of age.

D. States cannot deny the right to vote to American Indians on federal reservations.

SSUSH21c

5. Examine the information to answer the question.

- National television news programs show police using fire hoses and police dogs against peaceful demonstrators in Birmingham, Alabama
- National television news programs show police clubbing peaceful demonstrators marching in Selma, Alabama

What was the impact of national television coverage of these incidents?

A. Congress passed new laws to protect the civil rights and voting rights of minorities.

B. Alabama state government officials were arrested for violations of federal law.

C. Civil Rights leaders postponed their efforts until the safety of demonstrators could be better secured.

D. Based on evidence from this live coverage, the U.S. Supreme Court held that Alabama state officials had violated the U.S. Constitution.

SSUSH21b

6. Which program did President Lyndon B. Johnson introduce to end poverty in the United States?

A. New Deal

B. Great Society

C. Marshall Plan

D. Alliance for Progress

Chapter 17 | The Kennedy and Johnson Years

SSUSH21d

7. Which tactic was used by Cesar Chavez to further the goals of the United Farm Workers?

   A. voting for new laws to protect workers
   B. armed violence against rich farm owners
   C. civil disobedience by lying down in fields
   D. national boycotts of some types of crops

SSUSH21b

8. Use the graph to answer the question.

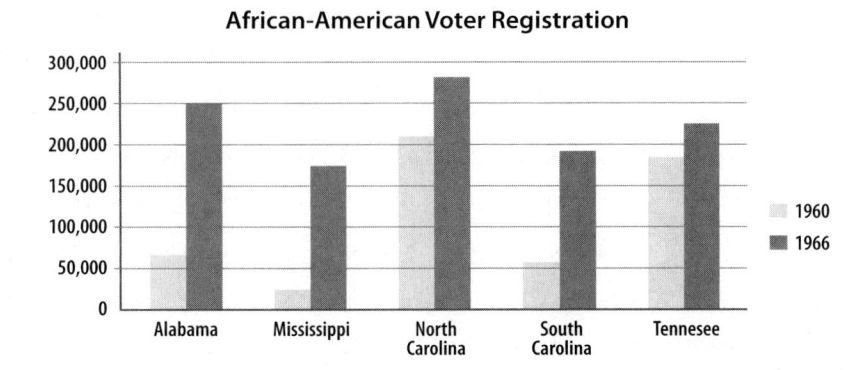

   African-American Voter Registration

   (Bar graph showing 1960 and 1966 voter registration for Alabama, Mississippi, North Carolina, South Carolina, and Tennessee)

   Which event MOST contributed to the changes shown in the graph?

   A. Congress passed the Voting Rights Act of 1965.
   B. Southern states enacted their own new voting laws.
   C. Desegregated restaurants and hotels made voting easier.
   D. Newly integrated schools encouraged African Americans to vote.

SSUSH21a

9. Use the diagram below to answer the question.

   (Diagram of falling dominoes labeled: China, Korea, Vietnam, Laos, Cambodia, Thailand, Malaysia, Indonesia, Burma, India)

   Which action was taken as a result of the theory illustrated by the diagram?

   A. Congress enacted the War Powers Act.
   B. The United States sent troops to South Vietnam.
   C. The United States attacked China during the Korean War.
   D. The United States distributed economic aid under the Marshall Plan.

Chapter 17 | The Kennedy and Johnson Years

SSUSH21a

10. Use the excerpt to answer the question.

> *The Congress approves and supports the determination of the President, as Commander in Chief, to take all necessary measures to repel any armed attack against the forces of the United States and to prevent further aggression.*
>
> —Gulf of Tonkin Resolution, August 7, 1964

What was the significance of this resolution?

A. Congress showed its support for a policy of isolationism.

B. Congress denied the President the revenues he needed to fight a war in Vietnam.

C. Congress provided the President with new constitutional powers to declare war.

D. Congress authorized the President to take military action in South Vietnam.

SSUSH21e

11. Which statement BEST explains the significance of the Tet Offensive?

A. It demonstrated the superiority of United States forces over the Vietcong in South Vietnam.

B. Its failure led to disagreements between the Vietcong and the government of North Vietnam.

C. It showed that the Vietcong could mount a successful attack on South Vietnamese cities and were not close to defeat.

D. United States and South Vietnamese troops were able to force the Vietcong to retreat to North Vietnam and Cambodia.

SSUSH21a

12. Which statement BEST summarizes one of the reasons why Americans were unable to win the conflict in Vietnam?

A. China intervened directly in the war.

B. South Vietnamese leaders decided to come to terms with North Vietnam.

C. The North Vietnamese and Vietcong were determined to unify Vietnam under their leadership.

D. American troops no longer possessed technological superiority over the North Vietnamese army.

SSUSH21e

13. Which event led to major rioting in many American cities in 1968?

A. news of the Tet Offensive

B. election of Richard Nixon

C. passage of the Civil Rights Act of 1968

D. assassination of Dr. Martin Luther King, Jr.

CHAPTER 18 The Presidency in Crisis: Presidents Nixon, Ford, and Carter

SSUSH22 What were the international and domestic policies of the Nixon, Ford, and Carter administrations, and how did their policies influence technological advances and social changes?

  a. What policies and actions were taken by the Nixon, Ford, and Carter administrations in response to the Cold War, including the establishment of diplomatic relations with China, the end of U.S. involvement in Vietnam, the War Powers Act, the Camp David Accords, President Carter's response to the 1979 Iranian Revolution, and the Iranian hostage crisis?

  b. What were the major domestic issues during these Presidencies and what were their social effects, including the creation of the Environmental Protection Agency (EPA), the emergence of the National Organization for Women (NOW), Nixon's resignation due to the Watergate scandal, and his pardon by President Ford?

Names and Terms You Should Know

Richard Nixon

"Peace with Honor"

Vietnamization

Draft

Cambodia

Antiwar movement

Doves

Hawks

Pentagon Papers

Kent State

Henry Kissinger

Paris Peace Accords

War Powers Act

Nixon's Visit to China

Environmental Protection Agency (EPA)

Watergate scandal

Women's Liberation Movement

Betty Friedan

National Organization for Women (NOW)

Gerald Ford

Pardon of Nixon

Inflation

Stagflation

Jimmy Carter

Presidential Election of 1976

Camp David Accords

Anwar Sadat

Menachem Begin

Iranian Revolution of 1979

Shah of Iran

Ayatollah Khomeini

Islamic Republic of Iran

Iranian Hostage Crisis

Election of 1980

Georgia "Peaches" of Wisdom

1. Presidents Nixon, Ford, and Carter faced problems they seemed unable to overcome. Many believed the Presidency itself was in crisis.

2. Nixon promised "peace with honor." Under his policy of "Vietnamization," American troops were gradually replaced with South Vietnamese. To place pressure on North Vietnam and the Vietcong, he increased bombing and sent troops into neighboring Cambodia.

3. Nevertheless, the war dragged on and on because Americans refused to withdraw, while North Vietnam and the Vietcong were committed to their cause. American public opinion became increasingly divided. "Doves" thought the war was immoral and had to be ended. "Hawks" wanted to continue the war to contain communism. In 1970, National Guards even fired on demonstrators at Kent State University, killing four students.

4. Meanwhile negotiations continued in Paris. In 1973, Dr. Henry Kissinger signed the Paris Peace Accords with North Vietnam. America withdrew its troops and North Vietnam freed American prisoners of war (POWs). In the course of the war, 58,000 Americans had died. South Vietnam eventually fell to communist forces in 1975 and North and South Vietnam were reunited.

5. Congress passed the War Powers Act, limiting the President's power to intervene abroad for more than 60 days without Congressional approval.

6. To place pressure on North Vietnam, President Nixon also sought détente—an easing of tensions—with the Soviet Union. Nixon greatly surprised the world by visiting communist China and starting the process of restoring diplomatic relations. This led to China's later admission into the United Nations and participation in the world community and economy. Many historians see this as Nixon's greatest achievement.

7. Nixon also signed the law creating the Environmental Protection Agency (EPA), which protects the environment.

8. The Watergate scandal ended Nixon's Presidency. Former CIA agents, working for the White House, were arrested while breaking into Democratic Party headquarters to set wiretaps. Nixon participated in an attempted cover-up. He was forced by the U.S. Supreme Court to hand over his tapes of White House conversations, which revealed that he had lied about the cover-up. Facing impeachment, Nixon resigned from office.

9. The Women's Liberation Movement aimed to achieve complete economic and social equality between women and men. In 1963, Betty Friedan published *The Feminine Mystique*, voicing the dislike of many middle-class women for their roles as housewives. In 1966, Friedan organized the National Organization for Women (NOW).

10. After Nixon's resignation, Vice President Gerald Ford became President. President Ford pardoned Nixon for his role in Watergate. This pardon was unpopular with many voters and may have cost Ford the next election.

11. Ford faced problems when Arab OPEC members boycotted the United States and oil prices soared. Ford was unable to stop "stagflation"—rising prices and high unemployment at the same time.

12. Governor Jimmy Carter of Georgia won the Presidential election of 1976. Carter came to Washington as an outsider who promised to restore the country's moral tone. He especially asserted morality in foreign policy. He signed a treaty agreeing to return the Panama Canal Zone to Panama. He invited the leaders of Egypt and Israel to Maryland, where he negotiated the Camp David Accords.

13. Like Ford, Carter was not able to solve the problem of stagflation and rising energy prices.

14. In 1979, the Shah of Iran was overthrown. Ayatollah Khomeini established the Islamic Republic of Iran. When Carter let the Shah come to the United States for medical treatment, students seized staff at the U.S. Embassy in Tehran. More than fifty embassy staff were held hostage for 444 days. Carter was unable to free them either by negotiation or military action.

15. Many Americans grew demoralized and Carter lost the election of 1980 to Ronald Reagan.

Chapter 18 | The Presidency in Crisis

In this chapter, you will learn about the domestic and foreign policies of three Presidents: Nixon, Ford, and Carter. Nixon believed in a strong Presidency with a focus on foreign affairs; however, he actually weakened the Presidency by overstepping its bounds. Despite his accomplishments, he was forced to resign from office. Ford and Carter faced crises at home and abroad that proved difficult to overcome, and both lost their bids to be elected for a second term. With so many difficult problems facing the nation, many Americans came to believe the Presidency itself was in crisis.

Nixon Continues the Vietnam War

In his election campaign, Richard M. Nixon had promised Americans an early end to the war, bringing "**peace with honor**." But in fact, the war continued for another four years. Like Johnson, Nixon did not want to become the first American President to lose a war.

The Historian's Apprentice

"I slept only about four hours my first night in the White House and was up at 6:45 a.m. While I was shaving, I remembered the hidden safe that Johnson had shown me during our visit in November. When I opened it the safe looked empty. Then I saw a thin folder on the top shelf. It contained the daily Vietnam Situation Report from the intelligence services for the previous day, Johnson's last day in office. I quickly read through it. The last page contained the latest casualty figures. During the week ending January 18, 185 Americans had been killed and 1,237 wounded. From January 1, 1968 to January 18, 1969, 14,958 men had been killed and 95,798 had been wounded. I closed the folder and put it back in the safe and left it there until the war was over, a constant reminder of its tragic cost."

— Richard Nixon, *The Memoirs of Richard Nixon*

1. What is a "memoir"?
2. What does this passage tell us about the responsibilities of being President in wartime?

Nixon pursued a policy of "**Vietnamization**": South Vietnamese troops took over the brunt of the fighting. As he had promised, Nixon began taking American combat troops out of Vietnam. By May 1972, there were fewer than 100,000 U.S. troops in Vietnam. This policy allowed Nixon to lower the number of men who were **drafted** (*required to serve in the armed services*). He was soon able to end the draft, realizing that the fear of being drafted was encouraging the antiwar movement.

While withdrawing American troops, Nixon increased both bombing missions over North Vietnam and the flow of U.S. military supplies and economic aid to South Vietnam. He believed the war could be shortened if supply routes from

528   Chapter 18 | The Presidency in Crisis

the North could be cut off. In 1970, American troops crossed the border into neighboring **Cambodia** to close North Vietnamese supply routes. The United States also began bombing locations in Cambodia and Laos.

These new steps greatly stimulated the **antiwar movement** in the United States. In November 1969, as many as 750,000 citizens participated in antiwar protests in major cities. Nixon had promised to end the war, but instead it seemed he was expanding it. In fact, Nixon was attempting a complex diplomatic strategy in which he increased the pressure on North Vietnam while holding out the possibility of American withdrawal. He hoped to bomb the North Vietnamese into submission and dramatically increased U.S. bombing missions. This was how Nixon planned to obtain a settlement that would give Americans "peace with honor."

Nixon also tried to place further pressure on the North Vietnamese by pursuing "détente" (*an easing of tensions*) with the Soviet Union and by visiting communist China. These efforts are described in more detail below.

The Home Front: Discontent and Division during the Vietnam War

By the time Nixon assumed office, Americans were deeply divided. "**Doves**" wanted the United States to withdraw from Vietnam. They saw the contest as a Vietnamese civil war in which Americans had no business. Many doves thought the war had become immoral. Americans were burning down so many villages and killing so many civilians that they were destroying Vietnam in order to save it. "**Hawks**," on the other hand, believed it was important to stop the spread of communism. They saw the war as the defense of South Vietnam, an independent country, against aggression from the North. Many hawks thought an all-out U.S. military effort in Vietnam could still bring victory.

Many younger Americans, especially college students, became frustrated at their inability to stop the war. They began to ask what kind of society could wage such a war. This led them to question fundamental values. Some concluded that the war had been caused by the American system of competitive capitalism. A new "counter-culture" emerged among those who rejected what they viewed as the callous materialism of American life. They did not wish to become cogs in a machine-like society. They were drawn instead to rock music, recreational drugs (marijuana and LSD), and the promise of greater freedom and personal fulfillment. They even adopted new fashions—such as long hair for men, bell-bottomed trousers, and colorful clothing—to set themselves apart. In August 1969, several hundred thousand of these young people, sometimes known as "hippies," gathered for a three-day outdoor concert at Woodstock, New York. The antiwar movement and the "counter-culture" reinforced one another.

My Lai Massacre

In March 1968, before Nixon took office, U.S. troops had fired on hundreds of unarmed men, women, and children in the South Vietnamese village of My Lai. A U.S. helicopter crew tried to save some of the villagers and reported the atrocity. The incident was only first reported in the news media in the fall of 1969. Disturbing photographs of the bodies of victims piled in a ditch appeared in newspapers and on television news in November 1969, just days before one of the largest demonstrations against the war. The platoon leader was later court-martialed and convicted. News of the My Lai massacre further enflamed feelings about the war.

Victims of My Lai massacre

The "Pentagon Papers"

Back in 1967, the U.S. Secretary of Defense had ordered a secret study of American involvement in Vietnam. The study contained hundreds of top-secret classified documents. These documents—known as the "Pentagon Papers"—revealed that U.S. officials thought there was little chance of winning the war but Presidents Kennedy and Johnson had not wanted to be seen as losing it. The study also provided numerous instances in which previous administrations had lied to the American public. Daniel Ellsberg, a government consultant, gave copies of the study to the *New York Times*, which published excerpts from the report. *The Washington Post* and other newspapers also reprinted the excerpts. Nixon attempted to prevent publication of the documents but was overruled by the U.S. Supreme Court on First Amendment grounds. The release of the "Pentagon Papers" further strengthened the case of opponents of the war.

Shootings at Kent State

When Nixon announced the invasion of Cambodia in the spring of 1970, antiwar demonstrations took place on college campuses across the country. At **Kent State University** in Ohio, students smashed windows and a campus building. The next day, the Governor of Ohio sent in the Ohio National Guard to control the demonstrators. Several of the inexperienced Guards fired, killing four students and wounding nine others. Two of those who died were not even demonstrators—they were just students on their way to class. The public was shocked that student protesters were being shot and killed. College students across the country shut down their campuses in protest. Millions of students went on strike.

End of U.S. Involvement in Vietnam

All this time, Nixon's National Security Adviser **Henry Kissinger** had been negotiating with the North Vietnamese in Paris. When the North Vietnamese delegates walked out of the negotiations in December 1972, Nixon authorized the heaviest bombing of North Vietnam of the entire war. The North Vietnamese returned to the negotiating table and in January 1973,

The Paris Peace Accords

- There would be an immediate cease-fire.
- The United States would withdraw all of its troops and advisers from Vietnam, and dismantle its bases.
- North Vietnam would release its American prisoners of war (POWs).
- North Vietnamese troops would be permitted to remain in South Vietnam.
- A "Council of Reconciliation," which included representatives from both the government of South Vietnam and the Vietcong, would arrange for future elections in the South.
- Foreign troops would be withdrawn from Cambodia and Laos.
- North and South Vietnam would eventually be peacefully re-united.

Kissinger and the North Vietnamese finally agreed to the **Paris Peace Accords**.

Nixon planned to continue providing military and economic assistance to South Vietnam. To show that he had not abandoned the South Vietnamese, he sent large amounts of supplies to South Vietnam.

After the American withdrawal, bitter fighting continued in Vietnam. Without direct military support from the United States, the government of South Vietnam proved unable to resist the North. Congress refused to permit further bombing of Vietnam. In April 1975, Cambodia and South Vietnam both fell to communist forces.

Consequences of the Vietnam War

The Vietnam War had important consequences:

- The greatest effects of the war were felt in Vietnam itself. At least 1.3 million Vietnamese were killed and a large proportion of the population of South Vietnam was left homeless. Herbicides destroyed rice paddies and forests. Cities were left in ruins.

- Almost 58,000 Americans were killed in the war. Their names are now inscribed on the Vietnam Veterans Memorial in Washington, D.C. Thousands of others experienced physical and psychological injuries. A large number suffered from exposure to American herbicides used during the war, especially "Agent Orange." Many Vietnam veterans felt their needs were ignored when they returned home.

- Vietnamese communists introduced repressive policies in South Vietnam. Many people, fearful of persecution, fled on small boats to neighboring non-communist countries. Some Vietnamese refugees immigrated to the United States.

- The extension of the Vietnam War into Cambodia led to the triumph of a radical faction of Cambodian communists, known as the "Khmer Rouge." In 1975–1976, the Khmer Rouge murdered between two and four million Cambodians.

- The expenses of the Vietnam War led to a reduction of the social welfare programs

Chapter 18 | The Presidency in Crisis

of Johnson's "Great Society." The war also caused rising **inflation** (*rising prices*).

- The failure in Vietnam led to widespread disillusionment in the United States. American leaders realized that there were limits to the exercise of American power. They grew fearful of over-extending commitments abroad, while the public became distrustful of their leaders and more isolationist.

The Historian's Apprentice

1. Watch one or more episodes of the PBS documentary, *Vietnam: A Television History* or *The Vietnam War* by Ken Burns and Lynn Novick. How does watching a documentary differ from reading a book? Is a television documentary more or less objective than a book? What do you think was the view of the producers of either of these documentaries? Explain your answers.
2. Imagine it is 1969. Hold a class debate between "Hawks" and "Doves" on this topic—"Resolved: the United States should immediately withdraw from Vietnam."
3. Using your school library or the Internet, find some newspapers from the 1960s. Look for opposing viewpoints on the war in Vietnam, expressed in editorials or articles. Then summarize the arguments you find in one of those editorials or articles.
4. Using your school library or the Internet, find out more information about Daniel Ellsberg and the "Pentagon Papers." What did they contain? Why was the federal government so concerned about their publication?
5. Interview a grandparent, relative, or neighbor who either fought in Vietnam or who participated in the antiwar movement. Be sure to formulate a series of good questions in advance. Then report the results of your interview to your class.
6. Why do you think the Vietnam War remains such a controversial topic today?

The War Powers Act

After the U.S. failure in Vietnam, Congress attempted to claim a greater role in formulating U.S. foreign policy. Both the Korean War and the war in Vietnam had been fought without a formal declaration of war by Congress.

In November 1973, Congress passed the **War Powers Act**. This act limited the President's power to commit U.S. troops overseas without Congressional approval. It requires the President, within two days of committing troops to combat, to make a report to Congress. The troops must then be withdrawn within 60 days, unless Congress authorizes a longer commitment.

The Historian's Apprentice

How did the War Powers Act (1973) differ from the earlier Gulf of Tonkin Resolution (1964)?

Nixon's Visit to China and Détente with the Soviet Union

To place additional pressure on North Vietnam, Nixon took two steps that surprised many. Ever since 1949, American leaders had refused to give diplomatic recognition to the communist government of China. No American politician was willing to be accused of being "weak" on communism. Nixon, a staunch anti-communist, decided to take the first steps towards reversing that policy.

This was at a time when China and the Soviet Union were already at odds. The two most populous communist countries had a dispute over their common border and were also in competition for leadership of the communist world. Nixon believed this Sino-Soviet split provided Americans with a unique opportunity.

As early as 1970, Nixon secretly asked the governments of Romania and Pakistan to let the Chinese government know that U.S. leaders were interested in entering into talks with them. In 1971, Kissinger made several trips to China, and in February 1972, Nixon and Kissinger (now the Secretary of State) visited Mao Zedong in Beijing, China's capital city. Television followed the President's week-long visit. Nixon began the process of normalizing diplomatic relations with the communist Chinese, although it would be several more years before full recognition was granted.

Nixon's reopening of relations with China had important repercussions. It opened the way for later trade with China, for the entry of communist China into the United Nations, and for the normalization of relations between China and the rest of the world. Most historians agree that Nixon's reopening of relations with China was one of his greatest accomplishments as President.

In May 1972, just months after his visit to China, Nixon also became the first U.S. President to visit Moscow, the Soviet capital. Nixon sought a "détente," or an easing of tensions, with the Soviet Union. While in Moscow, Nixon signed an agreement with Soviet leaders to limit the further development of nuclear arms, known as "SALT" (Strategic Arms Limitation Treaty).

Nixon hoped he could persuade Soviet and Chinese leaders to decrease their military and financial support of North Vietnam. This would place pressure on the North Vietnamese to negotiate an end to the war. The prospect of friendlier relations with the United States may also have kept the Soviet Union and China from protesting more vigorously when Nixon stepped up his bombing of Vietnam.

Domestic Policy under Nixon

Nixon was a moderate Republican. While he criticized the expansion of the role of the federal government, he showed flexibility in his domestic policies.

New Federalism/Revenue Sharing

Nixon opposed many of Johnson's Great Society programs and cut their funding, but he kept many of the most important ones, including Medicare, Medicaid, and Project Head Start. He actually increased aid to the poor and even proposed an early health insurance plan. Under Nixon, social security payments increased significantly. Nixon also strengthened "affirmative action": new rules required employers with federal contracts to set goals for the recruitment and hiring of women and minorities.

At the same time, Nixon opposed the further growth of the federal government in domestic matters. He introduced a policy of "New Federalism" in which the federal government gave back some of its revenues to state and local governments to spend on their own needs. Nixon required Southern states to enforce school desegregation to receive their revenue sharing funds, greatly speeding up the process.

Creation of the EPA

Conservationists had been making efforts to preserve our nation's resources ever since the days of John Muir and Theodore Roosevelt. In the postwar period, the threat to the environment from pollution became especially evident. In 1962, marine biologist Rachel Carson published her book *Silent Spring*, about the dangers of pesticide use, especially DDT. Congress passed a series of laws to protect the air, water, and land from pollution, including a Clean Air Act in 1963, a Wilderness Act in 1964, and a Clear Water Act in 1965. An Endangered Species Act was passed in 1966, requiring the Fish and Wildlife Service to list species of plants and animals that were threatened with extinction and to take steps to protect them, including protecting their habitats (*environments*).

Environmentalists copied the methods of the Civil Rights and antiwar movements to push for further protection of the environment. In January 1970, Nixon signed the law creating the **Environmental Protection Agency**, or "**EPA**." The EPA sets levels of acceptable air and water pollution and has the power to fine polluters. The EPA also requires builders to file an "Environmental Impact Statement" before undertaking any major new construction. EPA officials review the statement and determine whether the construction can go forward or whether it will be too damaging to the environment. Private citizens can also file lawsuits under the act against polluters.

Passage of the act was accompanied, in April 1970, by the first "Earth Day," in which millions of Americans demonstrated their concern for the environment. Nixon also signed subsequent laws protecting the environment, including a stricter Clean Air Act in 1970, and the Federal Water Pollution Control Act in 1972. He called for an expanded Endangered Species Act, which was passed in 1973.

Fighting Inflation

Mounting expenditures for the Vietnam War led to **inflation** (*rising prices*) in the United

States. Nixon attempted to fight inflation with a 90-day wage and price freeze, but this effort at government control proved ineffective. Nixon also took the United States off the gold standard (*the ability to convert U.S. dollars into a fixed amount of gold*) and permitted the dollar to be traded for other currencies at market rates. His goal was to make it easier for American companies to sell their goods abroad.

The Watergate Crisis and Nixon's Resignation

Nixon's foreign and domestic policy successes were overshadowed by the Watergate scandal shortly after the beginning of his second term.

After the leaking of the "Pentagon Papers," Nixon authorized the creation of a special unit in the White House to prevent further leaks, by unlawful means if necessary. During the Presidential election campaign of 1972, members of this special unit used an ex-CIA agent and four Cuban exiles to break into Democratic Party headquarters in the Watergate office complex in Washington, D.C., to photograph documents and set wiretaps. When they broke into the party headquarters a second time, a security guard spotted the unsecured doors and called the police, who arrested the burglars.

Two of the burglars had address books that listed a White House contact. One of them had deposited a large check from Nixon's campaign fund (to pay for their wiretapping expenses). When the FBI began tracing the check, Nixon gave his consent to his staff's proposal that the CIA be instructed to tell the FBI to call off their investigation. Nixon also later agreed to create a special "hush" fund to pay off the Watergate burglars, who faced imprisonment.

All this time, two young reporters at *The Washington Post* kept the story alive in the press. When the burglars faced sentencing for the break-in, one of them finally informed the judge that there had in fact been a high-level cover-up. Congress formed a committee to investigate the break-in, while the Attorney General appointed a special prosecutor to investigate.

The White House was now implicated in the cover-up, although Nixon still publicly denied knowing anything about it. At Congressional hearings, a former staff member accused the President of participating in the cover-up. It was then discovered that Nixon had taped all his conversations in the White House. The Congressional committee and special prosecutor both demanded access to the tapes. Nixon at first refused to hand over the tapes to investigators, claiming "executive privilege"—the need for the President, as the head of

Nixon leaving the White House on Marine One shortly before his resignation became effective, August 9, 1974

Chapter 18 | The Presidency in Crisis

the executive branch, to be able to freely explore alternatives without the interference of the other branches. Then Nixon gave investigators a highly edited version of some of the tapes. He later gave Congress typed transcripts of more of the tapes, which had been edited. His claims of "executive privilege" were finally denied by the U.S. Supreme Court, which unanimously ordered the President to hand over all of the requested tapes in their entirety. The tapes revealed that Nixon had indeed been behind the "cover-up" all along. Nixon resigned the Presidency when Republican leaders in Congress informed him that he faced certain impeachment.

The Historian's Apprentice

"A President and those who assist him must be free to explore alternatives in the process of shaping policies and making decisions, and to do so in a way many would be unwilling to express except privately. These are the considerations justifying a presumptive privilege for Presidential communications.... But this presumptive privilege must be considered in light of our historic commitment to the rule of law ... To ensure that justice is done, it is imperative to the function of courts that compulsory process be available for the production of evidence needed either by the prosecution or by the defense."

—*United States v. Nixon*, July 24, 1974

Only two weeks after the Court's decision, Nixon resigned as President. Congress had already prepared three articles of impeachment. In officially announcing his decision on television, Nixon told his viewers :

"I have never been a quitter. To leave office before my term is completed is opposed to every instinct in my body. But as President, I must put the interests of America first. America needs a full-time President, particularly at this time with [the] problems we face at home and abroad. To continue to fight through the months ahead for my personal vindication would totally absorb the time of both the President and the Congress ... Therefore, I shall resign the Presidency effective at noon tomorrow."

1. In *United States v. Nixon*, the Supreme Court weighed the President's need for confidentiality against the needs of the criminal justice system for evidence. Do you think they struck the right balance? Write a short essay giving your views on whether the Supreme Court was right in ordering Nixon to turn over the tapes.

2. Did Nixon admit to any wrongdoing in his announcement of resignation? Should he have done so?

3. Nixon negotiated an end to the war in Vietnam, re-opened relations with China, worked for détente with the Soviet Union, signed the law creating the EPA, and ended the draft. He also bombed Vietnam, Laos, and Cambodia, and tried to cover up the Watergate break-in. What rating would you give Nixon as President?

Origins of the Women's Liberation Movement

A major development in these years was the **Women's Liberation Movement**, which began in the 1960s and reached its peak during the Nixon Presidency. A century earlier, American women had struggled to achieve political and civil equality. Now they focused on achieving economic and social equality.

Origins of the Women's Liberation Movement (Feminist Movement)

In the postwar period, many educated, middle-class women felt the division of labor between men and women, both at home and in the workplace, was unfair and stifling. These women wanted to "liberate" themselves from traditional roles. They found a spokeswoman in **Betty Friedan**, who published *The Feminine Mystique* in 1963. The "mystique" was the belief that women always found happiness as housewives and mothers rather than in professional careers—a belief that Friedan challenged.

The Formation of NOW

The success of the Civil Rights Movement inspired these women to strive for greater equality with men. Many leaders of the Women's Liberation Movement had been active in the Civil Rights or antiwar movement. They adopted many of the same tactics to promote women's rights, such as forming organizations, lobbying, and engaging in demonstrations, boycotts, and strikes. In October 1966, Friedan and others formed the **National Organization for Women (NOW),** which became the chief voice of the modern women's movement. In 1972, Gloria Steinem founded a new monthly magazine, *Ms.*, devoted to women's issues.

The Historian's Apprentice

NOW's original "Statement of Purpose" was written by Betty Friedan:

Statement of Purpose

"We, men and women who hereby constitute ourselves as the National Organization for Women, believe that the time has come for a new movement toward true equality for all women in America, and toward a fully equal partnership of the sexes, as part of the world-wide revolution of human rights now taking place within and beyond our national borders.

The purpose of NOW is to take action to bring women into full participation in the mainstream of American society now, exercising all the privileges and responsibilities thereof in truly equal partnership with men . . .

WE BELIEVE that the power of American law, and the protection guaranteed by the U.S. Constitution to the civil rights of all individuals, must be effectively applied and enforced to isolate and remove patterns of sex discrimination, to ensure equality of opportunity in employment

Continued ▶

and education, and equality of civil and political rights and responsibilities on behalf of women, as well as for [African Americans] and other deprived groups."

—National Organization for Women, October 29, 1966

1. Based on this document, what were the original goals of NOW?
2. How did these goals differ from those of the women's suffrage movement fifty years earlier?
3. Why did these women feel it was necessary to create their own organization to further women's rights?

The goals of the Women's Liberation Movement were far-reaching. They demanded greater freedom and social and economic equality with men. One result was the Equal Opportunity in Education Act (1972), also known as **Title IX**, which prohibited universities and schools receiving federal aid from discriminating in their educational programs, including athletics, on the basis of sex. In the 1970s, the U.S. military academies (such as West Point) and all but a handful of colleges became co-educational (*both sexes were educated together*). High school gym classes in public schools, which had previously separated boys and girls, likewise became co-educational.

Meanwhile "affirmative action" programs promoted more hiring of women professors. A larger number of women began being admitted to law schools, medical schools, and graduate business schools.

The Equal Rights Amendment (ERA)

Feminists hoped to achieve many of their goals by passing a single constitutional amendment that guaranteed women equal rights with men. ("Equality of rights should not be denied . . . on account of sex.") The Equal Rights Amendment ("ERA") was first proposed in 1923. It was approved by both houses of Congress in 1972. First Lady Pat Nixon announced her support, but ERA was never ratified by enough states to become part of the Constitution.

The Ford Presidency

Nixon's Vice President, Spiro Agnew, had been guilty of taking bribes from contractors when he was Governor of Maryland. In a deal with prosecutors, the Vice President resigned from office rather than face imprisonment. **Gerald Ford**, a popular Congressman from Michigan, was appointed by Nixon in Agnew's place, with the support of Democrats and Republicans in Congress. Although Ford was never elected to the executive branch, he suddenly became President when Nixon resigned.

The Nixon Pardon

One step that Ford took after only a month in office was to grant a Presidential pardon to Nixon for all crimes he may have committed. This action was unpopular with many

Americans at the time and may have ultimately cost Ford the 1976 election. Ford felt he had to take this step to avoid the further division that placing Nixon on trial would have caused.

The Historian's Apprentice

Here is the actual text of Ford's pardon:

> "It is believed that a trial of Richard Nixon, if it became necessary, could not fairly begin until a year or more has elapsed. In the meantime, the tranquility to which this nation has been restored by the events of recent weeks could be irreparably lost by the prospects of bringing to trial a former President of the United States. The prospects of such trial will cause prolonged and divisive debate over the propriety of exposing to further punishment and degradation a man who has already paid the unprecedented penalty of relinquishing the highest elective office of the United States.
>
> *Now, Therefore, I, Gerald R. Ford,* President of the United States, pursuant to the pardon power conferred upon me by Article II, Section 2, of the Constitution, have granted and by these presents do grant a full, free, and absolute pardon unto Richard Nixon for all offenses against the United States which he, Richard Nixon, has committed or may have committed or taken part in during the period from January 20, 1969, through August 9, 1974."

1. Would you have agreed with Ford's reasoning in granting this pardon?
2. Why were so many Americans upset at Ford's action?

The Middle East and OPEC

In foreign policy, Ford kept Henry Kissinger as his Secretary of State. Ford and Kissinger continued Nixon's policy of détente with the Soviet Union. They faced new problems, especially in the Middle East. **OPEC**, the Organization of Petroleum Exporting Countries, had been formed in 1960. During the Arab-Israeli War of 1973, the Arab members of OPEC had boycotted the United States and other countries that traded with Israel. Even after the war ended, OPEC members continued to raise their oil prices, contributing to inflation in the United States at a time of high unemployment. The price for a barrel of crude oil in 1974 was almost four times what it had been just two years earlier, while the United States was importing 10% of its petroleum needs. By 1975, unemployment reached 9%, the highest since the Great Depression. High unemployment combined with inflation became known as **stagflation**.

The Fall of South Vietnam

President Ford was forced to stand by passively when North Vietnamese forces took over South Vietnam in April 1975. Congress refused to permit additional assistance. Movie cameras recorded the last American helicopters leaving the roof of the U.S. Embassy in Saigon. Those Vietnamese who had cooperated with the United States were left at the mercy of their sworn enemies, the Vietnamese communists.

Chapter 18 | The Presidency in Crisis

The Carter Presidency

In the 1976 Presidential election, Gerald Ford faced Democratic candidate **Jimmy Carter**, a former Governor of Georgia.

The practice of televised debates between candidates of the major parties, last seen between Kennedy and Nixon in 1960, was renewed by Ford and Carter. Carter won the election narrowly as a Washington "outsider." At a time when Americans were distrustful of politicians, Carter's campaign slogan was, "I'll never lie to you."

The 1976 Presidential Election

Candidate	Party	Popular Vote	Electoral Vote
Jimmy Carter	Dem.	40,831,881 (50.1%)	297
Gerald Ford	Rep.	39,148,634 (48.0%)	240

Domestic Policies and Stagflation

Carter began his Presidency with an exercise of the pardoning power: he pardoned draft evaders from the Vietnam War.

The most serious domestic problems Carter faced were continuing stagflation and an energy crisis. Americans had to wait in lines at gas stations because of fuel shortages, and many worried that the world's oil reserves might soon be exhausted. Smaller cars from Japanese and European manufacturers suddenly became popular with Americans as gas prices soared.

Carter cut taxes and increased spending to combat these problems, but these steps simply increased inflation, which reached as high as 12%. Mortgage rates reached 20%, making it impossible for most Americans to buy a house.

Jimmy Carter is the first Georgian to have been elected President. Born in the rural town of Plains, Georgia, in 1924, Carter went to the U.S. Naval Academy, became a submarine officer, and served on a naval nuclear reactor project. He was part of a team sent to Canada in 1952 to help clean up an accident when a nuclear reactor lost its coolant. Carter left the Navy in 1953 on the death of his father and returned to Georgia to manage the family peanut farm and business. At the time, Georgians were still arguing over racial segregation in schools. Carter strongly supported integration. He became interested in politics and served two terms in the state legislature. He lost his first bid to become Governor to a segregationist. Carter had strong religious faith and became a "born again" Christian. He was successful in his second campaign for the governorship in 1970. In his inaugural address, Carter attacked racism and segregation: "the time of racial discrimination is over... No poor, rural, weak, or [African-American] person should ever have to bear the additional burden of being deprived of the opportunity for an education, a job or simple justice." As Governor, Carter increased the number of African-American state employees, introduced administrative reforms, and encouraged the growth of industry. He drew attention as a liberal Southern Governor. In 1976, Carter decided to run for President. Although almost totally unknown outside of Georgia, Carter worked hard on his campaign and performed well in primary elections, giving him the Democratic nomination. He offered Americans the kind of honesty and sincerity they sought after Vietnam and Watergate.

Carter created a Cabinet-level Department of Energy and appealed to Americans to conserve energy. He also started filling the Strategic Petroleum Reserve, an emergency supply of oil that had been established during the Ford Presidency. But like Ford, Carter was never able to solve the problem of stagflation.

A New Approach to Foreign Policy: Panama and Camp David

In foreign policy, Carter believed it was necessary for Americans to take a more moral tone, especially in the defense of human rights. During the Cold War, American Presidents had been willing to back dictators to stop the spread of communism. Carter thought this was wrong. He tried to reassert American morality in foreign policy by signing a treaty with Panama in 1977. This agreement promised to hand over the Panama Canal to the government of Panama by 2000. Carter also refused to help anti-communist dictators like Anastasio Somoza in Nicaragua, even when they were friendly to the United States.

In the Middle East, Carter tried to bring Israelis and Arabs together. In November 1977, President **Anwar Sadat** of Egypt had dramatically flown to Israel to speak in the Israeli parliament. Sadat became the first Arab leader to set foot on Israeli soil. In 1978, Carter invited Sadat and Israeli Prime Minister **Menachem Begin** to Camp David in Maryland. At first, the invitation almost backfired. After a few days, Begin and Sadat were barely on speaking terms. Carter separated them and began his work as a mediator, going back and forth between the Israeli and Egyptian leaders. With Carter's help, the two leaders were finally able to reach an agreement. Carter persuaded Begin, for example, to agree

Egyptian President Anwar Sadat, Israeli Prime Minister Menachem Begin, and Jimmy Carter at Camp David in Maryland

to give up Israeli settlements on the Sinai Peninsula. Under the **Camp David Accords**, Egypt agreed to establish normal diplomatic relations with Israel and to permit Israelis to use the Suez Canal. In exchange, Israel agreed to return the Sinai Peninsula, which it had occupied since the 1967 War, to Egypt. The parties also pledged to eventual self-government for Palestinians in the West Bank and Gaza. It was the first time an Arab nation agreed to peace with Israel and demonstrated to other Arab states that negotiations could be conducted with Israel. The agreement was a triumph for Carter. Begin and Sadat won the Nobel Peace Prize in 1978, but Sadat was later assassinated by Islamic extremists who opposed peace with Israel.

U.S.-Soviet Relations

Relations with the Soviet Union deteriorated in the Carter years. President Carter and Soviet leaders signed an arms agreement in Vienna in June 1979. Only a few weeks later, the Soviet Union invaded Afghanistan, where Muslim rebels were attacking the pro-Soviet government. In retaliation, President Carter stopped U.S. grain sales to the Soviet Union and refused to let the United States participate in the 1980

Moscow Olympics. He also announced that the United States would act against any attempt by the Soviet Union to gain control of the Persian Gulf. Congress never ratified the arms agreement signed in Vienna, but both American and Soviet leaders continued to respect its terms.

The Iranian Revolution and the Hostage Crisis

In 1979, a popular revolution occurred in Iran. The pro-Western **Shah**, who had governed Iran since 1953, faced mass demonstrations against his rule when people filled the streets in Tehran and other cities. The Shah finally fled the country. A religious leader, **Ayatollah Khomeini**, returned from exile and established an Islamic Republic. Iran became a theocracy governed by Islamic law.

Khomeini blamed the United States and other Western powers for having supported the Shah. When the Shah sought medical treatment in the United States, Iranian students and other followers of Khomeini seized the staff at the U.S. Embassy in Tehran on November 4, 1979, and held just over 50 of them as hostages. They demanded that the United States send the Shah back to Iran for trial and punishment. President Carter was unable to obtain the hostages' release though negotiations, and the hostages were held captive for the rest of his Presidency (a total of 444 days). Americans grew demoralized at their nation's inability to rescue its own embassy staff. Carter made plans to free the hostages through a daring helicopter raid and attack on the embassy, but the mission was terminated when several of the helicopters had mechanical failures in the desert. One of the helicopters, caught by blowing sand, crashed into another, killing eight men.

In July 1980, the Shah died. Then in September 1980, Iraq invaded Iran. Secret talks between the United States and Iran opened in early November. In the last days of the Carter Presidency, details were worked out for the release of the hostages in exchange for the release of almost $8 billion in Iranian assets. At Khomeini's insistence, the hostages were not released until the moment when Carter was no longer President.

The 1980 Presidential Election

The hostage crisis and continuing problems with the economy at home caused Jimmy Carter to lose the Presidential election of 1980. His opponent was **Ronald Reagan**—a conservative, charismatic former actor and former Governor of California. Reagan promised to take a tough stand on the hostage crisis.

The failure in Vietnam, the Watergate scandal, the Iran Hostage Crisis, and the continuing stagflation all seemed to confirm the collapse of American power and the weakness of American leaders. The American Presidency was indeed in crisis as the new decade began.

The 1980 Presidential Election

Candidate	Party	Popular Vote	Electoral Vote
Ronald Reagan	Dem.	43,903,230 (50.7%)	489
Jimmy Carter	Rep.	35,480,115 (41.0%)	240

Chapter 18 | The Presidency in Crisis

For the Georgia Milestones EOC Assessment you should know that:

- [ ] President Nixon promised to end the war in Vietnam by giving Americans "peace with honor." He withdrew American troops through the process of Vietnamization, while increasing the bombing of North Vietnam and widening the war to neighboring Cambodia and Laos.

- [ ] The United States and North Vietnam finally agreed to a cease-fire in the Paris Peace Accords (1973): the United States withdrew its troops, North Vietnam released American POWs, and North Vietnamese troops were permitted to remain in South Vietnam.

- [ ] Congress passed the War Powers Act to strengthen Congressional influence on foreign policy and limit the President's ability to fight wars without their approval.

- [ ] Nixon visited communist China in 1972 and began the process of normalizing U.S.-Chinese relations. Nixon hoped this step might put pressure on North Vietnam. This development opened the way for later U.S.-China trade.

- [ ] Nixon approved the legislation creating the Environmental Protection Agency, or EPA.

- [ ] The Women's Liberation Movement sought equal opportunities for women. Supporters organized the National Organization for Women, or "NOW," which was founded in 1966.

- [ ] Nixon resigned the Presidency because of the Watergate scandal. Tapes of White House conversations showed he had participated in the cover-up and had attempted to pay off the Watergate burglars, who had broken into Democratic headquarters in the Watergate Complex in Washington, D.C.

- [ ] A month after becoming President, President Ford pardoned Nixon for any possible criminal activity he might have committed. The pardon was very unpopular.

- [ ] Jimmy Carter, the former Governor of Georgia, was elected President in 1976 as a Washington "outsider."

- [ ] President Carter asserted the importance of human rights in U.S. foreign policy. He brought Prime Minister Begin of Israel and Anwar Sadat of Egypt together at Camp David, Maryland, for twelve days, where they concluded the Camp David Accords. Egypt would establish diplomatic relations with Israel, and Israel would return the Sinai Peninsula to Egypt.

- [ ] In 1979, the Shah of Iran was overthrown in a popular revolt. Ayatollah Khomeini and other religious leaders took over and declared Iran to be an Islamic Republic.

- [ ] On November 4, 1979, students in Iran's capital city of Tehran seized the staff of the U.S. Embassy and held them hostage. Carter was unable to obtain their release through either negotiations or military action, weakening his Presidency.

- [ ] Carter lost the Presidential election of 1980 against Ronald Reagan.

Chapter 18 | The Presidency in Crisis

The Presidency in Crisis

Richard Nixon

Nixon and Vietnam
- Promised "Peace with Honor"
- "Vietnamization"
- "Doves" and "hawks"
- Increased bombing of North
- Spread of war into Cambodia
- Growing antiwar movement
- Pentagon Papers
- Kent State Shootings
- End of draft
- Kissinger and negotiations in Paris
- Paris Peace Accords—U.S. Withdrawal

Other Foreign Policies
- Détente with Soviet Union
- Visit to Communist China

Domestic Policies
- New Federalism
- Creation of the EPA—protects the environment

Watergate Scandal
- Break in to Democratic headquarters
- Cover up by Nixon administration
- Supreme Court orders Nixon to hand over tapes
- Nixon resigns rather than face impeachment

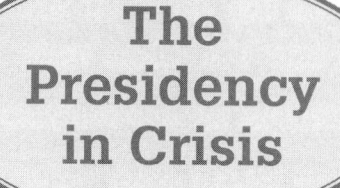

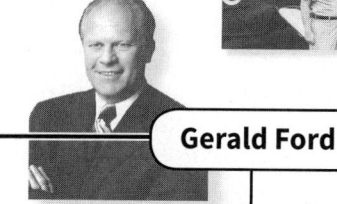

Gerald Ford
- Pardoned Nixon
- Arab OPEC boycott of U.S.
- Stagflation
- Fall of South Vietnam

Women's Liberation Movement
- Demand for social and economic equality
- Betty Friedan, *The Feminine Mystique*
- NOW: National Organization for Women
- Gloria Steinem, *Ms.* magazine
- Equal Rights Amendment (ERA)

Jimmy Carter
- Panama Canal Treaty
- Camp David Accords: Agreement between Egypt and Israel
- Energy shortages, high oil prices, and continuing stagflation
- Iranian Revolution—Ayatollah Khomeini proclaims Islamic Republic
- Hostage Crisis: US Embassy staff seized in Tehran and held 444 days

Chapter 18 | The Presidency in Crisis

Name _____

Complete the following chart about the topics in this chapter.

Event	Description or Explanation
Formation of the National Organization of Women (NOW)	
Nixon's Vietnamization policy	
Nixon's visit to China	
Creation of the EPA	
Paris Peace Accords	
Watergate Scandal	
War Powers Resolution	
President Ford's Pardon of Nixon	

Name _____

Complete the following chart about the topics in this chapter.

Event	Description or Explanation
Arab OPEC members boycott the United States	
Stagflation	
Election of Jimmy Carter	
Camp David Accords	
Iranian Revolution of 1979	
Iranian Hostage Crisis	

> "Scholars agree that the Watergate scandal marked a transformative moment in American politics and culture. As the historian Keith W. Olson contends, 'Watergate and Vietnam…contributed significantly to a fundamental distrust of government that has continued into the second decade of the twenty-first century.' … Historians have paid significant attention to the crisis of the American Presidency that unfolded during the 1960s and 1970s."
> —The Miller Center of the University of Virginia, "The Presidency in Crisis"

Why did the Presidencies of Nixon, Ford and Carter lead Americans to question the powers of the Presidency?

_____
_____
_____
_____

Chapter 18 | The Presidency in Crisis

What Do You Know?

SSUSH22a

1. Use the list to answer the question.

   - Experience in the Navy with energy issues
   - Successful record as a liberal Southern Governor
   - Election as an outsider to Washington
   - Success in bringing Egyptian and Israeli leaders together in the Camp David Accords.
   - Inability to stop inflation or rising energy prices
   - Inability to free Iranian hostages

   Which U.S. President is described by these characteristics?

   A. Bill Clinton
   B. Gerald Ford
   C. Jimmy Carter
   D. Ronald Reagan

SSUSH22b

2. Which of the following was a goal of the National Organization for Women (NOW)?

   A. the right to vote for women in all state and federal elections
   B. the full participation of women in society in equal partnership with men
   C. the duty to serve in combat positions in the armed services when citizens are drafted
   D. the right to a guaranteed number of top positions at universities and major corporations

SSUSH22a

3. Use the diagram to answer the question.

   - "Vietnamization"
   - Increased bombing missions over North Vietnam, Cambodia, and Laos
   - Negotiations with North Vietnamese
   → ?

   Which BEST completes the diagram?

   A. Paris Peace Accords
   B. Geneva Accords
   C. Gulf of Tonkin Resolution
   D. War Powers Act

Chapter 18 | The Presidency in Crisis

SSUSH22a

4. What did the War Powers Act (1973) seek to do?

   A. authorize the President to send troops to defend South Vietnam

   B. authorize the President to keep U.S. forces on the Korean Peninsula after the Korean War

   C. limit the President's ability to send troops overseas without the approval of Congress

   D. provide the President with special powers to deal with the emergency hostage crisis in Iran

SSUSH22a

5. Use the diagram to answer the question.

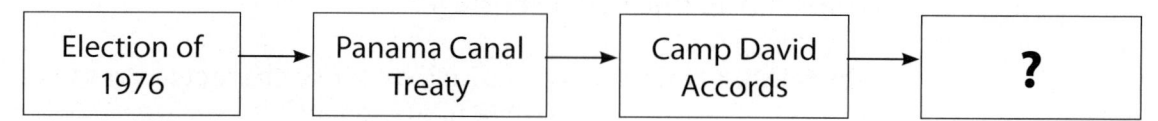

   Election of 1976 → Panama Canal Treaty → Camp David Accords → ?

   Which event BEST fits in the diagram?

   A. Iranian Revolution and Iranian hostage crisis

   B. Fall of South Vietnam

   C. Lower oil prices and economic recovery

   D. Resignation of the President to avoid impeachment

SSUSH22b

6. Which step did President Gerald Ford take that reduced his popularity?

   A. increased federal taxes

   B. took no steps during the fall of South Vietnam

   C. pardoned former President Richard Nixon for possible crimes

   D. signed an agreement in Helsinki that promoted human rights in Europe

SSUSH22a

7. Use the list to answer the question.

   - Publication of the "Pentagon Papers"
   - News reports of the My Lai massacre
   - Increased bombing of North Vietnam
   - Shootings at Kent State, Ohio

   What was the impact of these events?

   A. decline of the antiwar movement

   B. resignation of President Richard Nixon

   C. greater public opposition to the Vietnam War

   D. division among Nixon's Republican supporters

548   Chapter 18 | The Presidency in Crisis

SSUSH22a

8. Use the diagram to answer the question.

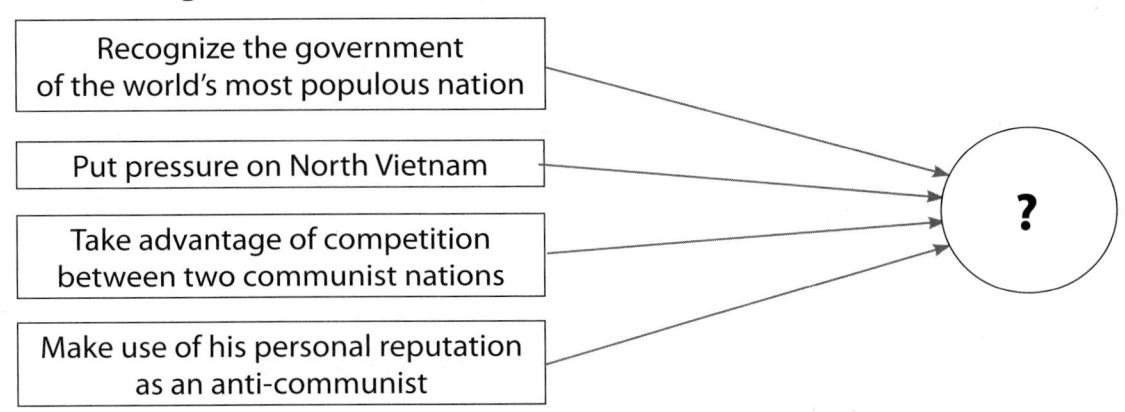

   - Recognize the government of the world's most populous nation
   - Put pressure on North Vietnam
   - Take advantage of competition between two communist nations
   - Make use of his personal reputation as an anti-communist

   → **?**

   Which statement BEST completes the diagram?

   A. Nixon visits Nationalist Chinese in Taiwan.
   B. Nixon opens relations with communist China.
   C. Nixon withdraws U.S. troops from Vietnam.
   D. Nixon increases U.S. bombing of North Vietnam.

SSUSH22b

9. Which steps does the federal government take through the Environmental Protection Agency?

   A. Maintain the national parks + Collect entrance fees from visitors to national parks

   B. Grant licenses for mining rights + Collect royalties from mining companies operating on federal land

   C. Establish rules for a safe working environment + Enforce workplace rules to ensure employee safety

   D. Set permissible pollution levels + Approve or deny all projects significantly affecting the environment

SSUSH22b

10. Which TWO factors MOST helped Jimmy Carter win the election of 1976?

    A. Voters thought Carter would better resist Soviet aggression.
    B. Voters were angry at President Ford's pardon of Richard Nixon.
    C. Voters blamed President Ford for the collapse of South Vietnam.
    D. Voters believed Carter would return the Panama Canal to Panama.
    E. Voters felt that Carter was more honest than Washington politicians.
    F. Voters believed Carter could better resolve conflicts in the Middle East.

Chapter 18 | The Presidency in Crisis

SSUSH22b

11. Use the diagram to answer the questions.

Ex-CIA members are arrested while breaking into Democratic headquarters → Nixon and White House staff secretly try to stop investigation → Congress and a special prosecutor launch investigations → White House tapes reveal Nixon was behind the cover-up → Nixon resigns rather than face impeachment

Part A

Which misconduct is described by these facts?

A. Teapot Dome Scandal
B. Watergate Scandal
C. Iran-Contra Affair
D. Hostage Crisis

Part B

What conclusion can BEST be drawn from these events?

A. Even the President is subject to the rule of law.
B. The President is above the law during his period in office.
C. Private discussions by those in power should always be made public.
D. Secrecy in the White House usually indicates wrongdoing of some kind.

SSUSH22a

12. Which statement BEST describes the long-term significance of President Nixon's visit to communist China in 1972?

A. It led to the reunification of Taiwan with communist China.
B. It persuaded Chinese leaders to introduce capitalism into the marketplace.
C. It showed that the Cold War between the "Free World" and communism was over.
D. It opened the way for China's entry into the United Nations and trade with the United States.

SSUSH22a

13. Use the list to answer the question.

- Demonstrations in the streets of Tehran
- The Shah flees from Iran
- Ayatollah Khomeini returns to Iran from exile

What was a direct consequence of these events?

A. Iran adopted a communist government.
B. Iran invaded neighboring Afghanistan.
C. Iran became an Islamic Republic.
D. The Soviet Union invaded Iran.

Chapter 18 | The Presidency in Crisis

CHAPTER 19 **America in Recent Times: Presidents Reagan, George H.W. Bush, Clinton, George W. Bush, and Obama**

SSUSH23 What political, economic, and technological changes took place during the Reagan, George H.W. Bush, Clinton, George W. Bush, and Obama Presidencies?

a. What challenges have been faced by recent Presidents, including the collapse of the Soviet Union, Clinton's impeachment, the attacks of September 11, 2001, and the war against terrorism?

b. What have been the economic policies of recent Presidents, including Reaganomics?

c. What has been the influence of technological changes on society, such as the personal computer, the Internet, and social media?

d. What was the historic nature of the Presidential election of 2008?

Names and Terms You Should Know

- Ronald Reagan
- Reaganomics
- Stagflation
- Deregulation
- Reagan Doctrine
- Strategic Defense Initiative
- Soviet Union
- Mikhail Gorbachev
- George H.W. Bush
- End of the Cold War

- Berlin Wall
- Bill Clinton
- Monica Lewinsky
- Impeachment of President Clinton
- George W. Bush
- Attacks of September 11, 2001
- World Trade Center
- Osama bin Laden
- Al Qaeda
- War on Terror

- War on Terrorism
- Department of Homeland Security
- Presidential Election of 2008
- Barack Obama
- Technology
- Personal Computer
- Internet
- Social Media
- Globalization

Georgia "Peaches" of Wisdom

1. In the 1980 election, President Reagan pledged to make America strong again. Reagan believed an over-extended federal government was at the root of many of the problems Americans faced.

2. To fight stagflation, he introduced "Reaganomics": tax rate cuts, reductions in federal spending on domestic programs, and the elimination of many federal regulations. Lower oil prices and increased military spending also helped the economy recover. Reaganomics had important long-term consequences: an increasing federal deficit and a growing gap between rich and poor.

3. Reagan wanted to roll communism back, not just contain it. Under the "Reagan Doctrine," he sent aid to anti-communists in Grenada, Nicaragua, and Afghanistan. Some U.S. officials secretly sold arms to Iran for freeing American hostages in Lebanon; money from Iran was then secretly given to the anti-communist contras in Nicaragua. The plan was discovered, leading to the "Iran-Contra" scandal.

4. Soviet leader Mikhail Gorbachev introduced important reforms in his country. Reagan's Strategic Defense Initiative led Gorbachev to meet with Reagan for several summit meetings. In 1986, the two leaders agreed to reduce their nuclear arms.

5. Gorbachev refused to use force against the Baltic states or countries of Eastern Europe, which asserted their independence. In 1989, the Berlin Wall, symbol of the Cold War, came down. Democratic elections were held in Eastern Europe.

6. While George H.W. Bush was President, the Cold War came to an end. Germany was reunited and the Soviet Union broke apart.

7. When Saddam Hussein, the dictator of Iraq, occupied Kuwait, Bush put together an international coalition to drive him out.

8. Bush was less successful in dealing with the U.S. economy, which experienced a temporary recession. He lost the 1992 election to Bill Clinton.

9. Under President Clinton, Americans enjoyed a "peace dividend" and prosperity. When ethnic conflicts arose in parts of the former Yugoslavia, Clinton intervened to prevent genocide.

10. Clinton became the second President to be impeached when he lied under oath about his relations with Monica Lewinsky, a White House intern. Congress voted along party lines and Republicans lacked enough votes to remove Clinton from office.

11. George W. Bush, the son of George H.W. Bush, came to power after a close election in 2000. A voting recount in Florida was halted by the U.S. Supreme Court.

12. On September 11, 2001, al Qaeda terrorists hijacked commercial planes and crashed them into the World Trade Center and Pentagon. President Bush declared a "War on Terror." U.S. forces invaded Afghanistan and overthrew the Taliban, which had sheltered al Qaeda. Bush also created the new Cabinet-level Department of Homeland Security.

13. Fearing Saddam Hussein was hiding weapons of mass destruction, Bush ordered an invasion of Iraq in 2003. Hussein was quickly defeated but U.S. forces found Iraq had become so unstable they could not immediately withdraw.

14. In the last two years of Bush's Presidency, Americans faced a severe economic recession triggered by shaky home loans.

15. The 2008 Presidential election was a historic contest. It took place at a time of economic crisis. The leading contenders for the Democratic nomination were an African American—Barack Obama—and a woman—Hillary Clinton. On the Republican side, another woman, Sarah Palin, became the second woman to be nominated by a major political party for Vice President. Obama won the Democratic nomination and in November became the first African American to be elected President—forty years after the death of Dr. Martin Luther King, Jr.

16. Americans saw their lives transformed in these years by advances in information technology: the personal computer, the Internet, and social media. These advances also contributed to globalization—the increased flow of goods, services, information, and people across national borders.

The Presidency of Ronald Reagan

In January 1981, **Ronald Reagan** took office as President. He pledged to take tough action to improve conditions for Americans at home and abroad. Reagan conveyed a sense of confidence that many Americans found reassuring.

On the day of Reagan's inauguration, Iran released its hostages from the U.S. Embassy. It may have been that Reagan sounded so tough Iranian leaders feared what would happen if they kept the hostages once he took office. But since President Carter had already negotiated their release, it is even more likely that, after the outbreak of the Iran-Iraq War, Iranian leaders wanted to end hostile relations with the United States and obtain the return of Iranian funds.

Even with the return of the hostages, Reagan faced major problems domestically and overseas. At home, the main problem was stagflation. Even though unemployment was high, prices were still rising. In foreign policy, Americans remained engaged in the Cold War against the Soviet Union.

Reaganomics

Reagan introduced far-reaching changes that brought a return to prosperity to many, although not to all Americans. Reagan felt that individuals and businesses were better able to solve economic problems by themselves rather than through government intervention.

Ronald Reagan (1911–2004) was raised in a poor family in Illinois. After college, he became a sportscaster on radio and then moved to Hollywood to become a successful movie actor. He became head of the Screen Actors Guild (the Hollywood actors' labor union), where he opposed the influence of communists during the McCarthy era. Reagan also resented paying up to 90% in taxes for what he earned in making a movie. When his movie career faded, Reagan became host to the General Electric Theater, a weekly television drama. For eight years, viewers enjoyed Reagan's calm, reassuring voice. Reagan began giving political speeches in G.E. factories and communities he visited while hosting the program. He was such a good speaker that he later became known as the "Great Communicator." Reagan came to see two evils plaguing America: communism and big government. In 1964, he gave a successful speech in support of conservative Republican Barry Goldwater. After that, Reagan was elected for two terms as Governor of California. As Governor, his style was to identify "big picture" ideas and rely on his team to carry them out. Reagan unsuccessfully sought the Republican nomination against Nixon and Ford in 1968 and 1976, but was nominated in 1980 to run against Jimmy Carter.

The Historian's Apprentice

In his Inaugural Address of 1981, Reagan presented his views on government:

> "In this present crisis, government is not the solution to our problem; government is the problem. From time to time we've been tempted to believe that society has become too complex to be managed by self-rule, that government by an elite group is superior to government for, by,

554   Chapter 19 | America in Recent Times

and of the people. Well, if no one among us is capable of governing himself, then who among us has the capacity to govern someone else? All of us together, in and out of government, must bear the burden. The solutions we seek must be equitable, with no one group singled out to pay a higher price."

1. What did Reagan mean by an "elite group"?
2. How did Reagan's approach differ from those of Presidents Franklin D. Roosevelt and Lyndon B. Johnson?
3. Would you have agreed with Reagan's approach if you had been a voter in 1980?

Reagan wished to reduce the federal government's role in the economy. He tried to solve the problem of stagflation by focusing on the supply of goods. His economic advisers believed that if the supply of goods could be increased, then prices for those goods would go down—ending stagflation. To increase the supply of goods, Reagan cut taxes and reduced government regulations (*rules that businesses must follow*). People called this new strategy **"Reaganomics."**

Shortly after an unsuccessful assassination attempt on his life, Reagan presented his economic program to Congress. Against this dramatic background, Congress approved his proposals—even though a majority of the House were Democrats.

The Key Measures of "Reaganomics"

Tax Rate Cuts
Reagan cut tax rates on businesses and the wealthy. He felt these tax rates were too high, stifling private initiative. His goal was to give people more incentive to produce and invest. In 1981, the maximum tax rates on individuals were reduced from 70% to 50%. Maximum tax rates were further reduced to 28% in 1986.

It was hoped that businesses and wealthy individuals would invest their tax savings in American businesses, raising productivity and increasing employment. This would then result in benefits that would "trickle down" to other groups. Reagan believed that as the economy expanded, government tax receipts would actually increase even at the lower tax rates.

Reductions in Domestic Spending
To finance these tax cuts, Reagan reduced spending on federal welfare programs. He also eliminated some tax "loop-holes" that had allowed certain groups to avoid taxes.

Deregulation
Reagan eliminated many federal regulations on industry, making it easier for new companies to compete. He ordered regulatory agencies to reduce new regulations and to allow businesses to have greater freedom. Reagan relaxed enforcement of the antitrust laws and allowed more business mergers. He also took steps against union rules in order to permit more flexible work practices. In Britain, his friend Prime Minister Margaret Thatcher took similar steps.

Chapter 19 | America in Recent Times

Other factors also contributed to the economic recovery during Reagan's Presidency:

▶ **Tightening the Money Supply**

To fight inflation (*rising prices*), the Federal Reserve raised interest rates. This reduced the supply of available money. Inflation, which was almost 15% in 1980, fell to 3% by 1983.

▶ **Increased Military Spending**

Reagan promised to reduce government spending, but he greatly increased military spending. Since he also cut tax rates, he financed this increased military spending through borrowing. This military spending stimulated the entire economy, creating a demand for many goods and services.

▶ **Lower Oil Prices and New Occupations**

In the 1980s, new supplies of oil from Alaska and the North Sea stabilized oil prices. Meanwhile the rise of the computer industry and improvements in health care created new jobs, such as in computer programming.

The Impact of Reaganomics

At first, Reagan's program led to higher unemployment. By 1983, however, the economy began to come out of the recession. Inflation also returned to more normal levels.

Reaganomics had other important consequences for the economy:

Federal Deficit and the National Debt

The **federal deficit** is the amount of money that the federal government spends beyond what it collects in taxes. Reagan had promised a "balanced budget" in which the government's expenditures were limited by the amount of taxes it raised. He thus reduced welfare programs that benefited the poor in order to reduce taxes. But because of military spending, Reagan actually increased the federal deficit. The federal deficit contributed to the **national debt** (*the total amount owed by the government*). During Reagan's two terms in office, the national debt more than doubled. At the same time, this "deficit spending" may have helped to end the recession.

A Growing Trade Imbalance

Higher interest rates at the start of Reagan's Presidency made a "stronger" dollar (*the dollar was worth more when exchanged for foreign currencies*). This made it harder to sell American goods overseas but made it easier for Americans to buy foreign goods. During the Reagan years, Americans bought more goods and services from abroad—especially from Japan—than they sold overseas. This "trade imbalance" led to the loss of jobs in manufacturing and the closing of American steel mills and auto plants.

An Increasing Gap between Rich and Poor

One of the most striking impacts of Reaganomics was an increasing gap between the rich, who profited from tax rate cuts, and the poor, who lost some of their welfare benefits.

The Historian's Apprentice

1. Why did Reagan believe that total tax receipts would increase, even at lower tax rates?
2. How high do you think maximum tax rates should be? Why?
3. Which factors were most important in defeating "stagflation"?

4. How has the "trade imbalance" continued even today? Should we be concerned about it?
5. With a partner, design a poster either for or against Reaganomics.
6. Make a chart showing the benefits and costs of Reaganomics. Then debate with your classmates whether Reaganomics was worthwhile, taking into account its many long-term consequences.

Reagan's Foreign Policy

President Reagan faced two chief problems in foreign policy—terrorism and the Cold War.

Terrorism

During Reagan's two terms in office, international terrorism became an increasing threat.

In 1982, the government of Lebanon appealed to the United Nations for help in a civil war. American and French troops were sent there as part of a U.N. peacekeeping mission. Opponents of the government used terrorist tactics to drive them out. In April 1983, a suicide bomber drove into the U.S. Embassy in Beirut, Lebanon. His truck exploded, killing 63 people. In October 1983, a second suicide bomber struck the U.S. Marine barracks in Beirut, killing 241 Americans. Four months later, Reagan withdrew remaining U.S. troops from Lebanon.

Although he withdrew from Lebanon, Reagan declared he would never negotiate with terrorists. When a bomb exploded in a West Berlin nightclub in 1986, Reagan launched punitive air strikes over Libya in retaliation. American officials believed the dictator of Libya had been behind the Berlin bombing.

The "Reagan Doctrine"

Reagan was a staunch anti-communist. He considered the Soviet Union to be an "evil empire." He was not satisfied with the goal of containment—Reagan wanted to "roll" communism back. He believed that other peoples around the world yearned to be free, just like the United States. This policy became known as the "Reagan Doctrine":

- **Afghanistan.** Reagan gave assistance to Islamic soldiers fighting the Soviet army.

- **Grenada.** When communists took over the small island of Grenada in the Caribbean, Reagan sent in U.S. troops.

- **Nicaragua.** In 1979, a socialist group—the Sandinistas—overthrew the country's dictator and seized power. Reagan gave support to anti-communist rebels in Nicaragua known as the "contras," who opposed the Sandinistas. When Congress prohibited further aid to the contras, members of Reagan's administration violated the law by giving them secret aid.

"Terrorists" use acts of violence to attract media attention or coerce governments. They strike "terror" in people to achieve their goals. Terrorists might take hostages, hijack or blow up airplanes, or explode bombs in places where ordinary citizens like to gather. They may threaten to explode a bomb or kill hostages if the government does not agree to their demands, such as to free political prisoners or to provide them with money. More recently, groups like al Qaeda and ISIS see themselves at war with the West and make no specific demands.

> Note: The Iran-Contra Affair will not be on the Georgia Milestones EOC Assessment, but it was an important event during the second term of Reagan's Presidency.

The Iran-Contra Affair

Several Americans had been kidnapped by terrorist groups in Lebanon. These terrorist groups had close ties to Iran. Iran was in the Iran-Iraq War and needed military supplies. In secret talks with Iran, some U.S. officials agreed to sell arms to Iran in return for the release of the American hostages in Lebanon. Money obtained from Iran in the secret arms sales was then turned over to the contras in Nicaragua.

When news of this secret transaction leaked out, Congress and the American public were shocked. Not only had American officials negotiated with terrorists, but they had also violated the Congressional ban on aiding the contras. Several prominent officials resigned and faced criminal charges, but President Reagan claimed he had no knowledge of the bargain. Since Reagan generally relied on his team to carry out the details of his policies, it is not clear whether they had actually informed him of the Iran-Contra plan.

Changes in the Soviet Union

During President Reagan's first term in office, the Soviet Union continued to suffer from economic stagnation. The Soviet economy had not kept pace with the West. Government officials dictated what was to be produced, which often did not correspond with people's real needs. Workers had little incentive to work hard, and alcoholism and corruption became chronic. People who were critical of the government were afraid of being arrested and jailed. Meanwhile, Soviet resources were being drained in an unpopular war in Afghanistan.

> In 1985, **Mikhail Gorbachev** assumed power as the new leader of the Soviet government. Gorbachev introduced new policies to deal with the problems his country faced. He established greater openness (*glasnost*) in Soviet society and government. For the first time, people were able to criticize the government and make suggestions without fear. Gorbachev also introduced a "restructuring" (*perestroika*) of the Soviet economy by allowing limited free enterprise. For example, he let peasants sell some of their crops in markets, permitted factory managers to set their own production levels, and authorized the opening of some private businesses. Finally, Gorbachev began withdrawing Soviet troops from the unpopular war in Afghanistan.

Gorbachev's policy of greater openness (*glasnost*) led to demands by some of the non-Russian peoples in the Soviet Union for independence. Rather than using force against the peoples of the Baltic States (Estonia, Latvia, and Lithuania), Gorbachev granted them their independence. The demand for greater freedom quickly spread to the other countries of Eastern Europe and to ethnic minorities within the Soviet Union itself.

> Note: you will not need to know the specific names of particular Soviet policies, like *glasnost* and *perestroika*, for the Georgia Milestones EOC Assessment. However you will need to know that the Soviet Union collapsed and that this had important consequences for U.S. foreign policy.

The Strategic Defense Initiative and Reagan-Gorbachev Summit Talks

Reagan did not like the idea of relying on the threat of massive retaliation to deter a nuclear attack. He wanted to be able to defend the United States against nuclear weapons. He therefore proposed the **Strategic Defense Initiative** (also known as "Star Wars") to develop an anti-ballistic missile defense system, perhaps using lasers, capable of withstanding a nuclear attack.

With the Soviet economy in shambles, Gorbachev knew that the Soviet Union could not afford to take similar steps. Soviet leaders feared Americans might even intend to launch a "first strike" nuclear attack since they would no longer have to worry about Soviet retaliation. Reagan's proposal for the Strategic Defense Initiative thus helped drive Gorbachev to seek discussions with the United States.

Reagan and Gorbachev met for the first time in Geneva, Switzerland, in November 1985. They met a second time in Reykjavik, Iceland, in October 1986. Surprisingly, they discussed dismantling their nuclear arsenals to make the world safer from the threat of nuclear war. Reagan and Gorbachev met several later times and signed an agreement to reduce the total number of nuclear missiles. Their agreement was the most successful arms reduction since the Cold War had begun.

By 1987, Reagan was looking forward to an end to the Cold War itself. Speaking in Berlin and pointing to the Berlin Wall, Reagan called on Gorbachev to "tear this wall down."

Reagan and Gorbachev signing an agreement to eliminate short and intermediate range nuclear missiles (1987)

The Historian's Apprentice

Reagan gave this speech standing near the Brandenburg Gate in Berlin:

> "We hear much from Moscow about a new policy of reform and openness. Some political prisoners have been released. Certain foreign news broadcasts are no longer being jammed. Some economic enterprises have been permitted to operate with greater freedom. Are these the beginnings of profound changes in the Soviet state? Or are they token gestures, intended to raise false hopes in the West? We welcome change and openness; for we believe that freedom and security go together. There is one sign the Soviets can make that would be unmistakable, [and] advance the cause of freedom and peace. General Secretary Gorbachev, if you seek peace, if you seek prosperity for the Soviet Union and Eastern Europe: Come here to this gate! . . . Mr. Gorbachev, tear down this wall!"

1. How did Reagan's stirring challenge at the Berlin Wall fit in with his earlier beliefs and policies?
2. How do you think Mikhail Gorbachev felt about this speech?

The Presidency of George H.W. Bush

After the difficulties experienced by Nixon, Ford, and Carter, Ronald Reagan's two terms seemed to demonstrate that a capable leader could indeed handle the problems faced by the office of President. Reagan's Vice President, George H. W. Bush, was elected President in 1988.

Bush's election meant four more years of Republican rule and a general continuation of Reagan's policies. Bush wanted to pursue the same policies but with greater sympathy for the underprivileged.

Bush's Foreign Policy

The central focus of Bush's Presidency was on foreign affairs.

The End of the Cold War

In 1989, the Cold War dramatically ended. Anti-government demonstrations spread throughout East Germany, Poland, and other Eastern European countries. Unlike earlier Soviet leaders, Gorbachev refused to use military power to prop up these unpopular regimes.

In June 1989, Poland became the first country behind the former Iron Curtain to elect a non-communist government. Then the **Berlin Wall**, the main symbol of the Cold War, came down in November 1989. Television screens around the world showed crowds of Germans cheering as they stood on and around the wall. The destruction of the wall meant that East and West Germans could pass back and forth freely. In October 1990, East and West Germany were reunited. Meanwhile, the other countries of Eastern Europe held democratic elections and installed non-communist governments.

> **George H.W. Bush** came from a wealthy family. His father had been a U.S. Senator. Bush himself had been of the youngest combat pilots in the U.S Navy during World War II. He had extensive foreign policy experience as U.S. Ambassador to the United Nations, Ambassador to China, Director of the CIA, and Vice President.

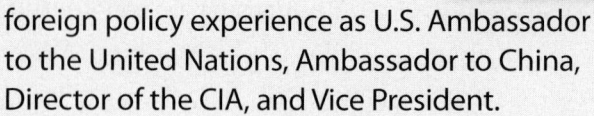

The Collapse of the Soviet Union

Even in the Soviet Union, various ethnic groups demanded greater freedom, including the Russians themselves. In the summer of 1991, hard-line Soviet military leaders attempted a coup (*a seizure of power; a strike or blow*) against Gorbachev's reformist government. They arrested Gorbachev while he was outside of Moscow. **Boris Yeltsin**, the President of Russia (the largest republic in the Soviet Union), occupied the Russian Parliament building and stood on top of a tank, where he called on all citizens to resist the illegal coup. After initial hesitation, President Bush gave Yeltsin his full support. Bush refused to recognize the coup leaders as a lawful government and demanded the release of Gorbachev. The coup quickly collapsed and the Soviet Communist Party lost all of its influence.

The **Soviet Union** was a federation of 15 republics of different nationalities that had replaced the Russian Empire. The largest of these republics was Russia itself. After the independence of the Baltic States and the countries of Eastern Europe, the different republics that made up the Soviet Union began demanding their own independence. At the end of 1991, the Soviet Union itself suddenly disintegrated.

Russia, led by Boris Yeltsin, left the Soviet Union and joined other former Soviet republics to form a loose association known as the Commonwealth of Independent States.

The Historian's Apprentice

"[T]he biggest thing that has happened in the world in my life, in our lives, is this: By the grace of God, America won the Cold War."

—President George H.W. Bush, State of the Union Address, January 28, 1992

1. Why was the end of the Cold War and the collapse of the Soviet Union such a historic event?
2. Who should get credit for ending the Cold War? Have a class discussion on this question: Did President Reagan's policies help to end the Cold War, or would Gorbachev have ended the communist system anyway, since the Soviet Union was already falling behind the West?

Note: The Persian Gulf War, U.S. actions in Panama and Somalia, NAFTA, Bush's domestic policies, Rodney King, and Ross Perot will not be tested on the Georgia Milestones EOC Assessment.

U.S. Intervention in Panama, Kuwait and Somalia

With the collapse of the Soviet Union, the United States became the world's only **superpower**. Many called for a "New World Order," based on democratic values. President Bush proved willing to use military power during these years to promote American national interests.

Shortly after becoming President, Bush sent U.S. forces into **Panama** to arrest the country's dictator, Manuel Noriega, who faced drug charges in the United States.

In August 1990, Iraqi dictator **Saddam Hussein** invaded **Kuwait**, a small neighboring country on the Persian Gulf with vast oil reserves. President Bush organized a large international coalition against the illegal Iraqi occupation. He sent U.S. troops to Kuwait as a major part of the coalition force. The United States and its allies quickly defeated Iraqi forces in the **Persian Gulf War**. Once the coalition chased the Iraqis out of Kuwait, however, Bush refused to use U.S. military power to depose Saddam Hussein in Iraq.

President Bush meeting troops in Saudi Arabia

In the final months of his Presidency, Bush sent U.S. troops into Somalia, a country in East Africa, on a humanitarian mission to help distribute food and save millions of people from starvation.

NAFTA

President Bush negotiated an agreement with Canada and Mexico, known as the **North American Free Trade Agreement**, or **NAFTA**, to create a trade association that would rival the European "Common Market" (a free-trade area of European states). The United States, Canada, and Mexico agreed to gradually reduce their tariffs on one another's goods and to carry out other forms of cooperation. This agreement, however, was not ratified by Congress until after Bush's Presidency.

Bush's Domestic Policy

Bush hoped to rely on increased voluntary efforts—which he called a "thousand points of light"—to improve people's lives. In an attempt to reduce the national debt, he also reached a compromise with the Democrats in control of Congress. Bush agreed to raise taxes slightly, despite an earlier pledge not to do so. The compromise cost him the support of many Republicans who opposed a tax increase. Bush also signed the Americans with Disabilities Act ("ADA"), which prohibited discrimination against individuals with disabilities and required businesses to create accessible pathways and spaces.

The Recession

The United States moved into a short recession by 1990. Increased oil prices from the Iraqi occupation of Kuwait were partly to blame. Greater foreign competition was also reducing the demand for some American products. The recession was accompanied by new racial tensions. Riots broke out in Los Angeles and other cities in 1992 when a jury found policemen not guilty even though they had been videotaped brutally beating Rodney King, a young African American.

The Election of 1992

The election of 1992 occurred just as the brief recession was coming to an end. Bush, whose main experience had been in foreign policy, seemed unable to improve economic conditions. Despite his successes in foreign affairs, many voters had the impression Bush was indifferent to their problems at home.

During the campaign, Bush was harshly criticized by third-party candidate **H. Ross Perot**, a Texas billionaire who opposed Bush's domestic policies, especially the increase in the national debt and NAFTA, which Perot predicted would lead to a loss of American jobs. The Democrats nominated **Bill Clinton**, the Governor of Arkansas. More than twenty years younger than Bush, Clinton attacked the President for being "out of touch" with middle-class Americans and their needs. Clinton defeated Bush in the election, while Perot attracted a surprising 19% of the popular vote.

Complete the chart below on the challenges faced by these two Presidents.

The Reagan and Bush Presidencies

Challenge	Description of the Challenge	How Reagan and Bush Responded
Stagflation		
Terrorism		
Soviet Union		

The Presidency of Bill Clinton

Bill Clinton was a "New Democrat," one of a group of moderates trying to attract former Reagan supporters together with traditional Democrats. New Democrats promised middle-class tax cuts, a reform of the welfare system, a balanced budget, and stronger law enforcement while remaining liberal on other issues.

A Prosperous Economy

The recession that cost Bush the election was short-lived. Clinton assumed the Presidency just as the Cold War ended. Americans reaped a "peace dividend," when Clinton closed military bases and reduced U.S. military expenditures. Defense spending decreased and taxes were cut. By the end of his Presidency the government was able to produce a small surplus that could be applied to the national debt.

Besides the benefits of the "peace dividend," Americans were undergoing a revolution in technology. The use of personal computers, first introduced in the early 1980s, was spreading rapidly. By 2000, 60 million American households owned a personal computer.

New companies, such as Microsoft, Intel, and Apple, reaped enormous profits. The introduction of the Internet, a global network of linked computers, also occurred in this decade. Public commercial use of the Internet was first made available in 1989. The "World Wide Web" was created in 1989 and became open to the public in August 1991.

An expansion of global trade further helped fuel American prosperity. Clinton was able to persuade members of Congress to ratify NAFTA, increasing trade with Canada and Mexico. The World Trade Organization was created in 1994 to encourage international trade and settle trade disputes. By the year 2000, the value of U.S. exports and imports reached 25% of the country's Gross National Product (GNP)—the total value of goods and services produced by American citizens in a single year.

As a result of these factors, Americans experienced one of their longest periods of uninterrupted prosperity. In the decade from 1991 to 2000, stock prices quadrupled. By 2000, unemployment reached a low of 4% and Americans were producing more than one fifth of the world's total goods and services. Almost every American household had one or more color television sets, while nearly half of them also owned a VCR or DVD player, a microwave oven, a clothes washer, and an electric dryer.

> **William Jefferson Clinton** was raised by his grandparents, mother, and stepfather in the small community of Hope, Arkansas. Clinton did well in school and earned scholarships to attend top universities—Georgetown, Oxford University in England, and Yale Law School. While at Georgetown, Clinton became an intern in the U.S. Senate. Clinton opposed the Vietnam War and after law school became active in politics. He was elected Governor of Arkansas in 1978 at the age of 32—making him the youngest governor in the country. After losing a bid for re-election, he was elected a second time in 1982 and served as governor for ten more years.

Some groups were left out of this prosperity, such as the residents of poor neighborhoods in inner cities, one-parent families, and American Indians on reservations. A large number of Americans also did not have health insurance. Clinton pledged to create a system of national health insurance during the election, but he was unable to get his plans passed by Congress and never delivered on this promise.

> Note: You will not need to know about the "Contract with America" or Clinton's foreign policy for the Georgia Milestones EOC Assessment. You will need to know about Clinton's impeachment.

In the 1994 elections, Republicans gained control of both houses of Congress. Newt Gingrich, a college history professor from Georgia, became Speaker of the House. Gingrich and other conservative Republicans promised voters a "**Contract with America**" if they were elected. The "Contract" proposed a balanced budget, social security reform, lower taxes for small businesses, tax credits for parents with children, an audit of Congress to reduce waste, the opening of Congressional committee meetings to the public, harsher sentencing for convicted criminals, and special requirements for new taxes. Republican control of Congress made it more difficult for Clinton to pass many of the measures he favored. Nevertheless he worked with Congress to pass a children's health care act and welfare reform, limiting the number of years that families could rely on welfare payments.

Clinton's Foreign Policy

The collapse of communism had brought an end to the Cold War but also created new challenges. Ethnic rivalries once held in check by communist governments tore some countries apart. In **Yugoslavia**, warfare broke out between different ethnic groups. Slovenia, Croatia, Bosnia-Herzegovina and Kosovo each declared its independence. Christian Serbs murdered Muslims in parts of Bosnia and Kosovo in a policy of genocide that became known as "**ethnic cleansing**." These conflicts brought bloodshed into the very heart of Europe. After some initial hesitation, Clinton stepped in to restore peace. Clinton used American air power against Serb positions in Bosnia. In December 1995, Serb and Bosnian representatives worked out an agreement in Dayton, Ohio. Fighting later shifted to Kosovo, a part of Serbia with a large Albanian population. Further NATO intervention was required before a final ceasefire could be achieved.

Another case of attempted genocide occurred in **Rwanda**, a small country in Central Africa. In 1994 one of its ethnic groups, the Hutus, began slaughtering another group, the Tutsis. The United States and other Western countries were slow to react, and as many as 850,000 people were killed.

Clinton supported democracy abroad. He maintained friendly relations with Russian leader Boris Yeltsin. When military leaders overthrew a democratically elected leader in **Haiti**, Clinton sent in American troops and restored the elected leader to power. Like Carter, Clinton was especially concerned with human rights. He pressured Chinese leaders to respect human rights in China, and encouraged other countries to show greater respect for women and individual civil rights.

Terrorism

Like previous Presidents, Clinton faced the continuing challenge of terrorism.

Oklahoma City Bombing

The most serious terrorist incident of Clinton's Presidency was domestic rather than foreign in

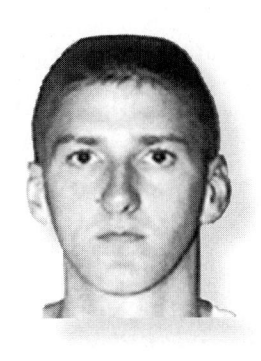

Timothy McVeigh and the wreckage of the federal building in Oklahoma City

origin. In April 1995, Timothy McVeigh and Terry Nichols, assisted by two others, blew up the federal building in downtown Oklahoma City. McVeigh was a Gulf War veteran who resented an attack by federal agents two years earlier on a religious compound in Texas. McVeigh and Nichols decided to bomb a federal building in revenge. They bought 40 bags of fertilizer, which they combined with other chemicals to create an explosive mixture. McVeigh then drove two tons of the explosive in a rented truck to Oklahoma City, parked the truck in front of the federal building, and set the bomb off on April 19, 1995. It killed 168 people, injured another 680, and caused $600 million in property damage. McVeigh and Nichols were both soon caught and convicted—McVeigh was executed while Nichols was sentenced to life imprisonment.

Al Qaeda Attacks

Osama bin Laden was a wealthy Saudi and Islamic Fundamentalist who had fought against the Soviets in Afghanistan. He greatly resented the arrival of U.S. troops in Saudi Arabia during the Persian Gulf War. Bin Laden founded **al Qaeda**, a terrorist organization that opposed Western influence in the Middle East. Bin Laden called for a *jihad*, or "holy war," against the United States. He found a favorable home for al Qaeda in Afghanistan, which had come under the rule of the **Taliban** (an Islamic Fundamentalist group). Bin Laden set up camps there for training anti-Western terrorists. In August 1998, al Qaeda terrorists attacked the U.S. Embassies in Kenya and Tanzania—two countries in East Africa. In October 2000, al Qaeda exploded a boat next to the U.S. Navy warship USS *Cole*. There seemed to be little that Clinton could do against such attacks, while U.S. intelligence services failed to recognize the great danger that al Qaeda posed.

Impeachment

With a booming economy, Clinton easily won re-election in 1996. However, a crisis occurred in his second term arising out of claims of earlier sexual harassment (*when an employer or person in power demands sexual favors or subjects an employee or colleague to unwanted physical contact*). A former state employee in Arkansas sued Clinton for having harassed her when he was Governor. Clinton tried to delay the lawsuit, but the U.S. Supreme Court ruled that the President could be subject to private lawsuits while still in office, so the case went forward.

Meanwhile a young White House intern, **Monica Lewinsky**, had a series of secret sexual encounters with the President. Lewinsky privately confided to a friend, Linda Tripp, about her affair. Tripp greatly resented the Clintons for having moved her job from the White House to the Pentagon. She recorded her conversations with Lewinsky and sent the tapes to the lawyers who were handling the sexual harassment case against Clinton.

As part of their case, the sexual harassment lawyers wanted to establish that Clinton had a pattern of abusing government employees. They added Lewinsky to their witness list. Lewinsky, however, denied having had any sexual relations with Clinton. Clinton also gave sworn testimony in the harassment case that he had had no sexual relations with Lewinsky.

Rumors leaked out to the press, and Clinton appeared on television in January 1998, when he told the public that he "did not have sexual relations with that woman, Miss Lewinsky." Eight months later, Clinton again swore under oath to a grand jury that he and Lewinsky were not having sexual relations.

Meanwhile, Tripp had sent another copy of her tapes to Kenneth Starr, the court-appointed independent counsel (*lawyer*) who was investigating the Clintons' real estate dealings. Starr obtained court permission to expand the scope of his investigation. He also gave Lewinsky immunity from prosecution. She now admitted that she had had sexual relations with the President. Her story was confirmed by evidence from her clothes. In August 1998, Clinton was forced to admit to the American public that he had lied—both to the American people and to his wife, Hillary.

Starr submitted a lengthy report to Congress detailing how Clinton had lied about his relations with Lewinsky under oath and how he had also attempted to obstruct justice in the sexual harassment case. Starr recommended that Congress impeach the President for "high crimes and misdemeanors." Republicans controlled the House of Representatives. A majority of the House voted for two articles of impeachment: (1) that Clinton had committed perjury (*lying under oath*); and (2) that he had been guilty of obstructing (*blocking; stopping*) justice.

The Historian's Apprentice

The following two articles were adopted by the House of Representatives:

RESOLUTION

"Resolved, That William Jefferson Clinton, President of the United States, is impeached for high crimes and misdemeanors, and that the following articles of impeachment be exhibited to the United States Senate:

ARTICLE I

In his conduct while President of the United States, William Jefferson Clinton, in violation of his constitutional oath . . . has willfully corrupted and manipulated the judicial process of the United States for his personal gain and exoneration, impeding the administration of justice, in that: On August 17, 1998, William Jefferson Clinton swore to tell the truth . . . before a Federal grand jury of the United States. Contrary to that oath, William Jefferson Clinton willfully provided perjurious, false and misleading testimony to the grand jury concerning . . . the nature and details of his relationship with a subordinate Government employee . . .

ARTICLE II

In his conduct while President of the United States, William Jefferson Clinton, in violation of his constitutional oath . . . has prevented, obstructed, and impeded the administration of justice, and has to that end engaged personally, and through his subordinates and agents, in a course of conduct or scheme designed to delay, impede, cover up, and conceal the existence of evidence and testimony related to a Federal civil rights action brought against him in a duly instituted judicial proceeding. . .

Wherefore, William Jefferson Clinton, by such conduct, warrants impeachment and trial, and removal from office and disqualification to hold and enjoy any office of honor, trust, or profit under the United States."

—House of Representatives, December 19, 1998

1. How would you have voted on each of these two articles of impeachment?
2. Clinton was the second President ever to have been impeached. The Constitution provides that the President and other officials "shall be removed from office on impeachment for, and conviction of, treason, bribery, or other high crimes and misdemeanors." Was Clinton's act of telling a lie under oath in a court proceeding sufficient grounds to remove him from office if he was otherwise doing a good job as President?

Although a simple majority of the House can impeach the President, a vote of two-thirds of the Senate is needed to remove him or her from office. Members in both Houses voted along party lines, and Republicans never had sufficient votes to remove Clinton from office. No Democrats voted to either impeach or remove Clinton. In the Senate, where the trial lasted over a month, a handful of Republicans joined with Democrats in voting not to remove Clinton.

While all this was going on, Clinton's legislative program stalled and the President had to deal with grave matters of national security. Some observers felt that the bickering between Republicans and Democrats that led to Clinton's impeachment was distracting government leaders from more urgent matters. In the same month that Clinton made his confession on television, al Qaeda terrorists blew up the U.S. Embassies in Kenya and Tanzania. Starr's investigation, which uncovered no wrongdoing in real estate transactions, cost taxpayers more than $60 million. Despite the impeachment, Clinton's approval rating as President remained high.

The Presidency of George W. Bush

The 2000 Election

The impeachment of Clinton may have hurt the chances of Vice President Al Gore to succeed Clinton in the White House. In the Presidential election of 2000, George W. Bush, the son of George H.W. Bush, was elected President after one of the closest contests in American history. On election night, it was still unclear who the winner was. Neither Bush nor Gore had enough electoral votes to win without those of Florida. However, it was unclear who had won Florida's votes because of inconsistencies in the voting process, especially on paper ballots. Bush's brother was the Governor of Florida and state election officials declared Bush to be the winner. Gore demanded a recount, which was in progress until it was stopped by the U.S. Supreme Court in *Bush v. Gore* (2000).

The Attacks of September 11, 2001

Bush was in office only nine months when an event occurred that would shape the rest of his Presidency. The terrorist organization **al Qaeda** had secretly sent some of their members to the United States to attend flight-training school. On September 11, 2001, the terrorists boarded

Chapter 19 | America in Recent Times

several commercial jets and used knives and box cutters they had smuggled on board to threaten passengers and hijack the planes. Then they flew the planes themselves into the **World Trade Center** in New York City and the Pentagon Building in Washington, D.C. A fourth plane was meant to crash into the White House, but the passengers on board learned of the other crashes and fought the hijackers, causing the plane to crash in a wooded area in Pennsylvania. The two towers of the World Trade Center collapsed, leading to almost 3,000 deaths and closing down much of New York City.

The "War on Terror"

President Bush quickly responded by declaring a "**War on Terror**" (also known as the "**War on Terrorism**"). Congress gave the President the authority to use "all necessary and appropriate force against those nations, organizations, or persons he determines planned, authorized, committed, or aided" the September 11th attacks.

Bush demanded that the **Taliban**— the Islamic Fundamentalist government of Afghanistan—turn over al Qaeda leader **Osama bin Laden**, the mastermind behind the September attacks. When the Taliban refused to surrender bin Laden, American forces invaded Afghanistan. They quickly overthrew the Taliban but failed to capture bin Laden. Americans became committed to restoring peace and stability to Afghanistan, and they found it difficult to withdraw their troops.

The "War on Terror" had effects on life within the United States as well as on U.S. foreign policy. Bush created the **Department of Homeland Security** to better coordinate the work of several federal agencies. The head of this department became a member of the Cabinet. New procedures were instituted at airports to screen passengers and baggage before boarding aircraft. The Transportation Security Administration (or TSA) was created to conduct these screenings. Congress also passed the USA PATRIOT Act. This act gave the President special powers to combat terrorism. The act made it easier for the government to set up wiretaps to eavesdrop on potential terrorists.

The Bush administration further adopted the use of harsh interrogation methods, such as "waterboarding" (*pouring water into a cloth on the face of a prisoner to create the sensation of drowning*) on high-level prisoners captured outside the United States. The administration maintained that, while these methods were harsh, they were not torture. Some suspected terrorists were sent to the U.S. military base on Guantanamo Bay, Cuba. Because Guantanamo Bay was not on American soil, the government argued that its prisoners did not have American "due process" rights.

The Historian's Apprentice

Nine days after the September attacks, President Bush addressed Congress and declared his "War on Terror":

> "On September the 11th, enemies of freedom committed an act of war against our country...

Americans have many questions tonight. Americans are asking: Who attacked our country? The evidence we have gathered all points to a collection of loosely affiliated terrorist organizations known as al Qaeda. They are the same murderers indicted for bombing American embassies in Tanzania and Kenya, and responsible for bombing the USS *Cole*.

Al Qaeda is to terror what the mafia is to crime. But its goal is not making money; its goal is remaking the world—and imposing its radical beliefs on people everywhere.

The terrorists practice a fringe form of Islamic extremism that has been rejected by Muslim scholars and the vast majority of Muslim clerics—a fringe movement that perverts the peaceful teachings of Islam. The terrorists' directive commands them to kill Christians and Jews, to kill all Americans, and make no distinction among military and civilians, including women and children.

This group and its leader—a person named Osama bin Laden—are linked to many other organizations in different countries . . .

Our war on terror begins with al Qaeda, but it does not end there. It will not end until every terrorist group of global reach has been found, stopped, and defeated. . . .

These terrorists kill not merely to end lives, but to disrupt and end a way of life. With every atrocity, they hope that America grows fearful, retreating from the world and forsaking our friends. They stand against us, because we stand in their way . . .

Americans are asking: How will we fight and win this war? We will direct every resource at our command—every means of diplomacy, every tool of intelligence, every instrument of law enforcement, every financial influence, and every necessary weapon of war—to the disruption and to the defeat of the global terror network. . . .

Our response involves far more than instant retaliation and isolated strikes. Americans should not expect one battle, but a lengthy campaign, unlike any other we have ever seen. It may include dramatic strikes, visible on TV, and covert operations, secret even in success. We will starve terrorists of funding, turn them one against another, drive them from place to place, until there is no refuge or no rest . . .

Our nation has been put on notice: We are not immune from attack. We will take defensive measures against terrorism to protect Americans. Today, dozens of federal departments and agencies, as well as state and local governments, have responsibilities affecting homeland security. These efforts must be coordinated at the highest level. So tonight I announce the creation of a Cabinet-level position reporting directly to me—the Office of Homeland Security . . .

These measures are essential. But the only way to defeat terrorism as a threat to our way of life is to stop it, eliminate it, and destroy it where it grows . . .

This is not, however, just America's fight. We ask every nation to join us. We will ask, and we will need, the help of police forces, intelligence services, and banking systems around the world. The United States is grateful that many nations and many international organizations have already responded — with sympathy and with support . . .

Continued ▶

> The civilized world is rallying to America's side. They understand that if this terror goes unpunished, their own cities, their own citizens may be next. Terror, unanswered, can not only bring down buildings, it can threaten the stability of legitimate governments. And you know what—we're not going to allow it."
>
> —President George W. Bush, Address to a Joint Session of Congress and the American People, September 20, 2011

1. What did Bush mean by a "war on terror"?
2. How did Bush see this war as different from other wars Americans had fought?
3. Why was Bush careful to distinguish between the al Qaeda terrorists—members of "a fringe form of Islamic extremism"—and other Muslims?
4. How would you have reacted to this speech if you had been a member of Congress at the time?

The War in Iraq

President Bush was also concerned about the actions of Iraqi dictator Saddam Hussein. His father had failed to depose Hussein after the Persian Gulf War in 1991. Bush suspected that Hussein was concealing chemical and biological weapons of mass destruction from U.N. weapons inspectors. Bush and his advisers especially feared that Hussein might make these weapons available to terrorists.

After presenting the American position to the U.N. Security Council and issuing a final warning to Hussein, President Bush ordered U.S. forces to invade Iraq in March 2003. As in Afghanistan, they quickly overthrew the government but soon found themselves in a new situation in which it was difficult to withdraw. Rival Iraqi groups competed for power, while former supporters of Hussein, radical Shiite Muslims allied to Iran, and other groups launched a resistance movement against the American occupation.

No weapons of mass destruction were ever found in Iraq, leading many critics in the United States and abroad to claim that the whole invasion had been a mistake. As time went on, the occupation became increasingly unpopular among many Americans.

The Financial Crisis and the Great Recession

George W. Bush's last year in office witnessed the country's worst economic crisis since the Great Depression. For decades, the federal government and Federal Reserve had been following policies to reduce swings in the U.S. economy. These efforts, combined with globalization, led to a financial crisis and a severe economic downturn known as the "Great Recession."

The roots of the crisis could be traced back to 2000, when there was a drop in stock market prices. The Federal Reserve lowered its interest rate to stimulate the economy. Many Americans took advantage of lower interest rates to obtain mortgages to buy new homes. Banks developed new types of "adjustable" loans, which often required low initial payments and higher interest payments later. Banks also began lending to borrowers who, based on their incomes, could not really afford the homes they were purchasing. Thousands of these shaky home loans were bundled together in packages with other investments and sold off to banks and investors, who did not really know what they were buying. These financial products were not closely regulated.

By 2007, overbuilding caused U.S. housing prices to fall. When interest rates started to rise again, many homeowners could no longer afford to make the payments on their adjustable-rate mortgages. There was a large increase in home foreclosures (*when a homeowner can no longer afford to make mortgage payments and the bank takes back the house to sell to recover the value of the loan*).

Loans lost their value when homeowners could not make their payments and the value of real estate sank. The investment banks, insurance companies, and other firms that had bought up bundles of these mortgage-backed securities also started to fail. Because of the crisis, banks stopped lending. Credit dried up. Investment firms went out of business. The economy was on the verge of a major collapse.

In his final months in office, President Bush and Congress provided direct federal government assistance to bail out several large companies. Congress approved a $700 billion bailout package. The Federal Reserve bought up government debt and troubled assets from banks. It made more money available and lowered interest rates. Government bailouts prevented the collapse of financial institutions, but the stock market still dropped and the country went into a major recession.

Complete the chart below on the challenges faced by these two Presidents.

The Clinton and George W. Bush Presidencies

Challenge	Description of the Challenge	How the President Responded
Impeachment		
Attacks of September 11, 2001		
Financial Crisis		

The Presidential Election of 2008

The Presidential election of 2008 took place against this background of economic crisis. Since George W. Bush had served two terms, Republicans had to choose a new candidate. They nominated Senator John McCain, a Vietnam veteran who had been a prisoner of war for several years. McCain was known as a "maverick" and free-thinker among Republicans. In

Chapter 19 | America in Recent Times

Congress, he had often been willing to cooperate with Democrats. To demonstrate a fresh approach, he chose Sarah Palin, the Governor of Alaska, as his running mate for the Vice Presidency. This was only the second time in history that a woman was nominated by a major political party for the Vice Presidency.

After eight years of Republican government, the unpopular war in Iraq, and the financial crisis, it seemed more than likely that the Democratic nominee would win the election in November 2008. Media attention was therefore focused on the Democratic primary elections. Here, the leading candidates were **Barack Obama**, the U.S. Senator from Illinois, and **Hillary Clinton**, the U.S. Senator from New York. The election contest was historic because this was the first time that the leading contenders from a major party were not white males. Barack Obama was an African American, while Hillary Clinton was a woman and former First Lady (the wife of Bill Clinton).

Hillary Clinton won the first primary in New Hampshire in January 2008, becoming the first woman to win a major party's state primary. On "Super Tuesday," February 5, 2008, Obama earned slightly more votes than Clinton. The contest continued neck-and-neck through most of the spring. Obama finally reached enough votes to win the nomination in early June, after more than a year of campaigning.

In the general election campaign that followed, Obama promised to establish a national health care system, to increase employment, to protect the environment, and to collaborate more closely with America's allies. He considered the invasion of Iraq to have been a great mistake and promised to withdraw U.S. troops as soon as possible.

Obama's election as President in November was historic. Obama became the first African-American President of the United States. His election came only forty years after Dr. Martin Luther King, Jr.'s assassination in 1968.

The Historian's Apprentice

On the news of his election as President in 2008, Barack Obama gave his victory speech in Grant Park, Chicago—the scene of mass protests and violence during the Democratic National Convention in August 1968. He reflected on the historic nature of his election:

> "If there is anyone out there who still doubts that America is a place where all things are possible; who still wonders if the dream of our founders is alive in our time; who still questions the power of our democracy, tonight is your answer....
>
> It's the answer spoken by young and old, rich and poor, Democrat and Republican, black, white, Latino, Asian, Native American, gay, straight, disabled and not disabled—Americans who sent a message to the world that we have never been a collection of Red States and Blue States: we are, and always will be, the United States of America.
>
> It's the answer that led those who have been told for so long by so many to be cynical and fearful and doubtful about what we can achieve, to put their hands on the arc of history and bend it once more toward the hope of a better day.

It's been a long time coming, but tonight, because of what we did on this day, in this election, at this defining moment, change has come to America...."

1. What made Barack Obama's election as President a historic moment?
2. Participants in Grant Park like Civil Rights leader Jesse Jackson and television celebrity Oprah Winfrey openly wept on television while Obama was giving this victory speech. Why did they have this reaction?

The Impact of Advances in Information Technology

In this chapter, you have learned about the foreign and domestic policies of Ronald Reagan, George H.W. Bush, Bill Clinton, and George W. Bush, and about the election of Barack Obama as President. While these events were taking place, Americans were also undergoing profound changes due to advances in information technology.

In the early twentieth century, electrical calculating machines were able to read cards with punched holes to perform calculations. During World War II, the British and Americans developed larger computing machines to break enemy codes. These machines were very large. For example the ENIAC computer, built in 1946, had 18,000 vacuum tubes and weighed 30 tons. It could add or subtract 5,000 times per second.

In the early 1950s, smaller transistors replaced vacuum tubes in computers. In 1963, the integrated circuit was invented. This circuit is a solid block made of different layers of silicon that either conduct electricity or act as insulators. An integrated circuit—also known as a silicon chip—does not have connecting wires. Its smaller size made personal computers possible.

Personal Computers

By the mid-1970s, computer hobbyists could buy computer kits, which had to be assembled. In 1977, Apple and two other companies started selling preassembled systems—the first true personal computers. IBM followed with the IBM PC in 1981. Microsoft designed the software that the IBM PC used, including its operating system, while Intel designed its microprocessor. Meanwhile, Apple developed the "graphical user interface" and introduced the use of a "mouse," making personal computers easier to use.

> **Technology** refers to the tools that people use and the ways that people do things. Major improvements in technology have included the discovery of fire, the development of farming, the invention of the wheel, the invention of the printing press, the Industrial Revolution, the invention of the electric light bulb and electrical appliances, and the invention of the internal combustion engine. In modern times, technology has been especially affected by our knowledge of science, mathematics and engineering. **Information technology** refers to the use of machines (computers) to store, transmit, and work with information (*data*).

Chapter 19 | America in Recent Times

Personal computers helped users to write papers, make calculations, and balance checkbooks. Each year, personal computers became faster, more powerful, and less expensive. Personal computers had especially dramatic effects on businesses and schools. Small businesses could use personal computers to keep records, do their correspondence and billing, track data on spreadsheets, and design their own advertising. Schools could have students collaborate and complete projects on computers. By 1990, a quarter of all American homes had a personal computer; by 2000, more than half did.

The Internet

The Internet was first developed by the U.S. government as a way for American scientists and the military to communicate, especially in the event of a nuclear war. This network was later connected to commercial users, leading to the Internet we have today. Email makes use of the Internet to connect computer users for instantaneous communication. The Internet also makes possible text messaging. The "World Wide Web" is the place on the Internet where web pages are stored.

With the introduction of the Internet and the World Wide Web, users can now contact one another instantly through text messages or email or can find useful information just by searching on the Internet with their computer. Businesses can create web pages providing information to potential customers and can even take customers' orders on their websites. Banking, paying bills, and many other tasks can now be performed more easily and quickly online.

Social Media

In the early twenty-first century, Facebook, Twitter, Instagram, Snapchat and other forms of "social media" have further increased the ways that computer users can interact with one another. Social media allow users to post information, such as photographs taken on vacation, so that other "friends" can have access to this information and comment on it. Later visitors can see both the original posting and how other visitors have responded in their comments. Users of social media also can form groups, or social networks, in which they share the same posts and comment to one another.

Social media can be used for political purposes. During the "Arab Spring," protestors used social media to call on fellow citizens to participate in anti-government demonstrations. Social media also have the potential to be misused. During the 2016 Presidential election, different interest groups deliberately planted false reports on Facebook and other social media to mislead voters.

Globalization

These advances in information technology have contributed to the phenomenon of globalization—the fact that the world today seems to be "shrinking." The flow of information across boundaries through personal computers, the Internet, and social media is helping to create a global culture. The Internet also makes it easier to buy and sell goods across frontiers. People travel and trade more today and share more information than at any other time in history.

* * *

Complete the chart below.

The Impact of Changes in Information Technology

Technology	Description of New Technology	Impact on Society and Government
The Personal Computer		
The Internet		
Social Media		

For the Georgia "Milestones" EOC Assessment, you should know that:

- ☐ President Reagan applied "Reaganomics" to fight stagflation: he lowered tax rates, reduced spending on welfare and other domestic programs, and cut back on government regulations. This was a turning point in the degree of government involvement in the economy.

- ☐ Reagan attempted to "roll back" communism. He proposed the Strategic Defense Initiative to defend Americans from a nuclear attack.

- ☐ Soviet leader Mikhail Gorbachev introduced reforms into Soviet society, including greater openness. His reforms led Eastern Europeans to demand their independence. Gorbachev refused to use force to suppress Eastern Europe, leading to the fall of the Berlin Wall and the end of the Cold War.

- ☐ Reagan met with Gorbachev several times and they began reducing the number of nuclear missiles.

- ☐ Following the example of Eastern Europe, the different republics of the Soviet Union, including Russia, also demanded their independence. This finally led to the collapse of the Soviet Union in 1991, when George H.W. Bush was President.

Continued ▶

- ☐ The focus of George H.W. Bush's Presidency was on foreign affairs. In his economic policies, he generally followed Reagan.
- ☐ During Bill Clinton's Presidency, Americans enjoyed prosperity caused by reductions in military spending, lower taxes, increased trade, and a revolution in information technology.
- ☐ President Clinton was impeached in the House of Representatives for having lied under oath about his relationship with a White House intern. The Senate did not have enough votes to remove him from office.
- ☐ George W. Bush, the son of George H.W. Bush, became President after one of the closest election contests in U.S. history.
- ☐ Shortly after Bush became President, al Qaeda terrorists crashed commercial jet planes into the World Trade Center in New York City and the Pentagon in Washington, D.C., leading to the deaths of about 3,000 people.
- ☐ In response to the September 11th attacks, President Bush called for a "War on Terror." This led him to launch an invasion of Afghanistan to topple the Taliban, to create the Department of Homeland Security, to conduct increased wiretapping and surveillance, and to invade Iraq in 2003.
- ☐ At the end of his Presidency, Bush faced a severe economic crisis. He authorized government bailouts and expenditures to prevent an even worse crash.
- ☐ The Presidential election of 2008 was historic because it showed an African American could be elected as President of the United States only 40 years after the assassination of Dr. Martin Luther King, Jr.
- ☐ During the years 1980 to 2008, Americans experienced a revolution in information technology—with the introduction of the personal computer, the Internet, and social media. These changed the ways in which Americans worked, entertained themselves, and communicated.

Conclusion

Now that you have completed your study of three centuries of American history, find the piece of paper on which you wrote one thing you wanted to learn in this course (see page xiii in the Introduction). How well have you met your objective? And how do you, as a well-informed citizen, now intend to apply your knowledge of American history?

America in Recent Times

Ronald Reagan
- Reaganomics: lower taxes, reduced domestic spending, and fewer regulations in order to stimulate production and end stagflation
- Increased military spending, which added to the federal deficit
- Air strike on Libya
- "Reagan Doctrine"—attempts to "roll back" communism: Grenada, Nicaragua, Afghanistan
- Iran-Contra Affair
- Strategic Defense Initiative
- Gorbachev tries to reform the Soviet Union and has talks with Reagan

George H.W. Bush
- End of Cold War
- Collapse of Soviet Union
- U.S. interventions: Panama, Somalia
- First Gulf War: Kuwait
- Recession in the United States

Impact of Advances in Information Technology
- The Internet: World Wide Web, search engines, email
- Social Media: Facebook, Twitter, Snapchat
- Globalization

Bill Clinton
- Economic recovery—"Peace Dividend"
- Growth of computer industry
- Congress approves NAFTA
- Domestic terrorism: 1995 Bombing of Federal Building in Oklahoma City
- Bosnia & Kosovo: "ethnic cleansing"
- Rwanda: genocide
- Embassy attacks by al Qaeda
- Impeachment of Clinton for perjured testimony

Barack Obama
- Historic Presidential election of 2008:
  - First African American elected as President
  - First time woman candidate almost won nomination of a major party (Hillary Clinton)
  - Second time a major party nominated a woman for Vice President

George W. Bush
- 2000 Election: Close election resolved by *Bush v. Gore*
- September 11, 2001: al Qaeda attacks on the World Trade Center and Pentagon with hijacked commercial aircraft
- "War on Terror" led to changes at home and abroad:
  - Taliban overthrown in Afghanistan
  - Department of Homeland Security
  - TSA: Screens all commercial air travelers
  - USA PATRIOT Act
- Iraq War
- Financial Crisis

Chapter 19 | America in Recent Times

Name _____

Complete the following chart about America in recent times.

Event	Description or Explanation
Reaganomics	
War on Terrorism	
Collapse of the Soviet Union	
Impeachment of President Bill Clinton	

Chapter 19 | America in Recent Times

Name _____

Complete the following chart about America in recent times.

Event	Description or Explanation
Terrorist Attacks on World Trade Center and Pentagon on September 11, 2001	
Influence of Personal Computer, Internet, and Social Media	
Presidential Election of 2008	

Chapter 19 | America in Recent Times

What Do You Know?

SSUSH23a

1. Use the diagram to answer the question.

[The Soviet Union falls behind the West in economic productivity] → [Mikhail Gorbachev introduces greater openness into Soviet society] → [President Reagan threatens to develop a new weapons system (Strategic Defense Initiative)] → [?]

Which statement best completes the diagram?

A. The Soviet Union and United States enter into a new arms race.

B. Reagan and Gorbachev hold a series of talks promising arms reductions.

C. Gorbachev reverses his policies to preserve the power of the Communist Party.

D. Reagan and Gorbachev join forces to resist the rising threat of global terrorism.

SSUSH23b

2. Use the excerpt to answer the question.

> *In this present crisis, government is not the solution to our problem; government is the problem.*
>
> —President Ronald Reagan, First Inaugural Address, January 1981

Which problems was President Reagan addressing in this speech?

A. Stagflation and excessive government regulation

B. Rising international competition and collapse of the banking system

C. Deflation and widespread unemployment

D. State resistance to federal civil rights programs

SSUSH23b

3. Which statement BEST describes how President Reagan believed tax cuts and deregulation would help the U.S. economy?

A. These steps would enable those from less privileged backgrounds to compete with others.

B. These steps would ensure greater competition by small businesses against larger ones.

C. These steps would protect workers from abuses by their employers.

D. These steps would give added incentive to individual enterprise.

SSUSH23b

4. Use the list to answer the question.

   - Tax cuts
   - Reductions in domestic spending
   - Deregulation
   - Increased military spending

   Which two Presidents MOST followed the policies on this list?

   A. Jimmy Carter and Bill Clinton
   B. Bill Clinton and Barack Obama
   C. Ronald Reagan and Barack Obama
   D. Ronald Reagan and George H.W. Bush

SSUSH23a

5. Use the excerpt to answer the questions.

   Our response involves far more than instant retaliation and isolated strikes. Americans should not expect one battle, but a lengthy campaign, unlike any other we have seen. It may include dramatic strikes, visible on TV, and covert operations, secret even in success . . .

   —President George W. Bush to Congress, September 20, 2011

   Part A

   Which event led to this speech?

   A. attacks on U.S. Embassies in East Africa
   B. fall of South Vietnam to Vietnamese Communists
   C. attack on the World Trade Center and Pentagon
   D. refusal of Saddam Hussein to hand over "Weapons of mass destruction"

   Part B

   Which step did President Bush take shortly after giving this speech?

   A. a raid in Pakistan to capture Osama bin Laden
   B. the invasion of Iraq to remove Saddam Hussein
   C. the invasion of Afghanistan to remove the Taliban
   D. landing of forces in Saudi Arabia to occupy Kuwait

Chapter 19 | America in Recent Times

SSUSH23a

6. Use the list to answer the question.

   - Explosion in U.S. Marine barracks in Beirut
   - Attacks on U.S. Embassies in Kenya and Tanzania
   - Attack on the World Trade Center and Pentagon

   What inference can be made from this list?

   A. Communist governments had served to prevent the spread of terrorism.

   B. Terrorism has become a growing threat to U.S. national security.

   C. Terrorists are not powerful enough to inflict damage on leading nation-states.

   D. Terrorists always have specific demands that accompany their acts of terror.

SSUSH23a

7. Which statement BEST describes how President Ronald Reagan's leadership helped to bring the Cold War to an end?

   A. U.S. military intervention in Eastern Europe led to a Soviet withdrawal.

   B. U.S. troop reductions led Soviet leaders to reduce their own troop levels.

   C. U.S. military strength encouraged Soviet leaders to pursue domestic reform and compromise in foreign policy.

   D. His actions frightened Soviet leaders by threatening nuclear war.

SSUSH23a

8. Examine the excerpt to answer the question.

   Resolved, that William Jefferson Clinton, President of the United States, is impeached for high crimes and misdemeanors...
   —House of Representatives, Articles of Impeachment, December 19, 1998

   Which "high crimes and misdemeanors" did this document claim the President had committed?

   A. receiving illegal bribes when he was Governor of Arkansas

   B. lying under oath in a legal proceeding and obstructing an investigation

   C. secretly trading arms for hostages in violation of a Congressional prohibition

   D. not taking sufficient measures to protect the U.S. Embassies in Kenya and Tanzania

SSUSH23b

9. Use the diagram to answer the question.

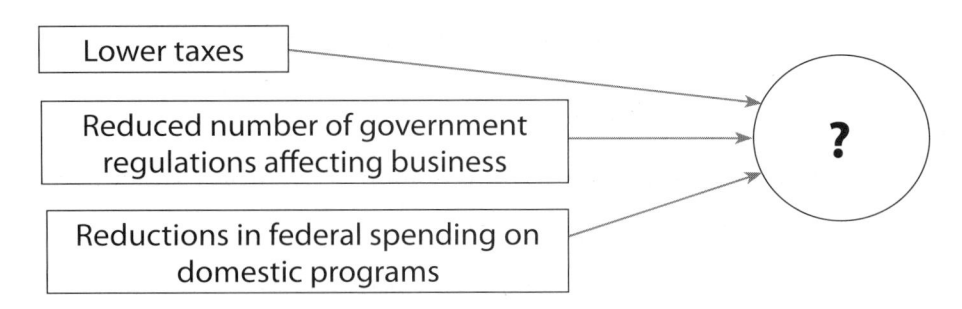

```
Lower taxes ─────────────────┐
                              ↘
Reduced number of government  →  ( ? )
regulations affecting business ↗
                              ↗
Reductions in federal spending on
domestic programs
```

Which word or phrase BEST completes the diagram?

A. Deficit spending

B. Reagonomics

C. Socialism

D. "New Democrat" Economic Policies

SSUSH23a

10. Use the photograph to answer the question.

New York City, September 11, 2001

What was the direct cause of this event?

A. Russian leaders decided to take revenge on the United States for their loss of the Cold War.

B. President Saddam Hussein of Iraq launched the attack as a warning to American leaders.

C. Islamic Fundamentalist terrorists organized the attack because of their hatred of America.

D. U.S. airplanes had more accidents after federal deregulation of the aviation industry.

Chapter 19 | America in Recent Times

SSUSH23a

11. Read the excerpt to answer the question.

> *They will hand over the terrorists or they will share in their fate.*
> —President George W. Bush speaking before Congress, September 20, 2001

Which government was President George W. Bush referring to in this speech?

A. the royal government of Saudi Arabia

B. the Taliban government of Afghanistan

C. the dictatorship of Saddam Hussein in Iraq

D. the government of Manuel Noriega in Panama

SSUSH23d

12. Use the list to answer the question.

- The election took place during a major financial crisis.
- American troops were actively engaged in combat overseas.
- A former First Lady was almost nominated by the Democratic Party.
- The first African American was elected as President.

Which statement also belongs in this list?

A. The Supreme Court halted a recount of close election results in Florida.

B. The two major candidates held identical views on health care.

C. The election occurred as the country started making an economic recovery.

D. One of the two major political parties nominated a woman for Vice President.

SSUSH23c

13. Use the diagram to answer the question.

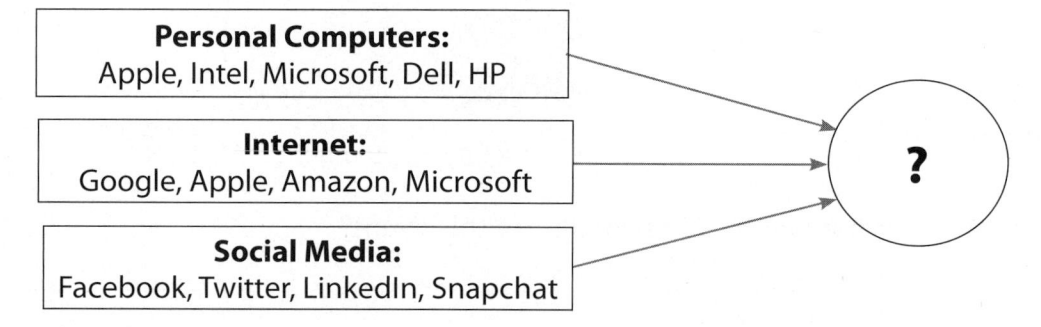

Personal Computers: Apple, Intel, Microsoft, Dell, HP

Internet: Google, Apple, Amazon, Microsoft

Social Media: Facebook, Twitter, LinkedIn, Snapchat

→ ?

Which phrase BEST completes the diagram?

A. Spread of democratic government to all nations

B. Increased job opportunities for unskilled workers

C. Improved communications and an information explosion

D. Narrower gap between the poorest and richest individuals

INDEX

Abolitionism, 155, 157, 159–161, 183, 189
Adams, John, 42, 47, 52, 57, 60, 63, 119–122
Alien and Sedition Acts, 120–122
American Federation of Labor (AFL), 244, 246, 299, 346
Angel Island, 250
Anti-Federalists, 98–100
Antietam, Battle of, 188–189, 194
Articles of Confederation, 76–83, 85–88
Atlanta, Battle of, 194
Atomic bomb, 440–441, 459, 467

Bill of Rights, English, 22
Bill of Rights, U.S., 76, 100–101, 116
Bill of Rights, U.S. states' bills of rights, 76
Black Codes, 212
Boston Tea Party, 43–44
Brown v. Board of Education (1954), 474–475
Brown, John, 183
Bush, George H.W., 560–562
Bush, George W., 567–571

Cabinet, 116, 397, 502, 541, 568
Camp David Accords, 541
Carnegie, Andrew, 237–239, 320
Carter, Jimmy, 540–542
Chavez, Cesar, 504–505
Cherokee Indians, 60, 148–149
Child labor, 242, 289, 293, 299, 399, 401
Chinese Exclusion Act, 250
Civil Rights Act of 1964, 499–500
Clay's "American System", 152
Clinton, Bill, 562–567
Cold War, 457–470, 493–495, 541, 559–560
Common Sense, 51
Communism, 362–363, 456–462, 464–470, 472–473, 494–495, 506–507, 514, 529, 533, 564
Compromise of 1850, 176–177
Containment, 461, 467, 557
Continental Congress, Second, 47–48, 52, 83
Cotton gin, 154, 179
Cuban Missile Crisis, 494–495

D-Day, 436
Daughters of Liberty, 41, 63
Davis, Jefferson, 184, 186, 195
Debs, Eugene, 298, 347
Declaration of Independence, 43, 52–55, 61–63, 76
Democratic-Republicans, 118, 122, 126
Douglass, Frederick, 159, 161, 189
Du Bois, W.E.B., 304
Dust Bowl, 392–394

Edison, Thomas, 234, 239, 371
Eisenhower, Dwight, 434, 456
Ellis Island, 248, 250
Emancipation Proclamation, 189, 195, 211
Environmental Protection Agency (EPA), 534
Espionage Act (1917), 347

Federal Reserve Act (1913), 298
Federalism, 95–96, 99
Federalist Papers, 99
Federalists, 98–100, 116, 118
Fifteenth Amendment, 214–215, 301, 501
Ford, Gerald, 538–539
Ford, Henry, 368, 370, 429
Fort Sumter, 184–185
Fourteen Points, 349–351
Fourteenth Amendment, 213–214, 302–303
Franklin, Benjamin, 37, 47, 52, 57, 60
Freedmen's Bureau, 210–211, 217
French and Indian War, 36–37, 40, 62
Friedan, Betty, 537

G.I. Bill of Rights, 470–471
Gettysburg, Battle of, 189–190, 194
Gompers, Samuel, 244, 320, 346
Grant, Ulysses S., 192, 214
Great Awakening, First, 22–25
Great Awakening, Second, 155–157, 159
Great Depression, 386–392, 396–405, 407, 420, 423
Great Migration, 348–349, 372
Great Society, 501–503, 534
Gulf of Tonkin Resolution, 508

Habeas corpus, 187
Hamilton, Alexander, 58, 82, 91–92, 99, 116–119
Harlem Renaissance, 371–374
Hayes, Rutherford B., 217–218
Hiroshima, 441
Hitler, Adolf, 420–422, 425, 433, 435–437
Hoover, Herbert, 345, 387, 390–392
Hooverville, 391–392

Immigration, 247–252, 364–365, 423, 502
Impeachment, 214, 536, 565–567
Imperialism, 316–327
Indian Removal Act, 148–150
Interstate Highway System, 472
Intolerable Acts, 43–44, 46
Iranian Hostage Crisis, 542, 554
Iron Curtain, 460

Jackson, Andrew, 129, 146–147, 149–153, 157
Jackson, Thomas "Stonewall", 186–187
Jefferson, Thomas, 47, 52, 62, 116–123, 125–126
"Jim Crow" laws, 301–303, 349
Johnson, Andrew, 210, 212–214
Johnson, Lyndon B., 499, 501–503, 508–510–513

Kansas-Nebraska Act, 176, 181–182
Kennedy, John F., 479, 492–497, 499, 501, 508
Kennedy, Robert F., 513–514
King, Jr., Dr. Martin Luther, 476, 496–497, 503, 513–514
Korean War, 465–467, 532
Korematsu v. U.S. (1944), 431
Ku Klux Klan, 217–218, 252, 304, 364, 373–374, 475, 497

Land Ordinance of 1785, 80
League of Nations, 350–352, 420, 425, 442
Lee, Robert E., 183, 186–190, 192, 194–195
Lend-Lease Act, 424
Lewis and Clark Expedition, 125

Lincoln, Abraham, 183–190, 192, 195–196, 211, 269
Louisiana Purchase, 122–123, 181–182

MacArthur, General Douglas, 438, 465–466
Madison, James, 81, 89–92, 97, 99, 116–118, 121, 126–128
Manhattan Project, 440–441
Manifest Destiny, 177–178, 319
Marshall Plan, 462–463, 471
McCarthy, Senator Joseph, 469
Medicare, 501–502, 534
Mercantilism, 3
Mexican War, 178–180
Mid-Atlantic Colonies, 7, 10, 13, 15, 17
Middle Passage, 11
Midway, Battle of, 439
Missouri Compromise, 176–177, 181–183
Monroe Doctrine, 130–131, 327
Muckraker, 289–292, 294

NAACP, 293, 304, 372, 474–476
NASA, 478
National Defense Education Act, 478–479
National Organization for Women (NOW), 537–538
NATO, 463–464
Neutrality, 119, 341, 423–424
New Deal, 394–395
New England Colonies, 7, 10, 12–13
New Federalism, 534
Nineteenth Amendment, 365–368
Nixon, Richard, 492, 515, 528–531, 533–536, 538–539
Northwest Ordinance of 1787, 79–81
Nullification Crisis, 150–151

Obama, Barack, 572
Oregon Territory, 125, 178

Paine, Thomas, 51
Palmer Raids, 363
Panama Canal, 325–327, 541
Paris, Treaty of (1763), 38
Paris, Treaty of (1783), 60–61
Pearl Harbor, 425–426
Philippines, 250, 316–318, 319, 322, 438, 440, 442

Plains Indians, 266, 269–273, 275
Plessy v. Ferguson (1896), 301–303, 474
Polk, James, 177–178
Proclamation Line of 1763, 39, 63
Progressive Movement, 288–290, 295
Prohibition, 366–368, 399

Radical Republicans, 212–215
Railroads, 153, 216–217, 230–232, 235–236, 238, 241, 250, 267–268, 270, 273–276, 294, 302, 346
Reagan, Ronald, 542, 554–560
Reaganomics, 554–557
Red Scare, 362–364
Reservations, 267, 269–271, 273, 275
Rockefeller, John D., 238–240, 290, 297
"Roosevelt Corollary", 327
Roosevelt, Eleanor, 396, 405–406, 443, 493
Roosevelt, Franklin D., 394–404, 423–426, 430, 432, 434–436, 438, 442
Roosevelt, Theodore, 296–298, 317–319, 326–327

Salutary Neglect, 22
Saratoga, Battle of, 56–57, 60
Scott v. Sandford (1857), 182
Seneca Falls Convention, 157
Shays' Rebellion, 82
Sherman Antitrust Act, 241
Sherman, William T., 192–193
Sinclair, Upton, 290–291, 297
Sioux Indians, 266, 269–270, 272
Slave rebellions, 159, 161–162, 176
Slave trade, 11, 158, 180
Social Security Act, 401
Socialism, 362
"Sons of Liberty", 40–41
Southern Colonies, 4, 6–7, 9–10, 12, 17–18
Soviet Union, 428, 433–435, 438, 440–442, 457–465, 467, 492, 494, 506, 510, 533, 541–542, 557–561
Spanish-American War, 316–320, 322–325
Sputnik, 477–479
Stamp Act, 40–41
Star-Spangled Banner, 129
Stock Market Crash of 1929, 387–388
Strike (labor), 238, 243, 245, 346, 362, 505

Tarbell, Ida, 290–291, 348
Tariffs, 151, 179, 298, 318, 368, 386, 562
Tea Act, 43
Telegraph, 153, 186, 233–236
Telephone, 233–236, 494–495
Teller Amendment, 318, 324
Temperance, 156, 289, 293, 366
Terrorism, 557–558, 564–565, 567–568
Tet Offensive, 512–513
Texas Republic, 177
Thirteenth Amendment, 211
Three-Fifths Compromise, 90
Tilden, Samuel, 217–218
"Trail of Tears", 148–150
Transcontinental railroad, 231, 249–250, 267–268, 270,
Trenton, Battle of, 50
Triangular trades, 14
Truman Doctrine, 461, 467
Truman, Harry S., 440–441, 456, 459, 461–462, 465–468, 473
Turner, Nat, 161–162

USS *Maine*, 317
United Nations, 442–443, 464, 533

Versailles, Treaty of (1919), 349–352
Vicksburg, Siege of, 192, 194
Vietnam, 505–515, 528–533, 539
Vietnamization, 528–529
Virginia and Kentucky Resolutions, 121–122
Voting Rights Act (1965), 503

"War on Terror," 568–570
War of 1812, 126–128, 130, 152
War Powers Act, 532
Washington, George, 36, 48–50, 56, 58–62, 81, 85, 91, 116–120
Washington's Farewell Address, 119–120
Watergate scandal, 535
Whiskey Rebellion, 119
Whitney, Eli, 154
Wilson, Woodrow, 298–299, 303, 341–352
Women's suffrage, 157, 292–293, 295, 367–368

Yalta Conference, 459
Yorktown, Battle of, 59–60

Zimmerman Telegram, 343